Ius Gentium: Comparative Perspectives on Law and Justice

Volume 140

Jaap de Zwaan, Erasmus University Rotterdam, Rotterdam, The Netherlands

Ius Gentium is a book series which discusses the central questions of law and justice from a comparative perspective. The books in this series collect the contrasting and overlapping perspectives of lawyers, judges, philosophers and scholars of law from the world's many different jurisdictions for the purposes of comparison, harmonisation, and the progressive development of law and legal institutions. Each volume makes a new comparative study of an important area of law. This book series continues the work of the well-known journal of the same name and provides the basis for a better understanding of all areas of legal science.

The *Ius Gentium* series provides a valuable resource for lawyers, judges, legislators, scholars, and both graduate students and researchers in globalisation, comparative law, legal theory and legal practice. The series has a special focus on the development of international legal standards and transnational legal cooperation.

Paolo Passaglia
Editor

European Legal Perspectives on Online Disinformation

Springer

Editor
Paolo Passaglia
Department of Law
University of Pisa
Pisa, Italy

ISSN 1534-6781 ISSN 2214-9902 (electronic)
Ius Gentium: Comparative Perspectives on Law and Justice
ISBN 978-3-032-25784-0 ISBN 978-3-032-25785-7 (eBook)
https://doi.org/10.1007/978-3-032-25785-7

This work was supported by University of Pisa.
CALL IIT SERICS SPOKE 1 No.1
Human-centered approach and Regulatory Dimension in Developing an Interoperable and Secure Cyberspace (HARD DISK)—CUP B53C22003950001

This Springer imprint is published by the registered company Springer Nature Switzerland AG
The registered company address is: Gewerbestrasse 11, 6330 Cham, Switzerland

Preface

This volume constitutes the outcome of an extensive and long-term collective research initiative involving a substantial number of legal systems of the Member States of the European Union. The project commenced in the autumn of 2024 and reached its conclusion with an international conference held in Pisa, Italy, on 20–21 November 2025. During this event, the participating scholars presented their respective national reports, each addressing some of the most significant legal issues associated with the phenomenon of online disinformation.

In recent years, an increasingly large body of scholarly literature has examined the subject of online disinformation from multiple disciplinary perspectives. Many of these contributions are of considerable value and represent meaningful advancements in the theoretical and empirical understanding of the topic. The present research project takes these earlier studies fully into account while seeking to offer additional insights and a more comprehensive legal analysis.

There are, in particular, four principal features that distinguish this research from previous investigations in the field.

First, all participants in the project are jurists. This is not intended to diminish the importance of contributions produced in other disciplines—such as computer science, sociology, economics, psychology, and related fields. On the contrary, the results of these disciplines are indispensable, as they provide the factual, conceptual, and methodological foundations upon which legal analysis must necessarily rely. The purpose of this project, however, is to approach online disinformation specifically from a legal perspective and to offer an analysis addressed primarily to legal scholars, practitioners, and policymakers.

Second, the scope of the research is not confined to a particular category of online disinformation (for example, political disinformation or disinformation aimed at electoral manipulation, etc.). Instead, the project adopts a broad and inclusive approach, examining online disinformation in all its manifestations. This includes forms of disinformation that may fall within the domains of criminal law or administrative law, that raise constitutional concerns, or that give rise to issues relevant to commercial, consumer, or civil law.

Third, the research focuses expressly on the European Union context. Its principal objective is to analyze the manner in which national legal systems transpose, interpret, and apply EU legislation and policy instruments. In this sense, the project may also be understood as an empirical illustration of legal system integration within the Union, and more broadly as a contribution to the scholarship on multilevel constitutionalism and the interaction between supranational and domestic legal orders.

Finally, it should be noted that this project does not constitute comparative law research in the strict methodological sense. More precisely, although the research is international in scope—since it encompasses contributions from scholars representing several national legal systems—each author focuses on the legal framework of her or his respective jurisdiction (with the sole exception of the rapporteur responsible for the analysis of EU law). The reports do not offer direct comparisons, nor do they attempt to identify convergences or divergences among the systems examined. Instead, the purpose is to lay the groundwork for subsequent comparative studies by assembling, within a single volume, detailed analyses of multiple national legal systems. To facilitate such future work, the national reports follow, wherever feasible, a uniform structure: they begin by defining the concept of online disinformation and distinguishing it from related notions; they then examine the relevant sources of law governing the phenomenon; and finally, they analyze the specific regulatory instruments applicable within each jurisdiction.

* * *

The decision to focus this research only on online disinformation derives from the recognition that, although the conceptual essence of disinformation remains constant across communicative environments, its operational dynamics, social impact, and normative implications vary profoundly when it occurs within the digital sphere. Substantively, disinformation retains the same capacity to distort public debate, manipulate individual perceptions, and influence collective decision-making irrespective of whether it appears offline or online. Accordingly, the definitional frameworks used to describe disinformation may, at least in principle, be applied uniformly across both contexts. Nevertheless, the regulatory and analytical significance of disinformation cannot be fully apprehended without careful attention to the environment in which it is produced and disseminated. It is at this contextual level that the transition from analog to digital communication generates a series of distinctive challenges that require systematic legal examination.

A broad interdisciplinary literature—spanning communication studies, political science, psychology, information systems, and computer science—has analyzed the transformation of information flows brought about by digital technologies. These scholarly contributions converge on the observation that the mechanisms governing the production, circulation, and reception of information online differ substantially from those that are characteristic of the physical world. The speed and scale of dissemination on the Internet, the algorithmic structures that curate and amplify content, and the architecture of social networks together create new conditions of visibility and credibility that are often decoupled from the accuracy of the information in question. The role of automation, the logic of virality, and the operation of opaque ranking systems have all been documented as critical factors in shaping contemporary information ecosystems. In this sense, the communicative environment of the digital sphere introduces variables that fundamentally alter the social and political significance of disinformation.

Situated within this interdisciplinary context, the present study adopts a specific legal perspective. Its central concern is the relationship between online disinformation and constitutional guarantees, with particular emphasis on the principle of freedom of expression. The reasons for the selection of this point of departure are self-evident: freedom of expression constitutes the normative foundation upon which legal approaches to information regulation must be built. Across the legal systems examined, the protection of expressive freedom functions as a structural guarantee of democratic governance rather than merely as an individual right. Constitutional jurisprudence consistently affirms that freedom of expression represents a primary safeguard against the arbitrary exercise of power. It enables individuals to articulate dissent, to contest authority, and to participate meaningfully in public deliberation. Such a safeguard necessarily requires formal legal protection embedded within an institutional framework that includes mechanisms of accountability and the presence of legitimate political opposition.

From this starting point, a crucial question arises: to what extent can the constitutional protections traditionally associated with freedom of expression be transposed into the digital sphere, particularly in relation to online disinformation? In purely abstract terms, the answer appears straightforward. Constitutional rights are formulated in general terms and apply broadly to all communicative acts irrespective of medium. Excluding digital expression from the scope of constitutional protection would therefore be incompatible with the universalist orientation of constitutional guarantees. This conclusion finds further support in an extensive body of legal scholarship and case law that recognizes the Internet as a space essential to the development of personal autonomy, social relations, and civic participation. Digital technologies now play a vital role in shaping the conditions under which individuals engage in public discourse, acquire information, and exercise democratic rights. Any regulatory intervention that affects speech in the digital sphere must therefore be scrutinized through the lens of constitutional principles that govern freedom of expression across all domains of social life.

However, this observation does not exhaust the inquiry. While it is clear that freedom of expression applies fully to digital communication, the specific characteristics of the online environment may require adjustments to the normative frameworks through which this right is interpreted and implemented. The distinctive features of digital communication—its speed, reach, algorithmic mediation, and reliance on privately governed platforms—raise questions that traditional legal tools may not adequately address. The unprecedented scale at which harm can be produced through the circulation of false information, the opacity of content moderation practices, and the concentration of communicative power in the hands of large technology companies all contribute to a regulatory landscape that differs markedly from that of the analog world. Consequently, one must ask whether the interpretation of freedom of expression requires recalibration in order to account for these new conditions—always provided that any such recalibration remains faithful to the constitutional constraints within which it must operate.

This conceptual framework guided the empirical and multinational components of the research. By examining in detail the legal systems of a significant number of Member States of the European Union, the research seeks to illustrate how different jurisdictions have confronted the challenge of online disinformation while maintaining fidelity to their constitutional traditions. The aim is to demonstrate that online disinformation is not a phenomenon whose regulation necessitates the creation of an entirely new legal paradigm. Rather, it is a challenge that must be incorporated into the existing constitutional structures governing expressive freedom, albeit with due recognition of the unique characteristics that distinguish digital communication from its analog counterpart.

The analysis of the national reports reveals a heterogeneous regulatory landscape. Although all Member States share a common commitment to protecting freedom of expression, the strategies adopted to address online disinformation differ in important respects. These differences reflect variations in constitutional traditions, historical experiences with information regulation, institutional arrangements, and political cultures. Nevertheless, a common tension emerges across all jurisdictions: the challenge of simultaneously ensuring the effective mitigation of harmful disinformation while safeguarding the constitutional essence of expressive freedom. This tension is particularly acute in the digital environment, where efforts to suppress harmful content clearly risk producing excessive or disproportionate restrictions on speech, and where the boundary between disinformation and unpopular or controversial opinion remains inherently difficult to draw.

European Union law plays a pivotal role in shaping the national regulatory responses examined in this study. Over the past decade, the EU has developed a multi-layered regulatory framework aimed at addressing the systemic risks posed by online disinformation. Instruments such as the Digital Services Act, the Code of Practice on Disinformation, and numerous communications and guidelines issued by the European Commission provide Member States with normative reference points that encourage harmonization while allowing for national adaptation. These instruments promote transparency obligations, platform accountability, cross-sector cooperation, and the protection of fundamental rights as central pillars of the EU's approach. At the same time, they leave considerable discretion to national authorities, resulting in a diverse array of regulatory models across the Union. Such discretion clearly emerges in the national reports.

Another feature emerging from the reports deserves special attention. A close reading of the chapters of this volume suggests that the legal solutions currently in place should be regarded as provisional rather than definitive. They represent initial or intermediate attempts to address a phenomenon that is both complex and rapidly evolving. The challenges posed by online disinformation—including the emergence of deepfakes, coordinated inauthentic behavior, algorithmic amplification, and microtargeted political advertising—are not yet fully understood even by the most advanced regulatory bodies and research institutions. Moreover, technological developments continue to evolve at a pace that outstrips the capacity of legal frameworks to respond effectively. In this context, national regulatory efforts remain fluid, contingent, and subject to ongoing revision.

Indeed, this provisional character may be regarded as one of the most relevant findings of the research. The analysis does not reveal a definitive or comprehensive legal solution to the problem of online disinformation. Instead, it exposes a regulatory landscape characterized by experimentation, incremental adaptation, and a deliberate caution informed by the need to preserve constitutional commitments. Member States are striving to craft regulatory responses that address genuine threats to democratic processes while avoiding undue interference with the fundamental principle of freedom of expression. Some emphasize cooperative mechanisms involving online platforms; others focus on transparency requirements, public awareness campaigns, media literacy, or administrative oversight. Across these diverse approaches, however, a shared recognition persists: the regulation of online disinformation must be carefully calibrated to ensure that the constitutional values underpinning democratic society are fully preserved.

Looking forward, the effectiveness and durability of the current regulatory frameworks will become more apparent in the coming years. As case law develops, as empirical evidence accumulates, and as technological and social conditions evolve, it will become possible to evaluate which of the existing measures have successfully mitigated the harms associated with online disinformation and which have proven inadequate or incompatible with constitutional principles. Until then, the legal system must remain adaptable, guided by constitutional norms and interpretations that must strive to be responsive to the unprecedented challenges introduced by the digital transformation of public discourse.

Pisa, Italy

Paolo Passaglia
paolo.passaglia@unipi.it

Contents

Introduction: The Notion of Disinformation and the Online World—Short Notes

Domenico Notaro

Abstract The chapter introduces the topic by presenting the issues addressed by the panel regarding the concept of disinformation and its potential legal implications. A description of disinformation, interpreted according to social parameters, is contrasted with a more detailed definition of the characteristics that can confer illicit relevance to the phenomenon. The primary focus is obviously on the potential use of online communication systems (particularly when they leverage artificial intelligence technologies) to commit acts of disinformation. The specific ways in which these practices are implemented and their growing threat to citizens could more easily justify the use of legal remedies, both preventive and punitive. However, these practices require careful discussion to select the cases in which to intervene and identify the most appropriate tools to respond, possibly including criminal law. The discussion concludes with a brief overview of the criminal provisions currently available in Italian law to counter the disinformation practices most easily implemented online.

It can certainly be said that defining the phenomenon of disinformation is as important as it is complex: information and disinformation are interconnected, and sometimes it is difficult to distinguish one from the other. Depending on the time period in which the news is spread and the beliefs shared by people, sometimes information may be both useful and useless (harmful): this perception depends also on the interpretation that people subsequently give to the news, based on their culture and sensitivity. Anyway, we must try to define the phenomenon under consideration to discuss measures that can be adopted to address it when appropriate. A likely advantage is that—presumably—the topic we are addressing presents connotations and challenges common to various national (and supranational) systems, especially when it comes to disinformation arising from the use of electronic tools—so we talk about online dis-information—, since thanks to them (the electronic tools), people

D. Notaro (✉)
Department of Law, Pisa University, Pisa, Italy
e-mail: domenico.notaro@unipi.it

P. Passaglia (ed.), *European Legal Perspectives on Online Disinformation*, Ius Gentium: Comparative Perspectives on Law and Justice 140,
https://doi.org/10.1007/978-3-032-25785-7_1

around the world interact, facing the same challenges, risks and obstacles. Therefore, the discussion on this topic from a comparative perspective appears interesting and very open.

When trying to identify effective cases of disinformation, it is essential to distinguish between disinformation as a *social* phenomenon and disinformation as a *legal* phenomenon.

As a social phenomenon, disinformation is considered relevant because it proves dysfunctional (dis-useful) with respect to the role recognized for information in connection with freedom (and need) of expression: without information, there is no discussion or exchange of ideas among people, and the very ability of individuals to choose their own behaviour is hindered. Disinformation as a social phenomenon includes (or can be compared to) cases of "misinformation" and "malinformation", which are often evoked alongside actual disinformation: in all these phenomena, we witness a use of communication that is not adequate to the social role of information.

As a legal phenomenon, otherwise, disinformation could constitute a problem deserving of legal responses, given its potential impact on the interests protected by legal systems. From this perspective, disinformation is distinguished from misinformation and malinformation. There are common views on the specific characteristics of disinformation as a legal problem: it occurs when false information is disseminated by the author with the knowledge of its falsity and with the intent to mislead interlocutors or recipients, and when its communication may offend other individuals or the public. As is well known, this definition appears in the European Commission's Action Plan specifically dedicated to combating disinformation.[1] These characteristics would highlight a phenomenon supported by a reprehensible attitude of the author of the disinformation and by recognizable undesirable effects—what in criminal law jargon are called "disvalue of action" and "disvalue of event"—so that legal remedies could be justified. Yet disinformation currently lacks specific legal recognition (in legislative texts) as a relevant phenomenon in itself; a first question to ask, therefore, is whether, in the long run, it should be considered so relevant.

From this perspective, it is necessary to consider whether the phenomenon's legal relevance can emerge only when disinformation targets and affects public or collective legal interests (state security, public order, electoral interests, common health, etc.) or also when it affects individual interests. It is perhaps in the answer to this question that the greatest differences in perspective between national legal systems can emerge. At the same time, the question is whether disinformation deserves to be considered an unpleasant phenomenon only when it affects certain interests and involves situations that more clearly offend them in terms of harm or danger. But here comes into consideration the other question of the unlawful relevance of disinformation as such in relation to its content or because it offends other interests. From this perspective, if disinformation deserves a legal response when it undermines other values, then it could also be countered when it offends individual interests. Another

[1] European Commission contribution to the European Council, *Action Plan against Disinformation*, 5 December 2018, available at: https://commission.europa.eu, last accessed 2025/12/08.

question, therefore, concerns the methods and measures to counter the phenomenon of disinformation: regulatory instruments, preventive measures, punitive sanctions.

The issues above mentioned are much more important when it comes to *online* disinformation. The reasons are well known, and they all stem from the technological capabilities of the online resources: (a) thanks to these tools, it is easier for people to create and spread disinformation, and these communications become much more insidious; (b) such communications can be spread much more quickly and widely than traditional ones, thus causing enormously greater damage; (c) given the context in which on-line information circulates, it is more difficult to counteract with traditional legal measures, and it is very difficult to remedy the damage caused. The birth and the development of artificial intelligence tools have increased the dangerousness of disinformation practices as they are more capable of deceiving the recipients and of conditioning public opinion in their own interests: the so-called deep fakes images and videos express this character very well. Given the above elements, it seems appropriate to *first* ask whether online disinformation practices can acquire and justify specific relevance as a legal problem, deserving of its own regulation. *Second*, we can discuss what types of requirements are necessary to assess the harmfulness of disinformation. From this perspective, it may be important to distinguish and select the online techniques used to spread messages, considering, for example, whether a false message is contained in a deepfake video or intended to be highlighted via a newsfeed feature.[2] Furthermore, when examining the practical application of the rules, it may be relevant, for example, whether the false message is followed by numerous "likes" or "posts", as Italian judges have ruled in several cases,[3] to assess the likely effects of the harmful message on readers. *Third*, it is important to determine which public or private actors (individuals or groups) can be charged with countering (preventatively or reactively) disinformation practices, so that they can be held accountable for violations of disinformation regulations. Here the well-known question arises as to the opportunity and conditions for asserting the liability of Service Providers for the content published and distributed on Internet sites.[4]

Based on these observations, we can therefore argue that, in some areas where the potential effects of distorting public opinion are more likely, the use of electronic resources makes (real) disinformation practices so fearsome as to require suitable and effective legal remedies. It is the case of communications that interfere with the conduct of electoral contests, the dissemination of information that undermines fundamental human values (such as dignity or collective health in the face of pandemic dangers), and the dissemination of ideas that attack the democratic foundations of our communities. Given these premises, online disinformation might also be considered illegal; however, it is still unclear what the most appropriate and effective

[2] Supreme Court of Cassation, Section I, December 6, 2021, n. 4534.

[3] Supreme Court of Cassation, Section V, September 25, 2017, n. 55418.

[4] Fiorinelli, G. (2022); Braschi, S. (2023); Guerini, T. (2020b): 2.

legal remedies are to combat it. Beyond regulatory provisions,[5] for example, it seems rather unlikely that criminal remedies are adequate to combat fake news.[6]

If we look at Italian criminal law, among the European systems, we find only a few provisions that criminalise disinformation practices: among these, the crimes of "publication or dissemination of false, exaggerated or tendentious news, capable of disturbing public order" (Article 656 of the Criminal Code) and "spreading false alarm among public authorities" (Article 658 of the Criminal Code) are often cited[7]; further crimes of political and economic "defeatism" (Articles 265 and 267 of the Criminal Code), can also be mentioned, but these only concern wartime and have therefore never been applied. According to the prevailing opinion of experts, disinformation cannot constitute a crime unless it is accompanied by an element of danger or is followed by a further harmful event. It is still possible to detect a potential crime of (pure) disinformation in the case of "propaganda and incitement to crime on the grounds of racial, ethnic, and religious discrimination" (Article 604-*bis* of the Criminal Code), which also punishes the dissemination of ideas based on racial or ethnic superiority or hatred. A true form of disinformation emerges when the propaganda is based, in whole or in part, on the denial, gross minimization, or apologia of the Holocaust or the crime of genocide, crimes against humanity, or war crimes.[8] Although this provision represents the clearest hypothesis of a crime of pure disinformation, it must also be emphasized that the penalty itself is linked to the prerequisite of the dissemination (through propaganda or incitement) of ideas that are in themselves illegal due to their discriminatory content, because the ideological contribution of so-called "negationism" constitutes only an aggravating factor of the aforementioned crime of propaganda.[9]

Furthermore, disinformation can constitute one of the ways to commit criminal offenses that involve broader forms of harm to third-party interests: for example, defamation (Article 595 of the Criminal Code) and false accusation (Article 368 of the Criminal Code), which punish various acts that harm the honor and reputation of others or that mislead the judicial authority in the exercise of its power of investigation and ascertainment of criminal liability. With particular regard to the crime of defamation, the Constitutional Court[10] has highlighted that so-called "disinformation campaigns"—characterized by the dissemination of allegations seriously damaging to the victim's reputation and committed with the perpetrators' knowledge of the objective falsity of the allegations, against individuals of public importance—represent one of those (few) exceptional cases (along with incitement to hatred and violence on racial or ethnic grounds) that deserve to be punished with a prison

[5] De Simone, F. (2018).

[6] Guerini, T. (2020a); De Flammineis, S (2020).

[7] Birritteri, E. (2020).

[8] Fronza, E. (2018).

[9] Macchia, A. (2022).

[10] Constitutional Court, July 12, 2021, n. 150.

sentence, even after the European Court of Human Rights[11] and the Italian Constitutional Court itself have recognized that defamation should generally be punished only by a fine, so as not to excessively discourage the activity of journalists by reducing ("chilling") their role of "watch-dogs" in democratic societies.

The rapid development of artificial intelligence has recently pushed the Italian Parliament to introduce new provisions and new types of crimes to combat innovative forms of harm also linked to disinformation practices. Among these provisions is the "Illicit dissemination of content generated or altered with artificial intelligence systems" (Article 612-*quater* of the Criminal Code), which came into force after a lengthy debate among experts.[12] This offence punishes anyone who, without the consent of the interested party, uses, transfers, publishes, or disseminates "deep fake" videos, photos, or audio, generated by artificial intelligence and capable of deceiving others, unfairly harming another person or a public authority. Deep fakes are considered highly insidious means of deceiving people, given their ability to create a false (and indistinguishable) appearance of reality, even in the most immediately perceptible aspects such as voice, facial expressions, and gestures. Therefore, they are much more suitable than other tools for carrying out public or individual disinformation operations or campaigns. Although the new criminal offence represents an interesting opportunity to qualify the misleading use of online tools, the criminal provision also requires the proof of damage caused to the subjects portrayed or abused by the document produced with the help of artificial intelligence.[13]

While there are numerous issues and challenges related to disinformation and new technologies, these must also be addressed at the legal and regulatory levels. The evolution of technological resources is increasingly interfering with communication systems, making it more difficult to ensure that information processes are useful to communities and individuals. It is therefore necessary to consider the possibility that the factors influencing communication processes are no longer simply malicious, but actually harmful to fundamental interests. This awareness has now gained traction among national legislators, and it is likely that in the future, legal instruments will increasingly be forced to adapt to new forms of aggression that exploit the weaknesses of modern communication systems. Perhaps it can be said that the way has been opened.

References

Birritteri, E. (2020): La disinformazione tra politica e diritto. Dimensione istituzionale, strategie preventive e dinamiche punitive, Diritto penale contemporaneo. Rivista trimestrale, (4), 317 (2020), available at: https://dpc-rivista-trimestrale.criminaljusticenetwork.eu, last accessed 2025/12/08.

[11] European Court of Human Rights, September 24, 2013, n. 43612/10, Belpietro v. Italy, § 115; European Court of Human Rights, March 7, 2019, n. 22350/13, Sallusti v. Italy, § 59.

[12] Fiorinelli, G. (2024).

[13] Caletti, G. M. (2024).

Braschi, S. (2023): Il nuovo Regolamento sui servizi digitali: quale futuro per la responsabilità degli Internet Service Provider?, Diritto penale e processo, (3), 367–375 (2023).

Caletti, G. M. (2024): *Habeas corpus* digitale. Lo statuto penale dell'immagine corporea tra privatezza e riservatezza, 160–162, Giappichelli, Torino, (2024).

Constitutional Court, July 12, 2021, n. 150.

De Flammineis, S. (2020): Diritto penale, beni giuridici collettivi nella sfida delle fake news: principio di offensività ed emergenze, Sistema penale, (6), 141–146, (2020), available at: https://www.sistemapenale.it, last accessed 2025/12/08.

De Simone, F. (2018): '*Fake news*', '*post truth*', '*hate speech*': nuovi fenomeni sociali alla prova del diritto penale, Archivio penale. Rivista web, (1), 16–42 (2018), available at: https://archiviopenale.it, last accessed 2025/12/08.

European Commission (2018) contribution to the European Council, *Action Plan against Disinformation*, 5 December 2018, available at: https://commission.europa.eu, last accessed 2025/12/08.

European Court of Human Rights, September 24, 2013, n. 43612/10, Belpietro v. Italy, § 115; European Court of Human Rights, March 7, 2019, n. 22350/13, Sallusti v. Italy, § 59.

Fiorinelli, G. (2022): L'attuale ruolo dei provider nella società digitale: modelli di responsabilità penale, La legislazione penale, (4), 258–286 (2022), available at: https://www.lalegislazionepenale.eu, last accessed 2025/12/08.

Fiorinelli, G. (2024): La violenza mediata dalla tecnologia. Dogmatica, profili politico-criminali e interpretazione della nozione di violenza nel diritto penale delle tecnologie digitali, 302–305, Giappichelli, Torino (2024).

Fronza, E. (2018): Il negazionismo di terza generazione. Dalla tutela della memoria alla tutela della verità?, Diritto penale contemporaneo. Rivista trimestrale, (4), 333, (2018), available at: https://dpc-rivista-trimestrale.criminaljusticenetwork.eu, last accessed 2025/12/08.

Guerini, T. (2020a): *Fake news* e diritto penale. La manipolazione del consenso nelle democrazie liberali, 194–200, Giappichelli, Torino, (2020).

Guerini, T. (2020b): La tutela penale della libertà di manifestazione del pensiero nell'epoca delle fake news e delle infodemie, Discrimen 15 June 2020, 63–66, available at: https://discrimen.it, last accessed 2025/12/08.

Macchia, A. (2020): Negazionismo, discriminazione e crimini d'odio: verso nuove frontiere?, Cassazione penale, 62, (1), 30, (2022).

Supreme Court of Cassation, Section V, September 25, 2017, n. 55418.

Supreme Court of Cassation, Section I, December 6, 2021, n. 4534.

The European Union's Legal Approach to Online Disinformation

Claas Friedrich Germelmann

Abstract Online disinformation poses a threat to the integrity of the democratic discourse and to fundamental rights. This challenge has been addressed by the EU legislator in a variety of legal acts and other measures in order to develop a working and coherent strategy for this pressing problem. The different legal acts and self-regulatory instruments address the providers of intermediary services and in particular platforms with significant market power. Some measures target illegal content, while other address legal, but potentially harmful content, which is untrue or misleading. For particularly powerful market players, the EU legislation focuses on the level of risk when dealing with different forms of online disinformation. Apart from that, it attempts to improve the situation for independent and pluralistic media in order to maintain a reliable information basis for the exchange of arguments and opinions in a democratic state. When adopting various restrictive legal measures, the EU is bound by the fundamental rights that require a balancing of the affected rights and interests, which is a complex and difficult endeavour in the concrete case.

I wish to thank Mr Danny Prieske, Leibniz Universität Hannover, for his valuable contribution and the exchange on the topic. All mistakes remain, of course, mine.

C. F. Germelmann (✉)
Leibniz Universität Hannover, Juristische Fakultät, Hannover, Germany
e-mail: claas.germelmann@jura.uni-hannover.de

P. Passaglia (ed.), *European Legal Perspectives on Online Disinformation*, Ius Gentium: Comparative Perspectives on Law and Justice 140,
https://doi.org/10.1007/978-3-032-25785-7_2

1 Introduction

Online disinformation is a major threat both to democratic political systems and to individual rights. As a consequence, it has received growing attention from the European institutions.[1] In the last years, the European Union has taken a multi-faceted approach to counter online disinformation. The dangers of manipulative content in the modern political discourse can hardly be overestimated. The fast development of technology, the constantly growing role of online services that disseminate information with a large range across borders, and the powerful position of gatekeepers that are able to control and influence the flow of information[2] make it difficult to limit and mitigate the effects of any untrue and misleading information. This is particularly relevant for the political sphere where the manipulation of information has always been a means of attaining or exercising power. A comparable, but less palpable situation exists in economic matters, where the rules on advertising have traditionally and quite successfully tried to contain the most detrimental forms of disinformation. While it will never be—and has never been—possible to guarantee an unreserved integrity of the political discourse and given the fact that disinformation has always been an issue in political life, the current settings of the information landscape make it easy for corrosive attempts to infiltrate and disintegrate a reasonable political discussion by means of powerful providers of disinformation in the sphere of the internet. Apart from that, in a free and democratic society, providing and receiving information is strongly protected by the fundamental rights which makes it difficult for a state to interfere and control the integrity of the facts that are being proposed and exchanged. This leads to a number of questions relating to online disinformation, spanning from the problem of who should be in charge of protecting the legitimate interest of society and of individuals to retain a fundamentally reliable system for the exchange of information. The most obvious choices are either the EU and its Member States or the private actors concerned. Furthermore, the proportionality standards that a public authority has to meet when restricting the exchange of information on grounds of disinformation have to be clarified. This rather complicated challenge has been addressed by the EU legislator in a variety of measures in order to develop a working and coherent strategy for the pressing problem of online disinformation.

---

[1] Joint Communication from the Commission and the High Representative to the European Parliament and the Council "Joint Framework on countering hybrid threats: a European Union response", JOIN (2016) 18 final, pp. 4 et seq.; Communications from the Commission to the European Parliament, the Council, the European Economic and Social Committee and the Committee of the Regions "Tackling online disinformation: a European Approach", COM (2018) 236 final; "On the European democracy action plan", COM (2020) 790 final, pp. 17 et seq.; "on Defence of Democracy", COM (2023) 630 final, pp. 13 et seq. See also Cavaliere (2022), p. 481.

[2] *Cf.* De Gregorio and Pollicino (2025), pp. 450 et seq.

2 The Notion of Disinformation

In several recent documents, the Commission has laid out a comprehensive approach to the problem of disinformation.[3] However, in European Union legislation, there is neither a legal definition nor an explicit reference to the term of "disinformation". The only place where it appears in the different legal acts are the recitals,[4] which are significant for interpreting the rules and provisions, but which are not in themselves binding. Hence, there is neither a precise and conclusive notion of disinformation nor a legally defined concept in EU law.

Nevertheless, the European Union understands the notion of disinformation broadly.[5] In its European democracy action plan, the European Commission addresses not only disinformation in the narrow sense, but also misinformation, information influence operations and foreign interference in the information space.[6] According to the definition as proposed by the Commission, disinformation relates to false or inaccurate representations that intend to mislead the users, while misinformation lacks the intentional element even though the incorrect content, from an objective point of view, can still be harmful. Information influence operations and foreign interferences share the element of a coordinated action with the objective to spread disinformation, which is often conducted by state actors and can constitute a part of hybrid attacks.

The legal acts addressing disinformation cover both legal and illegal information. They are therefore not dependent on the categories in which domestic law puts the relevant content. Obviously, drafting the Member States' obligations with a view to combating illegal contents might be easier than those concerning legal information, which nevertheless is misleading. The rationale lies in the fact that the current threats to democracy and fundamental rights not only stem from illegal content, but also follow from basically legal, but misleading information. This is particularly true when disinformation is being spread intentionally or even in the context of a hostile strategy by a foreign actor. The specific danger that nowadays lies in misleading, but formally legal information is rooted in the significant reach that current information technology can achieve and the high degree of concentration and market power of platforms and gatekeepers in the online world. In the core legal act in this field, the Digital Services Act (DSA), the majority of the service providers only face measures that target illegal content.[7] Only the duties of Very Large Online Platforms and Very

---

[3] Communication from the Commission to the European Parliament, the Council, the European Economic and Social Committee and the Committee of the Regions "Tackling online disinformation: a European Approach", COM(2018) 236 final, pp. 6 et seq.

[4] Peukert (2023), p. 279.

[5] For an overview of the variety in the terminology, *cf.* Peukert (2023), pp. 279 et seq.; Cavaliere (2022), pp. 484 et seq.; Caruso (2025); Husovec (2024), pp. 48 et seq.; Jungherr (2024), pp. 9 et seq. with a more narrow view.

[6] Communication from the Commission to the European Parliament, the Council, the European Economic and Social Committee and the Committee of the Regions "On the European democracy action plan", COM (2020) 790 final, pp. 17 et seq.

[7] *Cf.*, in more detail, Kuhlmann and Trute (2022), pp. 119 et seq.

Large Online Search Engines (VLOPs and VLOSEs) also cover systemic risks of formally legal disinformation, including actual or foreseeable negative effects for the exercise of fundamental rights, the democratic discourse, electoral processes, public security, the prevention of gender-based violence, the protection of public health and minors and serious negative consequences to the person's physical and mental well-being.[8] These more far-reaching measures are contained in Sect. 5 of the DSA, and in particular in Articles 34 and 35 DSA.[9] The European legislator therefore tries to take an approach that covers the majority of acts which are most likely to contain a danger for the democratic system or for fundamental rights.

The broad concept of disinformation leads to the necessity to distinguish it from comparable, but different phenomena so that legislation can be targeted and meaningful. This is even more relevant as the competences of the EU, under the principle of conferral,[10] require a sufficiently precise delineation of the subject of regulation. The distinction mainly relates to content that is illegal under national law and which falls under more specific measures. A major example is the legal framework for content that, in different legal orders, is described as "hate speech". The purpose of the rules and measures against disinformation is generally not only targeted at protecting individual rights and interests, but follows a more all-encompassing approach that relates to the integrity of the democratic discourse and the exchange of information. A particular focus lies on the integrity of the elections.[11] Even though the EU measures that combat disinformation are meant to protect fundamental rights as well as democratic procedures, they are rather conceived so as to prevent more general and systemic dangers for the state and the society, whereas phenomena like hate speech aim at protecting personality rights like personal honour from concrete and well-defined dangers. In any event, it cannot be excluded that the different forms of disinformation will, to a certain extent, overlap with concepts that are similar. However, it has to remain clear that the core objective of the fight against disinformation is the peaceful coexistence in a democratic society. Even though disinformation may also affect human rights and can, under certain circumstances, amount to hate speech, the two sets of rules and their purposes nevertheless differ as disinformation is the broader topic.

3 Sources of Law

As a consequence of this rather broad understanding of the notion and the different forms of online disinformation, it is difficult to establish a comprehensive and systematically coordinated legal toolbox for combating its negative effects on individual

---

[8] Article 34 para. 1 subpara. 2 DSA. See the examples in Bayer (2024b), pp. 20 et seq.; Peukert (2023), pp. 281 et seq.

[9] See, in more detail, *infra*, Sect. 4.2.

[10] See, *infra*, Sect. 3.2.

[11] See, *infra*, Sect. 3.1.3.

rights and the democratic process. On the contrary, the Union has taken quite a few initiatives in order to counter the adverse effects of online disinformation that are rather diverse and sometimes even stem from different regulatory approaches. They all range within the limits of primary Union law and in particular the fundamental rights that set up the framework for the rules which intend to prevent and restrict online disinformation. The major part of the Union's attempts to combat online disinformation consists of binding secondary law rules which are not always uniquely designed to cover online disinformation, but encompass broader fields like *e.g.* digital services in general.[12] In addition to the secondary law provisions, the European Commission resorts to soft law measures and policies in order to strengthen the resilience of the society and the individual user of digital services against the effects of online disinformation.[13]

3.1 Fundamental Rights Framework

The fundamental rights of the EU determine the framework for the Union's strategy against online disinformation. The information landscape is shaped by fundamental rights on different levels and in different aspects. The legislator has to implement their standards when drafting legal acts and both the EU and the Member States authorities have to follow them when putting the measures into action (Article 51 para. 1 CFR). The fundamental rights dimension of information as well as its relevance for the democratic process of decision-making lead to a proportionality test that is particularly strict when it comes to interferences with the right to freedom of speech or the right to receive information.[14] In setting the primary law framework for the EU measures on disinformation, not only the Charter of Fundamental Rights (CFR) of the EU has to be considered, but also the comparable provisions in the European Convention on Human Rights (ECHR) according to Article 52 para. 3 CFR. This proves to be particularly relevant in the context of disinformation since, compared to the case law of the Court of Justice of the European Union (CJEU), the case law of the European Court of Human Rights (ECtHR) is more extensive in this field. Although the majority of the decisions do not relate to cases having an online background, several basic lines can be deduced from the case law.

Fundamental rights are the core determining factor in the balancing act between the protective interest of the EU policy concerning disinformation and the legitimate interests of the market actors like service providers or online platforms which stem both from their fundamental freedoms and their fundamental rights. There is an

[12] *Infra*, Sect. 4.1.

[13] *Cf. supra*, note 2.

[14] *Cf.* ECtHR, 7 December 1976, no. 5493/72, § 49—*Handyside v. the United Kingdom*; 25 June 1992, no 13778/88, § 63—*Thorgeirson v. Iceland*; ECtHR (GC), 10 December 2007, no. 69698/01, § 105—*Stoll v. Switzerland*; ECtHR, 25 July 2019, no. 47542/07, § 53—*Brzeziński v. Poland*. See also, in more detail, Marauhn and Jaś-Nowopolska (2023), §§ 40 et seq.

inbuilt conflict between the objective of countering disinformation and the protection of fundamental rights, such as the freedom to conduct a business according to Article 16 CFR of platforms and other intermediaries as well as media outlets, the right to freedom of expression, and the right to receive information according to Article 11 para. 1 CFR.[15] The interest of the EU to restrict the potential impact of online disinformation also has a fundamental rights background, especially when disinformation can result in serious dangers for individual persons.[16] Furthermore, it intends to safeguard the integrity of the information that is available to everyone as a basis for the democratic process and the discourse in society. Media plurality (Article 11 para. 2 CFR) plays an important role in this context, too. The balancing act between these legal guarantees becomes even more difficult for the EU legislator if not only content that is clearly illegal or untruthful is hit with sanctions, but if permissible content is concerned that does not infringe any legal rules, but creates a danger or a risk by providing potentially misleading facts and opinions that have to be treated as online disinformation.

3.1.1 The Guarantee of Free Speech

In a free and democratic system, the dissemination of information is covered by both the guarantee of free speech and the right to unfettered information that are enshrined in Article 10 para. 1 ECHR and Article 11 CFR. Even though information that is untrue and not in good faith is not normally protected by these provisions,[17] it seems to be extremely difficult to distinguish it precisely from opinions that are related to these facts and which, as a matter of principle, enjoy the protection of the right to free speech. The only option to exclude it a priori from this protection lies in the prohibition of the abuse of this right as provided for in Article 17 ECHR and Article 54 CFR. These restrictions, however, are of limited relevance in this field as they require rather clear-cut cases and cannot be invoked lightly by the public authorities or the legislator.[18] This is even more true in the area which is covered by the freedom of expression as one of the core values and rights in a free and democratic system.

---

[15] *Cf.* De Gregorio and Pollicino (2025), pp. 453 et seq.; Jungherr (2024), pp. 14 et seq.; Shattock (2023), pp. 1326 et seq. *Cf.* CJEU, 8 December 2022, Case C-460/20—*Google (Déréférencement d'un contenu prétendument inexact)* on the weighing-up exercise between the rights according to Articles 7 and 8 CFR, on the one hand, and Article 11 CFR on the other relating to inaccurate information in the application of Art. 17 (3) lit. a GDPR.

[16] In particular the protection of fundamental rights such as the right to life (*cf.* Bayer [2024b], pp. 20 et seq.) and the integrity of democratic mechanisms, especially elections (*cf.* Datzer and Lonardo [2023], p. 752).

[17] *Cf.* ECtHR, 29 April 2014, no. 23605/09, § 47—*Salumäki v. Finland*. See, in more detail, Cavaliere (2022), pp. 505 et seq.

[18] *Cf.* ECtHR (GC), 23 September 1998, no. 24662/94, § 47—*Lehideux and Isorni v. France*; ECtHR, 24 June 2003, no. 65831/01—*Garaudy v. France*; ECtHR (GC), 16 March 2006, no. 58278/00, § 99—*Ždanoka v. Latvia*; 15 October 2015, no. 27510/08, §§ 113 et seq.—*Perinçek v. Switzerland*; ECtHR, 20 December 2022, no. 63539/19, § 61—*Zemmour v. France*. See, in more detail, Ehlers and Germelmann (2023a), § 92 and (2023b), § 118.

Therefore, the prohibition of abuse will mainly target statements which are directed against the values underlying the Convention,[19] but not for any kind of false or misleading facts, even if they can contribute to damaging the reliability or the proper functioning of the democratic discourse in society. However, if disinformation is being used in order to directly and demonstrably attack a right that is guaranteed by the Convention or the Charter with the aim of destroying or severely damaging it, it might lose its protection for being an abusive action in the concrete case.

In any event, the fundamental rights systems of the Convention and the Charter are not defenceless against actions that impede the democratic process and tarnish the factual basis of opinions and their exchange. The freedom of speech and the right to information can be restricted under Article 10 para. 2 ECHR and Article 52 CFR, if there are sufficient grounds of justification and if the proportionality test is met which, according to Articles 10 para. 2 ECHR and 52 para. 3 CFR, includes the requirement that the restriction is necessary in a democratic society. This may leave a relatively narrow scope only; however, the case law of the ECtHR has acknowledged that there are a number of matters of general interest and individual rights that can justify a restriction of the right to free speech if untrue and misleading information is concerned. This case law can be extended to the modern problem of online disinformation even if it originates in a time before the internet became prevalent.

3.1.2 Pluralism

It is obvious that pluralism is a fundamental requirement for a free society and for a democratic system.[20] This has been pointed out clearly by the ECtHR.[21] Hence, measures that contribute to safeguarding pluralism in general can constitute valid grounds of justification under Article 10 para. 2 ECHR and Articles 11 and 52 CFR. In a democratic and pluralistic society, media freedom is particularly important.[22] As Article 11 para. 2 CFR rightly emphasises, media freedom cannot be detached from media pluralism. Hence, the right to freedom of expression contains a "positive obligation to put in place an appropriate legislative and administrative framework to guarantee effective pluralism" for the state.[23] This obligation also applies to the online sphere where nowadays the majority of media services is being provided. In any event, the legislator has a wide margin of appreciation and a significant political

---

[19] ECtHR, 24 June 2003, no. 65831/01—*Garaudy v. France* (concerning the denial of the Holocaust).

[20] ECtHR, 7 December 1976, no. 5493/72, § 49—*Handyside v. the United Kingdom*; ECtHR (GC), 17 February 2004, no. 44158/98, §§ 89 et seq.—*Gorzelik and Others v. Poland*.

[21] ECtHR (GC), 13 February 2003, nos. 41340/98 and others, §§ 88 et seq.—*Refah Partisi (the Welfare Party) and Others v. Turkey*.

[22] ECtHR (GC), 5 April 2022, no. 48470/12, §§ 186 et seq.—*NIT S.R.L. v. the Republic of Moldova*; CJEU, 3 February 2021, Case C-555/19, §§ 54 et seq.—*Fussl Modestraße Mayr*.

[23] ECtHR (GC), 5 April 2022, no. 48470/12, § 186—*NIT S.R.L. v. the Republic of Moldova*.

discretion as to which protective measures are to be chosen and how they are to be implemented, provided that they are fair and not arbitrary.[24]

3.1.3 The Integrity of Democratic Elections

Equally important is the protection of the integrity of democratic elections and the defence of the personality rights of the candidates against false information. The ECtHR has ruled that this necessity can serve as a ground for justifying interferences with the right to freedom of expression under Article 10 ECHR.[25] According to the case law, positive obligations of the states to protect the fairness of elections follow from Article 3 of the First Protocol to the ECHR[26]; this includes the protection against disinformation by foreign actors.[27] Even if the Court has not explicitly extended this obligation to interferences from the internal sphere like, *e.g.*, internal political opponents or their supporters, and although it has not had the opportunity to clarify the role and obligations of market actors like platforms, it can be assumed from the Court's reasoning and the underlying values, which it refers to, that this obligation also encompasses disinformation from internal actors within the electoral process. The distinction between foreign interferences and internal actions that can be connected to or serve as a substitute for the foreign player is usually rather difficult to draw. Again, the state disposes of a wide margin of appreciation as to which measures to take.[28] In any event, it has to be borne in mind that the general weight of the guarantee of free speech will normally favour an approach that allows the free exchange of opinions on political matters or topics of general interest, especially in times before elections.[29] Regarding these matters, even statements made in good faith which may lack a sufficient factual basis are protected as legitimate expressions.[30] Therefore, the test whether a measure is necessary in a democratic society and proportionate has to keep in mind both the protection of the integrity of the electoral process and the importance of a free exchange of political views that are both elements of the democratic system.[31]

---

[24] ECtHR (GC), 5 April 2022, no. 48470/12, §§ 193 et seq.—*NIT S.R.L. v. the Republic of Moldova*.

[25] ECtHR, 14 October 2021, no. 20422/15, §§ 47 et seq.—*Staniszewski v. Poland*.

[26] ECtHR, 19 June 2012, no. 29400/05—*Communist Party of Russia and Others v. Russia*.

[27] ECtHR, 22 July 2025, no. 15653/22, §§ 130 et seq., 158 et seq.—*Bradshaw and Others v. the United Kingdom*.

[28] ECtHR, 22 July 2025, no. 15653/22, § 162—*Bradshaw and Others v. the United Kingdom*.

[29] ECtHR, 25 July 2019, no. 47542/07, §§ 53 et seq.—*Brzeziński v. Poland*; 9 January 2007, no. 51744/99, §§ 47 et seq.—*Kwiecień v. Poland*.

[30] ECtHR, 8 July 2008, no. 57659/00, §§ 43 et seq.—*Kita v. Poland*.

[31] *Cf*. ECtHR, 22 July 2025, no. 15653/22, §§ 158 et seq.—*Bradshaw and Others v. the United Kingdom*.

3.2 Union Competences

The Union measures in the area of online disinformation are, for the major part, secondary law which, according to the principle of conferral (Article 5 para. 2 TEU), has to be based on a specific EU competence. In this context, the main competence for measures against online disinformation is the general competence for internal market measures in Article 114 TFEU. As a matter of principle, regulating the permissible contents of online services and the tasks and duties of service providers is a form of market regulation that fits in with the more general objectives of the EU single market. Determining the roles of the market actors is a part of market design. Article 114 TFEU thus provides the legal basis for the measures that will be presented in more detail in the following parts,[32] namely, the DSA, the AVMSD, the AI Act, the EMFA, and the Regulation 2024/900.[33]

However, acting under the common market competence, the powers of the EU to counter disinformation are not unlimited. On the contrary, the fact that the EU uses its powers to harmonise the laws of the Member States in this field and creates new rules in previously unregulated areas like artificial intelligence, makes it necessary for every harmonising provision to prove its relevance for the common market. According to the case law of the CJEU, Article 114 TFEU requires a sufficiently concrete impact for the internal market: The measures must help to reduce market distortions or improve equal market conditions.[34] As far as measures against online disinformation are concerned, their market relevance follows, in particular, from the harmonising effect on the legal requirements for market actors like platforms and service providers. A diverging approach in the Member States that use their protective powers under the law of the fundamental freedoms would lead to unequal market conditions and therefore impede the proper functioning of the common market. However, in implementing its protective interests, the EU rules tend to go rather far and regulate questions that surpass the strict understanding of proper market conditions. Especially regarding the EMFA, Union competences have been a matter of contention as the Union is trying to safeguard not only the integrity of the market in the field of media, but also makes an attempt to protect the freedom of journalistic work and the plurality of the media landscape in general.[35] This is an objective that can be reached partially through rules against market relevant concentrations in the media sector. When it comes to the protection of the journalistic work, its contents and its independence in general, it is more difficult to identify a concrete market distortion if the protective rules of the Member States do not really create an unequal playing field. Hence, it is consequent that the EU rules refrain from a far-reaching harmonising approach in this area and resort to more nuanced solutions including

---

[32] *Infra*, Sects. 4.2–4.6.

[33] *Cf.* Bayer (2024b), pp. 23 et seq.

[34] CJEU, 14 October 2008, Case C-301/06—*Ireland v. European Parliament and Council of the European Union.*

[35] *Cf.* Sznajder (2024), pp. 69 et seq.; Bayer (2024a), pp. 111 et seq.; Malferrari (2023).

some core obligations in terms of substantive law, an institutional framework to support them, and a concentration control on the media market.[36]

Criminal law provisions concerning online content spreading disinformation are rare in EU law. This is partly because of the rather restrictive EU competences in the field of criminal law. Moreover, criminal law solutions are not in the focus of EU law relating to online disinformation.[37] Even though, according to the well settled case law of the CJEU, the main focus of the legal act is decisive[38] so that criminal law provisions can be enacted as parts of a wider set of rules that find a legal basis in a different treaty provision, the focus on regulatory instruments rather than on criminal sanctions prevails. The Anti-SLAPP[39]-Directive 2024/1069 is based on Article 81, para. 2, lit. f TFEU since it mainly deals with procedural law issues.

Restrictive measures to counteract external attempts to disseminate disinformation rely on the sanctions provision in Article 215 TFEU.[40]

4 Legislative Approaches

4.1 Secondary Law and Soft Law (Overview)

During the recent years, the EU has been developing a strategy for combating online disinformation that is detrimental to the exchange of information in a free society, the democratic discourse and the safeguard of fundamental rights in the societies of the Member States. This approach tends to be an integrated one which touches different aspects of disinformation and different situations in which it can appear or have an impact. Several communications by the Commission are laying out this strategy to combat disinformation in the interest of protecting democratic exchange and decision-making.[41] While these strategies form a part of the soft law of the European Commission, the EU legislator has enacted a number of legal acts that address online disinformation in different contexts. The most relevant instrument in the EU legislation is the Digital Services Act (DSA), which partly relies on self-regulation through codes of conduct,[42] including the 2022 Code of Conduct on Disinformation, which, in 2025, has been incorporated into the DSA as a code of conduct according to

---

36 *Cf.*, *infra*, Sect. 4.5.

37 *Cf.* De Gregorio and Pollicino (2025), p. 460.

38 CJEU, 10 December 2002, Case C-491/01, § 94—*British American Tobacco (Investments) und Imperial Tobacco.*

39 Strategic lawsuits against public participation.

40 GCEU, 27 July 2022, Case T-125/22, §§ 46 et seq.—*RT France*; 26 March 2025, Case T-307/22, §§ 41 et seq.—*A2B Connect BV*.

41 *Supra*, note 2.

42 Cavaliere (2022), pp. 486 et seq.

Article 45 DSA.[43] Further legal acts that target, among other threats, online disinformation are the Audiovisual Media Services Directive (AVMSD), the Artificial Intelligence (AI) Act, and the European Media Freedom Act (EMFA). Also relevant in the context for setting the framework of online disinformation are the Regulation 2024/900 on political advertising and the Directive 2024/1069 (Anti-SLAPP-Directive).

4.2 Digital Services Act

The Digital Services Act (DSA)[44] is one of the core legal acts of the EU that regulates the market and the providers of online services taking specifically into account the large service and platform providers that have a dominant position on the market. Even though its scope of application and the objectives of its rules are much broader, it forms the central element of the EU legislation in its attempt to fight online disinformation. According to its structure and its objectives, the DSA focuses on the role of the different market actors and sets up a number of obligations for them. As far as online disinformation is concerned, the DSA contains several requirements that mostly address the relevant market actors, but also affect the national legislator. In order to determine the scope of the obligations of the market actors, the DSA draws a distinction between different kinds of intermediary services, providers of hosting services, providers of online platforms and providers of VLOPs and VLOSEs. According to this distinction, the obligations for the different market actors differ. The DSA focuses in particular on the dominating platforms and service providers and increases the level of their obligations as compared to regular market participants. These obligations relate to mainly procedural measures.

The EU legislator distinguishes between content that is illegal under national or EU law standards, on the one hand, and, on the other hand, content that is only risky, thus creating a differentiated set of obligations. Online disinformation can fall into both categories as it is mainly characterised by being untruthful or misleading and not necessarily in breach of any legal provision. Its predominant danger follows from its disintegrating effects, but it seems virtually impossible to formally outlaw every kind of disinformation that is at least potentially harmful.

4.2.1 Orders to Act Against Illegal Content

According to the DSA, there are specific legal obligations which every intermediary service provider has to abide by if the content is deemed illegal based on national or Union law (Article 3 lit. h DSA) and if the national judicial or administrative

[43] Available online: https://digital-strategy.ec.europa.eu/en/library/code-conduct-disinformation.

[44] Regulation (EU) 2022/2065 of the European Parliament and of the Council of 19 October 2022 on a Single Market For Digital Services and amending Directive 2000/31/EC (Digital Services Act), OJ L 277, 27 October 2022, p. 1.

authorities have already issued an order to the effect that the content has to be removed or otherwise sanctioned.[45] In this case, all intermediary services have to follow these orders of the competent authority "on the basis of the applicable Union law or national law in compliance with Union law" to act against illegal content (Article 9 para. 1 DSA). Article 9 DSA contains the substantive and procedural legal requirements for such an order from the point of view of EU law. As the decisive factor for such an order lies in the illegality of the content, it not only targets disinformation in the narrow, but also in the broader sense if national law deems the content illegal.[46] Generally speaking, the provision covers content which is harmful, but not necessarily untruthful, thereby making it irrelevant if it amounts to disinformation at all. As a consequence of the breach of legal rules and in contrast to the situation of legal, but potentially harmful content, there is no provision concerning any dispute resolution mechanism between the provider and the authority.

4.2.2 General Due Diligence Obligations for All Intermediary Service Providers and Online Hosting Services

As far as legal, but potentially harmful content is concerned, the DSA distinguishes between the general obligations incumbent upon all intermediary service providers and the more specific and more far-reaching obligations that only Very Large Online Platforms (VLOPs) and Very Large Online Search Engines (VLOSEs) have to fulfil.

General Obligations

The general obligations which are compulsory for all providers of intermediary services are contained in the Articles 11–15 DSA and relate to potentially harmful content. They are therefore applicable to online disinformation in the narrow and in the broader sense as can be seen in the systematic structure of the DSA and, in particular, in its Chapter III which aims at creating a "transparent and safe online environment". These general obligations are chiefly institutional in nature (Articles 11–13 DSA) and, furthermore, include the obligation to "act in a diligent, objective and proportionate manner in applying and enforcing the restrictions" set out in the terms and conditions of the service provider in question, having due regard to the affected fundamental rights (Article 14 para. 4 DSA).[47] Hence, the fundamental rights framework as described before[48] determines the scope of the obligation in the concrete case.

---

[45] *Cf.* Kuhlmann and Trute (2022), pp. 118 et seq.

[46] Ó Fathaigh, Helberger and Appelman (2021), p. 15; Shattock (2023), p. 1323.

[47] *Cf.* Shattock (2023), pp. 1324 et seq.; Legner (2024), pp. 104 et seq.; Quintais, Appelman and Ó Fathaigh (2023).

[48] *Supra*, Sect. 3.1.

Further Obligations of Online Hosting Services and of Online Platforms

Online hosting services and online platforms have to fulfil several more detailed obligations under Articles 16–28 DSA.

Notice and Action Mechanism

Hosting service providers including online platforms have to put in place a notice and action mechanism according to Article 16 DSA in which any person or entity may give notice of the content which they consider illegal.[49] This can cover information which falls into the category of online disinformation, but the provision is, naturally, conceived more broadly than that. The providers of hosting services are obliged to take their decisions upon the notice "in a timely, diligent, non-arbitrary and objective manner" (Article 16 para. 6 DSA). There is no exact deadline for the decisions, but according to the rationale of the provisions, the provider has to act as soon as it can reasonably be expected. On top of that, Article 16 para. 3 DSA establishes an incentive for a timely reaction. According to Article 17 para. 1 DSA, the service provider has to notify the affected recipients and, at the same time, list the possible outcomes of the action that are being taken.

In the area of online platforms, the DSA creates a specific role for so-called "trusted flaggers" that have a particular expertise in a given area. If they inform the provider of problematic content, their notice must be given priority and has to be processed without undue delay according to Article 22 DSA. This provision attempts to make the action mechanism more focused and more professional in the case of online platforms and therefore increase its effectiveness.[50] By contrast, a provision on misuse prevention can be found in Article 23 para. 2 DSA. It deals with notices that are manifestly unfounded. It is the result of a balancing between the interest to suppress illegal content on the one hand and the fundamental right of freedom of expression on the other hand.

Internal Complaint-Handling System

Moreover, online platform providers have to provide an internal complaint-handling system according to Article 20 DSA which relates to decisions based on the grounds that content was deemed illegal or that it violated the terms and conditions of the provider (Article 20 para. 1 DSA). Disinformation can fall within both categories. As has been already mentioned, illegal content can, at the same time, amount to disinformation.[51] Similarly, misleading or untrue content can be in breach of the terms and conditions of the relevant service provider. In the case of its Article 20, the DSA refrains from defining risky content itself, but leaves the task to the terms

[49] *Cf.* Legner (2024), pp. 106 et seq.

[50] Kuhlmann and Trute (2022), p. 117.

[51] *Supra*, Sect. 4.2.1.

and conditions of the provider. The complaint shall be handled "in a timely, non-discriminatory, diligent and non-arbitrary manner" (Article 20 para. 4 sentence 1 DSA) and the deadline for a complaint is at least six months. If they deem the decision of the online platform unsatisfactory, users can either have the decision reviewed before the national courts according to Article 21 para. 1 subpara. 3 DSA or choose an out-of-court dispute settlement upon the complaint before a body which is certified by the national Digital Services Coordinator (Article 21 DSA). The provision on misuse prevention in Article 23 para. 2 DSA applies to the internal complaint-handling system, too.

4.2.3 Obligations for Very Large Online Platforms and Very Large Online Search Engines

A specific focus of the DSA lies on the VLOPs and VLOSEs, owing to their market power and their central role in disseminating information in the online world. The EU legislator subjects them to more stringent obligations as far as the transparency and the integrity of the content they distribute are concerned. The rules contained in the Articles 33–43 DSA concerning VLOPs and VLOSEs are therefore stricter and more far-reaching than the general rules concerning every provider of intermediary online services. The rules in Sect. 5 of the DSA cannot be extended to other providers of intermediary services. Article 8 DSA makes it clear that there are no general obligations to monitor the content and no duty to actively look for "facts or circumstances indicating illegal activity" for all intermediary service providers.[52] Given the specific position of the VLOPs and VLOSEs on the market and their significant impact on opinion making, the main difference compared to the general rules lies in the fact that these companies have certain duties to act even where there is no breach of law, but only a sufficient risk. These particular obligations apply to VLOPs and VLOSEs in addition to the general obligations which every service provider faces.

Risk Assessment and Mitigation (Articles 34 and 35 DSA)

The starting point for the obligations which VLOPs and VLOSEs have to fulfil is a compulsory risk assessment of their services and their systems. The assessment relates to the dissemination of illegal content or such content that poses a risk, *i.a.*, for fundamental rights or the democratic process. As a consequence, they have to mitigate the risks. Furthermore, they have to act accordingly as far as the systemic risks defined in Article 34 para. 1 subpara. 2 DSA are concerned. This is a particularly relevant extension with relation to online disinformation. The duties of the VLOPs and VLOSEs therefore are potentially the most effective tools to combat online

---

[52] *Cf.* CJEU, 3 October 2019, Case C-18/18—*Glawischnig-Piesczek v. Facebook Ireland* on Art. 15 E-Commerce-Directive, which was replaced by Art. 8 DSA (see Art. 89 DSA).

content which is not illegal, but misleading or untrue, and therefore creates risks for individual or societal interests.

The standard of the risk assessment which the VLOPs and VLOSEs are obliged to undertake is defined in Article 34 para. 1 subpara. 1 DSA. They have to "diligently identify, analyse and assess any systemic risks in the Union stemming from the design or functioning of their service and its related systems, including algorithmic systems, or from the use made of their services".[53] The obligation to mitigate any risks that the monitoring has identified includes the measures that are listed in Article 35 para. 1 DSA. The VLOP or VLOSE in question may be obliged to take a variety of internal actions concerning the design and functioning of the services. There are information and flagging obligations, but also, in particular, codes of conduct as defined in Article 35 para. 1 lit. h DSA.[54] These codes of conduct are highly specialised sets of rules which are not strictly speaking binding EU law provisions, but rather instruments of compulsory self-regulation which can, *de facto*, lead to a similarly effective implementation. The core problem in this regard concerns the enforcement of the self-regulatory rules which, in terms of content, contain sufficiently operative rules of conduct in preventing and fighting disinformation in the online sphere.[55] According to Article 37 DSA, an independent audit has to be performed annually for VLOPs and VLOSEs.

Crisis Protocols and Crisis Response Mechanism

Furthermore, the DSA provides for so-called crisis protocols that the Commission may draw up according to Article 48 DSA for situations affecting public security or public health. In its endeavour, the Commission is supported by the participation of the VLOPs and VLOSEs as well as the relevant Union bodies, offices and agencies. The crisis protocols can include, *i.a.*, "prominently displaying information on the crisis situation provided by Member States' authorities or at Union level, or, depending on the context of the crisis, by other relevant reliable bodies" (Article 48 para. 2 lit. a DSA),[56] and may require the adaption of "the resources dedicated to compliance with the obligations set out in Articles 16, 20, 22, 23 and 35 to the needs arising from the crisis situation" (Article 48 para. 2 lit. c DSA).

In the specific situation of a crisis according to Article 36 para. 2 DSA, the duties of the VLOPs and VLOSEs go even further and can be enforced by the Commission. Under the crisis response mechanism as set out in Article 36 DSA, the Commission may require VLOPs and VLOSEs to take one or more of the actions which are listed in Article 36 para. 1 DSA, including "specific, effective and proportionate measures,

---

[53] *Cf.* Legner (2024), pp. 108 et seq.

[54] *Cf.* Cavaliere (2022), pp. 486 et seq.; Datzer and Lonardo (2023), pp. 753 et seq.; Bayer (2024a), pp. 220 et seq.; De Gregorio and Pollicino (2025), pp. 465 et seq.; Brogi and De Gregorio (2024), pp. 40 et seq.

[55] See https://digital-strategy.ec.europa.eu/en/library/code-conduct-disinformation.

[56] *Cf.* Ferreau (2024), pp. 58 et seq.; Krönke (2023), pp. 151 et seq.

such as any of those provided for in Article 35(1) or Article 48(2)", *i.e.* a significant number of concrete mitigation measures within their service processes. Equally, the drawing up and the implementation of a specific crisis protocol can be required. In a situation of crisis, the duties of the VLOPs and VLOSEs therefore change their self-regulatory character and become directly enforceable. The Commission is monitoring the fulfilment of the obligations. Taking into account their fundamental rights dimension, the enforcement measures have to be proportionate and need to be revoked if necessary. The same applies to the definition of a crisis which is restrictive and requires "extraordinary circumstances [which] lead to a serious threat to public security or public health in the Union or in significant parts of it".[57]

4.2.4 Enforcement

Apart from the situations in which the crisis mechanism is applicable, the DSA provides for a complex enforcement structure, which includes national Digital Services Coordinators (Articles 49 et seq. DSA),[58] the Commission (Articles 66 et seq. DSA) and private enforcement including compensation in case of damage or loss (Article 54 DSA).[59] The last dimension is mainly governed by the codes of conduct for the VLOPs and VLOSEs. The enforcement powers of the Commission in relation to VLOPs and VLOSEs include non-compliance decisions according to Article 73 DSA, upon which it may impose fines (Article 74 DSA). An enhanced supervision procedure according to Article 75 DSA comprises an action plan in order to terminate or remedy the infringement. Again, the codes of conduct play a relevant role (Article 75 para. 2, 3 DSA). The plan has to be drawn up by the provider and the Commission has the task of monitoring it.

4.3 Audiovisual Media Services Directive

From a historical point of view, the oldest, but obviously not the most comprehensive set of rules which can have an impact on online disinformation can be found in the Audiovisual Media Services Directive (AVMSD).[60] Its framework regulation for

[57] *Cf.* recital 91 of the DSA: "Such crises could result from armed conflicts or acts of terrorism, including emerging conflicts or acts of terrorism, natural disasters such as earthquakes and hurricanes, as well as from pandemics and other serious cross-border threats to public health".

[58] See, for the VLOPs and VLOSEs, Article 40 DSA.

[59] *Cf.* Legner (2024), pp. 109 et seq.; Krönke (2023), pp. 136 et seq.; Husovec (2024), pp. 52 et seq. See also the compliance function in Article 41 DSA.

[60] Directive (EU) 2018/1808 of the European Parliament and of the Council of 14 November 2018 amending Directive 2010/13/EU on the coordination of certain provisions laid down by law, regulation or administrative action in Member States concerning the provision of audiovisual media services (Audiovisual Media Services Directive) in view of changing market realities, OJ L 303, 28 November 2018, p. 69.

platform responsibility has been called "the seeds of the future DSA".[61] The rules concerning video-sharing platforms were added in 2018. However, the AVMSD does not explicitly address online disinformation even though some of its protective provisions are applicable to this phenomenon as well. The starting point for the obligations of video-sharing platforms is the concept of "harmful content". This does not necessarily require an element of disinformation although a harm might result from untrue or misleading content that can either affect an individual person or group of persons or the democratic discourse in general. Apart from that, the rules of the AVMSD also target disinformation in the commercial field.

Generally speaking, Member States have to ensure that video-sharing platforms take the appropriate measures to protect users from certain particularly harmful content as defined in Article 28b para. 1 AVMSD. They shall also ensure that video-sharing platforms comply with the restrictions of commercial communications according to Article 9 para. 1 AVMSD (Article 28b para. 2 AVMSD). In this vein, Article 28b para. 3 AVMSD lists the kind of measures that platforms have to adopt in order to comply with their obligations under the directive. The Member States have to ensure the fulfilment of these obligations. The AVMSD therefore relies on a system of public enforcement. Nevertheless, codes of conduct can be a regulatory option, too, according to Article 28b paras. 4, 9, 10 AVMSD.

With this rather limited, but relevant set of rules, the AVMSD fits in the system of EU law countering online disinformation. However, contrary to the more modern and sweeping provisions of the DSA, the rules of the AVMSD are not tailored generally to systemic risks, but are more narrowly defined as they always require a degree of harmfulness.[62] Therefore, an assessment of the legal framework by the Council in 2025 is especially considering possible amendments to further counteract disinformation.[63]

4.4 AI Act

Another modern element in the EU law on disinformation is the new AI Act.[64] It is a piece of legislation that, for the first time,[65] tries to implement a regulatory concept for this rather fast evolving field in the European Union. Although it is based on the general EU competence for the internal market (Article 114 TFEU) and the legal basis for data protection measures (Article 16 TFEU), its relevance extends far beyond purely economic questions or data protection issues in a narrow

[61] Bayer (2024a), p. 105.

[62] Bayer (2024a), p. 106.

[63] Council conclusions on the assessment of the legal framework for audiovisual media services and video-sharing platform services, C/2025/2954.

[64] Regulation (EU) 2024/1689 of the European Parliament and of the Council of 13 June 2024 laying down harmonised rules on artificial intelligence [...] (Artificial Intelligence Act), OJ L, 2024/1689, 12 July 2024.

[65] See https://www.europarl.europa.eu/topics/en/article/20230601STO93804/eu-ai-act-first-regulation-on-artificial-intelligence.

sense. A core focus lies in the field of fundamental rights protection. Even though it intends to harmonise the legal requirements for the new technology on the entire single market, it clearly attempts to raise the overall standards for the safeguarding of fundamental rights such as free speech, non-discrimination, privacy and the rights of defence.[66] Artificial intelligence (AI) can, in particular, be used to create content which disseminates untrue or misleading facts. At the same time, AI is a very versatile means to enhance content targeting techniques.[67] Therefore, AI is a potentially risky and potent source of disinformation and its dissemination. At the same time, it can cause dangers for the freedom of speech and can enhance threats to the plurality and reliability of information. The AI Act therefore contains some elements of a framework, which complement the regulatory approach of the DSA. Like this legal act, it follows a risk level oriented approach with the exception of some "(h)orizontal requirements"[68] which apply to AI systems irrespective of their risk level, including the overall transparency requirement in Article 50 AI Act.

In line with this approach, Article 5 AI Act prohibits some particularly dangerous and manipulative applications of AI. Other high-risk AI creations are subject to the obligations according to Articles 8 et seq. AI Act.[69] They apply (with some exceptions) to AI "systems intended to be used for influencing the outcome of an election or referendum or the voting behaviour of natural persons in the exercise of their vote in elections or referenda" (Annex III No. 8 lit. b)[70] and consist in risk and quality management systems, conformity assessment procedures and transparency obligations. High-risk AI services have to undergo a fundamental rights impact assessment (Article 26 AI Act). The AI Act establishes a notification and monitoring system for which the national authorities are competent. It therefore clearly emphasises the potentially negative impact of AI generated content on the democratic process as well as on fundamental rights and intends to minimise the risks that are connected to it. Nevertheless, the special rules on the high-risk AI services will only cover a fraction of the creations that can be dangerous for an undisturbed and manipulation-free democratic exchange in society.

More generally, therefore, Article 50 AI Act sets an overall transparency standard so that AI which is intended to enter into a communication with natural persons or provides for synthetic audio, image, video or text content has to be recognisable as such. In the recent past, AI creations of that kind have significantly risen in number and they bear the risk of conveying false information or at least provoking misunderstandings among their users. The obligation of transparency thus is another element in the attempt of the EU legislator to reduce the danger of AI created content by publicly designating the potential doubts about its veracity and its authority. This

[66] See, European Commission, Proposal for a Regulation of the European Parliament and of the Council laying down harmonised rules on artificial intelligence (Artificial Intelligence Act) […], COM(2021) 206 final, pp. 7, 12–3.

[67] De Gregorio and Pollicino (2025), pp. 452 et seq.

[68] Almada and Petit (2025), p. 92.

[69] Cf. Latil (2024), pp. 571 et seq.

[70] De Gregorio and Pollicino (2025), p. 463.

transparency requirement is certainly a proportionate restriction of the fundamental rights of the creators of AI such as their economic freedom under Article 15 and 16 CFR or their right to free speech and artistic liberty[71] (Articles 11 and 13 CFR). It only puts a relatively moderate burden on them for the benefit of highly relevant societal and legal values. As far as the integrity of the democratic process is concerned, a particular danger follows from deep fakes, which, according to the definition of Article 3 para. 60 AI Act, appear to represent real people, but are generated by AI and may be used to distribute misleading content with the seemingly real authority of the person being imitated. An obvious example are fake statements by politicians.[72] AI generated deep fakes entail relatively high disinformation risks.[73] Consequently, the AI Act requires them to be labelled as such (Article 50 para. 4 AI Act). This obligation complements the obligation of VLOPs and VLOSEs under Article 35 para. 1 (k) DSA, which is also applicable to deep fakes. The personal scope of application of the AI Act, however, is different. A sanction mechanism is contained in Articles 99–101 AI Act which complements the transparency requirement. It is, however, by no means certain that the implementation and the enforcement of the obligations of the AI Act will be able to successfully reduce all the dangers that stem from this new technology in terms of the integrity of information exchange. In general, the AI Act therefore makes an important, but rather specific and limited contribution to the overarching objective of preventing disinformation from damaging the democratic process and from impairing the fundamental rights situation in the EU and its Member States.

4.5 *Protection of a Free and Pluralistic Media Landscape*

As online disinformation is developing into a constantly increasing threat to the democratic discourse which forms the basis of a democratic political system and its constitutional order,[74] the legislator of the European Union is focusing on the stability and the integrity of the media landscape in general. As it has been frequently acknowledged by the case law of the European Courts,[75] free and pluralistic media are of paramount importance for the functioning of a democratic society and its democratic institutions. While the measures of the DSA, the AVMSD and the AI Act, which focus on the risk level of the dissemination of content, mainly impose a variety of duties of monitoring and mitigation on the service providers, they only concern the transmission process. In addition to this strategy, several recent measures

[71] See also the exception in Article 50 para. 4, 3rd sentence: "Where the content forms part of an evidently artistic, creative, satirical, fictional or analogous work or programme, the transparency obligations set out in this paragraph are limited to disclosure of the existence of such generated or manipulated content in an appropriate manner that does not hamper the display or enjoyment of the work."

[72] *Cf.* De Gregorio and Pollicino (2025), p. 460.

[73] *Cf.* Almada and Petit (2025), pp. 107 et seq.; Flint (2024), pp. 587 et seq.

[74] De Gregorio and Pollicino (2025), pp. 459–60.

[75] *Supra*, Sect. 3.1.3.

of the Union intend to improve the general conditions for the media in order to reinforce their position in society and enable them to fulfil their constitutional role in safeguarding the integrity of the process of communication in society. According to the constitutional principles of liberal democracies, independent and pluralistic media are intended to counteract harmful disinformation by effectively providing a reliable factual basis for the democratic discourse. Therefore, the EU has taken several actions to strengthen "the essential role journalists play in informing citizens about the reality on the ground".[76] The EU legal acts in this area are complementary to the regulatory approach of the DSA, the AVMSD and the AI Act.

Among the most recent legal acts in the field of protecting the media for the benefit of an orderly democratic discourse is the European Media Freedom Act (EMFA).[77] According to Article 3 EMFA, Member States "shall respect the right of recipients of media services to have access to a plurality of editorially independent media content and ensure that framework conditions are in place in line with this Regulation to safeguard that right, to the benefit of free and democratic discourse".[78] The regulation provides for a rather broad set of rules that Member States have to follow in order to guarantee the independence and plurality of the media. The general focus of the act therefore lies on the framework which national law and practice have to establish in order to support the freedom, independence and plurality of the media.

Nevertheless, the EMFA acknowledges the central role which platforms and other intermediary service providers play in the modern media landscape. Media are dependent on these means of distribution. Flagging media content as inappropriate or misleading and thus barring it on the relevant platforms for dissemination would therefore result in a serious interference with the freedom of the media and, at the same time, could contribute to the spreading of disinformation if, in this manner, reliable media sources were to be excluded from the public discourse. The position of dominance that platforms have not only gives them the opportunity to spread disinformation themselves, but also to prevent corrections and to curtail opposing views. According to Article 18 para. 4 EMFA, VLOPs are therefore obliged to give certain media service providers the opportunity to object to a decision of the platform provider to bar its content from its platform prior to the implementation of this decision. They are entitled to give a statement of reasons before the decision to suspend the provision of the online intermediation services is put into action. This is aimed at preventing a premature or improper deletion of quality content of independent media providers. If no amicable solution is found, the media service provider may seek a mediation or an out-of-court settlement (Article 18 para. 7 EMFA). In order to enjoy these privileges and to benefit from the restrictions imposed on the VLOPs

---

[76] Communication from the Commission to the European Parliament, the Council, the European Economic and Social Committee and the Committee of the Regions "on Defence of Democracy", COM(2023) 630 final, p. 13. *Cf.* recital 14 of the EMFA: "Quality media services are also an antidote against disinformation and foreign information manipulation and interference."

[77] Regulation (EU) 2024/1083 of the European Parliament and of the Council of 11 April 2024 establishing a common framework for media services in the internal market and amending Directive 2010/13/EU (European Media Freedom Act), OJ L, 2024/1083, 17 April 2024.

[78] *Cf.* Cavaliere (2024), pp. 29 et seq.; Malferrari and Gerhold (2024), pp. 893 et seq.

by the EMFA, a media service provider has to give a declaration in accordance with the requirements of Article 18 para. 1 EMFA. The mechanism is in line with and complementary to the VLOPs' obligations under the DSA.[79]

Another recent legal act that pursues the objective of protecting media and journalists is the Directive 2024/1069 on protecting persons who engage in public participation from manifestly unfounded claims or abusive court proceedings ('Strategic lawsuits against public participation' - SLAPP).[80] It attempts to counter so-called cases that try to intimidate, discourage and therefore harm independent reporting by the media.[81] Its effects and its contribution to the European Union's strategy to counter disinformation are indirect and aim at the overall situation of media in the Member States. It has an indirect connection with online disinformation insofar as the risk of strategic lawsuits in the field of the distribution of content and, in particular, of information increases because of the boundless accessibility of online distribution.

Finally, a more general element in the Union's approach to disinformation that, however, does not have the character or the effect of a legal act, concerns the improvement of media literacy.[82] It attempts to better educate European citizens in order to enable them to detect and counter disinformation.

4.6 Regulation 2024/900 on the Transparency and Targeting of Political Advertising

Political advertising is an area which is particularly prone to online disinformation. Hence, the Regulation 2024/900 on the Transparency and Targeting of Political Advertising[83] has to be seen as another building block in the edifice of the European Union's strategy on online disinformation. This regulation is complementary to the DSA whose core obligations are applicable to political advertising as well (Article 2 para. 3 (i) Regulation 2024/900). This kind of advertising is already addressed by Article 39 DSA. According to this provision, VLOPs and VLOSEs have to publish

---

[79] *Cf.* Hennemann (2024), pp. 501 et seq.; Achleitner (2025).

[80] Directive (EU) 2024/1069 of the European Parliament and of the Council of 11 April 2024 on protecting persons who engage in public participation from manifestly unfounded claims or abusive court proceedings ('Strategic lawsuits against public participation'), OJ L, 2024/1069, 16 April 2024.

[81] See, in more detail, Allgayer (2025), pp. 138 et seq.; Hanna (2024).

[82] Communication from the Commission to the European Parliament, the Council, the European Economic and Social Committee and the Committee of the Regions "Tackling online disinformation: a European Approach", COM(2018) 236 final, pp. 12 et seq.

[83] Regulation (EU) 2024/900 of the European Parliament and of the Council of 13 March 2024 on the transparency and targeting of political advertising, OJ L, 2024/900, 20 March 2024. See, in more detail, Bayer (2022); Kalveram (2024); Brkan (2023); Flint (2024), pp. 586 et seq.; Cavaliere (2022), pp. 489 and 497; De Gregorio and Pollicino (2025), p. 464; Ó Fathaigh, Dobber, Zuiderveen Borgesius and Shires (2021).

a public repository in order to increase transparency in this field.[84] Article 13 of the Regulation 2024/900 adds a European repository for online political advertisements. This is part of several enhanced transparency obligations set out in the Articles 7–17, 21 of Regulation 2024/900 which can have an impact on the prevention of disinformation in the political sphere. In order to protect the integrity of the electoral process, Article 5 para. 2 Regulation 2024/900 establishes some restrictions on external political advertisement directly before elections. Finally, according to Article 18 Regulation 2024/900, the use of data for the purposes of political advertisement is restricted and profiling is prohibited.

4.7 *Protection from External Influences*

In its efforts to fight disinformation from external sources like foreign private or state actors,[85] the EU can resort to restrictive measures and sanctions under Article 215 TFEU. An example is the case of RT France where the General Court has upheld a decision of the Council on the basis of Article 29 TEU and a Regulation on the basis of Article 215 TFEU which banned the diffusion of RT France's programme that consisted chiefly in Russian state propaganda and was financed by the Russian state.[86] Apart from that, the Union is working on a conceptual approach for measures against Foreign Information Manipulation and Influence (FIMI) according to the requirements of the specific case in question.[87]

5 Conclusion

The EU approach for countering online disinformation consists in a diverse array of legal acts and strategies that attempt to both restrict the opportunities for disinformation and encourage and foster the independence and plurality of the media as well as of the integrity of the democratic process. The legal acts in this field target both the Member States and the intermediary service providers, in particular the VLOPs and VLOSEs. Apart from the rules that address illegal content, the EU legislation focuses on the level of risk when dealing with different forms of online disinformation. It imposes corresponding obligations on intermediary service providers. This

[84] *Cf.* De Gregorio and Pollicino (2025), p. 462.

[85] Datzer and Lonardo (2023), pp. 754 et seq. and 760.

[86] GCEU, 27 July 2022, Case T-125/22, §§ 46 et seq.—*RT France*; see also Gundel (2023); Lonardo (2023); Baade (2023).

[87] *Cf.* the Annex to the Communication from the Commission to the European Parliament, the Council, the European Economic and Social Committee and the Committee of the Regions "on Defence of Democracy", COM(2023) 630 final ANNEX, pp. 16 et seq.

approach, which has a precautionary element to it,[88] does not always involve legal enforcement mechanisms on the Member State or the Union level, but makes use of self-regulatory elements like, in particular, codes of conduct. Structurally, this seems to be a convincing choice since the entire field of the dissemination of information is highly predetermined by individual fundamental rights and necessitates solutions which comply with the principle of proportionality. While the fundamental rights give a clear direction in general and allow for restrictions in the interest of the integrity of the democratic discourse and the independence and plurality of the media, the case-by-case decisions are challenging in their balancing process and complex as far as the different legal rules are concerned. The overall effectiveness of the multilevel European strategy on online disinformation is difficult to predict. It depends significantly on the effectiveness of the combination of self-regulatory elements and the enforcement of the obligations under EU law which the large players on the market have to abide by. In this context, the balance between the different fundamental rights and interests is not static, but always open to adjustments by the legislator or the administrative practice if the situation of the protected interests changes.

References

Achleitner, R. A.: Das Medienprivileg im European Media Freedom Act: Schnittstellen und Wechselwirkungen mit dem Digital Services Act. Zeitschrift für das Recht der Digitalisierung, Datenwirtschaft und IT 28(2), 89-93 (2025).

Allgayer, P.: Europäisierung der Medienregulierung. Neue Juristische Wochenschrift 78(3), 135-9 (2025).

Almada, M., Petit, N.: The EU AI Act: Between the rock of product safety and the hard place of fundamental rights. Common Market Law Review 62(1), 85-120 (2025).

Baade, B.: EU Sanctions Against Propaganda for War—Reflections on the General Court's Judgment in Case T-125/22 (RT France). Heidelberg Journal of International Law 83(2), 257-82 (2023).

Bayer, J.: Digital Media Regulation within the European Union: A Framework for a New Media Order. Nomos, Baden-Baden (2024a).

Bayer, J.: The EU policy on disinformation: aims and legal basis. Journal of Media Law 16(1), 18-27 (2024b).

Bayer, J.: The Proposal for a Regulation on transparency and targeting of political advertising—The educated citizenry: A short overview. Zeitschrift für das Recht der Digitalisierung, Datenwirtschaft und IT 25(7), 535-40 (2022).

Brkan, M.: The regulation of data-driven political campaigns in the EU: from data protection to specialized regulation. Yearbook of European Law 41, 348-73 (2023).

Brogi, E., De Gregorio, G.: From the code of practice to the code of conduct? Navigating the future challenges of disinformation regulation. Journal of Media Law 16(1), 38-46 (2024).

Caruso, C.: Towards the Institutions of Freedom: The European Public Discourse in the Digital Era. German Law Journal 26(1), 114-37 (2025).

Cavaliere, P.: Freedom of expression after disinformation: Towards a new paradigm for the right to receive information. Journal of Media Law 16(1), 27-37 (2024).

[88] *Cf.* Peukert (2023), p. 279.

Cavaliere, P.: The Truth in Fake News: How Disinformation Laws Are Reframing the Concepts of Truth and Accuracy on Digital Platforms. European Convention on Human Rights Law Review 3(4), 481-523 (2022).

Datzer, V., Lonardo, L.: Genesis and evolution of EU anti disinformation policy: entrepreneurship and political opportunism in the regulation of digital technology. Journal of European Integration 45(5), 751-66 (2023).

De Gregorio, G., Pollicino, O.: The European Constitutional Way to Address Disinformation in the Age of Artificial Intelligence. German Law Journal 26(3), 449-70 (2025).

Ehlers, D., Germelmann, C. F.: § 2.1 Europäische Menschenrechtskonvention—Allgemeine Lehren. In: Ehlers, D., Germelmann, C. F. (eds.): Europäische Grundrechte und Grundfreiheiten, pp. 33–158. De Gruyter, Berlin and Boston (2023a).

Ehlers, D., Germelmann, C. F.: § 2.2 Grundrechte der Europäischen Union—Allgemeine Lehren. In: Ehlers, D., Germelmann, C. F. (eds.): Europäische Grundrechte und Grundfreiheiten, pp. 159–290. De Gruyter, Berlin and Boston (2023b).

Ferreau, J. F.: Crisis? What crisis? The risk of fighting disinformation with the DSA's crisis response mechanism. Journal of Media Law 16(1), 57-64 (2024).

Flint, J.: Staatsferne Regulierung als Lösungsansatz für Fake News auf Social Media: Vortrag im Rahmen des Symposiums "40 Jahre Privatrundfunk oder wie Regulierung (Rundfunk-) Freiheit sichert! Bestandsaufnahme, Best Practices und Ausblick" der Bayerischen Landeszentrale für neue Medien und des Instituts für Urheber- und Medienrecht am 19.4.2024 in München. Zeitschrift für Urheber- und Medienrecht 68(8/9), 583–91 (2024).

Gundel, J.: Europäischer Grundrechtsschutz für (dritt-)staatliche Propagandasender? – Anmerkung zum Urteil des EuG v. 27.7.2022, Rs. T-125/22 (RT France/Rat). Europarecht 58(1), 110–8 (2023).

Hanna, M.: SLAPPs: What are they? And how should defamation law be reformed to address them? Journal of Media Law 16(1), 118-45 (2024).

Hennemann, M.: Der European Media Freedom Act oder: Von Zielen und Mitteln des Medienrechts. Zeitschrift für Europäisches Privatrecht 32(3), 498-504 (2024).

Husovec, M.: The Digital Services Act's red line: what the Commission can and cannot do about disinformation. Journal of Media Law 16(1), 47-56 (2024).

Jungherr, A.: Foundational questions for the regulation of digital disinformation. Journal of Media Law 16(1), 8-17 (2024).

Kalveram, N.: Politisches Targeting – Gefahr für die demokratische Willensbildung? Neue Juristische Wochenschrift 77(51), 3702-7 (2024).

Krönke, C.: Die Europäische Kommission als Aufsichtsbehörde für digitale Dienste. Europarecht 58(2), 136-59 (2023).

Kuhlmann, S., Trute, H.-H.: Die Regulierung von Desinformationen und rechtswidrigen Inhalten nach dem neuen Digital Services Act. Zeitschrift für das Gesamte Sicherheitsrecht 5(3), 115-22 (2022).

Latil, A.: Le Règlement relatif à l'intelligence artificielle et l'approche par les risques: application d'une méthode législative structurante. Revue trimestrielle de droit européen, 563–85 (2024)

Legner, S.: Der Digital Services Act – Ein neuer Grundstein der Digitalregulierung. Zeitschrift für Urheber- und Medienrecht 68(2), 99-111 (2024).

Lonardo, L.: Censorship in the EU as a Result of the War in Ukraine. RT France v. Council of the European Union. European Law Review 48(6), 707–19 (2023).

Malferrari, L.: Der European Media Freedom Act als intra-vires-Rechtsakt. Europäische Zeitschrift für Wirtschaftsrecht 34(2), 49-50 (2023).

Malferrari, L., Gerhold, M.: Ein Unionsrecht auf Empfang pluraler Medien? Europäische Zeitschrift für Wirtschaftsrecht 35(19), 893-900 (2024).

Marauhn, T., Jaś-Nowopolska, M.: § 5.1 Schutz der Kommunikationsgrundrechte nach der EMRK. In: Ehlers, D., Germelmann, C. F. (eds.): Europäische Grundrechte und Grundfreiheiten, pp. 502–58. De Gruyter, Berlin and Boston (2023).

Ó Fathaigh, R., Helberger, N., Appelman, N.: The perils of legally defining disinformation. Internet Policy Review 10(4), 2–25 (2021).
Ó Fathaigh, R., Dobber, T., Zuiderveen Borgesius, F., Shires, J.: Microtargeted propaganda by foreign actors: An interdisciplinary exploration. Maastricht Journal of European and Comparative Law 28(6), 856–77 (2021).
Peukert, A.: Desinformationsregulierung in der EU – Überblick und offene Fragen. Juristenzeitung 78(7), 278-86 (2023).
Quintais, J. P., Appelman, N., Ó Fathaigh, R.: Using Terms and Conditions to apply Fundamental Rights to Content Moderation. German Law Journal 24(5), 881–911 (2023).
Shattock, E.: Lies, liability, and lawful content: Critiquing the approaches to online disinformation in the EU. Common Market Law Review 60(5), 1313-48 (2023).
Sznajder, M.: European Media Freedom Act and its Implications for Both Merger Control and Media Pluralism: The Polish Perspective. European Law Review 49(1), 66-77 (2024).

The National Legal Framework on Disinformation in Austria—An Overview

Florian Sebastian Werni

Abstract Disinformation, particularly online, is widely regarded as a threat to democratic societies. This chapter provides an overview of Austria's national legal framework on disinformation as of 1 December 2025. Its purpose is to present readers with a collection of relevant legislation, case law, legal literature, and other documents. Overall, there are only a few rules at the national level in Austria that explicitly focus on combating disinformation or online disinformation in particular. However, numerous legal provisions in various areas of national law, such as criminal law, civil law, and media law, may be relevant in this context. Recent federal legislation has primarily focused on better tackling online hate speech. Although the current federal government considers disinformation to be a fundamental threat to democracy, it has so far only provided a vague description of how this problem should be addressed at national level.

1 Notions of Disinformation

1.1 "Disinformation"

"Disinformation" *(Desinformation)* is not a specific legal term under Austrian law. It is not used in constitutional or statutory law. Case law mentions it very rarely and does not provide a definition.[1]

Austrian legal literature uses this term repeatedly, but only a few authors offer a definition. According to Gärner (2022, p. 93), the term "disinformation" refers to "all factual claims that are knowingly false and either made for ideological purposes

[1] See Constitutional Court *(Verfassungsgerichtshof)*, Judgment of 30 August 1994, W I- 6/94 (VfSlg. *[Ausgewählte Entscheidungen des Verfassungsgerichtshofs]* 13.839/1994); Supreme Court of Justice *(Oberster Gerichtshof)*, Judgment of 21 January 2025, 4 Ob 192/24z.

F. S. Werni (✉)
University of Vienna, Vienna, Austria
e-mail: florian.sebastian.werni@univie.ac.at

P. Passaglia (ed.), *European Legal Perspectives on Online Disinformation*, Ius Gentium: Comparative Perspectives on Law and Justice 140,
https://doi.org/10.1007/978-3-032-25785-7_3

(i.e. deception) or for economic reasons, disseminated in a way that is likely to mislead readers as to their truthfulness."[2] According to Kaschka "disinformation" is "false information spread with the intention to deceive"[3] (2024, p. 116 fn. 36). Other legal scholars use similar notions of the term, but do not make them explicit (e.g. Merli, 2019, Blaßnig, 2020, Pabel, 2020, Achleitner, 2022, Holoubek, 2022). Soldan (2025) has extensively analysed the notion of "disinformation" within the framework of European Union law. The problem of disinformation is also discussed in legal literature under the term "fake news" (e.g. Oberlaber, 2017; Noll, 2019; Gärner, 2022; Lewisch, 2025; Rohregger and Dumfarth, 2025).

Some public authorities in Austria have provided definitions of the term "disinformation" on their websites to inform the public about its dangers (see Sect. 2.6). According to the Federal Chancellery of Austria *(Bundeskanzleramt)*, disinformation is "the deliberate dissemination of untruths with the intention of deceiving or influencing individuals or groups"[4] (Federal Chancellery, no date). Similarly, the Austrian Regulatory Authority for Broadcasting and Telecommunications (*Rundfunk und Telekom Regulierungs-GmbH [RTR]*), describes disinformation as "the dissemination of false or misleading information that can harm the public, with the intention of deceiving others or capitalizing on it economically or politically"[5] (RTR, no date).

These definitions of disinformation share three elements:

- The information disseminated is false or at least misleading.
- The person disseminating the information must know that it is false.
- The person disseminating the information must have the intention of deceiving, influencing, or harming other people or the public.

These elements do not in and of themselves render disinformation illegal. Deliberately disseminating false information may be illegal under Austrian law, but not all deliberate dissemination of false information is necessarily subject to it (see Sect. 3).

1.2 "Online Disinformation"

In Austria, problems relating to disinformation are usually discussed in the context of online disinformation. However, there are no specific definitions of the term "online disinformation" in Austrian law, case law, or legal literature.

---

[2] My translation.

[3] My translation.

[4] My translation.

[5] My translation.

1.3 Similar Concepts ("Misinformation" and "Malinformation")

In legal contexts in Austria, some authors distinguish the notion of "disinformation" from the notions of "misinformation" *(Fehlinformation, Misinformation)* and "malinformation" *(Malinformation)* (Kaschka, 2024, p. 116; Soldan, 2025, pp. 153–154; Lewisch, 2025, p. 11; Nemeth, forthcoming).

Kaschka describes misinformation as "false information spread without the intention to deceive"[6] (2024, p. 116 fn. 37). According to the RTR, misinformation is "false or misleading information shared without the deliberate intent to cause harm but whose effects may be harmful"[7] (RTR, no date).

Kaschka also provides a definition of malinformation: It is "correct information disseminated with the intention of harming"[8] (2024, p. 116 fn. 38).

2 Sources of Law[9]

2.1 Constitutional References

The Federal Constitution of Austria *(Österreichische Bundesverfassung)* does not specify rules on disinformation or online disinformation. However, it grants several fundamental rights ("constitutionally guaranteed rights" *[verfassungsgesetzlich gewährleistete Rechte]*)[10] and provides various constitutional rules that may be relevant in this context.

It should be mentioned that the Federal Constitution of Austria is not a single document, but it is divided into numerous acts, including the core document, the Federal Constitutional Act *(Bundes-Verfassungsgesetz [B-VG])*,[11] and several other constitutional laws and constitutional provisions (Berka, 2021, pp. 22–24; Stelzer, 2022, pp. 20–21). The European Convention on Human Rights (ECHR) has constitutional status in Austria as well.[12] Therefore, the rights and freedoms enshrined in the ECHR are constitutionally guaranteed rights in Austria (Grabenwarter and Pabel, 2021, p. 16). The rights enshrined in the Charter of Fundamental Rights of the European Union (CFR) are not constitutionally guaranteed rights under the

---

[6] My translation.

[7] My translation.

[8] My translation.

[9] Austrian legislation and case law can be accessed via https://ris.bka.gv.at/, Accessed 1 Dec 2025. Certain Austrian laws are also available in an unofficial English translation; https://ris.bka.gv.at/defaultEn.aspx, Accessed 1 Dec 2025.

[10] Art. 144 B-VG.

[11] Federal Law Gazette *(Bundesgesetzblatt)* 1/1930 as amended by Federal Law Gazette I 89/2024.

[12] Federal Law Gazette 59/1964.

Federal Constitution of Austria, but the Constitutional Court *(Verfassungsgerichtshof [VfGH])* applies some CFR rights as constitutionally guaranteed rights[13] (Stelzer, 2022, pp. 184–187).

Freedom of communication. In Austria, freedom of communication is enshrined in several constitutional provisions.[14] It includes the right to express opinions and to share and receive information of any kind and in any form (Berka, Binder and Kneihs, 2019, pp. 661–667). Whether freedom of communication also includes a right to express and share untrue information is controversial in Austria.

Several legal scholars have argued that freedom of communication, in principle, protects the expression and sharing of untrue information (e.g. Bezemek, 2015, pp. 119–120; Pöschl, 2018, pp. 40–45; Struth, 2019, p. 369; Pabel, 2020, p. 103; Gärner, 2022, p. 111; Kaschka, 2025, pp. 29–30; Lewisch, 2025, p. 13; Rohregger and Dumfarth, 2025, p. 45; Soldan, 2025, p. 162). Similarly, the European Court of Human Rights (ECtHR) held in its judgment in the case of *Salov v. Ukraine* that "Article 10 of the Convention as such does not prohibit discussion or dissemination of information received even if it is strongly suspected that this information might not be truthful."[15]

More recently, some legal scholars (Grabenwarter and Pabel, 2021, p. 402; Hinghofer-Szalkay, 2025, para. 60) have pointed to recent ECtHR jurisprudence, according to which "statements which are based on (manifestly) untrue facts do not enjoy the protection of Article 10 […]."[16] Similarly, Austria's Supreme Court of Justice (*Oberster Gerichtshof*) held that negative value judgments based on untrue or insufficient factual claims do not fall within the scope of Article 10 of the ECHR.[17]

Due to the ambiguity of the case law, it is difficult to clearly determine the extent to which disinformation is protected by freedom of communication. Considering the aforementioned ECtHR jurisprudence, it can be concluded that the dissemination of information based on manifestly incorrect facts is not protected by freedom of communication.

Nevertheless, receiving incorrect information falls within the scope of Article 10 of the ECHR, even if the information received is manifestly incorrect.[18]

---

[13] Constitutional Court, Judgment of 14 March 2012, U 466/11 et al. (VfSlg. 19.632/2012).

[14] Art. 13 Basic Law on the General Rights of Nationals (*Staatsgrundgesetz über die allgemeinen Rechte der Staatsbürger [StGG]*), Imperial Law Gazette 142/1867 as amended by Federal Law Gazette 684/1988; Resolution of the Provision National Assembly of 30 October 1918 [on the abolition of censorship] (*Beschluss der Provisorischen Nationalversammlung vom 30. Oktober 1918 [über die Aufhebung der Zensur]*), State Law Gazette 3/1918; art. 10 ECHR.

[15] ECtHR, Judgment of 6 September 2005, no. 65518/01, *Salov v. Ukraine*, para. 113; see also ECtHR, Judgment of 26 February 2002, no. 29271/95, *Dichand and others v. Austria*, para. 49; for further references, see Ó Fathaigh, Helberger and Appelman 2021, p. 13.

[16] ECtHR, Judgment of 25 October 2018, no. 38450/12, *E.S. v. Austria*, para. 55 with further references.

[17] Supreme Court, Judgment of 25 April 2019, 6 Ob 235/18d with further references.

[18] Cf. ECtHR, Judgment of 22 July 2025, no. 15653/22, *Bradshaw and others v. United Kingdom*, para. 161.

Ban on censorship. The Federal Constitution of Austria stipulates an absolute ban on censorship.[19] This ban only applies to state-imposed pre-censorship and prohibits state authorities from exercising any form of preventive control over content prior to publication (Berka, Binder and Kneihs, 2019, p. 677). Preventive state control of communication for possible disinformation, whether online or not, would be unconstitutional in Austria but the ban does not apply to any subsequent repressive measures.

Fundamental rights against disinformation. Individuals who are affected by disinformation may invoke various fundamental rights, including the following:

- Article 8 of the ECHR guarantees the right to respect for private life (Berka, Binder and Kneihs, 2019, pp. 353–385). This right protects several aspects of a person's identity such as their image[20] and reputation.[21] Article 8 of the ECHR may be invoked by individuals whose personal identity is compromised by disinformation.
- § 1 of the Federal Act concerning the Protection of Personal Data *(Datenschutzgesetz [DSG])*[22] grants everyone a fundamental right to secrecy of personal data, to rectify incorrect data, and to erase of illegally processed data (Berka, Binder and Kneihs, 2019, pp. 386–405). These fundamental rights may be invoked by individuals combating disinformation involving their personal data.
- Article 6 of the Basic Law on the General Rights of Nationals *(Staatsgrundgesetz über die allgemeinen Rechte der Staatsbürger [StGG])* grants all nationals a fundamental right to practice any kind of gainful activity (Berka, Binder and Kneihs, 2019, pp. 473–494). Economic operators may invoke this fundamental right, for example, if their reputation is damaged by the dissemination of incorrect information.[23]

Right to free suffrage. Several provisions of the Federal Constitution grant the right to free suffrage in public elections.[24] This right prevents public authorities from interfering with election advertising and campaigns in an unobjective manner.[25] The right to free suffrage prohibits public authorities from disseminating false information during elections. Whether public authorities are generally obliged to tell the truth outside of such special situations is controversial in Austria (Feik, 2007; Merli, 2019; Storr, 2019).

---

[19] Resolution of the Provisional National Assembly of 30 October 1918 [on the abolition of censorship].

[20] See, for example, ECtHR, Judgment of 24 June 2004, no. 59320/00, *Hannover v. Germany*.

[21] See, for example, ECtHR, Judgment of 15 November 2007, no. 12556/03, *Pfeifer v. Austria*.

[22] Federal Law Gazette I 165/1999 as amended by Federal Law Gazette I 50/2025.

[23] See Constitutional Court, Judgment of 12 March 2009, G 164/08 (VfSlg. 18.747/2009) regarding warnings by public authorities.

[24] Art. 23a, 26, 60, 95, and 117 B-VG; art. 3 of the [First] Protocol to the ECHR.

[25] See Constitutional Court, Judgment of 30 August 1994, W I-6/94 (VfSlg. 13.839/1994); Constitutional Court, Judgment of 14 December 2004, W I-2/04 (VfSlg. 17.418/2004); Constitutional Court, Judgment of 16 June 2010, W I-4/09 et al. (VfSlg. 19.107/2010); Constitutional Court, Judgment of 28 June 2013, W III-2/2013 (VfSlg. 19.772/2013); Constitutional Court, Judgment of 1 July 2016, W I-6/2016 (VfSlg. 20.071/2016).

According to recent legal literature, the right to free suffrage also obliges public authorities to take action against any interference with the right to free suffrage by third parties (Pöschl, 2018, p. 53; Grabenwarter, 2019, pp. 92–93).[26] As Grabenwarter (2019) points out, this includes protection against intimidation, deception, the dissemination of false information, bribery, and other manipulations of elections. According to this view, the state is obliged to take action against disinformation by third parties to protect elections from manipulation. It is in this sense that the ECtHR judgment in the case of *Bradshaw and others v. United Kingdom* assumed that states have a duty to protect elections from disinformation by foreign agents.[27]

Independence of broadcasting. The Federal Constitutional Act on Guaranteeing the Independence of Broadcasting *(Bundesverfassungsgesetz über die Sicherung der Unabhängigkeit des Rundfunks [BVG Rundfunk])*[28] includes constitutional provisions on the independence of broadcasting services and their organization (Holoubek, Gärner and Grafl, 2019, pp. 1386–1388). It obliges federal legislation to enact provisions that ensure objective and impartial reporting by broadcasters.

Ban of National Socialism. The National Socialism Prohibition Act *(Verbotsgesetz 1947 [VerbotsG])*[29] lays down constitutional provisions on the prohibition of National Socialism. It also imposes a criminal ban on the dissemination of certain false statements regarding the crimes of National Socialism (see Sect. 3.1). The Act places constitutional limits on freedom of expression (Berka, Binder and Kneihs, 2019, p. 662 fn. 2875). Actions prohibited by the Act are therefore not protected by the right to freedom of communication.

2.2 *Implementation of EU Law*

In Austria, EU legal acts that tackle the problems of online disinformation[30] are typically implemented by federal legislation. The following list names the most important national laws in this regard:

- The Directive on Electronic Commerce[31] was implemented by the E-Commerce Act *(E-Commerce-Gesetz [ECG])*.[32]

---

[26] The Constitutional Court, however, took a different view in its Judgment of 1 July 2016, W I 6/2016 (VfSlg. 20.071/2020).

[27] ECtHR, Judgment of 22 July 2025, no. 15653/22, *Bradshaw and others v. United Kingdom*, para. 158–173.

[28] Federal Law Gazette 396/1974.

[29] State Law Gazette 13/1945 as amended by Federal Law Gazette I 177/2023.

[30] See the chapter by Claas Friedrich Germelmann in this volume.

[31] Directive 2000/31/EC of the European Parliament and of the Council of 8 June 2000 on certain legal aspects of information society services, in particular electronic commerce, in the Internal Market (Directive on electronic commerce).

[32] Federal Law Gazette I 152/2001 as amended by Federal Law Gazette I 182/2023.

- The Audiovisual Media Services Directive[33] was implemented by the Audiovisual Media Services Act *(Audiovisuelle Mediendienste-Gesetz [AMD-G])*.[34]
- The DSA Accompanying Act *(DSA-Begleitgesetz)*[35] lays down accompanying regulations for the implementation of the Digital Services Act (DSA).[36] The core document of this act is the Digital Services Coordinator Act *(Koordinator-für-digitale-Dienste-Gesetz [KDD-G])* (see Sect. 3.4).
- Accompanying regulations for the implementation of the Artificial Intelligence Act[37] have not yet been enacted.
- Accompanying regulations for the implementation of the Regulation on the transparency and targeting of political advertising[38] have not yet been enacted. However, in September 2025, the competent federal ministry presented a ministerial draft bill *(Ministerialentwurf)*.[39]

2.3 *Federal Laws*

The following overview lists relevant national federal laws that may be important in relation to (online) disinformation.

Criminal Law

- The Criminal Code *(Strafgesetzbuch [StGB])*[40] lays down rules on criminal offenses punishable by law. In certain circumstances, disseminating false information can constitute a criminal offense.
- The Code of Criminal Procedure *(Strafprozessordnung [StPO])*[41] lays down procedural rules for the prosecution of criminal offenses.

---

[33] Directive 2010/13/EU of the European Parliament and of the Council of 10 March 2010 on the coordination of certain provisions laid down by law, regulation or administrative action in Member States concerning the provision of audiovisual media services (Audiovisual Media Services Directive).

[34] Federal Law Gazette I 84/2001 as amended by Federal Law Gazette I 135/2023.

[35] Federal Law Gazette I 182/2023.

[36] Regulation (EU) 2022/2065 of the European and of the Council of 19 October 2022 on a Single Market For Digital Services and amending Directive 2000/31/EC (Digital Services Act).

[37] Regulation (EU) 2024/1689 of the European Parliament and of the Council of 13 June 2024 laying down harmonised rules on artificial intelligence and amending Regulations (EC) No 300/2008, (EU) No 167/2013, (EU) No 168/2013, (EU) 2018/858, (EU) 2018/1139 and (EU) 2019/2144 and Directives 2014/90/EU, (EU) 2016/797 and (EU) 2020/1828 (Artificial Intelligence Act).

[38] Regulation (EU) 2024/900 of the European Parliament and of the Council of 13 March 2024 on the transparency and targeting of political advertising.

[39] 49/ME, 28th legislative period (*Gesetzgebungsperiode*).

[40] Federal Law Gazette 60/1974 as amended by Federal Law Gazette I 50/2025.

[41] Federal Law Gazette 631/1975 as amended by Federal Law Gazette I 65/2025.

Civil Law

- The Civil Law Code *(Allgemeines bürgerliches Gesetzbuch [ABGB])*[42] lays down rules on the legal relationships between private individuals. In certain circumstances, an individual can make civil claims against another person for disseminating false information.
- The Copyright Act *(Urheberrechtsgesetz [UrhG])*[43] lays down rules on the protection of intellectual works in the fields of literature, music, art, and cinematography. It includes a right of the individual to one's own image (§ 78 UrhG).
- The Code of Civil Procedure *(Zivilprozessordnung [ZPO])*[44] lays down procedural rules for the enforcement of civil law claims.

Media Law

- The Media Act *(Mediengesetz [MedienG])*[45] lays down rules on the press and other published media. It includes specific rules on legal claims in the event of a violation of personal rights through such media.
- The Austrian Broadcasting Corporation Act *(ORF-Gesetz [ORF-G])*[46] lays down specific rules applying to the Austrian Broadcasting Corporation (*ORF*). The Austrian Broadcasting Corporation is a legal entity under public law.
- The Private Radio Broadcasting Act *(Privatradiogesetz [PrR-G])*[47] lays down rules for private radio services.

2.4 Repealed Federal Law: Communication Platforms Act

Austrian regulations on combating online hate speech were enacted recently in the Communication Platforms Act *(Kommunikationsplattformen-Gesetz [KoPl-G])*[48] (Fischer, Kettemann and Rachinger, 2020; Denk and Mischensky, 2022).

The Act was passed in December 2020 and entered into force on 1 January 2021.[49] The law aimed to combat the online dissemination of hate speech, including certain forms of disinformation.[50] It established various obligations for providers of online communication platforms. They were obliged to set up an effective and transparent procedure for dealing with and handling reports of allegedly illegal content available on the platform.[51] If illegal content was reported, the providers of communication

---

[42] Collection of Laws 946/1811 as amended by Federal Law Gazette I 25/2025.

[43] Federal Law Gazette 111/1936 as amended by Federal Law Gazette I 182/2023.

[44] Imperial Law Gazette 113/1895 as amended by Federal Law Gazette I 50/2025.

[45] Federal Law Gazette 314/1981 as amended by Federal Law Gazette I 182/2023.

[46] Federal Law Gazette 379/1984 as amended by Federal Law Gazette I 58/2025.

[47] Federal Law Gazette I 20/2001 as amended by Federal Law Gazette I 83/2023.

[48] Federal Law Gazette I 151/2020.

[49] § 14 KoPl-G.

[50] See the definition of "illegal content" in § 2, para. 8 KoPl-G.

[51] § 3 KoPl-G.

platforms were obliged to remove it.[52] The competent federal authority was authorized to enforce these obligations, for example, by imposing fines on providers of communication platforms.[53]

According to a judgment of the European Court of Justice in November 2023, the Communication Platforms Act was incompatible with the Country-of-Origin Principle (*Herkunftslandprinzip*) set out in the Directive on Electronic Commerce (Devlin and Steeneck, 2024).[54] Subsequently, the Communication Platforms Act was repealed with effect from 17 February 2024.[55]

2.5 *Case Law*

Constitutional Court. The Constitutional Court *(Verfassungsgerichtshof [VfGH])* has several competences,[56] including the competence to review federal and provincial laws for constitutionality.[57] The Constitutional Court also rules on the legality of elections and referendums.[58] It has repeatedly ruled on the question of whether the right to free suffrage protects against disinformation during elections.[59]

Supreme Court of Justice. The Supreme Court of Justice *(Oberster Gerichtshof [OGH])* is the highest instance in civil and criminal matters.[60] Its rulings have repeatedly addressed disinformation, particularly in civil law cases (see Sect. 3.2).

Supreme Administrative Court. The Supreme Administrative Court *(Verwaltungsgerichtshof [VwGH])* is, together with the Constitutional Court, the highest instance in matters of administrative law.[61] With respect to disinformation, the case law on the media's obligation to objectivity is of particular importance (see Sect. 3.3).

2.6 *Soft Law*

Government information. Public authorities have published legally non-binding documents on their websites to inform the public about the dangers of disinformation:

[52] § 3, para. 4 KoPl-G.

[53] §§ 8–11 KoPl-G.

[54] European Court of Justice, Judgment of 9 November 2023, no. C-376/22, *Google Ireland and others*.

[55] § 10, para. 1 KDD-G.

[56] Art. 137–145 B-VG.

[57] Art. 140 B-VG.

[58] Art. 141 B-VG.

[59] See, for example, Constitutional Court, Judgment of 30 August 1994, W I 6/1994 (VfSlg 13.839/1994); Constitutional Court, Judgment of 1 July 2016, W I 6/2016 (VfSlg 20.071/2016).

[60] Art. 92, para. 1 B-VG.

[61] Art. 133 B-VG.

- The "Action Plan Deepfake" *(Aktionsplan Deepfake)* provides an overview of the dangers posed by deepfakes and the measures that should be taken to mitigate them (Federal Ministry of the Interior, 2022).
- The flyer "Disinformation. What to do about it" *(Desinformation. Was kann ich dagegen tun?)* provides a brief overview of the dangers posed by disinformation and lists some relevant links (Federal Chancellery, 2024).
- The flyer "Tips for preventing online election manipulation" *(Tipps gegen Wahlmanipulationen im Netz)* gives recommendations on how to recognize online disinformation, especially AI-generated content and deepfakes (RTR, 2024).

Code of Honor (Austrian Press Council). The Austrian Press Council *(Österreichischer Presserat)* is a private association based in Vienna. It has published a Code of Honor *(Ehrenkodex)* laying down rules for good and responsible journalism (Press Council, no date). According to Sect. 2.1. of the Code of Honor, "conscientiousness and correctness in researching and reporting news and commentary are the foremost obligations of journalists."[62]

The Code of Honor is not legally binding. However, print media can become members of the Austrian Press Council and agree to abide by its rules and decisions.

3 The Legal Framework—Selected Regulations and Case Law

The following provides a brief overview of certain areas of Austrian law that may be relevant when it comes to combating disinformation. This overview is not exhaustive but focuses on a few selected regulations and cases.

3.1 Criminal Law

Relevant criminal offenses. In Austria, disinformation, whether online or not, is not punishable by law per se. However, in certain circumstances, disseminating false information can constitute a criminal offense.

Violation of personal rights. Disinformation can constitute a criminal offense if it violates the personal rights of individuals or affects them in a certain way. Important criminal offenses of this kind are:

- Persistent harassment involving telecommunication or computer systems *(Fortgesetzte Belästigung im Wege einer Telekommunikation oder eines Computersystems)* (§ 107c StGB),[63]

---

[62] My translation.

[63] "Any person who, using a telecommunication or computer system in a manner that can cause unreasonable interference with the lifestyle of another person.

- Deception *(Täuschung)* (§ 108 StGB),[64]
- Criminal defamation *(Üble Nachrede)* (§ 111 StGB),[65]
- Insult *(Beleidigung)* (§ 115 StGB),[66]
- Fraud *(Betrug)* (§ 146 StGB),[67] and
- False Accusation *(Verleumdung)* (§ 297 StGB).[68]

Influencing public elections or plebiscites. Disinformation can constitute a criminal offense if it is likely to influence public elections and plebiscites. Important criminal offenses of this kind are:

- Deception at elections or plebiscites *(Täuschung bei einer Wahl oder Volksabstimmung)* (§ 263 StGB),[69] and

1. commits an offense against the honour and reputation of a person in a manner noticeable by a larger number of people for a longer period of time or.

2. makes a fact or picture of the personal sphere of another available to a larger number of people for a longer period of time without the consent of the other person is liable to imprisonment for up to one year or a fine not exceeding 720 penalty units." (§ 107c, para. 1 StGB; translation in Schloenhardt, Höpfel and Eder, 2021, p. 112).

[64] "Any person who violates the rights of another for the purpose of causing a detriment to the other by deceiving the other person or a third person about material facts in order to cause the other person or the third person to do, acquiesce, or omit to do an act thus causing the detriment is liable to imprisonment for up to one year or a fine not exceeding 720 penalty units." (§ 108, para. 1 StGB; translation in Schloenhardt, Höpfel and Eder, 2021, p. 113).

[65] "Any person who accuses another person of a despicable characteristic or disposition, of dishonourable conduct, or of conduct against common decency in a way that the accusation is perceivable by a third person and in a manner capable of decrying or degrading the other person in the public opinion is liable to imprisonment for up to six months or a fine not exceeding 360 penalty units." (§ 111, para. 1 StGB; translation in Schloenhardt, Höpfel and Eder, 2021, p. 115).

[66] "Any person who publicly or in front of multiple other people insults or mocks another, does bodily harm to another or threatens another with bodily harm is liable to imprisonment for up to three months or a fine not exceeding 180 penalty units, unless this conduct is punishable by an offense with a more severe penalty." (§ 115, para. 1 StGB; translation in Schloenhardt, Höpfel and Eder, 2021, pp. 116–117).

[67] "Any person who by deceiving another about material facts causes the other person to do, acquiesce, or omit to do an act which causes a financial or other material loss to the other person or to a third person and who has the intention to gain an unlawful material benefit for himself, herself, or a third person is liable to imprisonment for up to six months or a fine not exceeding 360 penalty units." (§ 146, para. 1 StGB; translation in Schloenhardt, Höpfel and Eder, 2021, pp. 141–142).

[68] "Any person who puts another at risk of official prosecution by falsely suspecting the person of an offense requiring official prosecution or of violating official or professional duties, knowing (§ 5 para. 3) that the suspicion is false, is liable to imprisonment for up to one year or a fine not exceeding 720 penalty units; […]." (§ 297, para. 1 StGB; translation in Schloenhardt, Höpfel and Eder, 2021, p. 269).

[69] "Any person who by deception regarding material facts effects or attempts to effect that another errs about the content of his or her declaration when voting or casts an invalid vote against his or her will is liable to imprisonment for up to six months or a fine not exceeding 360 penalty units." (§ 263, para. 1 StGB; translation in Schloenhardt, Höpfel and Eder, 2021, p. 242).

- Disseminating false information at elections or plebiscites *(Verbreitung falscher Nachrichten bei einer Wahl oder Volksabstimmung)* (§ 264 StGB).[70]

Hate speech. Disinformation can also constitute a criminal offense if it involves certain forms of hate speech directed at certain groups. Important criminal offenses of this kind are:

- Hate speech *(Verhetzung)* (§ 283 StGB),[71] and
- Denial of National Socialist genocide and National Socialist crimes against humanity *(Leugnung des nationalsozialistischen Völkermords und der nationalsozialistischen Verbrechen gegen die Menschlichkeit)* (§ 3h VerbotsG).[72]

Repealed criminal offense. In the past, the dissemination of false, disturbing rumours *(Verbreitung falscher, beunruhigender Gerüchte)* (§ 276 StGB)[73] was a criminal offense. It was repealed in 2015 as it had no practical significance (Oberlaber, 2017, pp. 159–160). Some legal scholars have argued that abolishing this criminal offense may not have been a wise decision, considering the ongoing challenges posed by disinformation and fake news (Berka, 2018, p. 761; Schmoller, 2025, pp. 42–43; Zöchbauer, 2025, pp. 87–88).

---

[70] "Any person who publicly disseminates false information about a circumstance capable of preventing eligible voters from casting their vote or capable of influencing the exercise of their right to vote in a particular way at a point in time when a counter statement can no longer be effectively disseminated is liable to imprisonment for up to six months or a fine not exceeding 360 penalty units." (§ 264, para. 1 StGB; translation in Schloenhardt, Höpfel and Eder, 2021, p. 242).

[71] "Any person who publicly in a manner accessible to many people.

1. instigates the use of violence or incites hate against a church or religious community, or any other group of persons defined by existing or missing features relating to race, colour, language, religion or ideology, nationality, ancestry or national or ethnic origin, gender, impairment, age, or sexual orientation or any member of such group specifically because of the membership in such a group,

2. berates one of the groups listed in subpara. 1 or a person because of his or her membership of such a group with the purpose to violate the human dignity of members of the group or the person in a manner capable of decrying or degrading the group in the public opinion, or.

3. condones, denies, grossly downplays, or justifies felonies within the meaning of §§ 321 to 321f and § 321 k that have been determined with legal force by a domestic or international court, and if that conduct is specifically directed against one of the groups listed in subpara. 1 because of the membership in that group and is committed in a manner capable of inciting violence or hate against such a group or a member of such a group,

is liable to imprisonment for up to two years." (§ 283, para. 1 StGB; translation in Schloenhardt, Höpfel and Eder, 2021, pp. 259–260).

[72] "Any person who publicly denies, trivialises, endorses or seeks to justify the National Socialist genocide or other National Socialist crimes against humanity is liable to imprisonment for six months to five years, if the offense is not punishable under section 3g." (§ 3h, para. 1 VerbotsG; translation in https://www.ris.bka.gv.at/Dokumente/Erv/ERV_1945_13/ERV_1945_13.pdf, Accessed 1 Dec 2025).

[73] "Any person who, knowing (§ 5 para. 3) that it is false, disseminates a rumour which is likely to cause concern among a large number of people and thereby endanger public order, is liable to imprisonment for up to six months or a fine not exceeding 360 penalty units." (§ 276, para. 1 StGB; my translation).

In particular: Disseminating false information at elections or plebiscites (§ 264 StGB). According to § 264 of the Criminal Code, disinformation can constitute a criminal offense if it is likely to influence the behaviour of voters in public elections or plebiscites. In legal literature, this provision has been referred to as the "fake-news criminal offense" *(Fake News-Tatbestand)* (Lewisch, 2018, p. 89).

The scope of this criminal offense is limited in several ways (for more detail, see Lewisch, 2018, pp. 89–94). Firstly, it only applies to disinformation that is likely to influence public elections or plebiscites, not disinformation in general. Secondly, it only applies to the dissemination of false information, not propaganda or polemics (Eder-Rieder, 2024, para. 12). Thirdly, it only applies to public dissemination of false information. This requirement is met when the act is perceived by at least ten people.[74] Lastly, and most importantly, the act is only punishable if it is committed "at a point in time when a counter statement can no longer be effectively disseminated" (§ 264, para. 1 StGB). Since counter statements can be disseminated very quickly via the internet, this requirement will only be met if the false information is disseminated on the day before or the day of an election or plebiscite (Lewisch, 2018, p. 91).

Procedural rules. The following provides a brief overview of certain aspects of criminal procedure under Austrian law.

Subjects who can initiate criminal proceedings. Most of the criminal offenses mentioned above are prosecuted ex officio (*von Amts wegen*),[75] without the need for a formal complaint or claim by a victim or another person. Every person, including private individuals and public servants, regardless of their nationality, can report a criminal offense to the authorities. Once the authorities are aware of a criminal offense, it is solely their responsibility to conduct criminal proceedings.

Certain offenses against honour and reputation such as Criminal defamation (§ 111 StGB) and Insult (§ 115 StGB) are an exception. They are not prosecuted ex officio but only at the request of the victim (*Privatanklage*).[76]

Competent authorities. As part of investigative proceedings (*Ermittlungsverfahren*), the criminal investigation authorities (*Kriminalpolizei*) and the public prosecutor's office (*Staatsanwaltschaft*) are responsible for clarifying the relevant facts.[77] In the main proceedings (*Hauptverfahren*), the criminal courts (*Gerichte*) are responsible for deciding on the defendant's guilt and the penalty to be imposed.[78] The Supreme Court of Justice is the court of highest instance in criminal matters.[79]

---

[74] Supreme Court of Justice, Judgment of 8 February 1994, 11 Os 190/93.

[75] § 2, para. 1 StPO.

[76] § 71 StPO.

[77] § 2, para. 1 StPO.

[78] § 2, para. 2 StPO.

[79] Art. 92, para. 1 B-VG.

Sanctions. If someone is found guilty, the court imposes a penalty (imprisonment or fine).[80] Under certain circumstances, the court may also impose other sanctions,[81] such as the confiscation of property.[82]

3.2 Civil Law

Relevant civil law claims. Austrian civil law grants several claims that can be invoked by individuals who are affected by disinformation, such as the following:

- § 16 of the Civil Law Code[83] grants all persons certain "inherent [personal] rights", including e.g. the right to one's name, reputation, private sphere, and data security (Koch, 2023, para. 6–7). § 16 of the Civil Law Code is a programmatic provision which is specified by the following provisions.
- According to § 20, paragraph 1 of the Civil Law Code,[84] anyone who has suffered an infringement of a personal right or who fears that such infringement will be committed is entitled to an injunctive relief *(Unterlassung)* and claim for abatement and removal *(Beseitigung)* of the unlawful situation. If an intermediary is

[80] §§ 18–19 StGB.

[81] §§ 19a–31a StGB.

[82] § 19a StGB.

[83] "Every individual has inherent rights, already evident from common sense, and must thus be recognized as a person. Slavery or serfdom, and the exercise of any power in this regard, is prohibited in these countries." (translation in Esching and Pircher-Esching, 2021, p. 4).

[84] "(1) A person who has suffered an infringement of a right relating to personality or who fears that such infringement will be committed is entitled to an injunctive relief and claim for abatement and removal of the unlawful situation. The claim for injunctive relief also includes the claim for abatement and removal to remedy the unlawful situation caused by the non-compliance with the obligation to cease and desist from the infringing conduct. The persons specified in section 17a para 3 are also entitled to these claims subject to the requirements of section 17a para 3.

(2) If an employee or other staff suffers an infringement of his reputation or privacy in a medium in connection with the performance of his work and, provided that this conduct is capable to impair the employer's freedom to use the services of the respective employee or other staff not only to an insignificant degree or capable to materially infringe the reputation of the employee's or other staff's employer, the employer is entitled to file a claim for injunctive relief and claim for abatement and removal irrespective of the corresponding claim of the employee or other staff. This applies to volunteers and bodies of corporations accordingly. The employer's assertion of a claim does not require the consent of the employee or other staff. The employer has no duty to assert any claims at court in connection with the infringement of any of the employer's or other staff's right relating to personality, in particular not based on the employer's duty of care.

(3) If a person who has committed an infringement of a right relating to personality, of if an infringement is imminent based on the conduct of such person, uses the services of an intermediary for that purpose, a claim for injunctive relief and claim for abatement and removal can also be submitted at court against the intermediary. If the intermediary satisfies the requirements of the exemption from liability pursuant to the E-Commerce Act (*ECG*), the corresponding claims can only be brought against the intermediary following a prior warning. Service provider within the meaning of section 13 E-Commerce Act (ECG) do not qualify as intermediaries within meaning of para 3." (translation in Esching and Pircher-Esching, 2021, pp. 6–7).

involved, a claim for injunctive relief and claim for abatement and removal can also be submitted against the intermediary (§ 20, para. 3 ABGB).

- § 43 of the Civil Law Code[85] protects individuals from unauthorized use of their name *(Schutz des Namens)*. If a person is infringed by the unlawful use of his or her name, he or she is entitled to an injunctive relief and to claim for damages.
- As a general rule, § 1295 of the Civil Law Code[86] grants any person a claim for fault-based damages.
- § 1330 of the Civil Law Code[87] protects the honour *(Ehre)* and reputation of any person. If someone circulates facts that jeopardize the credit or income of another person and they knew or should have known that they are false, they are liable (§ 1330, para. 2 ABGB).
- § 78 of the Copyright Act[88] grants any person the right to their own image *(Bildnisschutz)*.

In particular: § 20, paragraph 3 ABGB. This provision was introduced in 2020 by the Online Hate Combating Act *(Hass-im-Netz-Bekämpfungs-Gesetz [HiNBG])*.[89] It was intended to provide victims of hate speech on the internet with effective legal remedies (Dokalik and Mokrejs-Weinhappel, 2021; Galla, 2021; Schoditsch and Brugger, 2021).

§ 20, paragraph 3 of the Civil Law Code explicitly clarifies that, in the event of a violation of personal right, the intermediary *(Vermittler)* can be sued for injunctive relief and removal. The term “intermediary” includes hosting service providers, such as deployers of online communication platforms (Dokalik and Mokrejs-Weinhappel,

[85] “If someone’s right to carry his name is challenged or he is infringed by the unlawful use of his name (alias), he is entitled to an injunctive relief, and in the case of fault, to claim for damages.” (translation in Esching and Pircher-Esching, 2021, p. 12).

[86] “(1) Everyone is entitled to claim compensation for damages from the damaging party who caused the damage at his fault; the damage may have been caused by breach of a contractual obligation or without reference to a contract.

(2) Whoever causes damages with malicious intent in a way which violates public policy is liable as well, however, if this happened when exercising a right, only if the exercise of the right obviously had the purpose of harming the other party.” (translation in Esching and Pircher-Esching, 2021, p. 465).

[87] “(1) If an actual damage or lost profit has been caused to someone by libel, he is entitled to claim compensation.

(2) This also applies if someone circulates facts which jeopardise the credit, the income or the progress of someone else and he knew or must have known the untruth of such. In this event the revocation and its publication can also be demanded. He is not liable for an announcement not made publicly, the untruth of which the announcing person did not know, if he or the recipient of the announcement had a legitimate interest in it.” (translation in Esching and Pircher-Esching, 2021, pp. 478–479).

[88] “(1) Pictures of persons may not be publicly displayed or distributed in any way that makes them accessible to the public if doing so would violate the legitimate interests of the person depicted, or, if that person is deceased, of a close relative, unless this has been authorized or ordered.” (My translation).

[89] Federal Law Gazette I 182/2020.

2021, p. 316). Hosting service providers can only be sued after they have been warned about the illegal content (§ 20, para. 3, last sentence ABGB).

Procedural rules. The following provides a brief overview of certain aspects of civil procedure under Austrian law.

Subjects who can initiate proceedings. In principle, anyone whose civil rights have been violated can file a lawsuit. Under certain conditions, public or private associations, such as the private Consumer Information Association (*Verein für Konsumenteninformation*),[90] may take legal actions against economic operators on behalf of consumers (*Verbandsklage*)[91] (Scholz-Berger, 2024; Schusser and Hotter, 2024/2025).

Competent authorities. Civil courts exercise jurisdiction over civil lawsuits.[92]

Sanctions. In principle, Austrian civil law has a compensatory function. It is intended to restore the lawful state and compensate for damage suffered. Depending on the respective civil law claims, civil courts may impose various sanctions on the unsuccessful party in a civil lawsuit such as:

- injunction *(Unterlassung),*
- removal *(Beseitigung),*
- revocation *(Widerruf),* and
- compensation for damages *(Schadenersatz).*

In particular: Proceedings for a substantial violation of personal rights within an electronic communication network *(Verfahren wegen erheblicher Verletzung von Persönlichkeitsrechten in einem elektronischen Kommunikationsnetz)* (§ 549 ZPO).[93] This provision was introduced in 2020 by the Online Hate Combating Act. It is intended to facilitate civil law proceedings against hate speech on the internet (Mokrejs-Weinhappel, 2021).

§ 549 of the ZPO provides for a simplified procedure *(Mandatsverfahren)* for individuals whose personal rights have been violated on the internet. The provision applies to significant violations of personal rights within an electronic communication network that impair the human dignity of a natural person. On the request of the person concerned, the court shall issue an injunction *(Unterlassungsauftrag)* without prior oral proceedings or hearing the defendant. This lawsuit may also be filed against

---

[90] Consumer Information Association, no date.

[91] See §§ 28–30 Consumer Protection Law *(Konsumentenschutzgesetz [KSchG]),* Federal Law Gazette 140/1979 as amended by Federal Law Gazette I 85/2024; §§ 619–635 ZPO; Qualified Entities Act *(Qualifizierte-Einrichtungen-Gesetz [QEG]),* Federal Law Gazette I 85/2024.

[92] § 1 Law on Court Jurisdiction *(Jurisdiktionsnorm [JN]),* Imperial Law Gazette 111/1895 as amended by Federal Law Gazette I 50/2025.

[93] "(1) In legal disputes concerning civil actions in which claims for injunctive relief are asserted exclusively on the grounds of a significant violation of personal rights within an electronic communication network that impairs the human dignity of a natural person, the court shall issue an injunction at the request of the plaintiff without prior oral proceedings or hearing the defendant if the claim can be conclusively derived from the information contained in the complaint. […].

[…]" (My translation).

hosting service providers, such as deployers of online communication platforms (Mokrejs-Weinhappel, 2021).

In judicial practice, this simplified procedure has so far been of limited significance (Koller, 2023).[94]

Case law. Rulings of the Supreme Court of Justice have repeatedly addressed problems of (online) disinformation in various civil law contexts. The following list provides an overview of some important rulings in recent years:

Supreme Court of Justice, Decision of 27 November 2019, 6 Ob 172/19s. This decision concerned posts on social networks (Facebook and Twitter), accusing a person of plagiarizing their doctoral thesis. The court held that the expression of untrue factual claims is not protected by freedom of expression. Given the seriousness of accusations of plagiarism, civil courts must thoroughly assess whether the accusations are true.

Supreme Court of Justice, Judgment of 2 July 2020, 4 Ob 31/20t. This judgment concerned a post by a politician on a social network (Twitter) that was written in the name of another politician. The court ruled that the post was likely to deceive the public, considering that people usually read online posts quickly. Since the post was not satirical, it violated the personal rights of the person concerned.

Supreme Court of Justice, Judgment of 30 August 2023, 6 Ob 166/22p. This judgment concerned a civil claim of a person living in Austria against an online social media company based in Ireland. The claimant demanded the worldwide removal of certain posts that defamed him. The court ruled in favour of the claimant. The court held that the Country-of-Origin Principle, as laid down in Article 3 of the Directive on Electronic Commerce, did not preclude the application of Austrian law because the claimant's human dignity had been violated.

Supreme Court of Justice, Judgment of 26 April 2024, 6 Ob 210/23k. The defendant shared a post on a social network (Facebook) defaming a police officer. The court held that a person who shares an online post may be held liable under civil law for damages, even if the resulting "shitstorm" was not caused solely by that person.

Supreme Court of Justice, Decision of 25 June 2024, 4 Ob 191/23a. This decision concerned a civil claim of the Austrian Broadcasting Corporation (*Österreichischer Rundfunk [ORF]*) against an online social media company based in Ireland. The claimant demanded the removal of a post that defamed it. The court held that the Country-of-Origin Principle, as laid down in Article 3 of the Directive on Electronic Commerce, does not permit the application of Austrian law in this case as it concerns the rights of a legal entity (the ORF).

Supreme Court of Justice, Judgment of 21 January 2025, 4 Ob 192/24z. A satirical magazine had used the name of a political party to send satirical letters to restaurants. The court ruled in favour of the political party's request for an injunction because the satirical nature of the letters was not evident. The court held that, without sanctions for disinformation, freedom of expression could be used to deliberately deceive and violate personal rights. Such behaviour is not protected by freedom of expression.

[94] See, however, Supreme Court of Justice, Judgment of 30 August 2023, 6 Ob 166/22p.

3.3 Media Law

Specific civil law claims. The Media Act lays down specific provisions enabling affected individuals to take legal action against the violation of their personal rights by media owners (Berka, 2019). These provisions can also be relevant when it comes to tackling disinformation in mass media (Zöchbauer, 2025). Individuals can invoke the following claims:

- Criminal defamation, insult, ridicule and false accusation *(Üble Nachrede, Beschimpfung, Verspottung und Verleumdung)* (§ 6 MedienG),[95]
- Violation of the strictly personal sphere *(Verletzung des höchstpersönlichen Lebensbereiches)* (§ 7 MedienG),[96] and
- Protection of the presumption of innocence *(Schutz der Unschuldsvermutung)* (§ 7b MedienG).[97]

Obligations to objectivity. Media law sets out various provisions requiring certain media services to report objectively. For example, the ORF must ensure an objective selection and presentation of information (Pöschl, 2014).[98] Private audiovisual[99] and radio services[100] must comply with the principle of objectivity and diversity of opinions (Eberhard, 2014).

Subjects who can initiate proceedings. The relevant laws entitle various persons to lodge a complaint *(Beschwerde)* for an infringement of these (and other) obligations with the authority,[101] including:

- A person who claims to have been directly damaged by the infringement of law,
- a person under certain circumstances if the complaint is supported by 120 persons (100 persons if it concerns private radio services), and
- an undertaking which is affected in its legal or economic interests by the alleged infringement.

---

[95] "(1) If the offense of criminal defamation, insult, ridicule or false accusation is committed in a medium, the person affected is entitled to claim from the media owner indemnity for the adverse personal effects suffered (§ 8 para 1)." (translation in https://www.ris.bka.gv.at/Dokumente/Erv/ERV_1981_314/ERV_1981_314.html, Accessed 1 Dec 2025).

[96] "(1) If a medium discusses or presents the strictly personal sphere of a person in a manner suited to compromise such person in public, the person affected is entitled to claim indemnity from the media owner for the adverse personal effects suffered (§ 8 para 1)." (translation in https://www.ris.bka.gv.at/Dokumente/Erv/ERV_1981_314/ERV_1981_314.html, Accessed 1 Dec 2025).

[97] "(1) If in any medium a person suspected of having committed an offense punishable by the courts but not yet finally convicted, is presented as having already been found guilty or as author of such punishable offense and not only as suspect, the person affected is entitled to claim indemnity from the media owner for the adverse personal effects suffered (§ 8 para 1)." (translation in https://www.ris.bka.gv.at/Dokumente/Erv/ERV_1981_314/ERV_1981_314.html, Accessed 1 Dec 2025).

[98] § 4, para. 5 ORF-G.

[99] § 41, para. 1 AMD-G.

[100] § 16, para. 1 PrR-G.

[101] § 36, para. 1 ORF-G; § 61, para. 1 AMD-G; § 25, para. 1 PrR-G.

The authority can also initiate proceedings ex officio.

Competent authority. The competent authority for deciding on violations of these obligations is the Austrian Communications Authority (*Kommunikationsbehörde Austria [KommAustria]*).[102] The KommAustria is an independent federal administrative authority responsible for numerous tasks in the field of media law (Kogler and Ulrich, 2024).[103] The RTR supports KommAustria in the performance of its tasks.[104]

Sanctions. The KommAustria determines whether any provision of the relevant laws has been violated and which facts form the basis of a violation.[105]

In the case of repeated and serious infringements of the law by a private audiovisual or radio service, the KommAustria shall initiate proceedings regarding withdrawal and prohibition of the license.[106]

Case law on the media's duties to objectivity. The following list provides an overview of some important rulings of the Constitutional Court and Supreme Administrative Court on the media's duties to objectivity in recent years:

Constitutional Court, Judgment of 10 December 2020, E 2281/2020 (VfSlg 20.427/2020). A political scientist labelled a politician as "batty" (*"plemplem"*) on an ORF news program. The court ruled that, with regard to freedom of expression, the anchor was not obliged to distance herself from this statement.

Supreme Administrative Court, Decision of 2 May 2020, Ra 2020/03/0009. The applicant, an Austrian sugar producer, claimed that the ORF had violated its duty to objectivity by broadcasting the special feature "Consciously Healthy: Sugar – the Sweet Poison" (*"Bewusst gesund: Zucker – das süße Gift"*). The court ruled that, although the title was polemical, the ORF had not exceeded its legal scope of discretion.

Supreme Administrative Court, Judgment of 15 May 2024, Ra 2023/03/0148. A commentator on a private television channel made misleading statements about the SARS-CoV-2 vaccine. The court ruled that the duty to objectivity may also be violated by a comment in a single episode of a television show.

---

[102] § 35, para. 3 ORF-G; § 66, para. 1 AMD-G; § 31, para. 2 PrR-G.

[103] § 2 KommAustria Act *(Komm-Austria-Gesetz [KOG])*, Federal Law Gazette I 32/2001 as amended by Federal Law Gazette I 50/2025.

[104] §§ 16–20 KommAustria Act.

[105] § 37, para. 1 ORF-G; § 62, para. 1 AMD-G; § 25, para. 3 PrR-G.

[106] § 63 AMDG; § 28 PrR-G.

3.4 Platform Law (Implementation of the DSA)

The DSA sets out several ways to tackle the dissemination of illegal content on the internet.[107] As a regulation, the DSA is directly applicable.[108] Austrian national law only lays down a few accompanying provisions for the national implementation of the DSA (Grafl, 2024; Paspalj, 2025):

Competent authorities. The competent authority responsible for performing the tasks of the Digital Services Coordinator *(Koordinator für digitale Dienste)*[109] is the KommAustria.[110] However, restrictions of access to intermediary services[111] shall be imposed by the Federal Administrative Court *(Bundesverwaltungsgericht)* on the request of the KommAustria.[112]

Fines and penalty payments. In accordance with Article 52 of the DSA, Austrian law lays down rules on fines and penalty payments *(Geldstrafen und Zwangsgeld)* applicable to infringements of the DSA.[113] The KommAustria is the responsible authority for imposing fines and penalty payments.[114]

These provisions can also be relevant in the context of tackling the dissemination of online disinformation. For example, if the provider of an online platform fails to establish a notice-and-action mechanism in accordance with Article 16 of the DSA, the provider may be punishable.[115] Fines and penalty payments can be imposed on both natural and legal persons (Grafl, 2024, pp. 134–135).

Under Austrian law, these fines and penalty payments are so-called administrative offenses *(Verwaltungsübertretungen)*. The Administrative Penal Act *(Verwaltungsstrafgesetz [VStG])*[116] sets out general procedural rules for the prosecution of administrative offenses (Hengstschläger and Leeb, 2023, pp. 399–540).

Right to lodge a complaint. In accordance with Article 53 of the DSA, the KommAustria has to decide on complaints against providers of intermediary services by issuing an administrative decision *(Bescheid)*.[117]

The specific modalities of this right are controversial in legal literature (for a German law perspective, see Schneider, 2023). Austrian law does not specify whether and what proceedings are to be conducted on the basis of a complaint, nor what legal effects an administrative decision has. Grafl has argued that the right to

[107] See the chapter by Claas Friedrich Germelmann in this volume.

[108] Art. 288 of the Treaty on the Functioning of the European Union *(Vertrag über die Arbeitsweise der Europäischen Union [AEUV])*.

[109] Art. 49 DSA.

[110] § 2 KDD-G.

[111] Art. 51, para. 3 (b) DSA.

[112] § 4 KDD-G.

[113] §§ 5–6 KDD-G.

[114] § 6 KDD-G.

[115] § 5, para. 2, subpara. 1 KDD-G.

[116] Federal Law Gazette 52/1991 as amended by Federal Law Gazette I 50/2025.

[117] § 2, para. 3, subpara. 11 KDD-G.

lodge a complaint constitutes an independent procedure concerning the violation of subjective rights of complainants (2024, p. 131).[118]

The General Administrative Procedure Act *(Allgemeines Verwaltungsverfahrensgesetz [AVG])*[119] sets out general procedural rules for the issuing of administrative decisions (Hengstschläger and Leeb, 2023, pp. 67–398).

4 Public and Private Reporting Offices

Several public and private reporting offices *(Meldestellen)* have been set up in Austria, to which anyone can report illegal content. These reporting offices may also be relevant when it comes to reporting disinformation. Reports do not necessarily result in legal proceedings. Instead, they are intended to provide information to the authorities or offer advice to those affected. Reporting offices of this kind are:

- Reporting Office National Socialist reactivation *(Meldestelle NS-Wiederbetätigung)*[120] (Directorate State Protection and Intelligence Service, no date),
- Reporting Office Extremism and Terrorism *(Meldestelle Extremismus und Terrorismus)*[121] (Directorate State Protection and Intelligence Service, no date),
- Reporting Office Cyber Crime *(Meldestelle Cybercrime)* (Criminal Intelligence Service, no date), and
- Advice Centre Against Online Hate *(Beratungsstelle GegenHassImNetz)* (Civil Courage and Anti-Racism Work, no date).

5 Conclusions and Perspectives

5.1 Few Explicit Rules but Various References to Disinformation

As the overview of the national legal framework in Sects. 2 and 3 has shown, there are few rules at the national level in Austria that explicitly focus on combating disinformation, and in particular, online disinformation. However, numerous legal provisions across various areas of law can be relevant in this context.

Disinformation can be illegal under both civil and criminal law if it infringes the rights of individuals. In certain circumstances, disinformation may also be illegal for

[118] My translation.

[119] Federal Law Gazette 51/1991 as amended by Federal Law Gazette I 50/2025.

[120] § 4, para. 2 State Protection and Intelligence Service Act *(Staatsschutz- und Nachrichtendienst-Gesetz [SNG])*, Federal Law Gazette I 5/2016 as amended by Federal Law Gazette I 54/2025.

[121] § 4, para. 2a SNG.

reasons of public interest, for example, if it could influence elections or if it involves hate speech. Furthermore, certain media providers (broadcasters) are obliged to ensure objectivity in their reporting. Apart from such special circumstances, however, the deliberate dissemination of false information is not illegal.

5.2 *Recent and Possible Future Legislation*

Recent legislation, such as the Communication Platforms Act (see Sect. 2.4) and the Online Hate Combating Act (see Sect. 3.2), has primarily focused on tackling online hate speech.

The current federal government's program addresses disinformation in several contexts:

- Under the heading "Packet of measures against online radicalization" *(Maßnahmenpaket gegen Onlineradikalisierung)*, the program calls for disinformation to be consistently combated and regulated (Federal Chancellery, 2025, p. 87).
- Under the heading "Fortified Democracy" *(Wehrhafte Demokratie)*, the program promotes measures to foster democracy education, strengthen the culture of debate, and encourage a science-friendly environment in order to actively combat disinformation (Federal Chancellery, 2025, p. 91).
- Under the heading "More Security for and through Europe" *(Mehr Sicherheit für und durch Europa)*, the program states that Austria is committed to strengthening its resilience to disinformation (Federal Chancellery, 2025, pp. 133–134).
- Under the heading "Reinforced Regulation and Control over Digital Platforms" *(Verstärkte Regulierung und Kontrolle über digitale Plattformen)*, the program calls for the examination of further national measures to combat disinformation, but does not explain them in detail (Federal Chancellery, 2025, p. 143).
- Under the heading "Combatting Fake News and Disinformation" *(Kampf gegen Fake News und Desinformation)* the program demands free access to Austrian digital media for pupils and apprentices (Federal Chancellery, 2025, p. 144).

As this overview shows, the current federal government of Austria apparently regards disinformation as a fundamental threat to national security and democracy. However, the federal government's program only provides a vague description of how disinformation should be tackled at a national level.

5.3 *Discussion in Legal Literature*

Legal scholars in Austria have repeatedly highlighted the dangers of disinformation, with respect to democracy in particular (Pöschl, 2018, pp. 35–36; Grabenwarter, 2019, pp. 90–91; Pabel, 2020, pp. 103–104; Gärner, 2022, pp. 93–96; Lewisch, 2025; Rohregger and Dumfarth, 2025; Soldan, 2025). In contrast, Kettemann (2025) argued that there is no empirical evidence which suggests disinformation has a significant impact on opinion-forming processes. While he acknowledges the challenges posed by disinformation, he denies that it poses an existential threat to democracy.

Some authors have argued in favour of legal amendments to better address the dangers of disinformation (for an overview of possible amendments, see Lewisch, 2025, pp. 29–35; Rohregger and Dumfarth, 2025, pp. 52–57; Zöchbauer, 2025, pp. 87–88). For example, Lewisch (2018) suggested amending the criminal offense "Disseminating false information at elections or plebiscites" (§ 264 StGB) to make it more effective in context of modern communication (see also Lewisch, 2025; Rohregger and Dumfarth, 2025). Noll (2019) addressed possible amendments to media law considering the increasing shift of communication to the internet. Gärner (2022) discussed whether less intrusive measures, such as fact-checks and warnings, might be useful to better tackle disinformation.

References

Achleitner R A (2022) Der Digital Services Act als risikobasierte Regulierung. Medien und Recht international (4): 114–121

Berka W (2018) Aktuelle Bedrohungen des Grundrechts auf Privatsphäre. Österreichische Juristenzeitung (17): 755–762

Berka W (2019) Vorbemerkungen §§ 6–8a. In: Berka W et al (eds) Mediengesetz Praxiskommentar, 4th edn. LexisNexis, Vienna

Berka W (2021) Verfassungsrecht, 8th edn. Verlag Österreich, Vienna

Berka W, Binder C, Kneihs B (2019) Die Grundrechte, 2nd edn. Verlag Österreich, Vienna

Bezemek C (2015) Freie Meinungsäußerung. Verlag Österreich, Vienna

Blaßnig M (2020) In Zeiten der Infodemie. Juridikum (4): 433–442

Denk S, Mischensky L (2022) Das Kommunikationsplattformen-Gesetz: eine öffentlich-rechtliche Bestandsaufnahme. Medien und Recht (3): 140–147

Devlin A, Steeneck J-H (2024) Keine generell-abstrakten Ausnahmen von Herkunftslandprinzip. Kommunikation und Recht (1): 18–21

Dokalik D, Mokrejs-Weinhappel C (2021) Die Bekämpfung von „Hass im Netz" mit den Mitteln des Zivilrechts. Österreichische Juristenzeitung (7): 309–318

Eberhard H (2014) Meinungsvielfältige Angebote im privaten Sektor. In: Berka W, Grabenwarter C, Holoubek M (eds) Meinungsvielfalt im Rundfunk und in den Online-Medien. Manz, Vienna

Eder-Rieder M (2024) § 264. In: Hinterhofer H (ed) Salzburger Kommentar zum Strafgesetzbuch. LexisNexis, Vienna

Esching P A, Pircher-Esching E (2021) Das österreichische ABGB – The Austria Civil Code, 2nd edn. LexisNexis, Vienna

Federal Chancellery *(Bundeskanzleramt)* (2024) Desinformation. Was kann ich dagegen tun https://www.bundeskanzleramt.gv.at/dam/jcr:50b2db5e-3457-4b58-bd67-d98f266cdd9b/flyer_desinformation_ueuw.pdf. Accessed 1 Dec 2025

Federal Chancellery *(Bundeskanzleramt)* (2025) Jetzt das Richtige tun. Für Österreich. https://www.bundeskanzleramt.gv.at/bundeskanzleramt/die-bundesregierung/regierungsdokumente.html, Accessed 1 Dec 2025

Federal Ministry of the Interior *(Bundesministerium für Inneres)* (2022) Aktionsplan Deepfake. https://www.bmi.gv.at/bmi_documents/2779.pdf, Accessed 1 Dec 2025

Feik R (2007) Öffentliche Verwaltungskommunikation. Springer, Vienna

Fischer G, Kettemann M C, Rachinger F (2020) Ein sanfter Riesenbändiger. Österreichische Juristenzeitung (23-24): 1064–1071
Galla F (2021) Hass im Netz. Facultas, Vienna
Gärner C (2022) Bekämpfung von Fake News. In: Grabenwarter C, Holoubek M, Leitl-Staudinger B (eds) Regulierung von Kommunikationsplattformen. Manz, Vienna
Grabenwarter C (2019) Die Freiheit der Wahl im „postfaktischen" Zeitalter. In: Berka W, Holoubek M, Leitl-Staudinger B (eds) Elektronische Medien im „postfaktischen" Zeitalter. Manz, Vienna
Grabenwarter C, Pabel K (2021) Europäische Menschenrechtskonvention, 7th edn. Beck, Munich
Grafl H (2024) Das Koordinator-für-digitale-Dienste-Gesetz – nationale Begleitmaßnahmen zum Digital Services Act. Zeitschrift für Informationsrecht (2): 130–135
Hengstschläger J, Leeb D (2023) Verwaltungsverfahrensrecht, 7th edn. Facultas, Vienna
Hinghofer-Szalkay S (2025) Art 10 EMRK. In: Korinek K, Holoubek M et al (eds) Österreichisches Bundesverfassungsrecht. Verlag Österreich, Vienna
Holoubek M (2022) Plattformregulierung aus grundrechtlicher Perspektive. In: Grabenwarter C, Holoubek M, Leitl-Staudinger B (eds) Regulierung von Kommunikationsplattformen. Manz, Vienna
Holoubek M, Gärner C, Grafl H (2019) Recht der Massenmedien. In: Holoubek M, Potacs M (eds): Öffentliches Wirtschaftsrecht. Band 1, 4th edn. Verlag Österreich, Vienna
Kaschka J (2024) Die Meinungsäußerungsfreiheit im Spannungsfeld staatlicher Gewährleistungspflichten. Journal für Rechtspolitik (2-3): 112–126
Kaschka J (2025) Die Risikominderungspflicht nach Art 35 DSA im Lichte der Kommunikationsfreiheit von Nutzern. In: Berger L B et al (eds) Recht innovativ – Das öffentliche Recht im (digitalen) Wandel. Jan Sramek, Vienna
Kettemann M C (2025) Desinformation in der Demokratie: Gefährdung oder Fehleinschätzung? https://www.derstandard.at/story/3000000257825/desinformation-in-der-demokratie-gefaehrdung-oder-fehleinschaetzung, Accessed 1 Dec 2025.
Koch B A (2023) § 16 ABGB. In: Bydlinski P, Perner S, Spitzer M (eds): Kommentar zum ABGB, 7th edn. Verlag Österreich, Vienna
Kogler M, Ulrich A (2024) Von der Transparenz über Terror, Vielfalt und Qualität zur KI – Die vielfältigen Aufgaben der KommAustria. In: Baumgartner G (ed) Jahrbuch Öffentliches Recht. Verlag Österreich, Vienna
Koller C (2023) § 549 ZPO. In: Kodek G, Oberhammer P (eds) ZPO-ON. Manz, Vienna
Lewisch P (2018) Meinungsfreiheit – Hassrede – Moderne Informationstechnologien: Das Strafrecht vor neuen Herausforderungen? In Koziol H (ed) Tatsachenmitteilungen und Werturteile: Freiheit und Verantwortung. Jan Sramek Verlag, Vienna
Lewisch P (2025) Fake News: Psychologische Grundlagen und rechtliche Einordnung. In: Benn-Ibler G, Lewisch P (eds) Fake News und Meinungsfreiheit. Manz, Vienna
Merli F (2019) Grenzen der Staatsinformation und staatlicher Propaganda. In: Berka W, Holoubek M, Leitl-Staudinger B (eds) Elektronische Medien im „postfaktischen" Zeitalter. Manz, Vienna
Mokrejs-Weinhappel C (2021) Zivilprozessuale Maßnahmen zur Bekämpfung von „Hass im Netz". Österreichische Juristenzeitung (2): 53–63
Nemeth, M (forthcoming) Kommunikationsfreiheit und staatliche Kommunikationspflicht in der Krise. Dissertation, University of Graz
Noll A J (2019) „Fake News" – grundrechtliche und rechtspolitische Aspekte. In: Berka W, Holoubek M, Leitl-Staudinger B (eds) Elektronische Medien im „postfaktischen" Zeitalter. Manz, Vienna
Ó Fathaigh R, Helberger N, Appelman N (2021) The Perils of Legally Defining Disinformation. Internet Policy Review 10(4): 1–25. https://doi.org/10.14763/2021.4.1584
Oberlaber J (2017) Fake News und der Ruf nach dem Strafrecht. Juridikum (2): 157–160
Pabel K (2020) Internet und Kommunikationsfreiheiten im Licht der EMRK. Journal für Rechtspolitik (2): 101–107
Paspalj F (2025) Talk of the town: Digital Services Act. juridikum (3): 314–325

Pöschl M (2014) Meinungsvielfalt im öffentlich-rechtlichen Rundfunk. In: Berka W, Grabenwarter C, Holoubek M (eds) Meinungsvielfalt im Rundfunk und in den Online-Medien. Manz, Vienna

Pöschl M (2018) Neuvermessung der Meinungsfreiheit? In Koziol H (ed) Tatsachenmitteilungen und Werturteile: Freiheit und Verantwortung. Jan Sramek, Vienna

Regulatory Authority for Broadcasting and Telecommunication *(Rundfunk und Telekom Regulierungs-GmbH)* (2024) Tipps gegen Wahlmanipulation im Netz. https://www.rtr.at/medien/was_wir_tun/DigitaleDienste/DownloadOrdnerDigitaleDienste/Broschuere_NRW_24.pdf, Accessed 1 Dec 2025

Rohregger M, Dumfarth T (2025) Grundrechtlicher Rahmen: Fake News vs Meinungsfreiheit. In: Benn-Ibler G, Lewisch P (eds) Fake News und Meinungsfreiheit. Manz, Vienna

Schloenhardt A, Höpfel F, Eder J (eds) (2021) Strafgesetzbuch. Austrian Criminal Code, 2nd edn. Neuer Wissenschaftlicher Verlag, Vienna

Schneider J-P (2023) Das verwaltungsrechtliche Beschwerderecht für Plattformnutzer gem. Art. 53 DSA. Computer und Recht 39(1): 45–52

Schmoller K (2025) 50 Jahre StGB – nachhaltiges Strafrecht für alte und neue Herausforderungen? Manz, Vienna

Schoditsch T, Brugger M (2021) Zivilrechtlicher Persönlichkeitsschutz im Internet – das neue HiNBG. Zeitschrift für Familien- und Erbrecht (3): 100–106

Scholz-Berger, F (2024) Kollektive Durchsetzung von Abhilfeansprüchen nach Umsetzung der VerbandsklagenRL in Österreich. ecolex (7): 583–588

Schusser S, Hotter A (2024/2025) Die neue Abhilfeverbandsklage: Kollektiver Rechtsschutz in Österreich nach Umsetzung der Verbandsklagen-RL. Juristische Ausbildung und Praxisvorbereitung (1): 46–51

Soldan M (2025) Making Europe Fit for the Digital Age? University of Vienna Law Review 9(2): 140–191. https://doi.org/10.25365/vlr-2025-9-2-140

Stelzer M (2022) The Constitution of the Republic of Austria, 2nd edn. Hart, Oxford, London, New York, New Delhi, Sydney

Storr S (2019) Darf der Staat lügen? Journal für Rechtspolitik (2): 75–86

Struth A K (2019) Hassrede und Freiheit der Meinungsäußerung. Springer, Berlin

Website Civil Courage and Anti-Racism Work *(Zivilcourage und Anti-Rassismus-Arbeit)*, https://www.zara.or.at/, Accessed 1 Dec 2025

Website Consumer Information Association *(Verein für Konsumenteninformation)*, https://verbraucherrecht.at/, Accessed 1 Dec 2025

Website Criminal Intelligence Service *(Bundeskriminalamt)*, https://www.bundeskriminalamt.at/, Accessed 1 Dec 2025

Website Directorate State Protection and Intelligence Service *(Direktion für Staatsschutz und Nachrichtendienst)*, https://www.dsn.gv.at/, Accessed 1 Dec 2025

Website Federal Chancellery *(Bundeskanzleramt)*, https://www.bundeskanzleramt.gv.at/themen/kampf-gegen-desinformation/kampf-gegen-desinformation-artikelseite.html, Accessed 1 Dec 2025

Website Press Council *(Presserat)*, https://www.presserat.at/, Accessed 1 Dec 2025

Website Regulatory Authority for Broadcasting and Telecommunications (*Rundfunk und Telekom Regulierungs-GmbH [RTR]*), DSA und Desinformation, https://www.rtr.at/medien/was_wir_tun/DigitaleDienste/DSA/Desinformation.html, Accessed 1 Dec 2025

Zöchbauer P (2025) Fake News, Medienfreiheit & more. In: Benn-Ibler G, Lewisch P (eds) Fake News und Meinungsfreiheit. Manz, Vienna

Online Disinformation in the Belgian Legal Framework: The Elephant in the Room?

Valentin Speleers and Marie Vanloocke

Abstract This chapter examines the current Belgian legal framework applicable to online disinformation. While no specific legislation currently exists, we find references to this topic in legislation related to media regulation and education. Nonetheless, tackling disinformation is currently possible through existing alternative legal tools, with mixed results.

1 Introduction

Disinformation has become an increasingly important topic in the past few years. The emergence of social media and its growing impact in so many aspects of our lives has undoubtedly brought a shift in this regard, as *online* disinformation spreads further and quicker than before. Its impact is yet to be fully understood, be it on public debate, trust in media and politics, or more broadly, democracy. However, tackling disinformation is far from an easy task. It raises many issues, namely the balance between limiting disinformation and ensuring freedom of expression. It also begs the question of the role of the State in regulating this phenomenon on platforms owned by private actors.

This contribution seeks to analyze the Belgian approach to regulating disinformation. After discussing the notion of disinformation and its differences with close concepts such as misinformation, malinformation and fake news (Sect. 2), we then turn to the Belgian legal framework on disinformation (Sect. 3). While the adoption of

V. Speleers (✉)
UCLouvain, Louvain-la-Neuve, Belgium

UCLouvain St-Louis Bruxelles, Bruxelles, Belgium
e-mail:valentin.speleers@uclouvain.be

M. Vanloocke
UCLouvain, Louvain-la-Neuve, Belgium

UCLouvain St-Louis Bruxelles, Bruxelles, Belgium
e-mail:marie.vanloocke@uclouvain.be

P. Passaglia (ed.), *European Legal Perspectives on Online Disinformation*, Ius Gentium: Comparative Perspectives on Law and Justice 140,
https://doi.org/10.1007/978-3-032-25785-7_4

specific legislation tackling the issue has been discussed, the current approach disfavors prohibitive measures. Freedom of expression is central to this debate, as its standards apply to any measure aimed at prohibiting (online) disinformation. Moreover, the Belgian Constitution prohibits any preventive limitation on freedom of expression. Nonetheless, references to disinformation can be found in other legislation, including media regulation, education and EU regulations.

The chapter finally considers which current legal tools may be leveraged against disinformation to compensate for the lack of specific measures against it (Sect. 4). Victims of disinformation can seek redress in courts, either through civil or criminal proceedings. Additionally, there exist reporting procedures—although not specifically designed against disinformation—which may prove useful, despite not leading to actual sanctions.

2 The Notion of Disinformation

Considering the lack of a specific legislation related to disinformation in Belgium, there is no official definition thereof. While specific pieces of legislation dealing with certain aspects of this topic exist, the notion is left undefined (see Sect. 3). Consequently, we must turn to non-legislative works and doctrinal references.

Beyond legislation per se, Belgian authorities sometimes refer directly to the definition given by the European Commission in its report on disinformation, *i.e.* "verifiably false or misleading information that is created, presented and disseminated for economic gain or to intentionally deceive the public, and may cause public harm" (European Commission 2018). This approach has been followed both by the Senate—in a proposal for resolution "concerning the problem of disinformation"[1]—and the Belgian experts' report commissioned by the Minister for Digital Agenda in 2018 (Alaphilippe et al. 2018).[2] Similarly, the National Crisis Center defines disinformation as "the deliberate dissemination of false, incorrect or misleading information to cause harm", the latter including "influenc[ing] opinions, mak[ing] money or harm[ing] society, public health or democracy, for example".

Therefore, disinformation consists of two main elements: it is voluntary (i), and accompanied by a specific intent (ii), the particulars of which may vary. For instance, the European Commission links disinformation specifically to political or economic gains (European Commission 2018, Hanot and Michel 2020). Alternatively, this intent can be framed as a general underlying objective to cause harm, without further

[1] "[...] la désinformation désigne les informations manifestement fausses ou trompeuses, créées, présentées et diffusées à des fins économiques ou destinées à tromper intentionnellement le public, pouvant dès lors causer un préjudice public." Proposition de résolution concernant la problématique de la désinformation, Développements, Doc. parl., Sén., sess. Ord. 2018–2019, n° 6–493/1, p. 1.

[2] "informations dont on peut vérifier qu'elles sont fausses ou trompeuses, qui sont créées présentées et diffusées dans un but lucratif ou dans l'intention délibérée de tromper le public et qui sont susceptibles de causer un préjudice public".

precision (Vercauteren, 2020) or with a non-exhaustive list of examples—as in the abovementioned definition from the National Crisis Center.

From this we can infer a working definition of disinformation as the (willing) creation or dissemination of fake or misleading information with a specific intent—either to cause harm, or more specifically for economic or political gain. It should be noted that the (il)legality of the content is irrelevant (Vercauteren 2020; European Commission 2018). While a certain behavior might constitute both disinformation and a criminal offense, it is not necessarily always the case (see Sect. 4).

This working definition allows us to distinguish disinformation from close concepts, such as misinformation and malinformation. The former may bring harm but unintentionally, *i.e.* when someone reposts erroneous information without knowing of its inaccuracy, while the latter refers to sharing accurate information specifically to cause harm—for instance, information that relates to someone's private life (National Crisis Center; Vercauteren 2020). Additionally, the term "fake news"[3] is sometimes still used. There is, however, a growing trend to discard this notion, due to its broadness and ambiguity (Vercauteren 2020), but also because disinformation can be caused by "misleading" information—that is, not entirely fake (Alaphilippe et al. 2018, National Crisis Center). Another issue is that it has become a sort of political tool to discredit information that political actors disagree with (Alaphilippe et al. 2018).

Finally, while the distinction between close concepts regarding the creation and diffusion of erroneous information is relevant in Belgium, the same cannot be said of the distinction between general and *online* disinformation. Rather, the use of online platforms—in particular social media—is seen as aggravating the problem of disinformation. As highlighted both by the Belgian experts' group (Alaphilippe et al. 2018) and the Senate,[4] it allows for further dissemination, to a previously unknown scale.

3 Legal Framework

Although it is not specifically the object of one regulation—except for an article from the criminal code that prohibits purposefully giving fake information regarding the existence of a risk of attack against people or goods (see Sect. 4)—disinformation is relevant in many areas of law.

First, constitutional law must be taken into consideration. In particular, any legislative proposal aiming to fight disinformation would have to operate an intricate balance with freedom of expression. Such legislation does not exist yet in Belgium, and its

[3] Also called "nepnieuws" in Dutch. While the term "fausses nouvelles" is sometimes used in French, it is quite rare.

[4] Proposition de résolution relative à la lutte contre les ingérences de puissances étrangères visant à saper les fondements de l'État de droit démocratique, Doc. parl., Ch. repr., sess. ord. 2024–2025, n° 56–873/1, p. 1.

adoption seems unlikely. Consequently, disinformation is currently tackled through existing legal means, such as civil liability or certain criminal offences (slander, libel, etc.). This will be explained in the next section.

While references to disinformation do exist in current legislation, it is with regards to media regulation and education. To this should be added recent EU regulation, with an underlying objective to fight disinformation.

3.1 Freedom of Expression

The right to express one's opinions "in all matters" is enshrined in article 19 of the Belgian Constitution, alongside freedom of religion. Under this provision, any interference in the exercise of freedom of expression shall stem from a legislative body, and can only be of a repressive nature, by exclusion of preventive measures. By "preventive measures", one should understand all measures that are imposed *before* the exercise of freedom of expression (Jongen & Strowel 2017; Tulkens 2011; Velaers 1991). Any regulation, including the ones that aim to prevent disinformation, are bound by that provision.

Article 25 of the Constitution guarantees freedom of the press, which is exclusively applicable to written forms of expressions,[5] either printed or digital. A specific repressive system is set up by article 150 for political and press misdemeanors. It endows the *Cour d'assises*—a specific criminal court, the only one involving a popular jury, assisted by a professional presiding judge and two lay assessors—with an exclusive competence in the matter, except when those misdemeanors (*wanbedrijf/délit*) are motivated by racism or xenophobia. Such cases are dealt with by the usual judges competent in criminal matters.

Although those provisions do not include a specific reference to disinformation, their application and use—namely by the Constitutional Court—is often linked to the application of their international equivalents (considering that their scopes form an 'indivisible whole'), such as article 10 of the ECHR, and consequently, the teachings of the Strasbourg's case-law. The European Court of human rights has ruled that the spread of fake news falls within the scope of article 10 ECHR.[6] As such, any legislation aiming to fight the spread of (to be distinguished from its creation, about which the Court hasn't ruled yet, to the best of our knowledge) disinformation would have to meet the criteria set by article 10, §2 (legality, legitimacy and proportionality) (Vercauteren 2020). Additionally, the application of available means of redress against disinformation by courts and tribunals—through civil liability and some criminal offences—must also be balanced with freedom of expression (see Sect. 4).

---

[5] The notion of « expression» encompasses any form of opinion, idea and information.

[6] European Court of Human Right, Salov v. Ukraine, 6 September 2005, §§104–107; see also Vercauteren 2020, pp. 646–647.

Adopting such legislation also comes with potential negative consequences in terms of censorship and chilling effect (Vercauteren 2020; Hanot & Michel 2020), although it is not impossible. The effect of such legislation has however not yet been examined concretely in Belgium. Nonetheless, an interesting parallel can be drawn with a recent case concerning measures against disinformation found in a private company's terms and conditions. Brussels' commercial tribunal saw a case brought against Google, because it had taken down videos posted on YouTube based on their terms of services, which prohibited spreading fake medical information related to Covid-19. The claimant's argument that this violated his freedom of expression was rejected, as the terms were clear and had been communicated beforehand (see 4.1).[7]

In any case, Belgian authorities do not seem to be particularly inclined to adopt a prohibitive legislation on the matter.

3.2 Lack of Prohibitive Legislation Regarding Disinformation

Under the impulse of the Minister for Digital Agenda, a group of experts was commissioned in 2018 to formulate recommendations and proposals for fighting disinformation.[8] Its main takeaway was to be cautious: while they do not entirely oppose adopting some form of repressive legislation, they do not recommend it. They rather encourage a cooperative model in which the legislative power would adopt a more supportive role, as a sort of facilitator (Alaphilippe et al. 2018).

This approach seems to be followed to this day, both at federal and federate levels. Concerning the former, although the latest coalition agreement recognizes the importance of fighting against disinformation and fake news and highlights their potential influence on elections and the democratic structure of the State, the strategy set forth does not include talk of sanctions or any form of repression least be noted. Instead, it relies on education (through awareness campaigns) and reinforced cooperation between public services, technological companies and media.[9] Similarly, federate entities—mostly Communities due to their competence regarding culture and education—insist on supporting initiatives furthering the population's media education and highlight the role of media services.[10]

---

[7] Trib. entr. Bruxelles (15e ch.), 7 mai 2024, A&M, 2025, p. 88. It should be noted, however, that the tribunal's appreciation of the legitimacy and proportionality of the measure were quite short.

[8] It should be noted that a public survey was carried out at the same time.

[9] Gouvernement fédéral, Accord de coalition fédérale 2025–2029, pp. 150–151. https://www.belgium.be/sites/default/files/resources/publication/files/Accord_gouvernemental-Bart_De_Wever_fr.pdf, last accessed 2025/10/30.

[10] Parlement de la Communauté française, Déclaration de politique communautaire 2024–2029, p. 70. https://archive.pfwb.be/1000000020d90cd, last accessed 2025/10/30; Vlaamse regering, Vlaamse regeerakkoord 2024–2029, pp 186 and 189. https://publicaties.vlaanderen.be/view-file/69476, last accessed 2025/10/30.

It is worth noting that a proposal for a resolution against "foreign interferences aimed at destabilizing the fundamentals of a democratic rule-of-law-abiding State" was brought before the federal Parliament in April 2025 and is still currently pending.[11] Under this proposal, disinformation is considered as one of the three main tools of foreign interferences.[12] Once again however, it highlights the importance of media education to reinforce the population's resilience against disinformation and does not—at least currently—envision any repressive measure.[13]

Consequently, the current legislative approach seems to favor cooperation with media—journalists and editors—as well as building resilience through education.

3.3 Legislative Regulation of Disinformation

To this day, the only explicit legislative regulation of disinformation in Belgium can be found in acts concerning regulation of audiovisual media and education. In view of the division of powers between the entities endowed with a legislative power in Belgium, both sets of matters fall under the competence of the Communities.[14]

As such, with regards to media regulation, norms (*décrets*) of the three communities—each for the audiovisual media falling under their competence—and a federal law (*loi*)—for the audiovisual media that are established in the bilingual region of Brussels and that cannot be exclusively linked to either the French-speaking or the Dutch-speaking community based on the language of its activities—are applicable.[15]

In the French Community, article 9.1.1–1. of the *décret SMA/SPV* (decree concerning audiovisual media services and video sharing services, adopted on February 4th, 2021) establishes the CSA (*Conseil supérieur de l'audiovisuel*) as the regulator of the audiovisual sector within the Community. The CSA is "composed of two colleges, an executive committee and an investigative secretariat".[16] One of its two colleges—the *collège d'autorisation et de contrôle*—must, in correspondence to the available means, take part in the realisation of studies and analyses, including

[11] It should be noted that a second legislative proposal refers to disinformation. It is, however, specifically aimed at greenwashing and only contains a brief reference to the fact that it can, in some instances, constitute disinformation. See Proposition de loi modifiant le Code droit économique, visant à lutter contre le greenwashing, Doc. parl., Ch. repr., sess. extr. 2024, n° 56–0224/1, p. 3.

[12] Proposition de résolution relative à la lutte contre les ingérences de puissances étrangères visant à saper les fondements de l'État de droit démocratique, Doc. parl., Ch. repr., sess. ord. 2024–2025, n° 56–873/1, p. 5.

[13] Proposition de résolution relative à la lutte contre les ingérences de puissances étrangères visant à saper les fondements de l'État de droit démocratique, Doc. parl., Ch. repr., sess. ord. 2024–2025, n° 56–873/1, p. 12.

[14] Const., art. 127, §1er, al. 1er; Loi spéciale du 8 août 1980 de réformes institutionnelles, M.B., 15 août 1980, p. 9434, art. 4, 6°.

[15] Const., art. 127.

[16] Décret Comm. fr. du 4 février 2021 relatif aux services de médias audiovisuels et aux services de partage de vidéos, M.B., 26 mars 2021, p. 29,036, art. 9.1.1–2.

recommendations, concerning education to the media and the fight against disinformation, in collaboration with the *Conseil de déontologie journalistique* and the *Conseil supérieur d'éducation aux médias*.[17] Similarly, Flemish media are regulated by the *Vlaamse Regulator voor de Media* (VRM),[18] and German-speaking media by the *Medienrat*.[19]

Additionally, specific rules apply to public media services—French-, Dutch- and German-speaking. For instance, the decree establishing the statute of the RTBF (public media service of the French speaking community), adopted on July 14th 1997, prohibits more specifically the production and the diffusion of emissions that are "contrary to the laws or the general interest, jeopardising human dignity, and namely containing incitation to discrimination, hatred or violence, particularly based on race, sex or nationality or aiming to denial, undermining, justification or approbation of the genocide committed by the German National Socialist regime during the Second World War or any other form of genocide".[20] The same provision states in its second paragraph that emissions taking part in information or education of the viewers and listeners must be made in a spirit of objectivity, without prior censorship or interference of any public or private authority.[21] In virtue of the same article, the administration board of the RTBF is required to adopt a bylaw specific to information processing and professional ethics for staff members, particularly journalistic ethics, to guarantee the objectivity and independence of information and those who provide it. Such regulation has been adopted in 1998, and although disinformation is not explicitly mentioned, some of its provisions clearly pursue this objective. Indeed, the *règlement d'ordre intérieur relatif au traitement de l'information et à la déontologie du personnel* contains several references to an exact and complete information,[22] as well as the abovementioned prohibition of certain contents.[23] Journalists of the RTBF also have an obligation to "respect the facts, to search the truth and to defend the freedom and independence of information, commentary and criticism. Their task is to collect and reveal facts and opinions without obstacle, by loyal means, and by only publishing information whose origin they are aware of. They cannot spread rumours,

---

[17] Décret Comm. fr. du 4 février 2021 relatif aux services de médias audiovisuels et aux services de partage de vidéos, M.B., 26 mars 2021, p. 29,036, art. 9.1.2–3, §1, 17°.

[18] Vlaamse decreet van 27 maart 2009 betreffende radio-omroep en televisie, M.B., 30 april 2009, p. 34,509, art. 215 et 218, §1er.

[19] Décret Comm. germ. du 1er mars 2021 relatif aux services de média et aux représentations cinématographiques, M.B., 12 avril 2021, p. 32,201, art. 112.

[20] Décret du 14 juillet 1997 portant statut de la Radio-Télévision belge de la Communauté française (RTBF), M.B., 28 août 1997, p. 22,018, art. 7, §1.

[21] Décret du 14 juillet 1997 portant statut de la Radio-Télévision belge de la Communauté française (RTBF), M.B., 28 août 1997, p. 22,018, art. 7, §2. Such a reference can also be found in other legislative norms regulating audiovisual media services.

[22] Règlement d'ordre intérieur relatif au traitement de l'information et à la déontologie du personnel, adopté par le Conseil d'Administration de la RTBF le 19 janvier 1998 et révisé par le Conseil d'Administration du 21 mars 2008, pts. 2 et 19.

[23] Règlement d'ordre intérieur relatif au traitement de l'information et à la déontologie du personnel, adopté par le Conseil d'Administration de la RTBF le 19 janvier 1998 et révisé par le Conseil d'Administration du 21 mars 2008, pt. 4.

delete essential information, nor alter the meaning of texts and documents. They commit themselves to the respect of privacy and to correct any inexact information (…)".[24]

References to principles such as the reliability and the objectivity of information can be found in a variety of subordinate acts relating to media regulation. While offering a complete overview of those norms in this contribution is impossible, it is important to highlight the explicit references to information within the management contracts (*contrats de gestion*) of the French- and Dutch-speaking public media services. These contracts refer to a diversity of measures to be taken by the media for it to play an essential role in fighting disinformation, including training journalists, media literacy, innovation, reinforcement of fact checking, etc.

Alongside media regulation, education plays an important role in preventing disinformation. Both the French and Flemish Communities have created a specific body whose role consists of furthering society's media education, which includes providing information and tools against disinformation. The *Kenniscentrum Digitale en Mediawijsheid*[25] and the *Conseil supérieur d'éducation aux médias*[26] both carry initiatives to educate on fake news, for instance through workshops and interventions in schools (Vercauteren 2020).

The integration of the topic of disinformation in education is mostly the result of subordinate acts. The basis for school curricula, as established by the French and Flemish authorities, includes educating students on disinformation and fake news, as part of their technical and digital training but also of their education to philosophy and citizenship.[27] Teachers can also benefit from training during their career, which may include how to teach students on this topic.[28]

---

[24] Règlement d'ordre intérieur relatif au traitement de l'information et à la déontologie du personnel, adopté par le Conseil d'Administration de la RTBF le 19 janvier 1998 et révisé par le Conseil d'Administration du 21 mars 2008, pt. 14. « Les journalistes de la RTBF doivent respecter les faits, rechercher la vérité et défendre la liberté et l'indépendance de l'information, et de la critique. Leur tâche est de recueillir et de révéler sans entraves, par des méthodes loyales, les faits et opinions en ne publiant que des informations dont l'origine est connue d'eux. Ils ne peuvent relayer les rumeurs, supprimer des informations essentielles, ni altérer le sens des textes et documents. Ils s'obligent à respecter la vie privée ainsi qu'à rectifier toute information publiée qui se révèle inexacte (…)».

[25] Programmadecreet van 16 december 2023 bij de begroting 2023, art. 2, §1, M.B., 29 décembre 2022, p. 102,610.

[26] Décr. Comm. fr. du 16 mai 2024 relatif à l'éducation aux médias, art. 3 & s., M.B., 12 septembre 2024, p. 107,434. It is interesting to note that this decree explicitly states that one of its main goals is fighting against disinformation (see art. 2, 5°).

[27] Référentiel de formation manuelle, technique, technologique et numérique de la Communauté française, http://www.enseignement.be/public/docs/r-f-rentiel-de-formation-manuelle-technique-technologique-et-num-rique-fmttn-.pdf; Référentiel d'éducation à la philosophie et à la citoyenneté, http://www.enseignement.be/public/docs/r-f-rentiel-d-ducation-la-philosophie-et-la-citoyennet-epc-.pdf. For the Flemish Community, see https://onderwijsdoelen.be/.

[28] Arrêté du Gouvernement de la Communauté française du 29 octobre 2020 portant approbation des orientations et thèmes prioritaires de la formation en cours de carrière de niveau interréseaux des membres du personnel de l'enseignement spécialisé, de l'enseignement secondaire ordinaires et des centres psycho-médico-sociaux pour l'année scolaire 2021–2022, art. 1er, M.B., 5 novembre 2020, p. 79,309; Arrêté du Gouvernement de la Communauté française portant approbation des

Other subordinate acts target disinformation in specific cases, for instance stating that the training of civil servants operating in intelligence and security must include "generalities […] on disinformation",[29] or that the establishment of neutral cigarette packs aim to reduce consumer's disinformation on the dangers of tobacco.[30] Such references are thus occasional and highly specific. The only one that tackles disinformation on a more general level is a circular of the federal minister for Interior. It concerns the policing of public space in case of events that might disturb public order and is addressed to police services and other civil servants called upon to ensure such policing. It highlights the changes in society which might impact the way societal conflicts and protest evolve, amongst which is disinformation.[31]

3.4 *Disinformation as an Underlying Objective of EU Regulations*

European law must also be considered with regards to tackling disinformation. The EU's response towards the latter has shifted in recent years from being based on autoregulation—thus relying on private actors' engagement—to an approach qualified as "descending coregulation": mainly regulated through legislative acts but still leaving room for adjustments by private actors (Poullet and Bontridder 2020). Consequently, while the EU and Belgium were on a similar path around 2018, the former seems to have somewhat modified its approach, while the latter has not. Although autoregulation remains relevant,[32] recent EU regulations—the most important being the Digital Services Act (DSA)[33]—include measures aimed to fight online disinformation. One can thus wonder if EU law might fill in the gap left within the Belgian approach to disinformation.

Within the DSA, recitals mention tackling disinformation as a key underlining objective, although the regulation itself does not contain any specific provision on the matter. Rather, the DSA introduces several obligations that aim, more indirectly, at

---

orientations et thèmes prioritaires de la formation en cours de carrière de niveau macro des membres du personnel des établissements d'enseignement fondamental ordinaire pour l'année scolaire 2021–2022, art. 1er, M.B., 5 novembre 2020, p. 79,312; Arrêté du gouvernement flamand du 23 juin 2000 définissant [les objectifs finaux spécifiques aux différentes branches] des deuxième et troisième degrés de l'enseignement secondaire ordinaire, M.B., 29 novembre 2000, p. 39,749.

[29] Arrêté ministériel du 17 janvier 2008 relatif au stage de certains agents civils du département d'état-majeur renseignement et sécurité, art. 4, M.B., 13 février 2008, p. 09,349.

[30] Arrêté royal du 13 avril 2019 relatif au paquet standardisé des cigarettes, du tabac à rouler et du tabac à pipe à eau, M.B., 17 mai 2019, p. 47,301.

[31] Circulaire CP 4bis du 30 janvier 2025 concernant la gestion négociée de l'espace public lors d'événements touchant l'ordre public.

[32] For instance, the 2022 Commission's Code of Practice on Disinformation was converted into a Code of Conduct in January 2025, in accordance with the DSA.

[33] Regulation (EU) 2022/2065 of the European Parliament and of the Council of 19 October 2022 on a Single Market for Digital Services and amending Directive 2000/31/CE (Digital Services Act).

reducing disinformation: obligations of transparency—with some additional obligations towards bigger platforms –, but also of evaluation and attenuation of systemic risks. Similarly, fighting disinformation is an underlying objective of other specific regulations—such as the EU AI Act, European Media Freedom Act and Regulation on the transparency and targeting of political advertising (Platon 2025).

Despite the change in the EU's approach towards disinformation, regulation remains rather light. Mostly, it establishes a framework within which private actors may regulate themselves such content—hence the aforementioned "co-regulatory" approach. However, this alone seems quite limited, and does not entirely replace State action, such as a coherent reporting procedure or means for redress—which Belgium lacks at the moment. A recent study analyzing Tiktok and Facebook's Statements of Reasons—that is, the explanation of why restrictions have been applied to content deemed illegal or incompatible with a platform's terms and conditions, regulated under the DSA –revealed that misinformation-related entries were scarce for the former, and even completely absent for the latter, although both platforms had clearly supported such content (De Meyere 2025). This illustrates the limits of a co-regulation approach, among which are transparency obligations.

The DSA, as well as the other mentioned acts, are regulations and thus do not require national transposition; they are directly applicable under Belgian law. Their implementation, however, does require some measure of action by Member States. The DSA, for instance, requires said States to designate one or more "competent authorities" to supervise and enforce application of the DSA, and amongst them one "Digital Services Coordinator".[34] Penalties for infringement of the DSA are also to be laid out by Member States, under the guidelines set forth by the regulation.[35]

This implementation is rendered more complex in Belgium due to the country's federal nature, as it may fall under the competence of different entities, federal or federate. This is the case regarding the DSA, involving both the federal level (regarding, amongst others, consumer's protection, commercial and corporate law, etc.) as well as the Communities (mainly under their competence for technical aspects and contents of media services). The chosen authorities to implement the DSA were pre-existing bodies on federal and federate levels, which were granted new competences. As such, the Digital Services Coordinator is the Belgian Institute for Postal Services and Telecommunications (BIPT), which is a *federal* regulatory body. Other competent bodies are on a *federate* level, one per Community—the aforementioned CSA for the French-speaking Community, VRM for the Dutch-speaking Community and *Medienrat* for the German-speaking Community. Each regulatory body is tasked with implementing parts of the DSA (including investigating complaints and eventually adopting penalties), depending on their relative competences, with the BIPT additionally acting as coordinator to ensure coherent monitoring and enforcement of the DSA. Each body's missions are defined by an act adopted by the competent

---

[34] Digital Services Act, art. 49.

[35] Digital Services Act, art. 52.

authority, completed by a cooperation agreement between the federal authority and the three Communities to ensure this system's coherence.[36]

Finally, the Belgian Constitution adds one last layer of complexity, as the previously mentioned ban on preventive measures (see Sect. 3.1) may be challenged by some of the obligations under the DSA.

4 Alternative Legal Avenues

Considering the lack of specific legislation meant to tackle disinformation, what are the available options in the current legal system? Claimants—and, in their wake, courts and tribunals—have not waited for such legislation to be adopted before embracing the issue. They however resort to more "indirect" means, such as civil liability or certain criminal offenses, in order to do so. Beyond judicial proceedings, reporting procedures can be leveraged to denounce disinformation although, once again, they were not created with this specific issue in mind.

4.1 The Role of Courts and Tribunals

When considering the role of courts and tribunals, it is useful to distinguish between supreme courts on the one hand, and ordinary courts and tribunals in the other.

4.1.1 Supreme Courts

Should any legislation aiming to tackle online disinformation be adopted (which has not been the case so far), the Constitutional Court would be competent to assess its compatibility with the fundamental rights enshrined in the Constitution (in combination and/or in light of their international equivalents), the federal division of powers and other constitutional provisions.[37]

Apart from the Constitutional Court, Belgium has two other supreme courts. They are the *Cour de cassation*, which ensures that courts and tribunals comply with the law when deciding cases, and the *section du Contentieux Administratif du Conseil d'Etat* (Administrative Litigation section of the Council of State), which mainly

---

[36] Accord de coopération du 3 mai 2024 entre l'État fédéral, la Communauté flamande, la Communauté française et la Communauté germanophone relatif à l'exécution coordonnée partielle du règlement (UE) 2022/2065 du Parlement européen et du Conseil du 19 octobre 2022 relatif à un marché unique des services numériques et modifiant la directive 2000/31/CE (règlement sur les services numériques), M.B., 30 décembre 2024, p. 143,703.

[37] Loi spéciale du 6 janvier 1989 sur la Cour constitutionnelle, M.B., 7 janvier 1989, p. 315, art. 1er et 26.

acts as the last instance in administrative cases as well as deciding on some specific matters (such as elections).

The former has recently been called to review the legality of disciplinary sanctions imposed onto professionals who had breached their respective code of deontology. All cases involved medical professionals—a pharmacist in one, and a doctor in the other two—who had spread disinformation about the Covid crisis on social media. In the first case, the Court rejected the argument that the pharmacist's freedom of speech could not be restricted through disciplinary proceedings and upheld the decision from the Pharmacist's order (*Raad voor Apothekers*).[38] In the second and third cases, it ruled that the principle of legality applied differently in disciplinary procedures—compared to criminal ones—and only required to be sufficiently precise as to infer that the professional had failed to uphold the honor or dignity of their profession. Consequently, it can sanction behavior that is not explicitly defined in law or deontological rules.[39] It remains to be seen whether this reasoning could be applied to other professionals subject to deontology—with potential disciplinary sanctions for breach thereof –, such as lawyers for instance. However, it should be noted that this does not apply to journalists: as will be further explained (Sect. 4.2), although they are subject to deontology, the bodies tasked with enforcing these rules—the *Conseil de déontologie journalistique* (CDJ) and the *Raad voor Journalistiek* (RvJ)—cannot impose disciplinary sanctions. This is meant to guarantee journalists' freedom of expression.

The *Conseil d'État* has not often been seized with cases concerning disinformation either. Claimants recently requested the annulment of local elections on the grounds that the media coverage of smaller political movements—in particular, citizen-led—amounted to their invisibilization. Consequently, they argued it amounted to disinformation regarding the political landscape. The judges however found this claim of "media discrimination" to lack any ground that would prove it may have influenced the results of the election, especially considering the diversity of other communication channels at the disposal of political candidates.[40]

Apart from this admittedly small case law, the bulk of judicial decisions in matters of disinformation stems from ordinary courts and tribunals. Despite the lack of specific legislation on the matter, redress against disinformation can be sought in court, as litigation may arise where a claimant seeks retribution for harm caused by the dissemination of fake information. This can lead to civil and/or criminal proceedings, the former based on civil liability regime, the latter on certain specific infractions (most often, slander, libel or forgery).[41]

---

[38] Cass., D.22.0011.N, 4 avril 2025, R.W., 2025–2026/3, p. 105.

[39] Cass. (1e ch.), D.22.0009.N, 27 juin 2025 and Cass. (1e ch.), D.22.0017.N, 4 avril 2025, R.W., 2024–2025/37, p. 1518.

[40] C.E., 31 janvier 2025, Elections communales de Charleroi, n° 262.208 et C.E., 31 janvier 2025, Elections communales de Thuin, n°262.209.

[41] In one case, the claimant tried proving that journalists had not only reported factually incorrect information, but that it was part of a broader disinformation campaign constitutive of hate speech. The judge however qualified the journalists' action as misinformation, and rejected the claim. Trib. corr. Dinant, 20 avril 2004, J.L.M.B., 2004, p. 799.

4.1.2 Subordinate Courts and Tribunals

There are two ways to seek redress against disinformation before courts and tribunals: civil liability or criminal proceedings. They may be pursued independently, or in parallel.

First, civil liability may be invoked where someone claims to have been wronged by the dissemination of fake information. This requires proving—amongst other conditions—misconduct or negligence from the author of disinformation. Furthermore, the specificity of online disinformation adds the complexity of identifying the author (Vercauteren 2020). Consequently, most cases concern journalists sued for spreading (alleged) disinformation, as they are easily identified. Such instances, however, require taking into account freedom of expression. In particular, judges will refer to the role of journalists and the importance of freedom of expression, considering that, while journalists have a duty to verify their information and be as truthful as possible, such duty is one of means and not of results (Hanot and Michel 2020). This leads to analyzing how journalists have conducted their research, and whether they have shown sufficient caution.

Additionally, courts have been called to analyze whether private actors can legally regulate or at least denounce disinformation, usually through civil proceeding.[42] This is a more recent strand of case-law, which two recent cases (from April and May 2024) illustrate. The first related to a series of articles published by a renowned journal, in which another small journal editor was presented as systematically publishing "counter-truths". Contrary to what was claimed, the judge found the articles had been written based on sufficient factual evidence and thus did not constitute disparagement.[43] The second upheld that terms of services (in this case, YouTube's) could be invoked to delete videos relaying fake news, as long as the user had been made aware of said terms.[44] This type of case law is peculiar because the parties are usually both considered as companies under Belgian law (two media services in the first instance, one media service and Google in the other). This brings two specificities: one, instead of relying on general civil liability, the claimant can invoke rules on unfair competition—specifically disparagement[45]—and two, such cases can be brought before commercial tribunals.[46]

---

[42] We have found one instance of criminal proceedings, where the claimant complained that the suppression of a petition they had submitted by the hosting website—because it relied on unfounded allegations about the effects of 5G—was constitutive of slander. The judge deemed the argument so unconvincing as to not require serious debate. Corr. Bruxelles (ch. cons.), 9 septembre 2021, A&M, 2021, p. 555.

[43] This specific claim was brought because both parties were corporation; consequently, the claimant relied on a specific provision of corporation law prohibiting disparagement between corporations. Trib. entr. Bruxelles (cess.), 17 avril 2024, A&M, 2025, p. 83.

[44] Trib. entr. Bruxelles (15e ch.), 7 mai 2024, A&M, 2025, p. 88.

[45] Interestingly, denigration does not require both parties to be actual competing companies. See Trib. entr. Bruxelles, 17 avril 2024, 2024, A&M, 2025, p. 83.

[46] See for instance Comm. Bruxelles fr. (cess.), ordonnance du 4 septembre 2024, A/24/01585.

Turning now to criminal law, and as stated before, the only *specific* prohibition related to disinformation concerns the diffusion of "fake information regarding a risk of attack against people or goods" (article 328 of the previous criminal code, article 234 of the new criminal code).[47] The aim is to target fake menaces of criminally punishable offences. A fake warning about an allegedly ongoing fire, for instance, does not fall under this prevention.[48] Furthermore, fake information should concern a *risk*, and not an already established attack. Case law is, however, not always consistent. One court of appeal considered that spreading information about a fake murder could not fall under this prevention, as the murder—although fake—would have already happened.[49] Another court of appeal however considered that a fake kidnapping did fall under this prevention.[50] This remains highly specific, and consequently not often applied. Let us then consider other offences, under which disinformation may be prevented.

First, disinformation can be constitutive of slander or libel[51]—although admittedly, it is not the fact that the information is fake which constitutes a criminal offence. Rather, both infractions require a specific intent to cause harm to the target, which is further complicated by the fact that penal law must be interpreted restrictively.[52] As seen above, while disinformation implies a certain goal which may be to cause harm, it is more broadly construed, as it could also aim to obtain economic or political gain.

Additionally, disinformation could also be construed as forgery[53] or more precisely data forgery[54]—two distinct infractions, both requiring a broader intent either to obtain some form of illegal gain (for oneself or someone else), or to cause harm.[55] The problem lies in the fact that forgery only applies if the altered act is "legally protected", meaning that it may be used as evidence to support a legal claim—the idea being that by altering said act, public trust was abused (Collin, France, Roggen and Spreutels 2021). To be constitutive of data forgery, it must be proven that the legal effect of the manipulated data was altered (Clesse et al. 2024). In both cases, further clarification of this notion depends on judges' appreciation and has sparked much debate, with inconsistencies in case-law. In one case (2010), the creation of a fake profile to impersonate someone else on a website has been considered as not altering any data's legal effect—and thus not constituting data forgery

---

[47] The articles pertaining to the criminal code in this contribution refer to the former code, in force until September 1st, 2026. However, the corresponding articles in the new criminal code will also be given.

[48] Corr. Marche-en-Fammenne, 16 mars 1988, J.L.M.B., 1991, p. 243.

[49] Bruxelles, 10 mars 2008.

[50] Gent, 30 octobre 2012, R.W., 2012–2013, p. 1109.

[51] Anc. Code pénal, art. 443–444 ; Code pénal, art. 240.

[52] Proposition de résolution concernant la problématique de la désinformation, Développements, Doc. parl., Sén., sess. ord. 2018–2019, n° 6–493/1, p. 4.

[53] Anc. C. pén., art. 193 ; C. pén., art. 451.

[54] Anc. C. pén., art. 210bis ; C. pén., art. 488.

[55] Cass., 11 décembre 2012, Pas., 2012, p. 2459.

(Clesse et al. 2024).[56] Another time (2017), the judges considered that, while the creation of a fake profile per se did not constitute data forgery, it did in this case as the aim was to give the impression that the profile belonged to a real person, thus altering the data of said profile's legal effect.[57]

Finally, anti-hate speech legislation may prohibit certain forms of disinformation. In Belgium, this depends upon several laws against discrimination, to which should be added one specific law prohibiting the denial, minimization, justification or approval of the genocide committed during the Second World War[58] (Cruysmans 2016).

Specifically, Belgian law prohibits inciting discrimination, hatred or violence against a person or group of persons, based on specific criteria. They relate to racism and xenophobia (nationality, alleged race, skin color or national or ethnic origins)[59]; sexism (sex, pregnancy, gender identity, etc.)[60]; or other forms of discrimination (age, sexual orientation, political, philosophical or religious conviction, disability, etc.).[61] While disinformation related to these topics may thus be prosecuted, it would not be enough to merely spread false information. The aim to "incite" requires a specific intent, interpreted quite restrictively by the Constitutional court: incitation "goes beyond information, ideas or critics", and requires "[…] encouragement, exhortation or instigation to discriminate"[62] (Vrielink 2014; Jongen and Strowel 2017). For instance, falsely reporting that underage foreigners were responsible of a specific infraction, even where emphasis is placed on the ethnicity of the alleged perpetrator, is not by itself sufficient, as there must be more concrete proof of an intent to *incite* hatred, discrimination or violence[63] (Vrielink 2014).

4.2 Reporting Procedures

Alongside courts and tribunals and existing legislation, there exist reporting procedures which, although not always designed specifically for disinformation, may be used in that regard.

First, EDMO Belux is a common platform for Belgium and Luxemburg, created to monitor, analyze and attenuate disinformation, along with promoting media

[56] Bruxelles (4e ch.), 22 juin 2010, inédit.

[57] Gent (10e ch.), 15 septembre 2017, R.W., 2018–2019, p. 351.

[58] Loi du 23 mars 1995 tendant à réprimer la négation, la minimisation, la justification ou l'approbation du génocide commis par le régime national-socialiste allemand pendant la seconde guerre mondiale, M.B., 30 mars 1995, p. 7996 and C. pén., art. 256.

[59] Loi du 30 juillet 1981 tendant à réprimer certains actes inspirés par le racisme ou la xénophobie, M.B., 8 août 1981, p. 9928 and C. pén., art. 250.

[60] Loi du 10 mai 2007 tendant à lutter contre la discrimination entre les femmes et les hommes, M.B., 30 mai 2007, p. 29,031 and C. pén., art. 250 and 257.

[61] Loi du 10 mai 2007 tendant à lutter contre certaines formes de discrimination, M.B., 30 mai 2007, p. 29,016 and C. pén., art. 250.

[62] C.C., n° 157/2004, 6 octobre 2004, B.49 and C.C., n° 17/2009, 12 février 2009, B.67.2.

[63] Gent (17e ch.), 5 mars 2013, A&M, 2014/3–4, p. 271.

education. Anyone can report a suspicion of online disinformation through their website, although not all complaints are analyzed.[64] This multidisciplinary platform is composed of disinformation analysts, fact-checkers, media education organizations and academics, and relies on a wider community of news agencies, research centers or universities, and administrative bodies. Their primary mission is fact-checking and investigation—through monthly reports, as well as more comprehensive studies—which they carry out based on the complaint they receive.

Second, journalists and media are subject to specific rules surrounding the way they collect and communicate information, some of which prevent disinformation. It should be noted that the journalists' code of deontology also applies where they publish information through social media platforms.[65] In Belgium, journalistic deontology is enforced by the *Conseil de déontologie journalistique* (CDJ) for French-speaking and German-speaking journalists, and the *Raad voor Journalistiek* (RvJ) for Dutch-speaking journalists. They complement the previously mentioned BIPT, CSA, VRM and Medienrat, tasked with monitoring audiovisual media.

Any person or organization (administrative body, civil society organization, corporation, etc.) can file a complaint to the CDJ, which can also initiate the procedure itself.[66] The claimant does not need to be the target of the reported news, or to prove any sort of personal interest. On the contrary, while the RvJ also takes complaints both from individuals and organizations, they must either be the subject of the reported news, thus invoking a personal interest, or be an organization working on a subject covered in the news, thus invoking a general interest.[67] Before both instances, complaints must be lodged within two months of the diffusion of the contentious material—which can be extended in case of serious and justified motives.

Complaints are analyzed by the CDJ and RvJ, which are composed of members representing the various actors involved. The CDJ is composed of 20 effective members (and 20 substitute), representing journalists (6 members), publishers (6), editors-in-chief (2) and civil society—who are themselves journalist, publishers or editor-in-chief (6). Similarly, the RvJ is composed of members representing journalists (12), publishers, broadcasters and other media companies (12), and 12 additional members. Both institutions follow a contradictory procedure, where parties are called to present their arguments.

However, neither the CDJ nor RvJ have any actual sanctioning competence. If they deem a complaint to be founded, they will ask the party responsible for the contentious material to publish their decision—usually on its website—within a certain time frame—7 days for the CDJ—starting from the communication of the decision. If the material is still online, the CDJ also requires a link to the decision

[64] https://belux.edmo.eu/fr/rapports-de-desinformation/. Accessed 30 Oct 2025.

[65] Conseil de déontologie journalistique (2010) Avis du Conseil de Déontologie Journalistique du 13 octobre 2010. https://www.lecdj.be/telechargements/10-10-13-Avis-sur-la-deontologie-et-les-reseaux-sociaux.pdf. Accessed 30 Oct 2025.

[66] Conseil de Déontologie Journalistique (2022) Règlement de procédure. https://www.lecdj.be/wp-content/uploads/2023-CDJ-Reglement-de-procedure-bis.pdf.

[67] Raad voor de Journalistiek, Werkingsreglement. https://www.rvdj.be/pagina/afdeling-iii-procedure#18.

to be added. Again, these are not obligations *stricto sensu*.[68] Consequently, there is no appeal against their decision, although the CDJ can decide to review its own decision if new elements are discovered within the year. Nonetheless, the CDJ and RvJ's decision can be invoked in front of a court or tribunal, for instance to engage a journalist's civil liability. While judges remain free to decide independently from the CDJ and RvJ's decisions, they tend to rely on them (Michel 2020).

5 Conclusion

A 2022 survey on disinformation, initiated by two major Belgian news outlets (one Dutch-speaking, one French-speaking) showed that nine Belgians out of ten consider the spread of disinformation to be a societal problem, of which online media were deemed responsible by 81%. Consequently, 45% of French-speaking and 35% of Dutch-speaking interviewees admitted they did not want to follow news because of the importance of fake news (Ryckmans 2022). The 2025 *Digital News Report* (supervised by the Reuters Institute) seems to confirm this trend, showing the overall level of trust towards news to be of 43%; while not incredibly high, it has remained quite stable since 2023. However, there is a significant gap between Dutch-speaking and French-speaking markets, their respective trust level being 51% and 35% (Picone 2025).

On the other hand, a more specific study concerning news' consumption by Dutch-speaking youth aged 12 to 26 showed a quite high level of trust in this population regarding news outlet. Interestingly, they present a higher level of trust in the media they choose to follow (overall 73%) than in media *in general* (overall 58%) (Arteveldehogeschool 2025, p. 38). The study also investigated the phenomenon of "news avoidance", where people purposefully avoid consuming news, in part because of disinformation leading to distrust. While 46% of the youth interviewed admitted to such behavior, this is a lower number compared to previous years. Moreover, the study highlights that such news avoidance does not mean they do not receive information, but rather that they choose to distance themselves in order to be more conscious of what they learn (Arteveldehogeschool 2025, p. 40).

These studies do not specifically address *online* disinformation as a separate problem. However, they highlight a growing use of online sources of news—according to the 2025 Digital News report, they make up 75% of news' consumption (Picone 2025). Distrust of news seems thus to be closely related to online news consumption and the potential disinformation that comes with it.

Although disinformation is perceived as an important issue, Belgium has not yet adopted any specific legislation on the matter. It should be kept in mind that tackling disinformation cannot be done at the expense of freedom of expression. Current case

[68] However, media which are members of the Association pour l'Autorégulation de la déontologie journalistique (AADJ), the legal structure that created the CDJ, have committed to this publication rule.

law demonstrates the difficulty of striking the right balance in that regard. While the relevance of prohibitive measures may thus be debated—and does not seem to be discussed in Parliament—the lack of a coherent reporting procedure, which may lead to more concrete measures, should at least be considered. To our best knowledge, this has not been discussed.

In the meantime, disinformation can currently only be tackled through broader, pre-existing legislation (such as civil liability or certain criminal offences). As such, not all cases of disinformation can be addressed.

One last difficulty in establishing such a procedure, highlighted throughout this chapter, is the federal nature of Belgium, as the issue of disinformation raises questions for which different entities have competence. Anything that relates to "audiovisual content" is to be regulated by the three Communities.[69] The federal authority is also competent when it comes to the other aspects of fighting disinformation. The establishment of a reporting procedure for disinformation would probably require four entities (one for each Community and a federal one, which could be the already existent CSA, VRM, Medienrat and BIPT) to work together. This would not only require each federal or federate entity to adopt a norm establishing the entity's competence, but also a cooperation agreement between the federal level and Communities.

References

Alaphilippe, A., De Marez, L., Gerlache, A., Lievens, E., Pauwels, T., Picone, I., Rouvroy, A.: Rapport du groupe d'experts belge sur les fausses informations et la désinformation (2018). https://www.droit-technologie.org/wp-content/uploads/2018/07/20180718_rapport_fakenewsFR.pdf, last accessed 2025/10/30.

Artevelde Hogeschool: Nieuws barometer 2025. https://www.arteveldehogeschool.be/nl/onderzoek-en-samenwerking/onderzoek/communicatie-media-design/nieuwsbarometer#barometer, last accessed 2025/10/30 (2025).

Clesse C.-E., Kennes, L., Carolus, P., Deckers, V., Fossion, L., Giacometti, M., Vansiliette, F., Veille, B.: Droit pénal des affaires. 2nd edn. Larcier-Intersentia, Bruxelles (2024).

Collin, J.-P., France, E., Roggen, F., Spreutels, J: Droit pénal des affaires. 2nd edn. Larcier, Bruxelles (2021).

Cruysmans, E. Racisme, blasphème et liberté d'expression – Aperçu de la jurisprudence « anti-hate speech » belge francophone. A&M. 2016/1, 71-90 (2016).

De Meyere J. Empty Transparency ? Assessing Platform Content Moderation of False Information Through the DSA Transparency Database. A&M. 2025/2, 149-158 (2025).

European Commission: Communication to the European Parliament, the Council, the European Economic and Social Committee and the Committee of the Regions, Tackling online disinformation : a European Approach. COM(2018) 236 final. https://eur-lex.europa.eu/legal-content/EN/TXT/?uri=celex:52018DC0236, last accessed 2025/10/30 (2018).

Hanot, M., Michel, A: Entre menaces pour la vie en société et risques réglementaires, les fakes news: un danger pour la démocratie? In: Poullet Y. (ed) Vie privée, liberté d'expression et démocratie dans la société numérique, pp. 155–208. Larcier, Bruxelles (2020).

Jongen, F. and Strowel, A. Droit des medias et de la communication. Larcier, Bruxelles (2017).

[69] Loi spéciale du 8 août 1980 de réformes institutionnelles, art. 4, 6°, M.B., 15 août 1980, p. 9434.

Michel, A.: L'influence grandissante du respect de la déontologie journalistique dans le cadre des actions judiciaires. R.D.T.I. 2020/1–2, 160–172 (2020).

National Crisis Center on Disinformation, https://crisiscenter.be/en/risks-belgium/security-risks/disinformation/disinformation, last accessed 2025/10/30.

Picone, I. Digital News Report 2025—Belgium. Reuters Institute. https://reutersinstitute.politics.ox.ac.uk/digital-news-report/2025/belgium, last accessed 2025/10/30 (2025).

Platon, S. La lutte contre la désinformation en Droit de l'Union européenne. In: Maubernard, C, Platon, S, Tinière, R (eds.). Les mutations de la liberté d'expression dans l'Union européenne, pp. 189–219. Bruylant, Bruxelles (2025).

Poullet, Y., Bontridder, N.: L'Union européenne et la régulation de l'information. R.D.T.I. 2020/4, 29–52 (2020).

Ryckmans, G.: Près de neuf Belges sur dix estiment que la diffusion de fausses infos est un problème pour notre société. RTBF. https://www.rtbf.be/article/pres-de-neuf-belges-sur-dix-estiment-que-la-diffusion-de-fausses-infos-est-un-probleme-pour-notre-societe-10965538, last accessed 2025/10/30 (2022).

Tulkens, F.: La liberté d'expression en général. In: Verdussen M. and Bonbled N. (ed) Les droits constitutionnels en Belgique. Les enseignements jurisprudentiels de la Cour constitutionnelle, du Conseil d'État et de la Cour de cassation (vol. 2), pp. 821–844, Bruylant, Bruxelles (2011).

Velaers, J., De beperkingen van de vrijheid van meningsuiting, Maklu, Antwerpen (1991).

Vercauteren, L.: Wetgeving als vaccin tegen de verspreiding van fake news. Een wettelijke regulering van fake news binnen België: heiligt het doel de middelen?. Jura Falc. 2020–2021(2), 601–665 (2020).

Vrielink, J. Cascade-aansprakelijkheid, onjuiste berichtgeving en de Antiracismewet. A&M. 2014/3-4, 210-220 (2014).

Ceci n'est pas une Information: Online Disinformation in Bulgaria Between Missing Constitution, Linguistic Games, and Post-modern Certainty About Uncertainty

Martin Belov and Stephan Anguelov

Abstract Online disinformation in Bulgaria is put in context and explored from legal and socio-legal perspectives. Disinformation, a term familiar but also elusive in Bulgarian constitutional jurisprudence, is presented as a multilayered phenomenon entrenched in a conceptual network with misinformation, information influence operations, and foreign interference in the information space, fake news, and propaganda. Some of these are legal concepts whereas others are doctrinal terms or concepts coined in the socio-legal discourses and narratives. The chapter explores the information and communication rights provided by the 1991 Constitution and other sources of constitutional law and their relevance for online disinformation. The information and communication rights serve not only as legal basis for communicative freedom and action but also as frameworks for legal interpretation and basis for various narratives. The analysis demonstrates the impact of global governance on the phenomenon of online disinformation and the epistemic, authority, and coordination issues resulting from it. The focus is on the constitutional framework. However, the chapter also presents the legislative foundations of the problem and provides extensive analysis of the relevant case-law of the Constitutional Court and the ordinary courts. The results are projected on the implementation of the EU related obligations of Bulgaria for countering online disinformation, partially elements of the "missing constitution". It offers several conclusions which point at the challenges that the phenomenon poses in the context of transnational and global governance, information and technology revolution, and post-modern deconstruction of truth claims.

M. Belov
Sofia University 'St. Kliment Ohridski', Sofia, Bulgaria

S. Anguelov (✉)
Sofia, Bulgaria
e-mail: stephan@anguelov-law.com

P. Passaglia (ed.), *European Legal Perspectives on Online Disinformation*, Ius Gentium: Comparative Perspectives on Law and Justice 140,
https://doi.org/10.1007/978-3-032-25785-7_5

1 Introduction

This chapter is devoted to the topic of online disinformation in Bulgaria put in broader geopolitical, conceptual, and socio-legal context. It explores the problem from legal and socio-legal perspectives. The legal analysis is presented in conjunction with the socio-political context in which it is embedded and which it is supposed to regulate. The chapter starts with an outline of the concept of disinformation necessary for the proper understanding of the case-study of the phenomenon. Disinformation is presented as a complex and multilayered phenomenon that is entrenched in a conceptual network that includes also misinformation, information influence operations, and foreign interference in the information space, fake news, and propaganda. Some of these phenomena are legal concepts whereas others are doctrinal terms or concepts coined in the socio-legal discourses and narratives.

The chapter explores the information and communication rights provided by the Bulgarian 1991 Constitution and the other sources of constitutional law. It shows the relationships between these rights, their restrictions provided by the Bulgarian law, as well as their relevance for the overall problem of online disinformation. The chapter shows that the information and communication rights serve not only as legal basis for communicative freedom and communicative action (Habermas, 1985) but also as frameworks for legal interpretation and basis for various narratives. Several groups of restrictions are outlined. Moreover, the analysis demonstrates the impact of global governance on the phenomenon of online disinformation and especially the epistemic, authority, and coordination issues resulting from it.

Special attention is devoted to the legal framework for prevention, protection, and fight against online disinformation in Bulgaria. The chapter explains and explores the sources of law that regulate these issues. Naturally, the focus is on the constitutional framework. However, the chapter also presents the legislative foundations of the problem and provides extensive analysis of the relevant case-law of the Constitutional Court and the ordinary courts.

The chapter explores the implementation of the EU related obligations of Bulgaria for combat against online disinformation despite the fact that they are still partially elements of the "missing constitution". It offers several conclusions which point at the challenges that the phenomenon poses in the context of transnational and global governance, information and technology revolution, and post-modern deconstruction of truth claims.

2 The Notion of Disinformation

The task of regulating disinformation is inherently complex, even due to the terminological difficulties in providing a clear definition of the term itself and distinguishing it from related concepts. According to Caroline Jack, "definitions of fake news, disinformation, misinformation, and propaganda are not mutually exclusive, and their meanings overlap, while the choice of term may depend on perspective…" (Jack, 2017).

Disinformation is not necessarily illegal content, such as material that infringes copyright and related rights or statements inciting hatred and violence (Ivanova, 2021). Nevertheless, practice shows that targeted propaganda campaigns often mix disinformation with unlawful incitement to violence and hatred against specific ethnic or social groups.[1] Such practices are usually related to politics of dark feelings (e.g. hatred, anxiety, despair) and especially to fear politics (Belov, 2021, 1). They altogether produce socio-legal context of radical uncertainty resulting in constitutional imaginaries of crisis and fear (Belov, 2025). Thus, they contribute to the promotion of dark constitutionalism (Belov, 2025).

In Bulgarian case-law so far, the concept mentioned above rarely appears, and in the few rulings of civil law courts, it is understood mostly as false information. For the first time, the Constitutional Court mentioned "disinformation" in 1993 in the dissenting opinions of five constitutional judges regarding a single court decision. They cited the reasoning of an act of the National Assembly (NA), which dismissed the Director General of the Bulgarian Telegraph Agency (BTA). According to the NA, the BTA under his leadership "made tendentious attempts at disinformation," gave publicity to false and deliberately distorted information. Certain facts were cited about the dissemination, mostly abroad, of "tendentiously selected and manipulated information which deliberately and in practice seriously damaged and compromised… the current government."[2] The five judges dissenting from the majority decision believed that these accusations against the former Director General could negatively affect his honor, dignity, and good name (Art. 32, para. 1, sentence 2 of the Constitution), which he should have been able to defend before the decision-making body—the National Assembly. The fact that the former BTA Director General had not been informed about the draft decision of Parliament, nor given the opportunity to state his position on it, in the view of the five judges amounted to a violation of the right to defense under Art. 56 of the Constitution and of democratic rules and values.[3] The majority of the other seven constitutional judges prevailed, and the decision of the National Assembly was not sanctioned. In their view, the legislative body exercises sovereign power in structuring the procedure for appointing and dismissing

---

[1] European Commission, Directorate-General for Communications Networks, Content and Technology, Digital Services Act – Application of the risk management framework to Russian disinformation campaigns, Publications Office of the European Union, 2023, https://data.europa.eu/doi/10.2759/764631.

[2] Dissenting opinion of the judge Neno Nenovski on Decision no. 15 of 28.09.1993 of the Constitutional Court of the Republic of Bulgaria on constitutional case no. 17/1993 [Особено мнение на съдията Нено Неновски по Decision no. 15 от 28.09.1993 г. на КС на РБ по к.д. № 17/1993 г.]

[3] Dissenting opinion of the judges Tsanko Hadjistoychev, Stanislav Dimitrov, Neno Nenovski, Nikolay Pavlov and Pencho Penev on Decision no. 15 of 28.09.1993 of the Constitutional Court of the Republic of Bulgaria on constitutional case no. 17/1993 [Особени мнения на съдиите Цанко Хаджистойчев, Станислав Димитров, Нено Неновски, Николай Павлов и Пенчо Пенев по Decision no. 15 от 28.09.1993 г. на КС на РБ по к.д. № 17/1993 г.]

the Director General of BTA, and the question of how the right to defense should be arranged in that procedure is not subject to judicial control.

Leaving aside the transgression that the state news agency dared to criticize the then government, the link between disinformation, false information, the deliberate distortion of meaning, and dissemination abroad sounds strikingly contemporary. Related concepts include defamation, the right to defense supported by democratic rules and values. It is curious that, ultimately, the measure to restrict the identified disinformation was taken by an act of the National Assembly—that is, the action was a public-law measure taken by a constitutionally empowered body.

Today, even when disinformation is mentioned, the term has no strictly defined meaning in Bulgaria and is perceived more as a given in the context of the European Union's efforts. Such approach opens the term for interpretative further-development and makes it prone to linguistic games of various narrators (Belov, 2024)—the courts, the Parliament, but also the media. Indeed, the term is hard to be rigorously defined due to range of factors: the socio-political dynamics, the emergence of various new information and communication technologies and platforms for shaping the meaning, the lack of monolithic and dominant public ethics in the context of radical conceptual pluralism and post-modern relativism, the role of the public sphere as battle field of multidirectional post-truths, etc.

The European Democracy Action Plan presents two definitions of disinformation—one broader and one more specific.[4] The broader one encompasses four distinct phenomena: misinformation, disinformation (in the narrow sense), information influence operations, and foreign interference in the information space.

Misinformation is "false or misleading content shared without intent to cause harm, although consequences may still be harmful, for example, when people share false information in good faith with friends and family."

Disinformation in the narrow sense is "false or misleading content spread with the intent to deceive or gain economic or political advantage, and which may harm the public interest."

Information influence operations are "coordinated efforts by domestic or foreign actors to influence target audiences through a set of deceptive means, including the suppression of independent information sources combined with disinformation."

Foreign interference in the information space — "often part of a broader hybrid operation, it can be defined as coercive and deceptive efforts by a foreign state actor or its agents to disrupt the free formation and expression of individuals' political will."[5]

[4] Communication from the Commission to the European Parliament, the Council, the European Economic and Social Committee and the Committee of the Regions On the European democracy action plan, COM/2020/790 final,
https://eur-lex.europa.eu/legal-content/EN/TXT/?uri=COM%3A2020%3A790%3AFIN&amp%3Bqid=1607079662423

[5] Communication from the Commission to the European Parliament, the Council, the European Economic and Social Committee and the Committee of the Regions On the European democracy action plan, COM/2020/790 final,

These four concepts are designed as gradations, listed in ascending order based on the intent to manipulate information and the origin of the actions. Different measures must be taken to address each phenomenon, with the last requiring the broadest and most coordinated EU-level approach (Pamment, 2020). In all four cases, the countermeasures are public-law in nature.

It must be noted, that substantive part of the problem related to the above phenomena stems from several structural issues of contemporary constitutionalism. These are the rise of governance in parallel to or even to detriment of government, the blurring of the 'public–private' distinction, the information and technological revolution and the decline of institutional trust and legitimacy. Transnational sources of information are hardly fitting in the regulative domain of national constitutional and administrative law. The spread of disinformation and misinformation on global scale via new technologies is both easier and more impactful. The imbalance of information games in favor of private actors produces inefficiency of governmental media policies that results in growing delegitimation and distrust. At the same time, globalization, de-institutionalization, and technological revolution allow for information pluralism. They grant unprecedented access to various information spread via a range of new forms of communication (e.g. social media, podcasts etc.) which increases the chances of pluricentric communication world and promotes information pluralism. These broader phenomena and issues are relevant also for the Bulgarian case due to the normative and socio-legal openness of the Bulgarian legal order, its exposure to global information governance, and embeddedness in informational and communicational globalization.

The specific definition of disinformation that is accepted by a substantial part of the doctrine (Strowel. De Meyere 2023) is the one that will serve as the principal definition in this text. It establishes three core criteria for disinformation. First, the information must be factually untrue or misleading. Second, there must be intent or deliberate purpose in its dissemination. Third, it must, or at least may, result in harm to society.

This definition, however, has not yet been incorporated into positive law, although it comes close. The European Democracy Action Plan is not legally binding. The Digital Services Act (DSA),[6] although it employs the term disinformation thirteen times in its preamble, neither defines it nor mentions it in its binding provisions. The definition, as cited above, is reproduced in the Code of Practice on Disinformation, which, as of 13 February 2025, has been approved under Article 45 of the Act and has been in force since 1 July 2025.[7] The Code of Practice is voluntary in nature and binds only the signatories. Thus, the notion of disinformation remains without

---

https://eur-lex.europa.eu/legal-content/EN/TXT/?uri=COM%3A2020%3A790%3AFIN&amp%3Bqid=1607079662423

[6] Regulation (EU) 2022/2065 of the European Parliament and of the Council of 19 October 2022 on a Single Market For Digital Services and amending Directive 2000/31/EC (Digital Services Act) (Text with EEA relevance), EUR-Lex, https://eur-lex.europa.eu/eli/reg/2022/2065/oj/eng

[7] European Commission: Directorate-General for Communications Networks, Content and Technology, Code of conduct on disinformation – As amended in October 2024, Publications Office of the European Union, 2025, https://data.europa.eu/doi/10.2759/5029213

a universally binding legal definition and, consequently, without clearly delineated boundaries. This creates a risk of fragmentation in the fight against disinformation across the Member States of the European Union.

It may be argued that the Digital Services Act employs two principal approaches to combating disinformation. First, the Regulation restricts the dissemination of illegal content. Second, it imposes enhanced due diligence obligations, particularly in relation to systemic risks, on a specific category of Internet service providers—namely, very large online platforms and very large online search engines. Thus, it tries to address the global information governance issues related to the transnational players in global, regional, or national (dis)information games.

The definition of "illegal content" in the Act further complicates the concept of disinformation, since it encompasses "information that, in itself or in relation to an activity, including the sale of products or the provision of services, is not in compliance with Union law or the law of any Member State which is in compliance with Union law, irrespective of the precise subject matter or nature of that law" (Art. 3, letter h, DSA). Illegal content is therefore determined by the EU legislature and separately by the legislatures of all Member States. In other words, it may vary across national jurisdictions. In this way, national legislatures have the opportunity to reflect more directly the public attitudes and needs in combating disinformation within their respective states. Over time, however, it has become evident that certain—but differing—types of disinformation are prohibited by national laws across the EU, which complicates the application of the Act from the perspective of platforms and service providers(Ó Fathaigh, Buijs, van Hoboken, 2025). This highlights again the coordination issues as one of the huge challenges of global constitutionalism and global governance. It also relates to the principle of proportionality as key element of vertical separation of competences in multilevel legal and constitutional orders. The proper balance between homogeneity and context adequacy in giving responses to global or regional issues such as disinformation in the age of information and technology revolution is of pivotal importance for the appropriate regulation of the phenomenon.

Within the Bulgarian regulatory framework, there is no specific legislation aimed at combating disinformation. As long as such efforts exist, they would necessarily be conceptualized as a restriction on the right to freely express and disseminate opinions, and on the right to seek, receive, and impart information—the so-called information and communication rights. The 1991 Bulgarian Constitution provides for these rights in its articles 39–41. The information and communication rights are systematically intertwined on constitutional level. However, the Constitution does not directly address the disinformation as separate constitutional phenomenon. Moreover, it shapes the constitutional parameters of the information and communication rights in a way that reflects the technological standing at the end of the 20th century while not specifically addressing contemporary information and communication technologies. The situation is not changed by the Constitutional Court's case law which is not addressing either contemporary challenges of disinformation or the overall impact of globalization, global governance, and technological innovation on the information and communication rights provided by the Bulgarian Constitution and the international and EU law that is binding for the country.

Restrictions on information and communication rights must always be prescribed by law.[8] They may be differentiated into constitutional and legislative restrictions with view to the source of law in which they are provided. Naturally, the legislative restrictions should be within the limits set by the constitution, although typically the constitution sets rather abstract provisions which are prone to interpretative further-development. The implementation of such restrictions is subject to proportionality control by the courts. Proportionality is also applicable in the case of balancing between human rights. In such case, other constitutional rights, e.g. honour, dignity and reputation, or privacy rights, can themselves serve as limitations and restrictions to information and communication rights. Restrictions imposed by EU law or international law must also observe the subsidiarity principle.

Substantially, the restrictions on communication rights can be divided into two groups.

The first group comprises information whose publication is prohibited and prosecuted by the state through the public prosecutor—for example, the advocacy of fascist or other anti-democratic ideologies, the violent alteration of the constitutionally established order, the incitement to terrorism, the advocacy or incitement to discrimination, violence, or hatred based on race, skin colour, origin, nationality or ethnic identity, or sexual orientation, the creation or dissemination of child pornography, the disclosure or other processing of classified information, the disclosure of personal data from the archives of the Ministry of Interior, and others. For this group, it is immaterial whether the disseminated information is factually true; its dissemination is prohibited outright, and it is prosecuted as a means of protecting a public value through the public prosecutor. These forms of information are part of the so called 'public order clause' which is the typical constitutional restraint of human rights. This clause, although relatively vague and thus prone to interpretation, is set as the ultimate limitation of constitutionally provided rights. It is the principle hurdle that human rights should meet in order to enjoy protection by the Bulgarian constitutional order.

The second group includes information directed against the rights and reputation of other citizens. In this case, the rights of the others (natural or legal persons) serve as limitation of the information and communication rights. Thus, they require proportionality and balancing test. This category encompasses insult and defamation under criminal law, as well as the broader notion of the protection of reputation under civil law. What these have in common is the protection of individual rights. Their judicial protection requires the aggrieved party to seek redress. At the same time, the person who has made a statement that potentially infringes these rights must prove that the statement is true. In other words, the criterion for determining the infringement is an assessment of factual truth. Evaluative statements are excluded, provided they are not insulting. As will be shown in the next section, the protection against defamation may also serve as a tool in the fight against disinformation, insofar

[8] Decision no. 7 of 04.06.1996 of the Constitutional Court of the Republic of Bulgaria 1/1996.

as it sanctions the dissemination of false information. However, defamation may be directed only against a specific natural person and potentially against a legal entity. This means that, at present, before the civil courts, only the harmed natural person may seek protection, while it remains debatable whether legal entities are entitled to such protection.[9] In any case, the "society" as a whole does not enjoy legal protection against harm caused by defamation. This marks the boundary between disinformation and reputational harm.

There is a single criminal offence that explicitly links the transmission of false content with prosecution by the state prosecutor: the transmission of false calls or misleading signals for assistance, accidents, or alarms. This concept comes closest to disinformation without fully encompassing it. It requires false information, dissemination with a degree of intentionality, and potential harm to society. However, the acts are limited to signals for assistance, accidents, or alarms, which can hardly capture the full potential of disinformation to shape perceptions, values, and political attitudes.

At the same time, restricting disinformation is comparable to censorship, which is, in principle, prohibited by the Constitution. It may be argued that, because censorship is prohibited as a principle, and because the legal approach relies on an assessment of factual truth, under Bulgarian law disinformation may be conceived only as false information or otherwise prohibited content. In this respect, Bulgarian law diverges from the concept in the European Democracy Action Plan, which provides that disinformation may also constitute "misleading content." The Bulgarian Constitution leaves no room for misleading content distinct from false content. This means that, if certain content is not expressly prohibited, in order for it to be sanctioned it must be proven factually false, with the restrictive measure proportionate to the infringement upon freedom of expression.[10]

3 The Sources of Law

3.1 Constitutional Provisions

The Constitution proclaims the right of every individual to express an opinion and to disseminate it through speech, defined in broad terms (Art. 39, para. 1). The limitations to this right are the infringement of the rights and reputation of others, and

[9] Interpretative case No. 1/2023 of the General Assembly of Judges of the Civil and Commercial Chamber of the Supreme Court of Cassation (SCC) and the First and Second Chambers of the Supreme Administrative Court (SAC) with an admitted question "Does our objective substantive law allow the award of compensation for non-pecuniary damages in favor of legal entities?" [Тълкувателно дело № 1/2023 г. на Общото събрание на съдиите от Гражданска и Търговска колегия на Върховния касационен съд (ВКС) и Първа и Втора колегия на Върховния административен съд (ВАС) с допуснат въпрос „Допуска ли обективното ни материално право присъждане обезщетение за.

неимуществени вреди в полза на юридическите лица? "].

[10] Decision no. 7 of 04.06.1996 of the Constitutional Court of the Republic of Bulgaria 1/1996.

calls for the violent alteration of the constitutionally established order, the commission of crimes, the incitement of hostility, or violence against the person (Art. 39, para. 2). Moreover, censorship of the press and other means of mass communication is prohibited (Art. 40). The suspension of a printed publication or another medium of information—which undoubtedly includes taking down of internet content—is permissible only on the basis of an act of the judiciary (Art. 40, para. 2). Everyone has the right to seek, receive, and disseminate information. The exercise of this right may not be directed against the rights and reputation of other citizens, nor against national security, public order, public health, or morality (Art. 41, para. 1). These, in short, are the three information and communication rights proclaimed by the Bulgarian Constitution (Belov, 2024, 2). Traditionally, they are considered to be part of the group of political rights by the predominant Bulgarian constitutional doctrine (Tanchev, 2003; Stoychev, 2002; Drumeva, 2013) despite the fact that they may concern also non-political information. This is due to the tradition of following the classical distinction between personal, political, and socio-economic and cultural rights by the Bulgarian scholarship. Nevertheless, these rights concern broader spectrum of objects beyond the purely political information. Thus, disinformation may have an impact beyond the strictly political information in the narrower sense.

The Constitutional Court, as early as 1996, adopted an interpretative decision[11] concerning these three rights, clarifying their substance and delineating the framework for their contemporary application. The foundation of these rights lies in constitutional imperatives "such as the dignity of the human person (Art. 4, para. 2), freedom of thought and freedom of conscience (Art. 37, para. 1), and political pluralism (Art. 11, para. 1)."[12] Some of these imperatives are constitutional principles, whereas others are human rights that form a network in which the information and communication rights are entrenched. Information and communication rights provide the individual with the opportunity for free expression of his or hers "essence and dignity as an equal participant in the social community."[13] They also guarantee the possibility for everyone to be informed about the socio-legal reality. At the same time, the Court observed, the free exchange of opinions shapes public opinion, which in turn creates the conditions for the existence and development of society.

The information and communication rights are mutually intertwined. The freedom to express and disseminate opinions lays at the center of this rights' network. It is not confined solely to speech but extends to sound, image, or any other form of expression (Art. 39, para 1). This fact must be highlighted in the context of the visual and emotional turn that is unfolding in contemporary constitutionalism (Belov, 2022, 2023). Indeed, the constitutional and political communication does not consist just in reading of legal texts. Rather, it is accomplished through various signifiers of constitutional and constitutionally relevant meaning that constitute forms of visual and performative constitutionalism.[14] Hence, the freedom of expression and all other

---

[11] Decision no. 7 of 04.06.1996 of the Constitutional Court of the Republic of Bulgaria 1/1996 г.

[12] Decision no. 7 of 04.06.1996 of the Constitutional Court of the Republic of Bulgaria 1/1996 г.

[13] Decision no. 7 of 04.06.1996 of the Constitutional Court of the Republic of Bulgaria 1/1996 г.

[14] Ibid.

information and communication rights protect all forms through which they are manifested, including art, architecture, performance, and the range of instruments for emotional exchange.[15] According to the Constitutional Court the freedom of expression "has the character of a generic concept which integrates the others and at the same time designates an independent right."[16] The Court emphasizes that the individual rights are regulated primarily as personal rights of the individual.

An exception is the freedom of the press and of the other means of mass communication, which is conceived more as an institutional right. Indeed, many rights serve also as crystallization core for the protection of the objective institution—in this case the media—via which it typically manifests itself. In the case of the freedom of the press and the means for mass communication the Constitution protects both the human right and its institutional reflection in the realm of the public sphere. Also, this right has to be interpreted extensively in order to include also the new means of communication, e.g. social platforms and networks, podcasts, social media channels, etc. resulting from the information and communication revolution. In the context of free media and free speech protection the Constitutional Court places the emphasis on the prohibition of censorship. "The explicit prohibition of censorship reflects the principle that any interference in the activities of the mass media by state authorities is impermissible—whether through the formal institutionalization of means of influence or through informal methods."[17] Although the Constitutional Court has not expressly commented on this point, formally speaking the prohibition of censorship applies only to the press and to the mass media, which excludes from its scope citizens and organizations that are not media entities. The Court has no explicit rulings on the protection against censorship in social media and the new forms and channels of communication nor does it have decisions on the constitutional protection of new media and transnational forms of speech facilitated via Internet. If in a future case the Court decides to adopt a reading closer to the original constitutional text, it may decide to carry out a distinction between some form of traditional media—"the press and the other mass information media" as Art. 40 reads—and other information channels. In such a case, only the former would benefit from the prohibition of censorship. For the others this would mean that they could be closed by an act which does not require judicial control. Furthermore, currently, certain groups of prohibited content like fraud or abuse under the Electronic Communications Act (Art. 138c), and malicious internet traffic—i.e., the source of a cyberattack under the Cybersecurity Act (Art. 14, para. 5 and Art. 15, para. 6) can be filtered or suspended based solely on a demand by the respective administrative authority without judicial control. When the demand for such filtering is addressed solely to an internet platform it has to comply and moderate the problematic content. There is no requirement for information to the sanctioned person under national law. This in turn means that the sanctioned person can only rely on redress mechanisms offered by the platform

---

[15] Ibid.

[16] Decision no. 7 of 04.06.1996 of the Constitutional Court of the Republic of Bulgaria 1/1996.

[17] Decision no. 7 of 04.06.1996 of the Constitutional Court of the Republic of Bulgaria 1/1996 r.

but not the Bulgarian state. This raises a risk of state-sponsored censorship which is both opaque and practically lacks judicial remedy.

Another interesting twist regarding online disinformation is that Article 9 of the DSA provides for acting upon orders against illegal content issued by any of the EU Member States' national judicial or administrative authorities. In all cases where such an order is issued by an administrative authority without an act by the judiciary it is potentially unconstitutional under the prohibition of censorship clause (Art. 40, para. 2 of the Constitution). A fortiori, the power of Digital Services Coordinators to order the cessation of infringements under Article 51, para. 2, letter b) of the DSA which is in essence a power of an administrative authority is again potentially unconstitutional under the prohibition of censorship clause (Art. 40, para. 2 of the Constitution).

From the perspective of restricting information and communication rights, the Constitutional Court stresses that these rights are not absolute. Limitations are permissible for the protection of other rights and interests that are also constitutionally protected, and may be imposed only on the grounds explicitly provided for in the Constitution.[18] Restrictions on the freedom to express and disseminate opinions must mandatorily be established by law. The potential for interference with this right is greatest when it is exercised in a manner that infringes the rights and reputation of others, since in this way the honor, dignity, and good name of the individual are safeguarded in accordance with Art. 4, para 2 and Art. 32, para 1, sentence 2 of the Constitution. Other possible restrictions follow thereafter. Nevertheless, the Court emphasizes that it does not find normative grounds for establishing a hierarchy of fundamental rights. This means that the freedom to express and disseminate opinions is not placed above other rights, but also that any restriction of a fundamental right requires an assessment in each concrete case and a determination of the proportionality of the interference. Naturally, this requires a proportionality and balancing test (Steiner, Netzer, Sulitzeanu-Kenan, 2022) to be accomplished in case of any limitations to information and communication rights either by act of public power or by another human right the latter stemming from the horizontal effect of human rights (Alexy, 1994).

This has been confirmed in a 2019 decision of the Constitutional Court,[19] which declared unconstitutional a provision of the Personal Data Protection Act introducing a list of criteria for processing personal data for journalistic purposes. The Court found that, in essence, such a legislative approach represented a step toward the establishment of a hierarchical ordering of fundamental rights, and that freedom of expression might thereby be subordinated to dignity and reputation or to the protection of public order and morality. According to the Constitutional Court, "such a hierarchy, however, runs counter to international treaties and to the national constitutions of contemporary democratic states governed by the rule of law, which establish the equivalence of rights and do not allow for the permanence of restrictive measures,

[18] Decision no. 7 of 04.06.1996 of the Constitutional Court of the Republic of Bulgaria 1/1996 г.

[19] Decision no. 8 of 15.11.2019 of the Constitutional Court of the Republic of Bulgaria on const. case no. 4 / 2019.

since that would be tantamount to their abrogation."[20] This is also the only decision of the Constitutional Court in which the notion of disinformation is mentioned, albeit briefly. The Court's view is that, for the purposes of journalistic activity, including in combating "deliberate pseudo-journalistic disinformation" that could serve as a tool for eroding trust in the media, self-regulation within the media industry and codes of conduct are preferable to statutory regulation.

3.2 Legislative Provisions

The constitutional principles are further specified at the statutory level in a number of legislative acts. The overview below is not intended to be exhaustive; rather, it highlights provisions that may have direct relevance for the application of the EU Digital Services Act (DSA). In the context of combating disinformation, the prohibited content regulated by Bulgarian law can be divided into per se prohibited content and false content.

3.2.1 Prohibited Content

The first category is subdivided into two groups.

The first group encompasses a number of provisions of the Criminal Code, which prohibit the proclamation of fascist or other anti-democratic ideology, or the violent alteration of the constitutionally established order (Art. 108); the incitement to commit terrorism (Art. 114L); the proclamation or incitement to discrimination, violence, or hatred based on race, skin color, origin, nationality or ethnic identity, or sexual orientation (Art. 162); among others. The Counter-Terrorism Act (Art. 32, para. 1) expressly empowers the Ministry of Interior and the State Agency for National Security (SANS) to request the Sofia City Court to suspend access to Internet pages whose content incites terrorism or disseminates knowledge about the commission of terrorist acts. Under the Markets in Financial Instruments Act (Art. 281), the Financial Supervision Commission, subject to review by the Sofia District Court, is granted a similar power with respect to internet pages offering investment services by persons not authorized to provide such services within the territory of the Republic of Bulgaria.

The second subgroup, however, includes several statutes that provide for the prohibition of certain online content without judicial authorization. Examples include the Markets in Crypto-Assets Act (Art. 28, para. 1, items 14 and 22) in cases of infringement of Regulation (EU) 2023/1114; the Gambling Act (Art. 88a), pursuant to Art. 9(1) of Regulation (EU) 2022/2065; and the Electronic Communications Act (Art. 138c), with regard to fraud or abuse. A particularly important case is found in the

[20] Decision no. 8 of 15.11.2019 of the Constitutional Court of the Republic of Bulgaria on const. case no. 4 / 2019.

Cybersecurity Act (Art. 14, para. 5 and Art. 15, para. 6), which grants the General Directorate for Combating Organized Crime of the Ministry of Interior and the State Agency for National Security the authority, solely upon notification and without judicial oversight, to impose filtering or suspension of malicious internet traffic—i.e., the source of a cyberattack. Such authority vested in the Ministry of Interior and SANS carries a high risk of concealed censorship.

3.2.2 False Content

The second category of statutory provisions—false content—is closest to the notion of disinformation. Here we find defamation under criminal law (Art. 147 of the Criminal Code) and under civil law in the form of non-pecuniary damages to reputation (Art. 45, para. 1 of the Obligations and Contracts Act), as well as the sanction for transmitting false calls or misleading signals for assistance, accidents, or alarms (Art. 326 of the Criminal Code).

For brevity, defamation—an established and long-standing legal institution—will not be addressed in detail here. Attention should instead be drawn to a significant recent development that departs from established practice and bears directly on the sanctioning of false content. Until recently, case-law had been based primarily on the provisions on insult and defamation in the Criminal Code (Arts. 146 and 147), which prescribe fines and public condemnation. In civil law, although the Obligations and Contracts Act (Art. 52) remains silent on the forms of compensation for tortious harm, the consistent case-law had long held that "non-pecuniary damages, by their very nature, cannot be repaired but may only be compensated through monetary redress by way of providing other goods."[21]

This position was altered by a decision of the Supreme Court of Cassation in April 2025, which directly addressed the question: "Does every citizen have a subjective right to protection against unlawful encroachments upon their rights by bringing a claim for the removal of an article published in an electronic media outlet containing defamatory statements and insults?"[22] The claimant in this case, a judge with an active civic profile, sought the removal from the website of an electronic publication of a number of articles containing offensive and defamatory statements concerning her. According to the Supreme Court of Cassation, "the primary civil law consequence of a tort is the emergence of an obligation on the part of the tortfeasor to repair the harm they have culpably caused to another… In interpreting Art. 45 of the Obligations and Contracts Act and resolving the question of what forms of protection it encompasses, it follows, by implication, that the rule of Art. 45 OCA on the "repair of harm"—in cases of publication of an article in an electronic media outlet containing insults and defamation—must also be interpreted in light of the principle enshrined in Art. 32, para. 1 of the Constitution of the Republic of Bulgaria, which guarantees every

[21] Ruling no. 195 of 09.03.2016 on commercial case no. 1696 / 2015 of the Supreme Court of cassation, Second Commercial Chamber.

[22] Decision no. 195 of 04.04.2025 of the SCC, civil case no. 3278 of 2023.

person the right to protection against infringements on their honor, dignity, and good name. Full protection would not be achieved if the right to seek restoration of the situation existing prior to the unlawful injury, through the removal of the respective article from the website of the electronic publication, were denied.

On the basis of the foregoing considerations, the question must be answered in the sense that any citizen whose personality has been harmed by an article in an electronic publication containing offensive and defamatory statements directed against them, has the right, pursuant to Art. 45 of the Obligations and Contracts Act, to bring, alongside the claim for monetary compensation for non-pecuniary damages, a claim requiring the owner of the electronic publication to restore the status quo ante the unlawful injury by removing the article from the site. This means of protection falls within the scope of the tortfeasor's obligation to "repair the damage" as provided in Art. 45 OCA."[23]

The departure from the Supreme Court of Cassation's established case law is as sharp as it is sparsely reasoned. It remains unclear what necessitated this break from precedent. No assessment is offered regarding the necessity and proportionality of the newly introduced form of redress. Understandable as the reasoning is for putting an end to the continued online presence of defamatory content, there is no consideration of the possibilities of dissemination, re-publication, or archiving of such publications. Once published and indexed by search engines, information never remains confined to its original address. Not least, while the justices cite the Constitution, they fail to take into account other protected rights. They overlook the fact that, regardless of its quality and the moral judgment it may deserve, an electronic publication is a medium of mass communication. The prohibition of censorship under Art. 40 of the Constitution, as well as the requirement that restrictions upon it be based on law, are omitted. The Obligations and Contracts Act does not expressly provide for a power to remove content. The question remains whether the panel of the Supreme Court of Cassation has not engaged in an excessively activist rewriting of the law. Time will show whether this jurisprudence will prove sustainable or will remain isolated.

The last norm referred to above is the closest to the notion of disinformation, albeit with a narrower scope of application. Art. 326 of the Criminal Code provides for punishment under two cumulative conditions. The first condition concerns the act itself—information must have been transmitted, even if no specific result has ensued. The second condition relates to the quality of this information—it must constitute "false calls or misleading signals for assistance, accident, or alarm." It is conceivable to further subdivide the quality of the information by distinguishing between false and misleading data, but for now this remains a merely hypothetical possibility. Case-law shows several cases in which sanctions have been imposed for the transmission of such information online. In each of them, criminal liability was replaced with administrative liability, leading only to the imposition of a fine.

In one case, through a video uploaded to a video-sharing platform, false alarm signals were disseminated regarding an impending natural disaster—namely, the

[23] Decision no. 195 of 04.04.2025 of the SCC, civil case no. 3278 of 2023.

flooding of a populated area by a dam.[24] According to the Oryahovo court, the content was delivered "in a threatening and even mocking tone."

In another case, the Gorna Oryahovitsa District Court sanctioned a citizen who, through his "Instagram" profile, disseminated misleading signals of an accident, namely, that a minor, presented as his daughter, had been struck by a car and had died, while the driver had fled the scene. A photograph of a child was also published, with the claim that it was the deceased.[25]

In the final example of sanctioning false content, the Kotel District Court, in 2020 during the COVID-19 pandemic, sanctioned a citizen who, through his Facebook profile in a group dedicated to the problems of the town of Targovishte, disseminated misleading signals of accident and alarm by posting the comment: "There is coronavirus in Targovishte officially since today."[26]

However, the lack of stability in judicial interpretation is underscored by three other cases related to the pandemic. In the first, also in 2020, a citizen was acquitted after transmitting, through the online social network Facebook in the group "Seen in Silistra," false and misleading signals of alarm, namely: "Three confirmed cases of coronavirus in Silistra. Sad but true!"[27] In this case, the court took into account that the information had been accessible for about fifteen minutes only to a limited circle of registered users on Facebook. At that moment, a state of emergency had already been officially declared in the country, and the spread of the disease was to be reasonably expected. With a touch of irony, the court observed that "the information that in Silistra there are sick people with the symptoms of this disease is unlikely to have caused particular alarm. Obviously, in this case, it impressed primarily the district prosecutor, but even here there is no categorical data that the information provoked anxiety in him; his reaction is rather a professional reflex."[28]

In another case, the Vidin Regional Court acquitted a citizen who had published in a Facebook group a video recording with a statement, accompanied by a textual comment, claiming that under instructions from the task force and the government, doctors and contacts of confirmed coronavirus patients were not being tested, and that this would lead to the spread of infection in Vidin.[29] The interesting point in this case is that the factual allegation was not proven as true. According to the district prosecutor's office in Vidin, the accused knew that doctors in the hospital had been tested. However, the statement in question was in fact a repetition of claims made by a third party—the director of the regional health inspectorate in Vidin—as well as information from various individuals and meetings with the RHI leadership. Referring to

---

[24] Decision no. 23 of 11.04.2016 on criminal case no. 94/2016 –of District Court – Oryahovo.

[25] Decision no. 161 of 03.08.2021 on administrative sanction case no. 513/2021 of District Court – Gorna Oryahovitza.

[26] Decision no. 260010 of 13.10.2020 on administrative sanction case no. 137/2020 – of District Court – Kotel.

[27] Decision no. 38 of 29.12.2020 on administrative sanction case no. 207/2020 of Silistra Regional Court.

[28] Decision no. 38 of 29.12.2020 on administrative sanction case no 207/2020 of Silistra Regional Court.

[29] Decision of 15.02.2021 on administrative sanction case no. 173 / 2020 of Vidin Regional Court.

the right to freedom of expression, the court held that the incriminated claims were not without basis, i.e., they were neither false nor misleading. It emphasized that the right to disseminate information also encompasses information that is disturbing.[30]

In another similar case, the Sofia City Court, acting as an appellate instance, acquitted the chairwoman of a professional pharmacists' organization, who had stated in interviews for national radio and television that "there are logistical problems even for medicines already in the country… there are logistical problems at the borders" and that "there are logistical problems, since many active substances for the production of medicines are purchased from India and China, which is not possible at present, and shortages of certain medicines are to be expected" (to Bulgarian National Radio), and that "shortages of medicinal products are to be expected, since many active substances used in the production of common medicines are purchased from China and India, which at the moment is impossible" (to Bulgarian National Television, Channel 1).[31] The court held that although not initially, the statements of the accused were subsequently proven true over time. Furthermore, her statements did not constitute misleading signals of alarm, since they were not assertions of accomplished facts but rather judgments, assessments, subjective interpretations, etc., connected with the informant's perception of a given event and its possible consequences for public life. The communication of publicly significant and truthful information does not amount to an alarm signal; rather, it constitutes a socially useful activity of informing society about events (even adverse ones) concerning the highest goods in modern society—human health and life.[32]

In fact, the latter two cases can also be read as attempts at censorship or at least pressure on civic activists by the prosecution under the pretext that they were sowing panic in society. Although the prosecutions did not succeed, these proceedings caused harm to the defendants.

In conclusion, it must be said that judicial practice under Art. 326 of the Criminal Code focuses on the examination of the truthfulness of the alleged facts, as well as on whether the claims can be verified for truth. This approach mirrors that used in the assessment of the existence of defamation. Although the statutory provision expressly provides for "misleading signals," the judges do not consider the substance of this element, but rather equate it, at least implicitly, with false content. At present, it is difficult to determine what the autonomous meaning—or even an example—of "misleading signals" would be. It is likely that this judicial hesitation will, by analogy, be carried over into the "misleading information" element of the definition of disinformation.

---

[30] Decision of 15.02.2021 on administrative sanction case no. 173 / 2020 of Vidin Regional Court.

[31] Decision no. 87 of 28.07.2021 on appellate administrative sanction case no. 1862/2021 of Sofia City Court, XIV appellate panel.

[32] Decision no. 87 of 28.07.2021 on appellate administrative sanction case no. 1862/2021 of Sofia City Court, XIV appellate panel.

4 The Regulation

The national legislation does not provide means to counter properly misleading content, even though some rules are aimed at sanctioning illegal content.

The Radio and Television Act grants certain supervisory and enforcement powers to the Council for Electronic Media (CEM), including competences to counter illegal audio-visual content (Articles 32 and 33 in conjunction with Article 10 of the Act). However, CEM is not responsible for monitoring or addressing other forms of disinformation that do not qualify as "illegal content."

A limited degree of oversight may be exercised through the Bulgarian Media Ethics Code, which constitutes a voluntary self-regulatory mechanism but does not have a proper sanctioning power.

Regarding the newer EU rules, Bulgaria adopted in late November 2025 national legislation implementing the requirements of the Digital Services Act (DSA).[33] Prior to that a decision of the Council of Ministers had designated the Communications Regulation Commission (CRC) as the Digital Services Coordinator.[34] The adopted act technically implements the EU regulation, however it falls short of introducing an effective legislative framework aimed at countering disinformation on the national level, despite the increasing relevance and even prevalence of this phenomenon. Put more succinctly: "Bulgaria: much disinformation, little counteraction." (Ognyanova, 2021).

Under the newly amended Electronic Communications Act (ECA), the role of Digital Services Coordinator is assigned to the CRC (Article 21, para. 6 of the act). The CRC is envisaged as being entrusted with the core tasks of monitoring compliance with the DSA, imposing enforcement measures, including those under Articles 9 and 10 DSA, applying sanctions, coordinating with other authorities, reporting, certifying out-of-court dispute settlement bodies, granting "trusted flagger" status, and accrediting "vetted researchers." The Council for Electronic Media (CEM) would act as the designated authority with specific responsibility regarding video-sharing platform services (Article 49d of the ECA).

The law introduces a special administrative procedure, distinct from the general Administrative Offences and Penalties Act, for establishing infringements of the DSA (Articles 323c–323v of the ECA). The declared aim of this procedure is to streamline the imposition of administrative fines or pecuniary penalties in order to ensure sanctions are "effective, proportionate and dissuasive," as required under Recitals 114 and 117 DSA. In practice, however, the proposed procedure risks duplicating the existing regime, introducing vague terminology and creating opportunities for delay.

---

[33] Law amending the Electronic Communications Act, State Gazette, issue 99, 21 November 2025, https://dv.parliament.bg/DVWeb/showMaterialDV.jsp?idMat=238812

[34] Council of Ministers of the Republic of Bulgaria, Decision No. 405 of 13 June 2024 [Решение No. 405 of 13 June 2024], Sofia, 13 June 2024, https://pris.government.bg/document/546ae73fc67664f8e2087e4c805894bc

The preliminary assessment of whether there are "reasonable grounds to presume an infringement" is carried out by either the CRC or CEM, depending on their competences. This assessment results in a report (Article 323d, para. 4 of the ECA), on the basis of which proceedings are either initiated or terminated. Only at this point is the provider concerned formally notified. During subsequent investigations, officials designated by the Chair of the CRC or by CEM enjoy the investigatory powers under Article 51(1) DSA, and providers are obliged to cooperate (Article 323 h of the ECA). However, no statutory deadlines are provided for the execution of these obligations, leaving scope for protracted procedures. Similarly, the CRC may request information pursuant to Article 51(1) DSA, but compliance deadlines are to be determined ad hoc by officials (Article 323i of the ECA), creating further risks of delay.

On-site inspections may be carried out by the CRC or CEM, subject to prior authorisation by a judge of the Sofia Region Administrative Court (Articles 323 k and 323 l). In cases of "sufficient data indicating an infringement, in urgent situations due to a risk of serious and irreparable harm," the CRC or CEM may impose interim measures, including suspension of the infringement, blocking of access to the service, or periodic penalty payments, within the meaning of Article 51(2)(b) and (d) DSA (Article 323o of the ECA). Appeals do not suspend enforcement in such cases. Yet the cumulative conditions, coupled with the use of undefined legal terms such as "sufficient data" or "serious and irreparable harm," create legal uncertainty and may undermine the stability of interim measures. Moreover, the administrative order to cease the infringement does not require judicial oversight and could thus be unconstitutional under the prohibition of censorship rule of Article 40, para. 2 of the Constitution.

The investigation concludes with a report, on which the provider has at least one month to comment (Article 323q). This again prolongs proceedings. Finally, the competent authority—CRC or CEM—adopts a decision in closed session, which may be appealed before the courts. In this case, appeals do suspend enforcement (Article 323r). Again, the final decision is in its nature an administrative act which if includes an order to cease the infringement does not require judicial oversight and could thus be unconstitutional under the prohibition of censorship rule of Article 40, para. 2 of the Constitution.

Overall, the proposed procedure does not appear substantially faster or more effective than the existing general administrative offence procedure. Risks of delay, ambiguity and judicial backlog remain, particularly given the exclusive jurisdiction conferred on the Sofia Region Administrative Court.

Crucially, the new law contains no provisions specifically targeting disinformation. The term itself is not mentioned. Disinformation is implicitly subsumed under the broader category of "illegal content," without recognition of its sui generis character as envisaged in European policy discourse. No mechanisms for coordination with other competent authorities are envisaged. In practical terms, therefore, nothing in the existing national framework would change. The approach to online disinformation is likely to remain narrowly confined to factual assessments of whether given content is "illegal," leaving misleading content—analogous to the "misleading signals" under Article 326 of the Criminal Code—outside the scope of the CRC and CEM.

The recently adopted law ensures that Bulgaria formally complies with the DSA requirement to designate and empower a national coordinator. However, several aspects warrant further debate. The draft amendments reflect only the minimum requirements of the DSA, without introducing substantive national measures against disinformation. Furthermore, an examination of Article 30 ECA shows that the CRC has traditionally functioned as a technocratic regulator concerned with competition and the functioning of electronic communications markets, rather than with the protection of fundamental rights such as human dignity, freedom of expression, privacy, or democratic processes, including free and informed elections. This raises the risk of limited institutional capacity to address disinformation, at least in the initial years of implementation.

5 Conclusions

The online disinformation is not anymore a new phenomenon. It exists since the emergence of Internet and the development of the web-based media channels, platforms, and networks. Initially, several decades ago, it might have seemed to be a continuation of the traditional disinformation accomplished via new technological means. However, the later developments have shown that online disinformation has much deeper repercussions and wider scope as well as incomparably bigger capacity to influence worldviews and mould the public opinion than the previous forms of disinformation. This is due to its reliance on time–space compression, its subsequent global and simultaneous outreach, and its enhanced ability to influence the minds and hearts of the people. The emotional engagement produced via digital means is incomparably stronger than the one resulting from traditional information and communication tools. The capacity for disinformation and misinformation has increased with the emergence of AI. The capacity of AI to produce augmented, if not fake reality is close to limitless. This brings the need to cope with online disinformation to a brand-new level.

Nevertheless, the current age creates not only perils, but also opportunities. The development and proliferation of new online channels for communication has diminished the state control, but also the state censorship and the hierarchically and centrally produced disinformation and misinformation. Thus, the emerging global transnational civil society has new epistemic and communication opportunities to produce genuine information via critical deliberation. Indeed, such deliberation does not function in sterile conditions. It can and is frequently distorted by national, supranational, international, and transnational actors having new models for influencing worldviews in the context of post-territorial and aterritorial forms of power (Belov, 2021, 2). Transnational private actors and more traditional sources of power can misuse the deliberative networks in order to impose their agenda in a hidden hierarchical manner. Moreover, AI can be a danger, but also aid in finding, sorting out, systematizing, and producing important and useful information. It can be a creator of fake news and even fake realities, but also instrument for combat against disinformation that can bring the human knowledge and human experience to a brand-new level.

Thus, we are in dire need not just of new tools for fight against online disinformation, but rather of genuinely novel framework for understanding and ordering the global, post-territorial, and transnational information and epistemic (dis)order. Such model must avoid, stop, or at least minimize the process of deconstitutionalization that is currently ongoing. With regard to online disinformation deconstitutionalization consists in the inability of the constitutional order to provide viable, efficient, and legitimate solutions, thus losing its role as normative framework of the socio-legal playground in which the power phenomena are unfolding. The visible processes of deconstitutionalization undermine the legitimacy of public power, including state power. The combat against deconstitutionalization in the sphere of online disinformation cannot be successful if accomplished locally. Transnational and global phenomena, such as online disinformation, require transnational and global means and responses. Hence, the prevention and fight against online disinformation in Bulgaria can be perceived only as part of a global puzzle that clearly goes beyond national and territorial borders.

Strategy and Coordination Gaps: Bulgaria lacks a national strategy on countering disinformation. There is no comprehensive policy document or action plan defining objectives, responsibilities, and measures to increase society's resilience to disinformation. This means efforts are reactive and fragmented. Various agencies (SANS, GDCOC, ministries) might address pieces of the problem, but without strategic coordination, important aspects fall through the cracks—for example, public awareness campaigns, systematic exposure of foreign influence networks, or support for independent media (Galev et al., 2025).

References

Belov, M. (2022): Constitutional semiotics. The Conceptual Foundations of a Constitutional Theory and Meta-Theory, pp. 107–241, Hart, Oxford.

Belov, M. (2024): Constitutional Imaginaries in Central and Eastern Europe – Layered Narratives on Symbolic-Imaginary Constitutionalism in a Region Marked by Semi-Permanent Transformation and Transition, in Review of Central and East European Law, Special issue, Volume 49, No. 2–4, also Martin Belov, The Constitutional Imaginaries of Crisis and Emergency: between Battle of Narratives and Entanglement in Quantum Constitutionalism in Belov, M. (ed) Constitutional Polycrisis and Emergency Constitutionalism, Palgrave, 2025 (forthcoming) and Martin Belov, Constitutional semiotics. The Conceptual Foundations of a Constitutional Theory and Meta-Theory, Hart, Oxford, 2022, 80–93.

Belov, M. (2024, 2): Constitutional Law in Bulgaria, pp. 225–226, Kluwer.

Belov, M (2025): Legal Imaginaries of Crisis and Fear. Dark Constitutionalism, pp. 1–334, Routledge, (forthcoming).

Drumeva, E. (2013): Constitutional Law, pp. 711, Ciela (in Bulgarian).

Galev, T. Malinov, S. O'Kelley, C. Dzhekova, R. Botan, M. (2025): Third evaluation report CoPD in Bulgaria and Romania. BROD. https://brodhub.eu/en/research/third-evaluation-report-copd-in-bulgaria-and-romania/

Habermas, J. (1985) Theory of Communicative Action, Volume 1: Reason and the Rationalization of Society, pp. 1- 465, Beacon Press.

Ivanova, I. (2021) Merki sreshtu desinformatsiyata i otgovornost na platformite v zakonodatelnitereformi na ES i Obedinenoto kralstvo. In: Desinfromatsiya: novite predizvikatelstva, pp. 119–150, University editions Sofia University 'St. Kliment Ohridski', Sofia (Иванова, Иглика. „Мерки срещу дезинформацията и отговорност на платформите в законодателните реформи на ЕС и Обединеното кралство". В. Сборник с доклади „Дезинформацията: новите предизвикателства", София: Университетско издателство СУ „Св. Климент Охридски", 2021, с. 119–150.)

Jack, C.: Lexicon of Lies: Terms for Problematic Information. Data & Society Research Institute. (2017)

Ó Fathaigh, R., Buijs, D., & van Hoboken, J. (2025): The Regulation of Disinformation Under the Digital Services Act. Media and Communication, 13, Article 9615. https://doi.org/10.17645/mac.9615

Ognyanova, N. (2021): Nyama da ima ministerstvo na istinata v ES, In: Desinfromatsiya: novite predizvikatelstva, pp. 119–150, University editions Sofia University 'St. Kliment Ohridski', Sofia (Огнянова, Нели. „Няма да има Министерство на истината в ЕС": по следите на едно обещание (политика на ЕС към дезинформацията). В. Сборник с доклади „Дезинформацията: новите предизвикателства", София: Университетско издателство СУ „Св. Климент Охридски", 2021, с. 92–118.)

Pamment, J. (2020): The EU's role in fighting disinformation: Taking back the initiative, Carnegie Endowment for International Peace Working Paper, available at: https://carnegieendowment.org/2020/07/15/eu-s-role-in-fighting-disinformation-taking-back-initiative-pub-82286.

See Alexy, R. (1994): Theorie der Grundrechte, pp. 475, Suhrkamp.

See Belov, M. (2021, 1) The Role of Fear Politics in Global Constitutional 'Ernstfall': Images of Fear under COVID-19 Health Paternalism in Belov, M. (ed.) Populist Constitutionalism and Illiberal Democracies. Between Constitutional Imagination, pp. 187–221, Normative Entrenchment and Political Reality, Cambridge, Intersentia.

See Belov, M. (2021, 2): Territory, Territoriality and Territorial Politics as Public Law Concepts in Belov, M. (ed.) Territorial Politics and Secession. Constitutional and International Law Dimensions, Palgrave, pp. 15–45.

See Belov M. (2023): Constitutional semiotics as a post-positivist and post-modern approach to constitution and constitutionalism based on the linguistic, visual and emotional turns, in Wagner, A. S. Marusek (eds) Research Handbook on Legal Semiotics, Oxford, Edward Elgar, p. 105–119

See Steiner, T., Netzer, L., Sulitzeanu-Kenan, R. (2022): Necessity or balancing: The protection of rights under different proportionality tests—Experimental evidence, International Journal of Constitutional Law, Volume 20, Issue 2, 642–663

Stoychev, S. (2002): Constitutional Law, pp. 254–255, Ciela, Sofia.

Strowel, Alain, De Meyere, Jean. (2023): „The Digital Services Act: transparency as an efficient tool to curb the spread of disinformation on online platforms?", 14 JIPITEC 66 para 1., https://www.jipitec.eu/issues/jipitec-14-1-2023/5708

Tanchev, E. (2003): Introduction in Constitutional Law, pp. 392. Sibi, (in Bulgarian).

Landscape of Disinformation Regulation in Czechia

Tina Mizerová

Abstract This chapter examines selected legal frameworks in Czechia that may be applied to address the proliferation of disinformation. It begins by clarifying how Czechia defines disinformation, followed by an analysis of relevant constitutional provisions, with a focus on the right to freedom of expression. The relevant legal provisions presented in the chapter include the protection of personality rights under civil law and key provisions of criminal law. Additionally, the chapter discusses other pertinent regulations, including those governing electoral campaigns, the blocking of disinformation websites, and international sanctions. Finally, the chapter assesses the implementation (or lack thereof) of the Digital Services Act and the Artificial Intelligence Act, while also addressing the ongoing policy debates surrounding them.

1 Introduction and Notion of Disinformation

This chapter presents Czech legal framework which targets (although indirectly) dissemination of online disinformation. The chapter is divided in three sub-chapters. The first sub-chapter presents constitutional provisions, with a particular focus on the right to the freedom of expression, as it sets the boundaries for any legal measures aimed at curbing the spread of online disinformation. The second sub-chapter focuses on national level, and discusses mainly the protection of personality rights under civil law and selected criminal offenses, as well as other notable regulation, such as the regulation of electoral campaigns or international sanctions that targets content from Russian media. The final sub-chapter addresses Czech implementation of key EU regulations governing the online environment: Digital Services Act and the Artificial Intelligence Act. Given that the process of their implementation is not yet completed, the chapter also considers the political debates shaping their implementation.

To begin, it is important to note that Czech regulation neither provides a legally binding definition of disinformation nor explicitly references the term. The

T. Mizerová (✉)
Institute of Law and Technology, Masaryk University, Brno, Czechia
e-mail: 471315@mail.muni.cz

P. Passaglia (ed.), *European Legal Perspectives on Online Disinformation*, Ius Gentium: Comparative Perspectives on Law and Justice 140,
https://doi.org/10.1007/978-3-032-25785-7_6

Ministry of the Interior, through its Center for Countering Terrorism and Hybrid Threats (which is responsible for monitoring hybrid threats including disinformation campaigns) defines disinformation as: "*Dissemination of deliberately false information, especially by state actors or their affiliates, aimed at other state or towards media with the aim of influencing opinions and decisions of those who receive the false information.*"[1] This definition reflects the Ministry's approach, shared by other state institutions, which frames disinformation primarily as a tool of influence operations and hybrid warfare. However, this perspective is narrow and overlooks actors who spread disinformation for financial gain or corporations that use disinformation campaigns to mislead the public on issues relevant to their interests.[2] Moreover, the definition is far from binding, as even the Constitutional Court in one of its recent decisions avoided its use. The Court refrained from offering a concrete definition of disinformation altogether, opting to reference Wardle and Derakhshan's widely cited report for the Council of Europe.[3]

2 Constitutional Provisions

At the constitutional level, the key provisions governing freedom of expression and its limitations are set out in the Charter of Fundamental Rights and Freedoms (further referred to as: "Charter"), particularly in its Article 17. Furthermore, ratified international human rights treaties are included in the constitutional order,[4] meaning that protections afforded to the freedom of expression under the Article 19 of the International Covenant on Civil and Political Rights, and especially under the Article 10 of the European Convention of Human Rights (further referred to as "ECHR") also constitute relevant constitutional provisions that apply to any legal limitation of freedom of expression in the context of disinformation. Given the focus of this chapter on the Czech legal framework, the following analysis will primarily center on the Charter.

Freedom of expression is classified in the Charter's second sub-part alongside other political rights such as the freedom of assembly and the right to vote and stand for election. Article 17, which enshrines freedom of expression, reads as follows (translated from Czech by the author):

1. Freedom of expression and the right to information are guaranteed.

---

[1] Definice dezinformací a propagandy - Centrum proti hybridním hrozbám (2020) Ministerstvo vnitra České republiky. Available via https://mv.gov.cz/chh/clanek/definice-dezinformaci-a-propagandy.aspx. Accessed 4 Nov 2025

[2] Hameleers M (2022) Disinformation as a context-bound phenomenon: toward a conceptual clarification integrating actors, intentions and techniques of creation and dissemination. Communication Theory 33(1), 1-10

[3] Wardle C Derakhshan H. INFORMATION DISORDER: Toward an interdisciplinary framework for research and policy making. Strasbourg: Council of Europe (2017).

[4] Decision of the Czech Constitutional Court from the 25th June 2002 file no. Pl. ÚS 36/01.

2. Everyone has the right to express their opinions in speech, writing, print, images, or other forms, as well as to freely seek, receive, and disseminate ideas and information without regard to state borders.
3. Censorship is prohibited.
4. The exercise of freedom of expression and the right to seek and disseminate information may be subject to such restrictions as are prescribed by law and are necessary in a democratic society for the protection of the rights and freedoms of others, state security, public safety, public health, or public morals.
5. State authorities and local government bodies are obliged to provide information about their activities in an appropriate manner. The conditions and implementation shall be determined by law.

A notable feature of Article 17 is its integration of freedom of expression with the right to seek and obtain information. This right manifests in two distinct ways: as an individual's right to seek and receive information (Art. 17(2)) and as the right to request public information and data in accordance with Act no. 106/1999 Sb., on Free Access to Public Information, in Art 17(5)). These rights extend to both individuals and legal entities, though their scope differs. Legal entities enjoy freedom of expression insofar as their nature permits. Most prominent examples are publishers and broadcasters, as the media channels serve as intermediaries in the dissemination of ideas and opinions. Without a subjective right to freedom of expression, media organizations would lack a legal basis to challenge restrictions on their activities, undermining their role in public discourse.[5]

Another distinctive feature is the explicit prohibition of censorship under Article 17(3). This prohibition reflects the Czechia's historical experience with totalitarian and authoritarian regimes which have systematically employed censorship as a tool of public control. The prohibition is directed at public authorities, who should refrain from any form of censorship. Censorship itself is not directly defined, it is generally understood as the preliminary review of content by state authorities, who possess the power to prohibit the publication and dissemination of content that they deem inappropriate.[6] Regarding online content, the Constitutional Court has ruled that the blocking of websites operating illegal gambling does not constitute censorship as such content is explicitly illegal and falls outside the protective scope of Article 17.[7] By analogy, this reasoning could potentially apply to the blocking of websites hosting foreign propaganda, such as content from Russian media outlets subject to EU sanctions. However, this remains speculative, as no such case has yet been adjudicated by the courts.

Article 17(4) of the Charter establishes the conditions under which freedom of expression may be limited, as this right is not absolute. The criteria for such limitations mirror those set out in Article 10(2) of the ECHR requiring that any limitation must: (1) be prescribed by law, (2) pursue a legitimate aim and (3) be necessary in

[5] Bartoň M. Svoboda projevu: principy, garance, meze. Leges, Prague (2010).

[6] Bartoň M (2021) Čl. 17. Svoboda projevu a právo na informace. In: Husseini, F. et al. (Eds.) Listina základních práv a svobod: komentář. C.H. Beck, Prague.

[7] Decision of the Czech Constitutional Court from the 14th February 2017, file no. Pl. ÚS. 28/16.

a democratic society. Any legal provision which restricts the freedom of expression must be specific, clear and predictable to prevent any arbitrary interference.[8] Legitimate aims refer to public interests that justify limiting freedom of expression. Both the Charter and the ECHR provide non-exhaustive lists of legitimate aims, restrictions may also be justified by other legitimate aims not explicitly enumerated in these texts.[9] Finally, the limitation must be necessary in a democratic society, meaning it must address concrete and pressing public interest, which cannot be achieved by any other mean that would not lead into the limitation of freedom of expression.[10]

Certain forms of expression, however, fall entirely outside the scope of protection under Article 17 of the Charter and the Article 10 of the ECHR. The reason lies in the principle of militant democracy, which is in the core of Czech legal and constitutional order. According to this principle, democratic states should protect themselves against attacks from those who seek to undermine fundamental democratic values and threaten the existence of democratic states.[11] This provision usually applies to extremist speech and hate speech that incites violence towards specific groups.[12] It may also extend to foreign propaganda.[13] However, such restrictions should be reserved only for the most severe cases of expression that are truly incompatible with democratic values.[14]

3 National Regulation

This sub-chapter is divided into four sections. The first presents civil law instruments, focusing on the protection of personality rights for both individuals and legal entities. The second presents relevant criminal offenses that may be applied to prosecute cases of online disinformation. Third section addresses regulatory provisions governing electoral campaigns and their enforcement. Fourth section presents three notable areas of jurisprudence, regulation and soft law: case law concerning blocking of disinformation websites, the implementation of international and EU sanctions targeting Russian disinformation and Methodical recommendation on public procurement to prevent the placement of advertisement on disinformation websites.

[8] Bartoň M (2021) Čl. 17. Svoboda projevu a právo na informace. In: Husseini, F. et al. (Eds.) Listina základních práv a svobod: komentář. C.H. Beck, Prague.

[9] Hanych M Pivoda M (2020) Disinformation and Fake News in Current Jurisprudence of the Strasbourg Court: An Unsolved Problem. In: Terzis G et al. (eds.) Disinformation and digital media as a challenge for democracy. Intersentia, Cambridge.

[10] Kasl F (2021) Labelling speech. In Gregor M Mlejnková P (eds.). Challenging online propaganda and disinformation in the 21st century. Palgrave Macmillan, Cham.

[11] Výborný Š (2013) Nenávistný internet versus právo. Wolters Kluwer, Prague.

[12] Kmec J et al. (eds) (2012) Evropská úmluva o lidských právech: komentář. C.H. Beck, Prague.

[13] Kasl F (2021) Labelling speech. In Gregor M Mlejnková P (eds.). Challenging online propaganda and disinformation in the twenty-first century. Palgrave Macmillan, Cham.

[14] Decision of the Constitutional Court from the 18th November 2011, file no. IV. ÚS 2011/10.

3.1 Civil Law

Czech civil law contains general legal instruments that permit restrictions of the freedom of expression to protect the rights of others, and which can be used to tackle online disinformation. These instruments mainly serve to safeguard personality rights. For individuals, the concept of personality (translated from Czech term *osobnost*) as the subject of private rights includes all external expressions of a person in relation to their surroundings. Private law protects individual's personality by offering legal safeguards for its different aspects.[15]

The existence of unlawful interference is the precondition for safeguarding personality rights. The unlawful interference may take the form of disinformation and violate specific aspect of individual's personality: most commonly their honor, dignity or their privacy. In such cases, affected individuals may bring legal action against the person responsible for the interference with their personality rights, seeking both the cessation of the interference and remedies for its consequences.[16] If the unlawful interference is intentional and threatens to harm individual's physical and moral integrity, the injured party can also claim compensations for non-pecuniary damage.[17]

When assessing whether the statement has violated personality rights or constitutes a criminal offense, courts apply different standards of evaluation depending on the nature of the statement. Jurisprudence recognizes three distinct categories: (1) Statements of facts, which contain claims that can be verified as true or false based on their correspondence with objective reality; (2) Value judgements, subjective opinions, which cannot be evaluated as true or false, but only as appropriate (or inappropriate) within the given context; (3) Hybrid statements, a combination of factual information and subjective opinion. Unlike certain criminal offenses (see below) all three categories of statements may potentially infringe upon personality rights.[18]

In practice, this instrument has already been used by Olga Richterová, member of Chamber of Deputies (the lower chamber of the Czech Parliament) for the Pirate Party. Richterová sued Nela Lisková, a pro-Russian online activist over two distinct claims. First Lisková shared a post containing a false allegation that Richterová and her political party planned to invite migrants from African countries and provide them with dedicated public housing. The post was designed to resemble a Pirate Party's official communication. Lisková shared this post twice, adding a comment on the second occasion that suggested she believed the false claim to be true. Second, after Richterová publicly shared death threats she has received, Lisková reposted Richetrová's message but falsely claimed that the death threats were directed at

[15] Lavický P (2014) Občanský zákoník. 1: Obecná část (§ 1 - 654) In: Lavický, P. (ed.). Velké komentáře: Občanský zákoník, Beck, Prague.

[16] § 82 of the Act no. 89/2012 Sb., Civil Code.

[17] Decision of the Supreme Court of Czechia from the 29th November 2007 file no. 30 Cdo 608/2007.

[18] Mizerová, T (2023) Právní nástroje boje proti dezinformacím na internetu. Diploma thesis, Masaryk University, Faculty of Law.

her (Lisková). She later reinforced this narrative by publishing an open letter which contained additional critical claims about Richterová. The court ruled that both claims constituted an infringement of Richterová's personality rights and emphasized that Lisková, as an individual with significant online following, should (akin to journalists) evaluate the accuracy of the claims that she shares. As a result, Lisková was ordered to remove all her posts containing false information about Richterová, publish a public apology and pay 50,000 CZK (approximately 2,100 EUR) as a compensation for non-pecuniary damage. The appellate court upheld the decision but modified the remedy, ruling that that personal apology (instead of public one) addressed to Richterová will suffice.[19]

In the author's view, the non-pecuniary damage awarded to Richterová should have been higher. Drawing on the Constitutional Court's jurisprudence regarding false defamatory claims in tabloid media, such violations are considered particularly grave, as they can intrude upon an individual's private and intimate sphere. In Court's view, non-pecuniary damages should serve not only a compensatory purpose but also have a preventive and punitive function, which ought to be reflected in the financial burden imposed on those responsible for the infringement.[20] However, this approach is highly controversial, as it is a matter of dispute whether civil law remedies should incorporate a punitive element at all.

Similar tool exists to protect legal entities from infringements of their reputation and privacy (see § 135(1) of the Act no. 89/2012 Sb., Civil Code). Any legal entity, that carries out its activities lawfully, may take legal actions against individual or legal entities who infringe its reputation. The reputation of legal entities is based on their conduct in business and, unless proved otherwise, all legal entities are presumed to have a good reputation.[21] To succeed in a claim, the legal entity must demonstrate that the interference was unlawful and that it infringes upon its privacy or reputation. As in the case of individuals, court may order the defendant to stop with the interference, remedy its consequences and provide non-pecuniary damage or lost profit (see § 135(1) of the Act no. 89/2012 Sb., Civil Code).

This instrument has already been applied in a case that involved proliferation of online disinformation. Online activist Jana Peterková posted claims alleging that several elderly patients had died after receiving a Covid-19 vaccine at an elderly care home. The care home subsequently sued Peterková for the infringement of their reputation. Since Peterková was absent from the hearing, the court issued a default judgement, ruling that her claims were false and caused a serious infringement of the care home's reputation. As a result, Peterková was ordered to remove all her online posts about the plaintiff, refrain from any further dissemination of such claims, apologize and pay 250 000 CZK (around 10 200 EUR) in non-pecuniary damages.[22]

---

[19] Decision of the District Court of Prague from the 12th of January 2023 file no. 22 Co 240/2022.

[20] Decision of the Czech Constitutional Court from the 6th of March 2012, file no. I. ÚS 1586/06.

[21] Lavický P (2014) Občanský zákoník. 1: Obecná část (§ 1 - 654) In: Lavický, P. (ed.). Velké komentáře: Občanský zákoník, Beck, Prague.

[22] Decision of the District Court of Prague from the 13th of January 2022 file no. 3 Cm 7/2021.

Both legal instruments are limited in scope: they address individual cases of serious disinformation rather than enabling broader restrictions on online disinformation content. Additionally, both can be only used ex-post, meaning they can only be applied after disinformation has been published and caused harm. A further limitation to the possible applications of civil law instruments to address online disinformation arises from the anonymity of the internet. Under Czech civil law, legal actions may only be filed against identified defendants. Consequently, the difficulty of identifying individuals responsible for creating or disseminating online disinformation negatively influences the use-case and effectiveness of these legal remedies.

3.2 *Criminal Law*

Within the Czech criminal law framework, there is no criminal offense that would directly address any form of disinformation. However, the dissemination of disinformation may be criminally prosecuted if it meets the criteria of other criminal offenses, particularly verbal crimes. The most relevant offenses include:

1. **Libel and false accusation.** Following up on previous chapter, libel constitutes a criminal infringement of personality rights. Libel involves the intentional disclosure of false information about an individual, which may jeopardize their reputation among fellow citizens, cause reputational damage to their professional career, disrupt their family relationships, or cause other serious harm (see § 184 of the Act no. 40/2009 Sb., Criminal Code, further referred to as „Criminal Code,“). This criminal offense is reserved only for individuals and cannot be used when the harmful information concerns legal entities. The crime of false accusation has even narrower scope, as the offense specifically addresses false claims that someone has committed a crime (see § 345 of Criminal Code). Both offenses can be committed only intentionally and may be applied to statement of facts and hybrid statements. Value judgements fall outside of the scope of both offenses. To the author‘s knowledge, neither offense has been used to prosecute the proliferation of disinformation.
2. **Spreading alarmist messages.** This offense addresses the intentional dissemination of false information to the public, provided that the false information induces serious concern among a specific population or within a particular location (see § 357(1) of Criminal Code). Falsity itself does not constitute a crime, an essential feature of this offense is the potential to raise serious concerns, which refers to an individual's mental state in which they feel fear, uncertainty or they feel threatened by the future. Online dissemination of alarmist message is considered an aggravated form of the offense, carrying a higher penalty. The Constitutional Court recently assessed the offense of spreading alarmist message in the context of a criminal prosecution of online disinformation. The defendant was (again) an online activist Ladislav Vrabel, who claimed that Czech government plans to provoke a nuclear war against Russia. The statement was presented as a part of his

critique of the government's purchase of F-35 fighter jets. Constitutional Court decided to revoke the judgements which have found Vrabel guilty of spreading alarmist messages, ruling that such prosecution violated his right to freedom of expression. In its decision, the Court emphasized the fundamental role of political speech in a democracy and drew a parallel between social media and the "marketplaces of ideas", where false claims can be countered through factual corrections and public debate. The Court further clarified that the offense of spreading alarmist messages may be applied only to statements of fact, explicitly excluding both value judgments and hybrid statements from its scope.[23] Prior to this ruling, online activist Jana Peterková (mentioned earlier) was also prosecuted and convicted for spreading alarmist messages after posting online videos in which she falsely claimed that NATO armies would invade Czechia and repeated her unfounded allegations about deaths caused by COVID-19 vaccinations. She received a two-year conditional prison sentence with a three-year probation period.[24]

3. **Hate Crimes.** This category encompasses crimes where the perpetrator and their actions are motivated by hate towards a certain group of individuals.[25] The criminal offenses include Defamation of a nation, race, ethnic or other group of individuals (see § 355 of Criminal Code), and Incitement to hatred against a group of individuals or to the restriction of their rights and freedoms (see § 356 of Criminal Code). Both offenses require public dissemination of the speech. If the speech is disseminated online, it constitutes an aggravated form of the offense, carrying a higher penalty. A key distinction between the two offenses is their scope: the first one applies to a narrower set of protected categories while the Incitement to hatred covers a broader range of groups. In both cases, the targeted group must share a common characteristic towards which the hate is targeted.[26] Both of these offenses apply to all three categories of speech: statements of fact, hybrid statements, and value judgments. Consequently, they may be used to prosecute the proliferation of online disinformation given that the disinformation include elements of hate speech offenses. Online activists Patrik Tušl and Tomáš Čermák were prosecuted for the offense of Incitement to hatred against a group of individuals or to the restriction of their rights and freedoms for statements they made during their anti-Ukrainian Facebook live stream. During the broadcast both men falsely accused Czech government of providing refugees from Ukraine with free phones and cars and incited their supporters to commit

[23] Decision of the Czech Constitutional Court from the 11th of March 2025, file no. I. ÚS 1927/24.

[24] ČT24: Soud uložil Peterkové za šíření poplašné zprávy dvouletou podmínku, Soud uložil Peterkové za šíření poplašné zprávy dvouletou podmínku (2022) Česká televize. Available via https://ct24.ceskatelevize.cz/domaci/3568070-soud-ulozil-peterkove-za-sireni-poplasne-zpravy-dvouletou-podminku. Accessed 11 Nov 2025.

[25] Provazník, J. „Pravé " verbální trestné činy z nenávisti. Časopis pro právní vědu a praxi 28(4), 657–694 (2020).

[26] Provazník, J. § 356 Podněcování k nenávisti vůči skupině osob nebo k omezování jejich práv a svobod. In: Ščerba, F. et. al. (eds.) Trestní zákoník. C. H. Beck, Prague (2022).

violent acts against Ukrainian refugees. Both men were convicted: Tušl received an unconditional sentence of 10 months, while Čermák was given a 6-month conditional sentence with two years of probation. Their status as repeat offenders influenced the severity of their sentences.[27] Final criminal offense in this category is the crime of Denial, questioning, approval, and justification of genocide (see § 405 of Criminal Code) which may be applied in cases where disinformation contains any form of approval, justification or apologetic tone towards genocide or when disinformation calls into question whether a genocide occurred. This offense was applied in case which involved three online activists, including Josef Skála, former member of Chamber of Deputies for the Communist Party. They were prosecuted and convicted for claims made during a livestream broadcasted on social media, in which they questioned and relativized soviet involvement in the Katyn massacre in 1940. The activists appealed their convictions, ultimately bringing their case to the Constitutional Court, which rejected their complaint. The Court ruled that they had ignored established historical facts and relied on biased evidence to downplay the undeniable responsibility of the USSR for the massacre. All three defendants received an 8-month suspended sentence with 18 months of probation.[28] However, one of the accused passed away during the legal proceedings.

4. **Terrorist criminal offenses.** The final category of criminal offenses applicable to the proliferation of disinformation consists of anti-terrorism offenses. Unlike the previously discussed offenses, these are considered particularly serious, with substantially higher baseline penalties for perpetrators. The two terrorism related offenses that may apply to online disinformation are Support and promotion of terrorism (see § 312e of Criminal Code) and the Threatening to commit terrorist offense (§ 312f of Criminal Code). However, their application is strictly limited to expressions in which the speaker either threatens to commit a terrorist act or approves a terrorist act that has already been committed. These offenses do not extend to general promotion or approval of terrorism as a concept. Tomáš Čermák, previously prosecuted for his anti-Ukrainian rhetoric (see earlier), was also charged with Support and promotion of terrorism, alongside another online activist, Zdeněk Strapina. The charges stemmed from livestreams in which they advocated for a violent coup d'état and incited violence against members of the Czech government and the Parliament. Strapina opted for a plea bargain[29] and received a two-year suspended sentence with five-year probation period and a monetary penalty of 30 000 CZK (around 1260 EUR). Čermák, however,

[27] Judgment of the District Court in Kladno from the 26th of October 2022, file no. 3T 139/2022. Judgment of the Regional Court in Prague from the 21st of December 2022, file no. 12 To 192/2022.

[28] Resolution of the Czech Constitutional Court from the 22nd October 2024, file no. II.ÚS 1593/24.

[29] Horák J Valášek L (2022) Patří na špagát, vymlátit to ven!" vyhrožoval terorismem parlamentu. Dostane trest. In: Aktuálně.cz Available via: https://zpravy.aktualne.cz/domaci/strapina-soud-do-hoda/r~3c917d0a2ea111edb1f50cc47ab5f122/. Accessed 11 Nov 2025.

was convicted and sentenced to an unconditional prison term of five and a half years. His appeals, including a final complaint to the Constitutional Court, were unsuccessful. The Court upheld the conviction, citing the principles of militant democracy and the state's obligation to protect itself against adversaries seeking to undermine democratic institutions.[30] The length of Čermák's sentence illustrates the significant disparity in baseline penalties for other verbal offenses and terrorism-related crimes. For context, the maximum baseline sentence for spreading alarmist messages and both two hate speech offenses (see earlier) is two years maximum. In contrast, support and promotion of terrorism carries a baseline sentence of 2 to 10 years, while threatening to commit a terrorist offense ranges from 3 to 12 years.

3.3 Regulation of Electoral Campaigns

The regulation of electoral campaigns is relevant because certain provisions may be applied to disinformation that is used within electoral campaigns. The regulation of electoral campaigns is currently fragmented across five separate acts each governing one of the six types of elections in Czechia: presidential, municipal, regional, European and parliamentary elections (with distinct electoral system for the Chamber of Deputies and the Senate). As of January 2026, new Act no. 234/2024 Sb., on electoral campaign and the transparency of political advertising (further referred to as Act on Electoral Campaign) will come into effect and consolidate the regulation of political campaigns into a single act. The Act on Electoral Campaign also contains the implementation of the Regulation (EU) 2024/900 on the transparency and targeting of political advertising. The Act on Electoral Campaign retains and unifies the following key principles (originally dispersed across the previous acts):

- The electoral campaign must be conducted honestly and fairly (see § 3(1) of the Act on electoral campaign),
- Publishing false or insulting information about other candidate or party is prohibited (see 3(2) of the Act on electoral campaign).

According to established case law, the principles of honesty and fairness of political campaign must be interpreted within the political context, which is characterized by intense conflict between different ideas and politicians, who seek to gain support for their programs and initiatives.[31] This context implies that political campaigns naturally involve more vigorous rhetoric than everyday discourse, a factor that courts must consider in their assessments of such cases.

Political candidates and public can challenge the campaigns and alleged breaches of these principles only post-election during the judicial review process. The only available remedy for breaching these requirements is the annulment of the entire

[30] Resolution of the Czech Constitutional Court from the 28th May 2025, file no. III.ÚS 692/24.

[31] Resolution of Supreme Administrative Court of Czechia from the 29th June 2025, file no. Vol 45/2006.

election or the election of a certain candidate. Courts may take this decision only if the following conditions are met: (1) there is a clear violation of these principles, (2) the violation influenced election results and (3) the violation is of a severe intensity (meaning that the candidate(s) would not have been elected if it was not for the violation). These requirements are very strict, and it is almost impossible to meet them, which illustrates cautious and restrained approach of Czech courts towards the issue of election annulment. The only instance of judicial election annulment (related to breach of the abovementioned principles) were Strakonice's 2018 Municipal elections, where the ruling coalition unlawfully restricted opposition candidates from advertising on municipal billboards and in the local newsletter.[32]

In the same year, the presidential campaign of candidate Miloš Zeman, who won the election, faced scrutiny, due to allegations of disseminating disinformation about his opponent. The Supreme Administrative Court reviewed two complaints, one focused on disinformation used directly by Zeman's campaign, the second was concerned with online disinformation that circulated during the election and its general impact on the result. The court dismissed both complaints, on the grounds that either the campaign claims did not exceed the requirement of honest and fair campaign or that the complaints did not meet the burden of proof to demonstrate that the disinformation constituted a severe breach of electoral law. At the same time, the Court recognised that online disinformation represents a new and influential form of political communication, capable of significantly impacting election results. It further noted that, going forward, courts must acknowledge the unique challenges in proving how digital communication affects results of an election, particularly when compared to traditional media.[33]

3.4 *Notable Regulation, Jurisprudence and Soft Law*

Blocking of Disinformation Websites After the Russian Invasion of Ukraine. Following the Russian invasion of Ukraine in February 2022, the Czech government and National Cyber Operation Center (the cyber defense unit of the Czech Armed Forces) called on domain administrators and mobile operators to block access to selected group of Czech disinformation websites.[34] This request was not grounded in any existing legal regulation. Administrative courts later characterized it as „*informal request*," as it lacked any enforceable mechanism and compliance was voluntary.

[32] Resolution of the Czech Constitutional Court from the 2nd April 2019, file no. I.ÚS 4178/18.

[33] Declaration of the Supreme Administrative Court of Czechia from the 21st of February 2018, file no. Vol 59/2018. Declaration of the Supreme Administrative Court of Czechia from the 21st of February 2018, file no. Vol 50/2018.

[34] Resolution of the Government of the Czech Republic No. 127 of February 25, 2022, on the government's statement on hybrid activities against the interests of the Czech Republic in connection with the Russian Federation's aggression against Ukraine (2022). In: Vlada České republiky. Available via: https://www.vlada.cz/assets/urad-vlady/poskytovani-informaci/poskytnute-informace-na-zadost/usneseni-vlady-c--127_1.pdf. Accessed 11 Nov 2025.

Consequently, due to its informal nature, the courts also determined that the government's request does not constitute unlawful interference by a public authority.[35] In contrast, AC24.cz, one of the blocked websites, sued T-Mobile, its service provider, for blocking access to the site. AC24.cz argued that T-Mobile has breached Article 3(3) of the Regulation (EU) 2015/2120 concerning open internet access.[36] The court ruled in favor of AC24.cz, finding that T-Mobile's actions breached the regulation. T-Mobile was also ordered to compensate AC24.cz for lost profits, primarily stemming from the loss of advertising revenue.[37]

In response to these events, rumors emerged regarding the preparation of a dedicated legal act that would authorize public authorities to block websites that pose a threat to national security. However, the government neither introduced such legislation, nor did it include legislative preparation of it among its legislative work schedules.[38] The Ministry of the Interior later released (following up on a request for information under the Act no. 106/1999 Sb., on the Free Access to Information) a draft proposal of such an act, emphasizing that the proposal is merely a preliminary outline.[39] Three years after the incident, no such regulation has been adopted. At the same time, it is highly unlikely that government will issue a similar informal request in the future.

Sanctions targeting Russian media. In summer 2025, the investigative website Voxpot revealed that Czech disinformation websites were publishing content directly sourced from Russian media subjected to EU sanctions. Approximately 250 articles published by Czech disinformation websites were taken directly from sanctioned Russian sources.[40] The EU sanctions targeting Russian media are based on the EU Council Regulation of the 1st March 2025, which amended Regulation (EU) 833/2014 concerning restrictive measures in view of Russia's actions destabilizing the

---

[35] Resolution of the Municipal Court in Prague from 29th June 2022, file no. 17 A 36/2022. Judgment of the Supreme Administrative Court from the 9th August 2023, file no. 7 As 22/2023. Resolution of the Municipal Court in Prague from the 24th June 2022, file no. 14 A 39/2022. Judgment of the Supreme Administrative Court from the 20th January 2023, file no. 4 As 206/2022.

[36] Regulation (EU) 2015/2120 of the European Parliament and of the Council of 25 November 2015 laying down measures concerning open internet access and amending Directive 2002/22/EC on universal service and users' rights relating to electronic communications networks and services and Regulation (EU) 531/2012 on roaming on public mobile communications networks within the Union.

[37] Pika T (2025) Blokace ‚konspiračního' webu AC24 byla nezákonná, řekl soud. T-Mobile mu musí zaplatit odškodné. Český rozhlas. Available via https://www.irozhlas.cz/zpravy-domov/konspiracni-web-ac24-uspel-u-soudu-t-mobile-mu-musi-zaplatit-za-nezakonnou_2510091327_pik. Accessed 11 Nov 2025.

[38] Cibulka J Pika T (2022) Jen bezpečnostní složky. Zákon proti dezinformacím vzniká bez veřejnosti, poradce váže mlčenlivost Český rozhlas. Available via https://www.irozhlas.cz/zpravy-domov/dezinformace-vnitro-zakon-legislativa_2207160500_cib Accessed 11 Nov 2025.

[39] Poskytnutí informace - zákon, dezinformace - Ministerstvo vnitra České republiky (2022). Ministerstvo vnitra České republiky. Available via https://mv.gov.cz/clanek/poskytnuti-informace-zakon-dezinformace.aspx. Accessed 11 Nov 2025.

[40] Boháč V Pecka V (2025) Ruská kampaň v Česku je mnohem větší, než jste si mysleli. VOXPOT: reportáže, které spojují Česko se světem. Available via https://www.voxpot.cz/ruska-kampan-v-cesku-je-mnohem-vetsi-nez-jste-si-mysleli/. Accessed 11 Nov 2025.

situation in Ukraine. This sanctions package introduced prohibition on broadcasting, facilitating or otherwise disseminating content produced by entities placed on the EU sanctions list (see Article 2f(1) of the Regulation (EU) 833/2014). The sanctioned media include outlets directly or indirectly controlled by the Russian government. By republishing content from sanctioned Russian media, Czech disinformation websites found themselves in violation of EU sanctions.

In Czechia, Act no. 69/2006 Sb., on the Implementation of International Sanctions (further referred to as Act on International Sanctions), governs compliance with and enforcement of international sanctions. The Financial Analytical Office is responsible for oversight and enforcement (§ 15 (1) of the Act on International Sanctions) and serves as the competent authority for conducting administrative proceedings related to sanctions violations (see § 15(1) of Act on International Sanctions). Under § 18(1)(b) of Act on International Sanctions, violating EU sanctions constitutes an administrative offense, punishable by fines of up to 4 million CZK (around 165 000 EUR). In cases of large-scale violations, such breaches may also qualify as criminal offense under § 410 of Criminal Code. According to Voxpot's reporting, relevant institutions are aware of the issue, but they lack political support needed to enforce these sanctions. Politicians are reportedly reluctant to act due to fears of imminent backlash from disinformation media and political opposition. At the same time, Czechia is not alone in struggling to enforce sanctions against Russian media. Institute for Strategic Dialogue has documented how content from sanctioned Russian media continues to circulate across Europe.[41] These outlets often evade sanctions by creating mirror websites on alternative domains[42], while blocking original domains remains an ineffective solution.[43] Moreover, these media outlets actively disseminate content designed to undermine trust and credibility in EU institutions and member state governments, reflecting a deliberate strategy by the Russian state. Given this context, ensuring robust enforcement of these sanctions should be a priority for the entire EU.

Methodological Recommendations for Purchasing Advertising. The Czech Ministry of Local Affairs and Development has issued methodological recommendations aiming at preventing public institutions from placing advertisements on disinformation websites. It is well known that some actors produce and disseminate disinformation primarily to generate advertisement revenue or secure financial

[41] Schafer, B. et al (2024) The Russian Propaganda Nesting Doll: How RT is Layered into the Digital Information Environment. Alliance For Securing Democracy. Available via https://securingdemocracy.gmfus.org/the-russian-propaganda-nesting-doll-how-rt-is-layered-into-the-digital-information-environment/. Accessed 11 Nov 2025.

[42] Balint K et. al. (2022) RT Articles are Finding their Way to European Audiences – but how?. Institute for Strategic Dialogue. Available via https://www.isdglobal.org/digital_dispatches/rt-articles-are-finding-their-way-to-european-audiences-but-how/. Accessed 11 Nov 2025.

[43] Maristany de las Casas, P (2025) Investigation Holding the line: Auditing the EU's ban of Russian state media 3 years on. Institute for Strategic Dialogue. Available via https://www.isdglobal.org/digital_dispatches/investigation-holding-the-line-auditing-the-eus-ban-of-russian-state-media-3-years-on/. Accessed 11 Nov 2025.

revenue from different resources.[44] Czech disinformation websites are no exception, as several operate purely on for-profit basis.[45]

The methodical recommendation advised that public procurement contractors may include a clause in their tender conditions to prohibit the placement of advertisements on websites that violate journalistic standards. This provision is legally grounded in § 37(1)(c) of the Act no. 136/2016 Sb. on public procurement. Notably, the document avoids using the terms "disinformation," or "disinformation media." Instead it refers to media outlets that consistently fail to meet journalistic standards (and advises not to place advertisement there) or advises the procurement contractors to be mindful about their brand security. The recommendations also reference the Nelež initiative, which seeks to prevent placing advertisement on disinformation websites and maintains a list of websites known for consistently publishing disinformation[46]. Information and data on whether and how the public procurement contractors adhere to this recommendation are not available.

4 European Law and (Non)implementation of DSA

This chapter was prepared in November 2025, in the immediate aftermath of the elections to the Chamber of Deputies, the lower house of the Czech Parliament. Andrej Babiš, leader of the ANO party and the winner of the election will almost certainly replace Petr Fiala as Prime Minister. This political shift will influence the ongoing process of implementation of key EU regulation, particularly the Regulation (EU) 2022/2065 on Single Market For Digital Services (Digital Services Act, further referred to as „DSA ") and the Regulation (EU) 2024/1689 laying down harmonized rules on artificial intelligence (Artificial Intelligence Act, further referred to as „AI Act ").

Czechia is one of five EU member states referred by the European Commission to the Court of Justice of the European Union for failing to effectively implement the DSA.[47] The outgoing government managed to designate Czech Telecommunications Office (further referred to as "CTO") as the National Digital Services Coordinator

[44] Allcott, H., Gentzkow, M. Social Media and Fake News in the 2016 Election. Journal of Economic Perspectives 31(2) pp. 211–236 (2017).

[45] Syrovátka, J. et al. (2020) Dezinformace jako byznys. Prague Security Studies Institute. Available via https://www.pssi.cz/download//docs/8207_751-dezinformace-jako-byznys.pdf. Accessed 11 Nov 2025.

[46] NELEŽ – Postav se za pravdu proti dezinformacím (2025). Nelež. Available via: https://www.nelez.cz/?utm_campaign=NELEZ_update_black_02&utm_medium=email&utm_source=leadhub&utm_lhm=f0ca32c80f85428ca80bac8757e64fc6#urcovani-dezinformacnich-webu. Accessed 11 Nov 2025.

[47] Lack of effective implementation of the Digital Services Act (2025) European Commission. Available via https://ec.europa.eu/commission/presscorner/detail/en/ip_25_1081. Accessed 11 Nov 2025.

and introduced the Act on Digital Economics. This Act was intended to implement the DSA, as well as Regulation (EU) 2022/868 on European data governance (Data Governance Act) and certain provisions of the Regulation (EU) 2019/1150 on promoting fairness and transparency for business users of online intermediation services (P2B regulation). The outgoing government submitted the Act on Digital Economics for a vote in the Chamber of Deputies, where it got sidelined until the end of the election period, thus preventing the final vote, which would lead to either its acceptance and advancement for further legislative proceedings in the Senate, or its rejection.[48] Political commentators attribute this situation to a lack of commitment on the government's side to actively implement the EU's digital agenda at the national level, combined with the obstructions by opposition parties. The opposition managed to frame DSA as a tool of "Brussels' censorship," succeeding in making the implementation part of the ongoing "culture wars."[49] On the other hand, a member of the CTO Council (CTO's supreme executive body) suggested that the Act was not voted on primarily due to time constraints.[50] With the dissolution of the previous Chamber of Deputies, the Act on Digital Economics is discharged and it must be resubmitted for a vote in the newly elected Chamber of Deputies (see § 121(1) of the Act no. 90/1995 Sb., on the Rules of Procedure of the Chamber of Deputies).

Additionally, the new government is under no obligation to resubmit the Act on Digital Economics and may instead introduce its own legislative proposal. Estimating the probabilities of this option is difficult. During the previous term, ANO representatives were among the most vocal critics of the DSA, openly declaring their intention to pressure the European Commission into revising the regulation.[51] The policy priorities published by the incoming government are notably vague. DSA is not directly mentioned, and the document includes only general statements about preventing "state repression of opinions," echoing the censorship claims.[52] The future of Czech implementation of DSA will depend on whether the new government chooses to politicize DSA. If it does, rhetorical clashes with the representatives of the EU and its institutions and a deliberate failure to fully implement the DSA may follow. If not, the Act on Digital Economics (or its alternative) could be approved quietly, without attracting significant political attention.

---

[48] Sněmovní tisk 776 (2025). Poslanecká sněmovna parlamentu České republiky. Available via https://www.psp.cz/sqw/text/historie.sqw?o=9&T=776. Accessed 11 Nov 2025.

[49] Soukeníková E (2025) Co je nelegální offline, má být nelegální i online. Zavádění pravidel EU se ale v Česku dál zpožďuje [online]. Český rozhlas. Available via https://www.irozhlas.cz/veda-technologie/technologie/co-je-nelegalni-offline-ma-byt-nelegalni-i-online-zavadeni-pravidel-eu-se-ale-v_2502100817_epo. Accessed 11 Nov 2025.

[50] Váš vztek je jejich zisk. Platí na sociálních sítích pravidla? (2025) Rušičky Podcast. Available via https://open.spotify.com/episode/60xrwJQ77zv5vpVYLu2xUC. Accessed 11 Nov 2025.

[51] Sněmovna přerušila druhé kolo debaty o zákonu o digitální ekonomice (2025). Česká tisková kancelář. Available via https://ct24.ceskatelevize.cz/clanek/domaci/zive-snemovnu-ceka-zakon-o-kyberneticke-bezpecnosti-i-pravidla-pro-volebni-kampane-357293. Accessed 11 Nov 2025.

[52] DOKUMENT: Programové prohlášení vlády Andreje Babiše (2025). iDNES.cz. Available via https://www.idnes.cz/zpravy/domaci/dokument-programove-prohlaseni-vlady-andreje-babise.A251103_110559_domaci_hejj. Accessed 11 Nov 2025.

In the meantime, CTO has begun fulfilling its obligations as the national Digital Services Coordinator. Its activities have included issuing guidance to the Czech-based intermediary services on their DSA compliance requirements, cooperating with the European Commission and establishing communication channels with Very Large Online Platforms and Very Large Online Search Engines. CTO also issued an annual report required by Article 50 of the DSA, processed complaints submitted under the Article 53 of the DSA and actively prepared to address any online influence campaigns that could have impacted the recent parliamentary elections.

The proposed Act on Digital Economics does not introduce any new definition of illegal content and it is not accompanied by any amendment to other regulation that would establish new categories of illegal content. Similarly, the Act does not contain any new definition of disinformation or specific provisions targeting online disinformation. The title of the Act and its association with the implementation of two other EU digital economy regulations suggest that the Czech approach to DSA prioritizes enforcing the rights of recipients of intermediary services rather than aiming to curb the proliferation of illegal or problematic content. Regarding content moderation rules or illegal content, the Act remains fully aligned with the DSA's existing legal framework.

Given that the AI Act is a more recent regulation than the DSA, its implementation process is less advanced. So far, the outgoing government adopted a strategy for the implementation of AI Act, though this document consists largely of vague declarations.[53] Prior to the elections, the government also approved the minimalistic draft of an Act which would implement AI Act into national law. The proposal designated CTO as the national supervisory authority, though at this stage, the assignment remains rather informal.[54] Additionally, the government's AI representative proposed a two-year suspension of AI Act rules, arguing that the private sector requires adequate time to prepare for compliance.[55] The incoming government has not included any concrete details regarding the implementation of AI Act in its policy priorities. Instead, it offers only a broad statement expressing its ambition to actively shape EU AI policies rather than passively accept regulation.[56]

Finally, the previous government successfully transposed the obligation to criminalize deepfake pornography, as required by the Directive (EU) 2024/1385 of the

---

[53] Další krok k rozvoji umělé inteligence v Česku. Vláda schválila návrh na zajištění implementace AI Aktu, novým gestorem je MPO (2025) Ministerstvo průmyslu a obchodu České republiky. Available via https://mpo.gov.cz/cz/rozcestnik/pro-media/tiskove-zpravy/dalsi-krok-k-rozvoji-umele-inteligence-v-cesku--vlada-schvalila-navrh-na-zajisteni-implementace-ai-aktu--novym-gestorem-je-mpo--287763/. Accessed 11 Nov 2025.

[54] Resolution of the Government of the Czech Republic No. 394 of May 28, 2025, on the proposal to implement the Artificial Intelligence Act in the Czech Republic.

[55] Zlom v AI regulaci? Silný český apel rezonuje, některé členské státy EU zvažují odklad částí AI aktu (2025). Česká asociace umělé inteligence. Available via https://asociace.ai/zlom-v-ai-regulaci-silny-cesky-apel-rezonuje-nektere-clenske-staty-eu-zvazuji-odklad-casti-ai-aktu/. Accessed 11 Nov 2025.

[56] DOKUMENT: Programové prohlášení vlády Andreje Babiše (2025). iDNES.cz. Available via https://www.idnes.cz/zpravy/domaci/dokument-programove-prohlaseni-vlady-andreje-babise.A251103_110559_domaci_hejj. Accessed 11 Nov 2025.

European Parliament and of the Council of 14 May 2024 on combating violence against women and domestic violence. New criminal offence called the Misuse of Identity for the Production and Distribution of Pornography (see § 191a of Criminal Code) was incorporated into the amended Criminal Code and is scheduled to enter into force on 1 January 2026.

5 Conclusion

Czech regulation does not directly target disinformation, and no legislative proposals currently exist that would specifically address its proliferation. At the constitutional level, all legal measures aimed at curbing online disinformation are constrained by constitutional protections of the freedom of expression, except in cases of extreme speech. Then, similarly as in the cases under Article 17 of the ECHR, and following the principle of militant democracy, such speech is not entitled to any protection.

Civil and criminal law provide legal instruments to address disinformation, but they can be applied only ex-post and if the disinformation violates personality rights (under civil law) or meets the criteria for an existing criminal offense. The application of these instruments is thus limited to individual cases of disinformation. Challenges in identifying online perpetrators and potential jurisdictional hurdles further complicate the effective use of these tools to combat online disinformation.

Czech law on electoral campaigns requires that political campaigns are conducted honestly and fairly. While this provision could, in theory, deter the use of disinformation in electoral campaigns, its enforcement is almost impossible, as the only available legal consequence for the violations of these principles is the annulment of the entire election or the election of a certain candidate.

Regarding EU regulation, Czechia has fallen behind in implementing DSA. This delay might be caused by unwillingness of politicians to address this agenda, as it could be controversial and costly. Following the recent elections, the Act on Digital Economics (which would implement key provisions of DSA) must be resubmitted to the newly elected Chamber of Deputies. The change in government has cast uncertainty over the future of the implementation process. The unwillingness of Czech executive to tackle online disinformation is further demonstrated by the non-enforcement of sanctions targeting content from sanctioned Russian media outlets and the failure to adopt regulation that would enable the blocking of disinformation websites that pose a threat to public security.

References

Allcott, H., Gentzkow, M. Social Media and Fake News in the 2016 Election. Journal of Economic Perspectives 31(2) pp. 211-236 (2017).

Balint K et. al. (2022) RT Articles are Finding their Way to European Audiences – but how?. Institute for Strategic Dialogue. Available via https://www.isdglobal.org/digital_dispatches/rt-articles-are-finding-their-way-to-european-audiences-but-how/. Accessed 11 Nov 2025.

Bartoň M. Svoboda projevu: principy, garance, meze. Leges, Prague (2010).

Bartoň M (2021) Čl. 17. Svoboda projevu a právo na informace. In: Husseini, F. et al. (Eds.) Listina základních práv a svobod: komentář. C.H. Beck, Prague.

Boháč V Pecka V (2025) Ruská kampaň v Česku je mnohem větší, než jste si mysleli. VOXPOT: reportáže, které spojují Česko se světem. Available via https://www.voxpot.cz/ruska-kampan-v-cesku-je-mnohem-vetsi-nez-jste-si-mysleli/. Accessed 11 Nov 2025.

Cibulka J Pika T (2022) Jen bezpečnostní složky. Zákon proti dezinformacím vzniká bez veřejnosti, poradce váže mlčenlivost Český rozhlas. Available via https://www.irozhlas.cz/zpravy-domov/dezinformace-vnitro-zakon-legislativa_2207160500_cib Accessed 11 Nov 2025.

ČT24: Soud uložil Peterkové za šíření poplašné zprávy dvouletou podmínku, Soud uložil Peterkové za šíření poplašné zprávy dvouletou podmínku (2022) Česká televize. Available via https://ct24.ceskatelevize.cz/domaci/3568070-soud-ulozil-peterkove-za-sireni-poplasne-zpravy-dvouletou-podminku. Accessed 11 Nov 2025.

Decision of the Constitutional Court from the 18th November 2011, file no. IV. ÚS 2011/10.

Decision of the Czech Constitutional Court from the 25th June 2002 file no. Pl. ÚS 36/01.

Decision of the Czech Constitutional Court from the 6th of March 2012, file no. I. ÚS 1586/06.

Decision of the Czech Constitutional Court from the 14th February 2017, file no. Pl. ÚS. 28/16.

Decision of the Czech Constitutional Court from the 11th of March 2025, file no. I. ÚS 1927/24.

Decision of the District Court of Prague from the 13th of January 2022 file no. 3 Cm 7/2021.

Decision of the District Court of Prague from the 12th of January 2023 file no. 22 Co 240/2022.

Decision of the Supreme Court of Czechia from the 29th November 2007 file no. 30 Cdo 608/2007.

Definice dezinformací a propagandy - Centrum proti hybridním hrozbám (2020) Ministerstvo vnitra České republiky. Available via https://mv.gov.cz/chh/clanek/definice-dezinformaci-a-pro pagandy.aspx. Accessed 4 Nov 2025

Hameleers M (2022) Disinformation as a context-bound phenomenon: toward a conceptual clarification integrating actors, intentions and techniques of creation and dissemination. Communication Theory 33(1), 1-10

Hanych M, Pivoda M (2020) Disinformation and Fake News in Current Jurisprudence of the Strasbourg Court: An Unsolved Problem. In: Terzis G et. al (eds.) Disinformation and digital media as a challenge for democracy. Intersentia, Cambridge.

Horák J Valášek L (2022) Patří na špagát, vymlátit to ven!" vyhrožoval terorismem parlamentu. Dostane trest. In: Aktuálně.cz Available via: https://zpravy.aktualne.cz/domaci/strapina-soud-do-hoda/r~3c917d0a2ea111edb1f50cc47ab5f122/. Accessed 11 Nov 2025.

Judgment of the District Court in Kladno from the 26th of October 2022, file no. 3T 139/2022.

Judgment of the Regional Court in Prague from the 21st of December 2022, file no. 12 To 192/2022.

Judgment of the Supreme Administrative Court from the 9th August 2023, file no. 7 As 22/2023.

Judgment of the Supreme Administrative Court from the 20th January 2023, file no. 4 As 206/2022.

Kasl F (2021) Labelling speech. In Gregor M Mlejnková P (eds.). Challenging online propaganda and disinformation in the 21st century. Palgrave Macmillan, Cham.

Kmec J et al. (eds) (2012) Evropská úmluva o lidských právech: komentář. C.H. Beck, Prague.

Lack of effective implementation of the Digital Services Act (2025) European Commission. Available via https://ec.europa.eu/commission/presscorner/detail/en/ip_25_1081. Accessed 11 Nov 2025.

Lavický P (2014) Občanský zákoník. 1: Obecná část (§ 1 - 654) In: Lavický, P. (ed.). Velké komentáře: Občanský zákoník, Beck, Prague.

Maristany de las Casas, P (2025) Investigation Holding the line: Auditing the EU's ban of Russian state media 3 years on. Institute for Strategic Dialogue. Available via https://www.isdglobal.org/digital_dispatches/investigation-holding-the-line-auditing-the-eus-ban-of-russian-state-media-3-years-on/. Accessed 11 Nov 2025.

Mizerová, T (2023) Právní nástroje boje proti dezinformacím na internetu. Diploma thesis, Masaryk University, Faculty of Law.

NELEŽ – Postav se za pravdu proti dezinformacím (2025). Nelež. Available via: https://www.nelez.cz/?utm_campaign=NELEZ_update_black_02&utm_medium=email&utm_source=leadhub&utm_lhm=f0ca32c80f85428ca80bac8757e64fc6#urcovani-dezinformacnich-webu. Accessed 11 Nov 2025.

Pika T (2025) Blokace ‚konspiračního' webu AC24 byla nezákonná, řekl soud. T-Mobile mu musí zaplatit odškodné. Český rozhlas. Available via https://www.irozhlas.cz/zpravy-domov/konspiracni-web-ac24-uspel-u-soudu-t-mobile-mu-musi-zaplatit-za-nezakonnou_2510091327_pik. Accessed 11 Nov 2025.

Poskytnutí informace - zákon, dezinformace - Ministerstvo vnitra České republiky (2022). Ministerstvo vnitra České republiky. Available via https://mv.gov.cz/clanek/poskytnuti-informace-zakon-dezinformace.aspx. Accessed 11 Nov 2025.

Provazník, J. „Pravé" verbální trestné činy z nenávisti. Časopis pro právní vědu a praxi 28(4), 657–694 (2020).

Provazník, J. § 356 Podněcování k nenávisti vůči skupině osob nebo k omezování jejich práv a svobod. In: Ščerba, F. et. al. (eds.) Trestní zákoník. C. H. Beck, Prague (2022).

Regulation (EU) 2015/2120 of the European Parliament and of the Council of 25 November 2015 laying down measures concerning open internet access and amending Directive 2002/22/EC on universal service and users' rights relating to electronic communications networks and services and Regulation (EU) 531/2012 on roaming on public mobile communications networks within the Union.

Resolution of the Czech Constitutional Court from the 2nd April 2019, file no. I.ÚS 4178/18.

Resolution of the Czech Constitutional Court from the 22nd October 2024, file no. II.ÚS 1593/24.

Resolution of the Czech Constitutional Court from the 28th May 2025, file no. III.ÚS 692/24.

Resolution of the Government of the Czech Republic No. 127 of February 25, 2022, on the government's statement on hybrid activities against the interests of the Czech Republic in connection with the Russian Federation's aggression against Ukraine (2022). In: Vlada České republiky. Available via: https://www.vlada.cz/assets/urad-vlady/poskytovani-informaci/poskytnute-informace-na-zadost/usneseni-vlady-c--127_1.pdf. Accessed 11 Nov 2025.

Resolution of the Government of the Czech Republic No. 394 of May 28, 2025, on the proposal to implement the Artificial Intelligence Act in the Czech Republic.

Resolution of the Municipal Court in Prague from 29th June 2022, file No. 17 A 36/2022.

Resolution of the Municipal Court in Prague from the 24th June 2022, file no. 14 A 39/2022.

Resolution of Supreme Administrative Court of Czechia from the 29th June 2025, file no. Vol 45/2006.

Schafer, B. et al (2024) The Russian Propaganda Nesting Doll: How RT is Layered into the Digital Information Environment. Alliance For Securing Democracy. Available via https://securingdemocracy.gmfus.org/the-russian-propaganda-nesting-doll-how-rt-is-layered-into-the-digital-information-environment/. Accessed 11 Nov 2025.

Sněmovna přerušila druhé kolo debaty o zákonu o digitální ekonomice (2025). Česká tisková kancelář. Available via https://ct24.ceskatelevize.cz/clanek/domaci/zive-snemovnu-ceka-zakon-o-kyberneticke-bezpecnosti-i-pravidla-pro-volebni-kampane-357293. Accessed 11 Nov 2025.

Sněmovní tisk 776 (2025). Poslanecká sněmovna parlamentu České republiky. Available via https://www.psp.cz/sqw/text/historie.sqw?o=9&T=776. Accessed 11 Nov 2025.

Soukeníková E (2025) Co je nelegální offline, má být nelegální i online. Zavádění pravidel EU se ale v Česku dál zpožďuje [online]. Český rozhlas. Available via https://www.irozhlas.cz/veda-technologie/technologie/co-je-nelegalni-offline-ma-byt-nelegalni-i-online-zavadeni-pravidel-eu-se-ale-v_2502100817_epo. Accessed 11 Nov 2025.

Syrovátka, J. et al. (2020) Dezinformace jako byznys. Prague Security Studies Institute. Available via https://www.pssi.cz/download//docs/8207_751-dezinformace-jako-byznys.pdf. Accessed 11 Nov 2025.

Váš vztek je jejich zisk. Platí na sociálních sítích pravidla? (2025) Rušičky Podcast. Available via https://open.spotify.com/episode/60xrwJQ77zv5vpVYLu2xUC. Accessed 11 Nov 2025.
Výborný Š (2013) Nenávistný internet versus právo. Wolters Kluwer, Prague.
Wardle C Derakhshan H. INFORMATION DISORDER: Toward an interdisciplinary framework for research and policy making. Strasbourg: Council of Europe (2017).
Zlom v AI regulaci? Silný český apel rezonuje, některé členské státy EU zvažují odklad částí AI aktu (2025). Česká asociace umělé inteligence. Available via https://asociace.ai/zlom-v-ai-regulaci-silny-cesky-apel-rezonuje-nektere-clenske-staty-eu-zvazuji-odklad-casti-ai-aktu/. Accessed 11 Nov 2025.
§ 82 of the Act no. 89/2012 Sb., Civil Code.

Disinformation, Defamation, and Fundamental Rights in Estonia's Legal Framework

Carri Ginter and Mirjam Orav

Abstract This chapter provides an in-depth analysis of Estonia's legal framework governing disinformation and defamation across private, criminal, and public law. Although Estonian legislation does not distinguish between online and offline disinformation, digital communication—particularly user-generated content—has intensified the relevance of judicial interpretation. The chapter outlines how the Law of Obligations forms the core of civil remedies, offering mechanisms for addressing both incorrect factual statements and unjustified value judgments. Criminal law regulates only exceptional cases, such as defamation of state officials or courts, while public law requires a clear statutory basis for reputationally harmful actions taken by public authorities. Case law plays a central role in clarifying key concepts, distinguishing facts from value judgments, and balancing reputation with freedom of expression. Landmark decisions, including Delfi v. Estonia, continue to shape digital liability standards. Despite available remedies, Estonia lacks a dedicated disinformation oversight body, placing much of the burden on courts and online platforms. Ongoing EU infringement proceedings related to hate speech highlight gaps in transposition and signal the need for reform. The chapter concludes by identifying structural challenges and recommending clearer definitions, enhanced procedural safeguards, and more coherent institutional support for tackling disinformation.

C. Ginter (✉) · M. Orav
School of Law, University of Tartu, Tartu, Estonia
e-mail: carri.ginter@ut.ee

M. Orav
e-mail: mirjamorav@gmail.com

C. Ginter
International Dispute Resolution Team, Law Firm Sorainen, Tallinn, Estonia

M. Orav
M&A and Private Equity Team, Law Firm Sorainen, Tallinn, Estonia

P. Passaglia (ed.), *European Legal Perspectives on Online Disinformation*, Ius Gentium: Comparative Perspectives on Law and Justice 140,
https://doi.org/10.1007/978-3-032-25785-7_7

1 The Notion of Disinformation

This chapter provides an overview of the definitions of disinformation and similar concepts.

1.1 Definitions

Pursuant to Estonian law, disinformation is regulated under private, public and criminal law depending on who the subject of the disinformation is, how the harm was caused, and what the nature of the harm caused was. Under Estonian private law disinformation can be either defamation of a person or disclosure of incorrect information. In public law, the concept of disinformation is derived from its definitions in private law. Private law also differentiates the unlawfulness of incorrect opinions of experts, which falls outside the scope of this analysis. Criminal law differentiates between insult and defamation with defamation falling within the scope of this legal analysis.

Private law differentiates between defamation and disclosure of incorrect information. Thus, this section focuses on the definitions of defamation and incorrect information.

1.2 Definitions Distinction Between Close Concepts (E.G. Disinformation / Misinformation / Malinformation, Etc.)

In Estonian law, the concept of defamation is framed similarly in both private and criminal law. The definitions in private and public law are the same, as confirmed by case law in public law. In private law, defamation is set out in § 1046 of the Law of Obligations (hereinafter 'LOA').[1] The topic of defamation is a subjective assessment, not a fact. Defamation includes passing undue value judgement, defaming a person by the unjustified use of the name or image of the person, or by breaching the inviolability of the private life or another personality right of the person. Although it is possible to justify a value judgment, it is not possible to prove the truth or falsity of its content.[2] One mainly assesses whether there were justifications for passing such a value judgement.

Disclosure of incorrect information is objective—a factual mistake that can be checked. § 1047 of the LOA sets out the unlawfulness of disclosure of incorrect information. Article 1047 states: 'The violation of personality rights or interference with the economic or professional activities of a person by way of disclosure of

[1] Law of Obligations.—RT I, 04.07.2024, 18.

[2] RKTKo, 21.12.2010, 3-2-1-67-10, para. 17.

incorrect information or by the incomplete or misleading disclosure of factual information concerning the person or the activities of the person is unlawful unless the person who discloses such information proves that, upon the disclosure thereof, the person was not aware and was not required to be aware that such information was incorrect or incomplete.' This means that the information provided can be proven to be true or false.

The publication of incorrect information is a general term that also covers the publication of incomplete and misleading information. In court practice, information is understood to mean factual statements, i.e. statements whose truth value can be verified. The Supreme Court has clarified that published factual statements (information) must be taken as they are, i.e. in the event of a dispute, the court must determine what the defendant, from the perspective of a reasonable person, intended to disclose to the public. The court must determine what the person disclosed to the public according to the understanding of a reasonable person and whether, in addition to factual statements, a value judgment was also made and whether this value judgment is damaging to the reputation of another person.[3]

Incorrect information may also include so-called indirect factual statements.[4] Indirect factual statements may also be refutable false information, i.e. factual statements that are not explicitly stated in the defendant's publication but can reasonably be inferred from it. A person may be misrepresented to the public by presenting indirect circumstances from which reasonable conclusions can be drawn about the claimant. In such a case, the claimant may demand that the publisher refute the conclusion drawn from the publication at the publisher's expense.[5] Thus, the factual claim that the person is seeking to refute does not have to have been expressly stated by the respondents, but can be deduced from, among other things, the context.

In conclusion, a factual statement is, in principle, verifiable and its truth or falsity can be proven in court; a value judgment is expressed in an assessment, which, due to its content or form, may have a derogatory meaning in a specific cultural environment—although it is possible to justify a value judgment, but not the truth or falsity of its content.[6] In case of a value judgement, the court checks whether or not facts supported the passing of such a value judgement.

Estonian criminal law regulates special cases of defamation, e.g. defamation of representative of state authority or a court. Criminal law differentiates defamation and insult. Defamation is the presentation or dissemination of a factual statement (i.e., not a value judgment) that is false and may damage the reputation of the victim in the eyes of the public (so-called external honour). Defamation does not occur if the factual statement being disseminated is shameful but true, or false but not shameful.[7] In the case of presenting false factual claims, insulting someone is different from

---

[3] RKTKo, 21.12.2010, 3-2-1-67-10, para. 21.

[4] Võlaõigusseadus IV. kommentaarid. § 1047, para. 3.1.

[5] RKTKo, 31.05.2006, 3-2-1-161-05, para. 12.

[6] RKTKo, 21.12.2010, 3-2-1-67-10, para. 17.

[7] J. Sootak, P. Pikamäe. Karistusseadustik. Kommenteeritud väljaanne. § 247, para. 3.2.

defamation because in the first case, the factual claim is made to the person who is being insulted, while in the second case, it is made to a third party.[8]

Notably, there is no relevant court practice regarding the definition of defamation in criminal law by the Supreme Court. However, the county court has noted the following. Under § 305-1(1) of the Penal Code, only statements of fact, but not value judgments, can be considered defamation.[9] Otherwise, the scope of punishability of the criminal offense provided for in § 305-1(1) of the Penal Code would become excessively broad and it would be virtually impossible to distinguish it from the misdemeanour of insult of court provided for in § 305(1) of the Penal Code. This could lead to a conflict with the principle of criminal law as a last resort and the requirement of precision laid down in § 23(1) of the Constitution and § 2(1) of the Penal Code. Defamation of court must be less subjective and have a significantly more harmful effect on the administration of justice than the insulting of court.[10] The court ruled that calling the appealed court order a mess and the assessment that the judge lacks basic legal knowledge are both value judgments that do not constitute defamation of the court under § 305-1(1) of the Penal Code.[11]

The parliament decided to differentiate between defamation and insult of representative of state authority for the following reason. While insulting a representative of authority is often committed spontaneously, due to a conflict situation and alcohol consumption, defamation, on the other hand, is a conscious and deliberate act that may be motivated by revenge or self-interest.[12] Thus, pursuant to criminal law defamation is a conscious act of presenting a factual statement that is false and shameful.

1.3 Specificity (if Any) of Online Disinformation

There is no difference whether the disinformation was presented on- or offline. The courts frequently handle cases where disinformation was published on social media. Also, frequently, the same information has been published on paper and on the web-portal of a newspaper.

The Supreme Court has found that an online news platform can be held liable for defamatory comments posted by readers under articles published on its platform. In the case of Delfi AS v. Estonia,[13] the Estonian courts held Delfi, a leading internet news portal in Estonia, liable under the LOA for defamatory third-party comments posted in the comments section of its articles. Delfi filed an application with the

---

[8] Ibidem. § 247, para. 3.3.

[9] TrRKm, 13.06.2025, 1-24-5461, para. 8; J. Sootak, P. Pikamäe. Karistusseadustik. Kommenteeritud väljaanne. § 247, para. 3.2., § 305-1 para. 4.

[10] TrRKm, 13.06.2025, 1-24-5461, para. 8.

[11] TrRKm, 13.06.2025, 1-24-5461, para. 9.

[12] Eelnõu 554 (Riigkogu XII koosseis) teise lugemise seletuskiri (Karistuseadustiku kommenteeritud väljaanne § 275-1, para. 1).

[13] CASE OF DELFI AS v. ESTONIA, *Application no. 64569/09,* 16 June 2015.

European Court of Human Rights (ECtHR), arguing that the ruling violated its right to freedom of expression under Article 10 of the European Convention on Human Rights. The Grand Chamber of the ECtHR ruled in favour of the State, following the Supreme Court's reasoning that Delfi had not taken sufficient measures to remove the anonymous comments, which clearly amounted to hate speech and incitement to violence. The ECtHR took into account the fact that the defamatory comments clearly amounted to hate speech and incitement to violence and that Delfi was a large commercial news platform. The ECtHR developed criteria for assessing the liability of a news platform for user-generated comments in similar cases (e.g. Index.hu Zrt v. Hungary).

In the case Index.hu Zrt v. Hungary,[14] the ECtHR found that the Hungarian courts' ruling, which held two major Hungarian internet news providers liable for offensive user-generated comments, constituted a violation of Article 10. The ECtHR reasoned that, unlike in Delfi AS v. Estonia, the comments did not amount to clearly unlawful speech, and one of the applicant platforms was also non-commercial. Consequently, the ECtHR found that the State's interference had not been proportional. In both cases, the ECtHR applied the general principles regarding whether an interference with freedom of expression is necessary in a democratic society. In particular, the Court considered the context of the comments, the measures applied by the applicant company in order to prevent or remove defamatory comments, the liability of the actual authors of the comments as an alternative to the intermediary's liability, and the consequences of the domestic proceedings for the applicant company.' Accordingly, the courts should take both judgments into account when applying the "Delfi" principles.

2 The Sources of Law

This chapter provides an overview of the sources of law applicable in Estonia regarding online disinformation.

2.1 Constitutional References

The Constitution lays out many fundamental rights that are related to freedom of expression. Sections 17, 19 and 45 hold special significance. The Supreme Court has stated that an administrative measure that infringes fundamental rights set out in the Constitution can only be lawful if it is based on a legal basis provided for by

---

[14] CASE OF MAGYAR TARTALOMSZOLGÁLTATÓK EGYESÜLETE AND INDEX.HU ZRT v. HUNGARY, *Application no. 22947/13*, 2 February 2016.

law, complies with procedural and substantive law, and is necessary in a democratic society, i.e. proportionate.[15]

Section 17 states: 'No one's honour, or good name shall be defamed.' This section protects honour and reputation, and it is worded without reservations, but this does not mean that the fundamental right established in § 17 is absolute. Pursuant to § 19(2) of the Constitution, everyone must, in exercising their rights and freedoms and in fulfilling their obligations, respect the rights and freedoms of others and observe the law. Even fundamental rights without a limitation clause may be restricted if the restriction is based on the conflicting fundamental right of a third party or some other constitutional value.[16]

Regarding section 17, the Supreme Court has found that information disseminated in any manner or form that contains or allows for disparaging assessments is damaging to honour and good name.[17]

A prerequisite for defamation is that the act be committed in public.[18] Disinformation does not need to be widely published in order to be considered defamation. The assessment of unlawfulness may be influenced by whether the allegations defaming the claimant were made to a narrow circle of persons and whether the information or opinions allegedly defaming the claimant were directed specifically against the claimant or against a group of persons to which the claimant belongs.[19]

Actions that damage a person's reputation or good name are also considered unlawful between individuals, e.g. between members of a housing association or within a workplace collective. However, in certain cases—such as with the chairperson of a housing association—persons must accept the possibility that members of the association may criticize their actions, even if such criticism is unjustified. In these situations, criticism expressed through the disclosure of incorrect factual statements or inappropriate value judgments may not necessarily be unlawful.[20]

A person's dignity may also be damaged in situations where the act is not committed in public or in front of a third party. If an act that degrades dignity (such as spitting in someone's face or other degrading acts) is committed privately between two persons, it does not constitute defamation or damage to reputation, but rather degradation of a person's dignity.[21]

The state has a positive obligation to protect a person's honour and good name. This means that individuals must be able to protect their honour and good name both from public authorities in the public sphere (vertical effect) and from private individuals in the private sphere (horizontal effect).[22]

---

[15] RKHKo, 12.06.2012, 3-3-1-3-12, para. 20.

[16] Põhiseadus.—Kommenteeritud väljaanne, § 17, para. 3.

[17] RKHKo, 12.06.2012, 3-3-1-3-12, para. 17.

[18] Põhiseadus.—Kommenteeritud väljaanne, § 17, para. 4.

[19] RKTKo 16.11.2022, 2-19-8673/96, para. 11; RKTKo, 12.01.2009, 3-2-1-127-08, para. 16; RKTKo 11.02.2004, 3-2-1-11-04, para. 11.

[20] RKTKo 31.05.2006, 3-2-1-161-05, para. 15.

[21] Põhiseadus.—Kommenteeritud väljaanne, § 17, para. 4.

[22] Põhiseadus.—Kommenteeritud väljaanne, § 17, para. 5.

Section 17 provides protection to all natural persons whose honour and good name have been defamed. With regard to legal persons, it should be noted that defamation is inherent only to natural persons, i.e. human beings. However, the protection of reputation, i.e. good name, extends beyond natural persons to legal persons, such as companies or other entities established under the law.[23] The legal remedies for legal persons are more limited. A legal person cannot, by virtue of its nature, be subject to claims for compensation for non-patrimonial damage resulting from defamation.[24] However, a legal person has other remedies, which are explained in Sect. 2.3.1.

Section 45 of the Constitution defines the right to freedom of expression. However, this right is not absolute and may be restricted by a law to protect public order, morals, or the rights and freedoms, health, honour and good name of others. The Constitution differentiates between information and ideas, as does Article 10 of the European Convention on Human Rights. This distinction means that freedom of expression is not limited to the presentation of verifiable, factual, or measurable information, but also includes the expression of opinions, ideas, beliefs, criticisms, assessments, thoughts, and images.[25]

In addition to the previous constitutional rights, sections 11 and 19 (necessary restrictions of rights), 12 (principle of equality), 31 (right to engage in enterprise), 38 (freedom of science and art), 40 (freedom of conscience, religion and thought) and 41 (right to remain faithful to own opinions and beliefs) are also relevant.

2.2 *EU Law and Its Implementation*

The effect EU law has regarding Estonian approach to defamation comes from the EU Charter of Fundamental Rights, data protection regulations (GDPR, DSA) and the impact that the Court of Justice of the EU (CJEU) case law has had.

As of June 2023, the Estonian Parliament (Riigikogu) has been processing a law to amend the Penal Code, the Code of Criminal Procedure, and the Code of Misdemeanour Procedure in order to align national legislation with the Framework Decision on Combating Racism and Xenophobia (2008/913/JHA). This legislative initiative follows a letter of formal notice from the European Commission, which stated that Estonia's national laws do not fully or accurately transpose the EU rules on combating certain forms of expression of racism and xenophobia through criminal law.[26]

---

[23] Põhiseadus.—Kommenteeritud väljaanne, § 17, para. 6.

[24] RKTKo, 27.03.1997, 3-2-1-35-97.

[25] Põhiseadus.—Kommenteeritud väljaanne, § 45, para. 10.

[26] Ginter, C., Soo, A. The 'Public Order' Parachute in Combating Racism and Xenophobia. - Juridica International 31/2022, pp 48–58, accessed 05.08.2025: Issue article - www.juridicainternational.eu.

2.3 *Legislative Acts*

Disinformation is regulated under different norms depending on whether the action falls inside the scope of private, criminal or public law.

2.3.1 Disinformation and Private Law

In private law, the LOA[27] regulates claims regarding unlawful disclosure of incorrect information. Notably, the section is part of tort law, which means that the pre-requisite of using the legal rights set out, is that there is no contract between the parties. Otherwise, the potential claims might be based on the contractual obligations and rights between the parties.

Chapter 53 'Unlawful causing of damage' sets out the rules regarding unlawfulness of damaging personality rights (§ 1046), unlawfulness of disclosure of incorrect information (§ 1047) and unlawfulness of incorrect opinion of expert (§ 1048). Since § 1048 falls outside the scope, the prerequisites for that section are not analysed. The potential damages for all the articles largely overlap, but certain differences are still present.

The legal basis is formed by § 1043 together with § 1045 (1) 4). For a successful claim and compensation regarding disinformation, the following requirements set out in §§ 1043-1050 must be met: 1) a violation of a personal right and damages have occurred and there is a causality between them; 2) the act is unlawful pursuant to § 1046-§1047; 3) the person is culpable pursuant to § 1050. The prerequisites of LOA §§ 1046 and 1047 are now examined individually.

Pursuant to LOA § 1046 the violation has occurred if personal rights have been damaged.

The second condition for a successful claim is the unlawfulness of the act. Section 1046(1) establishes the principle that an act that violates the personal rights of another person is presumed to be unlawful on the basis of its objective characteristics. However, it follows from the second sentence of subsection 1 that the unlawfulness of a violation of a personal right requires a value judgment, which must take into account the nature of the violation (i.e., which personal right was violated and in what manner), the cause and motive of the violation (e.g. whether the violation was caused or motivated by the victim's own actions and whether the act of the perpetrator, the legality of which is being assessed, is an adequate and permissible response to the victim's actions), as well as the relationship between the objective pursued by the violation and the severity of the violation.[28] The second sentence of paragraph 1 allows courts not to consider minor violations that a person must reasonably tolerate in certain situations as unlawful.[29]

---

[27] Law of Obligations.—RT I, 04.07.2024, 18.

[28] RKTKo, 29.03.2017, 3-2-1-153-16, paras. 35–36.

[29] RKTKo, 31.05.2006, 3-2-1-161-05, para 15.

The first sentence of paragraph 2 stipulates that a violation of personal rights is not unlawful if the violation is justified, taking into account other interests protected by law and the interests of third parties or the public. The second sentence of paragraph 2 stipulates that in such cases, the determination of unlawfulness must be based on a comparative assessment of the various protected interests and benefits.[30] Thus, LOA § 1046 obliges the court to make a value judgment in every case of a violation of personal rights in order to assess the unlawfulness of the violation.

Pursuant to LOA § 1047 the violation of a personal right has occurred if incorrect information has been disclosed. Disclosure is, within the meaning of § 1047 of the LOA, the communication of data to third (unrelated) parties.[31] In court practice, the disclosure of data is considered to be the disclosure of data in a television program,[32] in the press,[33] in the student newspaper,[34] on the internet,[35] including in comment sections,[36] in books,[37] on posters displayed in public spaces,[38] in master's theses,[39] and in public procurement documents.[40] The publication of incorrect factual statements and inappropriate value judgments may also occur in a situation where a person is applying for a job and the new employer asks for an assessment of the person's work experience and suitability from their previous employer.[41]

Section 1047 also outlines the second prerequisite—unlawfulness. It states that disclosing incorrect information or sharing factual information in a misleading or incomplete way, is considered unlawful. This applies when such disclosure harms a person's personality rights or interferes with their economic or professional activities. However, the person who disclosed the information can avoid liability if they prove they did not know—and were not expected to know—that the information was incorrect or incomplete. Additionally, sharing defamatory facts or facts that could negatively affect someone's financial situation is also unlawful. In these cases, the person who disclosed the facts must prove that the information is true.

The third and last condition for both sections 1046 and 1047 is that the person who committed the act is culpable. Pursuant to section 1050 culpability is the basis

[30] RKTKo, 18.02.2015, 3-2-1-159-14, para. 11.

[31] RKTKo, 21.12.2010, 3-2-1-67-10 para. 16. P. Varul jt. Võlaõigusseadus. Kommenteeritud väljaanne III. Tallinn: 2009.—§ 1047 komm 3.1. lg 3. Võlaõigusseadus. Kommenteeritud väljaanne IV. Tallinn: 2020.—§ 1046 komm 3.2. lg 3.

[32] RKTKo 18.02.2015, 3-2-1-159-14.

[33] For example RKeKo 05.12.1997, 3-2-1-99-97; RKTKo, 15.04.2015, 3-2-1-24-15; RKTKo 19.02.2008, 3-2-1-145-07.

[34] RKTKo 13.06.2002, 3-2-1-63-02 para. 8.

[35] RKTKo, 25.09.2013, 3-2-1-80-13.

[36] RKTKo 31.10.2007, 3-2-1-73-07.

[37] RKTKo 29.03.2017, 3-2-1-153-16.

[38] RKTKo 21.12.2010, 3-2-1-67-10.

[39] RKTKo 19.03.2019, 2-17-17140/47 para. 14.

[40] TrtRnKo 15.06.2020, 2-18-2988.

[41] TlnRnKo, 17.01.2017, 2-15-9284.

for liability. The form of culpability is assessed. The types of culpability are carelessness, gross negligence, and intent. Objective culpability pursuant to § 104 means committing an unlawful act either intentionally or through negligence, i.e. because of failing to exercise the due care required in the circumstances. Together with the form of culpability the possible restrictions on liability are assessed. Section 1052(1) sets out that a person under 14 years of age shall not be liable for damage caused by himself or herself. In that case, the parents or curators are liable. Additionally, a person shall not be liable for damage caused by himself or herself if he or she caused the damage in such a condition that he or she could not understand the meaning of or direct his or her actions.

Lastly, distinguishing factual statements and value judgments is important, as the legal remedies applicable to them differ. If the victim is a physical person, the victim may claim compensation for the patrimonial or non-patrimonial damage caused to them in both cases, and, regardless of whether a claim for compensation has been made, demand that the offender cease the unlawful conduct pursuant to § 1055 of the LOA if the infringement is continuing, or to refrain from threatening to do so if there is reason to fear that the infringement will be repeated (e.g. a claim for the removal of incorrect information published on the internet). A value judgment can only be declared unlawful in conjunction with the aforementioned claims.[42]

Notably, section 1047 allows the victim to demand that the person who disclosed incorrect information refute the information or publish a correction at the person's expense regardless of whether the disclosure of the information was unlawful or not. The claim under § 1047(4) cannot be made in relation to value judgments. The Supreme Court has also rejected the reversal of an inappropriate value judgment in cases where the value judgment is based on incorrect assumptions or factual claims.[43]

Legal remedies for legal persons are the following. Firstly, a legal person may have a claim for compensation for financial loss against a person who causes it financial loss by unlawfully and culpably publishing incorrect information about it.[44] The Supreme Court has explained that causing damage by disclosing incorrect information about a legal person may be unlawful, particularly if such disclosure interferes with the legal person's economic or professional activities, violates a legal obligation, or is intentionally contrary to good morals. For example, the damage may consist of loss of turnover, customer departures, or difficulties in concluding new contracts, including hiring employees.[45]

Secondly, under LOA § 1055(1), a legal person may demand the prohibition on performance of damaging acts in order to protect its reputation. This remedy can be applied in two main situations: first, when an unlawful act corresponding to the general tort liability requirements has already been committed and is of a continuing nature, or there is a risk that such an unlawful act will be committed again in the

---

[42] RKTKo, 31.05.2006, 3-2-1-161-05 para. 10.

[43] P. Varul jt. Võlaõigusseadus. Kommenteeritud väljaanne IV. Tallinn: 2020.—§ 1047 komm 3.5.2. lg 2.

[44] RKTKo, 09.08.2023, 2-20-5869/87, para. 14.

[45] RKTKo, 09.08.2023, 2-20-5869/87, paras. 14, 21.

future; and second, when there is a threat of unlawful harm, even if the harmful act has not yet occurred.[46] For example, courts have recognized that leaving false factual statements or damaging value judgments about a company online constitutes ongoing harm, which can be ordered to be removed.[47] Importantly, the Supreme Court has clarified that the violation does not need to be ongoing—proof of a risk of recurrence is sufficient, as once an infringement has occurred, the likelihood of repetition is presumed.[48] Furthermore, if a threat of unlawful harm exists, it is not necessary to establish that an unlawful act has already taken place; it is enough that the threat itself creates the danger of such an act.[49] The claim under LOA § 1055(1) allows the injured party to require the wrongdoer to take measures to eliminate harmful consequences, such as filing requests with search engines to remove defamatory content, which must be submitted properly (e.g., signed applications) to be effective.

§ 1047 of the LOA addresses issues related to the publication of incorrect information about both natural persons and legal persons. If false information about a natural person's business or professional activities is published, it may constitute a violation of their personal rights under § 1045(1)(4), § 1046, and § 1047(1-3). According to § 1045(1)(6), the legal interest protected primarily concerns the business of an entrepreneur or other professional. Therefore, the protection provided by these provisions extends to all business owners (see also § 1045(3)(7)). This protection also applies to non-profit associations, foundations, and apartment and housing associations.[50]

2.3.2 Disinformation and Criminal Law

In criminal law, the Penal Code regulates claims regarding defamation. In case the subject of the disinformation is a representative of state authority, a court, judge or a lay judge, the Penal Code regulates the potential consequences. Both in theory and in practice, there is limited information available on how disinformation is addressed within the framework of criminal law.

The Penal Code lays out possible repercussions if the subject of the disinformation is: a person enjoying international immunity (§ 247), state authority representative (§ 275 and § 275-1), a court (§ 305 and § 305-1), judge (§ 305 and § 305-1), or lay judge (§ 305 and § 305-1). The consequences include a potential fine, detention or even imprisonment. The provisions differentiate between insults and defamation. Section 247 sets out the same repercussions for either defaming or insulting persons enjoying international immunity, where the penalty is either a pecuniary punishment or up to two years' imprisonment. For a state authority representative, court, judge and lay judge, the punishments depend on whether the person has been defamed or

[46] P. Varul jt. Võlaõigusseadus. Kommenteeritud väljaanne IV. Tallinn: 2020.—§ 1055 komm 3.1.

[47] TlnRnKo, 17.10.2023, 2-21-13,323, para. 88 and para 3.3 from the resolution.

[48] RKTKo, 17.06.2021, 2-16-17,491/80, para. 20.2, RKTKo, 21.06.2022, 2-19-10,047, para. 13.

[49] RKTKo, 09.12.2009, 3-2-1-104-09, para. 15.

[50] Võlaõigusseadus IV. kommentaarid. § 1047, 1.

insulted. Insult is considered a misdemeanour and is punishable by a fine of up to 300 fine units or by detention. Defamation is a criminal offence and is punishable by a pecuniary punishment or up to two years' imprisonment.

Regarding the subjective element, all aforementioned paragraphs presuppose intent with regard to all objective circumstances of the composition. The composition is fulfilled if the person acts with at least indirect intent.

Regarding the objective elements, the following can be noted. Regarding defamation of persons enjoying international immunity set out in § 247 the objective element includes (a) defamation or (b) insult of an internationally protected person or a member of their family. The composition is very broad. At the same time, it would be technically complicated and impractical to establish precise criteria for when, how, and which internationally protected persons may be defamed or insulted. Therefore, the paragraph in question must be interpreted narrowly, weighing, on the one hand, the protectability of the legal interest and the extent of the harm caused and, on the other hand, the freedom of expression necessary in a democratic society.[51] Notably, there is no relevant court practice regarding § 247 of the Penal Code.

The objective element of defamation of representative of state authority set out in § 275-1 consists of defamation of a public official in connection with the performance of his or her official duties. This section protects all public officials, not only those who protect public order. At the same time, it should be noted that defamation of a court or judge is criminalised separately as an offense against the administration of justice in § 305-1.[52] Notably, there is no relevant court practice regarding § 275-1 either.

Defamation of court set out in § 305-1 includes publicly defaming the court as an institution or spreading false information about an individual judge or lay judge. Defamation of a judge or lay judge as a person is protected by law only to the extent that the defamation concerns their professional activities. The motive or object of the defamation is a decision or ruling made by the judge, or their conduct in the course of administering justice.[53] Notably, there is only one relevant country court decision regarding this section, which focused on the definition of defamation as laid out under chapter 1.

2.3.3 Disinformation and Public Law

In cases where the source of the disinformation is a public body exercising its public obligations, the Administrative Procedure Act[54] (hereinafter APA) and the State

[51] J. Sootak, P. Pikamäe. Karistusseadustik. Kommenteeritud väljaanne, § 247, para. 4.

[52] Ibidem, § 275-1, para. 4.

[53] Ibidem, § 305-1, para. 3.1.

[54] Administrative Procedure Act. - RT I, 06.07.2023, 31 Administrative Procedure Act-Riigi Teataja - www.riigiteataja.ee.

Liability Act[55] (hereinafter SLA) apply. Notably, state liability does not extend to cases where a public authority acts in a private capacity; the performance of public tasks must take place in a public capacity.[56]

The prerequisites for a successful claim are largely aligned with those established under private law, though certain distinctions do exist. When assessing the legality of administrative measures that damage a person's honour and reputation, section 107 of the APA must be the primary basis, but in disputes over damage caused by such measures, sections 1046 and 1047 of the LOA must also be applied in accordance with section 7(4) of the SLA, insofar as they do not conflict with administrative law.[57]

When it comes to administrative activities more broadly, this encompasses not only the issuance of administrative acts, but also other forms of public authority conduct, such as factual actions and procedural steps taken in the course of performing public duties. Pursuant to section 7(1) of the SLA, a person whose rights have been violated in a public legal relationship by an unlawful act of a public authority in a public law relationship may claim compensation for the damage caused to them if the damage could not have been avoided and cannot be remedied by protecting or restoring their rights in the manner provided for in SLA sections 3, 4, and 6 (primary legal remedies). Section 9 of the SLA regulates the claims for a monetary compensation for non-pecuniary damage in cases of intentional defamation or damage to reputation of a natural person.

The Supreme Court emphasized that in public law, there must be a legal basis for making statements that damage a person's honour and good name, i.e. the legality of the publication is not sufficient on the basis of the mere fact that factual statements and value judgments are in accordance with sections 1046 and 1047 of the LOA.[58] Section 3 of the APA stipulates that in administrative procedure, the fundamental rights and freedoms or other subjective rights of a person may be restricted only pursuant to law; and administrative decisions and measures shall be appropriate, necessary and proportionate to the stated objectives. The court must first determine whether the administrative authority had a sufficient legal basis for making the disputed statements. Only thereafter does the court assess whether the statement constitutes a fact or a value judgment, and whether its disclosure was lawful under the LOA. Compensation for damage is provided in accordance with § 7 of the SLA.

The Supreme Court has emphasized that the choice of words used by public officials when informing the public is of great importance—particularly in the case of higher officials, whose statements carry significant weight in society. Specifically, the Supreme Court found that a statement made by the prosecutor at a press conference contained an undue value judgment, which created the incorrect impression that

[55] Riigivastutuse seadus. - RT I, 07.05.2025, 19. State Liability Act-Riigi Teataja - www.riigiteataja.ee

[56] Section 2 of the State Liability Act.

[57] RKHKo, 03.10.2023, 3-19-1565/46, para. 15.

[58] RKHKo, 12.06.2012, 3-3-1-3-12, para. 41.

the applicants had accepted bribes, thereby unlawfully undermining the presumption of innocence.[59] Therefore, individuals performing public law functions—especially representatives of state power—have an elevated obligation of diligence when making negative statements about persons. This duty includes verifying the legal and factual basis for making such statements, as well as whether disclosure of such information is proportionate to the legitimate objective of the administrative measure. If statements are made without legal basis and contain defamation or incorrect information within the meaning of the LOA, the State may be held liable under the SLA.

2.4 *The Role of Case Law*

Case law plays an important role in the application of legal acts concerning defamation in Estonia, as it helps interpret and clarify how statutory provisions should be understood and enforced in practice. As such, case law serves as a crucial complement to written legislation, shaping the development of defamation law in Estonia over time.

2.4.1 Case Law in Private Law

The role of Supreme Court's case law is significant. While Estonia lacks a system of precedents, the decisions carry a significant weight as role models.

For example, the Supreme Court has clarified the definitions of undue value judgments and incorrect factual statements and has established principles for distinguishing between them. The Supreme Court has noted that factual statements can be verified by the court, but value judgments can be only justified and not proved.[60] The Supreme Court has also added that any statement that includes data or information about a person can be considered a factual statement.[61] For example, the Supreme Court has held that stating a person has committed criminal offences constitutes a factual statement, not an expression of opinion.[62]

The Supreme Court has explained that disclosure of incorrect information within the meaning of § 1047 of the LOA refers to the communication of information to third parties. For example, the Court found that if data is published in the media, then in addition to the media outlet, the person who provided the data to the media may also be regarded as the disclosing party.[63] Information is also considered disclosed when

[59] RKHKo, 03.10.2023, 3-19-1565, paras. 15, 18, 21, 22, 23.

[60] RKTKo, 29.03.2017, 3-2-1-153-16, para. 28.

[61] RKTKo, 31.05.2006, 3-2-1-161-05, para. 10.

[62] RKTKo, 18.02.2025, 3-2-1-159-14, para. 10.

[63] RKTKo, 21.12.2005, 3-2-1-95-05, para. 25.

a person shares a press release issued by someone else on social media.[64] According to the Supreme Court, a factual statement can also be disclosed indirectly.[65] In such a case, the court will use a reasonable person as a standard and determine how such a person would interpret the published statements, considering the manner and context of the disclosure. Then, the court will decide whether the defendant's statements constitute a factual statement.[66] The Supreme Court held, however, that expression of approval of a comment published by another person on a social media platform cannot be considered an indirect disclosure of a factual statement. Such approval can only be deemed unlawful in exceptional cases, where mere endorsement of another person's statement results in a serious infringement of the victim's right to honour and reputation.[67]

The Supreme Court has established several principles by which it assesses whether an infringement of a person's honour and reputation is unlawful under the LOA, when weighed against another individual's right to freedom of expression.

According to Supreme Court practice the deliberate disclosure of false information about a person is never lawful. The Court has emphasised that the disclosure of a factual statement that corresponds to reality, even if it damages the reputation of a person, is not in itself unlawful.[68]

In the case of a negative value judgment, the disclosing person's freedom of expression is significantly broader and depending on the circumstances, a person must tolerate negative value judgments directed at them, as such statements cannot automatically be considered defamatory or unlawful. The Supreme Court found that under § 1046 of the LOA, minor violations that a person must reasonably tolerate in certain situations—such as those arising from the manner of publication, context, or content—should not be considered unlawful. Not every negative value judgment published in the press warrants an award of damages. For example, the claim that a person is encouraging others to enter transactions of dubious content should not be considered more than a minor insult to that person's honour.[69] In such case the Court decided that such an assessment does not exceed the threshold of unlawfulness set out in § 1046(1) of the LOA and was not of a nature that is degrading, humiliating or ridiculous.[70] The Court has noted that it may also be relevant to consider whether the article containing defamatory statements was published solely in print or also online, where it is presumed to reach a significantly larger audience than a print publication.[71]

The Supreme Court has explained that, when assessing the unlawfulness of certain statements that infringe upon a person's honour and reputation, certain individuals

64 RKTKo 18.05.2022, 2-20-12,495, para. 11.

65 RKTKo 10.04.2024, 2-20-3847, paras. 12–13; RKTKm, 01.12.2021, 2-15-18661, para. 11.

66 RKTKm, 01.12.2021, 2-15-18661, para. 11.

67 RKTKo 10.04.2024, 2-20-3847, para. 12–13.

68 RKTKo, 21.12.2010, 3-2-1-67-10, para. 18.

69 RKTKo, 10.04.2024, 2-20-3847, para. 11; RKTKo 03.07.2024, 2-20-2328, para. 12.

70 RKTKo, 10.04.2024, 2-20-3847, para. 11.

71 RKTKo, 26.06.2013, 3-2-1-18-13, para. 28.

are expected to tolerate a higher level of criticism. According to the prevailing view of the Supreme Court, public figures are subject to greater public scrutiny and must therefore also expect greater criticism.[72] Depending on the nature and scope of their activities, public figures may vary and, as a result, the degree of legitimate public interest in their private lives may also vary.[73]

The circumstances that allow a person to be considered a public figure depend on the nature of that person's activities and the nature of their public exposure. Therefore, no one can be considered a public figure in the abstract; each case must be considered individually. This means that if the claimant is a public figure, this fact must be taken into account when applying § 1046(1) and (2) of the LOA as one of the circumstances relevant for the application of other provisions.[74]

For example, the heightened interest of the public in the personality of a politician or a senior public official exercising executive power and in his or her political and professional activities is justified.[75] On the other hand, the mere fact of being a sworn advocate does not constitute grounds for considering a person to be a public figure.[76] Among other things, public figures must tolerate unjustified public criticism to a greater extent than other persons.[77]

At the same time, the Supreme Court has clarified that a person does not necessarily have to be a public figure to be subject to a higher standard of tolerance. For example, the Court found that the chairperson of an apartment association is not a public figure *per se*, but must accept the possibility that members of the association may criticize their actions, even if such criticism is unjustified. In such cases, criticism expressed through the disclosure of incorrect factual statements or inappropriate value judgments may not necessarily be unlawful.[78]

The Supreme Court has confirmed that legal persons have the right to demand refutation of false information under § 1047(4) of the LOA. The court stated that the right to make a claim under § 1047(4) of the LOA is not dependent on whether the claimant has fundamental rights capacity. The law does not restrict the circle of claimants to natural persons or private legal entities. A fundamental right is an important right or freedom enshrined in the constitution that protects individuals and enables them to exercise their rights. This can be understood in different ways—either as all rights enshrined in the constitution, only civil liberties, or rights that cannot be easily changed by parliament.[79] The legislature can grant the right to make a claim to any person, regardless of their fundamental rights. The law does not restrict the

[72] RKTKo, 13.05.2005, 3-2-1-17-05, para. 20.

[73] RKTKo, 26.06.2013, 3-2-1-18-13, para. 15.

[74] RKTKo, 18.05.2022, 2-20-12,495, para 15.

[75] RKTKo, 30.10.1997, 3-2-1-123-97.

[76] RKTKo, 18.05.2022, 2-20-12,495, para 15.

[77] RKTKo, 26.06.2013, 3-2-1-18-13, para. 15, RKTKo, 18.05.2022, 2-20-12,495, para 15.

[78] RKTKo 31.05.2006, 3-2-1-161-05 para. 15.

[79] See Põhiseaduse kommenteeritud väljaanne, ptk 2 "Sissejuhatus" EESTI VABARIIGI PÕHISEADUS - pohiseadus.ee.

circle of claimants to natural persons or private legal entities.[80] This principle also applies to legal person in public law.[81]

2.4.2 Case Law in Administrative Law

The Supreme Court has established how the legality of administrative acts that damage a person's honour and reputation must be assessed.

When assessing the legality of administrative acts that damage honour and reputation, the first point of reference is Section 107 of the APA. In disputes over damage caused by such acts, section 1046 and 1047 of the LOA are also applicable pursuant to section 7(4) of the SLA, insofar as they do not conflict with administrative law provisions. The Supreme Court emphasized that in public law, there must be a legal basis for making statements that damage a person's honour and good name.[82] That is to say that the legality of the publication is not sufficient on the basis of the mere fact that the factual statements and value judgments are in accordance with sections 1046 and 1047 of the LOA.

Notably, one case regarding potential damage to the reputation of a judge also reached the European Court of Human Rights. In Shuvalov v. Estonia,[83] the applicant, a sitting Estonian judge, was criminally investigated on suspicion of accepting bribes. During the investigation, the public prosecutor issued press releases and made statements to the media about the case, noting that a judge was under suspicion and later confirming that an indictment had been filed. The applicant considered these disclosures damaging to his reputation and a breach of his rights, arguing that they portrayed him as guilty before any conviction. Relevant domestic law included section 9 from SLA (non-pecuniary damages), LOA sections 1046, 1047 and 1055.

He brought actions before the Estonian courts seeking to have the statements declared unlawful, but the Tallinn Administrative Court and the Court of Appeal found that the disclosures were lawful, proportionate, and justified by strong public interest in transparency given the position he held. The Supreme Court refused to hear his appeal.

Before the ECtHR, the applicant claimed violations of the presumption of innocence under Article 6 § 2, his right to respect for private life under Article 8, and the absence of an effective domestic remedy under Article 13. The ECtHR held that the disclosures did not breach Articles 6 or 8, as they were proportionate, derived from official records, and framed in a way that preserved the presumption of innocence. While acknowledging that available domestic remedies were limited, the Court found no sufficient basis to establish a violation of Article 13 in the circumstances.

---

[80] RKTKo, 17.12.2015, 3-2-1-144-15, para 11.

[81] RKTKo, 17.12.2015, 3-2-1-144-15.

[82] RKHKo, 12.06.2012, 3-3-1-3-12, para. 41.

[83] CASE OF SHUVALOV v. ESTONIA, *(Applications nos. 39820/08 and 14942/09), 29.05.2012.*

2.4.3 Case Law in Criminal Law

The Supreme Court also plays an important role in interpreting the Penal Code. For example, the Supreme Court of Estonia clarified the application of § 275 (1) of the Penal Code, which deals with the defamation or insult of a representative of state authority.[84] This provision protects the honour and dignity of such officials, including prison guards and other prison staff, who exercise public authority over detainees. The court emphasized that the insult does not need to occur in a public place or be perceived by unrelated third parties. In addition, when attributing the objective elements of § 275(1) of the Penal Code, it must be established whether the conduct of the person under investigation violated the honour and dignity of the representative of state authority and whether the insult took place in connection with the performance of their official duties. This case highlights the role of judicial practice in shaping the interpretation of the Penal Code.

2.5 The Impact of Soft Law

There are two Estonian Code of Ethics for the Press for journalists and the press that the courts have referred to.[85] The codes are almost identical, with some minor typos and different wording present. However, the publishers are different: the Estonian Media Companies Association[86]and the Public Word Council (*Avaliku Sõna Nõukogu* in Estonian).[87] Pursuant to the Supreme Court, the Public Word Council assesses the compliance with the requirements of the Estonian Code of Ethics for the Press.[88]

In 1998 the Estonian Media Companies Association established the Estonian Code of Ethics for the Press[89] to which the court sometimes refers to. The Code sets out basic ethical principles for journalists and media companies as well as affirms some of the principles laid out in legal acts and supported by the court practice. For example, section 1.4 sets out that the media organization shall ensure that no inaccurate, distorted or misleading information is published. The Code defines a public person open for more criticism as follows: (1) people who hold political and economic power and control information that is important to the public and (2) those who earn their living by exposing themselves or their work. This means that the definition is broader than that of the courts— courts have not named the latter

---

[84] RKKKo, 13.04.2016, 3-1-1-31-16, para 10.

[85] For example RKTKo, 26.06.2013, 3-2-1-18-13; RKTKo, 04.10.2017, 2-15-16,007, para. 16.

[86] Eesti ajakirjanduseetika koodeks. Established in 29.01.1998 by the Estonian Media Companies Association.

[87] Eesti ajakirjanduseetika koodeks. The Public Word Council (*Avaliku Sõna Nõukogu* in Estonian).

[88] RKTKo, 13.05.2005, 3-2-1-17-05, para. 28.

[89] Eesti ajakirjanduseetika koodeks. Established in 29.01.1998 by the Estonian Media Companies Association.

as public persons. The Supreme Court has referred to the Code when discussing the definition of a public person.[90] In the same decision, the Court also referred to section 4.7 of the code which states that disputes between parents over child custody are not generally reported in the media.[91]

The potential of disinformation is regulated by stating that news material should be based on verifiable and evidence-based factual information. Lastly, section 5.3 states that in the event of incorrect information being published, a correction must be published.

2.6 *Influence (if Any) of Foreign Legal Solutions*

The influence of foreign legal solutions is limited to the EU legislation and court practice of the CJEU and ECtHR The most influential case has been Delfi AS v. Estonia,[92] which was discussed under Sect. 1.3 of this analysis.

2.7 *Possible Legal Reforms*

The European Commission initiated infringement proceedings against Estonia in 2020 because, in its opinion, the Estonian Penal Code does not adequately regulate hate speech and is contrary to the European Union Framework Decision.[93] The Commission noted that Estonia has not transposed the criminalisation of specific forms of hate speech, particularly the public condoning, denial, or gross trivialisation of international crimes and the Holocaust, when intended to incite violence or hatred. Furthermore, Estonia's legislation fails to adequately criminalise hate speech by excluding public incitement to violence or hatred against groups and by not prescribing appropriate penalties. Lastly, the Estonian Penal Code does not ensure that racist or xenophobic motives are treated as aggravating circumstances, thereby hindering the effective prosecution of such offences.

Currently, the possible legal reforms regarding the infringement proceedings are in the making. The process has been delayed as both the public as well as the parties in the parliament lack a uniform understanding of what should be covered by these amendments. The latest development took place in 2023 when the parliament

---

[90] RKTKo, 26.06.2013, 3-2-1-18-13, para. 15.

[91] RKTKo, 26.06.2013, 3-2-1-18-13, para. 16.

[92] CASE OF DELFI AS v. ESTONIA.

[93] 'October infringements package: key decisions', EU Commission, 30.10.2020. Link: https://ec.europa.eu/commission/presscorner/api/files/document/print/GA/inf_20_1687/INF_20_1687_EN.pdf.

approved the first reading of the legal draft.[94] The changes would include amending the Penal Code, Code of Misdemeanour Procedure and the Code of Criminal Procedure. Pursuant to the draft law, the aggravating circumstances for the imposition of punishment would also include committing an offense against a person on the basis of their nationality, race, skin colour, gender, disability, language, origin, religion, sexual orientation, political beliefs, or financial or social status. The section 151 on incitement of hatred set out in the Penal Code would also be amended. Changes in the Code of Misdemeanour Procedure and the Code of Criminal Procedure include simply updating the legal references to the Penal Code.

3 The Regulation: Reporting Procedure and Other Ways to Tackle Online Disinformation

There are no specificities regarding online disinformation in Estonia. However, in practice, all the main media portals have implemented a reporting functionality largely due to the Delfi vs Estonia case mentioned above.

Although personal data breaches can be reported to the Data Protection Inspectorate pursuant to Article 33 of the General Data Protection Regulation (EU) 2016/679, there is no similar institution that specifically tackles reports regarding disinformation.

If defamation takes place on a social media platform, similarly to other countries, a person has a chance to ask the platform to take down the comment as defaming content most likely contradicts the user policies of the platform. However, there are no other specific remedies or institutions in Estonia that focus on tackling disinformation. Thus, a person has a chance to file a claim in the court. In case disinformation may include elements of a threat, or the target is a state authority representative, a court, judge or a lay judge, a person may contact the police and start criminal proceedings against the potential suspect.

4 Conclusions

Estonia's legal framework for addressing disinformation is multifaceted, encompassing private, criminal, and public law. While the law does not distinguish between online and offline disinformation, online disinformation is increasingly perceived as a societal and legal concern—particularly in light of landmark cases such as Delfi v. Estonia. The most developed legal remedies are found in private law, especially under the Law of Obligations, where courts have clarified the distinction between factual statements and value judgments. Factual inaccuracies must be corrected regardless

[94] Karistusseadustiku, kriminaalmenetluse seadustiku ja väärteomenetluse seadustiku muutmise seadus (vaenu õhutamine ja vaenumotiiviga kuriteod). Draft law, 24.05.2023.

of culpability, whereas value judgments are assessed based on their justification and context. This distinction is crucial, as it determines the applicable legal remedies and the threshold for unlawfulness. Courts have also emphasized proportionality, especially when balancing freedom of expression with the protection of personal rights.

Despite the availability of legal tools, the overall effectiveness of Estonia's disinformation regulation is mixed. Criminal law is reserved for exceptional cases, and public law requires a clear legal basis for reputational harm caused by state actors. The absence of a centralized authority or reporting mechanism for disinformation limits enforcement, leaving courts and platforms to fill the gap. Key challenges include the complexity of legal definitions, limited remedies for legal persons, and the high threshold for proving unlawfulness in public law. From a *de jure condendo* perspective, Estonia would benefit from clearer statutory definitions, enhanced procedural safeguards, and specialized institutions to handle disinformation claims. Ongoing EU infringement proceedings and proposed reforms—particularly regarding hate speech—present an opportunity to strengthen the legal framework. As digital communication evolves, Estonia's legal system must continue adapting to ensure both the protection of reputation and the preservation of democratic freedoms.

References

Commentary

J. Sootak, P. Pikamäe: Karistusseadustik. Kommenteeritud väljaanne. Juura, Tallinn (2021).
P. Varul and others: Võlaõigusseadus. Kommenteeritud väljaanne III. Juura, Tallinn (2009).
P. Varul and others: Võlaõigusseadus. Kommenteeritud väljaanne IV. Juura, Tallinn (2020).
Eesti Vabariigi Põhiseadus. Kommenteeritud väljaanne. 2020. Link: https://pohiseadus.ee/, last accessed 2025/11/27.

Court Practice

CASE OF DELFI AS v. ESTONIA, Application no. 64569/09, 16 June 2015, available on https://hudoc.echr.coe.int/eng#{%22fulltext%22:[%2264569/09%22],%22languageisocode%22:[%22ENG%22],%22documentcollectionid2%22:[%22GRANDCHAMBER%22,%22CHAMBER%22],%22itemid%22:[%22001-155105%22]}, last accessed 2025/11/27.
CASE OF MAGYAR TARTALOMSZOLGÁLTATÓK EGYESÜLETE AND INDEX.HU ZRT v. HUNGARY, Application no. 22947/13, 2 February 2016, available on https://hudoc.echr.coe.int/eng#{%22itemid%22:[%22001-160314%22]}, last accessed 2025/11/27.
CASE OF SHUVALOV v. ESTONIA, (Applications nos. 39820/08 and 14942/09), 29.05.2012, available on https://hudoc.echr.coe.int/eng#{%22appno%22:[%2214942/09%22]}, last accessed 2025/11/27.
RKeKo 05.12.1997, 3-2-1-99-97, https://www.riigikohus.ee/et/lahendid?asjaNr=3-2-1-99-97, last accessed 2026/05/06.

RKHKo 12.06.2012, 3-3-1-3-12, https://www.riigikohus.ee/et/lahendid?asjaNr=3-3-1-3-12, last accessed 2026/05/06.
RKHKo 03.10.2023, 3-19-1565/46, https://www.riigikohus.ee/et/lahendid?asjaNr=3-19-1565/46, last accessed 2026/05/06.
RKTKo 27.03.1997, 3-2-1-35-97, https://www.riigikohus.ee/et/lahendid?asjaNr=3-2-1-35-97, last accessed 2026/05/06.
RKTKo 30.10.1997, 3-2-1-123-97, https://www.riigikohus.ee/et/lahendid?asjaNr=3-2-1-123-97, last accessed 2026/05/06.
RKTKo 13.06.2002, 3-2-1-63-02, https://www.riigikohus.ee/et/lahendid?asjaNr=3-2-1-63-02, last accessed 2026/05/06.
RKTKo 11.02.2004, 3-2-1-11-04, https://www.riigikohus.ee/et/lahendid?asjaNr=3-2-1-11-04, last accessed 2026/05/06.
RKTKo 13.05.2005, 3-2-1-17-05, https://www.riigikohus.ee/et/lahendid?asjaNr=3-2-1-17-05, last accessed 2026/05/06.
RKTKo 21.12.2005, 3-2-1-95-05, https://www.riigikohus.ee/et/lahendid?asjaNr=3-2-1-95-05, last accessed 2026/05/06.
RKTKo 31.05.2006, 3-2-1-161-05, https://www.riigikohus.ee/et/lahendid?asjaNr=3-2-1-161-05, last accessed 2026/05/06.
RKTKo 31.10.2007, 3-2-1-73-07, https://www.riigikohus.ee/et/lahendid?asjaNr=3-2-1-73-07, last accessed 2026/05/06.
RKTKo 19.02.2008, 3-2-1-145-07, https://www.riigikohus.ee/et/lahendid?asjaNr=3-2-1-145-07, last accessed 2026/05/06.
RKTKo 12.01.2009, 3-2-1-127-08, https://www.riigikohus.ee/et/lahendid?asjaNr=3-2-1-127-08, last accessed 2026/05/06.
RKTKo 09.12.2009, 3-2-1-104-09, https://www.riigikohus.ee/et/lahendid?asjaNr=3-2-1-104-09, last accessed 2026/05/06.
RKTKo 21.12.2010, 3-2-1-67-10, https://www.riigikohus.ee/et/lahendid?asjaNr=3-2-1-67-10, last accessed 2026/05/06.
RKTKo 26.06.2013, 3-2-1-18-13, https://www.riigikohus.ee/et/lahendid?asjaNr=3-2-1-18-13, last accessed 2026/05/06.
RKTKo 25.09.2013, 3-2-1-80-13, https://www.riigikohus.ee/et/lahendid?asjaNr=3-2-1-80-13, last accessed 2026/05/06.
RKTKo 18.02.2015, 3-2-1-159-14, https://www.riigikohus.ee/et/lahendid?asjaNr=3-2-1-159-14, last accessed 2026/05/06.
RKTKo 15.04.2015, 3-2-1-24-15, https://www.riigikohus.ee/et/lahendid?asjaNr=3-2-1-24-15, last accessed 2026/05/06.
RKTKo 17.12.2015, 3-2-1-144-15, https://www.riigikohus.ee/et/lahendid?asjaNr=3-2-1-144-15, last accessed 2026/05/06.
RKTKo 29.03.2017, 3-2-1-153-16, https://www.riigikohus.ee/et/lahendid?asjaNr=3-2-1-153-16, last accessed 2026/05/06.
RKTKo 04.10.2017, 2-15-16007, https://www.riigikohus.ee/et/lahendid?asjaNr=2-15-16007, last accessed 2026/05/06.
RKTKo 19.03.2019, 2-17-17140/47, https://www.riigikohus.ee/et/lahendid?asjaNr=2-17-17140/47, last accessed 2026/05/06.
RKTKo 17.06.2021, 2-16-17491/80, https://www.riigikohus.ee/et/lahendid?asjaNr=2-16-17491/80, last accessed 2026/05/06.
RKTKm 01.12.2021, 2-15-18661, https://www.riigikohus.ee/et/lahendid?asjaNr=2-15-18661, last accessed 2026/05/06.
RKTKo 18.05.2022, 2-20-12495, https://www.riigikohus.ee/et/lahendid?asjaNr=2-20-12495, last accessed 2026/05/06.
RKTKo 21.06.2022, 2-19-10047, https://www.riigikohus.ee/et/lahendid?asjaNr=2-19-10047, last accessed 2026/05/06.

RKTKo 16.11.2022, 2-19-8673/96, https://www.riigikohus.ee/et/lahendid?asjaNr=2-19-8673/96, last accessed 2026/05/06.
RKTKo 09.08.2023, 2-20-5869/87, https://www.riigikohus.ee/et/lahendid?asjaNr=2-20-5869/87, last accessed 2026/05/06.
RKTKo 10.04.2024, 2-20-3847, https://www.riigikohus.ee/et/lahendid?asjaNr=2-20-3847, last accessed 2026/05/06.
RKTKo 03.07.2024, 2-20-2328, https://www.riigikohus.ee/et/lahendid?asjaNr=2-20-2328, last accessed 2026/05/06.
RKTKo 18.02.2025, 3-2-1-159-14, https://www.riigikohus.ee/et/lahendid?asjaNr=3-2-1-159-14, last accessed 2026/05/06.
TlnRnKo 17.01.2017, 2-15-9284, https://www.riigiteataja.ee/kohtulahendid/koik_menetlused.html?otsinguNr=2-15-9284, last accessed 2026/05/06.
TlnRnKo 17.10.2023, 2-21-13323, https://www.riigiteataja.ee/kohtulahendid/koik_menetlused.html?otsinguNr=2-21-13323, last accessed 2026/05/06.
TrRKm 13.06.2025, 1-24-5461, https://www.riigiteataja.ee/kohtulahendid/koik_menetlused.html?otsinguNr=1-24-5461, last accessed 2026/05/06.
TrtRnKo 15.06.2020, 2-18-2988, https://www.riigiteataja.ee/kohtulahendid/koik_menetlused.html?otsinguNr=2-18-2988, last accessed 2026/05/06.

Legal acts

Law of Obligations.—RT I, 04.07.2024, 18. Link: https://www.riigiteataja.ee/en/eli/528072025003/consolide, last accessed 2025/11/27.
State Liability Act.—RT I, 07.05.2025, 19. State Liability Act-Riigi Teataja. Link: https://www.riigiteataja.ee/en/eli/516052025004/consolide, last accessed 2025/11/27.
Administrative Procedure Act.—RT I, 06.07.2023, 31. Link: https://www.riigiteataja.ee/en/eli/505122023003/consolide, last accessed 2025/11/27.

Legal articles

Ginter, C., Soo, A. The 'Public Order' Parachute in Combating Racism and Xenophobia.—Juridica International 31/2022, pp 48-58. Issue article—www.juridicainternational.eu, last accessed 2025/11/27.

Other

Eelnõu 554 (Riigkogu XII koosseis) teise lugemise seletuskiri (Karistuseadustiku kommenteeritud väljaanne § 275-1, para. 1).
Eesti ajakirjanduseetika koodeks. Established in 29.01.1998 by the Estonian Media Companies Association.
Eesti ajakirjanduseetika koodeks. The Public Word Council (Avaliku Sõna Nõukogu in Estonian).
October infringements package: key decisions', EU Commission, 30.10.2020. Link: https://ec.europa.eu/commission/presscorner/api/files/document/print/GA/inf_20_1687/INF_20_1687_EN.pdf, last accessed 2025/11/27.
Karistusseadustiku, kriminaalmenetluse seadustiku ja väärteomenetluse seadustiku muutmise seadus (vaenu õhutamine ja vaenumotiiviga kuriteod). Draft law, 24.05.2023.

Disinformation and Freedom of Expression in Finland: Regulatory Approaches, Digital Challenges, and Future Directions

Päivi Korpisaari

Abstract This chapter examines Finland's approach to disinformation within the broader European regulatory landscape. While Finland consistently ranks among the most resilient countries in Europe in terms of media literacy and public trust, it faces the same structural challenges posed by an evolving information environment, hybrid influence operations, and emerging regulation such as the Digital Services Act (DSA) and the AI Act. The chapter outlines the constitutional and legislative framework relevant to false or misleading information, explores the role of media self-regulation, and discusses procedural avenues for redress. It then evaluates the European Court of Human Rights' first disinformation-related judgment, *Avagyan v. Russia*, and draws lessons for rights-respecting regulation. The chapter concludes by analysing future challenges posed by AI-driven content manipulation, and by emphasising the central importance of trust, transparency, and media literacy for democratic resilience.

1 Introduction: The Finnish Media Landscape and the Concept of Disinformation

In recent years, Finland has received considerable international attention as a high-trust country that has also been successful in its efforts to counter disinformation.[1] Nearly 70 per cent of Finns feel that they can trust the news, and during the COVID-19 pandemic, trust in the news media even increased.[2] Our country ranks year after year at the top of the European media literacy index, which measures the ability of states to resist disinformation.[3]

[1] Bjola and Papadakis (2021).

[2] Newman (2024).

[3] Lessenski (2023).

P. Korpisaari (✉)
Faculty of Law, University of Helsinki, Helsinki, Finland
e-mail: paivi.korpisaari@helsinki.fi

P. Passaglia (ed.), *European Legal Perspectives on Online Disinformation*, Ius Gentium: Comparative Perspectives on Law and Justice 140,
https://doi.org/10.1007/978-3-032-25785-7_8

According to a recent study, trust in traditional news media in Finland is relatively high. Trust is lowest among men, people with lower levels of education, and supporters of the so-called True Finns Party. An interesting detail is that among individual media outlets, trust in the public service broadcaster YLE is particularly strong, with some 56 per cent expressing complete trust. In turn, traditional news media are trusted more than social media as a news source. Only 10 per cent trust social media completely as a news source, while 34 percent do not trust it at all. Of course, "social media as a news source" is a vague category, as social media platforms vary widely, and respondents may also understand the concept in different ways.[4]

Finland's Ministry for Foreign Affairs has correctly considered that combating disinformation is important from the perspective of realisation of human rights. According to the Ministry, Finland's strength lies in high public trust in institutions and the media as well as in teaching media literacy.[5]

Actors seeking to influence public debate through disinformation often rely on a range of mutually reinforcing tactics. They may try to increase polarisation by promoting extreme viewpoints that heighten conflicts and make constructive democratic discussion more difficult. Genuine content—such as photos or videos edited to change their meaning—can be manipulated, or entirely fabricated content may be produced to mimic trustworthy sources, including fake websites, deepfake-style videos, or AI-generated audio. Disinformation campaigns also create false narratives, impersonate individuals or institutions, and misuse diplomatic or official social media accounts to appear credible. Another common strategy is to erode trust in reliable sources by taking information out of context or casting doubt on established expertise. To maximise the impact of these messages, the visibility of disinformation is often artificially boosted through coordinated networks of bots or trolls. In some cases, cyber tools—including hacking and other digital intrusions—are used to steal, alter, or invent information, giving false claims an appearance of authenticity.[6]

The harms of disinformation are well known.[7] Disinformation undermines the foundations of a democratic society by eroding public trust in institutions and the media, threatening the integrity of elections, reducing citizens' capacity to make informed choices, and distorting the conditions for genuine freedom of expression. This is why the European Union and its Member States are intensifying their efforts to counter the activities of actors who disseminate disinformation with the aim of destabilising societies and democratic institutions, exploiting crises, and endangering citizens' safety.[8]

---

[4] Matikainen et al. (2025), pp. 144–145, 151.

[5] Ministry of Foreign Affairs of Finland (2021).

[6] European Council (2025).

[7] However, in some cases, criticism may have been exaggerated, vague, short-sighted, or deliberate. See Heikkilä (2025).

[8] European Commission (2024).

As for Finland, no statutory definition of disinformation has been formulated.[9] The concept appears mainly in policy documents and soft law instruments. The Government Report on Human Rights Policy[10] defines disinformation as deliberately publicly disseminated false and harmful information. Unlike many other definitions, this context does not associate the concept of disinformation with consequences of any kind.

At the end of 2020, the Freedom Online Coalition (FOC) adopted a statement on the spread of disinformation, which Finland prepared together with the United Kingdom. The statement emphasises the importance of respecting freedom of expression and other human rights obligations, as well as the responsibility of states and business actors and international cooperation. Finland promoted international action against disinformation, particularly in its role as chair of the FOC in 2021.

In an FOC paper, disinformation is defined as "the deliberate creation and dissemination of false and/or manipulated information that is intended to deceive and mislead audiences, either to cause harm or for personal, political or financial gain."[11] In turn, the European Commission has defined disinformation as "false or misleading content that is spread with an intention to deceive or secure economic or political gain, and which may cause public harm."[12] Seemingly, in most definitions the concept of disinformation includes an intention to cause harm, annoyance, or damage, or to promote the interests of the speaker or the entity they represent.

In this chapter the concept of disinformation is used in a narrow sense. This means that disinformation is intentional dissemination of false or misleading information. An intention to cause harm or gain some benefit is not associated with it.

Disseminating false information—whether on purpose or without intent—is prohibited under many laws, as will be examined in more detail later. Considering the definition of disinformation, the illegality of the expression is not inherent to it. This means that the content of disinformation as such can be legal or illegal. It is also worth noting that many forms of false or misleading information remain protected under freedom of expression, unless they specifically violate criminal or civil law provisions. In other words, illegality arises from the content, its effects or consequences when a legal provision prohibits such content, effects, or consequences. As a result, dissemination of disinformation as such is not prohibited. To summarise, dissemination of false information may be punishable or otherwise prohibited or under tort liability under legal rules in specific contexts.

---

[9] The concept of disinformation is not defined in DSA either, even though the word disinformation is mentioned in preambles thirteen times. Regulation (EU) 2022/2065 of the European Parliament and of the Council of 19 October 2022 on a Single Market For Digital Services and amending Directive 2000/31/EC (Digital Services Act) (Text with EEA relevance), EUR-Lex, https://eur-lex.europa.eu/eli/reg/2022/2065/oj/eng. Accessed 29 Oct 2025.

[10] Finnish Government (2022), p. 79.

[11] Freedom Online Coalition (2020), p. 1. The development of this statement was led by the governments of Finland and the United Kingdom with input from other Coalition member states and the multi-stakeholder FOC.

[12] European Commission (2025).

As no regulation exists on disinformation, there is no specific regulation concerning online disinformation either. In general, Finnish regulation respects the principle of technological neutrality, according to which freedom of expression is regulated the same way, regardless of the medium.

Disinformation should not be confused with misinformation. No statutory definition of misinformation exists either, but in literature and policy reports it is considered inaccurate information disseminated without intent to deceive. The European Commission defines misinformation as "false or misleading content shared without harmful intent though the effects can be still harmful".[13] In this article, the concept of misinformation is defined as unintentional dissemination of false or misleading information. This refers to situations where the disseminator of the information is unaware that it is false.

2 Freedom of Expression and Access to Information as Fundamental Rights

Section 12 of the Constitution of Finland (Suomen Perustuslaki, 731/1999) regulates Freedom of expression and the right of access to information. It reads as follows:

> *Section 12 - Freedom of expression and the right of access to information*
>
> Everyone enjoys freedom of expression. Freedom of expression entails the right to express, disseminate and receive information, opinions and other communications without prior restraint by anyone. More detailed provisions on exercising freedom of expression are laid down by an Act. Provisions on restrictions relating to pictorial programmes that are necessary for protection of children may be laid down by an Act.
>
> Documents and recordings in the possession of the authorities are public, unless their publication has for compelling reasons been specifically restricted by an Act. Everyone has the right of access to public documents and recordings.

The main principle in Finland is that expression is permitted unless expressly prohibited by law. Prohibition of prior restraint stands at the heart of freedom of expression. According to this principle, no expression may be prohibited in advance. However, if an expression proves to be unlawful, consequences such as punishment or damages may follow afterwards.

According to the Finnish Constitution, fundamental rights belong to every human being. As a starting point, protection of fundamental rights does not apply to legal entities such as companies and associations. However, in terms of freedom of expression, the preparatory works of the Constitution refer to protection of journalistic work, which means that the provision can be interpreted so that publishing and broadcasting companies, as well as other legal entities, also enjoy the constitutional protection of

[13] Ibid.

freedom of expression.[14] Media companies are also protected by protection of property under Section 15 of the Constitution and freedom to engage in commercial activity under Section 18 of the Constitution.

The status of freedom of expression as a fundamental right influences Finnish jurisprudence in two principal ways. First, it must be considered during the legislative process, ensuring that any statutory provisions respect constitutional guarantees. Second, it shapes interpretation and application of the law in individual cases, guiding courts towards rights-consistent outcomes. In Finland, constitutional protection of a fundamental right implies that the scope for restricting it is exceptionally narrow—if not entirely excluded.

Since prohibiting dissemination of disinformation restricts the fundamental right to freedom of speech, an acceptable reason for it must be given in each case under the Finnish system of fundamental rights. Restrictions on freedom of expression must also be compatible with Finland's international human rights obligations, such as the European Convention on Human Rights. Any restriction of fundamental rights is only possible if all the following preconditions set by the Finnish Constitutional Law Committee are fulfilled[15]:

1. The restriction is prescribed by law. This means that legislative powers should not be delegated to a lower level than the law.
2. The law is precise and clearly defined.
3. The restriction is acceptable in relation to the objective pursued. When assessing this, the European Convention on Human Rights and other international human rights treaties may also be relevant.
4. Proportionality of the restriction: a restriction is permissible only if the objective cannot be achieved by less intrusive means. Moreover, the restriction must not go beyond what is justified, in view of the importance of the interest underlying the restriction when compared to that of the interest subject to the restriction. Interest in limiting a fundamental right must be balanced against interest in protecting some other right.
5. Immunity of the core area of a fundamental right: restriction of the core content of a fundamental right cannot be achieved by an ordinary law. This means that fundamental rights cannot be limited to the extent that would invalidate their core content, unless the constitution is changed.
6. Sufficient legal protection: when fundamental rights are infringed, the state must guarantee adequate legal protection, such as the right to appeal.
7. Compliance with the obligations of human rights: infringements of fundamental rights must not conflict with Finland's international human rights obligations. As a result, the interpretative harmonisation of fundamental and human rights is considered important.[16]

[14] Alén-Savikko and Korpisaari (2021).

[15] See Constitutional Law Committee Report (PeVM 25/1994 vp).

[16] Freedom of expression is also guaranteed as a human right in Article 19 of the United Nations Universal Declaration of Human Rights, in Article 10 of the European Convention on Human

The laws contain various restrictions on freedom of expression, which will be discussed later.

The Act on the Exercise of Freedom of Expression in the Mass Media (Laki sananvapauden käyttämisestä joukkoviestinnässä, 460/2003)[17] contains more detailed provisions on exercising freedom of expression in the mass media. It applies to all forms of mass media: printed publications, radio, television, and the Internet. According to Section 1 of the Act, in the application of the Act, interference with the activities of the media is legitimate only in so far as it is unavoidable, taking due note of the importance of freedom of expression in a democracy subject to the rule of law.

While the Act on the Exercise of Freedom of Expression in the Mass Media does not define which expressions are lawful or unlawful in terms of content, it does regulate—among other things—the obligation to appoint an editor-in-chief for periodical publications, as well as the obligations of publishers and programme operators. Chapter 3 provides sections for the right to reply and correction and the duty to publish a reply or correction.[18]

According to Section 9, a private individual, a corporation, a foundation, and a public authority have the right to have erroneous information on them or their operations contained in a periodical, network publication, or programme corrected in the same publication or in a programme by the broadcaster in question, unless such correction is manifestly unnecessary owing to the minor significance of the error.

According to Section 10, the responsible editor must publish a reply or correction, free of charge and without undue delay, appropriately extensively and in the same manner as the message on which the demand for a reply or correction is based. The contents of the reply or correction must not be illegal or offensive. Where necessary, the responsible editor should assist in the technical realisation of the reply.

As it reads in the Sections, the right to reply is applicable only if the expression is published in a periodical, network publication, or programme. Those are mediums that need to have an editor-in-chief, whose task it is to decide about publication of a reply or correction. So, if false information has been published in an online site such as Facebook, Instagram, or YouTube that has no editor-in-chief, there is no right to reply or correction. The same applies to web discussion forums. However, regarding web discussion forums that are related to a periodical, network publication, or programme, good journalistic ethics might require certain action from the editorial staff.

Media companies as well as other companies enjoy freedom to engage in commercial activity as guaranteed in Section 18, Subsection 1 of the Finnish Constitution, which states that “everyone has the right, as provided by an Act, to earn his or her

Rights, and in Article 11 of the EU Charter of Fundamental Rights. Those are not discussed further here.

17 Act available online at https://finlex.fi/fi/lainsaadanto/2003/460 (in Finnish). Unofficial English translation available at https://www.finlex.fi/en/legislation/translations/2003/eng/460. Accessed 27 Oct 2025.

18 For more information on Finnish media law, see Alén-Savikko and Korpisaari (2021).

livelihood by the employment, occupation or commercial activity of his or her choice. The public authorities shall take responsibility for the protection of the labour force." The right to freedom of enterprise has not been considered as a very significant argument within the case law concerning exercise of freedom of expression. This follows from the fact that, in these types of cases, a need usually arises for the court to strike a balance between many different fundamental rights.

Section 10 of the Finnish Constitution guarantees the right to privacy. It reads as follows:

> *Section 10 - The right to privacy*
>
> Everyone's private life, honour and the sanctity of the home are guaranteed. More detailed provisions on the protection of personal data are laid down by an Act.
>
> The secrecy of correspondence, telephony and other confidential communications is inviolable.
>
> Limitations of the secrecy of communications may be imposed by an Act if they are necessary in the investigation of crimes that jeopardise the security of the individual or society or the sanctity of the home, at trials and security checks, during deprivation of liberty, and for the purpose of obtaining information on military activities or other such activities that pose a serious threat to national security. (817/2018, entry into force 15.10.2018)

The first Subsection of Section 10 guarantees the right to honour. This means that the state has an obligation to protect its citizens against attacks against their honour.

According to Section 22 of the Finnish Constitution, the public authorities will guarantee observance of basic rights, liberties, and human rights. Consequently, fundamental and human rights possess significance in legal relationships between private entities in addition to being relevant in relations between the state and an individual. This is because—due to the provision—the state must not only refrain from violating the fundamental and human rights of its citizens but must also take active measures to ensure that these rights are upheld. This may require, for example, introduction or maintenance of criminal penalties for defamation or establishing liability for damage caused by a violation of fundamental or human rights.

The rights to freedom of expression and to privacy possess equal normative status under both constitutional and human rights law. Accordingly, whether in the legislative process or in the interpretation and application of legal provisions, a fair balance must be struck between these competing rights in accordance with fundamental and human rights standards. This requirement has become especially salient in defamation proceedings and in cases concerning dissemination of private or personal information.

Since Finland has no constitutional court, cases concerning freedom of expression are decided in general courts and ultimately in the Supreme Court of Finland, which acts as the final instance in civil and criminal matters.

3 Regulation Relevant to Disinformation

These constitutional principles are further elaborated in Finnish legislation. In relation to addressing the spread of disinformation, the guiding principle has been that regulation of platform companies should aim to primarily address manipulative behaviour rather than the content of messages, which is regarded as important in terms of freedom of expression.[19]

The following overview does not aim to be exhaustive; rather, it highlights legislative provisions particularly relevant to tackling the spread of disinformation while also taking into consideration the implementation and application of the EU Digital Services Act (DSA).[20]

Concerning the DSA, disinformation is not mentioned in the articles, but it is mentioned in recitals 2, 9, 69, 83, 84, 88, 95, 104, 106, and 108. DSA Article 16 contains a notice and action mechanism, which requires providers of hosting services to put in place mechanisms to allow notifications of illegal content. This regulation is implemented in Finland by the Act on the Supervision of Online Intermediary Services (18/2024).[21] The Act includes provisions on competent authorities, penalties for storage service providers and online platform providers, and blocking access to services. The competent authorities are the Finnish Transport and Communications Agency, the Consumer Ombudsman, and the Data Ombudsman.[22]

Further, the AI Act[23] contains some articles that can be relevant in relation to regulation of disinformation. For example, Article 5(1)(a) of the AI Act prohibits placing on the market, putting into service, or using an AI system that "deploys subliminal techniques beyond a person's consciousness or purposefully manipulative or deceptive techniques, with the objective or the effect of materially distorting the behaviour of a person or a group of persons by appreciably impairing their ability to make an informed decision, thereby causing them to take a decision that they would not have otherwise taken in a manner that causes or is reasonably likely to cause that person, another person or group of persons significant harm." Legislation on national implementation of the AI Act has not yet been passed. However, a legislative proposal concerning implementation is currently being considered by the Finnish parliament.[24]

---

[19] Finnish Government (2022), p. 80.

[20] For a comprehensive database on Finnish disinformation regulation see Hard Disc 2025.

[21] Laki verkon välityspalvelujen valvonnasta. Act available online at https://www.finlex.fi/fi/lainsaadanto/2024/18 (in Finnish). Accessed 29 Oct 2025.

[22] For more details see Sections 1–3.

[23] Regulation (EU) 2024/1689 of the European Parliament and of the Council of 13 June 2024 laying down harmonised rules on artificial intelligence and amending Regulations (EC) No 300/2008, (EU) No 167/2013, (EU) No 168/2013, (EU) 2018/858, (EU) 2018/1139 and (EU) 2019/2144 and Directives 2014/90/EU, (EU) 2016/797 and (EU) 2020/1828 (Artificial Intelligence Act).

[24] Government bill to Parliament on legislation supplementing the EU Artificial Intelligence Regulation (HE 46/2025 vp). Available online at https://www.eduskunta.fi/valtiopaivaasiat/HE+46/2025 (in Finnish). Accessed 01 Dec 2025.

4 Criminal and Civil Liability for False Information

The Criminal Code of Finland[25] contains several provisions according to which dissemination of incorrect or false information is punishable. The provisions can be divided into two groups, based on whether they apply to a specific person or generally to a group of people or society. We will first examine the second category.

Chapter 11, Section 10 (511/2011) on *Agitation against a population group* criminalises dissemination or making available or keeping available to the public such information, an opinion or other message where a certain group is threatened, defamed, or insulted on the basis of its race, colour, descent, national or ethnic origin, religion or belief, sexual orientation, or disability or on another comparable basis. The purpose of the provision is to condemn hate speech and to safeguard equality and human dignity. It is not intended to condemn disinformation, but it also applies to situations where false information is presented about, for example, an ethnic or religious group.

Chapter 12, Section 2 (578/1995) of the Criminal Code of Finland criminalises *Incitement to war.* The provision states that "[i]f a person in Finland or a Finnish citizen outside of Finland, during an ongoing or imminent military crisis or international political crisis concerning Finland, for the purpose of causing Finland to be at war or become the target of a military operation, [...] 3) systematically disseminates manifestly unfounded or misleading information on Finland's national defence or the military or defence policy intentions of Finland so that the act clearly increases the risk of Finland being at war or becoming the target of a military operation, the person shall be sentenced for incitement to war to imprisonment for at least one year and at most ten years."

Additionally, some forms of disseminating images or recordings that depict sexual indecency in a realistic or truthful manner are criminalised as *distributing sexually offensive images* in Chapter 17, Section 18 (650/2004) of the Criminal Code.[26]

Marketing offences involve a slightly different type of misrepresentation. Chapter 30, Section 1 (475/1999) on marketing offences states that "A person who, in the professional marketing of goods, services, real estate, bonds and securities of a private limited liability company, or other commodities, gives false or misleading information that is significant from the perspective of the group at which the marketing is directed shall be sentenced for a marketing offence to a fine or to imprisonment for at most one year."

---

[25] Rikoslaki (39/1889). Act available online at https://www.finlex.fi/fi/lainsaadanto/1889/39-001 (in Finnish). Unofficial English translation available at https://www.finlex.fi/en/legislation/translations/1889/eng/39-001. Accessed 01 Dec 2025.

[26] "*Distribution of a sexually obscene image*—A person who manufactures, offers for sale or for rent or otherwise offers or makes available, keeps available, exports from, imports to or transports through Finland to another country, or otherwise distributes images or visual recordings that in a sexually obscene manner, either factually or realistically, depict a child, violence or. bestiality. shall be sentenced for distribution of a sexually obscene image to a fine or imprisonment for at most two years. (540/2011) An attempt is punishable." (Unofficial translation by the Ministry of Justice). See also Chapter 10, Section 7 (723/2022) on unauthorised distribution of sexual images.

Unfair competition offences are criminalised in Chapter 30, Section 2 (769/1990) of the Criminal Code. According to that section "A person who in business activities uses a false or misleading expression concerning his or her own business or the business of another and thus causes damage to another trader shall be sentenced for an unfair competition offence to a fine or to imprisonment for at most one year". *Market manipulation*, in turn, is criminalised in Chapter 51, Section 3, Subsection 2 (521/2016) of Criminal Code, which states that "A person who manipulates the market in order to obtain economic benefit for himself or herself or another person, by disseminating information through the media or by any other means, which gives false or misleading signals as to the supply of, demand for, or price of a financial instrument or a related spot commodity contract, or secures the price of a financial instrument or a related spot commodity contract at an abnormal or artificial level, shall be sentenced for market manipulation to a fine or to imprisonment for at most two years." An aggravated form of market manipulation appears in Chapter 51, Section 4.

Chapter 34, Section 10 (578/1995), for its part, criminalises a *false report of a danger.* According to the provision, a person "who makes a false report about a bomb, fire, distress at sea, major accident or other equivalent distress or danger, which is conducive to leading to rescue or safety measures being taken or the arousal of panic, shall be sentenced for a false report of a danger to a fine or to imprisonment for at most one year."

The Criminal Code of Finland also includes provisions on criminalisation of an *information offence concerning the securities market* (Chapter 51, Section 5, 1235/2018).

The Consumer Protection Act (38/1978, Kuluttajansuojalaki) Chapter 2, Section 6, Subsection 1 (561/2008) contains a *prohibition on providing false or misleading information.*[27] According to that Section "In marketing or a customer relationship, false or misleading information shall not be provided if the information is likely to lead to a consumer making a purchasing decision or other decision relating to a consumer good or service that the consumer would not have made without the information provided." The aim of the Section is to combat forms of disinformation that appear in a commercial context. In doing so, it promotes integrity and trust in both digital and physical market environments.

An example of crimes against individuals is *defamation*, which is criminalised in Chapter 24, Section 9 (879/2013) of the Criminal Code. It reads as follows:

A person who

1. presents false information on or a false insinuation against another person so that the act is conducive to causing damage or suffering to that person or subjecting that person to contempt, or
2. disparages another person in a manner other than that referred to in paragraph 1

---

[27] Act available online at https://www.finlex.fi/fi/lainsaadanto/1978/38 (in Finnish). Unofficial English translation available at https://www.finlex.fi/en/legislation/translations/1978/eng/38. Accessed 29 Oct 2025.

> shall be sentenced for defamation to a fine.
>
> A person who presents false information on or a false insinuation against a deceased person, so that the act is conducive to causing suffering to a person to whom the deceased was particularly close, shall also be sentenced for defamation.
>
> Criticism that is directed at a person's activities in politics, business, public office or position, science, art, or in other comparable public activity and that does not clearly exceed what can be deemed acceptable does not constitute defamation referred to in subsection 1, paragraph 2.
>
> Presenting information for the purpose of dealing with a matter of general importance shall also not be considered defamation, if presenting the information, considering its content, the rights of others, and other circumstances, does not clearly exceed what can be deemed acceptable.

An aggravated form appears in Chapter 24, Section 10. Defamation can be interpreted as a form of disinformation, especially when false information is disseminated through the press or social media.

Honour has traditionally been afforded a high level of protection in Finland. Following several judgments issued by the ECtHR against Finland for violations of freedom of expression, the courts have adopted a more favourable stance towards freedom of expression. The last Subsection of the provision came into force at the beginning of 2014. Its purpose is to limit the scope of punishability and emphasise the importance of weighing and balancing the right of freedom of expression against the right to private life and honour, as expressed in the practice of the ECtHR. Prior to amendment of the provision, the maximum penalty for defamation was six months' imprisonment, but because the ECtHR considered that in many cases it is unacceptable for journalists to face the risk of imprisonment, the penalty was reduced to fines. The maximum penalty for aggravated defamation is two years' imprisonment.

As stated in the provision, defamation may be committed by presenting false information, or a false insinuation about another person, in a manner that is likely to cause harm or suffering to that person or to expose them to contempt. Defamation may also concern a deceased person if the act is liable to cause suffering to an individual who was particularly close to the deceased. Defamation can only be directed at a person. For instance, a company or association cannot be the target of defamation, so presenting false information about them would not be punishable as defamation at all. However, the act may fulfil the criteria for another crime or illegal act.

Assessment of whether a statement is conducive to causing damage, suffering, or contempt in a defamation case is objective, considering both the content of the expression and the surrounding circumstances. A person of particularly sensitive disposition does not enjoy a higher level of protection than an average individual. In certain instances, however, the victim's profession or social role may be relevant, as some statements may have greater defamatory potential in specific contexts. For example, accusing an individual of being a racist may be considered defamatory if that person works with immigrants or in a profession that requires impartiality and equality, whereas the same statement may not be defamatory when directed at a politician advocating for restrictive immigration policies, or at a member of a motorcycle club publicly known for anti-immigrant views.[28]

In Supreme Court case KKO 2010:88[29] a television programme had claimed that three of the individuals named on the programme were members of a group that finances a terrorist organisation operating abroad. According to information that the journalist had obtained from Finland, the individuals in question were detained in Iraq on suspicion of being involved in terrorist activities. They had since been released. The allegations and insinuations made in the programme were based mainly on interview statements from eight people, whose identities the interviewing journalist did not disclose. During the case, the journalist explained how they had tried to verify the information presented. However, the court held that, considering the inadequacy of the explanation of the sources and information received, which called into question the reliability of the sources, and the facts known to the journalist, it must have been clear that there were insufficient grounds to support the programme's claims and insinuations. On that basis, the editor and editor-in-chief of the programme were found guilty of defamation and ordered to pay damages.

5 Self-Regulation and Professional Standards

The Guidelines for Journalists[30] are designed for self-regulation by the media. The guidelines apply to all journalistic work and editorial content in all publication channels used by the editorial office. According to the introduction, "Editorial content means material produced, commissioned, edited or highlighted by the editorial office, regardless of the medium or how it is presented or the technology used to produce it. Decision-making power must always rest with the editorial office." The guidelines stipulate, among other things, that:

> 7. The journalist has a duty to seek truthful information.
>
> 9. Information must be checked as thoroughly as possible – even if it has been previously published.
>
> 11. The public must be able to distinguish fact from opinion and fictional material.
>
> 12. Information sources must be approached critically. This is particularly important when the matter is controversial or when the source of the information may be intended for personal gain or to damage others.

---

[28] See Supreme Court decision KKO 2011:71, in which the charges were nevertheless dismissed, as the statement in question was general in nature and directed at such a broad group of people that it could not reasonably be regarded as referring to any specific individual, including the complainant who was employed at a refugee reception centre. The precedent available at https://www.finlex.fi/fi/oikeuskaytanto/korkein-oikeus/ennakkopaatokset/2011/71 (in Finnish). Accessed 27 Oct 2025.

[29] The decision available at https://www.finlex.fi/fi/oikeuskaytanto/korkein-oikeus/ennakkopaatokset/2010/88 (in Finnish). Accessed 27 Oct 2025.

[30] Council For Mass Media in Finland (2024) Journalists Guidelines. https://jsn.fi/journalistin-ohjeet/ (in Finnish.). English translation of the Guidelines also available at https://jsn.fi/en/journalists-guidelines/. Accessed 30 Oct 2025.

Any person who believes that the press, radio, or television has breached good professional practice may submit a complaint to the Council for Mass Media (CMM).[31] The CMM is a self-regulatory body founded by publishers and journalists in the field of mass communication. Its purpose is to interpret and promote good professional practice and to safeguard freedom of speech and publication. The Council also considers the methods by which journalists obtain information. Although it has no legal jurisdiction or public authority, its decisions carry considerable weight and are widely respected and observed within the media sector.

The Council may also consider complaints concerning online material, provided that the content in question is deemed to have been published by an online medium falling within its remit. A complaint does not need to concern the complainant personally; however, if the case involves an identifiable injured party, that person's consent is required for the matter to be processed.

If the Council finds that a media outlet has violated good professional practice, it issues a notice of opinion, which the outlet concerned is obliged to publish promptly. Should the media organisation fail to do so, the notice will be made public by other means. The complaint procedure is free of charge.

Most Finnish media outlets have signed the Council's Basic Agreement, authorising the CMM to handle complaints directly concerning their activities. In addition, when a case involves matters of significant ethical or professional principle, the Council may initiate proceedings on its own initiative.

The Council has no authority over websites or discussion forums. However, following the amendment adopted on 17 March 2026, journalistic social media influencers may be accepted as members of the Council for Mass Media if they publish a sufficient amount of journalistic content and have an editor-in-chief. In addition, the media must undertake to comply with the Guidelines for Journalists and the Basic Agreement of the Council for Mass Media.

6 Reporting Procedures and Other Mechanisms for Addressing False Information

If dissemination of false information constitutes a criminal offence against a specific individual, the injured party must request an investigation by the police. This is the case, for example, if someone considers themselves to be the victim of defamation. According to Chapter 10, Section 2, Subsection 1 of the Criminal Investigation Act (Esitutkintalaki, 805/2011), the police will then investigate and refer the matter to the prosecutor for consideration of charges or for the issue of a summary penal judgment or summary penal fine. However, there are some exceptions to this. According to the Criminal Investigation Act, Chapter 3, Section 10 the prosecutor may, upon the recommendation of the investigator in charge, decide not to conduct a preliminary

[31] English overview of the CMM's function and tasks see: https://jsn.fi/en/what-is-the-cmm/. Accessed 28 Nov 2025.

investigation or to terminate it if, pursuant to Chapter 1, Sections 7 or 8 of the Act on Criminal Proceedings, or other corresponding provisions of law, the prosecutor would be required to refrain from bringing charges and no important public or private interest requires that charges be brought.[32]

The prosecutor may also decide, on the recommendation of the investigator in charge, to terminate the preliminary investigation if the costs of continuing the investigation would be clearly disproportionate to the nature of the matter under investigation and the penalty that could be expected, or if, on the basis of the preliminary investigation measures already carried out, it is highly probable that the prosecutor would have to refrain from bringing charges on grounds other than those mentioned in paragraph 1. Termination of the preliminary investigation also requires that no important public or private interest requires continuation of the preliminary investigation.

According to Chapter 10, Section 2, Subsection 1 of the Criminal Investigation Act on the conclusion of the criminal investigation, the matter shall be submitted to the prosecutor for the consideration of charges or for the issue of a summary penal judgment or summary penal fine.

According to the Criminal Procedure Act[33] the prosecutor decides whether to bring charges based on evidence gathered during the pre-trial investigation. It is the prosecutor who determines whether the suspect should be formally accused of a crime. If charges are filed, the prosecutor prepares an application for a summons, which sets out the offence in question and forms the basis for the case in court. If the prosecutor decides not to press charges, they issue a written decision explaining why no prosecution will follow.

A prosecutor must refrain from bringing charges if the evidence is insufficient to establish a probable case against the suspect. When there are probable grounds to believe the suspect committed the offence, charges are normally required. However, even in such situations, the prosecutor may choose not to prosecute—for example when the offence is minor, the suspect is a minor, or when imposing a punishment would be unreasonable or serve no useful purpose.[34]

The limitation period for prosecution depends on the maximum penalty prescribed by law for the offence in question. As a rule, the limitation period begins to run from the date of the offence. The limitation period is usually 2–20 years. The limitation period is interrupted when the defendant is served with a summons to appear in court. Limitation periods are stated in Chapter 8 of the Criminal Code of Finland.

In its judgment KKO 2024:3, the Supreme Court examined the issue of limitation. In that case, an individual was charged with defamation for presenting false information or insinuations about another person in a Facebook post and its comments section or otherwise disparaging that person. Both the post and the discussion section were

---

[32] An unofficial translation by the Ministry of Justice: https://www.finlex.fi/fi/lainsaadanto/saadoskaannokset/2011/eng/805. Accessed 30 Oct 2025.

[33] Laki oikeudenkäynnistä rikosasioissa (689/1997). Available at https://www.finlex.fi/fi/lainsaadanto/saadoskokoelma/1997/689. Accessed 30 Oct 2025.

[34] See Sections 5–8 of the Act.

available to read until the charges were brought. On the grounds stated in its ruling, the Supreme Court considered that the limitation period for bringing charges should be calculated from the date of publication of the posts. The Supreme Court stated that, unlike incitement against a group of people, keeping the statement available was not punishable. Only presenting the statement was punishable. Additionally, the Court ruled that the manner and method of expression could affect the conclusion that actions constituting a crime against honour do not necessarily end when the information or suggestion that defames another person or otherwise disparages them is first published. Due to the diversity of methods, it is also possible to pay attention in the assessment to what actual opportunities the perpetrator had to remove the offensive or derogatory expression from public access and how the perpetrator used that opportunity. In this case, however, the defendant was not said to have republished his writings or taken any other active steps to attract new readers or maintain their visibility after publication.

Consumers who have suffered damage due to misleading or incorrect marketing may demand that the incorrect product be repaired, the price be reduced, or that compensation be paid for damage. The Consumer Ombudsman may also demand that misleading marketing be stopped in accordance with the Consumer Protection Act. The Consumer Ombudsman may also impose a penalty payment on the party responsible for misleading marketing. Since July 2020, the Consumer Ombudsman has had the right to request the Market Court to impose a fine on a business operator who acts to the detriment of consumers intentionally or through negligence and violates or neglects the fundamental rights of consumers.[35]

The legislation makes it possible to try to identify the sender of the message in some cases. However, in many cases, the service provider does not know the identity of the sender of the message. According to Section 17, Subsection 1 of the Act on the Exercise of Freedom of Expression in the Mass Media (460/2003) "On the request of an official with the power of arrest, as referred to in Chapter 1, Section 6(1), of the Coercive Measures Act (450/1987), a public prosecutor, or an injured party, a court may order the keeper of a transmitter, server, or other similar device to release the information required for identification of the sender of a network message to the requester, provided that there are probable reasons to believe that the contents of the message are such that providing it to the public is a criminal offence. However, the identifying information may be ordered to be released to the injured party only in the event that they have the right to bring a private prosecution for the offence. The request must be filed with the District Court of the domicile of the keeper of the device, or with the District Court of Helsinki, within three months of publication of the message in question. The court may reinforce the order by imposing a threat of a fine."

An unlawful message may be ordered to be removed. According to Section 18, Subsection 1 of the same Act "On the request of the public prosecutor, the head of a pre-trial investigation, or the injured party, a court may order that the publisher, broadcaster or keeper of a transmitter, server or other comparable device is to cease

[35] See Consumer Protection Act Chapter 2, Sections 15a-20.

the distribution of a published network message, if it is evident on the basis of the contents of the message that providing it to the public is a criminal offence. The court shall deal with the request as a matter of urgency. Before issuing a cease order, the court shall reserve the intended addressee of the order and the sender of the network message an opportunity to be heard, unless the urgency of the matter otherwise necessitates." According to the first sentence of Subsection 3 "The person who has been issued with a cease order, as well as the sender of the network message, have the right to apply for the reversal of the cease order from the court that originally issued it." According to Section 22, Subsection 3 "The court may order that a network message whose contents have been found unlawful be rendered unavailable to the public and destroyed. The provisions on procedure relating to forfeiture apply to such proceedings, in so far as appropriate."

The Finnish Transport and Communications Agency Traficom[36] may impose a fine on the mere conduit, caching or hosting service provider for a violation of the DSA.[37]

7 Discussion and Future Perspectives: Rights-Respecting Governance in a High-Trust Society

Disinformation is a complex and evolving phenomenon. False or misleading content can cause real harm to individuals, institutions, and democratic processes. Yet measures aimed at countering it may themselves endanger freedom of expression, potentially generating harms greater than the disinformation in question. Any regulatory response must therefore be both evidence-based and carefully proportionate.

The DSA reflects this dilemma. It does not ban disinformation outright; instead, it requires VLOPs to assess and mitigate systemic risks, including those linked to disinformation, while at the same time safeguarding fundamental rights.[38] This risk-based approach acknowledges that disinformation is not a uniform category: false statements can range from trivial misunderstandings to coordinated manipulation; they may originate from credible or non-credible sources; and their impact depends on context, audience reach, and intent. A one-size-fits-all prohibition would be incompatible with democratic debate.

The ECtHR's recent judgment in *Avagyan v. Russia*—its first case directly addressing "disinformation legislation and its application"—illustrates the dangers of overbroad or poorly applied restrictions. The applicant, who used Instagram mainly to advertise her nail salon, questioned the accuracy of COVID-19 data and government transparency. She was convicted of disseminating "false information" and fined.

---

[36] Liikenne- ja viestintävirasto Traficom.

[37] See Laki verkon välityspalvelujen valvonnasta 18/2024 (Act on the Supervision of Network Intermediary Services), Sections 14–17 and 20.

[38] See, for example, DSA recitals 79–88.

The Strasbourg Court found violations of both Article 6 and Article 10. Crucially, the domestic courts had not established the legally required element of deliberate falsehood; instead, they shifted the burden of proof to the applicant. They also overlooked that her comments concerned matters of public interest, shared with a very small audience and promptly challenged by another user. The absence of a prosecuting party further undermined procedural fairness. The ECtHR held that the interference was neither necessary nor proportionate and carried a chilling effect on public debate.

The judgment underlines several issues relevant for future regulation: the need to prove intention or knowledge of falsehood; the importance of context, reach, and actual risk; and the requirement that courts safeguard open debate, especially during crises when information is fluid and public scrutiny is vital. It also shows that disinformation cannot be effectively regulated through strict-liability or punitive models that suppress debate rather than address harm.

Looking forward, the DSA's harmonised framework is a constructive step in addressing cross-border information flows and platform power. However, regulatory intervention alone cannot solve the disinformation challenge. Over-regulation risks silencing legitimate criticism and weakening democratic resilience. The most sustainable defence is likely to be a combination of transparency obligations, platform accountability, robust procedural safeguards, and strengthened media literacy and critical thinking skills. Empowering users to recognise, question, and contextualise information is a long-term solution that supports, rather than constrains, freedom of expression.

8 Conclusions

The Finnish approach to disinformation rests on a clear normative foundation: the right to information is an essential component of freedom of expression, and protecting that right requires the state both to uphold open access to reliable information and to avoid actions that might facilitate the spread of false or manipulative content. Finland's human rights policy therefore emphasises that measures to counter disinformation must never undermine the very rights they aim to protect. Restrictions must remain transparent, proportionate, and grounded in clear lines of responsibility, while overall management of the information environment must be open to public scrutiny. Strengthening citizens' skills—including media literacy, critical reasoning, and the capacity for informed participation—remains central to this strategy.[39]

At the European level, Finland is an active contributor to the development of robust, rights-respecting tools for addressing disinformation. This includes engagement in EU strategic communication, cooperation on platform regulation and initiatives aimed at safeguarding electoral processes and public debate from foreign influence. The Finnish government emphasises that regulation should target manipulative behaviour rather than the content of speech, reflecting a longstanding constitutional

[39] Finnish Government (2022), pp. 79 – 80.

commitment to technology-neutral, content-neutral regulation and the primacy of freedom of expression.[40]

Finland's internal security assessments acknowledge the increasing scale and sophistication of hostile information influence. As a member of the EU and NATO, Finland faces coordinated, multi-layered operations that aim to destabilise democratic institutions, manipulate public attitudes and erode societal cohesion. Hybrid influencing blends political, economic, cyber and information tools, and may also exploit humanitarian issues such as migration. While these developments pose challenges, the Finnish authorities consider the country's trust-based and highly literate society to be comparatively resilient. Countering such influence demands cross-sector cooperation, strong legislative frameworks and close international coordination, alongside efforts to raise awareness and improve media literacy among the population.[41]

According to the Government Report on Internal Security, hybrid influencing has increased, and its range of methods is broad. It includes political, diplomatic, economic, and military means as well as information and cyber operations. Hybrid influencing can also involve the use of migration, refugees, or citizens of countries engaged in hybrid activities who are residing in other nations. Combating hybrid influencing requires a cross-administrative approach and close cooperation with the private and third sectors. Legislative measures, as well as international and EU cooperation, are also used to counter hybrid threats. In countering information influence, raising awareness among citizens and the media, along with media literacy, plays a key role. Authorities' presence on social media aims to limit the space and opportunities for actors spreading targeted disinformation and attempting to create societal instability. Some social media companies have also taken steps to prevent the spread of disinformation.

Recent research, however, shows that trust is not evenly distributed across institutions or demographic groups. This unevenness underscores the need for sustained investment in civic education, societal dialogue, and long-term efforts to reinforce shared democratic values. Since effective information influence operates by gradually shaping worldviews rather than relying on individual falsehoods, Finnish policy must remain attentive to broader structural vulnerabilities in the information environment.

The main challenge is not individual disinformation campaigns. Effective information influence is typically long-term: it reinforces certain narratives and worldviews over time, shaping people's thinking on a subconscious level. The aim is to weaken the target society's ability to function and make sound decisions.[42] A society's resilience depends heavily on people's trust—trust in democracy, in public institutions and in one another. This trust helps shield society from vulnerabilities and strengthens its psychological preparedness in times of crisis. However, recent research in Finland shows that levels of trust vary between institutions and that there are noticeable differences across regions and demographic groups. Countering

[40] Ibid. pp. 80 – 81.

[41] Finnish Government (2025), pp. 22 – 23.

[42] Ibid., p. 23.

information influence therefore requires broad cooperation across society, including active efforts to maintain and strengthen citizens' critical media literacy.[43]

Open, proactive, and strategically coordinated communication from public authorities is central to countering the influence of information. Effective communication can strengthen public trust, promote civic participation, and reinforce social cohesion—all of which are essential components of a society's overall resilience. Considering the rapidly evolving security and information landscape, Finland must be able not only to anticipate, but also prevent, information influence. This work must be seamlessly integrated into the authorities' broader security management and support national leaders' decision-making processes.

Finally, public authorities' strategic communication plays a decisive role in resilience. Timely, transparent, and coherent communication strengthens trust, supports informed civic participation and enhances psychological preparedness during both normal times and crises. To remain effective, strategic communication must be grounded in situational awareness, coordinated across sectors, and aligned with clear objectives. In an era of rapidly evolving hybrid threats, Finland's ability not only to respond to but also to anticipate and prevent information influence is essential. Maintaining a high-trust society is therefore both a security imperative and a human rights commitment—and requires continuous, inclusive and rights-respecting cooperation throughout society.[44]

Looking ahead, Finland will face new challenges as communication technologies evolve. Tools powered by artificial intelligence can now create highly convincing images, videos, and messages that look real even when they are not. As these tools become more common, it will become harder for people to judge what information is trustworthy. This means Finland will need not only updated regulation, but also stronger "information resilience": the skills, habits and public institutions that help people evaluate information responsibly and make informed decisions.[45]

Finland is in a strong position because of its high level of media literacy and trust in public institutions. However, maintaining this advantage will require long-term investment in education, transparent and reliable public communication, close cooperation within the EU, and continuous monitoring of new technological risks. The challenge is no longer only to stop intentionally false information, but also to ensure that the overall information environment remains healthy, open, and supportive of democratic participation. In other words, countering disinformation is not just about reacting to problems—it is about shaping future conditions in which democracy and public trust can continue to thrive.

[43] Ibid.

[44] Ibid., pp. 23 – 24.

[45] Ibid., pp. 22 – 23.

References

Alén-Savikko A, Korpisaari P (2021) International Encyclopaedia of Media Law Finland, 2nd edn. Kluwer Law International, Netherlands

Bjola C, Papadakis K (2021) Digital propaganda, counterpublics, and the disruption of the public sphere: The Finnish approach to building digital resilience. In: Clack T, Johnson R. (eds) The World Information War. Routledge, London

Council for the Mass Media in Finland (2025) What is the CMM. https://jsn.fi/en/what-is-the-cmm/. Accessed 28 Nov 2025

European Commission (2024) A strengthened EU Code of Practice on Disinformation. https://commission.europa.eu/strategy-and-policy/priorities-2019-2024/new-push-european-democracy/protecting-democracy/strengthened-eu-code-practice-disinformation_en. Accessed 29 Oct 2025

European Commission (2025) Tackling online disinformation. https://digital-strategy.ec.europa.eu/en/policies/online-disinformation. Accessed 29 Oct 2025

European Council (2025) Disinformation and democratic resilience. https://www.consilium.europa.eu/fi/policies/disinformation-and-democratic-resilience/. Accessed 12 Dec 2025

Finnish Government (2022) Government of Finland Report on Human Rights. Publications of the Finnish Government 2022:10. Finnish Government, Helsinki. Available via Valto. https://urn.fi/URN:ISBN:978-952-383-637-2. Accessed 25 Oct 2025

Finnish Government (2025) Government Report on Internal Security. Publications of the Finnish Government 2025:87. Finnish Government, Helsinki. Available via Valto. https://urn.fi/URN:ISBN:978-952-383-766-9. Accessed 25 Nov 2025

Freedom Online Coalition (2020) FOC Joint Statement on Spread of Disinformation Online. Available via Freedom Online Coalition. https://freedomonlinecoalition.com/document/foc-joint-statement-on-spread-of-disinformation-online/. Accessed 28 Nov 2025

HARD DISC (Human centered approach and regulatory dimension in developing an interoperable and secure cyberspace) (2025) Comparative Research on Online Disinformation. University of Pisa, Department of Law. https://harddisc.jus.unipi.it/database/. Accessed 28 Nov 2025

Heikkilä, T (2025) Harhaanjohtavan viestinnän kiistellyt vaarat: Integroiva kirjallisuuskatsaus mis- ja disinformaation ongelmanmäärittelyjen kritiikkiin. Media & viestintä 48(1):112–140 (2025). https://doi.org/10.23983/mv.148332

Lessenski M (2023) "Bye, bye, birdi": Meeting the Challenges of Disinformation. The Media Literacy Index 2023. Open Society Institute, Sofia. Available via Open Society Institute. https://osis.bg/wp-content/uploads/2023/06/MLI-report-in-English-22.06.pdf. Accessed 30 Nov 2025

Matikainen J, Horowitz M, Tuomola S (2025) Luottamuksen rooli informaatiohäiriöiden torjunnassa: Suomalaisten mediakuluttajien kokemus medialuottamuksesta ja mediaitseluottamuksesta. Media & viestintä 48(1):141–159. https://doi.org/10.23983/mv.148376

Ministry of Foreign Affairs of Finland (2021) Countering disinformation to defend human rights. https://valtioneuvosto.fi/-/disinformaation-torjunta-on-ihmisoikeuksien-puolustamista?languageId=en_US. Accessed 28 Nov 2025

Newman N (2024) Overview and Key Findings of the 2024 Digital News Report. Reuters Institute for the Study of Journalism, https://reutersinstitute.politics.ox.ac.uk/digital-news-report/2024/dnr-executive-summary. Accessed 30 Nov 2025

Disinformation in France: Regulation Over Punishment

Coralie Richaud

Abstract French law addresses the issue of online disinformation through a plurality of pre-existing legal regimes—ranging from the 1881 Press Law and criminal law, to electoral law (the 2018 law on information manipulation) and consumer law—thereby targeting the specific manifestations and unlawful consequences of false information (such as disturbances to public order or undermining the sincerity of the vote). French law does not directly define what online disinformation is and relies on an aggregate of legal provisions and administrative and criminal sanctions framing online disinformation. By emphasizing regulation and associated sanctions, the French regime appears to address the consequences of online disinformation rather than its causes.

1 The French News and Disinformation Landscape

The French news ecosystem is characterized by a diverse media landscape encompassing public and private television and radio broadcasters, national and regional print outlets, and a growing presence of digital news platforms. Traditional media, including leading newspapers such as *Le Monde*, *Le Figaro*, and *Libération*, continue to play a central role in shaping public debate, while online news portals, social media platforms, and independent digital outlets have expanded the dissemination channels available to the public. This plurality of sources contributes to a robust information environment but also presents challenges in ensuring accuracy and reliability.

Disinformation has emerged as a significant concern within this ecosystem, particularly in the context of political elections, public health crises, and international conflicts. False or misleading content can spread rapidly on social media platforms and messaging applications, amplified by algorithms that prioritize engagement over accuracy. In France, authorities have identified several key vectors of disinformation,

C. Richaud (✉)
CERCOP, University of Montpellier, Montpellier, France
e-mail: coralie.richaud@umontpellier.fr

P. Passaglia (ed.), *European Legal Perspectives on Online Disinformation*, Ius Gentium: Comparative Perspectives on Law and Justice 140,
https://doi.org/10.1007/978-3-032-25785-7_9

including fabricated news articles, manipulated multimedia content, and coordinated online campaigns designed to influence public opinion or sow societal discord.

The French government and regulatory bodies have responded with a combination of legislative, administrative, and voluntary measures aimed at mitigating the impact of disinformation. Legal instruments, such as the SREN Law (2024) and the LCEN (2004), establish obligations for platforms to remove illegal content and protect vulnerable populations, while soft law instruments, including codes of conduct and guidelines aligned with the European Digital Services Act (DSA) promote best practices for content moderation and transparency. Regulatory authorities, notably the Autorité de Régulation de la Communication Audiovisuelle et Numérique (ARCOM), oversee compliance, particularly during electoral periods, ensuring that both platforms and content producers adhere to legal and ethical standards.

2 The Notion of Disinformation

2.1 Definition

In 2018, the French Language Enrichment Commission proposed recommendations regarding the terms to use for referring to methods that contribute to public disinformation. Although the term "fake news" was not adopted by the legislator, the Commission suggested using terms already present in the French legal corpus. It stated that "when referring to false or deliberately biased information—spread, for example, to favor one political party over another, to damage the reputation of an individual or company, or to contradict established scientific truth—the term 'fallacious information' or the neologism 'infox,' derived from the words 'information' and 'intoxication,' may be used." Additionally, the recommendation emphasized the use of terms already present in the legal framework: "false news," "fake news," "false information," or "fake information."

Although French law does not directly use the term "disinformation," the legal framework governs the act of providing false, manipulated, or misleading information within the context of voluntary dissemination. Initially, on the occasion of the adoption of the law on the Press (Law 07/1849), by the Legislative National Assembly under the Second Republic, the text referred to the "publication or reproduction made in bad faith of false news, fabricated documents, falsified or wrongly attributed to third parties, when such news or documents are likely to disturb public peace." Subsequently, this provision was taken up by the Press Law (Law 06/1881). Its Article 27 provides for a criminal offense for the "publication, dissemination, or reproduction, by any means, of false news, fabricated documents, falsified or wrongly attributed to third parties, when, made in bad faith, it has disturbed public order or was likely to disturb it." Under this law, Article 29 defines defamation as the allegation or imputation of a specific fact that harms the honor or consideration of a person. Meanwhile, insult is defined as a contemptuous or outrageous expression toward a person.

While these texts initially targeted the press sector, other provisions have since enriched French law regarding false information related to commerce and consumption. The Commercial Code, modified in 2002, introduced a criminal offense for companies "disseminating, by any means, false or defamatory information". The Consumer Code also considers a commercial practice to be misleading "when it is based on false allegations, indications, or presentations, or is likely to mislead." Similarly, Article L.121-3 of the Consumer Code states that "a commercial practice is also misleading if, considering the limitations of the communication medium used and the circumstances surrounding it, it omits, conceals, or provides ambiguous, unintelligible, or untimely substantial information, or does not indicate its true commercial intent when it is not already clear from the context." This idea is also reflected in Article L.465-3-3 of the Monetary and Financial Code, which sanctions the transmission of false or misleading data or information, particularly in the context of financial indices. In criminal matters, it is primarily Article 322-14 of the Penal Code that sanctions "the act of communicating or disseminating false information with the intent to make people believe that a destruction, degradation, or dangerous deterioration for persons is about to occur or has occurred," punishable by two years' imprisonment and a fine of €30,000. There is also Article 226-10, which relates to false accusations.

However, it is in electoral matters that the notion of false information is most present. The provisions of Article L.97 of the Electoral Code have provided since the 2000s that "those who, through false news, slanderous rumors, or other fraudulent maneuvers, have surprised or diverted votes, or determined one or more voters to abstain from voting, shall be punished by one year's imprisonment and a fine of €15,000." In 2018, the legislator adopted the first law on combating information manipulation, marking the first time the terms "information manipulation" appeared in the French legal framework. The 2018 law introduced a new summary procedure mechanism during national elections (presidential, legislative, European, and referendums). This mechanism aims to quickly halt the massive dissemination of information that must meet the following criteria:

- The false news must be manifestly false.
- It must have been disseminated massively and artificially.
- It must be likely to disturb public order or undermine the sincerity of the vote.

More recently, the French legislature adopted a law to "secure and regulate the digital space," aimed in particular at strengthening the legal framework governing information manipulation by extending it beyond the electoral context. The law thus introduced specific mechanisms to combat the production and dissemination of falsified content, including content generated by artificial intelligence technologies. This text, which complements the Digital Services Act, incorporates certain of its requirements at the national level. In seeking to address the challenges posed by disinformation and the proliferation of hate speech, the legislation adopted by Parliament in 2024 provides for a stricter criminal framework governing manipulated content.

French criminal law now penalizes the creation or dissemination of falsified content likely to disturb public order or infringe upon human integrity. These sanctions are accompanied by measures requiring the accelerated removal of manifestly unlawful content (including hate speech, terrorist material, or child sexual abuse material) within 24 hours of its being reported.

2.2 *Distinction Between Close Concepts: Disinformation, Misinformation and Malinformation*

The term "fake news" has been gradually abandoned because it is imprecise, lacks legal basis, and is subject to political misuse. The French legislator, in the law of 22 December 2018, relating to the fight against the manipulation of information, uses only the term "fausse information" (false information), defined in Article L. 163-2 of the Electoral Code. As mentioned above, French law only recognizes the concepts of "nouvelle fausse" (false news), "fausse nouvelle" (false report), "information fausse" (false information), or "fausse information" (false information), and since 2018, "manipulation de l'information" (manipulation of information). Under current law, misinformation is not considered an offense and is not subject to criminal penalties. The absence of intent is the marker that prevents these actions from being covered by French criminal law.

The concept of malinformation, although not named as such in French law, is nevertheless regulated, particularly within the framework of commercial law and consumer law, as the law penalizes deceptive or misleading information, whether online or offline. In this context, the legal understanding of these terms is directly linked to the information communicated by companies regarding the products or services they market.

Finally, the bill proposed by MP Laetitia Avia in 2020 aimed to strengthen the contribution of digital operators in the fight against certain manifestly hateful online content. In this regard, the proposal did not target disinformation, malinformation, or misinformation, as its objective was to combat manifestly illegal content. The bill, as passed by Parliament, required online platform operators and search engines to remove manifestly illegal content—such as incitements to hatred, racist or anti-religious insults—within 24 hours. For terrorist or child sexual abuse content, this deadline was to be reduced to 1 hour. Struck down by the Constitutional Council in its decision of 18 June 2020, these provisions therefore did not come into effect.

2.3 Application of the Notion of Disinformation in the Different Areas of the French Legal Order

The scope of the concept of disinformation is very broad. Although French law does not explicitly use this term, the idea it conveys has diverse applications. As previously mentioned, the legal framework for disinformation initially focused on the field related to the press, particularly to ensure the maintenance of public order. For this reason, the legislator early on created the offenses of defamation and insult to penalize the circulation of false information deliberately used against third parties. Subsequently, the scope of application expanded to the economic domain, understood in a broad sense (consumer law, distribution law, and commercial law). The challenge here is to curb misleading commercial practices. Criminal law is no exception, as it also regulates the offense of false accusation and prohibits the act of spreading false information, for example, to make people believe in a destruction that could lead to a disturbance of public order.

2.4 Specificity of Online Disinformation

The specificity of French law regarding online disinformation was initially closely linked to electoral matters. The law adopted on 22 December 2018, significantly modified the provisions of the electoral code. At least five innovations are worth noting.

First, the new Article L. 163-1 of the Electoral Code, created by Article 1, imposes several transparency obligations on online platform operators. The operators concerned are those defined in Article L. 111-7 of the Consumer Code, whose activity exceeds a certain threshold of connections on French territory. This definition covers search engines (such as Google or Qwant), referencing sites (such as Lafourchette or Tripadvisor), marketplaces (such as Amazon or Leboncoin), and social networks (such as Facebook or Twitter). Since this system is justified by the need to protect the integrity of elections, these obligations apply during a limited period: the three months preceding the first day of the month of general elections and extending until the date of the final round of voting. The obligations imposed on these operators are threefold. They must:

- Provide users with "loyal, clear, and transparent information" about the identity and quality of persons paying for the promotion of "informational content related to a debate of general interest," as well as the identity of the persons on whose behalf these payments are made, if applicable (1° of Article L. 163-1).
- Provide the same users with "loyal, clear, and transparent information" on the use of their personal data "in the context of promoting informational content related to a debate of general interest" (2° of Article L. 163-1).
- Publicly disclose the amount of remuneration received in exchange for promoting such content when it exceeds a threshold set by decree (3° of Article L. 163-1).

The information provided must be aggregated in a register made available to the public electronically and regularly updated.

Next, the law introduced a summary procedure whereby "During the three months preceding the first day of the month of general elections (…) when inaccurate or misleading allegations or claims (…) are disseminated deliberately, artificially, automatically, and massively (…) the emergency judge may order any proportionate and necessary measures to stop this diffusion." The emergency judge must rule within 48 hours of being seized. Additionally, the law requires platform operators to implement an "easily accessible and visible" reporting mechanism for the targeted information. It also mandates complementary measures, which may include:

- Transparency of algorithms,
- Promotion of press content,
- Combating accounts that massively spread false information,
- Informing users about the identity of advertisers,

These measures, along with the allocated resources, must be made public. Each platform must send an annual declaration to the ARCOM on the implementation of these measures. These obligations also apply in certain overseas territories. Finally, the law significantly strengthened the powers of the ARCOM because it can also issue recommendations to platform operators to improve their fight against "false information" and must publish periodic reports on the application of these measures.

Although these provisions specifically target online content, a major criticism can be made regarding the period covered. Article L. 163-2 of the Electoral Code only applies during the three months preceding general elections, which limits the scope of the summary procedure and does not aim to prevent information manipulation outside electoral periods.

2.5 *The Relevance of Illegal Contents on the Definition*

The relevance of illegal content sanctioned by French law is twofold. It is indeed possible to distinguish between two cases of application in which illegal content is suppressed.

In the first scenario, this primarily concerns products or services that can be commercialized, and thus mainly relates to economic and commercial stakes. While this aspect is important, it diverges from what is directly understood as online disinformation. In this first context, the issue of disinformation falls primarily under the scope of misleading commercial practices. However, it is predominantly under the second case of application that the relevance of illegal content can be noted. This concerns two aspects: the electoral field since 2018 and, more recently since 2024, online hate speech.

In the electoral sphere, the suppression of illegal content is primarily justified given the risks and potential harm to the sincerity of elections (scrutins). The underlying principle is to ensure the integrity of the vote as a condition for the democratic ideal.

Since 2024, however, the legal framework has been strengthened under the effect of the Digital Services Act (DSA), introducing mechanisms aimed at combating the proliferation of online hate speech in particular. Although the objective of the law was to combat the phenomenon of disinformation, this specific term does not appear in the text. The SREN Law (Law 05/2024) nonetheless regulated the production and dissemination of manipulated content, thereby extending the framework already initiated in 2018 concerning electoral matters.

3 The Sources of Law

3.1 Constitutional Law

The invocable constitutional sources are numerous and find their origins both in the constitutional text and in its preamble.

First, the constitutional protection of freedom of expression and communication is based on Article 11 of the 1789 Declaration, which states: "The free communication of ideas and opinions is one of the most precious rights of man: every citizen may therefore speak, write, and print freely, but shall be responsible for the abuse of this liberty in the cases determined by law." Freedom of expression and communication applies to online public communication services, including the internet.

Next, the principle of legality of offenses and penalties is based on Article 8 of the Declaration of the Rights of Man and of the Citizen, which states: the law shall establish only penalties that are strictly and evidently necessary, and no one shall be punished except by virtue of a law established and promulgated prior to the offense and legally applied.

Furthermore, the freedom to undertake, which is based on Article 4 of the Declaration of the Rights of Man and of the Citizen, states: "Liberty consists in the ability to do whatever does not harm others: thus, the exercise of the natural rights of each man has no limits other than those which ensure to the other members of society the enjoyment of these same rights. These limits can only be determined by law."

Finally, the principle of pluralism is based on Article 4 of the Constitution, which states: the law guarantees the pluralistic expression of opinions and the equitable participation of parties and political groups in the democratic life of the Nation.

3.2 EU Law and Its Implementation

The French domestic framework is increasingly harmonized with European Union regulations designed to govern digital services and political transparency. The primary instruments shaping this landscape include:

- Digital Services Act (DSA)—Regulation (EU) 2065/2022, which establishes a comprehensive liability and safety regime for online intermediaries.
- Audiovisual Media Services Directive—Directive No. 2018/1808, amending Directive 2010/13/EU (AVMSD), implemented by Ordinance No. 2020–1642 of 21 December 2020.
- Artificial Intelligence Act—Regulation (EU) 2024/1689, addressing the risks associated with AI-generated content.
- Regulation (EU) 2024/900, which enhances transparency in the targeting and delivery of political advertising.
- General Data Protection Regulation (GDPR) (EU) 2016/679 and The Code of Conduct on Disinformation— 13 February 2025, the latter providing non-binding yet influential ethical and data protection standards.

3.3 Legislative Acts

The French legal framework governing freedom of expression, information, and digital communication is structured around a set of complementary legislative instruments that progressively adapt constitutional principles to technological and societal developments. Together, these laws establish a balance between the protection of fundamental freedoms, the prevention of abuses, and the regulation of digital spaces.

At the core of this framework, the Press Law (Law 07/1881) constitutes the foundational pillar of freedom of expression in France. It affirms the principle of freedom of the press while simultaneously defining its legal limits through offenses such as defamation, insult, and provocation to hatred, discrimination, or violence. By clearly identifying the responsibilities of authors, editors, and publishers, this law provides a long-standing normative framework that reconciles freedom of expression with the protection of public order, individual dignity, and reputation.

In parallel, the CNIL Law (Law 01/1978) on information technology, data files, and civil liberties complements this framework by addressing the relationship between freedom of expression and the protection of personal data. It establishes a specific derogatory regime for journalistic, academic, artistic, and literary activities, ensuring that data protection rules do not unduly restrict freedom of information. At the same time, it preserves the applicability of civil, criminal, and press law provisions intended to safeguard privacy, reputation, and the right of reply, thereby maintaining accountability for abuses committed in the exercise of expressive freedoms.

With the development of online communication services, the Confidence in the Digital Economy Law (Law 06/2004) introduced a liability regime adapted to digital intermediaries. It distinguishes between content publishers and hosting providers, limiting the liability of the latter provided they act expeditiously to remove illegal content once notified, while explicitly excluding any general obligation to monitor user-generated content. This law laid the legal foundations for platform regulation in France and aligned national law with emerging European standards for intermediary liability.

In response to the growing impact of online disinformation on democratic processes, the manipulation Law (Law 12/2018) specifically addresses the risks posed during electoral periods. It grants judicial authorities the power to order the removal or dereferencing of demonstrably false information disseminated deliberately and on a massive scale, with the objective of safeguarding the integrity of elections while preserving freedom of political debate.

Subsequently, the Law (Law 06/2020) strengthened the obligations imposed on online platforms with regard to the reporting and removal of manifestly illicit content. It introduced clear definitions of hate-based content and imposed strict deadlines for its removal following notification, reinforcing the role of platforms in preventing the dissemination of racist, antisemitic, sexist, and discriminatory speech in digital environments.

In the same normative trajectory, the Data Republic Law (Law 08/2021) strengthening respect for the principles of the Republic further reinforced the repression of hate speech and threats, particularly when directed at public officials or linked to religious or ethnic discrimination. This law reflects an increased emphasis on protecting public institutions and social cohesion against forms of expression that undermine republican values.

More recently, the Law (01/2022) on the regulation and protection of cyberspace expanded the legal response to online harms by explicitly addressing cyberbullying and digital harassment. It introduced aggravated penalties for harassment committed through online public communication services, recognizing the specific severity and persistence of digital forms of violence.

Finally, in alignment with the evolving European regulatory framework, the SREN Law (05/2024) on securing and regulating the digital space represents a significant evolution of French digital law. It implements elements of the Digital Services Act and strengthens measures to combat online hate, disinformation, and the dissemination of manipulated content, including deepfakes. It also introduces mechanisms to protect minors, notably through age verification requirements for access to pornographic content, and expands regulatory oversight of digital economic activities.

3.4 The Role of Case Law

3.4.1 Courts

The French Constitutional Council has consistently recognized freedom of expression and communication as a constitutional principle, grounded in Article 11 of the 1789 Declaration of the Rights of Man and of the Citizen and reaffirmed by the Preamble to the 1946 Constitution. This constitutional protection extends to online public communication services, including the internet, reflecting the evolution of communication technologies and their role in contemporary democratic societies.

In the Constitutional Council, case 84-181/1984 (11 October 1984), the Constitutional Council affirmed that the right to free communication and the freedom to speak, write, and publish constitute a fundamental freedom. It emphasized that this freedom is of particular importance insofar as its exercise constitutes one of the essential guarantees for the protection of other rights and freedoms, as well as for the preservation of national sovereignty.

This approach was further developed in the Constitutional Council, case 2009-580/2009 (10 June 2009), in which the Council reiterated that freedom of expression and communication is a prerequisite for democracy and a key safeguard for other fundamental rights. The Council held that any restriction on the exercise of this freedom must satisfy the requirements of necessity, appropriateness, and proportionality in light of the objectives pursued. By articulating these criteria, the Council subjected legislative limitations on freedom of expression to its highest level of constitutional scrutiny, namely a full proportionality review.

In the same decision, the Constitutional Council expressly acknowledged the central role of online public communication services in democratic life and in the dissemination of ideas and opinions. It concluded that freedom of expression necessarily entails the freedom to access such services. On this basis, the Council declared unconstitutional a legislative provision authorising administrative disconnection from internet access, including from a private residence, as a sanction for breaches of intellectual property law.

In the Constitutional Council, case 2011-625/2011 (10 March 2011), the Council upheld legislative provisions empowering an administrative authority to restrict access to online public communication services disseminating child pornography, for the purpose of protecting internet users. The Council considered that the legislature had not committed a manifest error of assessment in adopting such measures and reaffirmed that it does not substitute its own assessment for that of Parliament, provided that the means chosen are not manifestly inappropriate to the intended objective. It further emphasized that the administrative authority's powers were strictly limited, subject to full judicial review, and proportionate to the constitutional objective of safeguarding public order.

In the Constitutional Council, case 2018-773/2018 (20 December 2018), the Constitutional Council examined the constitutionality of an expedited judicial procedure intended to halt, during the three months preceding a general election, the dissemination of false information on online public communication services where such dissemination was likely to undermine the sincerity of the electoral process. Subject to an interpretative reservation, the Council concluded that this mechanism was compatible with constitutional requirements.

Finally, in the Constitutional Council, case 2004-496/2004 (10 June 2004), although freedom of expression was not explicitly invoked, the Constitutional Council addressed its implications in relation to the liability regime applicable to hosting providers. The Council upheld the constitutionality of provisions governing the civil and criminal liability of hosting providers for failure to remove illegal content, subject to an interpretative reservation specifying that such liability cannot arise where the illegal nature of the content is not manifest or where its removal has not been ordered by a judicial authority.

The French judicial system has also played a central role in delineating the scope of freedom of expression, particularly with regard to defamation, insults, and incitement to hatred, while also defining the limits of administrative restrictions on this fundamental right.

The Cour de cassation has consistently clarified that freedom of expression is not absolute and does not extend to speech that infringes upon the rights of others or threatens public order. In the Cour de cassation, Criminal Chamber, case of Jean-Marie Le Pen (12 July 2000), the Court upheld the conviction for Holocaust denial, ruling that such statements fall outside the protection of freedom of expression and constitute an offense under Article 24 bis of the Press Law (Law 07/1881). Similarly, in the Cour de cassation, case of Dieudonné (1 July 2020), the Court confirmed the conviction for incitement to hatred, holding that racist or antisemitic remarks, including symbolic gestures such as the "quenelle," are not safeguarded by freedom of expression. More recently, in the Cour de cassation, case of Éric Zemmour (3 November 2021), the Court ruled that discriminatory statements, in this instance directed against Muslims, remain unprotected even when articulated in the context of public debate. In the Cour de cassation, case concerning the "Yellow Vests" movement (15 June 2022), the Court held that calls for violence disseminated on social media, even if metaphorical or indirect, may be subject to sanction, thereby reinforcing the principle that public expression cannot threaten the security of others.

The Conseil d'État has similarly addressed the permissible limits of administrative interventions affecting freedom of expression. In CE, case Benjamin (19 May 1933), the Council recognized that administrative authorities may impose restrictions on public expression to preserve public order, provided that such measures are proportionate in terms of time and space. In CE, case Charlie Hebdo (27 October 1995), the Council annulled a prefectural ban on distributing a blasphemous issue of the magazine, affirming the primacy of freedom of expression over arbitrary administrative restrictions. In CE, case concerning burkinis (9 November 2016), the Council suspended municipal bans on wearing burkinis on beaches, ruling that the measures constituted excessive restrictions on freedom of expression and individual liberties. Most recently, in CE, case concerning protests against police violence (6 August 2020), the Council reiterated that bans on demonstrations must be justified by a demonstrable risk of public disorder, underscoring the necessity of proportionality in administrative limitations of expressive freedoms.

Collectively, these judicial decisions illustrate a careful balancing approach in French law, which seeks to reconcile the protection of fundamental freedoms with the prevention of harm, discrimination, and threats to public order, both in the criminal and administrative spheres.

3.4.2 Supervisory Authorities

The legal landscape in which France addresses online disinformation is fundamentally shaped by the jurisprudential framework of the European Court of Human

Rights, particularly through its evolving interpretation of Article 10 of the European Convention on Human Rights. Although the Court has not yet established disinformation as a standalone legal category, its rulings on intermediary liability and the limits of expressive freedom serve as the primary normative reference for French national courts and legislative bodies. This judicial oversight ensures that any domestic measures, such as those found in the 2018 Law on Information Manipulation or the 2024 SREN Law, adhere to the strict European standards of legality, necessity, and proportionality within a democratic society.

Central to this framework is the balance between the state's interest in protecting public order and the individual's right to receive and impart information. The Court has repeatedly affirmed that Article 10 protection extends to digital communication, yet it acknowledges that false statements or misleading information may be subject to restriction when they infringe upon the rights of others or threaten societal stability. In the landmark Grand Chamber judgment of Sanchez v. France (European Court of Human Rights, case no. 45581/15, 15 May 2023), the Court upheld the criminal conviction of a French politician for failing to promptly remove third-party hate speech from his social media page. This decision is particularly significant as it clarifies that the interference with freedom of expression can be justified when the objective is to prevent incitement to hatred, thereby informing how French law addresses the intersection of disinformation and harmful content.

The Court's reasoning in Sanchez builds upon an established trajectory of case law regarding the heightened responsibilities of professional online actors. For instance, in the case of Delfi AS v. Estonia (European Court of Human Rights, case No. 64569/09, 16 June 2015), the Court affirmed that professional publishers hosting user-generated content bear a specific duty of care to prevent the dissemination of clearly unlawful material. While these precedents do not always deal with disinformation in its purest form, they provide the essential criteria for assessing platform liability and the proportionality of administrative or judicial interventions. Consequently, the French regulatory model remains deeply anchored in this European standard, which prioritizes a rights-oriented approach and requires that any limitation on digital expression be narrowly tailored and supported by relevant and sufficient reasons. This consistent application of European principles acts as a safeguard against potential state overreach or arbitrary censorship in the digital space.

The jurisprudence of the European Court of Human Rights (ECtHR) provides the essential interpretative framework for Article 10 of the European Convention on Human Rights, influencing how French authorities balance the fight against disinformation with the protection of fundamental freedoms. While the Court has not conceptualized "disinformation" as a standalone legal category, its rulings on intermediary liability serve as a primary reference for national courts.

3.5 *The Impact of Soft Law*

The Munich Charter of 1971 establishes fundamental principles regarding the rights to information, free expression, and criticism. Its preamble affirms that the right to information, free expression, and criticism constitutes one of the fundamental freedoms of every human being. By articulating this broad conception of expression and access to information, the Charter situates freedom of expression as a cornerstone of democratic societies and underscores its universality as a human right.

Although the Munich Charter is not legally binding, it carries significant normative weight and has influenced both national and international standards on media freedom, transparency, and the protection of journalists. It provides ethical guidance for the development of policies and legal frameworks aimed at promoting accountability, civic participation, and the free exchange of ideas.

In the contemporary context, particularly with regard to the regulation of online platforms and the fight against disinformation, the Charter serves as a reference for ensuring that measures targeting false or harmful content respect the fundamental right to information and the ability of individuals to express and receive opinions freely. Its principles inform European soft law initiatives and national guidelines on media responsibility, content moderation, and public access to information.

4 Reporting Procedure and Other Ways to Tackle Online Disinformation

France does not rely on a single, standalone anti-disinformation law. Instead, it combines multiple legal frameworks—press law, data protection (GDPR), civil/criminal liability, and platform regulation (LCEN/DSA)—to address misleading content, enforce transparency, and provide ex-post remedies (right of reply, rectification, damages, sanctions) without prior restraints.

4.1 *Subjects Who Can Report*

Two main categories of actors are empowered to report disinformation on online platforms. The first category comprises private individuals, who are entitled to notify platforms of content they consider misleading or false. This right is guaranteed under the Digital Services Act (DSA), which obliges hosting service providers to implement accessible and transparent mechanisms for reporting and addressing illegal content. Article 16 of the DSA specifies that providers of hosting services shall establish notice and action procedures allowing any individual or entity to notify them of the presence of specific items of illegal content. This provision ensures that users can actively participate in the moderation of online information and contributes to the accountability of digital platforms.

The second category consists of public authorities, which in France include the ARCOM. ARCOM has the capacity to report illegal or misleading content, particularly in contexts where public interest is high, such as during electoral periods. For example, Article 1, I of the SREN Law entrusts ARCOM with the responsibility to ensure that certain content, including pornographic material, is not accessible to minors and to establish a reference framework setting minimum technical requirements for age verification systems. By extension, ARCOM's mandate allows it to intervene in the reporting of content that may be illegal, misleading, or otherwise harmful, reinforcing the regulatory oversight of online information.

Together, these mechanisms reflect a dual approach in France to countering disinformation, combining the vigilance of individual users with the regulatory authority of public institutions to ensure that online platforms operate in compliance with both legal and ethical standards.

4.2 Subjects Who Decide on the Report

Three main types of entities are responsible for evaluating reports of disinformation and determining the appropriate follow-up measures. The first category comprises online platforms themselves. Major platforms, such as Facebook, Twitter (X), and YouTube, are required to assess user reports and to remove content that is manifestly illegal. Article 14 of the Digital Services Act (DSA) stipulates that providers of intermediary services shall, upon obtaining actual knowledge of illegal content, act expeditiously to remove or disable access to such content. This obligation ensures that platforms play a proactive role in moderating harmful or unlawful material while complying with the standards of the DSA.

The second category consists of administrative authorities. In France, the ARCOM is empowered to order the removal of illegal or misleading content, particularly during periods of heightened public interest, such as elections. Article 1, II of the SREN Law authorizes ARCOM to formally request that entities granting access to content, including pornographic material, comply with established technical and regulatory standards within a specified timeframe. This provision reinforces the capacity of regulatory bodies to intervene when online platforms fail to address problematic content effectively.

The third category comprises the judiciary. Civil, criminal, and administrative courts in France are competent to adjudicate disputes or appeals arising from removal decisions. According to Article 834 of the Code of Civil Procedure, judicial courts have jurisdiction over requests aimed at halting manifestly illegal disturbances, thereby providing a legal recourse for affected parties and ensuring that decisions on content removal are subject to independent review.

Together, these mechanisms establish a multi-layered framework for addressing disinformation online in France, combining the operational responsibilities of platforms, the supervisory authority of regulators, and the adjudicatory role of courts. This structure seeks to balance the protection of freedom of expression with the need to limit harmful or unlawful content in the digital environment.

4.3 *Means to Establish the Falsehood of the Contents and the Related Responsibilities*

Establishing the falsity of content and determining responsibility in cases of online disinformation involves multiple actors and mechanisms. Fact-checking constitutes a central element of this process. Platforms are required to implement fact-checking measures, either internally or in cooperation with independent organizations, to assess the veracity of reported content. Articles 34 and 35 of the Digital Services Act (DSA) mandates that very large online platforms take measures to assess and mitigate risks, including by using trusted flaggers for the identification of illegal content. This requirement ensures that platforms actively verify information and identify potentially false or misleading material before it can cause harm.

Platforms themselves bear significant responsibility for addressing false or misleading content, particularly when it has the potential to influence judicial or electoral proceedings. Under Article 12 of the SREN Law, hosting service providers must promptly remove content reported as being disseminated in violation of rights or regulatory provisions. This provision establishes a clear obligation for platforms to act decisively in mitigating the impact of disinformation.

Authors of disinformation are also held accountable under French law. The Penal Code and the Press Law (Law 07/1881) impose criminal penalties for publishing or disseminating false news, fabricated documents, or information wrongly attributed to third parties, particularly when such content constitutes defamation, incitement to hatred, or manipulation of information. Article 27 of the Press Law specifies that individuals engaging in these acts may be subject to prosecution, reinforcing personal responsibility for content creation.

Furthermore, the use of false informational elements to influence civil, criminal, or administrative proceedings is explicitly prohibited. Article 226-8-1 of the Penal Code, as amended by the SREN Law (Law 05/2024), criminalizes acts such as presenting sexual montages or manipulated images or words of an individual without consent, imposing penalties of imprisonment and fines. This provision underscores that disinformation is not limited to textual falsehoods but also encompasses manipulated multimedia content intended to deceive or harm.

4.4 Deadlines for the Decision

Deadlines for processing reports of disinformation and illegal content are a critical component of France's regulatory framework for online platforms. Platforms are obligated to remove content that is manifestly illegal within a strict timeframe to prevent further harm. Under the SREN Law, hosting service providers must act promptly, ensuring that content reported as illegal is removed within twenty-four hours of notification. This requirement underscores the importance of rapid intervention in mitigating the potential impact of disinformation and other harmful online content.

In addition to the removal of content, procedural safeguards exist for individuals or entities wishing to contest platform decisions. Article 17 of the Digital Services Act (DSA) establishes that providers of online platforms must communicate a reasoned decision to complainants without undue delay and, in any case, within a reasonable period. These provisions ensure that affected parties have timely access to remedies, maintaining a balance between rapid enforcement against harmful content and the protection of freedom of expression through effective avenues of appeal.

4.5 Forms of Protection for the Authors of Allegedly Illegal Content or Disinformation

Authors of allegedly illegal content or disinformation in France benefit from specific forms of protection that aim to safeguard their rights while ensuring accountability. One such protection is the right of reply, which allows individuals named or referenced in a publication to publish a response or correction. Article 13 of the Law of 29 July 1881 stipulates that any individual identified in a periodical publication has the right to insert a reply therein. This mechanism ensures that individuals can defend their reputation and correct misleading information in a public forum.

Legal protection also extends to the possibility of contesting sanctions or content removal decisions before the courts. Under Article 531 of the Code of Civil Procedure, any interested party may file a third-party opposition to a judgment. This provision guarantees that authors of content, even if accused of disseminating false or harmful information, have access to judicial remedies and procedural safeguards, maintaining a balance between enforcement and the protection of freedom of expression.

When disinformation is detected, sanctions may be imposed on both authors and platforms. Criminal sanctions targeting authors of false information include fines and imprisonment. Article 27 of the Law of 29 July 1881 provides for penalties of up to one year of imprisonment and a fine of 45,000 euros for publishing or disseminating false news. Administrative sanctions may also be applied to online platforms that fail to remove illegal content. Article 52 of the Digital Services Act empowers the European Commission to impose fines of up to six percent of the total worldwide annual turnover of very large online platforms that fail to comply with their content moderation obligations.

4.6 *Sanctions in Case of Detection of Disinformation*

Sanctions for disinformation in France are designed to address both the actions of individual authors and the responsibilities of online platforms. Criminal sanctions target authors who publish or disseminate false information, with penalties including fines and imprisonment. Article 27 of the Press Law (Law 07/1881) provides that those found guilty of publishing false news may be subject to up to one year of imprisonment and a fine of 45,000 euros. These measures aim to hold content creators personally accountable for acts of disinformation that can harm public trust, influence public debate, or violate the rights of others.

Administrative sanctions complement criminal measures by targeting platforms that fail to remove illegal content in accordance with their obligations. Under Article 52 of the Digital Services Act (DSA), the European Commission is empowered to impose fines on very large online platforms of up to six percent of their total worldwide annual turnover if they do not comply with content moderation requirements. This provision underscores the responsibility of digital intermediaries to implement effective mechanisms for detecting and removing disinformation, thereby reinforcing systemic accountability in the online environment.

4.7 *Sanctions in Case of Unfounded Reports or Complaints*

Users who submit false or malicious reports of disinformation are subject to sanctions under platform governance frameworks. Online platforms reserve the right to suspend or terminate the accounts of individuals who repeatedly submit inaccurate or misleading reports. For instance, the terms of service of major providers, such as Meta and Google, explicitly state that accounts may be suspended or terminated in cases of repeated false reporting. This mechanism serves both to maintain the integrity of content moderation processes and to discourage the misuse of reporting tools, ensuring that the systems established for identifying and addressing disinformation are not undermined by bad-faith actions.

4.8 *Review of Previous Decisions*

Mechanisms for reviewing decisions related to disinformation in France operate at multiple levels, providing safeguards for individuals and ensuring accountability in content moderation. Platforms themselves are required to establish internal appeal procedures, allowing users to contest decisions regarding the removal of content. Article 20 of the Digital Services Act (DSA) stipulates that providers of online platforms must maintain an internal complaint-handling system, ensuring that users have the opportunity to seek reconsideration of moderation outcomes.

Administrative appeals represent a second layer of oversight. In France, affected parties may seize regulatory authorities such as the Autorité de Régulation de la Communication Audiovisuelle et Numérique (ARCOM) to challenge content removal or other enforcement measures. Article 1, V of the SREN Law grants the right to request that the president of the administrative court annul measures taken under the authority of ARCOM, providing a formal mechanism for administrative review.

Finally, judicial appeals offer the possibility of contesting decisions before the courts. Article 834 of the Code of Civil Procedure provides that judicial courts have jurisdiction over requests aimed at halting manifestly illegal disturbances, thereby granting affected parties access to independent judicial scrutiny. Together, these internal, administrative, and judicial review mechanisms establish a robust system of checks and balances, ensuring that content moderation decisions are subject to accountability and respect for procedural rights.

4.9 Sanctions for Private Entities or Administrative Bodies Who Rendered Erroneous Decisions

Sanctions in the French regulatory framework for online disinformation extend not only to content authors but also to platforms and administrative authorities. Platforms that fail to comply with their moderation obligations may be subject to significant administrative penalties. Article 52 of the Digital Services Act (DSA) empowers the European Commission to impose fines on very large online platforms of up to six percent of their total worldwide annual turnover in cases of non-compliance. This measure ensures that platforms are incentivized to implement effective content moderation mechanisms and to act promptly in response to reports of illegal or harmful content.

Administrative authorities are also subject to liability when their decisions are arbitrary, erroneous, or the result of gross negligence. Article 12 of Law No. 2000-321 of 12 April 2000 provides that administrative bodies may be held liable for their decisions in such circumstances. This principle of accountability ensures that regulatory interventions, including those by ARCOM or other supervisory authorities, are exercised in a careful, reasoned, and proportionate manner, maintaining trust in the administrative oversight of online content.

Together, these sanctions establish a dual system of accountability that reinforces both the operational responsibilities of platforms and the procedural integrity of administrative authorities, contributing to a balanced and enforceable framework for addressing online disinformation in France.

5 Conclusions

The French approach is characterized by a strong attachment to freedom of expression as a constitutional and conventional principle, combined with a progressive adaptation of legal tools to address the risks posed by false, misleading, or manipulated information in the digital environment.

Rather than relying on a unified legal definition of disinformation, French law addresses the phenomenon indirectly through a plurality of legal regimes, including press law, criminal law, electoral law, consumer protection, and digital regulation. This fragmented construction reflects a deliberate choice to avoid the establishment of a generalised regime of content control, in line with constitutional requirements and the jurisprudence of the European Court of Human Rights. At the same time, it results in a regulatory framework whose scope of application remains uneven, both materially and temporally, with the most specific mechanisms historically confined to electoral periods or to clearly defined categories of illegal content.

Recent legislative developments, particularly the adoption of the SREN Law and the implementation of the Digital Services Act, mark a significant evolution in the governance of online content. These instruments strengthen platform obligations, enhance transparency and reporting mechanisms, and reinforce the role of regulatory authorities such as ARCOM. However, they continue to focus primarily on manifestly unlawful content rather than on disinformation as a distinct legal category, thereby limiting their capacity to address more diffuse or structural forms of information manipulation.

Judicial oversight plays a central role in maintaining the balance between the fight against disinformation and the protection of fundamental rights. The consistent application of principles of legality, necessity, and proportionality by French courts and by the European Court of Human Rights constitutes a key safeguard against excessive restrictions on freedom of expression. Soft law instruments further complement this framework by promoting ethical standards and best practices, although their effectiveness depends largely on voluntary compliance and institutional support.

Overall, the French model illustrates a cautious and rights-oriented approach to online disinformation, privileging targeted interventions and procedural safeguards over broad substantive regulation. While this approach mitigates the risks of censorship and arbitrary interference, it also exposes structural limitations in addressing rapidly evolving and technologically sophisticated disinformation practices. The ongoing challenge for the French legal order lies in developing a more coherent and forward-looking regulatory response, capable of enhancing democratic resilience while remaining firmly anchored in constitutional and European human rights standards.

References

ARCOM (2023) Annual report on the fight against information manipulation. Autorité de Régulation de la Communication Audiovisuelle et Numérique, Paris

Commission for the Enrichment of the French Language (2018) Recommendation on the vocabulary of computer science and the internet. Journal Officiel de la République Française.

Constitutional Council (1984) Decision No. 84-181 DC of 11 October 1984. Journal Officiel de la République Française.

Constitutional Council (2004) Decision No. 2004-496 DC of 10 June 2004, Law on confidence in the digital economy (LCEN). Journal Officiel de la République Française.

Constitutional Council (2009) Decision No. 2009-580 DC of 10 June 2009, Law favoring the distribution and protection of creation on the Internet (Hadopi I). Journal Officiel de la République Française.

Constitutional Council (2018) Decision No. 2018-773 DC of 20 December 2018, Law on the fight against the manipulation of information. Journal Officiel de la République Française.

Constitutional Council (2020) Decision No. 2020-801 DC of 18 June 2020, Law aimed at fighting hateful content on the internet (Avia Law). Journal Officiel de la République Française.

Constitutional Council (2024) Decision No. 2024-866 DC of 17 May 2024, Law aimed at securing and regulating the digital space. Journal Officiel de la République Française.

Council of State (1933) Case Benjamin, 19 May 1933. Recueil Lebon.

Council of State (1995) Case Charlie Hebdo, 27 October 1995. Recueil Lebon.

Council of State (2016) Case concerning burkinis, 9 November 2016. Recueil Lebon.

Council of State (2020) Case concerning protests against police violence, 6 August 2020. Recueil Lebon.

Court of Cassation, Criminal Chamber (2000) Case of Jean-Marie Le Pen, 12 July 2000. Bulletin Criminel, no. 200.

Court of Cassation (2020) Case of Dieudonné, 1 July 2020. Bulletin Criminel, no. 169.

Court of Cassation (2021) Case of Éric Zemmour, 3 November 2021. Bulletin Criminel, no. 220.

Court of Cassation (2022) Case concerning the "Yellow Vests" movement, 15 June 2022. Bulletin Criminel, no. 150.

Declaration of the Rights of Man and of the Citizen (1789) Articles 4, 8, and 11. National Assembly, Paris.

European Court of Human Rights (2015) Delfi AS v. Estonia. Application no. 64569/09, 16 June 2015.

European Court of Human Rights (2023) Sanchez v. France. Application no. 45581/15, 15 May 2023.

European Union (2016) Regulation (EU) 2016/679 (GDPR). Official Journal of the European Union.

European Union (2018) Directive (EU) 2018/1808 (AVMSD). Official Journal of the European Union.

European Union (2022) Regulation (EU) 2022/2065 (Digital Services Act). Official Journal of the European Union.

European Union (2024) Regulation (EU) 2024/900 on the transparency and targeting of political advertising. Official Journal of the European Union.

European Union (2024) Regulation (EU) 2024/1689 (Artificial Intelligence Act). Official Journal of the European Union.

European Union (2025) Code of Practice on Disinformation. European Commission, Brussels

French Republic (1881) Law of 29 July 1881 on the Freedom of the Press. Journal Officiel de la République Française.

French Republic (2018) Law No. 2018-1202 of 22 December 2018 on the manipulation of information. Journal Officiel de la République Française.

French Republic (2024) Civil Code. Articles 1240-1241. Légifrance.

French Republic (2024) Consumer Code. Article L.121-1. Légifrance.

French Republic (2024) Criminal Code. Articles 226-8-1, 226-10, 322-14. Légifrance.

French Republic (2024) Electoral Code. Articles L.97, L.111-7, L.163-1 and L. 163-2. Légifrance.
French Republic (2024) Law No. 2024-449 (SREN Law) on securing and regulating the digital space. Journal Officiel de la République Française.
Munich Charter (1971) Charter of Munich on the rights and duties of journalists. International Federation of Journalists, Munich.

The Legal Mosaic of Fighting (Online) Disinformation in Germany

Antje von Ungern-Sternberg, Pia Diemath, Nicolaj Feltes, and Fabian Hoffmanns

Abstract Regulation of (online) disinformation in German law is rather fragmented. Freedom of expression provides a strong constitutional protection of statements made by private actors, but its reach has certain limits. Three main areas limiting disinformation can be identified: personality rights, economic interests, and the democratic order. These legal interests are protected by various instruments: criminal offences, civil law injunctions, media due diligence obligations as well as laws protecting the constitutional order. This chapter provides an overview of the most relevant rules of criminal, civil and public law while aiming to create a comprehensive picture of the mosaic formed by these provisions.

1 Freedom of Expression and the Fight Against (Online) Disinformation[1]

1.1 Introduction: Freedom of Expression and Disinformation

Attempting to regulate online disinformation is first and foremost an issue of freedom of expression. Spreading false or misleading facts and opinions will, at least in Germany, generally fall within the scope of freedom of speech. Thus, it is crucial

---

[1] Written by Antje von Ungern-Sternberg.

A. von Ungern-Sternberg (✉) · P. Diemath · N. Feltes · F. Hoffmanns
Digital Law Institute Trier (IRDT), Trier University, Trier, Germany
e-mail: lsvonungern@uni-trier.de

P. Diemath
e-mail: diemath@uni-trier.de

N. Feltes
e-mail: feltes@uni-trier.de

F. Hoffmanns
e-mail: hoffmannsf@uni-trier.de

P. Passaglia (ed.), *European Legal Perspectives on Online Disinformation*, Ius Gentium: Comparative Perspectives on Law and Justice 140,
https://doi.org/10.1007/978-3-032-25785-7_10

to explain the corresponding German right under Article 5 Basic Law (Sect. 1) before exploring more specific legal norms organized according to the three pillars of German law, i.e. criminal law (Sect. 2), civil law (Sect. 3), and public law (Sect. 4).

Disinformation is defined, in the EU Code of Conduct on Disinformation with reference to the European Commission Communication on the European Democracy Action Plan, to be "false or misleading content that is spread with an intention to deceive or secure economic or political gain and which may cause public harm" (European Union 2025, fn. 8). This definition can also be relied upon in the German context where a similarly authoritative legal definition of disinformation does not exist. In short, the definition relies on three characteristics: (1) false or misleading content, (2) malicious intent by the person disseminating the content which leaves open the questions of whether this person, in addition to striving for personal gain, also needs to be aware that the content was false or misleading, and (3) the possible consequence of public harm as opposed to private harm or no harm at all. Online disinformation stands for disinformation disseminated in an online surrounding. The velocity and wide reach of online communication, together with the possibility to address highly defined audiences based on profiling, the modalities to conceal the true authors of communication, and the disinhibiting effect of certain online fora create specific risks for the common good and make online disinformation a particularly pressing research topic.

In German law, (online) disinformation is partially legal and partially illegal. In addition to banning certain forms of disinformation, the law also provides other forms of regulation related to disinformation, e.g. due diligence obligations, the victim's rights, or responses to legal forms of dissemination directed against the constitution. This chapter seeks to show the larger picture of a mosaic composed of many individual legislative pieces prohibiting or regulating disinformation. As all of these laws must pass a test of constitutionality, we will briefly outline the relevant constitutional guarantees. Spreading disinformation can be protected by freedom of expression (Art. 5 (1) (1st sentence) Basic Law), freedom of press and broadcasting (Art. 5 (2) (2nd sentence) Basic Law), freedom of science (Art. 5 (3) Basic Law), freedom of occupation (Art. 12 (1) Basic Law), and other fundamental rights. The following outline focuses on freedom of expression as the most important fundamental right in the context of disinformation.

Art. 5 (1) (1st sentence) Basic Law, reads: "(1) Every person shall have the right freely to express and disseminate his opinions in speech, writing and pictures and to inform himself without hindrance from generally accessible sources. Freedom of the press and freedom of reporting by means of broadcasts and films shall be guaranteed. There shall be no censorship. (2) These rights shall find their limits in the provisions of general laws, in provisions for the protection of young persons and in the right to personal honour." Due to freedom of expression, as interpreted and developed in the Federal Constitutional Court's case law, any state measure banning or restricting disinformation will have to pass a three-step test of constitutionality involving the scope of freedom of expression (1), a state interference (2) and its possible justification (3). The test requires answering the following questions: (1) Is disseminating a particular piece of disinformation protected by the scope of freedom of expression?

This question could be answered in the negative if, for example, intentional lies were not protected under Art. 5 Basic Law. (2) Does the state measure qualify as an interference in the constitutional freedom? This requirement is easily met if criminal law sanctions, civil law prohibitions or public law obligations are at stake, as is the case with the legal norms presented in the following sections. (3) Is this interference justified? This third step includes several aspects and usually encompasses a very detailed assessment. First, any state measure must be based on a legal ground, i.e. a 'general law' as Article 5 (2) Basic Law stipulates (the other limitations not being of practical relevance). A 'general law' is characterised by not being directed against a specific opinion. A general law might, for example, ban incitement to hatred as such (§ 130 StGB, see below), but not right-wing extremist incitement to hatred. Furthermore, the 'general law' also needs to pass a proportionality test which means that it protects a legitimate aim and is suitable, necessary, and appropriate to reach this aim. Second, if an individual state measure is based on this 'general law', for example a criminal fine, a civil injunction, or an administrative act, the proportionality requirement also has to be met.

To make things more complex, the Federal Constitutional Court (hereinafter BVerfG) has also acknowledged that, apart from limiting freedom of expression based on a 'general law', another exceptional limit is drawn directly by the constitution. The Court held that provisions which impose boundaries on the 'propagandistic condonation of the National Socialist Regime between the years 1933 and 1945' (§ 130 (4) StGB, see below) can be—exceptionally—justified as the Federal Republic of Germany was to be understood as an 'antithesis' of 'the injustice and the horror of Nazi rule' (BVerfGE 124, 300 (327 seqq.) 2009 *Wunsiedel Case*; for a general overview on the German case law on freedom of opinion cf. Nußberger 2025). Finally, fundamental rights do also apply in private-law relationships by means of the so-called indirect 'horizontal effect'. This implies that private law norms regarding disinformation will be interpreted in the light of fundamental freedoms, namely freedom of expression.

1.2 Protecting Disinformation? Facts, Opinions, and Due Diligence

In Germany, the scope of freedom of expression also encompasses the dissemination of disinformation. At first glance, the BVerfG seems to establish the opposite. For the Court distinguishes 'opinions' (which cannot be proven to be true or false) from 'facts' (which can be proven to be true or false) and only deems the dissemination of 'opinions', not 'facts' to be protected by freedom of expression (BVerfGE 90, 241 (247) 1994 *Auschwitz Lie*). What's more, the Court has explicitly stated on several occasions that 'incorrect information' does not deserve the protection of Art. 5 Basic Law. Thus, 'incorrect quotations' (BVerfGE 54, 208 (219) 1980 *Böll*), the 'deliberate assertion of untrue facts' (BVerfGE 61, 1 (8) 1982 *'CSU NPD Europas'*), and the 'expression of proven false factual claims' (BVerfGE 90, 241 (249) 1994 *Auschwitz Lie*) do not fall within the scope of freedom of expression.

A closer look reveals, however, that this only rarely applies. Very often, it will be rather difficult to separate facts from opinions, particularly if facts are used to support opinions. In these cases, asserting facts is also protected by freedom of expression (BVerfGE 61, 1 (8 et seq.) 1982 *'CSU NPD Europas'*). When interpreting the meaning of a statement, the courts must also give due regard to all relevant factors such as the context or the audience. This also leads to a large scope of freedom of expression. "All soldiers are murderers", for example, means that soldiers have to kill in war, but does not necessarily imply that soldiers are technically accused of the crime of murder (BVerfGE 93, 266 (297 et seqq.) 1995 *Soldiers are Murderers*). "Germany pays 370 Mill. Euros of development aid to the Taliban" can be understood to mean that the Taliban government indirectly profits from aid paid to other recipients, even if German money is not transferred directly to the Taliban government (BVerfG NJW 2024, mn. 37 et seq.). Most importantly, it will often be complicated to establish the truth. If potential speakers were only protected after verifying every single fact of an assertation this would severely hamper the free exchange of ideas, as the BVerfG acknowledges (BVerfGE 99, 185 (197) 1998 *Scientology*). As a result, many incorrect statements will fall within the scope of freedom of expression. In practice, the protection of freedom of expression is only refused if a speaker uses a misquote or denies the Holocaust (BVerfGE 54, 208 (219) 1980 *Böll;* BVerfGE 90, 241 (249) 1994 *Auschwitz Lie*). However, if the wrongfulness of a statement is established, it will be easier to justify restrictions on freedom of speech (e.g. the public assertion that a person belongs to Scientology, BVerfGE 99, 185 (197) 1998 *Scientology*).

As a consequence, the focus shifts to due diligence in verifying facts that speakers must exercise before disseminating a statement. These due diligence obligations vary according to the person of the speaker and to the context. As will be shown below, public statements by authorities and public officials are bound by the principle of neutrality and objectivity which includes relying on established facts. In the context of journalism, professional due diligence obligations have evolved that bind traditional media (press, broadcasting) as well as modern forms of media (telemedia, bloggers). Specific rules apply for 'suspicion-based reporting', i.e. media reports on alleged (criminal) offences that are being investigated but have not been clarified yet. In contrast to state officials or journalists, private individuals do not have to verify facts that have been disseminated by the media (BVerfGE 99, 185 (199) 1998 *Scientology*). As the boundaries of traditional journalism and other forms of online mass communication, authored by 'ordinary' but highly visible users, are blurring, begging the question if due diligence obligations of these influential users also need to increase due to these users' reach and impact.

1.3 Why and How to Respond to Disinformation? Freedom of Expression and Conflicting Interests

It was shown that although the BVerfG does not deem disinformation to be worthy of protection, even possibly false assertations fall within the scope of freedom of expression as it is difficult to establish the truth. Nevertheless, there are several rules to be found in German statutory and case law prohibiting or at least responding to particular forms of disinformation. These rules could be grouped according to the protected legal interest, to the area of law they originate in, to the type of speech or disinformation they relate to, or to the rules' addressees. The following sections are organised along the three main pillars of the German law system, i.e. roughly along areas of law. We will outline criminal law which sanctions offences (potentially) including disinformation, we will then continue with civil law which encompasses a general protection of individuals against disinformation as well as rules for specific areas of law (journalism, economic competition), and we will conclude with public law which comprises rules of media law as well as constitutional provisions protecting electoral integrity or militant democracy, or limiting public statements made by public officials. However, apart from distinguishing rules targeting particular types of speech or disinformation (e.g. transparency rules on social bot, see below) or particular groups of people (e.g. different due diligence obligation, see above), it is particularly helpful to ask which legal interests are protected by a provision concerning disinformation.

From a constitutional point of view, these legal interests constitute the legitimate aim necessary to justify a restriction on freedom of expression. The legal interests are typically grounded in the constitution and thus influence, by means of 'constitutional interpretation', the reading of the 'ordinary' criminal, civil, and public law provisions (cf. Herdegen 2025 mn. 90 et seqq.). Due to their importance, these legal interests are protected across the different areas of law even if this cannot be illustrated in detail in the limited space of this chapter. As a general rule, legal interests protected by criminal offences are also protected in civil and public law. This means, for example, that a (possible) violation of a criminal offence can allow for a civil injunction under § 823 (2) BGB (see below) or give rise to an administrative act, e.g. imposing requirements on public assemblies which prohibit the use of certain slogans.

German provisions on disinformation protect at least four legal interests: personality rights, economic interests, public peace, and the democratic order. First of all and most importantly, individuals are protected against disinformation concerning their honour (in the more traditional criminal law terminology) or their general right to personality (in the constitutional and civil law terminology; this right is based on human dignity, Art. 1 Basic Law, and the personality right, Art. 2 (1) Basic Law). Spreading lies and other forms of disinformation about a person can thus be punished as criminal offences like malicious gossip, defamation, or insult. But personality rights can also be claimed by means of civil injunctions, and they justify public laws establishing journalistic due diligence or the right to reply. In addition to that, economic interests can be protected against disinformation by criminal offences like fraud but also by laws against unfair competition or misleading commercial practices (see below). Increasingly, these laws also apply to online activities. Buying Facebook-likes for an online review, for example, is not allowed (LG Bonn WRP 2021, 392, 305).

It is less established in jurisprudence, however, that disinformation needs to be fought in favour of other legal interests. But due to the phenomenon of online disinformation, these interests have gained more attention in recent times. The criminal offence 'incitement of the masses' protects public peace (and human dignity, see below). It is thus meant to prevent, at an early stage, developments leading up to acts of violence, for example against refugees, which might be caused by online posts falsely claiming that refugees have raped a girl. Finally and on a more general level, (online) disinformation can threaten our democratic order. Legal norms are gradually being adapted to this challenge. In criminal law, a particular provision protecting politicians against certain forms of disinformation (§ 188 StGB, see below) and provisions protecting the integrity of the electoral process and the free electoral vote (§ 107a and § 108a StGB, see below), are increasingly invoked in practice. In civil law, state actors might also defend themselves against disinformation based on the interest of the 'functioning of state institutions' (BVerfG NJW 2024, 1868, 1869, 1870). Furthermore, the balancing of freedom of expression and personality rights also takes the public (democratic) interest of disseminating a particular piece of information into account. In public and constitutional law, standards of electoral integrity are being developed, and rules of due diligence and transparency are created for (online) communication in the interest of a meaningful democratic discourse. In addition, instruments of militant democracy such as the surveillance of anti-constitutional activities by the Office for the Protection of the Constitution or the prohibition of anti-constitutional associations also respond to anti-constitutional disinformation. The question remains whether the fight against disinformation should be continued in this incremental, piecemeal fashion, or if democracy deserves a more thorough protection against disinformation. On the one hand, freedom of expression places a particular burden on anyone arguing in favour of limiting disinformation on a broader scale. On the other hand, the value of a fair democratic discourse can be compared to the value of fairness and integrity in the economic sphere where corresponding rules have already been established; they could serve as a model for the protection of democracy against disinformation.

2 Online Disinformation in German Criminal Law[2]

Criminal law is considered to be the most potent instrument within the German legal system. In the context of disinformation, three distinct categories of criminal offences can be delineated.

---

[2] Written by Fabian Hoffmanns.

The first category of offences protects a person's reputation or personal rights against false or misleading statements, i.e. malicious gossip (§ 186 Strafgesetzbuch / Criminal Code, hereinafter: StGB), defamation (§ 187 StGB), insult (§ 185 StGB), and insult, malicious gossip and defamation directed at persons in political life (§ 188 StGB). The second category serves, in part alongside the protection of personal honour, primarily to safeguard public order, e.g. the offence of incitement of the masses is contained in § 130 StGB. The third category is intended to protect electoral processes and the freedom of voters from the propagation of false information, particularly the fraud in connection with elections (§ 107a StGB) and the deceiving voters (§ 108a StGB).

2.1 Malicious Gossip

2.1.1 Legal Ground: § 186 *StGB*

> Whoever asserts or disseminates a fact about another person which is suited to degrading that person or negatively affecting public opinion about that person, unless this fact can be proved to be true, incurs a penalty of imprisonment for a term not exceeding one year or a fine and, if the offence was committed publicly, in an assembly or by disseminating content (§ 11 (3)), a penalty of imprisonment for a term not exceeding two years or a fine.

Explanation: In accordance with § 186 StGB, the deliberate propagation of a fact that is demonstrably false, whether with the intention of defamation or not, is subject to legal sanction. The purpose of this provision is to protect against acts of disrespect from others, thereby safeguarding the victim's honour, or—in more contemporary terminology—their right of personality. (BGH NJW 1958, 797; MüKo StGB/Regge/Pegel, § 186 mn. 1 et seq.). It is imperative that the statement be made to a third party, rather than to the victim. (BayObLG NJW 1959, 57; MüKo StGB/Regge/Pegel, § 186 mn. 2). In contradistinction to value judgments, § 186 StGB offers protection exclusively to factual claims, that is to say, statements that are capable of being proven. (Leipziger Kommentar StGB/Hilgendorf, § 186 mn. 6; Rengier 2025, § 29 mn. 3, 4). In cases that involve both facts and value judgements, the interpretation of the text is pivotal in determining the predominance of the factual statement (Rengier 2025, § 29 mn. 4). It is important to note that criminal liability is ruled out in the event that the fact is proven to be true (MüKo StGB/Regge/Pegel, § 186 mn. 24; Rengier 2025, § 29 mn. 14). The veracity of the aforementioned fact is to be determined by the court through a trial proceeding (BeckOK StGB/Valerius, § 186 mn. 20 et seq.; Rengier 2025, § 29 mn. 14). The pivotal consideration is the accuracy of the basis of the statement (BGH NJW 1963, 665). In the absence of substantiating evidence, the individual making the statement is at a disadvantage (BGH NJW 1958, 797; BeckOK StGB/Valerius, § 186 mn. 20 et seq.). It is the prevailing opinion that the impossibility of proving a fact should not be attributed to the perpetrator's intention. (Rengier 2025, § 29 mn. 12 et seq.).

Example: In a public Facebook post, A states: "Be careful of the new employee Mara M. at company XY—she stole from her last job. Everyone here knows that!" A is asserting a fact. If the truth of this fact cannot be proven, A is liable to prosecution under § 186 StGB, regardless of whether he knows that the fact is incorrect.

2.2 Defamation

2.2.1 Legal Ground: § 187 StGB

Whoever, despite knowing better, asserts or disseminates an untrue fact about another person which is suited to degrading that person or negatively affecting public opinion about that person or endangering said person's creditworthiness incurs a penalty of imprisonment for a term not exceeding two years or a fine, and, if the act was committed publicly, in an assembly or by disseminating content (§ 11 (3)), a penalty of imprisonment for a term not exceeding five years or a fine.

Explanation: The concept of defamation encompasses more than mere malicious gossip, as it requires the element of falsehood to be intentionally perpetuated by the perpetrator (BGH NJW 1964, 1148, 1149; Leipziger Kommentar StGB/Hilgendorf § 187 mn. 4). This corresponds to a significantly higher penalty (up to five years imprisonment or a fine; for malicious gossip up to two years imprisonment or a fine). § 187 StGB encompasses not only the protection of the victim's honour or right to a good reputation, but also the protection of the victim's creditworthiness (MüKo StGB/Regge/Pegel, § 187 mn. 1).

Example: A student deliberately posts on Instagram "The teacher Mr. Müller sells drugs to his students!" even though she knows that this claim is false and there is no evidence to support it.

2.3 Insult

2.3.1 Legal Ground: § 185 StGB

The penalty for insult is imprisonment for a term not exceeding one year or a fine and, if the insult is committed publicly, in an assembly, by disseminating content (§ 11 (3)) or by means of an assault, imprisonment for a term not exceeding two years or a fine.

Explanation: The purpose of § 185 StGB is also to protect the victim's honour or personality right (MüKo StGB/Regge/Pegel, § 185 mn. 1). In contrast to §§ 186 and 187 StGB, the term "insult" as defined in § 185 StGB refers to the expression of one's own contempt, disdain, or disrespect. An insult may take the form of either a defamatory statement of fact or a value judgement. According to the prevailing view, in the case of a statement of fact, the untruthfulness of that statement is an essential element of the offence (Rengier 2025, § 29 mn. 38). If this is accepted, the statement cannot be a criminal offence if it is true (Rengier 2025, § 29 mn. 37).

Furthermore it is important to note that the legal process of prosecuting insults is typically initiated upon the request of the individual who has been insulted. This is outlined in § 194 StGB.

Example: Someone writes in an Instagram comment: "You're so stupid, you'd better not post anything anymore!" This statement constitutes a defamatory remark against another individual, thereby amounting to an insult as defined by § 185 StGB. The statement does not claim that an individual has performed a specific action (i.e. it is not a statement of fact), but rather it directly disparages the person. The veracity of the statement is not pertinent; the salient issue is the disrespect or disparagement of the person themselves. In accordance with § 185 StGB, the application of this legislation must be undertaken with meticulous consideration of the freedom of expression of the perpetrator (BVerfG NJW 2019, 2600).

A blogger writes on Facebook about a politician's statement on the topic of paedophilia, calling the politician a "paedophile slut" and "brain-dead", and disseminating a misquote made up of the politician's (true) statement and an additional half-sentence not spoken by the politician. This statement is more challenging to evaluate as it combines a value judgement and the erroneous citation of a politician's statement. The court ruled that erroneous quotations should not be accorded robust protection under the umbrella of freedom of expression. Consequently, the Facebook post was deemed to be an affront. This reasoning also applies if a blogger disseminates a misquote created by a third party that is readily identifiable as a false quotation (KG NJW 2023, 161).

2.4 *Insult, Malicious Gossip and Defamation Directed at Persons in Political Life*

2.4.1 Legal Ground: § 188 StGB

(1) If an offence of insult (§ 185) is committed publicly, in an assembly or by disseminating content (§ 11 (3)) against a person involved in the political life of the nation on account of the position that person holds in public life and if the offence is suited to making that person's public activities substantially more difficult, the penalty is imprisonment for a term not exceeding three years or a fine. The political life of the nation reaches down to the local level.

(2) Malicious gossip (§ 186) under the same conditions incurs a penalty of imprisonment for a term of between three months and five years and defamation (§ 187) under the same conditions incurs a penalty of imprisonment for a term of between six months and five years.

Explanation: In accordance with § 188 StGB, the offence of insulting someone under § 185 StGB is subject to a maximum custodial sentence of three years, provided that the insult is directed at an individual engaged in political life and pertains to their public function, thereby substantially hindering their public activities. Furthermore, the penalty is increased to a prison sentence of a minimum of three months for malicious gossip (§ 186 StGB) and a minimum of six months for defamation (§ 187 StGB). The requirements for reputation protection are stricter in this case because it involves politically active individuals who may be subject to hostility (BayObLG NJW 1982, 2511).

Example: Someone publicly posts on Twitter/X: "Member of Parliament Ms. X is definitely corrupt and secretly takes money from corporations to influence legislation." Ms. X is a person involved in political life (Member of Parliament). Thus, this example of malicious gossip or defamation will result in a more severe punishment.

2.5 *Safeguarding Legitimate Interests*

2.5.1 Legal Ground: § 193 StGB

> Critical opinions about scientific, artistic or commercial achievements, similar statements […] which are performed to exercise or protect rights, or to safeguard legitimate interests […] only entail criminal liability to the extent that the existence of an insult results from the form of the statement or the circumstances under which it was made.

Explanation: In addition to the general grounds for justification under criminal law, criminal offences against honour and personality rights can also be justified if the corresponding statement pursues legitimate interests that take precedence after weighing up the relevant factors (BGH NJW 1963, 665; Rengier 2025, § 29 mn. 45). It is evident that this ensures the safeguarding of freedom of expression (BVerfG NJW 2020, 2622 et seqq., 2629 et seqq., 2631 et seqq., 2636 et seqq.; Rengier 2025, § 29 mn. 55 et seq.)

Example: A journalist publishes the following in an online article: "During his term in office, the mayor has repeatedly wasted public funds and made decisions that have damaged the city's reputation." The statement could in principle be considered as constituting defamation (§ 186 StGB) or even insult (§ 185 StGB) due to its damaging effect on reputation. In this particular instance, § 193 StGB could provide a legitimate justification for the statement, as it constitutes an objective critique of a public figure, addressing a matter of public interest (the expenditure of taxpayers' funds).

2.6 *Incitement of Masses / Incitement to Hatred*

One of the key criminal offences pertaining to expression is that of incitement of the masses. This is a provision designed to protect public order and the dignity of the victim (MüKo StGB/Anstötz, § 130 mn. 2 et seq.; Leipziger Kommentar StGB/Krauß § 130 mn. 8).

2.6.1 Legal Ground: § 130 StGB

> (1) Whoever, in a manner suited to causing a disturbance of the public peace,
>
> 1. incites hatred against a national, racial, religious group or a group defined by their ethnic origin, against parts of the population or individuals on account of their belonging to one of the aforementioned groups or sections of the population, or calls for violent or arbitrary measures against them or.
>
> 2. violates the human dignity of others by insulting, maliciously maligning or defaming one of the aforementioned groups, parts of the population or individuals on account of their belonging to one of the aforementioned groups or parts of the population.
>
> incurs a penalty of imprisonment for a term of between three months and five years. [...].
>
> (3) Whoever publicly or in an assembly approves of, denies or downplays an act committed under the rule of National Socialism of the kind indicated in § 6 (1) of the Code of Crimes against International Law in a manner suited to causing a disturbance of the public peace incurs a penalty of imprisonment for a term not exceeding five years or a fine.
>
> (4) Whoever publicly or in an assembly disturbs the public peace in a manner which violates the dignity of the victims by approving of, glorifying or justifying National Socialist tyranny and arbitrary rule incurs a penalty of imprisonment for a term not exceeding three years or a fine.

Explanation: § 130 (1) StGB makes it an offence to incite or instigate violence, as well as to use abusive language, malicious contempt or defamation that undermines human dignity. The definitions of insult, defamation and malicious gossip are the same as those for offences in the first category (MüKo StGB/Anstötz, § 130 mn. 53; Tübinger Kommentar StGB/Sternberg-Lieben/Schittenhelm, § 130 mn. 5d). Furthermore, the act must be committed on the grounds of membership of the aforementioned groups and must be likely to disturb the public peace, the interest protected by § 130 StGB. Moreover, section (3) stipulates that denying the Holocaust is a criminal offence. In this regard, section (3) constitutes a specific legal provision intended to address the unique experience of persecution, notably endured by the Jewish people (Tübinger Kommentar StGB/Sternberg-Lieben/Schittenhelm, § 130 mn. 16). In this context, the term 'denial' is employed to denote the historical act of rejecting or refuting the Holocaust. (Tübinger Kommentar StGB/Sternberg-Lieben/Schittenhelm, § 130 mn. 16, 19).

Example: In a public forum, user A posts: "All Syrian refugees are criminal parasites and rapists who are destroying our country. We must expel them all, by force if necessary!" This constitutes incitement to hatred under § 130 (1) (1) StGB because this maliciously maligns or defames a certain section of the population defined by their nationality (Syrian refugees) and the statement is likely to disturb the public peace. As set out in § 130 (2) StGB, the penalty for such an act is increased if it is committed in public.

2.7 *Fraud in Connection with Elections*

2.7.1 Legal Ground: § 107a StGB

> (1) Whoever votes without being entitled to do so or brings about an incorrect election result or falsifies the result in another way incurs a penalty of imprisonment for a term not exceeding five years or a fine. Whoever, in the capacity as a permissible assistant, casts a vote which is contrary to the choice of the person entitled to vote or without the person entitled to vote having expressed their choice also votes without being entitled to do so.
>
> (2) Whoever incorrectly announces an election result or causes it to be incorrectly announced incurs the same penalty.

Explanation: § 107a StGB serves the public interest by ensuring that elections are conducted in accordance with the law (BGH NJW 1981, 588; MüKo StGB/Anstötz § 130 mn. 2.). The statute delineates three distinct scenarios: the first pertains to the act of casting a vote without the necessary eligibility, the second involves the fabrication of results, and the third encompasses the generation of false outcomes through other means. Furthermore, the falsification of the decision of an individual to whom assistance in voting is permitted is subject to legal sanction. The question of whether the action resulted in erroneous outcomes is not pertinent to the evaluation of criminal culpability. it is sufficient that the election was not conducted in accordance with the applicable legislation (OLG Zweibrücken NStZ 1986, 554, 555).

Example: An IT administrator for a local authority manipulates the software used for the digital counting of postal vote results. As a result, Party Z receives 2,000 additional votes while the votes for Party Y are reduced accordingly. It is evident that the determination of the election result is deliberately influenced in an incorrect manner. The manipulation in question occurs within the framework of an electoral procedure, in this case digital vote counting. The act is subject to criminal prosecution irrespective of the perpetrator's eligibility to vote.

2.8 *Deceiving Voters*

2.8.1 Legal Ground: § 108a StGB

> (1) Whoever, by means of deception, causes another to be mistaken as to the content of their declaration upon casting their vote or, against their will, not to vote or to cast an invalid vote incurs a penalty of imprisonment for a term not exceeding two years or a fine.

Explanation: The formation of opinion is not immune to the influence of political campaigning and advertising. § 108a StGB is intended to protect the electoral freedom of the electorate and to prevent an erroneous election result (BGH NJW 1956, 1485; Tübinger Kommentar StGB/Eser/Schuster, § 108a mn. 1 et seq.). It is a criminal offence to mislead voters by making false statements or concealing relevant facts. The deception must result in an error when casting a vote.

Example: Shortly before a federal election, a group spreads fake online ads and social media posts claiming: "Voters for Party X must also sign their vote on the ballot, otherwise their vote will be invalid!" The objective of these actions is to minimise the number of votes for Party X, since the act of signing a ballot paper will render it invalid. In the event of success, the attempt fulfils § 108a StGB. Nevertheless, the publication of a sentence such as "Only idiots vote for Party XY!" may be considered distasteful by some, however, it is protected by the right to freedom of expression and does not fall under the category of deception about the voting process or the explanation of how to cast a vote.

3 Online Disinformation in German Civil Law[3]

German civil law does not provide a single, exhaustive regime to address online disinformation. Instead, regulatory responses are fragmented across several doctrinal pillars. In particular, civil-law remedies may be invoked from the general right of personality, for example where disinformation is disseminated in the context of suspicion-based reporting. In addition, claims may arise from protective (criminal) provisions such as §§ 185 ff. StGB via § 823 (2) Bürgerliches Gesetzbuch / German Civil Code (hereinafter: BGB). Finally, disinformation might also be prohibited according to the rules of unfair competition under the Gesetz gegen unlauteren Wettbewerb / Act against Unfair Competition (hereinafter: UWG) if disinformation is spread in a commercial context.

[3] Written by Nicolaj Feltes.

3.1 General Right of Personality

3.1.1 Legal Ground: Art. 1 Basic Law for the Federal Republic of Germany (Hereinafter: Basic Law)

(1) Human dignity shall be inviolable. To respect and protect it shall be the duty of all state authority. [...]

3.1.2 Legal Ground: Art. 2 Basic Law

(1) Every person shall have the right to free development of his personality insofar as he does not violate the rights of others or offend against the constitutional order or the moral law. [...]

3.1.3 Legal Ground: § 823 BGB

(1) A person who, intentionally or negligently, unlawfully injures the life, limb, health, freedom, property or some other right of another person is liable to provide compensation to the other party for the damage arising therefrom.

(2) The same duty is incumbent on a person who commits a breach of a statute that is intended to protect another person. If, according to the contents of the statute, it is possible to violate it also without fault, then liability to compensation only exists in the case of fault.

3.1.4 Legal Ground: § 1004 BGB

(1) If the ownership is interfered with by means other than removal or retention of possession, the owner may demand that the disturber remove the interference. If there is the concern that further interferences will ensue, the owner may seek a prohibitory injunction. [...]

Explanation: The general right of personality (*allgemeines Persönlichkeitsrecht*), derived from Art. 2 (1) and Art. 1 (1) Basic Law, is an uncodified constitutional right shaped by case law. In civil law, injunctive relief claims are based on § 1004 (1) i.c.w. § 823 (1) BGB, while damages are pursued under § 823 (1) BGB. It encompasses various personality rights, such as the right to one's own image or the right to self-determination. In the context of the right to self-determination, the BVerfG has held that a violation of the general right of personality occurs especially where words are put into someone's mouth that were never uttered by that person, undermining their self-determined claim to social recognition (BVerfGE 54, 148, (155) 1980 *Eppler*).

Not every interference with the general right of personality constitutes a violation thereof, as the right is classified as a framework right. Rather, it is necessary to conduct an interest-balancing exercise that accounts for both the legitimate interest of the opposing side—in particular their freedom of expression—and the general right of personality of the party affected by the alleged personality violation (settled case-law, e.g. BGH NJW 1987, 2667). Expressions of opinion, which are characterised by elements of judgement or subjective belief (BVerfGE 66, 116 (149) 1984 *Springer/Wallraff*), are fundamentally constitutive due to their paramount importance for a democratic and liberal constitutional order (BVerfGE 35, 202 (221) 1973 *Lebach*). True factual statements fall within the scope of the right to freedom of expression only insofar as they support opinion formation (BVerfGE 85, 1 (15) 1991 *Bayer Aktionäre*). In contrast, incorrect statements of fact cannot serve the accurate opinion formation and are therefore not protected by the right to freedom of expression (BVerfGE 54, 208 (219) 1980 *Böll*).

Visual forms of disinformation—particularly deceptive deepfakes—may, in cases where the depicted person has not given consent, be enforced via § 823 (1) BGB on the basis of § 22 Kunsturhebergesetz (Act on Copyright and Related Rights, hereinafter: KUG) (see Kumkar and Rapp 2022, p. 204). The "right to one's image" laid down in § 22 KUG likewise forms part of the general right of personality.

Example: B creates and distributes fake private messages allegedly from politician P, containing fabricated statements where the politician appears to make racist remarks. These fake messages are shared across social media platforms, presented as "leaked" authentic correspondence. Through the fabricated text message, B attributes words to P that P never uttered, impairing his self-determined claim to social recognition. However, as a framework right, mere impairment of this right does not automatically create a claim, as B's right to freedom of expression could predominate. Here, the content does not indicate that it is satirical or inauthentic, causing recipients to perceive it as "genuine". Based on this belief, they cannot form an accurate opinion about P's alleged actions—therefore, the factual claim falls outside B's freedom of expression. Accordingly, P's interests prevail, and his general right of personality is infringed.

3.2 Civil Action in Response to Criminal Offences

3.2.1 Legal Ground

Civil claims can also be brought for violations of criminal provisions under § 1004 BGB by analogy i.c.w. § 823 (2) BGB. A prerequisite is that the criminal provision qualifies as a protective law (*Schutzgesetz*). A protective law under § 823 (2) BGB is any legal provision that is intended to protect an individual or a specific group of persons against the infringement of a particular interest. This is especially the case with provisions concerning offences against personal honour, such as §§ 185 ff. StGB.

Explanation: In assessing offences against personal honour (§§ 185 ff. StGB), it is—similarly to the general right of personality—crucial to determine whether the statement in question constitutes an expression of opinion or a statement of fact. This is particularly relevant when a state institution is the 'victim' of the statement in question, as these institutions cannot invoke the general right of personality, which is a fundamental right afforded exclusively to natural persons. Instead, the state can rely on § 1004 BGB by analogy i.c.w. 823 (2) BGB and §§ 185 ff. StGB to act against defamatory and false statements.

Additionally, in cases of attribution confusion caused by the unauthorised use of names or official designations, a more limited but targeted form of protection can be obtained under § 12 BGB, enforced via § 1004 BGB by analogy and § 823 (1) BGB, including situations in which the unauthorised use occurs through the dissemination of (deceptive) deepfakes that create the false impression of official communication (LG Berlin II, GRUR-RS 2024, 25902).

Example: Journalist J publishes a tweet on X, stating that Germany has paid "370 MILLION EUROS in development aid to the TALIBAN!" over the past years, followed by strong criticism of the federal government, calling it a "historically unique madhouse." The tweet included a link to an article titled "Germany resumes development aid to Afghanistan", visible in the tweet preview. The corresponding Federal Ministry (BMZ) wants to take action against the tweet (BVerfG, NJW 2024, 1868).

The state cannot invoke fundamental rights to protect its reputation. Therefore, unlike holders of personality rights, the state needs to tolerate even polemical criticism (BVerfG, NJW 2024, 1868, 1869) as such criticism is protected under Art. 5 (1) Basic Law. That said, there is no constitutional protection for false statements of fact or mere vituperative criticism. If a statement combines factual and evaluative elements that cannot be separated without distorting its meaning, it must be treated as an expression of opinion to protect fundamental rights effectively (e.g. BVerfGE 61, 1, (8) 1982 *'CSU NPD Europas'*). Here, J stated in a tweet that Germany has paid development aid to the Taliban, whereas in fact the funds were allocated for projects in Afghanistan. Accordingly, the question arises whether this constitutes a false statement, given that no direct payments were in fact made to the Taliban, or whether it is to be regarded as a deliberately exaggerated expression of opinion. The isolated consideration of the statement "Germany paid 370 million euros to the Taliban" may at first appear to be a false statement of fact, as the assertion implies a direct payment of development aid to the Taliban—which is not the case. However, the headline of the linked article "Germany resumes development aid to Afghanistan" must also be taken into account, as it was readily visible without clicking on the link. Additionally, it must be considered that assertions can contain both expressions of opinions and statements of fact. The criticism expressed may concern the fact that development aids, while not benefiting the Taliban directly, may nevertheless do so indirectly (BVerfG NJW 2024, 1868, 1871). As a result, the statement constitutes a permissible expression of opinion. It does not give rise to a legal claim.

3.3 Suspicion-Based Reporting

3.3.1 Legal Ground

The permissibility of suspicion-based reporting is also evaluated pursuant to the provisions of (§ 1004 (1) BGB by analogy i.c.w.) § 823 (1) BGB i.c.w. Art. 2 (1) Basic Law and Art. 1 (1) Basic Law, as the person under suspicion may invoke his general right of personality.

Explanation: According to consistent case law, a factual allegation whose truth has not been clarified and which concerns a matter of substantial public interest may not be prohibited as long as the person asserting or disseminating it may regard it as necessary for the protection of legitimate interests. Therefore, judicial precedent has established criteria for assessing the permissibility of suspicion-based reporting: there must be a minimum evidential basis, no prejudgment of the affected person, an opportunity for them to comment, and the matter must be of significant public interest (settled case-law, e.g. BGH NJW 2023, 3233, 3236 et seq.).

Example: Credible evidence suggests that Chief Executive B has misappropriated company assets. On Thursday morning, journalist J attempts to contact B to offer her the opportunity to comment on the allegations. Instead, the call is answered by B's co-shareholder, C. J informs C that he plans to publish the article the following day and emphasizes the urgency of a response from B. Despite this, B does not return the call. J publishes an article stating that, based on the available evidence, B is likely to have committed embezzlement.

Whether J was permitted to publish the article depends on the criteria for suspicion-based reporting. The existing "credible" evidence satisfies the requirement for a foundational basis of supporting the veracity of information. Furthermore, J's reporting characterizes the conduct as "likely" embezzlement, which presents the matter as suspicion rather than an established fact. However, it is questionable whether J's call satisfies the requirement to give B an opportunity to submit a statement. It is already doubtful whether conveying the information to a third party can, in itself, be sufficient to meet the requirements for offering an opportunity to comment (BGH ZUM 2019, 472, 476). Even if B was aware that her co-shareholder had spoken with J—and thereby became aware of the underlying suspicion—this does not render the opportunity to comment dispensable. Rather, a waiver of the opportunity to give a statement can only be assumed if the person concerned is aware of the specific allegations made against them (BGH ZUM 2019, 472, 476).

3.4 Protection of Competitors

3.4.1 Legal Ground: § 3 UWG

(1) Unfair commercial practices are illegal. [...]

3.4.2 Legal Ground: § 4 UWG

Unfairness is deemed to have occurred where a person.

asserts or disseminates facts about the goods, services or business of a competitor or about the entrepreneur or a member of the management of the business, such facts being suited to harming the operation of the business or the credit of the entrepreneur, to the extent that the facts are not demonstrably true; if the communications are confidential and if the person making or receiving the communication has a legitimate interest therein, the action is only unfair where facts are asserted or disseminated contrary to the truth; [...]

3.4.3 Legal Ground: § 8 UWG

(1) Whoever engages in an illegal commercial practice pursuant to section 3 or section 7 can be sued for elimination and, in the event of the risk of recurrence, to cease and desist. The claim to cease and desist already pertains in the event of the risk of such infringement of section 3 or section 7.

(2) Where the infringements are committed in a business by a member of staff or by a person exercising a mandate, the claim to cease and desist and the claim to elimination are also deemed to apply in relation to the owner of the business.

(3) The claims under subsection (1) vest in.

any competitor which supplies or demands goods or services not only to an insignificant extent and not only occasionally; [...]

3.4.4 Legal Ground: § 9 UWG

(1) Whoever, while acting with intent or negligently, engages in an illegal commercial practice pursuant to section 3 or section 7 is obliged to compensate competitors for the damage arising therefrom.

(2) Whoever, while acting with intent or negligently, engages in an illegal commercial practice pursuant to section 3 and thereby causes consumers to take a transactional decision which they would otherwise not have taken is obliged to compensate the damage arising therefrom. [...].

Explanation: The UWG transposes relevant EU directives, including the "Unfair Commercial Practices Directive", into German law, ensuring their standards apply nationally. Its core provision, § 3 (1) UWG, prohibits unfair commercial practices. §§ 3a–6 UWG then specify when a practice is considered "unfair". In this context, § 4 UWG protects competitors and covers cases where a market participant disseminates false facts about a competitor.

Example: A runs a cosmetics company that has been struggling ever since competitor B entered the market. In response, A publishes a post on social media falsely claiming B's skincare products contain harmful chemicals. The allegation is entirely unfounded and solely serves to deter potential customers from purchasing B's products.

Under § 3 (1) UWG, commercial practices are unlawful if they are deemed "unfair" within the meaning of §§ 3a to 6 UWG. Pursuant to § 4 no. 2 UWG, unfairness occurs when false factual claims are made about a competitor's goods, services or business. Both A and B supply their customers with cosmetic products, operating in the same market sector, and are thus considered "competitors". Moreover, the asserted facts about B's goods are deliberate falsehoods, satisfying the criteria set out in § 4 no. 2 UWG. A is required to delete the social media post pursuant to § 8 (1) UWG and to compensate B for the resulting damage under § 9 (1) UWG.

3.5 *Misleading Commercial Practices*

3.5.1 Legal Ground: § 5 UWG

> (1) Unfairness is deemed to have occurred where a person engages in a misleading commercial practice which is suited to causing the consumer or other market participant to take a transactional decision which he or she would not have taken otherwise.
>
> (2) A commercial practice is regarded as misleading if it contains false statements or other information suited to deception regarding the following circumstances:
>
> the main characteristics of the goods or services, such as their availability, nature, execution, benefits, risks, composition, accessories, method or date of manufacture, delivery or provision, fitness for purpose, uses, quantity, specification, after-sale customer assistance, complaint handling, geographical or commercial origin, the results to be expected from their use, or the results or material features of tests carried out on the goods or services;
>
> the reason for the purchase, such as the existence of a specific price advantage, the price or the manner in which the price is calculated, or the conditions on the basis of which the goods are supplied or the services are provided; (…).

Explanation: Similarly to § 4 UWG, § 5 UWG defines when a commercial practice is "unfair" and therefore illegal within the meaning of § 3 (1) UWG. According to § 5 (1) UWG, "unfairness" encompasses misleading commercial practices likely to lead the customer to take a decision they would otherwise not have made. § 5 (2) UWG lists a catalogue of circumstances that, if misrepresented or falsely conveyed in a manner likely to deceive, render a commercial practice "misleading". This catalogue covers deceptive practices relating to the main characteristics of the good, such as its availability (no. 1); the reason for the purchase, such as the existence of a specific price advantage (no. 2) or attributes of the entrepreneur (no. 3). Additionally, § 5a UWG prohibits cases in which misleading commercial practices occur by omission.

Example: B, who runs an online coffee machine store, sends an e-mail newsletter, reading: "20% off the entire order – only today*." This was followed by a section of the e-mail with visuals repeatedly highlighting the 20% discount. At the end, the asterisk note was explained in a very small print: "Does not apply to […] coffee machines." C, needing a coffee machine, buys one on B's website, believing he must take advantage of the discount that is available for today only (LG Hamburg GRUR-RS 2021, 44500).

As in the example mentioned above, commercial practices are unlawful under § 3 (1) UWG if they are considered unfair within the meaning of §§ 3a–6 UWG. In this case, advertising with an e-mail reading "20% off – today only", despite excluding coffee machines—the main product category in B's assortment—merely via a small-print asterisk note may constitute a misleading commercial practice. The phrase "20% off the entire order" in the newsletter could amount to a false or deceptive statement within the meaning of § 5 (2) No. 2 UWG, as it relates to the existence of a special price advantage. The Regional Court (LG) of Hamburg affirmed that the statement in question was deceptive regarding a particular price advantage. In the court's view, an asterisk disclaimer is inadmissible if significant parts of the product range are excluded from the advertised offer. While consumers may anticipate some limitations indicated by an asterisk, these are typically understood as conditions, such as the discount not being combinable with other offers (LG Hamburg, GRUR-RS 2021, 44500). Accordingly, B's newsletter was "unfair" and therefore unlawful within the meaning of § 3 (1) UWG. While § 8 (3) UWG does not grant consumers the right to seek injunctive relief, C may claim damages under § 9 (2) UWG for intentional unlawful commercial practices that influenced their transactional decisions.

4 Online Disinformation in German Public Law[4]

German Public Law encompasses a variety of different constitutional, statutory, and other laws dealing with (online) disinformation. A first set of rules by the Interstate Media Treaty (hereinafter: IMT) covers media activities: It extends both journalistic due diligence obligations to verify facts and the right to reply of a person affected by public reporting—already established in the traditional context of press and journalism—to broadcasting and telemedia. Furthermore, the IMT also creates transparency obligations for the use of social bots. Another set of legal provisions is found in the constitution and implemented by statutory laws. The constitution very fragmentarily protects the integrity of the electoral process, thereby relying on limits to electoral campaigning and speech as defined by criminal law. The Basic Law, designed as a militant democracy, also erects safeguard against anti-constitutional activities which might also consist in spreading disinformation; as a consequence, these activities might give rise to surveillance by the Federal Office for the Protection of the Constitution or to a ban of an association if it is actively agitating against the constitutional order. Finally, constitutional law also binds public officials to the principle of neutrality and objectivity.

[4] Written by Pia Diemath.

4.1 IMT: Due Diligence Obligations for Broadcasting and Telemedia with Journalistic-Editorial Offers

The Interstate Media Treaty contains the principal regulatory framework for the organisation and the offer, the transmission, and the provision of broadcasting and telemedia in Germany. Broadcasting is defined in Art. 2 (1) sentences 1 and 2 IMT as "a linear information and communication service; it means the provision and transmission of journalistic-editorial offers for the general public for simultaneous reception in moving images or sound along a schedule using telecommunication. The term includes offers which are transmitted in encrypted form or can be received against special payment." Telemedia is defined in Art. 2 (1) sentence 3 IMT as "all electronic information and communication services", as far as they are not telecommunication services pursuant to § 3 No. 61 of the Telecommunications Act (hereinafter: TKG), which consist entirely of the transmission of signals, or telecommunications-based services pursuant to § 3 No. 63 TKG, or broadcasting pursuant to sentences 1 and 2.

4.1.1 Legal Ground: Art. 6 (1) IMT (Broadcasting)

> Reporting and information programmes must conform to accepted journalistic standards, also where virtual components are employed. They must be independent and objective. Prior to transmission, news must be verified regarding their truthfulness and origin in accordance with the attention to accuracy and source required by the circumstances. Comments must be clearly separated from the reports and must be identified as such giving the name of the author.

Explanation: Art. 6 IMT stipulates due diligence obligations for broadcasting. Traditionally, broadcasting as defined in the IMT includes private and public broadcasting services via TV or radio, especially as opposed to the printed press (BeckOK InfoMedienR/Martini, MStV § 2 mn. 21). In the online context, the streaming of the regular, linear broadcasting programme via the internet also falls within the scope of the broadcast (BeckOK InfoMedienR/Martini, MStV § 2 mn. 25), resulting in the application of the duties of Art. 6 IMT to this case (Beck RundfunkR/Flechsig, MStV § 6 mn. 11). According to Art. 6 (1) sentence 1 IMT reporting and information programmes must conform to 'accepted journalistic standards'. These standards are stipulated within the IMT itself or to be found in the sum of legal provisions regulating the legality and permissibility of information procurement and information dissemination through broadcasting in general (Beck RundfunkR/Flechsig, MStV § 6 mn. 27).

Art. 6 (1) sentence 3 IMT explicitly names two principles with relevance to the phenomenon of online disinformation. Art. 6 (1) sentence 2 IMT states that reporting and information programmes must be independent and objective. Furthermore, Art. 6 (1) sentence 3 IMT states that prior to their transmission, news must be verified regarding their truthfulness and origin in accordance with the attention to accuracy and source required by the circumstances. Where the news concern personal rights of individuals, the scope of these obligations equals the standards elaborated by civil and criminal law courts (BeckOK InfoMedienR/Fiedler, MStV § 6 mn. 2). But where the news concerns a subject not related to personal rights, reporting a wrongful information also may present an infringement of Art. 6 (1) sentence 3 IMT (BeckOK InfoMedienR/Fiedler, MStV § 6 mn. 3).

Example: B regularly watches the linear live stream programme of the public-service broadcasting service 'A2Z' online. The streamed shows she watches cover the topics of solar energy and house construction. They highlight supposed ways of reducing energy consumption in the home. B believes that this information is untrue and that those responsible for the programmes were aware of this. As the content of the programme does not address her personality rights, she cannot pursue civil action. B seeks redress through administrative law proceedings. Even though it is possible that this kind of reporting sheds a too positive light on possibilities of house owners to save energy to a degree that includes possibly wrong factual statements on this topic and hereby violates the accepted journalistic standards (BeckOK InfoMedienR/Fiedler, MStV § 6 mn. 3), B does not have the possibility to legally challenge this reporting. While the provision formulates programme principles and objectives, compliance and implementation thereof cannot be personally enforced by every viewer or listener by means of administrative proceedings (VG Köln, Urt. v. 18.11.2007 – 6 K 2/07, BeckRS 2012, 50839).

4.1.2 Legal Ground: Art. 19 (1) IMT (Telemedia with Journalistic-Editorial Offers)

> Telemedia with journalistic-editorial offers, particularly in which the entire or partial content of periodical print materials is reproduced in text or image, must comply with recognised journalistic principles. The same applies to other commercial, journalistic-editorial telemedia offers, which regularly contain news or political information and which do not fall under sentence 1. Before they are disseminated, news stories are to be checked by the provider for content, origin, and truth with the due diligence required for the circumstances.

Explanation: Art. 19 (1) IMT obliges telemedia with journalistic-editorial offers to comply with recognised journalistic principles. 'Offers' are to be defined as media products, free or paid, for a specific target group (BeckOK InfoMedienR/Lent, MStV § 17 mn. 12). These offers are 'journalistic-editorial' if they have a certain degree of formal and content-related preparation and if they give users the impression of directly serving the formation of individual and public opinion in the present day within the projected social relevance. This can include professional or citizen journalism (Beck RundfunkR/Grosche, MStV § 19 mn. 24). Art. 19 (1) IMT also targets online journalism offers. Traditionally, this includes digital versions of printed newspapers or magazines as well as original e-journals distributed via various channels, e.g. websites, social media pages or app stores. But blogs can also constitute telemedia with journalistic-editorial offers if they fulfil the criteria above, especially in distinction from (excluded) blogs serving personal presentation, where for example merely personal political opinions in relation to other journalistic offers are presented (BeckOK InfoMedienR/Lent, MStV § 17 mn. 17 et seq.).

Art. 19 (1) IMT refers to the 'recognised journalistic principles', which are to be found along the lines of the relevant civil law jurisprudence and, where appropriate, with the interpretation aid of the German Press Code (Beck RundfunkR/Grosche, MStV § 19 mn. 32). One central due diligence obligation explicitly mentioned in Art. 19 (1) sentence 3 IMT is the 'duty to truth'. Providers need to check published news—meaning factual assertations, not value judgments – for truthfulness with the due diligence required by the circumstances. When they report unconfirmed reports, rumours and suppositions, they need to be identified as such. However, this is not an absolute obligation for truth, but a due diligence obligation, as the media may otherwise not be able to fulfil their role in public control anymore (BeckOK InfoMedienR/Lent, MStV § 19 mn. 5).

Example: A is a social media influencer regularly posting news on domestic politics at the federal level. After reading in a news article that members of the right-wing party work for the well-known podcast B, A publishes a post repeating this information. A makes no effort to verify the information but relies on the original news article before she publishes her post. Due to the continuity and the context of her activity, A falls within the scope of Art. 19 (1) IMT. The due diligence obligations therein include the duty to conduct their own research into the veracity of the information spread, even when taking information from other media. However, A simply trusted that the uncontested reports from the news articles were accurate and therefore violated Art. 19 (1) IMT (Jennessen/Schlossarczyk 2025, pp. 430 et seq.; BVerfG ZUM-RD 2000, 271).

4.2 *IMT: Right to Reply*

4.2.1 Legal Ground: Art. 20 (1), (2) IMT

> (1) Providers of telemedia including journalistic edited offers which, in particular, prior to distribution, completely or partially reproduce texts or visual contents of periodical print media are required to include in their offers without delay the reply of the person or institution who is affected by an assertion of fact made in their offer at no cost to the person affected. The reply must be provided without insertions and omissions in the same layout as the assertion of fact. The reply must have the same length as the assertion of fact and be provided in direct conjunction with it. If the assertion of fact is no longer provided or if the offer is discontinued before the reply can be included, the reply must be provided in a comparable position for the same duration as the assertion of fact originally provided. A response to the reply must be limited to factual information and must not be directly linked to the reply.
>
> (2) No obligation to include the reply pursuant to (1) arises if:
>
> 1. the affected party has no legitimate interest in the reply,

2. the reply inappropriately exceeds the extent of the assertion of fact being refuted,

3. the reply is not restricted to factual information or includes contents which are liable to prosecution, or

4. the reply, in writing and signed by the affected party or its legal representative, is not made available to the provider against whom a right of reply is claimed, without delay, at the latest within six weeks following the last day of the offer including the refuted text being available, but in any event three months after the offer was first made available.

Explanation: Addressees of Art. 20 IMT are the providers of periodical digital press, including hybrid or merely digital periodical press as well as blogs of amateur press that continuously amend their offer with articles and videos on demand that are part of a periodical media offer (BeckOK InfoMedienR/Fiedler, MStV § 20 mn. 4 seqq.; 15). They are "required to include in their offers without delay the reply of the person or institution who is affected by an assertion of fact made in their offer at no cost to the person affected." The reply of the person or institution affected must (also) be a fact, not a value judgment, see Art. 20 (2) No. 3. It is to be noted that this requirement is not linked to a violation of rights by the provider but also applies in case the reported fact is true and lawful (BeckOK InfoMedienR/Fiedler, MStV vor § 20). However, the right to reply is excluded for example where the affected party has no legitimate interest in the reply (No. 1), which is the case e.g. if the reply is manifestly or judicially known to be untrue or if the addressee already published a correction that is recognisable as such (BeckOK InfoMedienR/Fiedler, MStV § 20 mn. 1).

Example: German Newspaper A posts a video on YouTube in which it states that politician C has been a member of a right-wing party for five years before she eventually joined her current, more liberal party. Politician C asserts her right to reply, ordering the newspaper to publish a counterstatement, stating that she has not actively engaged in any party action of said conservative party. The counterstatement needs to be published in the "same format", in order to ensure that it can generate the same attention and reach the same addressees. In this case C has originally stated the facts via spoken word in a video, therefore the counterstatement has to be published as a spoken text as well (KG MMR 2024, 961).

4.3 IMT: Transparency Obligation for the Use of Social Bots

4.3.1 Legal Ground: Art. 18 (3) IMT

In the case of content or messages created automatically by means of a computer programme (sic), providers of telemedia in social networks are obligated to specify the fact of automation, provided that the user account used for this purpose appears to have been made available by natural persons.

It must be made legibly clear, with or before the content or the message, that it was automatically created and sent using a computer program that controls the user account.

'Creation' within the meaning of this provision does not only mean when content and messages are automatically generated immediately before they are sent, but also when prefabricated content or pre-programmed message is used automatically with the transmission.

Explanation: Art. 18 (3) IMT carries a special importance in the context of online disinformation as it obliges providers of telemedia in social networks to clarify the usage of "social bots". The definition of telemedia according to Art. 2 (1) sentence 3 IMT is a rather broad one. The addressees of Art. 18 (3) IMT, i.e. the providers of telemedia, are the holders of the accounts used for the purpose of spreading automatically created content or messages (Siara 2020, p. 372). They have to act in social networks, which for this purpose are to be defined as platforms that are operated for profit on the Internet and are intended for users to share any content with other users or make it available to the public. This excludes platforms with their own journalistic-editorial offers, platforms that merely serve individual communication and platforms used for spreading specific content (von Ungern-Sternberg 2022, pp. 107 et seq.). A central condition for the obligation is the optical deception of identity implying that the account is used by a natural person (BeckOK InfoMedienR/Lent, MStV § 18 mn. 20). If this is the case, automatically generated content or messages must be clearly labelled by the addressed holders of the account with information concerning its automated origin. The violation of Art. 18 (3) IMT presents an administrative offence, see Art. 115 (1) sentence 2 No. 2 IMT.

Example: A German political candidate has poor poll ratings among voters in Germany with Turkish heritage. The candidate uses bots on the social media platform X carrying Turkish-sounding names and generating posts exclusively by automated means containing positive statements about her. These bots are constructed to mimic the behaviour of natural persons, deceiving users into believing they are real people. By using the social bots this way, the candidate violates her obligation according to Art. 18(3) IMT.

4.4 Constitutional Protection of the Electoral Process

4.4.1 Legal Ground: Art. 41 Basic Law

(1) Scrutiny of elections shall be the responsibility of the Bundestag. It shall also decide whether a Member has lost his seat.

(2) Complaints against such decisions of the Bundestag may be lodged with the Federal Constitutional Court.

Explanation: German Public Law lays down rules regarding speech in the specific context of elections. From a constitutional law perspective, the scrutiny of elections (Art. 41 Basic Law) is decisive for the examination of potential irregularities in elections on a federal level. There is no set of consolidated rules for the review of these elections, leaving considerable space for the development of such rules in practice and academia (Dürig/Herzog/Scholz/Klein/Schwarz GG, Art. 41 mn. 12). Both the BVerfG and the German Federal Administrative Court (hereinafter: BVerwG) have elaborated basic rules that help distinguish between lawful and unlawful influence and can gain relevance in the area of online disinformation. The BVerfG notably distinguishes between private and state actors.

As regards private third parties, including political parties and individual candidates, an unlawful influence occurs, according to the BVerfG, where these parties have influenced the election decision by means of coercion or pressure, or if the formation of voter opinion has been influenced in a similarly serious manner without there being sufficient opportunity to defend against this—for example with the help of the courts or the police—or to compensate for it, for example by means of electoral competition (BVerfGE 124, 1 (20 et seq.) 2009 *Nachwahl*). The BVerfG emphasises the role of the public communication process as a means to counter private influence on the election. This will likely mean that permissible activities by private individuals are only limited by criminal offences such as § 108 StGB (coercion of voters) or § 240 StGB (coercion) (for more examples, see above; Dürig/Herzog/Scholz/Klein/Schwarz GG, Art. 41 mn. 122). Furthermore, the BVerwG has ruled that as private actors are not bound by the principle of democracy, electoral freedom according to Art. 28(1) sentence 1, 2 Basic Law or the fundamental rights, private dissemination of deception and lies does not constitute an electoral error (BVerwG Beschl. v. 5.6.2012—8 B 24.12, BeckRS 2012, 210,267, mn. 12).

The BVerfG case law for state influence on election is stricter (Dürig/Herzog/Scholz/Klein/Schwarz GG, Art. 41 mn. 128). It states that state influence on elections is unlawful—to the point that it may jeopardise the validity of the election –, if, in the run-up to the election state authorities have exerted a more than insignificant degree of partisan influence on the formation of the will of the voters (BVerfGE 124, 1 (20) 2009 *Nachwahl*; BVerfGE 103, 111 (132 et seq.) 2001 *Wahlprüfung Hessen*; BVerfGE 122, 304 (315) 2009 *Wahlprüfungsbeschwerde nach Bundestagsauflösung*).

Example: Such a form of undue influence could occur if state financial resources are used in election campaigns to pay for social bots that specifically promote a particular party. This could be the case if a member of the federal government used his ministry's funds during an election campaign to finance social bots on X that deliberately mislead voters into believing that a particularly large number of voters of Turkish origin have a particularly positive opinion of the candidate (von Ungern-Sternberg 2019, p. 21).

4.5 *Militant Democracy and Anti-Constitutional Disinformation*

If online disinformation is directed against the core principles of the German constitution, it might also lead to a response by German authorities—as part of the so-called militant democracy—intended to safeguard the constitution from its enemies. Two examples can illustrate this: the activities of the Federal Office for the Protection under the Federal Constitution Protection Act and the possible prohibition of anti-constitutional associations.

4.5.1 Legal Ground: § 3 (1) Federal Constitution Protection Act (Hereinafter: BVerfSchG)[5]

> (1) The task of the federal and state constitutional protection authorities is to collect and evaluate information, in particular factual and personal information, news and documents, about
>
> 1. efforts directed against the liberal-democratic constitutional order, the existence or security of the Federation or a state, or aimed at unlawfully impairing the functioning of the constitutional organs of the Federation or a state or their members (...).

Explanation: According to § 1 (1) BVerfSchG, the protection of the constitution serves to protect the liberal-democratic constitutional order, the existence and security of the Federal Republic and the federal states. § 3 BVerfSchG further defines the specific areas in which the Office for the Protection of the Constitution (BfV) takes action. Depending on the severity of a suspicion that an anti-constitutional behaviour is taking place, the authorities can take various measures. These measures range from gathering information from general sources to surveillance measures and internet monitoring (Wöhlert 2024, pp. 645 et seqq.). In addition, there are reporting obligations to the interior ministries and the public, cf. § 16 BVerfSchG. Although online disinformation is not explicitly mentioned in this legal framework, it is relevant for measures taken by the BfV.

Example: In 2024, the yearly report of the BfV on its activities included explicit remarks on the topic of online disinformation by the Russian Federation's intelligence and security services in Germany. The report referred to the case of the pro-Russian news portal 'Voice of Europe', which presented itself as an international news portal while spreading narratives in line with Russian foreign policy. This Russian influence organisation was uncovered and stopped by the BfV and other European intelligence services in the run-up to the European Parliament elections on 9 June 2024. This case was highlighted in connection with Russia's general efforts to influence political discourse in Germany in favour of pro-Russian positions. According to the report, the dissemination of state propaganda and disinformation, particularly on social media,

---

[5] Our translation.

has intensified with the 2022 war against Ukraine (Bundesministerium des Innern 2024).

4.5.2 Legal Ground: Art. 9 Basic Law

> (2) "Associations whose aim or activities contravene the criminal laws or that are directed against the constitutional order or the concept of international understanding shall be prohibited."

Explanation: The German Constitution in combination with German ordinary law provides for the prohibition of associations that are directed against the constitutional order or the principle of international understanding. The 'constitutional order' in the sense of Art. 9 (2) Basic Law encompasses not the constitution as a whole, but its core consisting of the central principles of human dignity, democracy, and the rule of law (BeckOK GG/Cornils, Art. 9 mn. 26). Art. 9 (2) Basic Law is part of the principle of 'militant democracy', which is set up in the Basic Law to ensure that enemies of the constitution do not endanger, impair or destroy the constitutional order or the existence of the state by invoking the freedoms granted by the Basic Law (BVerfGE 144, 20 (164) 2017 *NPD-Verbotsverfahren*). While these provisions do not have an explicit link to online disinformation, past cases have shown that online disinformation is a considerable factor in the prohibition of associations.

Example: In 2025, the Federal Minister of the Interior prohibited the "Königreich Deutschland e.V.". This association is considered the biggest association of "Reichsbürger", i.e. individuals negating the existence of the Federal Republic of Germany and rejecting its legal system. Instead, the members of this association believe in the existence of a "Königreich Deutschland", a monarchical-absolutist kingdom of Germany. The association aggressively claims its own statehood to the outside world and questions the Federal Republic's monopoly on the use of force. The Federal Ministry of Interior has found that the "Königreich Deutschland e.V.", amongst other aspects, has continuously propagated antisemitic conspiracy-theoretical narratives delegitimising state institutions in an unconstitutional manner. To spread its ideology, the "Königreich Deutschland e.V." has been active on social media platforms such as YouTube and Telegram. The ban of the "Königreich Deutschland e.V." comes along with the blocking of the online platforms of the association and its sub-organisations (Bundesministerium des Innern 2025).

4.6 *The Constitutional Principle of Neutrality and Objectivity for Public Officials*

4.6.1 Legal Ground: Article 21 Basic Law

> (1) Political parties shall participate in the formation of the political will of the people. They may be freely established. Their internal organisation must conform to democratic principles. They must publicly account for their assets and for the sources and use of their funds.

Explanation: In Germany, the state cannot invoke Art. 5 (1) Basic Law vis-à-vis its citizens (Cf. e.g. BVerwG NVwZ 2018, 433, 435). Therefore, different standards apply for statements made by state actors in the exercise of their official duties. Generally, there are two basic principles that significantly shape the dogma surrounding the right of public officials to express their opinions: The principle of neutrality and the principle of objectivity. The principle of neutrality implies neutrality by public officials regarding political parties. According to the case law of the BVerfG, this principle finds its constitutional basis in the principle of democracy, Art. 20 (1) Basic Law, the principle of free elections, Art. 38 (1) Basic Law, and the right of political parties to equal opportunities under Art. 21 (1) Basic Law (BVerfGE 44, 125 (138 et seqq.) 1977 *Öffentlichkeitsarbeit*). The latter protects the equal chances of political parties to participate in the process of forming the opinion and the will of the people and is violated when organs of the state—either to the benefit or to the detriment of a political party or an election candidate – interfere in an election campaign (BVerfGE 44, 125 (144 et seqq.) 1977 *Öffentlichkeitsarbeit*; BVerfGE 136, 323 (333) 2014 *Spinner*) or the political debates and competition in general (BVerfGE 140, 225 (227) 2015 *Rote Karte*). The principle of equal opportunities under Art. 21 (1) Basic Law also carries a requirement of objectivity, prohibiting government statements about parties that are distorting or disparaging and therefore unobjective, discriminatory or defamatory as they constitute an "impermissible one-sided stand in political competition" (BVerfGE 148, 11 (30) 2018 *Chancengleichheit politischer Parteien*). Furthermore, when the Federal Government publicly assesses a political party as anti-constitutional, such assessment becomes impermissible when "(…) the assessment is no longer understandable to the point that it must be concluded that the assessment rests on irrelevant considerations and arbitrarily impairs the right of the party concerned to equal opportunities in political competition" (cf. BVerfGE 162, 207 (246) 2022 *Äußerungsbefugnis Bundeskanzlerin*). Neutrality is also required for statements on the web page or social media account of the government or its members (Cf. von Ungern-Sternberg 2025).

More generally, but closely related, German constitutional law stipulates a principle of objectivity for state action (BVerfGE 57, 1 (8) 1981 *NPD*; BVerfGE 105, 252 (272) 2002 *Glykol*). This rule also finds its roots in the principle of democracy, Art. 20 (1), (2) sentence 2 Basic Law, requiring an *electoral* decision of the people that is free and independent of any state influence (*Suslin/Brockmann* 2024, p. 883; BVerfGE 44, 125 (140) 1977 *Öffentlichkeitsarbeit*; BVerwG NVwZ 2018,

433, 435 et seq.) While this does not mean that public officials cannot communicate in the political sphere at all, the BVerwG argues that, as democracy lives off the exchange of objective argumentation, public officials who do participate in the political debate need to construct their statements around the rule of rational and objective discourse (BVerwG NVwZ 2018, 433, 436). Additionally, resulting from the constitutional prohibition of arbitrariness, statements by public officials in the form of value judgments must be based on a core of facts that is essentially accurate or at least appropriate and justifiable and must not exceed the limits of what is objectively necessary (BVerwG NVwZ 2018, 433, 435).

Example: In the context of recently published AfD plans for "remigration" in January 2024, the then Minister President of Rhineland-Palatinate, Malu Dreyer, published a statement on her Instagram profile. She pointed out—among other things—that the term 'remigration' obscured the fact that the AfD is planning the expulsion and deportation of millions of people for racist motives. The Court ruled that this assessment "is not incomprehensible when viewed objectively" and is based on a sufficient factual basis and therefore not arbitrary. Furthermore, according to the Court, the contested statements also comply with the requirement of objectivity, as the statements "do not contain any defamatory or deliberately discriminatory assessments. (…) Despite the pointed wording, the statements maintain an objective tone overall and limit themselves to specifically pointing out the perceived dangers to the liberal-democratic constitutional order." Therefore—at least from the point of arbitrariness and of objectivity—the posted statement did not interfere with the right of the political parties to equal opportunities (VerfGH RhPf NVwZ 2025, 921).

References

Binder R, Vesting T (eds) (2024) Beck'scher Kommentar zum Rundfunkrecht. 5th edn. Beck, München.

Bundesministerium des Innern (2024) Verfassungsschutzbericht 2024. https://www.verfassungsschutz.de/SharedDocs/publikationen/DE/verfassungsschutzberichte/2025-06-10-verfassungsschutzbericht-2024.pdf?__blob=publicationFile&v=4. Accessed 22 Dec 2025.

Bundesministerium des Innern (2025) Pressemitteilung vom 13.05.2025. https://www.bmi.bund.de/SharedDocs/pressemitteilungen/DE/2025/05/verbot-koenigreich-deutschland.html. Accessed 22 Dec 2025.

Circener G et al (eds) (2023) Leipziger Kommentar, vol 10. 13th edn. De Gruyter, Berlin.

Eisele J et al (eds) (2025) Tübinger Kommentar Strafgesetzbuch. 31st edn. Beck, München.

Epping V, Hillgruber C (eds) (2025) Beck'scher Online-Kommentar Grundgesetz. 63rd edn. Beck, München.

European Union (2025), Code of Conduct on Disinformation. https://digital-strategy.ec.europa.eu/en/library/code-conduct-disinformation. Accessed 22 Dec 2025.

Gersdorf H, Paal B (eds) (2025) Beck'scher Online-Kommentar Informations- und Medienrecht. 50th edn. Beck, München.

Herb G et al (eds) (2021) Leipziger Kommentar. vol 8. 13th edn. De Gruyter, Berlin.

Herdegen M (2025) The Basic Law in the Context of Western Constitutionalism. In: Herdegen / Masing / Poscher / Gärditz (eds), Constitutional Law in Germany, Beck, München, 3–47.

Herdegen M et al (eds) (2025) Dürig/Herzog/Scholz Grundgesetz. 108th edn. Beck, München.
Jennessen J, Schlossarcyk M (2025) Äußerungen von Influencern im Spannungsfeld von Laienprivileg und journalistischen Sorgfaltspflichten. Zeitschrift für Urheber und Medienrecht (ZUM) 69(6):426–437.
Kumkar L, Rapp, J (2022) Deepfakes. Zeitschrift für Digitalisierung und Recht (ZfDR) 2(3):199–229.
Lent W (2020), Paradigmenwechsel bei den publizistischen Sorgfaltspflichten im Online-Journalismus – Zur Neuregelung des § 19 Medienstaatsvertrag. Zeitschrift für Urheber- und Medienrecht (ZUM) 64(8/9):593–600.
Nußberger A (2025) Communication-Related Freedoms. In: Herdegen / Masing / Poscher / Gärditz (eds.), Constitutional Law in Germany, Beck, München, 981–1019.
Rengier R (2025) Strafrecht Besonderer Teil II. 26th edn. Beck, München.
Sander G (ed) (2025) Münchener Kommentar zum Strafgesetzbuch, vol 4. 5th edn. Beck, München.
Schäfer J (ed) (2025) Münchener Kommentar zum Strafgesetzbuch, vol 3. 5th edn. Beck, München.
Siara C (2020) Der Medienstaatsvertrag und die „neuen“ Medien“. Zeitschrift für das Recht der Digitalisierung, Datenwirtschaft und IT (MMR) 23(6):370–373.
Suslin A, Brockmann T (2024) Äußerungen staatlicher Funktionsträger im Spannungsfeld von Meinungsfreiheit und Neutralitätsgebot. Neue Zeitschrift für Verwaltungsrecht (NVwZ) 43(12):882–888.
von Heintschel-Heinegg B, Kudlich H (eds) (2025) Beck'scher Online-Kommentar StGB. 67th edn. Beck, München.
von Ungern-Sternberg A (2019) Demokratische Meinungsbildung und künstliche Intelligenz. In: Unger / von Ungern-Sternberg (eds), Demokratie und künstliche Intelligenz, Mohr Siebeck, Tübingen, 3–31.
von Ungern-Sternberg A (2022) Mehr Lauterkeit für Online-Kommunikation – Kennzeichnungspflichten zum Schutz der Demokratie vor Social Bots. Rechtswissenschaft (RW) 13(1):94–125.
von Ungern-Sternberg A (2025) Öffentlichkeitsarbeit als Verfassungsschutz – Der Verfassungsgerichtshof Rheinland-Pfalz sicht Ausnahmen vom Neutralitätsgebot. Verfassungsblog, 7.4.2025. https://verfassungsblog.de/offentlichkeitsarbeit-als-verfassungsschutz/. Accessed 22 Dec 2025.
Wöhlert M (2024) Der Verfassungsschutz – Struktur, Aufgaben und rechtliche Grundlagen. Juristische Schulung (JuS) 64 (7):644–648.

Beyond the Lie: Ireland's Fragmented Response to Online Disinformation and Future Legal Reforms

Martin Démas, Emiliya Taushanska, and Edoardo Celeste

Abstract The Irish legislator's approach to online content focuses predominantly on harmful or illegal material, leaving disinformation to be prosecuted only when it constitutes an existing offence under domestic law. This results in a sparse regulatory landscape where explicit measures targeting disinformation are scattered, mainly addressing the electoral context and conducts regulated by EU law. The overall lack of direct legal concepts such as 'disinformation', 'misinformation', or 'fake news', with the exception of the Electoral Reform Act 2022, highlights a legislative gap, as online disinformation does not inherently constitute a punishable offence. However, critically, several of the disinformation-related provisions of the Electoral Reform Act 2022 are currently suspected by the EU Commission of being inconsistent with EU law and will likely lead to a legislative recast. The chapter therefore concludes that the Irish regulatory landscape is poised for major, indirect or direct, legislative updates that will reshape its approach to online disinformation.

1 *Bréagaisnéis*: The Notion of Disinformation

In Irish Gaelic, *bréagaisnéis*, composed of *bréag*, untruthful, and *aisnéis*, information (An Foclóir Nua Béarla-Gaeilge 2025), is the closest equivalent of the English word *disinformation,* which is defined as the act of "disseminating deliberately false information" (Oxford English Dictionary 2025). The Irish context has been—and unfortunately still is—characterised by this phenomenon. Historically, during the so-called "Troubles", psychological operations were conducted by the British Army

M. Démas (✉) · E. Taushanska · E. Celeste
Dublin City University, Law and Tech Research Cluster, School of Law and Government, Dublin, Ireland
e-mail: martin.demas2@mail.dcu.ie

E. Taushanska
e-mail: emiliyaemilova.taushanska2@mail.dcu.ie

E. Celeste
e-mail: edoardo.celeste@dcu.ie

P. Passaglia (ed.), *European Legal Perspectives on Online Disinformation*, Ius Gentium: Comparative Perspectives on Law and Justice 140,
https://doi.org/10.1007/978-3-032-25785-7_11

and the Royal Ulster Constabulary (RUC)[1] to influence opinions (Bamford 2005). Today, this threat has dramatically changed in scale as online outlets have surpassed TV as the main source of news (Coimisiún na Meán 2025a). Despite a generally high level of trust in the media (Eurostat 2022), Ireland has known emblematic cases of disinformation, which heavily relied specifically on the use of social media platforms (Culloty 2023, p. 4). They concerned issues related to the Covid-19 pandemic (Culloty 2023, pp. 4–5), the conditions of war refugees and asylum-seekers fleeing Ukraine (Smyth 2024), the LGBTQ+ community (Culloty 2023, pp. 4–5), and the Palestinian genocide (Coimisiún na Meán 2024c, p. 122; United Nations Human Rights Council 2025). These trends have been accompanied by an increase in general attacks towards mainstream media through "cross-platform mobilisation" (European Digital Media Observatory Ireland 2023), i.e. when extreme audiences become active across multiple platforms. Disinformation in Ireland is also facilitated via online groups, such as Facebook and private WhatsApp chats (European Digital Media Observatory Ireland 2023, p. 17). Alternative media sources like Gettr and Gab, mainly focused on promoting far-right values, have also grown in popularity (Gallagher et al. 2023, p. 7).

In Ireland, the concept of disinformation is broadly defined as the intentional provision of false information to shift narratives around sensitive themes, particularly through the use of digital technology (Joint Committee on Tourism, Culture, Arts, Sport and Media 2024, pp.16–18). More precisely, Ireland's Media regulator, Coimisiún na Meán, supports the definition provided in the National Counter Disinformation Strategy (Department of Culture, Communications and Sport, 2023) and the 2020 European Democracy Action Plan, qualifying disinformation as "false or misleading content that is spread with an intention to deceive or secure economic or political gain and which may cause public harm" (Joint Committee on Tourism, Culture, Arts, Sport and Media, 2024, p. 15). In practice, according to a recent report by An Garda Síochána, Ireland's police force (Joint Committee on Tourism, Culture, Arts, Sport and Media 2024), disinformation can take many forms, such as false survey results, deliberately inaccurate reporting, misleading and purposely decontextualized statements, and imposter accounts on social media.

The Act does not address "malinformation" explicitly, but regulates "manipulative or inauthentic behaviour, including the use of undisclosed bots" in the context of elections,[2] defining this type of behaviour as "tactics, techniques and procedures that (a) constitute the deceptive use of services or features provided by an online platform, […], (b) are likely to influence the information visible to other users of that platform, (c) by reason of their nature and character, context or any other relevant circumstance, give rise to the inference that they are intended to result in the dissemination, publication or increased circulation of false or misleading online electoral information, and (d) may cause public harm".[3]

[1] State police force in Northern Ireland, established in 1922, and superseded by the Police Service of Northern Ireland in 2001 as part of the Belfast ('Good Friday') Agreement (1998).

[2] Electoral Reform Act 2022 (no. 30 of 2022), Section 150.1 c).

[3] *Ibid.*, Section 144.

While the concept of "disinformation" is only currently present in a single piece of Irish legislation,[4] disinformation could potentially be prosecuted if it relates to a broad array of offences, such as defamation (Department of Justice, Home Affairs and Migration 2022, p. 6),[5] cyber harassment,[6] incitement to violence, hatred or public disorder,[7] or election interference (Shattock 2025).

The Online Safety and Media Regulation Act 2022 (OSMR)[8] and the EU Digital Services Act (as transposed into Irish law per the Digital Services Act 2024)[9] impose obligations on online platforms to address certain forms of 'online harmful content'. Under Irish law, disinformation itself is not always classified as an 'online harmful content'. Therefore, unless the content is illegal on the ground of other offences (Coimisiún na Meán 2025g), the obligations relating to illegal content will not apply. Furthermore, the Electoral Reform Act does not distinguish between online and offline disinformation. A distinction can only be inferred as "online" is mentioned in Parts 4 and 5 of said Act.

The Irish police force is not compelled to take down content if that content is not illegal (Joint Committee on Tourism, Culture, Arts, Sport and Media 2024, p. 14) as sharing false information is not a crime in Ireland, unless it can be qualified as a specifically sanctioned conduct, such as harassment, incitement, or defamation. Even when taking into consideration deepfakes, while they can be a means of disinformation, Irish law currently targets the harmful effects (such as harassment or abuse) rather than the mere creation or sharing of false content. Nevertheless, online disinformation leading to harmful content or abuse can constitute an offence and could be investigated under several provisions (Joint Committee on Tourism, Culture, Arts, Sport and Media, 2024).

This chapter explores the phenomenon of online disinformation in Ireland, from its conceptual foundations to its legal framing, focusing on the practical implications within the Irish media ecosystem. After introducing the notion of *bréagaisnéis* and outlining the evolving definition of disinformation and its nuances, the chapter analyses the Irish approach within the broader framework of European Union law (Sect. 2). The interplay between EU regulatory initiatives and national legislation is strongly highlighted. The chapter subsequently focuses on two key national legal instruments: the Online Safety and Media Regulation Act (OSMR Act) and the Electoral Reform Act, assessing their role in countering disinformation, which in Ireland appears to be explicitly defined only within the electoral context (Sect. 3). The chapter then addresses the procedural aspects related to enforcement, oversight, and institutional responsibilities in implementing EU and national law related to disinformation, highlighting existing issues of conformity with EU law. Section 5

---

[4] *Ibid.*

[5] Defamation Act 2009 (no. 31 of 2009), Section 6.2.

[6] Harassment, Harmful Communications and Related Offences Act 2020 (no. 32 of 2020), Section 4.

[7] Incitement to Hatred Act 1989 (no. 19 of 1989), Section 2 (1).

[8] Online Safety and Media Regulation Act 2022 (no. 41 of 2022) ('OSMR Act').

[9] Digital Services Act 2024 (no. 2 of 2024).

concludes explaining how the Irish legal system will likely be subject to legal reforms to address such incompatibilities.

2 The Preeminent Role of EU Law in the Irish Legal Toolbox

European law offers the most significant part of the legal arsenal available to Ireland on disinformation. The Charter of Fundamental Rights of the EU (CFR) enshrines the principles that are mostly affected by online disinformation, namely the rights to respect for private and family life,[10] to protection of personal data,[11] to freedom of expression and information,[12] to free elections,[13] and the provisions on the scope and limitations of said rights.[14] These norms must be observed and guaranteed by the Union and its Member States when implementing EU law and reflect analogue principles enshrined in the European Convention on Human Rights.[15]

Following the spread of online forms of disinformation, in 2018 the Union introduced the Action Plan against Disinformation as a key pillar advocating an expansion of resources and capacities to detect and tackle this issue.[16] Similarly, a Rapid Alert System (European External Action Service 2019)—notably put to test amid Covid-19 disinformation (Stolton 2020) – was created to strengthen coordination between EU institutions, Member States, and other relevant stakeholders (Jas-Koziarkiewicz & Dobrowolska, 2024). Initiatives on behalf of both the Union and its Member States were also proposed in the areas of media literacy (Government of Ireland 2025,

[10] Charter of Fundamental Rights of the European Union ('CFR'), Article 7.

[11] *Ibid.*, Article 8.

[12] *Ibid.*, Article 11.

[13] *Ibid.*, Article 39 (2).

[14] *Ibid.*, Article 52 (1) and (3), Article 54.

[15] *Ibid.*, Article 51.

[16] EU Commission, Joint Communication to the European Parliament, the European Council, the Council, the European Economic and Social Committee and the Committee of the Regions – Action Plan against Disinformation, JOIN(2018)36 final, 5.12.2018.

p. 22), targeted political advertising,[17] audiovisual media services (including online services),[18] and independent, high-quality journalism.[19]

Proposed as a major follow-up to this strategy, the Digital Services Act (DSA) serves as a broad regulatory canvas, as it aims to harness a range of actors, including very large online platforms (hereinafter "VLOPs") and search engines (hereinafter "VLOSEs").[20] Under this framework, codes of conduct are seen as useful means of tackling disinformation, so long as the content in question is deemed 'illegal' according to national law, while ensuring a certain level of accountability for large online platforms (European Parliament: Directorate-General for Internal Policies of the Union 2021). Two codes of conduct, respectively on disinformation (European Commission, 2025) and on countering illegal hate speech online (European Commission, 2025), have been developed and integrated into the DSA framework.[21] Notably, the code of conduct on disinformation, voluntarily signed by 42 actors, VLOPs and VLOSEs (European Commission, 2025)—with the exception of X (ex-Twitter)[22]—established a "Rapid Response System" (Disinformation Code Transparency Centre, 2024; European Digital Media Observatory, 2024) for swift cooperation between institutions, online platforms, and other stakeholders (including fact-checkers) during key periods like elections or crises. Recent reports nevertheless point out mixed results during the last EU elections, with a very high percentage of content removal instead of providing labels and additional context (Disinformation Code Transparency Centre, 2024; European Digital Media Observatory, 2024).

Several initiatives have been adopted to tackle the spread of online disinformation through artificial intelligence (Munich Security Conference, 2024).[23] However, despite regulatory obligations and voluntary commitments placed upon VLOPs and

---

[17] Regulation (EU) 2024/900 of the European Parliament and of the Council of 13 March 2024 on the transparency and targeting of political advertising, OJ L, 2024/900, 20 Mar 2024.

[18] Directive (EU) 2018/1808 of the European Parliament and of the Council of 14 November 2018 amending Directive 2010/13/EU on the coordination of certain provisions laid down by law, regulation or administrative action in Member States concerning the provision of audiovisual media services (Audiovisual Media Services Directive) in view of changing market realities, OJ L 303, 28.11.2018, pp. 69-92; Statutory Instrument No. 557/2024 - European Union (Audiovisual Media Services) Regulations 2024, Iris Oifigiúl, no. 86, 25.10.2024, p. 1522.

[19] Regulation (EU) 2024/1083 of the European Parliament and of the Council of 11 April 2024 establishing a common framework for media services in the internal market and amending Directive 2010/13/EU (European Media Freedom Act), OJ L, 2024/1083, 17 Apr 2024.

[20] Regulation (EU) 2022/2065 of the European Parliament and of the Council of 19 October 2022 on a Single Market For Digital Services and amending Directive 2000/31/EC (Digital Services Act) ('DSA'), OJ L 277, 27.10.2022, p. 1–102.

[21] DSA (*Ibid.*), Article 45.

[22] *Ibid.*

[23] Regulation (EU) 2024/1689 of the European Parliament and of the Council of 13 June 2024 laying down harmonised rules on artificial intelligence and amending Regulations (EC) No 300/2008, (EU) No 167/2013, (EU) No 168/2013, (EU) 2018/858, (EU) 2018/1139 and (EU) 2019/2144 and Directives 2014/90/EU, (EU) 2016/797 and (EU) 2020/1828 (Artificial Intelligence Act), OJ L, 2024/1689, 12.7.2024; Commission Guidelines for providers of Very Large Online Platforms and Very Large Online Search Engines on the mitigation of systemic risks for electoral processes pursuant to Article 35(3) of Regulation (EU) 2022/2065, OJ C., C/2024/2537, 26.4.2024.

VLOSEs, it seems that many of these AI-powered contents are not labelled and flagged with consistency, leading to potential disinformation spikes, especially in electoral contexts (Schueler, Romano, et al., 2024). Specific adjustments have been introduced to ensure better protection and an easier pursuit of cases against non-consensual sharing of intimate or manipulated content, cyber-harassment, and cyber incitement to violence or hatred.[24] Finally, a recent directive is seeking a more adequate protection of persons engaging in public participation, in areas such as fighting disinformation, from manifestly unfounded or abusive strategic lawsuits such as defamation claims.[25]

In light of the current geopolitical context, a series of initiatives has been adopted by the EU in the context of the Russian aggression war on Ukraine, with the notable involvement of the European Parliament.[26] Partly developed in collaboration with the Member States in the context of the Common Foreign and Security Policy (European External Action Service, 2025),[27] these measures aim to counteract the amplification of hybrid threats, such as "Foreign Information Manipulation and Interference", referred to as "FIMI" (European External Action Service, 2025; Bentzen, 2024), which are most notably presented in the form of intentionally deceptive and actively distributed disinformation across the Union.[28] The initiative for a 'European Democracy Shield', (European Parliament, 2025; Burke, 2025) as part of the European Democracy Action Plan (European Parliament, 2025), currently at the proposal stage, aims at tackling this issue, along with the reinforcement of existing measures.

In line with this legal enhancement, the Court of Justice of the EU has refined its previously relatively scarce (Shattock, 2025) case law regarding the restrictions of

---

[24] Directive (EU) 2024/1385 of the European Parliament and of the Council of 14 May 2024 on combating violence against women and domestic violence, OJ L, 2024/1385, 24.5.2024, Articles 5, 7, and 8.

[25] Directive (EU) 2024/1069 ('Strategic lawsuits against public participation', or 'SLAPP'), OJ L., 2024/1069, 16.4.2024.

[26] European Parliament resolution of 8 February 2024 on Russiagate: allegations of Russian interference in the democratic processes of the European Union (2024/2548(RSP)), P9_TA(2024)0079, OJ C., C/2024/6343, 7.11.2024; European Parliament decision of 18 December 2024 on setting up a special committee on the European Democracy Shield, and defining its responsibilities, numerical strength and term of office (2024/2999(RSO)), P10_TA(2024)0065, OJ C/2025/1981, 11.4.2025; European Parliament resolution of 23 January 2025 on Russia's disinformation and historical falsification to justify its war of aggression against Ukraine (2024/2988(RSP)), P10_TA(2025)0006, OJ C/2025/2147, 23.4.2025; CJEU (Grand Chamber), 27 July 2022, RT France v. Council of the European Union (Case T-125/22).

[27] Council Regulation (EU) 2022/350 of 1 March 2022 amending Regulation (EU) No 833/2014 concerning restrictive measures in view of Russia's actions destabilising the situation in Ukraine, OJ 2022 L 65, p. 1–4, 2.3.2022; Council Decision (CFSP) 2022/351 of 1 March 2022 amending Decision 2014/512/CFSP concerning restrictive measures in view of Russia's actions destabilising the situation in Ukraine, OJ L. 65, p. 5–7, 2.3.2022.

[28] CJEU (Second Chamber), 4 July 2019 (request for a preliminary ruling from the Vilniaus apygardos administracinis teismas - Lithuania), Baltic Media Alliance Ltd v Lietuvos radijo ir televizijos komisija (Case C-622/17); CJEU, 27 July 2022, RT France v. Council (*op. cit.*), §§ 56, 145, 211.

freedom of expression,[29] of the right to inform and be informed,[30] and concerning the extent of the platforms' obligations under the DSA.[31] It is of interest to note that these restrictions, sanctioned by the case law of the CJEU, are in line with the case law of the ECtHR, the latter being much more extensive regarding the freedom of expression and proportionate restrictions in cases of abuse of rights,[32] and notably in the political and electoral context (Shattock, 2025).

3 The National Legal Framework: A Focus on the Electoral Context

No provision within the Irish Constitution explicitly mentions disinformation. Article 40.6 enshrines the right to freedom of expression and media and establishes that "[t]he publication or utterance of seditious [i.e. material undermining the authority of the State or advocating for the overthrow of the State (Citizens' Information, 2025)] or indecent matter is an offence which shall be punishable in accordance with law".

Irish courts have not formally applied the concepts of 'disinformation', 'misinformation', 'malinformation', or 'fake news', which appear only in parties' statements or evidence. Few cases reference these terms, mostly in matters such as defamation, incitement to hatred and/or violence, or cyberbullying. A notable recent case on abusive lawsuits,[33] called 'Strategic Lawsuits Against Public Participation' ('SLAPPs'), saw an Irish High Court propose 29 indicia to identify abusive proceedings,[34] consistent with Directive (EU) 2024/1069[35] and drawing reference from Section 195 of the UK Economic Crime and Corporate Transparency Act 2023 (UK Parliament, 2023). Among them is when defendants engage in 'activities to combat disinformation',[36] potentially guiding or supplementing Ireland's future transposition of the directive. The Defamation (Amendment) Bill 2024 (Houses

[29] CJEU, 4 July 2019, Baltic Media Alliance (*op. cit.*); CJEU, 27 July 2022, RT France v. Council (*op. cit.*).

[30] CJEU, 27 July 2022, RT France v. Council (*Ibid.*); CJEU (Grand Chamber),8 December 2022 (request for a preliminary ruling from the Bundesgerichtshof - Germany) - TU, RE v Google LLC (Case C-460/20).

[31] Order of the Vice-President of the Court of 27 March 2024 - European Commission v. Amazon Services Europe Sàrl (Case C-639/23 P(R)).

[32] ECtHR (Grand Chamber), 13 February 2003, Refah Partisi (The Welfare Party) and others v. Turkey, Appl. Nos. 41340/98, 41342/98, 42343/98 and 42344/98, § 99.

[33] These 'SLAPP' proceedings are brought to court to restrict activities of common interest carried out often by citizens against more powerful actors.

[34] The High Court Planning & Environment, 15 April 2024, Glenveach Homes Limited v. Pat Lynch and Denise Leavy, H.P.2023.0001353, §62.

[35] Directive (EU) 2024/1069.

[36] *Ibid.*, §53 in relation with §62.

of the Oireachtas, 2025) aims to transpose and extend the EU 'SLAPP' directive, introducing a 'serious harm' threshold for corporate plaintiffs and authorising identification orders in anonymous defamation cases.

The main Irish legislative acts dealing with disinformation are the Online Safety and Media Regulation Act and the Electoral Reform Act, which will be explained in the following subsections.

3.1 The Online Safety and Media Regulation Act 2022: The Creation of Coimisiún Na Meán

The 2022 Online Safety and Media Regulation Act (OSMR Act) transposed the EU Audiovisual Media Services Directive into national law (EUR-Lex, 2025). It established an Online Safety Commissioner and a Media Commission—*Coimisiún na Meán* in Irish (O'Neill, 2022, p. 1)—with powers to enforce compliance, sanction platforms, block services, prosecute offences, and impose fines (Kirk, Farris & Shankar, 2021). The Act regulates broadcasters and audiovisual on-demand service providers, defined as suppliers of programme compilations transmitted through electronic networks for simultaneous or near-simultaneous public reception.[37] It mandates their registration with Coimisiún na Meán[38] and governs user-generated content moderation.

Section 46 J(1)(a)-(e) prohibits disseminating content that causes harm or undue offence or promotes crime. Section 2(2) of the Harassment, Harmful Communications and Related Offences Act, referenced by the OSMR Act, defines 'harm' as intentional or reckless interference with privacy causing alarm or distress, with provisions for future expansion through consultation among Coimisiún na Meán, the Minister for Communications, and a Joint Oireachtas Committee (Kirk, Farris & Shankar, 2021).[39] Section 139A(1) establishes two definitions for harmful content. First, it refers to offence-specific categories from Schedule 3, notably 'content inducing hatred',[40] 'harassment through persistent unwanted contact or communication',[41] and 'threatening or grossly offensive communications intended to harm'.[42] Second, it includes content constituting or promoting acts of bullying, humiliation, eating disorders, self-harm, or suicide.[43] Content also qualifies as harmful if it poses reasonably foreseeable risk to life or significant physical or mental health harm.[44] Such a

[37] Broadcasting Act 2009 (no. 18 of 2009), Section 2.

[38] OSMR Act 2022, Section 46A.

[39] Oireachtas is the Irish word for 'parliament'.

[40] Prohibition of Incitement to Hatred Act 1989, Section 2(1).

[41] Non-Fatal Offences against the Person Act 1997 (no. 26 of 1997), Section 10(1).

[42] Harassment, Harmful Communications and Related Offences Act 2020 (*op. cit.*), Section 4(1).

[43] OSMR Act 2022, Section 139A(3).

[44] *Ibid.*, Section 139A(4).

categorisation should be implemented in practice using a 'balance of probabilities' standard.[45]

Additionally, Coimisiún na Meán adopted an Online Safety Code in October 2024 (Coimisiún na Meán, 2024a), introducing obligations for Irish-based video-sharing platforms to protect users—especially minors—from harmful content, emphasising user media literacy tools and education that these platforms shall provide their users with (Coimisiún na Meán, 2025b, p. 16).

3.2 *From the Broadcasting Act 2009 to the Electoral Reform Act 2022: Proportionality Issues*

Ireland's decision to regulate disinformation in the electoral context stemmed from two observations. On the one hand, the country already partially covered the issue of what constitutes legal advertising in the Broadcasting Act 2009.[46] On the other hand, online political advertising, which constitutes an important part of the electoral competition, remained unregulated (Cousins & Lynch, 2022, p. 37). The Broadcasting Act provided only that "a broadcaster shall not broadcast, and a relevant media service provider shall not make available [...], an advertisement which (a) is directed towards a political end or has any relation to an industrial dispute [...]".[47] Online political advertising lacked the basic transparency requirements applicable to "traditional" broadcasting media, leaving citizens unable to properly assess these advertisements and their funding (Cousins & Lynch, 2022, p. 50). This opaqueness blurred the boundaries between an apparent advertisement and paid political promotion through content that at first sight cannot be identified as such (Cousins & Lynch, 2022, p. 38).

A report produced by the Institute for Strategic Dialogue highlights that between May 26th and June 12th, 2024, there have been 162 posts across X, Telegram, Facebook, YouTube, and TikTok claiming election interference surrounding Irish local and European elections. A more specific example of this relates to a series of articles published by the Irish Channel, seen as interfering with said elections as they contained "factual errors, fictitious quotes and inexistent interviewees" (O'Connor, 2024, p. 5), thereby falsely reporting about 'vote rigging' activities allegedly conducted by a competing political party. However, despite this case of disinformation, these articles ended up being promoted among online communities (O'Connor, 2024).

The Electoral Reform Act was adopted in 2022 to fill this legal void. It is characterised by a much broader approach than the DSA, as it applies to most forms of disinformation, and not merely to 'illegal content'. However, criticism has been raised against Parts 4 and 5 of the legislation, as its risk-based approach, which focuses

[45] *Ibid.*, Section 139A(5).

[46] Broadcasting Act 2009 (*op. cit.*); Electoral Act 1997 (no. 25 of 1997).

[47] Broadcasting Act 2009 (*Ibid.*), Section 41.3.

neither on the 'intention to deceive' nor on 'material evidence', may compel VLOPs and VLOSEs to restrict the right to access information when considering potentially legitimate communications and genuinely held opinion, so long as communications are suspected of falsity (Government of Ireland, 2025, p. 22; Shattock, 2025).

Parts 4 and 5 of the Electoral Reform Act have not been implemented yet by the Government due to suspicions of incompatibility with EU law, the Charter of Fundamental Rights (CJEU Research and Documentation Directorate, 2018), and the ECHR (CJEU Research and Documentation Directorate, 2018), and will likely be amended. Part 4 obliges online platforms to verify advertisers' identities and withhold political ads in the emergence of 'reasonable grounds' to suspect breaches. This potentially lays the ground for a lower liability threshold than the E-commerce Directive's threshold of 'actual knowledge'. A lower threshold could arbitrarily restrict lawful content and limit access to information that should be available (European Commission, 2022a, 2022b; Shattock, 2025, p. 2). Part 5 does not distinguish disinformation from misinformation and seems to fail in differentiating between deliberate deception and good-faith errors (Shattock, 2025, p. 5). It has also been criticized for allowing intermediaries to restrict content based on potential risk rather than actual influence, ignoring whether dis- or misinformation is likely to affect voters' choice effectively (Shattock, 2025, p. 23).

In 2024, Coimisiún na Meán strengthened broadcasting regulation (Coimisiún na Meán, 2024e) by adopting a series of Guidelines in Respect of Coverage of Elections (Coimisiún na Meán, 2024d). These Guidelines apply primarily to Irish broadcasters but also invite foreign broadcasters whose content targets Irish audiences to comply voluntarily (Coimisiún na Meán, 2024d, p. 3). They govern airtime allocation, viewpoint diversity, public participation, and conflicts of interest (Coimisiún na Meán, 2024d, p. 6). The 2024 revision abolished the prior 24-h broadcast moratorium, replacing it with a 'critical election period' beginning 24 h before polling and lasting until closure, requiring careful handling of electoral content and promotion of fact-checking to counter disinformation. This amendment followed comparative reviews of 'electoral silence' regimes abroad and seeks to support broadcasters' fact-checking during elections (Coimisiún na Meán, 2024b). The Guidelines exclude print media, social media, and on-demand or online audiovisual content (Coimisiún na Meán, 2024b, p. 3), as they are generally considered online platforms or intermediaries governed under different legal frameworks,[48] yet acknowledge broadcasters' key role in countering misinformation and disinformation. Broadcasters are urged to verify social media sources and avoid amplifying false or AI-generated content, including deepfakes (Coimisiún na Meán, 2024d, p. 8).

[48] Cf. DSA and OSMR Act (*op. cit.*).

3.3 Proposals for Legal Reforms: Literacy, Deepfakes and Hate Speech

Irish legal reforms related to disinformation currently focus on three domains: literacy, deep fakes and hate speech. The National Counter Disinformation Strategy (2025), structured around five action pillars (21 Noticias, 2025) seeks to counter disinformation (Government of Ireland, 2025, pp. 9–10) and uphold freedom of expression by promoting media literacy to enhance public resilience on the long-term (Government of Ireland, 2025, pp. 4, 35).

The Protection of Voice and Image Bill 2025 proposes criminal sanctions for the misuse of personal characteristics through AI or other digital means, addressing deepfake-related harms, possibly through automated means or AI (Houses of the Oireachtas, 2025; Pinsent Masons, 2025). A Danish bill is proposing the first European ban on deepfakes (Bryant, 2025), criminalising the dissemination of digital imitations of personal traits. Its approach could shape Ireland's Protection of Voice and Image Bill 2025, under discussion in the Dáil Éireann, particularly in view of Denmark's 2025 EU Council Presidency (Houses of the Oireachtas, 2025).

Lastly, the Prohibition of Incitement to Hatred Act 1989, subject to EU infringement procedures (European Commission, 2024; European Commission, 2025)[49] for non-compliance with the 2008 framework decision on combating racism and xenophobia,[50] may be revised after criticism from the EU Commission over its omission of provisions on 'Holocaust denial and condoning of international crimes' (European Commission, 2024; European Commission, 2025). A previous attempt to reform the Irish legislation on hate speech, initially including a comprehensive project on hate offences,[51] was abandoned at the end of 2024 amid controversy (O'Halloran, 2024).

4 Countering Disinformation in Ireland: Procedural Aspects

The following section highlights the procedural aspects related to the implementation of EU regulations and national acts related to disinformation.

---

[49] EU Commission (2024) Infringement procedure no. INFR(2024)2205.

[50] Council Framework Decision 2008/913/JHA of 28 November 2008 on combating certain forms and expressions of racism and xenophobia by means of criminal law, OJ L 328, 6 Dec 2008, pp. 55-58.

[51] Criminal Justice (Hate Offences) Act 2024 (no. 41 of 2024).

4.1 *Digital Services Act: The Key Role of* Coimisiún Na Meán

The provisions contained in Chapter II to IV of the DSA outline how complaints about illegal content conducted, cached, or hosted by online platforms[52] are handled by said platforms and the relevant 'Digital Services Coordinator' (DSC).[53] Throughout the recitals of the DSA, online disinformation is characterised as a potential systemic risk, presenting a threat of societal harm. It does not, however, constitute an offence per se, and shall be characterised as 'illegal content' to be taken down.[54] The DSA decentralises the fight against disinformation in the hands of the end-users and other relevant stakeholders. It provides for a comprehensive notice mechanism through which users may flag content they deem illegal to the hosting platform.[55] A fast-track route is also enabled for 'trusted flaggers'.[56] These bodies, certified by Coimisiún na Meán, shall eventually report their actions to the Irish media regulator and publish their results, thereby increasing scrutiny and public trust into platforms.

Upon receipt of said notice, the platform shall then take a decision in a timely manner, with priority given to those submitted by trusted flaggers and, if the content is found illegal, may impose several restrictions on its users and the content uploaded or shared.[57] In order to enable informed appeals, a decision shall in any case be accompanied by a comprehensive statement of reasons, detailed in a clear, precise and specific manner.[58] Users may then choose to appeal moderation decisions through a complaint addressed directly to the platform, within six months upon receipt of the first instance decision.[59] This appeal mechanism shall be reviewed internally and free of charge.[60]

Alternatively, users may submit their complaint to Coimisiún na Meán, seek redress before Irish courts, or select any certified out-of-court dispute settlement bodies. The latter are available EU-wide, and the content may be submitted in most spoken EU languages. However, the dispute itself may only be communicated in ten EU languages to one of the six currently certified bodies EU-wide (Coimisiún na Meán, 2025c),[61] a list the Irish language is not part of (European Commission, 2025). Additionally, providers of hosting services shall notify the law enforcement (i.e. An Garda Síochána in Ireland) or judicial authorities of the relevant member

52 DSA (*op. cit.*), Articles 4 to 6.

53 *Ibid.*, Article 3 (n), Article 3 (o).

54 *Ibid.*, Article 3 (h).

55 *Ibid.*, Article 16.

56 *Ibid.*, Article 22.

57 *Ibid.*, Article 17 (1) (a) to (d).

58 *Ibid.*, Article 17 (3), (4).

59 *Ibid.*, Article 20.

60 *Ibid.*, Article 20 (1).

61 'Appeals Centre Europe', registered in Ireland and certified by Coimisiún na Meán, reviews disputes regarding the application and enforcement of terms and conditions of Facebook, Instagram, TikTok and YouTube.

state as soon as they become aware of any 'information giving rise to suspicions of criminal offences' involving a 'threat to the life or safety' of one or more persons,[62] and give their full effect to any subsidiary order to act against illegal content, or to provide information about specific individuals, issued by said national authorities.[63]

Lastly, regarding the redress mechanisms and sanctions applicable to intermediary services and platforms found to be in breach of their DSA obligations, the European Commission may request information, order access to the VLOPs' and VLOSEs' data and algorithms, or eventually reach for the support and cooperation of Coimisiún na Meán and other relevant DSCs[64] to conduct further investigation at the VLOPs' premises.[65]

Coimisiún na Meán plays a particularly important role in the implementation of the DSA as 15 of the total 25 VLOPs and VLOSEs listed by the EU Commission are established in Ireland, notably Google Search, YouTube, LinkedIn, Facebook, Instagram, Bing, TikTok, and X.

4.2 Between Terrorist Content and Disinformation

Regulation (EU) 2021/784 addresses the online dissemination of terrorist content.[66] The regulation defines 'terrorist content' as online material that may incite the commission of terrorist offences, such as their glorification, solicit persons to commit or contribute to their commission, participate in the activities of terrorist groups, or even constitute a threat to commit terrorist offences.[67] These types of content may simultaneously represent a form of disinformation.

In those cases, pursuant to this regulation and to the DSA,[68] online service providers and platforms shall promptly notify the Gardaí or the Irish judicial authorities as soon as they become aware of the presence of any information giving rise to suspicions of terrorist offences, and shall cooperate with said authorities when ordered to provide additional information as part of investigative proceedings.[69]

An Garda Síochána is the only authority in Ireland vested with the power to oblige a platform to take down terrorist content through the issuance of a removal order.[70]

[62] DSA (*op. cit.*), Article 18.

[63] *Ibid.*, Articles 9 and 10.

[64] *Ibid.*, Article 60.

[65] *Ibid.*, Chapter IV, Section 4.

[66] Regulation (EU) 2021/784 of the European Parliament and of the Council on addressing the dissemination of terrorist content online, OJ L. 172, 17.5.2021, pp. 79–109.

[67] *Ibid.*, Article 2 (7)(a) to (e).

[68] DSA (*op. cit.*), Article 18.

[69] *Ibid.*, Article 10.

[70] Regulation (EU) 2021/784 (*op. cit.*), Article 3 (1); DSA (*op. cit.*), Article 9.

In case of a systematic or persistent failure the maximum fine is 4% of the hosting service provider's annual global turnover.[71]

4.3 Coimisiún Na Meán *and the Classification of Illegal Online Content*

The OSMR Act 2022 includes implementation measures of both the Audiovisual Media Services Directive[72] and the DSA,[73] with additional specificities applicable to Ireland. The provisions contained in its Sections 139R to 139V outline how complaints related to harmful online content are handled by Coimisiún na Meán. In its dedicated webpage, Coimisiún na Meán mentions only "illegal or harmful content" (Coimisiún na Meán, 2025f), without explaining whether disinformation is included in these categories. According to Section 139S, Coimisiún na Meán can only consider a case if the user has first complained to the provider of the designated online service, hereinafter called 'provider' (Coimisiún na Meán, 2025d),[74] and more than two days have passed since then. Moreover, the provider must have an approved complaint-handling process, which the user must have reasonably tried to address. Nevertheless, even if those conditions are not met, Coimisiún na Meán may still act in light of the principles of fair handling contained in Section 139U.

If the content is potentially of criminal nature, i.e., "offence-specific", Coimisiún na Meán must notify An Garda Síochána, the user and the video-sharing platform, and can only proceed if the police decline to act.[75] Lastly, according to Section 139T, Coimisiún na Meán may decide to: refer the complaint back to the provider with advice/support; send the complaint to another appropriate body; or issue a formal content limitation notice under enforcement powers. Through the latter, Coimisiún na Meán can order platforms to remove, restrict, or limit access to harmful online content, either immediately, if discovered during general monitoring actions, or after investigation, if linked to a suspected legal breach (in this case, it must wait until investigation is complete and confirmed).[76] When issuing this notice, the Commission considers the nature and scale of the service, the technical capabilities of the provider, the risk of harm (especially to children), the rights of the provider, uploader, users, and those affected by the content and the proportionality of the action. Moreover, this notice can require some limitations to be imposed on the flagged content such as: restricting access to the content to persons who have attained the age of 18 years, including a warning/information label on the online content, reducing the

[71] Regulation (EU) 2021/784 (*Ibid.*), Article 18 (3).

[72] Directive (EU) 2018/1808 (*op. cit.*).

[73] DSA (*op. cit.*).

[74] OSMR Act 2022 (*op. cit.*), Section 3(f).

[75] *Ibid.*, Section 139S(3).

[76] *Ibid.*, Section 139ZZD.

interaction with the content (e.g. by disabling comments) or ensuring that prominence is not given to the content, or the content is not recommended to users.[77]

With regards to the content of the notice, Section 139ZZE provides that the notice must clearly identify the content in question, specify the category of harmful online content it falls under, and provide the reasons for its classification. The notice must include sufficient information to allow the platform to locate and act on the content, detail the specific action required (such as removal or restriction), define its territorial scope, and set a timeline for compliance. The notice must also allow at least 28 days for both the provider of a designated online service and, where applicable, the uploader of user-generated content to make submissions in response. The provider is required to inform the uploader within two days of receiving the notice and report back to Coimisiún na Meán on the steps taken. Coimisiún na Meán may then direct the provider to take additional steps if necessary. After considering any submissions, it shall either confirm the notice (with amendments and a new compliance deadline) or revoke it entirely.

Finally, under Section 139ZZF, the provider of a designated online service or the uploader of user-generated content may appeal a confirmed content limitation notice to the Circuit Court within 28 days. The court may set aside the notice, replace it with a new one, or send it back to Coimisiún na Meán for reconsideration with specific directions. Appeals can be made on grounds such as legal error, irrational reasoning, or procedural unfairness. Coimisiún na Meán has the right to dismiss complaints if it concludes that the content does not qualify as harmful online content, or is no longer available on the designated service, as well as if the complaint is "frivolous or vexatious".[78]

On its website, Coimisiún na Meán presents a useful scheme concerning what constitutes "illegal" content (Coimisiún na Meán, 2025h), reconstructing the patchwork of applicable legislation. If an online service has failed to comply with its obligations under the relevant Irish online safety framework (DSA / Online Safety Code / Terrorist Content Online Regulation), the person submitting a complaint shall provide all details of the communication with the platform. Upon receipt by Coimisiún na Meán, the complaint may be passed to the Competition and Consumer Protection Commission—if the complaint relates to online trading—or to the European Commission—if the complaint relates to VLOPs or VLOSEs (Coimisiún na Meán, 2025e). After confirming a contravention, Coimisiún na Meán determines the sanction, with regards to the gravity, harm caused, cooperation, intent, and previous history.[79]

[77] *Ibid.*, Section 139ZZD(4).

[78] *Ibid.*, Section 139T(1) d,e.

[79] *Ibid.*, Section 139 ZW.

4.4 *Implementing the Electoral Reform Act: Legislation Under Scrutiny*

Part 5 of the Act, for which the EU Commission has expressed concerns on potential incompatibility with EU law (European Commission, 2022a; European Commission, 2022b; Shattock, 2025, pp. 2, 5, 23), currently sets out rules for online platforms[80] on how to limit the dissemination of false and misleading electoral communications (Shattock, 2025, p. 22). It also empowers the Electoral Commission to 'monitor, investigate, identify, and combat' the dissemination of misleading 'online electoral information' and 'online electoral process information' (Shattock, 2025, p. 6).

Under Section 148, online platforms shall notify the Electoral Commission "without undue delay" if they become "satisfied" that their services are being used to disseminate false electoral communications during an election campaign period. Additionally, platforms with over a million monthly users are required to submit written reports outlining significant risks to election integrity, including disinformation, misinformation, or manipulative behaviour.[81] Section 149 obliges online platforms to implement notification mechanisms allowing "any individual, entity or person to notify it of the presence on their service of specific activities or behaviours in respect of online electoral information that the individual or entity considers may amount to manipulative or inauthentic behaviour".[82] Moreover, platforms shall, without undue delay, assess, process and determine the validity of the raised concerns,[83] and maintain records of the received notifications and the outcome of the determination for a period of 2 years following the end of the electoral period concerned.[84] These records need to be available to the Electoral Commission for inspection on reasonable notice.[85]

During electoral periods, the Electoral Commission may issue several notices of compliance to platforms (i.e. seek the removal of content deemed disinformation, correct or label content, block access to disinformation, or publish a statement informing users about the presence of manipulative or inauthentic behaviour).[86] If deemed necessary, it may also apply to Ireland's High Court to enforce their compliance.[87] Additionally, the Electoral Commission may establish a direct reporting facility on its website,[88] enabling the public to report suspected acts of disinformation or misinformation. While Section 161 establishes an appeals mechanism for any individual or platform to contest the abovementioned notices, it does not provide

[80] Electoral Reform Act 2022 (*op. cit.*), Section 144.

[81] *Ibid.*, Section 148 (2).

[82] *Ibid.*, Section 149 (2).

[83] *Ibid.*, Section 149 (4).

[84] *Ibid.*, Section 149 (5).

[85] *Ibid.*, Section 149 (6).

[86] *Ibid.*, Sections 153 to 157.

[87] *Ibid.*, Section 158.

[88] *Ibid.*, Section 160.

for the inclusion of independent expertise, as the appeal panel shall only involve 'one or more' members of the Electoral Commission (Shattock, 2025, p. 6). Lastly, Section 166 sanctions the deliberate dissemination of disinformation during an electoral or campaign period aimed at influencing election outcomes or undermining electoral integrity. This offence is severely punished, either by a fine, imprisonment for a term not exceeding two years, or both.

5 Conclusions: An Evolving Legal Landscape

The fight against disinformation, especially online, seems to be increasingly part of the public debate in Ireland. The Covid-19 pandemic, a catalyst for Irish interest in the media, has also highlighted the need for greater vigilance regarding the accuracy of information. Although the recent years have seen a growth of social media as online sources of information, traditional media, such as TV, radio and newspapers via their online publications have regained momentum as frequently used and trusted news sources (Coimisiún na Meán, 2025a, p. 21–22). Interest in news is on the rise in Ireland (from 53 to 56% over the 2024–2025 period), far exceeding the EU average (45%, constant over the same period)—a trend positively confirmed by a relatively high overall level of trust (50%), ahead of the EU level (39%) (Coimisiún na Meán, 2025a, p. 20). Furthermore, although the level of occasional or frequent news avoidance is on the rise, that of trust in traditional media outlets and brands (public broadcasters such as RTÉ[89] and local and regional news outlets) remains quite strong ranging from 65 to 72% (Coimisiún na Meán, 2025a, p. 27).

This high level of trust in traditional media outlets is coupled with recent trends showing a larger share of people informing themselves primarily through TV over the past year, along with an increasingly notable audience agreeing to pay for news (from 12% in 2020 up to 20% in 2025), well above the EU average (which only plateaued around 15% over said period) (Coimisiún na Meán, 2025a). It thus seems that increased audience awareness about online disinformation (around 68%, albeit higher among the elderly and lower among those aged 18–24) (Coimisiún na Meán, 2025a, p. 34) fuels a need for reliable sources.

The Irish legislator's concern has primarily been to target harmful or illegal online content, thus leaving disinformation to be prosecuted so long as it is included in these two concepts and thereby constitutes an offence under Irish law. Disinformation in Ireland is only explicitly addressed in the electoral context, in case of conducts

[89] RTÉ (for Raidió Teilifís Éireann) is Ireland's public television and radio broadcaster.

regulated by EU law[90] or through scattered pieces of Irish legislation[91] and guidelines,[92] thus resulting in a fragmented regulatory landscape. With the exception of the Electoral Reform Act 2022, the overall absence of the concepts of 'disinformation', 'misinformation', 'malinformation' or 'fake news' may legitimately raise questions about the extent to which online disinformation is regulated, given that it does not in itself constitute a punishable offence. However, this concern may also extend to the Electoral Reform Act 2022 itself, as several of its provisions, pertaining to disinformation during electoral periods, are suspected by the EU Commission of being inconsistent with EU law, in particular with regards to the right to freedom of expression, and will potentially lead to a legislative recast.

Indeed, from a *de iure condendo* perspective, the Irish regulatory landscape is likely to face several updates which will directly or indirectly reshape its approach to online disinformation. The recently adopted Directive (EU) 2024/1385 on combating violence against women and domestic violence,[93] which criminalises the non-consensual sharing of intimate or manipulated material, cyber-harassment, and cyber-incitement to violence or hatred, must still be transposed into Irish law (EUR-Lex, 2025).[94] As said, the Irish Electoral Reform Act 2022 (namely its Parts 4 and 5) is currently under scrutiny by the European Commission for potential incompatibility with EU law on freedom of expression and is likely be amended. Similarly, the Irish legislation on hate speech and related offences, and notably the Prohibition of Incitement to Hatred Act 1989, is now the subject of an infringement procedure for suspected non-compliance with the EU Framework Decision 2008/913/JHA[95] and is undergoing a revision process. The outcome of this reform could expand the scope of prohibited hate speech, thus addressing the dissemination of disinformation targeting protected groups.

References

An Foclóir Nua Béarla-Gaeilge (2025) Disinformation. In: An Foclóir Nua Béarla-Gaeilge. Available via https://www.focloir.ie/ga/dictionary/ei/disinformation. Accessed 04 Dec 2025

Bamford BWC (2005) The role and effectiveness of intelligence in Northern Ireland. In: Intelligence and National Security 20(4):581–607. https://doi.org/10.1080/02684520500425273

---

[90] Cf. Regulation (EU) no. 2021/784, no. 2022/2065, no. 2024/1083, no. 2024/1689; Directive (EU) no. 2024/1069, no. 2024/1385; EU codes of conduct on 'Countering Illegal Hate Speech Online + ' and on 'Disinformation' (*op. cit.*).

[91] Cf. Prohibition of Incitement to Hatred Act 1989; Non-Fatal Offences against the Person Act 1997; Broadcasting Act 2009; Defamation Act 2009; Competition and Consumer Protection Act 2014; Harassment, Harmful Communications and Related Offences Act 2020; OSMR Act 2022 (*op. cit.*).

[92] Cf. Online Safety Code; Guidelines in Respect of Coverage of Elections; Code of Fairness, Objectivity, and Impartiality in News and Current Affairs (*op. cit.*).

[93] Directive (EU) 2024/1385 (*op. cit.*), Articles 5, 7, and 8.

[94] *Ibid.*, Article 49 (1).

[95] Council Framework Decision 2008/913/JHA (*op. cit.*).

Bentzen N (2024) Information integrity online and the European democracy shield. In: European Parliamentary Research Service, PE 767.153. Available via https://www.europarl.europa.eu/thinktank/en/document/EPRS_BRI(2024)767153. Accessed 04 Dec 2025

Bryant M (2025) Denmark to tackle deepfakes by giving people copyright to their own features. In: The Guardian. Available via http://theguardian.com/technology/2025/jun/27/deepfakes-denmark-copyright-law-artificial-intelligence. Accessed 04 Dec 2025

Burke H (2025) European Democracy Shield Explored. In: Institute of International and European Affairs. Available via https://www.iiea.com/images/uploads/resources/Democracy_shield_explainer_final.pdf. Accessed 04 Dec 2025

Citizens' Information (2025) Fundamental rights under the Irish Constitution. In: Citizens Information. Available via https://www.citizensinformation.ie/en/government-in-ireland/irish-constitution-1/constitution-fundamental-rights/. Accessed 04 Dec 2025

Coimisiún na Meán (2024a) Coimisiún na Meán adopts final Online Safety Code. https://www.cnam.ie/coimisiun-na-mean-adopts-final-online-safety-code/. Accessed 4 Dec 2025

Coimisiún na Meán (2024b) Coimisiún na Meán removes traditional broadcast moratorium for election coverage. https://www.cnam.ie/coimisiun-na-mean-removes-traditional-broadcast-moratorium-for-election-coverage/. Accessed 04 Dec 2025

Coimisiún na Meán (2024c) Digital News Report Ireland 2024. In: Coimisiún na Meán. Available via https://www.cnam.ie/app/uploads/2024/06/20240607_DNR-2024_DMB.pdf. Accessed 04 Dec 2025

Coimisiún na Meán (2024d) Guidelines in Respect of Coverage of Elections. In: Coimisiún na Meán. Available via https://www.cnam.ie/app/uploads/2024/11/Coimisiun_na_Mean_Broadcast_Guidelines_Nov2024.pdf. Accessed 04 Dec 2025

Coimisiún na Meán (2024e) Media Service Code. Code of Fairness, Objectivity & Impartiality in News and Current Affairs (Radio and Television Broadcasters). In: Coimisiún na Meán. Available via https://www.cnam.ie/industry-and-professionals/codes-legislation/codes-and-rules/code-of-fairness-impartiality-and-objectivity/. Accessed 04 Dec 2025

Coimisiún na Meán (2025a) Digital News Report Ireland 2025. In: Coimisiún na Meán. Available via https://www.cnam.ie/digital-news-report-ireland-2025/. Accessed 04 Dec 2025

Coimisiún na Meán (2025b) Online Safety Code. In: Coimisiún na Meán. Available via https://www.cnam.ie/industry-and-professionals/online-safety-framework/online-safety-code/. Accessed 04 Dec 2025

Coimisiún na Meán (2025c) Out-of-court dispute settlement bodies. https://www.cnam.ie/industry-and-professionals/online-safety-framework/certifications-schemes/out-of-court-dispute-settlement-bodies/. Accessed 04 Dec 2025

Coimisiún na Meán (2025d) Register of designated online services. https://www.cnam.ie/industry-and-professionals/online-safety-framework/online-safety-code/register-of-designated-online-services/. Accessed 04 Dec 2025

Coimisiún na Meán (2025e) Report to us. https://www.cnam.ie/general-public/report-complain/something-i-saw-or-experienced-online/report-to-us/. Accessed 04 Dec 2025

Coimisiún na Meán (2025f) What can I report? https://www.cnam.ie/general-public/report-complain/something-i-saw-or-experienced-online/what-can-i-report/. Accessed 04 Dec 2025

Coimisiún na Meán (2025g) What is harmful content? In: Coimisiún na Meán. Available via https://www.cnam.ie/general-public/online-safety/what-is-harmful-content/. Accessed 04 Dec 2025

Coimisiún na Meán (2025h) What is illegal content? https://www.cnam.ie/general-public/online-safety/what-is-illegal-content/. Accessed 04 Dec 2025

Cousins C. and Lynch C. (2022) Bill Digest - Electoral Reform Bill 2022. In: Houses of the Oireachtas - Library & Research Service. Available via https://data.oireachtas.ie/ie/oireachtas/libraryResearch/2022/2022-09-27_bill-digest-electoral-reform-bill-2022_en.pdf. Accessed 14 June 2025

Culloty E (2023) Disinformation landscape in Ireland. In: EU Disinfo Lab. Available via https://www.disinfo.eu/publications/disinformation-landscape-in-ireland/. Accessed 04 Dec 2025

Court of Justice of the European Union - Research and Documentation Directorate (2018) Field of application of the Charter of Fundamental Rights of the European Union. In: CJEU - Research and Documentation Directorate. Available via https://curia.europa.eu/jcms/upload/docs/application/pdf/2018-05/fiche_thematique_-_charte_-_en.pdf. Accessed 04 Dec 2025

Department of Culture, Communications and Sport (2023) Multi-stakeholder Working Group established to develop a National Counter Disinformation Strategy. In: Government of Ireland. Available via https://www.gov.ie/en/department-of-culture-communications-and-sport/press-releases/multi-stakeholder-working-group-established-to-develop-a-national-counter-disinformation-strategy/. Accessed 04 Dec 2025

Department of Justice, Home Affairs and Migration (2022) Summary Review of the Report of the Review of the Defamation Act. In: Government of Ireland. Available via https://www.gov.ie/en/department-of-justice-home-affairs-and-migration/publications/report-of-the-review-of-the-defamation-act-2009/. Accessed 04 Dec 2025

Disinformation Code Transparency Centre (2024) Code of Practice Signatories implement the Code's commitment for a Rapid Response System ahead of EP elections. In: Disinformation Code Transparency Centre. Available via https://disinfocode.eu/eu-elections-2024/. Accessed 04 Dec 2025

EUR-Lex (2025) National Transposition Measures communicated by Ireland concerning Directive (EU) 2018/1808 of the European Parliament and of the Council of 14 November 2018. In: EUR-Lex. Available via https://eur-lex.europa.eu/legal-content/EN/NIM/?uri=CELEX%3A32018L1808. Accessed 04 Dec 2025

EUR-Lex (2025) National Transposition Measures communicated by the Member States concerning Directive (EU) 2024/1385 of the European Parliament and of the Council of 14 May 2024 on combating violence against women and domestic violence. https://eur-lex.europa.eu/legal-content/EN/NIM/?uri=oj:L_202401385. Accessed 04 Dec 2025

European Commission (2022a) Electoral Reform Bill 2022 (Draft Heads of Bill—new Part 4A), 2022/0376/IRL. In: European Commission. Available via https://technical-regulation-information-system.ec.europa.eu/en/notification/15799/print. Accessed 04 Dec 2025

European Commission (2022b) Electoral Reform Bill 2022 (Part 4—sections 117 to 139 inclusive), 2022/0184/IRL. In: European Commission. Available via https://technical-regulation-information-system.ec.europa.eu/en/notification/17149. Accessed 04 Dec 2025

European Commission (2024) October infringements package: key decisions. In: European Commission. Available via https://ec.europa.eu/commission/presscorner/detail/en/inf_24_4561. Accessed 04 Dec 2025

European Commission (2025) May infringements package: key decisions. In: European Commission. Available via https://ec.europa.eu/commission/presscorner/detail/en/inf_25_982. Accessed 04 Dec 2025

European Commission (2025) Code of Conduct on Disinformation. In: European Commission. Available via https://ec.europa.eu/newsroom/dae/redirection/document/112678. Accessed 04 Dec 2025

European Commission (2025) Code of Conduct on Countering Illegal Hate Speech Online +. In: European Commission. Available via https://ec.europa.eu/newsroom/dae/redirection/document/111777. Accessed 04 Dec 2025

European Commission (2025) Out-of-court dispute settlement bodies under the Digital Services Act (DSA). In: European Commission. https://digital-strategy.ec.europa.eu/en/policies/dsa-out-court-dispute-settlement. Accessed 04 Dec 2025

European Commission (2025) Signatories of the 2022 Strengthened Code of Practice on Disinformation. https://digital-strategy.ec.europa.eu/en/library/signatories-2022-strengthened-code-practice-disinformation. Accessed 04 Dec 2025

European Digital Media Observatory Ireland (2023) EDMO Ireland Hub Briefing Report. In: EDMO. Available via https://edmo.eu/wp-content/uploads/2022/09/2023_EDMO-Ireland-Briefing-Report-2023.pdf. Accessed 04 Dec 2025

European Digital Media Observatory (2024) EDMO's Assessment of the Rapid Response System of the Code of Practice on Disinformation. In: EDMO. Available via https://edmo.eu/publications/edmos-assessment-of-the-rapid-response-system-of-the-code-of-practice-on-disinformation/. Accessed 04 Dec 2025

European External Action Service (2019) Factsheet: Rapid Alert System. In: European External Action Service. Available via https://www.eeas.europa.eu/sites/default/files/ras_factsheet_march_2019_0.pdf. Accessed 04 Dec 2025

European External Action Service (2025) Information Integrity and Countering Foreign Information Manipulation & Interference (FIMI). https://www.eeas.europa.eu/eeas/information-integrity-and-countering-foreign-information-manipulation-interference-fimi_en. Accessed 04 Dec 2025

European Parliament (2025) European Democracy Shield, Legislative Train Schedule. https://www.europarl.europa.eu/legislative-train/package-european-democracy-action-plan/file-european-democracy-shield. Accessed 04 Dec 2025

European Parliament (2025) Package European Democracy Action Plan, Legislative Train Schedule. https://www.europarl.europa.eu/legislative-train/package-european-democracy-action-plan. Accessed 04 Dec 2025

European Parliament: Directorate-General for Internal Policies of the Union (2021) The fight against disinformation and the right to freedom of expression. In: Publications Office of the European Union. Available via https://data.europa.eu/doi/https://doi.org/10.2861/305. Accessed 04 Dec 2025

Eurostat (2022) Flash Eurobarometer - Media & News Survey 2022. In: Eurostat. Available via https://europa.eu/eurobarometer/api/deliverable/download/file?deliverableId=82692. Accessed 04 Dec 2025

Gallagher A, O'Connor C, Visser F (2023) Uisce Faoi Thalamh: Summary Report. In: Institute for Strategic Dialogue. Available via https://www.isdglobal.org/isd-publications/uisce-faoi-thalamh-summary-report/. Accessed 04 Dec 2025

Government of Ireland (2025) National Counter Disinformation Strategy. In: Government of Ireland. Available via https://assets.gov.ie/static/documents/20250416_National_Counter_Disinformation_Strategy_-_EN_-_Final.pdf. Accessed 04 Dec 2025

Houses of the Oireachtas (2025) Defamation (Amendment) Bill 2024 (Bill no. 67 of 2024). In: Houses of the Oireachtas. Available via https://www.oireachtas.ie/en/bills/bill/2024/67/. Accessed 04 Dec 2025.

Houses of the Oireachtas (2025) Protection of Voice and Image Bill 2025 (Bill no. 11 of 2025). In: Houses of the Oireachtas. Available via https://www.oireachtas.ie/en/bills/bill/2025/11/. Accessed 04 Dec 2025

Jas-Koziarkiewicz M, Dobrowolska J (2024) Recommendations of the fact-checkers regarding the EU's system for tackling disinformation. Przegląd Europejski 2024(1):27-45 https://doi.org/10.31338/1641-2478pe.1.24.2

Joint Committee on Tourism, Culture, Arts, Sport and Media (2024) The State's response to online disinformation and media/digital literacy, including social media and fake news. In: Houses of the Oireachtas. Available via https://data.oireachtas.ie/ie/oireachtas/committee/dail/33/joint_committee_on_tourism_culture_arts_sport_and_media/reports/2024/2024-11-06_the-state-s-response-to-online-disinformation-and-media-digital-literacy-including-social-media-and-fake-news_en.pdf. Accessed 04 Dec 2025

Kirk N, Farris E, Shankar K (2021) Ireland's Online Safety and Media Regulation Bill: Too Little, Too Soon? In: UCD Centre for Digital Policy. Available via https://digitalpolicy.ie/explainer-irelandsonline-safety-and-media-regulation-bill/. Accessed 04 Dec 2025.

Munich Security Conference (2024), A Tech Accord to Combat Deceptive Use of AI in 2024 Elections. In: Munich Security Conference. Available via https://securityconference.org/en/aielectionsaccord/. Accessed 04 Dec 2025

Noticias (2025) The Irish Minister O'Donovan Welcomes Publication of National Counter Disinformation Strategy. In: 21 Noticias. Available via https://21noticias.com/2025/04/17/the-irish-minister-odonovan-welcomes-publication-of-national-counter-disinformation-strategy/. Accessed 04 Dec 2025

O'Connor C. (2024) The Irish Channel: Investigating an Irish Misinformation Hub, Political Connections and AI hallucinations. In: Institute for Strategic Dialogue. Available via https://www.isdglobal.org/isd-publications/the-irish-channel-investigating-an-irish-misinformation-hub-political-connections-ai-hallucinations/. Accessed 04 Dec 2025

O'Neill B (2022) Ireland's Online Safety and Media Regulation Act 2022. Leibniz Institut für Medienforschung - Hans-Bredow-Institut (HBI), CO:RE - Children Online: Research and Evidence. doi.org/https://doi.org/10.21241/ssoar.83520

O'Halloran M. (2024) Controversial hate speech provisions removed from criminal justice legislation as Bill passed in Seanad. In: The Irish Times. Available via https://www.irishtimes.com/politics/oireachtas/2024/10/16/controversial-hate-speech-provisions-removed-from-criminal-justice-legislation-as-bill-passed-in-seanad/. Accessed 04 Dec 2025

Oxford English Dictionary (2025) Disinformation. In: Oxford English Dictionary. Available via https://www.oed.com/dictionary/disinformation. Accessed 04 Dec 2025

Pinsent Masons (2025) Image rights in Ireland. In: Pinsent Masons. Available via https://www.pinsentmasons.com/out-law/guides/image-rights-ireland. Accessed 04 Dec 2025

Schueler M, Romano S, et al. (2024) Artificial Elections: Exposing the Use of Generative AI Imagery in the Political Campaigns of the 2024 French Elections. In: AI Forensics. Available via https://aiforensics.org/uploads/Report_Artificial_Elections.pdf. Accessed 04 Dec 2025

Shattock E (2025) Knowledge, deception, and freedom of expression: a critical examination of Ireland's approach to disinformation under the Electoral Reform Act 2022. International Review of Law, Computers & Technology, 39(3):344-373, https://doi.org/10.1080/13600869.2024.2428145.

Smyth C (2024) Ireland's asylum debate has turned violent thanks to the spread of misinformation and disinformation. The Conversation. doi.org/https://doi.org/10.64628/AB.q5dmkqvgp

Stolton S (2020) EU Rapid Alert System used amid coronavirus disinformation campaign. In: Euractiv. Available via https://www.euractiv.com/section/tech/news/eu-alert-triggered-after-coronavirus-disinformation-campaign/. Accessed 04 Dec 2025

The Library Association of Ireland (2025) Launch of Public Consultation on National Counter Disinformation Strategy. In: The Library Association of Ireland. Available via https://www.libraryassociation.ie/launch-of-public-consultation-on-national-counter-disinformation-strategy/. Accessed 04 Dec 2025

UK Parliament, Section 195 of the Economic Crime and Corporate Transparency Act 2023 (UK), https://www.legislation.gov.uk/ukpga/2023/56/section/195/enacted. Accessed 04 Dec 2025

United Nations Human Rights Council (2025), A/HRC/60/CRP.3, 16 Sept 2025, https://www.un.org/unispal/document/commission-of-inquiry-report-genocide-in-gaza-a-hrc-60-crp-3/. Accessed 04 Dec 2025

Disinformation in the Italian Legal System

Gian Luca Conti and Sara Riccardi

Abstract This chapter provides a detailed analysis of disinformation within the Italian legal framework, examining the constitutional basis, relevant legislation, and enforcement mechanisms. The investigation begins with the acknowledgment that Article 21 of the Italian Constitution, which protects freedom of expression, is not absolute but must be balanced against other fundamental interests. The chapter then reviews the main legal sources aimed at combating disinformation, with particular focus on its treatment within the criminal justice system. It highlights that the dissemination of false information is criminalized only when it infringes specific legal interests, such as public order, public health, the market, rather than the concept of truth itself. The discussion further extends to disinformation in economic and political spheres, addressing the various procedural and regulatory tools designed to mitigate these risks. Particular attention is given to the limited liability of Internet Service Providers (ISPs) for unlawful content, especially considering the new European Digital Services Act (DSA) and its implications for content regulation. Finally, the chapter explores the complex challenges posed by judicial disinformation, where media coverage of ongoing trials can blur the line between public information and prejudicial reporting. This "media trial" phenomenon risks undermining the presumption of innocence and threatens the fairness of the judicial process, raising significant concerns for the democratic system as a whole.

Sections 1.1, 1.2 and 2.2. were written by Gian Luca Conti; Sects. 2.1, 2.3, 2.4, 3.1 and 3.2. were written by Sara Riccardi. Section 4.1 was jointly discussed by the authors and drafted by Sara Riccardi.

G. L. Conti (✉) · S. Riccardi
Department of Law, University of Pisa, Pisa, Italy
e-mail: gianluca.conti@unipi.it

S. Riccardi
e-mail: sara.riccardi@phd.unipi.it

P. Passaglia (ed.), *European Legal Perspectives on Online Disinformation*, Ius Gentium: Comparative Perspectives on Law and Justice 140,
https://doi.org/10.1007/978-3-032-25785-7_12

1 Disinformation in the Legal System of the Italian Republic

1.1 Freedom of Expression and Constitutional Framework

The first issue to be addressed concerns the identification of the constitutional coordinates that come into play when discussing disinformation. Disinformation may be regarded as a specific form of expression through which a certain "truth" is narrated with the purpose of shaping public opinion by reinforcing—or inducing—a distorted perception of reality (Nicita 2021; Pitruzzella and Pollicino 2020; Vigevani and Bassini 2017; Manetti 2023).

It is commonly argued that disinformation cannot be equated with the constitutional right to freedom of expression, since a form of expression whose purpose is to distort, rather than enrich, the free marketplace of ideas cannot be protected (Barile 1962; Manetti 2022). Accordingly, the constitutional framework governing disinformation reflects the general principles of criminal law, as inferred from Articles 13, 25, and 27 of the Italian Constitution. These provisions grant the legislature wide discretion in defining unlawful conduct.

This seems to be the interpretive framework of current law, which penalizes conduct amounting to disinformation. Yet, from a constitutional standpoint, such an approach implies a functional view of freedom of expression that this paper does not support (Esposito 1959).

Freedom of expression deserves to be taken seriously not merely because it is the cornerstone of a democratic society organized through voting or other forms of participation that require a minimum degree of awareness, but because it represents each individual's right to freely express their personality through thought. This individual right falls within the broad protection guaranteed by Article 2 of the Constitution, according to which the Republic recognizes, rather than creates, the fundamental rights of the person, acknowledging their existence as inherent in a state of nature that precedes both law and the regulation of means of communication.

Freedom of expression is therefore grounded in the same ideal rationale that justifies the recognition of the intrinsic value of the human person. It follows that democracy is a consequence of this freedom, not its precondition (Esposito 1959). Hence, those who claim that it is constitutionally permissible to limit freedom of expression in order to protect the "free marketplace of ideas" are mistaken.

Nevertheless, Article 21 of the Constitution, after proclaiming that everyone has the right to freely express their thoughts, also establishes several equally significant principles: the press cannot be subjected to authorization or censorship (paragraph 2); printed materials may be seized only in cases of violation of the law governing the press or in the absence of an identified responsible editor (paragraph 3); preventive seizure is permitted, but in such cases it must be carried out by judicial police officers, with the requirement that validation be requested within 24 hours and that a judge rule within the following 24 hours (paragraph 4). Furthermore, the legislator may require the disclosure of sources of funding for periodical publications (paragraph

5). Lastly, publications, performances, and other manifestations contrary to public decency are prohibited, and the legislator must establish adequate measures to prevent and suppress such violations.

Even more generally, Article 68, paragraph 1, of the Constitution exempts members of Parliament from any form of liability for opinions expressed and votes cast in the exercise of their functions. This provision would make little sense if there were no constitutionally admissible circumstances in which the expression of certain opinions could be prohibited. Thus, freedom of expression cannot be regarded as absolute.

At the same time, both the third and fourth paragraphs of Article 21 presuppose that the press law may establish criminal offences allowing for the seizure of printed materials, and that such seizure may occur when the responsible editor is not indicated. This confirms that the legislature enjoys a certain discretion in defining which expressive behaviors may be prohibited and sanctioned under criminal law.

However, authorization or censorship may never be imposed on the press. Debate persists on whether this safeguard applies only to printed media or also to online expression. Jurisprudence generally extends constitutional protection to registered online periodicals and, later, to all communication operators under the Electronic Communications Code, that is Legislative Decree No. 259/2003 (Melzi d'Erile 2011).

This case law limits the constitutional scope of press freedom to media formally registered under press legislation. Only these outlets benefit from guarantees against authorization and censorship, the criminal rule requiring an editor's identification, seizure regulations, and funding disclosure obligations. All other forms of expression fall within the general legal framework derived from Articles 13, 25, and 27 of the Constitution, and are therefore subject to the broad legislative discretion recognized therein. From this perspective, the protection of freedom of expression under the Italian Constitution appears less robust than is often suggested by a superficial reading of Article 21, paragraph 1.

It is commonly asserted that freedom of expression may be restricted whenever it conflicts with another constitutional value of comparable rank, requiring a balancing of interests. In other words, one may freely express one's thoughts unless such freedom becomes an abuse (Pace and Manetti 2006).

However, this prevailing view is untenable for three reasons. First, it neglects the innovative intent of Article 21 compared with the pre-constitutional regime. Second, it is logically inconsistent to treat a primary constitutional value as "absolute" while simultaneously subjecting it to legal balancing, since all values are ultimately defined by law and therefore cannot be absolute. Third, Article 21(1) protects the freedom to express one's personality through thought—by any medium—but not an unconditional right to publish any content. In this sense, individuals must remain free to express themselves and use any medium to communicate, without persecution for their ideas. Yet transferring thought from the private to the public sphere is a distinct activity, which may constitute a commercial or communicative enterprise rather than a personal expression, as it often involves disseminating others' ideas. Accordingly, the final clause of Article 21, prohibiting expressions contrary to public decency, should be read in this light. Historically, this referred to acts offending public modesty or decency, and such an interpretation remains valid (Barile 1975).

At the same time, the Constitution cannot be read solely through its 1948 meaning. While the framers' intent is authoritative, it cannot confine the evolving interpretation of constitutional norms, including the final paragraph of Article 21. Accordingly, the prohibition of expressions contrary to public decency requires deeper analysis. One interpretative line reflects the Constituent Assembly's broad consensus against obscene or immoral expressions. The notion of "public decency" must rest on shared social values, not on political majorities, and jurisprudence has recognized its evolving character as shaped by collective moral sensitivity free from ideological bias (Supreme Court, judgment Labour Section, No. 2014/2018).

The second interpretative approach views "public decency" in light of its 1948 context, when it reflected society's moral recovery from fascist repression. It cannot be reduced to a majoritarian expression of political will but serves as a substantive limit on the legislature: any restriction on expression must rest on values shared by the whole civil community, not on partisan ideology. While in 1948 such prohibitions targeted offenses against sexual morality, today they relate to safeguarding a healthy and trustworthy infosphere, protecting democracy and especially the most vulnerable from the harms of disinformation.

1.2 Beyond the Boundaries of Freedom of Expression: Pluralism

Much of the jurisprudential debate on freedom of expression has concerned the regulation of broadcasting (Barile et al. 1980; Zaccaria 2019). Indeed, the Constitutional Court has exercised a broad interpretative latitude, elaborating principles that transcend the mere protection of freedom of expression as an individual right to self-realization through the externalization of thought. The notion of pluralism—whether internal or external—within the broadcasting sector reflects the State's constitutional duty to ensure an informational environment conducive to the free formation of individual opinions through open confrontation among diverse perspectives. Such pluralism thus represents an objective constitutional value, instrumental to the democratic process. In this framework, public economic intervention seeks to achieve social objectives through coordinated public–private action under Articles 3(2), 41, 42, and 43 of the Constitution. Article 21(1) functions as a guiding principle, ensuring that enterprise serves the social utility of democratic circulation of ideas.

Constitutional jurisprudence initially addressed the technical limits to a free broadcasting market, which justified a public monopoly. The Court held that the national broadcaster must be governed pluralistically, independent from the ruling majority and reflective of parliamentary representation (Caretti and Cardone 2024).

The shift from internal pluralism to external pluralism occurred once a technically feasible path toward a genuinely free broadcasting market emerged. The Court held that when the information market operates on commercial grounds, it must be balanced by educational and citizen-oriented content. This led to a model based on external pluralism—multiple broadcasters—and to continued public intervention aimed at safeguarding pluralistic, non-profit-driven information (Italian Constitutional Court, judgment No. 420, 1994). This principle seems to belong to a bygone era and, in hindsight, can be said to have had limited success in reshaping the marketplace of ideas to foster pluralism.

The interpretative framework acquires new relevance in a context diametrically opposed to that considered in Constitutional Court Decision No. 103/1975. At that time, the constitutional concern was to open the marketplace of ideas to civil society and to limit the dominance of the public broadcasting monopoly. Today, by contrast, the information ecosystem is controlled by global platforms, and its evolution increasingly depends on artificial intelligence. In this environment, pluralism and the circulation of ideas are not the primary objectives of economic activity but collateral outcomes of business models financed by targeted advertising and sustained by algorithmic profiling, which fosters informational segregation. The State's role has thus been reduced to that of a regulatory intermediary, charged mainly with implementing European measures designed to contain the market power of non-European platforms. Antitrust tools are structurally unable to restore pluralism in the infosphere, dominated by unassailable platforms such as Alphabet, Meta, and ByteDance. Algorithmic systems reinforce homogeneity, and search engines optimize relevance rather than diversity. This context calls for "outside-in pluralism," promoted by public intervention to sustain pluralism within the digital sphere. Contemporary broadcasting services largely maintain traditional programming models, yet public broadcasters possess the resources and institutional mandate to evolve into communication operators capable of competing within the platform economy, guided by the constitutional principle of pluralism. The digital environment, exemplified by platforms such as YouTube illustrates the marginalization of conventional television and the growing dominance of global networks capable of aggregating users through pervasive data-driven profiling. In this context, the public service mission of broadcasters like RAI acquires renewed significance: it should not be confined to linear programming but directed toward ensuring pluralistic access to information within the digital sphere, where the formation of public opinion increasingly occurs.

2 Sources of Law Countering Disinformation

2.1 Disinformation in the Criminal Code

Reviewing the various areas in which disinformative conduct is relevant, it seems appropriate to start from the Criminal Code. Indeed, numerous provisions give relevance to the dissemination of false, tendentious, or exaggerated information (Perini

2017; Guerini 2020; Costantini 2019; Biritteri 2021). This does not imply that criminal law attributes criminal relevance to online disinformation itself, understood as the dissemination of intentionally manipulated content aimed at obtaining economic benefit or misleading the public; rather, in light of the principles of subsidiarity, and consistent with our premises, the false information is punished only when it proves instrumental to harming legal interests protected by the criminal legal system, such as public order, property, market protection, and individual honor (Wardle et al. 2017).

It would not be possible to examine all the provisions in which the dissemination of mendacious content assumes criminal relevance. Therefore, following the notion of disinformation given by EU Code of Practice on Disinformation, according to which disinformation is a "*set of verifiable false content and misleading information which is created and disseminated for economic gain or to intentionally deceive the public and may cause public harm, intended as threats to democratic political and policymaking processes as well as public goods (citizens' health, environment, security),*" this report will primarily focus on offenses aimed at protecting goods of collective relevance.

Among the relevant provisions, Article 656 and Article 658 of the Criminal Code stand out, both aimed at protecting public order, that is the legal order upon which social coexistence is founded (Caraccioli 1962). While Article 656 punishes "*whoever publishes or disseminates false, exaggerated or tendentious news, by which public order may be disturbed,*" Article 658 punishes anyone who "*by announcing non-existent disasters, accidents or dangers, causes alarm with the Authority, or with entities or persons exercising a public service.*" In light of the broad notion of "dissemination", understood as divulgation of news by any means to a plurality of persons, such provisions encompass also the propagation of *fake news* through the internet (Costantini 2019). Article 656 of the Criminal Code must be interpreted as a danger crime, which requires that the content of the news is able to *give rise to widespread disturbance (apprehension, agitation, distrust) capable of reflecting upon public order*, as it has been established by the Penal Supreme Court, judgment No. 19367, 2020; Article 658 is, instead, a common offense of event and bound form, requiring the proof that the conduct has aroused genuine alarm with the authority.

Article 656 of the Criminal Code may also apply to the dissemination of mendacious news referring to vaccines and medicines produced by pharmaceutical companies, spread online by people motivated by feelings of skepticism and intolerance. As just noted, Article 656 of the Criminal Code requires the existence of a concrete danger; therefore, such conduct can fall within the scope of Article 656 only if it is capable of undermining public confidence in the safety of healthcare treatments (Grignolio 2016).

A different scenario arises where pharmaceutical companies themselves engage in the dissemination of misleading or fraudulent information about their products. In such cases, the conduct does not fall under Article 656, but constitutes crimes against the public administration, offenses against public health, and crimes provided under Article 123(1) and (3), as well as Article 147(5) of Legislative Decree no. 219 of 24 April 2006, which penalize "*anyone who, in the course of information and promotional activities regarding medicinal products directed at physicians, offers or promises prizes, pecuniary advantages, or benefits in kind*." Similarly, Article 170 of Royal Decree no. 1265 of 27 July 1934 punishes *physicians who accept, for themselves or for others, money or other benefits for the purpose of facilitating, through medical prescriptions or in any other way, the dissemination of pharmaceutical specialties or other medicinal products*. Also applicable are Articles 41 et seq. of Legislative Decree no. 200 of 2007, which *penalize anyone who, for authorization purposes or publication, produces, prepares, or submits data that are not consistent with reality, thereby potentially affecting the assessment of the submitted material* (Vallini 2018).

The dissemination of fake news may also fall within the concept of "deception" under Article 294 of the Criminal Code, which punishes "*whoever with violence, threat or deception prevents in whole or in part the exercise of a political right, or determines someone to exercise it in a manner contrary to their will*." Originally intended to protect political rights as instrumental to safeguarding the personality of the State, the provision has been reinterpreted in light of constitutional principles. Today, it is regarded as a guarantee of the fundamental rights and freedoms that citizens enjoy by virtue of their membership in the community (Padovani 1982; Pelissero 2010). As Penal Supreme Court pointed out (judgment No. 51722, 2016), this is an event crime, requiring verification that the deception or threat has made the exercise of the political right impossible. This requirement, when applied to the context of *online* disinformation, makes such criminalization practically inoperative, as it is quite difficult to prove that false information has coercively induced the citizens to exercise their political right (for example, the right to vote) in a manner contrary to their real intention.

The provision was recently amended by Law No. 132 of 2025, containing provisions and delegations to the Government on matters of artificial intelligence, implementing Regulation (EU) 2024/1689 on Artificial Intelligence (the so-called AI Act). As is well known, artificial intelligence represents a new and powerful tool for the automated creation of false or misleading content, characterized by a previously unimaginable degree of realism and by an extremely rapid capacity for mass dissemination. In order to counter such outcomes, the law has introduced, in paragraph 2 of Article 294 of the Criminal Code, a special aggravating circumstance, aimed at punishing more severely the conduct of anyone who commits deception through the use of artificial intelligence systems.

Online disinformation may also assume relevance in the offense of Article 501 of the Criminal Code, commonly called "market manipulation". This provision protects market competition by punishing anyone who, by disseminating "*false, exaggerated or tendentious news*," causes an increase or decrease in the price of goods or securities negotiable in the public market. The offense will be examined in the paragraph dedicated to financial disinformation.

Finally, the dissemination of false news may be part of a disinformation campaign aimed at fostering discriminatory attitudes toward particular minorities. In the domestic legal system, such phenomena are addressed under Article 604-bis of the Criminal Code, which punishes conduct of propaganda or instigation for racial, ethnic, national or religious motives (so-called *hate speech*). Strictly speaking, this provision is independent of the truth or falsity of the narrated fact; nonetheless, the importance of "objective" truth, or at least historical truth, emerges in the aggravating circumstance of "*negationism*" provided for in the final paragraph. It attaches criminal relevance to Holocaust denial, as well as to the denial of acts of genocide, crimes against humanity, and war crimes, as defined respectively in Articles 6, 7, and 8 of the Statute of the International Criminal Court. Within this framework, online disinformation assumes particular relevance where the fake news is used to disseminate content denying historical facts, such as the genocide of Jews during World War II. Unlike other provisions, here it is less clear the legal interest protected by the provision, different from mere truthfulness of the news. According to some scholars, the provision seems to underlie concepts, especially those of historical truth and memory, that are undefined and imprecise, whose content is inevitably influenced by value judgments (Fronza 2012; Cavaliere 2016; Galluccio 2020).

In addition to harming interests of collective relevance, disinformative conduct—particularly when carried out in the exercise of the right to report—may also amount to defamation under Article 595 of the Criminal Code. In this area, it is therefore necessary to recall the limits developed by case law, starting from the well-known 'journalist's decalogue' established by the Civil Supreme Court (judgment No. 5259, 1984), which excludes the liability of journalists who, in exercising the rights of reporting, critique, or satire, disseminate information detrimental to others' reputations. Focusing specifically on the right to report, the information disseminated must have social utility; it must comply with the principle of restraint (i.e., it must not employ clearly offensive language or unduly harsh or biting expressions); and it must be presented as truthful. With regard to this latter requirement, case law demands a strict correspondence between the reported facts and what actually occurred, requiring journalists to conduct a thorough verification of sources. The so-called putative justification is recognised only where the journalist's error arises despite a careful and diligent effort to verify the information (Gullo 2013).

Recently, Law No. 132 of 29 September 2025 introduced a new criminal offense aimed at combating the phenomenon known as "*deep fake*." Specifically, the new Article 612-quater of the Italian Penal Code, entitled "Unlawful dissemination of content generated or altered by artificial intelligence systems," criminalizes the manipulation or generation of content through AI, encompassing both entirely AI-created materials and real content altered by AI. According to this provision, it is not sufficient for the content to be falsified; rather, it must be capable of misleading third parties into believing it to be authentic, thereby requiring the potential to deceive. Furthermore, the dissemination of such false content must cause harm to the victim, which may be of any kind, including reputational, moral, psychological, or economic.

2.2 *Information in the Political, Commercial and Financial Fields*

The regulation of information in political, commercial, and financial domains still reflects insights long advanced by Coase in the field of *law and economics* (Coase 1974; J. Marchetti 2022). A tension persists between those who, while supporting regulation of the goods and services market to secure its social function, oppose intervention in the marketplace of ideas, and those who take the opposite view. Information affecting the economic sphere is subject to detailed regulation intended to prevent distortions of market behaviour, whereas information in the political domain remains largely unregulated. In the financial sector, the key concern is market abuse, governed by Regulation (EU) No. 596/2014 and, in Italy, by Article 186-ter of the *Testo Unico della Finanza*, which sanctions conduct capable of providing false or misleading indications on the supply, demand, or price of financial instruments. Such cases include both action-based and information-based manipulation, that is behaviour that fails to offer a "true and fair view" of market reality.

Beyond the complex relationship between EU law and its national implementing provisions, it is clear that supervisory authorities are responsible for pursuing such conduct at the administrative level, while the criminal courts impose sanctions—according to a "dual-track" system that is not uncommon in the economic sphere (Vizzardi 2006). In the goods and services market, information regulation primarily addresses market failures in self-regulation. This has led to a model centred on autonomous supervisory authorities, empowered to define the content, timing, and modalities of market disclosure.

These bodies act to correct the deficiencies of economic morality through stringent administrative oversight. The underlying objective is to foster a culture of informational fair play, whereby market success is perceived as inseparable from reputational integrity. Such fair play is reinforced by independent actors (auditing firms and credit-rating agencies) that perform verification and certification functions analogous to those of fact-checkers within the Digital Services Package.

Auditors ensure compliance with accounting standards that enable comparability across entities, while rating agencies certify the reliability of market participants, thereby facilitating transparent access to capital markets. Increasingly, these institutions are being called upon to assess environmental and social sustainability, thus assuming a foundational role in aligning market dynamics with broader public policy objectives. As is well known, the Preliminary Programme of the European Economic Community for a Consumer Protection and Information Policy, adopted on 25 April 1975, established the safeguarding of five fundamental consumer rights as its primary objective. These rights include: (a) the right to the protection of health and safety; (b) the right to the protection of economic interests; (c) the right to compensation for damages; (d) the right to information and education; and (e) the right to representation (the right to be heard). This framework naturally pertains to informational advertising rather than to advertising aimed solely at promoting brand awareness.

Directive 84/450/EEC prohibited misleading advertising and was implemented by Legislative Decree No. 79/1992, while Directive 97/55/EC authorised comparative advertising, deemed capable of enabling consumers to make more informed choices. Directive 89/522/EEC on broadcasting services prohibited advertising messages not clearly recognisable as such, as well as subliminal advertising. These prohibitions were extended to all forms of advertising by Article 4 of Legislative Decree 79/1992. Subsequently, Directive 2005/29/EC prohibited all forms of unfair commercial practice, defined in Article 5 as any conduct which "*contravenes the requirements of professional diligence and materially distorts or is likely to materially distort the economic behaviour of the average consumer*" with respect to a product. The same definition was almost identically transposed into Article 20 of Legislative Decree 206/2005 (the so-called *Consumer Code*), which, in the following provisions, prohibits both misleading and aggressive advertising.

Within this framework, the advertising message forms part of a structurally asymmetrical relationship between trader and consumer: advertising a product is lawful insofar as it defines the characteristics of that product or its manufacturer (*branding*), but where it promotes a particular good, it encounters the limit of *fairness*—the consumer's right not to be manipulated through practices that distort their capacity for judgment. The distortion of judgment is manifest in aggressive advertising, which, through harassment, coercion (including physical force) or undue influence, "significantly limits or is likely to limit the average consumer's freedom of choice or conduct with regard to a product and thereby causes or is likely to cause them to take a transactional decision they would not otherwise have taken." What immediately comes to mind is *behavioural advertising*—that is, online advertising based on users' browsing data and, to put it simply, showing to those interested in a given market sector advertisements tailored to their interests.

Behavioural advertising is a tool capable of manipulating user behaviour far more effectively than any traditional display advertising. It is admissible only to the extent that users themselves consciously consent to being targeted, receiving advertising messages on matters of personal interest.

In any event Article 41 of the Constitution follows a distinctive path: the advertising message is an expression of the entrepreneur's freedom of economic initiative, which may not harm either social utility or human dignity. Accordingly, the *fair play* rules should ensure the reasonable fairness of the relationship between trader and consumer, who has the right to make an informed choice because they have been "pleasantly" informed.

Branding, by contrast, encounters no limits other than that of unfair competition through imitation: Article 41 of the Constitution encompasses, within the freedom of enterprise, the manner in which consumers perceive the uniqueness of the *business name* under which the entrepreneur operates.

Within this model, freedom of enterprise naturally includes the right to define, protect, and enhance one's trade name and reputation as instruments of market positioning.

Over time, however, the brand has transcended its purely commercial nature, acquiring symbolic value as a marker of identity and social belonging. Strong brands not only identify an entrepreneur but enable consumers to define themselves through affiliation with particular communities—sometimes as an assertion of pride against those who despise or deem them inferior. Hence the growing adoption of branding strategies by actors once distant from commercial communication, who now employ such tools to reclaim vitality and recognition within a fragmented social landscape.

Communication in the political field remains substantially governed by Law No. 28 of 22 February 2000, as later amended by Law No. 313/2003 and by the 2004 Ministerial Decree introducing a self-regulation code for local broadcasters. The regulation applies essentially to electoral periods, from the calling of the elections to the end of the electoral campaign. It applies primarily to media service providers as defined by Legislative Decree No. 208 of 8 November 2021. Two provisions (Articles 7 and 8) concern the daily and periodical press, while none apply to the internet.

The protection of principles concerning pluralism of information, fairness, completeness, impartiality, objectivity, integrity, and openness to different political opinions and tendencies—laid down by Legislative Decree 208/2021 and by Laws No. 28/2000 and No. 515/1993—is entrusted to the *Autorità per le Garanzie nelle Comunicazioni* (AGCOM) under Law No. 249/1997.

AGCOM has established a Technical Working Group for the Guarantee of Pluralism and Fairness of Information on Digital Platforms (Resolution No. 423/17/CONS), which, among other tasks, seeks to counter disinformation.

This framework, hitherto rather limited and therefore supplemented mainly through self-regulatory commitments adopted by individual communication operators, has been enriched by Regulation (EU) 2024/900 on the transparency of political communication. On 8 October 2025, the European Commission adopted non-binding guidelines for its implementation.

None of the provisions concerning political communication explicitly refers to the *truthfulness* of messages disseminated to promote a particular candidate or the issues characteristic of a given ideological platform.

The focus is instead on ensuring that political communication is clearly recognisable as such, that it is properly archived in dedicated repositories, that campaign sponsors are explicitly identified, and that cross-border political communication is prohibited—preventing foreign entities from influencing electoral or referendum campaigns within a given legal order.

2.3 Liability and Obligation of Internet Service Providers

The role of Internet Service Providers (ISPs) and, more generally, of digital intermediaries, has become central in the fight against online disinformation. Since most *online* content circulates through platforms managed by private subjects the issue has arisen of whether, and to what extent, such actors may be held liable for unlawful conduct committed by users through their services (Ingrassia 2012; Panattoni 2018; D'Agostino 2021).

For many years, the regulatory framework was defined by Directive 2000/31/EC on electronic commerce, which identified three categories of intermediaries: *mere conduit* providers, responsible for data transmission; *caching* providers, enabling temporary storage to improve efficiency; and *hosting* providers, who store user-generated content and make it publicly accessible. The issue of intermediary liability has primarily arisen with regard to hosting providers, whose indexing activities enhance the visibility and accessibility of uploaded material. Article 14 of the Directive established a regime of limited liability: providers are exempt from responsibility for unlawful content if they lack actual knowledge of its illegality and act promptly to remove it once aware. This framework was transposed into Italian law by Legislative Decree No. 70/2003, which reaffirmed the exemption (Art. 16) and excluded any general monitoring obligation (Art. 17).

Accordingly, Italian law does not impose liability preemptively; rather, liability arises only after the fact, specifically when providers fail to remove illegal content upon becoming aware of it. From a criminal law perspective, Internet Service Providers (ISPs) may be held liable under Article 388 of the Criminal Code (willful non-execution of a judge's order), when a removal order is issued pursuant to a judicial provision; under Article 650 of the Criminal Code, which penalizes non-compliance with provisions issued for reasons of justice or public security; and potentially under Article 378 of the Criminal Code, which, according to established case law, may encompass omissions constituting a breach of a legal duty to act. This principle was notably affirmed by the Supreme Penal Court in judgment no. 5494 of 2016, which held an ISP liable for contributing to the crime of defamation on the basis that the provider had knowingly maintained the defamatory content. More debated, however, is the extent to which an ISP can be held liable for omissive participation in the commission of the offense by the user (Seminara, 1998; Flor, 2010).

More than twenty years after the e-commerce directive, technological evolution and the growing impact of digital platforms have imposed a revision of the legal framework. With the Digital Services Act (EU Regulation 2022/2065), the Digital Market Act (Regulation 2022/1925) and the regulation on Artificial Intelligence (Regulation 2024/1689), the European Union has overcome the idea of pure technical neutrality of intermediaries, introducing a system based on the active responsibility of operators. The DSA confirms the absence of a general surveillance obligation and the limited liability structure, but complements it with a set of duties of diligence and cooperation that significantly affect content management. Adopting a risk-based approach, obligations are tailored in light of the size and impact of platforms. For very large platforms (so-called VLOPs and VLOSEs) reinforced obligations are provided, such as systemic risk assessment concerning disinformation, adoption of mitigation measures, and submission to audits (Biritteri 2023). Among the most innovative aspects, we underline the notice and action mechanisms (Article 16), according to which receipt of a reliable report by a user or authority attributes to the provider "*effective knowledge*" of illicit content and creates the obligation to remove or disable it. This clarification resolves interpretative doubts on "effective knowledge" under Italian law. Article 16 of Legislative Decree No. 70/2003, establishing ISP liability for unlawful content, requires removal "upon notification by the competent authorities," raising the question whether the duty arises only from official notices or also from reports by the injured party.

We also note an obligation of justification (Article 17), requiring providers to clearly inform users of moderation decision, strengthening transparency and user protection guarantees. Still, the DSA encourages action on complaint procedures and extrajudicial remedies (Article 18), so as to reduce the risk of arbitrary decisions by platforms.

These innovations show how the DSA enhances their active role in content management, particularly in the face of phenomena such as online disinformation. In Italy, no specific law has yet been adopted to implement the DSA and, in parallel, Article 3, paragraph 4, of Legislative Decree No. 50/2024 has repealed those provisions provided by Legislative Decree 70/2003 regarding ISP liability (Articles 14–17). As a consequence, Regulation No. 2065/2022 (DSA) has become the main reference for regulation of the matter, being directly applicable in the Italian legal system.

2.4 *Judicial Malinformation*

Among the various manifestations of the freedom of expression, a particular role is assumed by the freedom of judicial reporting. It is a shared feature of democratic systems that the administration of justice should not take place in secrecy, but rather through procedures that ensure public scrutiny by those who are subject to its effects (Spagnolo 2014). This principle finds constitutional confirmation in Article 101 of the Italian Constitution, which provides that justice is administered "*in the name of the people*".

However, the right to inform cannot receive unconditional protection, as it must be balanced against the fundamental rights of the individuals involved in criminal proceedings. At stake are, above all, the presumption of innocence, the impartiality, and the free conviction of the judge. The Italian Constitutional Court (judgment No. 25, 1965 and judgment No. 18, 1981) has repeatedly affirmed that the freedom of expression meets the limit of the proper administration of justice, and that it lies within the discretion of the legislature to regulate the relationship between justice and the media.

In this respect, the Italian Code of Criminal Procedure of 1988 lays down, in Articles 114, 115 and 329, a detailed framework governing investigative secrecy and the publication of procedural acts. In essence, it establishes an absolute prohibition on the publication of acts covered by secrecy – mainly investigative acts as identified in Article 329(1) c.p.p. – as well as on the disclosure of their content. The subsequent provisions introduce relative prohibitions: while the publication of acts no longer covered by secrecy (the so-called "accessible acts") remains forbidden, their content may be reported in summary form, without textual reproduction (Colamussi 2021).

To safeguard these rules, both criminal and disciplinary sanctions are provided. Article 684 of the Criminal Code criminalises the unauthorised publication of acts of a criminal proceeding; furthermore, Article 2(1)(u) of Legislative Decree No. 109/2006 classifies as a disciplinary offence the disclosure – even through negligence – of acts covered by secrecy or subject to a publication ban.

Yet, daily practice has long contradicted these prohibitions, to the point of producing a genuine "collapse of legality" (Giostra 1989; Triggiani 2022). In Italy, the principle of publicity in judicial proceedings—originally intended to ensure democratic oversight of justice—has gradually evolved into a mechanism that fosters the premature presumption of guilt in public opinion (Casiraghi 2021).

Although the phenomenon is far from new – one need only recall the notorious *Dreyfus affair* – it has assumed peculiar traits in the Italian context, marked by the persistent celebration of criminal trials in parallel media fora (press, social media, talk shows), the so-called *media trial* (Mantovani 2011; Manes 2022; Bruti Liberati 2022). The most critical distortion arises when the media publish acts and documents still covered by secrecy, often before they have been served to the parties concerned, thus contributing to the public vilification of suspects (Giostra 2007). This phenomenon entails the unauthorised transfer of confidential materials from the actors of the criminal process – judges, police officers, lawyers, consultants, or witnesses – to "trusted" journalists who ensure their immediate dissemination. It is not uncommon for defendants to discover the very existence of proceedings against them through the press, or to read in newspapers excerpts of wiretaps involving their own conversations.

Such distortions stem, at least in part, from the different logics governing criminal proceedings and mass communication. Criminal justice unfolds through formalised and time-consuming procedures aimed at ensuring accuracy and due process, whereas information follows the logic of speed and immediacy: news is an ephemeral commodity that must be captured before it fades. Consequently, media attention tends to focus on the pre-trial phase, exerting constant pressure on investigators and prosecutors (Giostra 2007).

Moreover, procedural truth, which is critical, formal and bounded by the rules of adversarial procedure, differs profoundly from media truth, which is instantaneous, partial and often shaped by prosecutorial hypotheses, enriched with sensational or moralising elements designed to engage public emotion (Manes 2022).

The adverse effects of this situation emerge on multiple levels. First, it undermines the presumption of innocence enshrined in Article 27 of the Constitution, as the dissemination of confidential information often generates public expectations of guilt. The ensuing trial may thus acquire a "spurious" character, directed more at satisfying collective perceptions than at ensuring a fair adjudication.

Closely connected is the issue of the judge's free conviction, an essential component of the right to a fair trial under Article 6 ECHR. The trial judge should be in a condition of "cognitive virginity", safeguarded by the strict separation between the investigation file and the trial file. However, extensive media coverage can compromise this condition, as judges may be exposed, through the press, to materials that should have remained confidential.

The Italian Penal Supreme Court (judgment No. 268529, 2016) when addressing the possibility of transferring proceedings (*rimessione del processo*) under Article 45 c.p.p. in cases of excessive *strepitus fori* (media clamour), has held that media attention should be considered a "neutral element", being an expression of freedom of expression and an instrument of transparency in the exercise of criminal justice. A significant strand of legal scholarship, however, has criticised this stance, arguing that media pressure can indeed influence judicial reasoning and, ultimately, the outcome of trials (Albertario and Castellini 2012).

The repercussions extend to the democratic sphere. Media reporting tends to privilege cases in which someone has an interest in leaking information, and such leaks follow opaque and discretionary channels. Journalists then perform a second selection, deciding which stories reach public attention (Giostra 2007). This dynamic contributes to a broader erosion of public trust in the judiciary: when final judgments are delivered long after the facts and diverge from the "verdict" already pronounced by public opinion, they are often perceived as surprising, unreliable, or unjust.

This problematic landscape has prompted numerous supranational initiatives aimed at regulating communication between prosecutorial offices and the media. Among the most significant is Recommendation (2003)13 of the Council of Europe, which provides that where an accused person can demonstrate that the information released is likely to prejudice the right to a fair trial, an effective legal remedy should be available.

A key instrument in this regard is Directive (EU) 2016/343, on the strengthening of certain aspects of the presumption of innocence, which obliges Member States to prevent public authorities from presenting suspects as guilty. Italy implemented the Directive through Legislative Decree No. 188/2021 which focused in particular on the relationship between judicial authorities and the media (Castellaneta 2022). It has introduced significant amendments to the Code of Criminal Procedure: notably, Article 115-bis c.p.p., prohibiting references to suspects as guilty, and Article 114(6-bis) c.p.p., forbidding the publication of orders imposing precautionary measures until the completion of the preliminary investigation or the preliminary hearing.

In addition, Article 5 of Legislative Decree No. 106/2006 was amended to require that the Chief Public Prosecutor maintain relations with the press exclusively through official statements or press conferences, which must be expressly justified by reasons of public interest.

Following these reforms, the High Council of the Judiciary (CSM) adopted, in 2018, detailed guidelines on judicial communication, reaffirming the defendant's right not to learn from the media information that should be formally communicated, and the duty of prosecutors to express disagreement with judicial decisions solely within the proper procedural framework.

Nevertheless, the Italian reality has remained largely unchanged. Many provisions of Legislative Decree No. 188/2021 still await full implementation by individual prosecutor's offices, and only a few virtuous models of institutional communication have emerged. Unsurprisingly, the European Commission has recently initiated infringement proceedings against Italy for the defective transposition of Directive 2016/343/EU, highlighting serious shortcomings regarding the presumption of innocence, the public display of coercive measures, and the ineffectiveness of remedies available in case of violation.

3 Procedures to Counter Disinformation

3.1 The Seizure of Information in Print and Online Newspaper

Article 21, paragraph 3, of the Constitution subjects the seizure of the press to a dual guarantee: (1) a "jurisdiction reservation", which excludes seizure interventions by administrative authorities; (2) a "statutory reservation", whereby preventive seizure may be imposed solely in the specific cases expressly provided for by statute. This dual mechanism reflects the constitutional intent to protect press freedom by limiting both the actors and the circumstances under which restrictions may be imposed. As is well known, the seizure referred to in Article 21, paragraph 3, of the Constitution constitutes a measure of real coercion, designed to prevent the free availability of objects related to a crime from aggravating or prolonging its consequences, or from facilitating the commission of further crimes. Focusing on the reservation of law, seizure is admitted in cases involving obscene or indecent printed materials (Article 2 of Royal Decree-Law May 31, 1946, No. 561); violation of press law provisions on registration and identification of the responsible director of a newspaper or other periodical (Articles 3 and 16 of Law February 8, 1948, No. 47); apology for fascism committed through newspapers, publications or printed matter (Article 8 of Law June 20, 1952, No. 645); violation of norms protecting copyright (Article 161 of Law April 22, 1941, No. 633).

The discipline has raised a significant debate regarding the possibility of applying the guarantees provided by Article 21, paragraph 3, of the Constitution to news published on the *web* by online newspapers (Costanzo 2011). In this case, seizure requires intervention on the service provider, who must prevent access to the site or individual web page or arrange for deletion of the incriminated *file*.

In this regard, Article 1 of the press law (Law February 8, 1948, No. 47) identifies two conditions for qualifying press: an objective requirement, namely that "*all typographical reproductions or those obtained by mechanical or physico-chemical means*" constitute press, and a subjective requirement, meaning that the publication is intended for dissemination to an indeterminate number of recipients. Initially, the differences between "traditional" press and online newspapers, especially the absence in the latter of a typographical product, led jurisprudence and doctrine to deny the extension of guarantees provided by Article 21, para. 3, of the Constitution to online newspapers.

For instance, the seizure of an article published in an online newspaper, where such content was defamatory within the meaning of Article 595 of the Criminal Code, was considered legitimate, as online publications were not covered by the constitutional safeguard against seizure provided by Article 21(3) of the Italian Constitution.

The question also arose in light of Law March 7, 2001, No. 62, which introduced a notion of *editorial product* such as to include also *online* publications. In a landmark 2015 decision, the Supreme Court adopted an evolutionary interpretation of the Constitution, affirming the equivalence between traditional and online newspapers.

A publication qualifies as a newspaper when it has a masthead, a responsible editor, regular periodicity, and registration with the competent tribunal. The Court (especially Penal Supreme Court, United Sections, judgment No. 31022/2015) further held that online newspapers meet the objective requirement through public accessibility of content and the subjective requirement through the dissemination of journalistic information on the web. In following years, constitutional and legitimacy jurisprudence (such as Penal Supreme Court, judgment No. 20644/2021) specified that the guarantees of Article 21, paragraph 3, both Constitution and Supreme Court do not extend to *blogs, social networks, forums, newsgroups*, or *newsletters*, not presenting the characteristics of an editorial product. They will therefore be subject to ordinary preventive seizure pursuant to Article 321 of the Criminal Procedure Code.

3.2 *Procedures for the Removal of Unlawful Content by Internet Service Providers: A Self-Regulation Approach*

The European Union has promoted instruments of self-regulation, based on the idea that platforms themselves should take an active role in combating disinformation. This approach was first adopted with respect to online hate speech (*The EU Code of conduct on countering illegal hate speech online)*, when, on 31 May 2016, the European Commission invited major web platforms, social media, and search engines to subscribe to a common *Code of Conduct*. By signing it, Microsoft, YouTube, Facebook, and Twitter committed to removing or disabling access to illicit content within 24 h.

Following this path, in 2018 the *Code of Practices on disinformation* was introduced, signed by major technology companies including *Facebook, Google, Twitter, Microsoft* and *TikTok*. It represents the first global attempt to create a *soft law* framework specifically dedicated to disinformation, providing voluntary commitments regarding transparency of political advertising, limitation of monetization of disinformative content and promotion of independent *fact-checking* (Monti 2019). In 2022 the Code was revised to reinforce reporting duties and to introduce stricter commitments on the use of algorithms and automated moderation, with the aim of becoming recognised as a Code of Conduct under the Digital Services Act (DSA).

For our purposes, it is important to highlight how the self-regulatory approach has effectively empowered digital services to implement quasi-sanctioning mechanisms, including measures such as content removal, temporary suspension of user activities, and even account elimination (Flaminio 2022). Naturally, although the Code of Practice provides a common legal framework, it does not eliminate the differences between the internal policies of individual platforms, as evidenced by the community standards of major services such as *Facebook, Google (YouTube)*, and *Twitter* (Bonini 2020).

Self-regulation instruments have also been adopted at the domestic level. In 2017, the Italian Communications Authority (AGCOM) established a "*Technical table for guaranteeing pluralism and correctness of information on digital platforms*". Within this context, Guidelines for equal access to online platforms during the electoral campaign for the 2018 political elections were promoted.

The self-regulation model raises significant criticalities among Italian and foreign doctrine. First, it entails the risk of a *privatization of censorship*, as private actors, often driven by economic interests, assume para-jurisdictional functions in evaluating the lawfulness of contents. Secondly, the use of *fact checkers* risks compromising informational pluralism and control neutrality, as these actors are often influenced by specific political ideas (Monti 2017); no fewer criticalities arise from algorithmic moderation, which often operate according to opaque and often discriminatory logic, raising problems of transparency and *accountability* (Pitruzzella 2018).

4 Conclusion

4.1 Summary Framework and **De Jure Condendo** *Perspective*

After examining the main sectors in which disinformation acquires legal relevance, it is possible to outline its defining features within the Italian legal order and to draw, from the peculiarities we intend to highlight, some *de jure condendo* considerations.

It appears evident that the approach to countering disinformation in the Italian legal system largely mirrors the models adopted in other Member States of the European Union. One may consider, for instance, the regulation of Internet Service Providers, misleading advertising and unfair commercial practices. Overall, therefore, much of the Italian response to disinformation is substantially consistent with that adopted by other Member States.

This observation does not exclude the existence of certain peculiarities specific to the Italian context, especially in light of the constitutional protection afforded to freedom of expression. As we have already pointed out, this freedom is intimately linked to the implementation of the personalist principle enshrined in Article 2 of the Italian Constitution. From this starting point, it becomes possible to provide unity and systemic coherence to the multiple aspects examined in this study (*supra*, §1).

First and foremost, the protection accorded to freedom of expression has led constitutional case law, particularly in the field of broadcasting, to recognise the value of pluralism, initially internal and subsequently external. In the current context dominated by large digital platforms, pluralism must be reinterpreted in an *"outside-in"* sense: a pluralism promoted by the public sphere, which, together with the support of the State, ensures genuine diversity of information within the network. The objective, in accordance with Article 21 of the Constitution, is to uphold pluralism as the (sole) instrument capable of enabling the formation of a free and informed opinion, through an open and dynamic confrontation of ideas (*supra*, §2).

A second consequence concerns the distinction between *thought* and *news*. While Article 21 protects the free expression of thought, the same cannot be said of the dissemination of news. In other words, one thing is the individual activity through which thought takes shape; quite another is the activity of those who transmit that thought into the public sphere. This distinction allows us to understand the textual limitation contained in the final paragraph of Article 21, which prohibits publications, performances, and other expressions "contrary to public morality". In an evolutionary reading, *public morality* has been understood as a constraint imposed upon the legislator whenever they intend to restrict the freedom to publish one's thought: the legislator must ask whether the restriction responds to a concern genuinely shared by civil society as a whole, rather than by a particular political faction. In this light, policies against disinformation should aim to safeguard a healthy informational environment that protects vulnerable individuals rather than abstract notions of truth. (*supra*, §1).

The distinction between thought and news also reveals a common feature across all the sectors analysed: the Italian legal order displays a substantial indifference towards the protection of "truth" as an autonomous value. The legislator is not concerned with safeguarding truth; rather, disinformation is sanctioned only to the extent that it infringes upon other constitutionally relevant interests — such as market integrity, consumer rights, or public order. Even in the realm of *judicial malinformation*, the (in)accuracy of a piece of news is not, in itself, decisive; what matters is its potential to compromise the presumption of innocence and, more broadly, the relationship of trust between the public and the administration of justice.

This approach of "disinterest" towards truth also explains why many measures to counter disinformation are primarily aimed at ensuring the *impartiality* of information. Consider, for example, communication in the economic and financial sectors, where supervisory authorities play a crucial role in determining which information may be disclosed to the market, as well as the timing and modalities of such disclosure.

This framework also helps to clarify the differences between constitutional jurisprudence on pluralism and case law concerning the limits of the right to report news. As is well established, three conditions must be met for journalistic activity to be deemed lawful: (1) public interest in the knowledge of the reported facts; (2) the truthfulness of the information, understood as putative objective truth; and (3) the *continence* of expression, that is, the use of correct and measured language.

The limits placed on the right to report call for particular attention to the field of judicial malinformation. The problematic relationship between prosecutorial activity and communication has repercussions on two levels: first, upon the criminal process itself, undermining the presumption of innocence; and second, upon the democratic order as a whole, generating tensions between public opinion and the administration of justice. These characteristics make judicial reporting the sector in which disinformation in Italy takes on its most distinctive and representative form. Yet it remains largely unregulated: existing provisions are weak and often ignored, while the High

Council of the Judiciary's guidelines, being soft law, have had minimal practical effect. (*supra*, §2.4).

In this context, the distinction between freedom of thought and dissemination of news may offer useful insights for addressing the existing regulatory gap. The pluralism governing the marketplace of ideas cannot be extended to the sources of judicial information, particularly when such sources are subject to confidentiality regimes essential to safeguarding the right to a fair trial. Without undermining the fundamental role of the right to report within democratic systems, it appears necessary to introduce procedural mechanisms governing the dissemination of judicial information, capable of ensuring transparency, traceability, and equal access to sources for those seeking to bring criminal justice matters into the public sphere.

To effectively achieve these objectives, it is not implausible to envisage, *de jure condendo*, the creation of an institutional single channel of judicial information, that is, a genuine *legal monopoly* of judicial communication. This could take the form of legislation requiring public prosecutors' offices to issue an "official bulletin" reporting on ongoing investigations and disclosable procedural acts no longer covered by secrecy. Such an instrument would enable the public to be informed about prosecutorial activities and to expose potential distortions in the exercise of prosecutorial discretion. It could also reveal tendencies to direct investigations toward politically exposed individuals, thereby subtly shaping public opinion and ultimately undermining the impartiality that underpins the mandatory exercise of criminal action in the Italian legal system.

A mechanism of this nature would acquire the status of an *authoritative source*, serving as the only channel from which reliable judicial information may emanate, in a manner comparable to the publication of laws in the *Gazzetta Ufficiale*. The proposed measure should also be accompanied by stricter rules on procedural secrecy and by effective sanctions for its violation, in accordance with recent recommendations issued by the European Union in the context of ongoing infringement proceedings.

References

Albertario, E., Castellini, G.N.: La ricostruzione di cronaca giudiziaria nei media. In: Montagna, M. (ed.) L'assassinio di Meredith Kerker. Anatomia del processo in Perugia, 51–74. Aracne, Roma (2012).

Barile, P.: La libertà di espressione del pensiero e le notizie false, esagerate e tendenziose. Foro it 5, 855–864 (1962).

Barile, P.: La libertà di manifestazione del pensiero. Cedam, Padova (1975).

Barile, P., Cheli, E., Zaccaria, R.: La radiotelevisione pubblica e privata in Italia. Il Mulino, Bologna (1980).

Biritteri, E.: Punire la disinformazione: il ruolo del diritto penale e delle misure di moderazione dei contenuti delle piattaforme tra pubblico e privato. Dir. pen. cont. riv. trim. 4, 304–330 (2021).

Biritteri, E.: Contrasto alla disinformazione, Digital Services Act e attività di private enforcement: fondamento, contenuti e limiti degli obblighi di compliance e dei poteri di autonormazione degli operatori. Media Laws 2, 52–87 (2023).

Bruti Liberati, E.: Delitti in prima pagina. La giustizia nella società dell'informazione. Raffaello Cortina, Milano (2022).
Casiraghi, R.: Informazione giudiziaria, processo mediatico e imparzialità del giudice. Arch. Pen. 3, 1–15 (2021).
Castellaneta, M.: L'attuazione della direttiva sulla presunzione d'innocenza: atto dovuto o occasione per limitare la libertà di stampa? Media Laws 1, 74–98 (2022).
Cavaliere, A.: La discussione intorno alla punibilità del negazionismo, i principi di offensività e libera manifestazione del pensiero e la funzione della pena. Riv. it. dir. proc. pen. 3, 999–1015 (2016).
Colamussi, M.: Il libero convincimento del giudice tra divieto di pubblicazione degli atti e diritto all'informazione. Processo penale e giustizia 1, 279–292 (2021).
Costantini, A.: Istanze di criminalizzazione delle fake news al confine tra tutela penale della verità e repressione del dissenso. Dir. pen. cont. riv. trim. 2, 60–80 (2019).
Costanzo, P.: La stampa telematica (tuttora) tra ambiguità legislative e dissensi giurisprudenziali. In: D'Amico, M., Randazzo, B. (eds.) Alle frontiere del diritto costituzionale. Scritti in onore di Valerio Onida, 519–540. Giuffrè, Milano (2011).
D'Agostino, L.: Disinformazione e responsabilità delle piattaforme. Obblighi di attivazione e misure di compliance. Dir. pen. cont. riv. trim. 4, 282–303 (2021).
Esposito, C.: La libertà di manifestazione del pensiero nell'ordinamento italiano. Giuffrè, Milano (1959).
Flaminio, S.: Lotta alle fake news: dallo stato dell'arte a una prospettiva di regolamentazione per il "vivere digitale" a margine del Digital Services Act. Riv. it. inform. dir. 2, 75–94 (2022).
Flor, R.: Tutela penale e autotutela tecnologica dei diritti d'autore nell'epoca di Internet. Cedam, Padova (2010).
Fronza, E.: Il negazionismo come reato. Giuffrè, Milano (2012).
Galluccio, A.: Punire la parola pericolosa. Pubblica istigazione, discorso d'odio e libertà di espressione nell'era di Internet. Giuffrè, Milano (2020).
Giostra, G.: Processo penale e informazioni. Giuffrè, Milano (1989).
Giostra, G.: Processo penale e mass media. Criminalia 2, 57–69 (2007).
Grignolio, A.: Chi ha paura dei vaccini? Codice Edizioni, Torino (2016).
Guerini, G.: Fake news e diritto penale. La manipolazione digitale del consenso nelle democrazie liberali. Giappichelli, Torino (2020).
Gullo, A.: Diffamazione e legittimazione dell'intervento penale. Contributo a una riforma dei delitti contro l'onore. Aracne, Roma (2013)
Ingrassia, A.: Il ruolo dell'ISP nel ciberspazio: cittadino, controllore o tutore dell'ordine? In: Luparia, L. (ed.) Internet provider e giustizia penale. Modelli di responsabilità e forme di collaborazione processuale, 15–65. Giuffrè, Milano (2012).
Manes, V.: Giustizia mediatica. Gli effetti perversi sui diritti fondamentali e sul processo. Il Mulino, Bologna (2022).
Manetti, M.: Paolo Barile e la diffusione di notizie false, o Fake news. In: Quaderni del Circolo Fratelli Rosselli, 93–106 (2022).
Manetti, M.: Internet e i nuovi pericoli per la libertà di informazione. Quad. cost. 3, 525–544 (2023).
Mantovani, G.: Informazione, giustizia penale e diritti della persona. Jovene, Napoli (2011).
Melzi d'Eril, C.: La complessa individuazione dei limiti alla manifestazione del pensiero in Internet. Dir. inform. 4–5, 571–589 (2011).
Monti, M.: Fake news e social network: la verità ai tempi di Facebook. MediaLaws 1, 79–90 (2017).
Monti, M.: Il Code of Practice on Disinformation dell'UE: tentativi in fieri di contrasto alle fake news. MediaLaws 2, 320–324 (2019).
Nicita, A.: Il mercato delle verità. Come la disinformazione minaccia la democrazia. Il Mulino, Bologna (2021).
Padovani, T.: Bene giuridico e delitti politici. Contributo alla critica e alla riforma del Titolo I, libro II c.p. Riv. it. dir. proc. pen. 3, 3–41 (1982).

Panattoni, B.: Il sistema di controllo successivo: obbligo di rimozione dell'ISP e meccanismi di notice and take down. Dir. pen. cont. riv. trim. 5, 249–263 (2018).
Pelissero, M.: Reati contro la personalità dello Stato e contro l'ordine pubblico. Giappichelli, Torino (2010).
Perini, C.: Fake news e post-verità tra diritto penale e politica criminale. Dir. pen. cont. 1, 1–14 (2017).
Pitruzzella, G.: La libertà di informazione nell'era di Internet. MediaLaws 1, 19–47 (2018).
Pitruzzella, G., Pollicino, O.: Disinformation and Hate Speech. A European Constitutional Perspective. Egea, Milano (2020).
Seminara, S.: La responsabilità penale degli operatori su internet. Dir. inform. 4–5, 745–774 (1998).
Spagnolo, P.: Il segreto giornalistico nel processo penale. Giuffrè, Milano (2014).
Triggiani, N.: E' la stampa, bellezza! E tu non puoi farci niente! Niente! (... neppure con il soccorso della presunzione di innocenza). Informazione e giustizia penale. In: Triggiani, N. (ed.) Dalla cronaca giudiziaria al "processo mediatico", 1–54. Cacucci Editore, Bari (2022).
Vallini, A.: Vaccine hesitancy ed obbligo vaccinale. Un dilemma medico-giuridico nell'epoca della "post-verità". La questione della responsabilità penale. Riv. it. med. leg. 1, 187–215 (2018).
Vigevani, G.E., Bassini, M.: Primi appunti su fake news e dintorni. Riv. dir. dei media 1, 11–22 (2017).
Vizzardi, M.: Manipolazione del mercato: un doppio binario da ripensare. Riv. it. dir. e proc. pen. 2, 704–731 (2006).
Wardle, C., Derakhshan, H.: Information Disorder: Toward an Interdisciplinary Framework for Research and Policy Making. Council of Europe Report DGI(2017)09 (2017).
Zaccaria, R.: Rai. Il diritto e il rovescio. Il servizio pubblico oggi. Passigli, Firenze (2019).

Tackling Disinformation Online in the Dutch Legal System

Marco Bassini and Maria Francesca Cavalcanti

Abstract This chapter analyses how the Dutch legal system addresses online disinformation, focusing on the interaction between national law and European Union law. It first clarifies the conceptual distinctions used in Dutch policy documents between disinformation, misinformation, and related phenomena, noting that disinformation is not a legal term of art in Dutch law. Rather than relying on a dedicated anti-disinformation statute, the Netherlands tackles harmful falsehoods through a combination of criminal, civil and administrative law provisions that apply when disinformation overlaps with unlawful conduct such as defamation, hate speech, or serious threats to public order. The Dutch constitutional framework is characterised by the absence of constitutional review of acts of Parliament and the key role of international human rights law, especially Article 10 ECHR, in shaping freedom of expression standards. The chapter further examines the key role of Dutch case law, highlighting a harm- and context-based approach that strongly protects political speech while permitting targeted interventions against manifestly false and harmful campaigns. Overall, the Dutch model reflects a deliberate preference for proportionality, platform accountability, and caution against content-based bans on disinformation.

M. Bassini (✉)
Tilburg Institute for Law, Technology, and Society, Tilburg University, Tilburg, Netherlands
e-mail: M.Bassini@tilburguniversity.edu

M. F. Cavalcanti
Department of Public Law and Governance, Tilburg University, Tilburg, Netherlands
e-mail: M.F.Cavalcanti@tilburguniversity.edu

P. Passaglia (ed.), *European Legal Perspectives on Online Disinformation*, Ius Gentium: Comparative Perspectives on Law and Justice 140,
https://doi.org/10.1007/978-3-032-25785-7_13

1 The Notion of Disinformation

1.1 Key Concepts on Disinformation in the Dutch Legal System

Disinformation (‘*desinformatie*’) generally refers to false or misleading information spread deliberately with malign intent, often to deceive the public or cause harm (National Coordinator for Counterterrorism and Security; Government of the Netherlands).

In the Dutch government’s terminology, disinformation is defined as the intentional dissemination of misleading information, usually with a malicious intent—for example to influence opinions, profit financially, or damage society, democracy, or public health (National Coordinator for Counterterrorism and Security).

Disinformation does not necessarily consist of false information: it often involves a combination of facts and fabricated information, or events taken out of context. This concept implies an element of intent to mislead or harm, which is absent in misinformation.

Misinformation (‘*misinformatie*’) covers false or misleading information that is shared without the intent to deceive—e.g. a person unknowingly forwarding an inaccurate news item out of concern (National Coordinator for Counterterrorism and Security).

According to governmental reports, the expression ‘fake news’ (‘*nepnieuws*’) typically means wholly fabricated news-style content not produced by professional or genuine journalists. This wording is used colloquially to label falsehoods and poor journalism (National Coordinator for Counterterrorism and Security).

Dutch authorities distinguish these concepts to better target their responses: if false information is not spread with the intent to mislead or harm, it is treated as misinformation rather than disinformation.

Also, if truthful information is weaponized to cause harm (for instance, by leaking it out of context), it can be seen as ‘malinformation’ (Wardle and Derakhshan 2017; Ó Fathaigh, Helberger, and Appelman 2021).

1.2 Disinformation in the Dutch Legal System

‘Disinformation’ itself is not a term of art in Dutch law—there is no specific crime or act named as such. Instead, the Dutch legal system addresses the phenomenon indirectly through various areas of law when disinformation overlaps with unlawful content or conduct.

In criminal law, for example, certain maliciously false statements are punishable under general offences like defamation, hate speech, or electoral fraud. Dutch criminal provisions on defamation (‘*smaad*’/‘*smaadschrift*’) impose penalties for deliberately harming someone’s honour or reputation by public accusations of specific acts.

If the speaker knew the accusation was false, it becomes the more serious offence of '*laster*' (slander) punishable by up to two years imprisonment.

Likewise, spreading falsehoods that incite hatred against a protected group could fall under hate speech laws—e.g. Article 137c of the Dutch Criminal Code criminalizes public insults of a group based on race, religion, sexual orientation, etc., and Article 137d criminalizes incitement to hatred or violence against such groups.

These provisions, while not targeting disinformation per se, can apply when false or grossly misleading claims cross into the realm of unlawful hate propaganda or group defamation.

In Dutch civil law, intentionally spreading falsehoods about individuals or entities can be addressed as an '*onrechtmatige daad*' (unlawful act) under Article 6:162 of the Civil Code, enabling victims to seek compensation of damages.[1] Indeed, Dutch courts have granted civil injunctions to stop certain false and harmful campaigns, treating them as unlawful falsehoods injurious to reputation or public interests. For instance, in a 2025 case, an organization obtained a court order against a group that disseminated a 'Black Book' linking that organization to paedophilia without any factual basis: the court found these accusations *unlawful* and ordered the materials to be retracted (Central Netherlands Court—April 17, 2025- ECLI:NL:RBMNE:2025:1778).

In administrative law, disinformation as such has not been explicitly codified; however, broadcasting regulators uphold standards of journalistic accuracy and may act if a public broadcast contains demonstrably false harmful statements.

Under the Media Act 2008 (implementing the EU Audiovisual Media Services Directive), video-sharing platforms are obliged to take measures against certain harmful content like incitement to violence or hatred. While this does not directly mandate removal of 'disinformation' in general, it means that disinformation which qualifies as hate speech, terrorist propaganda, or other illegal material must be addressed by platforms. Furthermore, administrative bodies like the Dutch Authority for Consumers & Markets (ACM) now have a role in overseeing online platforms' content moderation processes under the Digital Services Act, which indirectly covers how platforms handle problematic content including disinformation (which may not necessarily be illegal but equally qualify as harmful).

In election law, specific acts of spreading false information are not per se outlawed unless they breach existing provisions (e.g. defamation of candidates or coercion of voters). The Dutch Criminal Code, however, contains election-related offences that could intersect with disinformation in elections. There is no blanket ban on 'fake

---

[1] Article 6:162 Definition of a 'tortious act'.

A person who commits a tortious act (unlawful act) against another person that can be attributed to him, must repair the damage that this other person has suffered as a result thereof.

As a tortious act is regarded a violation of someone else's right (entitlement) and an act or omission in violation of a duty imposed by law or of what according to unwritten law has to be regarded as proper social conduct, always as far as there was no justification for this behavior.

A tortious act can be attributed to the tortfeasor [the person committing the tortious act] if it results from his fault or from a cause for which he is accountable by virtue of law or generally accepted principles (common opinion).

news' in campaigns, reflecting caution not to police political speech too broadly. Instead, the approach relies on general laws (like defamation or incitement) if false statements violate rights, and on transparency measures (as introduced by EU law on political advertising) to mitigate disinformation in campaigns.

Therefore, the notion of disinformation in Dutch law is present across various legal areas: it is addressed when it constitutes another recognized conduct/activity (libel, hate speech, fraud, etc.) or via regulatory obligations on platforms and media, rather than as a standalone concept.

1.3 Specificity of Online Disinformation

While false or misleading information is not new, the online environment gives disinformation unique scale and impact. Dutch authorities acknowledge that digital platforms and social media greatly amplify the speed and reach of misleading content.

Algorithms create 'filter bubbles' (Pariser 2012) and echo chambers (Sunstein 2009) that can reinforce false narratives (Government of the Netherlands 2021; isdatechtzo.nl). The government's public information campaigns note that not everyone sees the same information online due to personalization and profiling, and popular or sensational false stories can spread widely before they are debunked.

Moreover, the advent of generative AI has escalated concerns: the government observed that since around 2023, the rise of AI-generated text, images, and deepfakes has increased the volume of online disinformation (Government of the Netherlands 2024) so that the latter has grown in scope and intensity. Also, by virtue of digital technologies, online disinformation can be disseminated anonymously or from abroad.

These facets differentiate online disinformation from traditional media falsehoods, which tended to be easier to identify and rectify. As a result, the regulatory focus has shifted to online platforms—the primary venues of viral falsehoods—and to bolstering digital media literacy. The Netherlands' approach emphasizes that responses to online disinformation must uphold internet users' freedoms while addressing the cross-border and decentralized nature of the threat.

The problem is also seen as a security issue: the National Coordinator for Counterterrorism and Security (NCTV) sees large-scale online disinformation, particularly by state actors, as a potential threat to national security and social stability (National Coordinator for Counterterrorism and Security). In a 2024 governmental call-to-action (Government of the Netherlands 2024), four key domains were flagged as especially crucial to protect from online disinformation campaigns: (1) democratic processes (elections), (2) public health (e.g. vaccine misinformation), (3) social cohesion and public order, and (4) international security. In all these domains, the online context makes disinformation more pervasive and potentially more dangerous, prompting new solutions (like platform accountability and fact-checking networks) tailored to the digital environment.

1.4 Disinformation and Illegal Content

A crucial distinction in policy is that disinformation itself is often lawful content, even if harmful (HLEG on fake news and online disinformation 2018). Unlike other pieces of content—which are illegal both offline and online—false or misleading statements are not automatically against the law.

The prevailing European view, echoed in the Netherlands, is that disinformation typically is outside already illegal forms of speech such as defamation, hate speech or incitement (Ó Fathaigh, Helberger, and Appelman 2021). In other words, if a piece of disinformation does not slander a person, does not constitute hate propaganda, and does not otherwise violate a specific law, disseminating it cannot be penalized simply for being false.

The EU's High-Level Expert Group on fake news and online disinformation stressed that while disinformation can be very harmful, it is not necessarily illegal and thus requires responses other than blanket prohibition. This understanding is reflected in the Netherlands' approach: the government and courts carefully distinguish unlawful content from lawful but harmful content. For example, a conspiracy theory that incites harassment or violence can be dealt with as an unlawful threat or libel, but a groundless opinion or unproven theory, however misleading, is generally protected by freedom of expression.

Dutch case law illustrates this line of reasoning. In one case, a court declined to force Twitter to pre-emptively remove all tweets about a local conspiracy concerning a paedophile-satanic network allegedly existing in Bodegraven for many years, reasoning that a blanket filter would also take down lawful content (The Hague District Court—October 4, 2022 - ECLI:NL:RBDHA:2022:10082). This underscores the reluctance to over-remove merely false (but not illegal) expressions. The Dutch government likewise has emphasized that any measures against disinformation must keep fundamental rights paramount, especially freedom of expression (Ministry for Internal Affairs and Kingdom Relations 2022).

2 The Dutch Legal Framework Applicable to Disinformation

2.1 Constitutional Framework and Fundamental Rights

The position of fundamental rights within the Dutch Constitution ('*Grondwet*') is traditionally described as formally central yet functionally weak.

The Constitution contains a detailed catalogue of fundamental rights, encompassing both classic liberty rights and equality rights. However, this Bill of Rights does not operate as a standard for assessing the validity of Acts of Parliament, since Article 120 of the *Grondwet* expressly prohibits courts from subjecting parliamentary legislation to constitutional review (Adams and van der Schyff 2017). This means that, while courts are barred from applying the Constitution to Acts of Parliament, they are nonetheless required to review all legislation for compatibility with provisions of international law that are binding on all persons (van der Schyff and Meuwese 2013).

Within the Dutch constitutional order, the idea that binding provisions of international law automatically become part of the domestic legal system, namely, by virtue of their status as international law and without the need for further implementing measures, is deeply internalised. While Article 120 of the Constitution prohibits courts from ruling on the constitutionality of Acts of Parliament, Article 93 provides that those provisions of treaties and of decisions of international organisations which, by virtue of their content, are binding on all persons acquire binding force after publication. Article 94 complements this framework by codifying a position that had already existed in unwritten constitutional law, according to which any statutory provision must be set aside insofar as it is incompatible with such binding international norms (Uzman 2011).

Consequently, by virtue of these provisions, Dutch courts are required to set aside domestic legislative norms that are incompatible with self-executing treaty obligations, even where such norms could not be reviewed under the Constitution itself. Through this mechanism, international human rights law, and the ECHR in particular, assumes a role that is de facto equivalent to that of a justiciable bill of rights.

Within the Dutch legal order, it is therefore not possible to identify a body of domestic constitutional case law on fundamental rights. The development of the content and limits of rights takes place predominantly through reference to the ECHR and the case law of the European Court of Human Rights. That said, the Dutch Supreme Court has frequently ruled on fundamental rights issues; it has done so, however, by adopting the ECHR and the corresponding European jurisprudence as its primary normative point of reference. The protection of rights in the Netherlands is thus marked by a pronounced externalisation: rights discourse is legally internal, yet conceptually and methodologically external.

This dynamic emerges with particular clarity in the field of freedom of expression. Article 7 of the *Grondwet* does not frame freedom of expression as a general and abstract principle, but rather as a sector-specific regulation of different forms of communication, with a historically rooted emphasis on the prohibition of prior censorship (van Schooten 2003). As a result, the substantive definition of freedom of expression, its scope, its limits, and the applicable balancing criteria, is largely entrusted to Article 10 ECHR and the corresponding European case law. It is through the necessity and proportionality tests developed by the Strasbourg Court that Dutch judges assess the legitimacy of restrictions, especially in cases involving the media, investigative journalism, and political debate (Voorhoof et al. 2015).

Any analysis of the legal issues relating to disinformation must therefore necessarily take as its point of departure the principles laid down in the Constitution, as interpreted in light of European Union law. In this sense, freedom of expression does not enter the Dutch legal order as a fully articulated constitutional right, but rather as a conventional standard whose concrete scope is mediated through the assessment by national courts of its direct applicability in the circumstances of the specific case.

Article 7(1) provides that 'no one shall require prior permission to publish thoughts or opinions through the press' and by extension prohibits prior restraint in other media as well. This means the government cannot institute a system of pre-approval or licensing for speech. Even for non-press communications, Article 7(3) forbids requiring advance submission of opinions for approval before dissemination, reaffirming that censorship is not allowed in the Netherlands. This principle has direct significance for disinformation: it prevents any law that would, for example, require pre-screening or filtering of social media posts for accuracy before they are published (in accordance with the absence of a general monitoring obligation for hosting providers under EU law). However, Article 7 also notes that individuals remain responsible under the law for what they express, as it applies without prejudice to the responsibility of every person under the law.

As anticipated, the constitutional framework must necessarily be aligned with that set out in Article 10 ECHR. Within the Dutch constitutional system, the relationship between Article 7 of the *Grondwet* and Article 10 ECHR is marked by a clear functional asymmetry. Although Article 7 of the Constitution formally enshrines freedom of expression, it does not conceptualise this freedom as a general and abstract principle. Rather, it structures it as a regulation of the different forms of communication, historically centred on the prohibition of prior censorship ('*censuurverbod*') and on a media-specific approach (the press, broadcasting, and other means of communication). This 'rule-based' design limits the capacity of Article 7 to operate as a substantive benchmark for rights balancing, constraining its effectiveness primarily in relation to the legislature and in addressing emerging forms of digital communication.

By contrast, Article 10 ECHR assumes a substantively constitutive function within the Dutch legal order, supplying the normative criteria through which freedom of expression is concretely defined, restricted, and balanced. It follows that, while Article 7 of the *Grondwet* continues to perform a structural role as a safeguard against prior censorship, it is Article 10 ECHR that operates as the substantive benchmark for assessing restrictions on freedom of expression, complementing domestic constitutional protection and decisively shaping Dutch judicial practice.

The Netherlands therefore accepts the ECHR as part of its legal order. As is well known, Article 10 ECHR allows interference with freedom of expression only if it is prescribed by law, pursues a legitimate aim (such as public safety, health, morals, or protection of others' rights), and is necessary in a democratic society.

Another relevant right enshrined in the Convention is Article 8 ECHR, which safeguards private life and reputation. In disinformation disputes—especially defamation or privacy cases—courts have to balance Article 10 and Article 8 rights. Dutch jurisprudence often mirrors the Strasbourg Court's approach in landmark cases like *Axel Springer* (ECtHR, *Axel Springer AG v. Germany,* app no 39954/08, 7 February 2012) and *Von Hannover* (ECtHR, *Von Hannover v. Germany (I),* app no 59320/00, 24 June 2004), weighing factors such as public figure status, public interest, factual basis of the allegations, and intent.

For example, in a 2024 case, a claimant argued that false statements in a broadcast violated her Article 8 rights; the court had to balance those against the broadcaster's Article 10 rights (Central Netherlands Court—July 17, 2024—ECLI:NL:RBMNE:2024:4378). Ultimately that claim was dismissed, indicating the speech was within the permissible boundaries of journalistic expression.

Besides speech rights, other constitutional or fundamental principles play a role. Freedom of information is considered part of freedom of expression (and explicitly mentioned in ECHR 10 and EU Charter Article 11) and also includes the right to receive information. This means any regulatory action (even well-intended, like removing disinformation) implicates not just the speaker's rights but also the public's right to access information.

Media freedom and pluralism are also protected under the ECHR and the EU Charter of Fundamental Rights, cautioning authorities against actions that unduly pressure news outlets or online platforms' editorial decisions.

Additionally, while not framed as a constitutional right in the Netherlands, freedom to conduct business and property rights can be relevant. Dutch courts have recognized that platforms like YouTube may invoke their economic freedom and property rights when defending their moderation decisions. For instance, in a 2021 ruling, the Amsterdam District Court (Amsterdam District Court—ECLI:NL:RBAMS:2021:5117) upheld YouTube's removal of a politician's video under its COVID-19 misinformation policy, noting that YouTube's freedom to conduct a business (and, thus, to manage its service) and property rights were factors to consider alongside the user's speech rights.

2.2 *European Union Law and Its Implementation in the Netherlands*

EU law significantly influences the Netherlands' approach to online disinformation, both through binding regulations and directives and through coordinated policies.

To this end, one major instrument is the Digital Services Act (DSA)—Regulation (EU) 2022/2065—which creates a comprehensive framework governing online intermediaries. The DSA, in force since November 2022 and became applicable between 2023 and 2024, imposes new duties on online platforms regarding content management, transparency, and systemic risk mitigation.

Although the DSA, far from introducing any specific content regulation, does not outlaw disinformation, it explicitly addresses the issue as part of the systemic risks that very large online platforms (VLOPs) must assess and mitigate (Article 34 DSA). It also establishes mechanisms for notice-and-action on illegal content and requires platforms to establish terms of service governing content moderation that are respectful of fundamental rights.

The Netherlands, as an EU Member State, directly applies the DSA. To facilitate its enforcement, it passed the Digital Services Regulation Implementation Act

(*Implementatiewet Digitale Diensten*) on 29 January 2025.[2] This Act has designated the Authority for Consumers and Markets (ACM) as the Digital Services Coordinator for the Netherlands.[3] The ACM now serves as the primary regulator supervising online platforms' compliance with DSA obligations, including those indirectly relevant to disinformation (e.g. ensuring platforms have functioning notice systems and conduct risk assessments for societal harms).

The Dutch Data Protection Authority (AP) is also designated as competent authority to address personal data aspects (for instance, disinformation that involves profiling or microtargeting falls partly under data regulation).[4]

Under the DSA, users in the Netherlands can report illegal content to platforms, and if dissatisfied, can complain to the ACM, even about platforms based abroad. Such cross-border cooperation is crucial given the international nature of online disinformation. The DSA also encourages codes of conduct for matters like disinformation (Article 45 DSA), and in February 2025 the EU Code of Practice on Disinformation was formally integrated into the DSA framework as a Commission-endorsed Code of Conduct (European Commission 2025).

Originally a voluntary commitment by online platforms since 2018 and strengthened in June 2022, the Code includes measures such as demonetizing false content, transparency in political advertising, and support for fact-checkers. As of 13 February 2025, platforms' adherence to the Code will serve as a benchmark for regulators when assessing compliance with the applicable obligations. In practical terms, major platforms operating in the Netherlands have signed onto this Code.

Another pertinent EU law act is the Audiovisual Media Services Directive (AVMSD) (Directive 2010/13/EU, as amended by Directive (EU) 2018/1808). The AVMSD, implemented in the Netherlands via the Media Act 2008, extends certain content regulation to video-sharing platforms.

Under the AVMSD rules, these platforms must take appropriate measures to protect the public from videos containing incitement to violence or hatred and other illegal content, and to protect minors from harmful content. While AVMSD does not mention disinformation explicitly, it indirectly covers some disinformation that falls into those categories (e.g. videos spreading hate-based false narratives). The Dutch Media Authority ('*Commissariaat voor de Media*') oversees compliance with these obligations.

For instance, if a Dutch user flagged a video on a platform containing illegal hate speech disguised as 'news', the platform's obligations under the Media Act (transposing the AVMSD) would require it to put in place mechanisms to review and, if warranted, restrict access to that video. The Media Act also encourages media literacy programs, aligning with AVMSD provisions that promote public awareness of disinformation and other online risks.

Furthermore, new EU legislation is on the horizon that touches on disinformation. The Regulation on transparency and targeting of political advertising (Regulation

---

[2] https://www.autoriteitpersoonsgegevens.nl/en/about-the-ap/digital-services-act-dsa.

[3] See Artikel 2.1 ('aanwijzing Autoriteit Consument en Markt als digitaledienstencoördinator').

[4] See Artikel 3.1 and Artikel 3.2.

(EU) 2024/900) imposes transparency requirements on online political advertising. This is directly relevant to disinformation because it aims to shed light on 'who is behind' political messages online, thus countering covert influence or microtargeted falsehoods in elections. The Netherlands will enforce this regulation to ensure that political advertising carries disclaimers of its sponsor, funding, and targeting criteria, mitigating one avenue of organized disinformation (e.g. foreign-funded misleading campaign ads).

Additionally, the EU Artificial Intelligence Act (Regulation (EU) 2024/1689) includes provisions about AI-generated content. It requires transparency for deepfakes—e.g. artificially generated images or videos—to address concerns that AI could fuel disinformation. Dutch policymakers already flagged deepfakes in the 2023 government-wide vision on generative AI, emphasizing the need to label AI content to maintain trust in information.

2.3 Countering Disinformation Through Dutch Law

The Netherlands relies on a patchwork of national statutes to address various facets of disinformation. As noted, there is no specific 'anti-disinformation law'; instead, existing laws are applied where relevant. Key legislative sources include the Dutch Criminal Code ('*Wetboek van Strafrecht*') and the Dutch Civil Code ('*Burgerlijk Wetboek*').

2.4 Criminal Law

Several provisions in the Dutch Criminal Code can criminalize forms of false information dissemination in specific contexts:

- Defamation, libel and slander: Article 261 defines defamation ('*smaad*') as intentionally attacking someone's honor or reputation by alleging a specific fact, with the clear aim of publicizing it. This offence is punishable by up to 6 months imprisonment or a fine. If done in writing or images made public (libel, '*smaadschrift*'), the penalty can increase to 1 year imprisonment. Article 262 further provides that if the perpetrator knew that the allegation was false, the offence becomes '*laster*' (slander), which is punished by up to two years imprisonment. These provisions are directly relevant when disinformation takes the form of personal unfounded accusations. However, they include a safe harbour: no defamation is committed if the speaker acted in good faith believing the statement true and in the public interest. This defence protects those who share misinformation without intent to defame (echoing the misinformation/disinformation distinction in legal terms). In practice, criminal defamation charges in the Netherlands are relatively rare; more often, these articles serve as a basis for civil claims or are invoked in exceptional cases (such as orchestrated hate campaigns).

- Group insult and hate speech: Article 137c criminalizes publicly making insulting statements about a group of people based on characteristics like race, religion, sexual orientation, or disability. Article 137d criminalizes incitement to hatred, discrimination or violence against such groups. The maximum penalty is 1 year imprisonment (or two years if done as a habitual offence or in concert with others; up to 4 years imprisonment for organized incitement). These provisions have been relied upon to prosecute hate propaganda, genocide denial, etc. If disinformation involves false claims about protected groups—for instance, a fabricated story vilifying an ethnic group—it could fall under these prohibitions. The law thereby covers a subset of disinformation that overlaps with hate speech or discriminatory rumours. Notably, Article 137c explicitly punishes even gross trivialization or denial of certain facts when done with intent to insult a group, which could encompass some forms of historical disinformation.
- Election-related offences: The Dutch Criminal Code also protects electoral integrity. Articles 125–129 make it illegal to use violence, threats, or bribery to influence someone's vote, or to fraudulently interfere with the casting or counting of votes. While these do not explicitly mention false information, they could in theory cover certain disinformation strategies. Article 127 criminalizes any fraudulent act that causes a vote to be recorded incorrectly or declared invalid; deliberately spreading misinformation about voting procedures might be captured if it results in spoiled ballots. However, there is no broad offence of 'spreading fake news during elections' outside these specific manipulative acts. The emphasis is on tangible interference (violence, buying votes, falsifying results) rather than speech. The Dutch approach thus refrains from criminalizing general political lies, relying on the political process and counter-speech to sort truth from falsehood, except where the lies entail defamation or illegal coercion.

2.5 *Civil and Administrative Law Provisions*

In the Dutch Civil Code, Article 6:162 provides that 'a person who commits an unlawful act (tortious act) against another that can be attributed to them must repair the damage that this other person has suffered as a result thereof'. A tortious (i.e., unlawful) act includes a violation of someone else's right and an act or omission in violation of a duty imposed by law or of what according to unwritten law has to be regarded as proper social conduct, as far as there is no justification applicable to the behaviour. So framed, tort liability is broad enough to encompass the spreading of damaging falsehoods. Many disinformation-related disputes can be handled from a civil law perspective under this rubric. For instance, individuals or organizations falsely accused can ask for a court order to remove online posts and sometimes for a retraction or damages. Dutch courts, in applying Article 6:162 to speech, perform the usual balancing test: is the statement unlawful (e.g. defamatory or privacy-invading) considering factors such as context, truth, public interest, intent, etc.?

The Media Act 2008 implemented the AVMS Directive. It sets duties for media services and video sharing platforms. For instance, video platforms must have mechanisms for users to report content and for restricting content that is illegal. The Media Act also empowers the Media Authority (‘*Commissariaat voor de Media*’) to conduct oversight. While not directly about ‘disinformation’, if a disinformation video crosses into prohibited territory (hate speech, etc.), the Media Act comes into play. Additionally, the Media Act contains rules for broadcast media—e.g. the national public broadcaster has an editorial role requiring accurate and unbiased news; the Media Authority can admonish or ultimately cut funding for serious breaches of journalistic standards, but direct intervention in content is rare due to the need to safeguard editorial independence.

The Elections Act (‘*Kieswet*’)[5] regulates electoral campaigns, but it does not contain explicit rules against spreading falsehoods about candidates or issues. Campaign advertising on public broadcast is regulated for equal access but not for truthfulness.

The Dutch approach leans on self-regulation by political parties and fact-checking by media during campaigns, rather than legal enforcement of truth (aside from extreme cases covered by defamation or existing criminal law).

2.6 *Disinformation at the Bar: Dutch Case Law*

Court precedents have become key in the absence of specific disinformation legislation. Dutch courts at various levels—ordinary courts (district and appellate courts) and the Supreme Court (Hoge Raad)—have been adjudicating disputes that effectively set the contours of lawful and unlawful speech in the context of false information.

It must be preliminarily noted that there is no constitutional court in the Netherlands, and—as noted—courts cannot invalidate ordinary laws and statutes for conflicting with the Constitution; however, they can enforce international treaties protecting human rights and interpret national laws in each case, thus shaping how disinformation is handled.

At the level of the Supreme Court, there have not yet been landmark rulings squarely on disinformation as a general phenomenon. More concrete developments come from the district courts (‘*Rechtbanken*’) and Courts of Appeal, which have handled urgent cases through summary proceedings (‘*kort geding*’) and merits cases. A survey of recent case law illustrates the judiciary’s approach.

In political speech cases involving COVID-19-related disinformation, courts have sometimes intervened against platforms on behalf of users and sometimes not,

[5] Act of 28 September 1989 containing new provisions governing the franchise and elections (Elections Act).

indicating a nuanced balance. In 2021, the North Holland District Court ruled in favour of a Dutch politician whose entire LinkedIn profile was removed due to alleged misinformation concerning COVID-19 (North Holland Court—October 6, 2021-ECLI:NL:RBNHO:2021:8539). The court found that while the specific posts amounted to disinformation according to the platform's policy (and did not order those reinstated), the platform had not provided clear standards in its policy about what constituted 'misinformation' and had not acted with sufficient care in applying the ultimate sanction of deleting the user's account. The profile was ordered to be restored. This case highlights that platforms must adhere to principles of fairness and clarity even in private content moderation, especially when political speech is at stake. The court emphasized that LinkedIn's policy was insufficiently informative about where the line was drawn between posts that 'completely contradict' health authority guidelines and posts that merely offer critical commentary on those guidelines.

A series of cases involving YouTube's COVID-19 disinformation policy illustrates the courts' approach to balancing public health protection with freedom of expression.

In September 2020, the Amsterdam District Court ruled the removal by YouTube of videos containing interviews about hydroxychloroquine as a COVID-19 treatment (Amsterdam District Court—September 9, 2020—ECLI:NL:RBAMS:2020:4435). The court held that while a strict application of YouTube's policy to allow only content aligned with WHO (World Health Organization) and RIVM (The National Institute for Public Health and the Environment) views was too narrow and incompatible with freedom of expression, the specific videos in question constituted dangerous medical misinformation and could be removed. The court found that the interviews, which claimed hydroxychloroquine works against COVID-19, were presented as medical advice without sufficient scientific basis and could be harmful to public health. This decision established an important principle: while platforms cannot simply defer to government health authorities to define all permissible speech, they may remove content that makes specific medical claims contradicting scientific consensus when such claims pose health risks.

The Amsterdam District Court sided with YouTube in a case where a Member of Parliament's speech critical of COVID measures was removed as misinformation (Amsterdam District Court—September 15, 2021—ECLI:NL:RBAMS:2021:5117). The court held that YouTube's removal, based on its COVID misinformation policy, was not unacceptable according to the standards of reasonableness and fairness under Dutch tort law. It was also not contrary to societal norms in the sense of Article 6:162. The judgment acknowledged YouTube's rights (property and freedom to conduct business) and found that the platform's enforcement of its terms of service, in that case, did not disproportionately infringe the MP's expression rights. The court noted that the politician had alternative channels to express his views, including the official parliamentary channel Debat Direct, and that YouTube was not obligated to serve as a megaphone for all political speech.

Similarly, another 2021 decision held that Google was not required to reinstate a removed video featuring a political party leader's parliamentary speech on COVID-19 (Amsterdam District Court—August 18, 2021—ECLI:NL:RBAMS:2021:4308). The court confirmed the legitimacy of the removal, noting that there is no 'must-carry' obligation for platforms to host all political content. The video contained claims that COVID-19 was merely a 'flu variation' and statements contradicting established health guidance. The court held that while political expression enjoys strong protection, YouTube was entitled to enforce its community guidelines against medical misinformation, even when such disinformation appeared in a parliamentary speech. The decision underscored that parliamentary immunity (Article 71 of the Constitution) protects MPs from legal consequences for statements made in Parliament, but does not obligate private platforms to disseminate those statements.

These decisions suggest that Dutch courts generally do not override platform content decisions unless an important public interest in the speech outweighs the platform's rationale. Courts apply a case-by-case proportionality test.

As far as conspiracy and extremist content cases are concerned, courts have shown willingness to issue restraining orders to stop the spread of falsehoods when they constitute incitement or cause serious harm to identifiable individuals. The Bodegraven cases represent the most prominent example of judicial intervention against organized disinformation campaigns. In July 2021, the The Hague District Court granted an order to cease and desist against three individuals spreading claims of a satanic paedophile network allegedly operating in the municipality of Bodegraven-Reeuwijk. The defendants had used social media to name specific individuals as perpetrators, victims, or accomplices in ritual satanic child abuse (The Hague District Court—July 2, 2021—ECLI:NL:RBDHA:2021:6769).

The court found these accusations were based solely on one defendant's purportedly 'recovered memories' and had no factual foundation whatsoever. The judge held that protecting individuals from such groundless and serious accusations and protecting public order outweighed the defendants' freedom of expression. The court ordered the defendants to remove such statements from their websites, online platforms and social media. This case established that the cumulative harm of coordinated disinformation campaigns—including disturbance of public order, harassment of named individuals, and violation of peace of the graves—justifies strong judicial intervention; and that courts will consider the broader societal impacts, not just individual harms, when assessing whether to restrict speech.

The Bodegraven litigation continued with a case against Twitter in October 2022 (The Hague District Court—October 4, 2022—ECLI:NL:RBDHA:2022:10082). The municipality sought an order requiring Twitter to proactively remove all content similar to the unlawful statements already identified in the earlier judgment. The court held that Twitter had done enough by permanently suspending the main account spreading the conspiracy theory and removing all retweets of that account's posts. However, the court declined to order Twitter to implement automated filters to detect and remove similar content from other users, reasoning that not all mentions of 'Bodegraven' and 'child abuse' were necessarily unlawful (some might be neutral journalistic coverage of the controversy itself); and that requiring Twitter to autonomously assess whether each post was unlawful would impose a prohibited general monitoring obligation under EU law. In the court's view, the municipality could use the notice-and-takedown procedure to flag specific unlawful tweets, which Twitter would then be obligated to remove promptly. This decision illustrates the limits of judicial orders against platforms: courts will not compel platforms to engage in broad content filtering, but will require them to respond effectively to concrete notices of unlawful content.

A subsequent Bodegraven-related case in 2024 (Gelderland Court—August 26, 2024—ECLI:NL:RBGEL:2024:5750) involved a new defendant who had taken up spreading the same conspiracy theory after the original defendants were convicted. The court again granted an injunction, prohibiting the defendant from making statements linking named persons or the municipality to satanic paedophile crimes, and ordering removal of such content from websites and social media. The court reiterated that the conspiracy theory had no factual basis and that continuing to spread it violated both the rights of individuals and public order. These cases collectively demonstrate that Dutch courts treat organized disinformation campaigns targeting specific persons or communities as actionable torts, particularly when the claims are demonstrably false, seriously harmful, and incite real-world consequences (such as harassment or public disturbances).

Additionally, courts have directed platforms to cooperate in such scenarios: this exemplifies a measured approach, where courts seek to halt the unlawful disinformation at its source and ensure platforms respond to notices, but avoid imposing general monitoring obligations that conflict with EU law and freedom of expression principles.

In media defamation cases, courts have dealt with situations where mainstream outlets or websites are accused of spreading false or unverified claims. In June 2022, the District Court Midden-Nederland (RB Midden-Nederland) found that a TV program (*Pointer*, produced by the public broadcaster KRO-NCRV) had made an unlawful statement by alleging that a climate-sceptic organization was funded by the oil industry without sufficient evidence (Central Netherlands Court—June 7, 2022—ECLI:NL:RBMNE:2022:2136). The broadcaster had based this claim on circumstantial connections (such as the organization's founder having worked on oil-industry-funded research projects and some authors having received oil industry money), but could not demonstrate that the organization itself received such funding. The court held the claim about funding unsupported and thus defamatory, requiring rectification. This case indicates that even reputable media can be held liable for disinformation if journalistic diligence fails—thus emphasizing that truth and verification standards are legally expected.

Broadcasters must ensure factual claims are adequately supported and must include relevant rebuttals, especially when making serious allegations about an organization's integrity or funding sources. In a 2024 case (Central Netherlands Court—July 17, 2024—ECLI:NL:RBMNE:2024:4378), a journalist sued a broadcaster for statements made about her in a television program. The program had featured individuals who monitor and criticize online conspiracy theorists, and they showed a clip of the plaintiff's video and commented that she was 'completely crazy' and 'anti-Ukraine'. The plaintiff argued these were false and defamatory. The court dismissed the claim, holding that the statements were value judgments with sufficient factual basis (the plaintiff's own video), that the program was addressing a topic of public interest (the online information war), and that the plaintiff, as someone who actively participates in public debate with strong language herself, must tolerate robust criticism.

Another media case from 2025 involved a dispute over a 'Black Book' publication by an organization (Civitas) alleging that a sexual education foundation (Rutgers) was sexualizing children and linked to paedophilia (Central Netherlands Court—April 17, 2025—ECLI:NL:RBMNE:2025:1778). This decision underscores that participants in heated public debates—especially those who themselves use provocative rhetoric—are expected to accept sharp criticism. The court found that Civitas had systematically misrepresented Rutgers' educational materials by taking quotes out of context and framing them as evidence of promoting sexual activity among children, when in fact the materials were designed to teach children about boundaries and prevent abuse. The court held that accusing Rutgers of having a 'paedophile agenda' had no factual basis and that the accusations were unlawful. The court ordered Civitas to stop distributing the Black Book, remove the defamatory statements from websites and social media, and send a court-mandated correction to everyone who had received the book.

A 2025 case involving a dispute between two activists on social media (Amsterdam District Court—July 3, 2025 ECLI:NL:RBAMS:2025:4628) further illustrates the high threshold for judicial intervention in online debates. The plaintiff sought removal of posts calling her transphobic and accusing her of spreading disinformation about transgender persons. The court refused, holding that both parties actively participated in a heated public debate about gender issues, that the defendant's statements were value judgments rather than factual assertions, and that the plaintiff herself used strong language that others would find offensive. The court applied the principle that 'those who throw stones can expect the ball back' ('*wie kaatst, kan de bal verwachten*'), emphasizing that active participants in polarized debates must accept robust counter-speech.

Another case concerned fake online advertisements using a celebrity's name/likeness in false endorsements (Amsterdam District Court—May 18, 2022—ECLI:NL:RBAMS:2022:2638). The case involved fraudulent bitcoin investment advertisements that used the image and name of a well-known Dutch media personality without permission. Victims who clicked on these ads were led to fake news articles claiming the celebrity had made money with bitcoin, and ultimately to fraudulent investment platforms where they lost money. The court addressed whether Google, as the advertising platform, could be held liable for hosting these deceptive ads. The court found that Google had taken reasonable measures to combat such fraud and that the scale of fraudulent ads on Google's network was limited (only 17 ads were identified from the examples provided). The court held that Google was not liable for the ads themselves, as it qualified for the hosting safe harbour under the E-Commerce Directive, having acted promptly to remove the ads once notified.

However, the court did order Google to provide the celebrity with identifying information (name, address, email, bank account) of the advertisers behind those ads, so that the celebrity could pursue legal action against the actual fraudsters. This decision illustrates the approach to commercial disinformation: platforms are not strictly liable for every fraudulent ad, but they must have systems in place to address fraud and must cooperate with victims. The case also shows the limits of platform liability, as imposing monitoring obligations would be technically difficult and risk over-blocking legitimate content.

In the absence of a comprehensive and specific legislative framework on disinformation, Dutch courts have assessed the phenomenon through an incremental, case-by-case development of case law. Judicial intervention does not seek to define disinformation in abstract terms; rather, it aims to delineate ex post the boundary between lawful and unlawful expression by relying on private-law instruments, fundamental-rights standards, and proportionality tests. This role is structurally conditioned by the Dutch constitutional settlement. The absence of constitutional review of legislation, combined with the direct applicability of international human rights law, steers judicial reasoning towards Article 10 ECHR as the primary substantive benchmark.

The case law reveals a clearly differentiated approach depending on the nature of the speech and the interests at stake. Political speech and expression on matters of public interest enjoy particularly robust protection, even when controversial or contested, whereas disinformation taking the form of manifestly false factual assertions, defamation, incitement, or serious individual harm is more readily classified as unlawful. This confirms a judicial preference for harm- and context-based assessments rather than for content-based prohibitions as such.

In the future, higher courts may further refine these principles, especially as new kinds of disputes arise under the DSA. But already, the judiciary is a key regulator of disinformation indirectly, by drawing boundaries of lawful speech and by ensuring that private censorship by platforms can be reviewed if it overreaches or is procedurally unfair. Courts have consistently emphasized that any restriction on speech—whether by the state or by powerful private platforms—must be necessary, proportionate, and procedurally fair, with particular scrutiny applied when political discourse is at stake.

2.7 *Soft Law and Self-Regulatory Measures*

Alongside hard law, the Netherlands heavily employs soft law and policy initiatives to combat online disinformation. These actions do not create enforceable legal rules but guide behavior and often precede or supplement legislation.

In December 2022, the Dutch Cabinet released a government-wide strategy against disinformation (Ministry for Internal Affairs and Kingdom Relations 2022), coordinating the efforts of three ministries (Interior; Economic Affairs/Media; Foreign Affairs). This strategy, detailed in a Parliamentary letter (‘*Kamerbrief*’), outlined a multi-pronged approach focusing on resilience, education, and cooperation with private platforms. It explicitly stated that no new laws banning disinformation would be introduced, in line with preserving free speech, and instead emphasized enhancing society's defences.

In June 2024, the government issued a follow-up letter to Parliament on the progress of this strategy and new actions (Ministry for Internal Affairs and Kingdom Relations 2024). This letter announced a significant new package of measures including: increasing support for fact-checking and research, through the allocation of additional funding to BENEDMO, the Belgium-Netherlands Digital Media Observatory, which is part of a European network of fact-checkers and academic researchers, and the funding of media literacy projects and initiatives to boost the availability of reliable information in key areas (e.g., health-related matters); measures targeting repeated disinformation distributors, including by exposing networks of fake accounts, public-awareness campaigns about foreign influence, and possibly working with social media to ban recidivist offenders.

Furthermore, in 2024 the Ministry of Interior issued guidelines for local governments on dealing with misinformation (Ministerie van Binnenlandse Zaken en Koninkrijksrelaties, 2024). These guidelines instruct officials to neither overreact nor remain passive: for example, if a false rumour about a municipality is circulating, the guidance is to proactively provide correct information via official channels and only consider legal action if the misinformation clearly crosses into unlawful domains.

In essence, soft law fills the gaps left by hard law in the disinformation domain. It allows a responsive and evolving approach—funding fact-checkers, promoting digital literacy, creating channels for complaints and dispute resolution—without immediately resorting to punitive regulation that might infringe speech.

The Dutch government perceives disinformation as a long-term societal challenge where building resilience is as important as enforcement. Indeed, a public survey in 2022 indicated a sizable portion of Dutch citizens are concerned about disinformation's impact on society (e.g. 47% worried it leads to greater societal divides and erodes trust in democracy) (National Coordinator for Counterterrorism and Security 2022). Soft measures are aimed at addressing those concerns by empowerment rather than censorship. The Netherlands' stance remains that freedom of expression must remain paramount, and thus it prefers solutions like 'more speech' (counter-narratives, quality journalism) to 'less speech' (bans), except against clearly unlawful content.

3 Conclusion

In the Netherlands, online disinformation is recognized as a serious problem. Public sentiment shows significant concern: nearly half of Dutch citizens believe they frequently encounter disinformation and are worried about its effects on society. The Dutch government regards disinformation as a threat to values such as the integrity of democracy, public health, and national security. Comparatively, disinformation in general (including offline) has long existed but the online variant is perceived as more acute due to its speed and reach.

However, the public debate also acknowledges that while disinformation is harmful, overreacting by limiting speech could be more damaging. This is reflected in a careful approach: the government stresses that countering disinformation must not undermine freedom of expression. Thus, the perception is that disinformation is a problem to be solved in a way consistent with democratic values.

In comparison to disinformation in general (offline), online disinformation is seen as more pervasive yet also more visible and trackable.

The degree of perception of online disinformation as a problem in the Netherlands is high and has grown in recent years. It is taken seriously at the highest levels of government and by the public, particularly regarding vulnerable domains like elections and health. Yet, this concern is balanced with a conscious effort not to let the cure become worse than the disease. The approach remains to treat disinformation as a condition to manage through targeted intervention, rather than as an excuse to curtail civil liberties broadly.

References

Adams M, van der Schyff, G (2017) Constitutional Culture in The Netherlands: A sober affair. In: Adams, M, Meuwese, A, Hirsch Ballin, E (eds) Constitutionalism and the Rule of Law: Bridging idealism and realism. Cambridge U.P., Cambridge

European Commission, 'The Code of Conduct on Disinformation', 13 February 2025, at https://digital-strategy.ec.europa.eu/en/library/code-conduct-disinformation

Government of the Netherlands, 'Disinformation, misinformation and fake news', at https://www.rijksoverheid.nl/onderwerpen/desinformatie-nepnieuws/oorzaken-redenen-nepnieuws-op-internet-social-media

Government of the Netherlands, 'Cabinet presents robust new measures to tackle disinformation', 17 June 2024, at https://www.rijksoverheid.nl/onderwerpen/desinformatie-nepnieuws/nieuws/2024/06/17/kabinet-presenteert-stevige-nieuwe-maatregelen-voor-aanpak-desinformatie

High-Level Expert Group on fake news and online disinformation (2018) Final report of the High-Level Expert Group on Fake News and Online Disinformation

isdatechtzo.nl, 'Stap jij uit je filterbubbel?', at https://www.isdatechtzo.nl/hoe-wordt-nepnieuws-verspreid/filterbubbels-algoritmes/zit-jij-in-je-eigen-filterbubbel/, 25 January 2021

Minister for Internal Affairs and Kingdom Relations, Cabinet tackles disinformation, 23 December 2022 at https://www.rijksoverheid.nl/regering/bewindspersonen/hanke-bruins-slot/nieuws/2022/12/23/kabinet-pakt-desinformatie-aan.

Ministry for Internal Affairs and Kingdom Relations, 'Letter to Parliament about progress of the government-wide strategy for the effective approach to disinformation and announcement of new actions', 17 June 2024

Ministerie van Binnenlandse Zaken en Koninkrijksrelaties, 'Omgaan met misinformatie voor medeoverheden', 25 November 2024, at https://www.kennisopenbaarbestuur.nl/site/binaries/site-content/collections/documents/2024/11/25/handreiking-omgaan-met-misinformatie-voor-medeoverheden/Handreiking+Omgaan+met+misinformatie+voor+medeoverheden.pdf

National Coordinator for Counterterrorism and Security, 'Public survey on disinformation. Outcomes and initial communication insights guideline on foreign disinformation', 28 October

2022, at https://english.nctv.nl/binaries/nctv-en/documenten/publications/2022/10/28/public-survey-on-disinformation/221207+NCTV+Desinformatie+A4+EN.pdf
National Coordinator for Counterterrorism and Security, 'Disinformation', at https://www.nctv.nl/onderwerpen/d/desinformatie
Ó Fathaigh, R, Helberger, N, Appelman, N (2021) The perils of legally defining disinformation. Internet Policy Review 10(4).
Pariser, E (2012) The Filter Bubble: What The Internet Is Hiding From You. Penguin Books, London
Sunstein, C (2009) Republic.com 2.0. Princeton University Press, Princeton
Uzman, J (2011) The Dutch Supreme Court: A Reluctant Positive Legislator. In Brewer-Carías AR (ed) Constitutional Courts as Positive Legislators: A Comparative Law Study. Cambridge University Press, Cambridge. 645
van der Schyff, G, Meuwese, A (2013) Dutch Constitutional Law in a Globalizing World. Utrecht Law Review 9(2)
van Schooten H (2003) Freedom of Expression in the Dutch Constitution: Censorship and Sense Construction. International Journal for the Semiotics of Law 16(2): 139-154
Voorhoof et al. (2015) Freedom of Expression, the Media and Journalists, IRIS Themes, European Audiovisual Observatory
Wardle C, Derakhshan, H (2017) Information Disorder: Toward an interdisciplinary framework for research and policy making. Report DGI(2017)09, Council of Europe

The Legal Framework and Constitutional Challenges Related to Combating Online Disinformation in Poland

Monika Florczak-Wątor

Abstract This chapter analyses the legal and constitutional challenges of countering online disinformation in Poland. It demonstrates that one of the main barriers to the successful application of legal instruments developed so far in practice is a lack of a transparent and effectively applicable legal definition of disinformation. The chapter examines how Polish legal doctrine and jurisprudence define the notion of disinformation and distinguish it from related concepts such as misinformation, malinformation, or propaganda. It indicates the constitutional basis for the protection of truth and reliable information, focusing on the relevant provisions of the 1997 Constitution of the Republic of Poland, in particular those concerning freedom of speech, access to public information and personal data protection. The case law of the Polish Constitutional Tribunal shows that truth is a value deeply rooted in the constitutional order and constitutes one of the prerequisites for democratic governance and the informed participation of citizens in public life. The chapter also presents a multi-level legal framework for countering disinformation in Poland, covering criminal, civil, press, electoral and administrative law at the statutory level. It describes the practical effectiveness of these mechanisms and identifies significant regulatory gaps in combating contemporary forms of digital information manipulation.

1 Introduction

This chapter analyses the understanding of disinformation, including online disinformation, in Polish legal doctrine and jurisprudence, as well as its legal regulation and the application of these regulations in practice. It argues that the undefined legal status of the concept of disinformation in Polish law complicates the consistent application of existing provisions and, consequently, the attribution of responsibility for disseminating false or misleading information.

M. Florczak-Wątor (✉)
Jagiellonian University, Krakow, Poland
e-mail: m.florczak-wator@uj.edu.pl

P. Passaglia (ed.), *European Legal Perspectives on Online Disinformation*, Ius Gentium: Comparative Perspectives on Law and Justice 140,
https://doi.org/10.1007/978-3-032-25785-7_14

The chapter is divided into three parts. The first part presents the definitions of disinformation and related concepts, including misinformation, malinformation and propaganda. It emphasises the importance of the speaker's intent and awareness and outlines the main manipulation techniques. The second part of the chapter analyses the constitutional basis for the protection of truth and reliable information, as well as constitutional regulations limiting various rights and freedoms, while also serving to protect them. In particular, this part refers to several provisions of the Polish Constitution of 1997,[1] including those that guarantee the protection of personal data (Article 51), freedom of expression (Article 54) and the right to public information (Article 61). The third part of the chapter discusses statutory and soft law regulations that indirectly address disinformation. It incorporates mechanisms from criminal, civil, administrative, press and electoral law, as well as relevant case law, to reconstruct legal standards for reliable communication and effective responses to false information.

2 Conceptual Ambiguity of Disinformation: Methods, Techniques, and Strategic Patterns

In the Polish legal system, the concept of disinformation lacks a clear and uniform definition, which complicates the interpretation and application of the relevant legislation. Academic scholarship does not resolve this ambiguity, as definitions formulated in the literature vary considerably, particularly with respect to the intentionality of the message, the speaker's knowledge and the purpose of the communicative act.[2] This definitional inconsistency contributes to conceptual uncertainty and limits the effectiveness of regulatory or interpretative efforts.

Significant divergences also appear across academic disciplines. Legal scholars seek to define disinformation as precisely as possible, basing their analyses on existing normative frameworks.[3] Experts in security studies, by contrast, adopt a broader understanding of this concept that includes the dissemination of both true and false information, whether intentional or inadvertent.[4] Political scientists focus primarily on the practical mechanisms and dynamics of spreading disinformation, rather than clarifying its normative contours.[5] This disciplinary fragmentation makes it difficult to develop a coherent and constructive debate on how disinformation should be understood and regulated.

Against this background of competing conceptualisations, the present chapter adopts the legal studies approach, which is also reflected in the relevant Polish

---

[1] The Constitution of the Republic of Poland as adopted on 2 April 1997 (Journal of Laws No 78, item 483, with amendments).

[2] See e.g. Konieczny (2022: 172), Halagiera (2024: 27–44).

[3] See e.g. Domalewska (2024), Bień-Kacała, Kacała (2023), Konieczny (2022).

[4] Legucka (2020), Wachowicz (2019), Kacała (2015).

[5] Domalewska (2024). See also Freelon, Wells (2020), Jerit, Zhao (2020), Mckay, Tenove (2020).

regulatory framework. Under this definition, disinformation is understood as the intentional dissemination of false or manipulated information designed to produce a specific effect on the recipient. This implies that the speaker must be aware of the falsehood of the message and must act with the intention of misleading the recipient.[6] Disinformation thus involves presenting fabricated, misleading or otherwise distorted content as truth in order to confuse or deceive its audience.[7]

Disinformation, understood in this way, relies on a variety of recurring techniques, methods and strategies of manipulation, many of which are well-documented in communication studies.[8] The primary method is the denial of facts, which involves negating and rejecting information that is supported by reliable evidence, even though the available empirical data, scientific research or expert findings clearly indicate that the information is true. Another method of disinformation is distorting, modifying or reversing facts, which involves presenting reality in a way that alters its meaning by adding, omitting or misrepresenting essential elements. As a result, the audience receives an account of events that does not correspond to what actually happened. The most extreme form of this practice is fact reversal, in which facts are presented in a manner entirely opposite to the truth. Another common strategy is obscuring information, which means the deliberate introduction of excessive, irrelevant or marginal details that dilute the main message. This technique often takes the form of 'informational overload', making it difficult for recipients to distinguish essential facts from secondary or fabricated elements, thereby fostering cognitive fatigue and confusion. Disinformation is also often based on generalisation, which involves taking isolated or exceptional events and presenting them as representative of a broader reality, thereby creating the impression of systemic problems or widespread tendencies where none exist. A closely related technique is that of illustration, in which carefully selected examples, often atypical or emotionally charged, are used to suggest the existence of trends that are not supported by reliable evidence.

Another strategy is unequal representation, where one side of a dispute is given significantly less space to present its arguments or where its statements are selectively edited to appear weaker, inconsistent or unconvincing. This creates a false sense of imbalance, implying that one position dominates by virtue of its supposed strength, rather than as a result of manipulation. In the later stages of coordinated campaigns, disinformers may shift to equal representation, presenting two positions as equally credible, even when one is grounded in verified facts and the other is demonstrably false. This technique aims to blur the distinction between truth and misinformation, fostering doubt and relativising well-established findings.

A particularly effective method of disinformation is mixing truth with falsehood, in which genuine, verifiable facts are combined with manipulated, exaggerated or entirely fabricated elements. The presence of factual fragments lends credibility to the overall narrative, making it considerably more difficult for an average recipient to recognise the manipulation and disentangle truth from deception.

[6] Halagiera (2024: 45–46).

[7] Kacała (2015: 51), Domalewska (2024: 361–362).

[8] Mazur (2021: 79).

Disinformation campaigns rely heavily on narrative strategies, such as reversal (turning accusations back onto the accuser), appropriation (adopting the opponent's language to undermine their narrative), denigration (systematically discrediting individuals or institutions) and legitimisation (using apparent authority or expert status to strengthen the intended message). These strategies are often supported by rhetorical devices, such as insinuations, accusations of hypocrisy and moral framing, all designed to redirect attention away from substantive critique and towards emotionally charged reactions. Daniel Arce identifies additional disinformation strategies, namely leaking, lying, seeding, and smearing.[9] Leaking consists of the strategic disclosure of true information at a carefully chosen time and through selected channels in order to influence perceptions or gain a political or strategic advantage. Lying involves the intentional dissemination of false statements presented as factual with the aim of misleading the target audience. Seeding refers to the deliberate introduction of information (whether true, false or mixed) into the information environment in order to initiate its diffusion and shape subsequent narratives. Smearing denotes the spread of damaging claims or insinuations, often combining truthful and false elements, designed to undermine the reputation and credibility of individuals, groups or institutions.

Together, these methods, techniques and strategies aim to produce cognitive confusion, undermine the recipient's ability to independently assess the reliability of information and ultimately shape attitudes or behaviours in ways that serve the interests of those disseminating the disinformation. Their effectiveness increases in situations of social uncertainty, crisis or diminished trust in state institutions, when the public is particularly vulnerable to simplified narratives, emotional appeals and manipulated content.

3 Conceptual Boundaries of Disinformation: Related Concepts and the Post-Truth Phenomenon

Disinformation should be distinguished from the related concepts of misinformation and malinformation, which differ in both the intent and the truthfulness of the content.[10] Misinformation refers to false or inaccurate information spread without the intention to deceive; it typically results from error, misunderstanding or insufficient verification of the information provided.[11] Its impact stems from the fact that people unknowingly amplify inaccuracies, believing them to be true. Disinformation, by contrast, involves the intentional creation or dissemination of false or grossly misleading content in order to deceive recipients and achieve a specific objective that is often political or social in nature. Malinformation, on the other hand, concerns genuine information that is shared in a harmful or unethical way, for example, by

---

[9] Arce (2024).

[10] Broda, Strömbäck (2024), Tandoc et al. (2018), Fetzer (2004).

[11] Halagiera (2024: 57–60), Broda, Strömbäck (2024: 141).

exposing private data or releasing true material out of context to damage a person or institution.[12] It becomes harmful not because the content is false, but because truthful information is weaponised to produce negative consequences. While malinformation relies on truthful content used to cause harm, disinformation operates through false or manipulated content designed to mislead.

The term 'propaganda' is often used interchangeably with 'disinformation', even though the two have different meanings. Propaganda may contain both true and false content, and its primary aim is to influence attitudes and behaviours.[13] Rather than rejecting the truth entirely, propaganda uses truthful elements in a deliberate and systematic manner to shape perceptions and elicit specific reactions from recipients that serve the interests and intentions of the entity disseminating it.[14] In academic literature, propaganda is broadly defined as 'the systematic, one-sided, institutionalised, emotional and intellectual influence on the consciousness of individuals or social groups, exercised through persuasive and manipulative methods and aimed at altering or maintaining their attitudes or behaviours in accordance with the interests of those directing the propaganda'.[15] The relationship between disinformation and propaganda remains a matter of debate. Some researchers treat them as distinct phenomena, while others regard disinformation as a component or instrument of propaganda.[16] 'Fake news' and 'deepfakes', on the other hand, are understood differently—as specific examples of false content used in disinformation processes, that is, as the subject matter of communication. Fake news refers to deliberately fabricated or heavily distorted information presented in the style of a news report in order to trigger specific emotions, mislead audiences or influence their opinions.[17] This is content that imitates credible journalism, while, in reality, it has no basis in fact. Deepfakes, by contrast, are synthetic audio or video recordings created using advanced artificial intelligence technologies that realistically depict people saying or doing things they never actually said or did. Their purpose is most often to manipulate recipients by producing a highly convincing yet entirely false representation of reality.

Despite their differing intentions and forms, all of these phenomena contribute to the emergence of a post-truth environment in which the distinction between truth and falsehood is becoming increasingly blurred.[18] The notion of post-truth is defined in various ways in the Polish academic literature,[19] yet its essence lies in the observation that people's perceptions of reality are often shaped not by facts or reliable information, but by emotions and personal beliefs. Consequently, the importance of

---

[12] Halagiera (2024: 60–63). See also Ireton, Posetti (2018: 44), Wardle, Derakhshan (2017: 27).

[13] Benkler, Faris, Roberts (2018), Jowett, O'Donnell (1999).

[14] Bień-Kacała, Kacała (2023: 13).

[15] Bartoszewicz (2019: 86).

[16] Martin (1982: 47).

[17] Łódzki (2017: 21–23). See also Tandoc et al. (2018: 147–148), Lazer et al. (2018: 1094–1096).

[18] McIntyre (2018), Lewandowsky (2017).

[19] Kawka (2019: 11).

truth as an objective measure of reality and as a value that deserves protection is gradually decreasing.[20] The spread of post-truth is facilitated by communication via the internet and social media. The mass circulation of information, the declining sense of responsibility for its accuracy and reliability and the anonymity of those who create and share it all significantly limit the effectiveness of verifying its truthfulness, sometimes precluding it entirely. Post-truth is also a by-product of the rise of populism, accompanied by an increase in social tolerance for disseminating information that is 'not entirely true', but which is anticipated or desired for various reasons.[21]

Disinformation is never an end in itself, but rather a tool used to achieve specific objectives, for example, within the framework of state policy.[22] Its purpose is instrumental: Actors who disseminate disinformation do so to influence public attitudes, destabilise institutions, shift the balance of power or manipulate social behaviour in ways that serve their strategic interests. This is particularly evident in areas such as national security,[23] where disinformation can erode trust in public authorities or disrupt social cohesion; in the protection of electoral processes,[24] where it may distort voter perceptions or undermine confidence in the integrity of elections; in crisis management, including pandemics,[25] where misleading narratives can obstruct effective responses; and in information warfare,[26] where disinformation is a deliberate component of hybrid operations intended to confuse adversaries and destabilise democratic societies.

In the digital environment, disinformation has far greater reach and impact than traditional media. Unlike earlier forms of disinformation, which relied on limited channels of distribution and were easier to attribute to specific actors, online disinformation spreads within a decentralised, high-velocity ecosystem in which content can be replicated, modified and disseminated instantaneously across borders.[27] The anonymity of broadcasters, the use of automated bots, the algorithmic amplification of false content and deepfake technology pose various threats to the rule of law and the quality of public debate, as they enable manipulation on a scale and with a degree of precision that was not previously attainable. Online social platforms play an ambivalent role in this regard, providing space for expression and discussion while simultaneously serving as powerful vehicles for disinformation due to their design, business models and engagement-driven ranking systems. These factors create an environment in which false content can outcompete verified information, undermining trust in institutions, experts and democratic processes.[28] This underscores

---

[20] Florczak-Wątor (2023:74).

[21] Ibid.

[22] Legucka (2020: 171).

[23] See e.g. Legucka (2020), Kacała (2015).

[24] See e.g. Bader (2018).

[25] See e.g. Gutiérrez-Coba, Coba-Gutiérrez, Gómez-Díaz (2020), Liu, Huang (2020), Basch, Meleo-Erwin, Fera, Jaime, Basch (2021).

[26] See e.g. Kacała (2015), Bień-Kacała, Kacała (2023).

[27] Humprecht, Esser, Van Aelst (2020).

[28] Hameleers, Powell, Van Der Meer, Bos (2020).

the need for appropriate regulation, including transparency obligations, accountability mechanisms and safeguards for users' rights, in order to limit the systemic risks posed by online disinformation.

4 The Multi-Level Legal Framework for Countering Disinformation

The legal sources that regulate or relate to disinformation within the Polish legal system are fragmented and do not constitute a coherent or comprehensive body of legislation. To interpret them, it is necessary to examine multiple branches of law, including constitutional, civil, criminal, press, administrative and electoral law. As a cross-border digital phenomenon, disinformation transcends traditional legal categories. This means that its legal assessment depends on the context, including the purpose of the act, the nature of the content, the communication channel used and its social and individual effects. In practice, this requires the simultaneous application of provisions that safeguard personal rights, electoral integrity, state security, public order and the reliability of information.

4.1 The Constitutional Dimension: Truth, Freedom of Expression and the Right to Information

Although the Constitution of the Republic of Poland does not explicitly grant citizens the right to truth, this does not mean that such a right is not protected within the constitutional framework.[29] As the Constitutional Tribunal noted in one of its rulings, 'truth is a value embedded in the axiology of the Constitution.'[30]

In the Preamble to the Polish Constitution, truth is identified as one of the fundamental values alongside goodness, beauty and justice, reflecting its role as a common ethical reference point for society. The framers of the Constitution recognised truth as a universal value deriving from the shared moral foundations embraced by the Polish Nation—by citizens who believe in God as the source of truth, justice, good and beauty, as well as by those who do not share this faith but ground these universal values in other sources. In a democratic state governed by the rule of law, respect for and protection of the truth are the primary prerequisites for the proper functioning of public life.[31] Safeguarding truth in public discourse becomes a constitutional imperative, as it underpins the legitimacy of democratic institutions and enables citizens to participate meaningfully in the collective decision-making process.

---

[29] Florczak-Wątor (2023: 75–77), Dobrzeniecki (2020: 73), Zajadło (2016: 327).

[30] Judgment of the Constitutional Tribunal of 12 May 2008, ref no SK 43/05.

[31] See e.g. Bayer (2019), Cyuńczyk (2004).

The Polish Constitution is therefore the starting point for any consideration of measures aimed at countering the spread of disinformation, particularly in the context of freedom of expression, the right to information and the protection of personal rights. Article 14 of the Constitution guarantees freedom of the press and other means of social communication in the Republic of Poland. In contrast, Article 54(1) protects the freedom to express opinions and to seek and disseminate information. While these freedoms are fundamental to the functioning of a democratic state, they are not absolute. Article 31(3) of the Constitution allows for restrictions to be placed on these freedoms when necessary to protect state security, public order, environment, health, public morals or the rights of others. This authorises the legislator to create legal instruments to combat disinformation, provided that the principles of proportionality and respect for the essence of freedom of expression are upheld. In this context, efforts to counter the dissemination of false information should be viewed as measures to safeguard freedom of expression from abuse and the distortion of public debate, rather than as limitations.

Against this constitutional backdrop, particular attention should be given to Articles 47 and 51 of the Polish Constitution, which establish additional safeguards of particular relevance to combating disinformation. Article 47 guarantees the protection of private life, honour and one's good name, thereby shielding individuals from the reputational harm caused by the dissemination of false or misleading content. Article 51, in turn, regulates the protection of personal data and includes, in paragraph 4, a constitutional right to request the rectification or removal of information that is false, incomplete or collected in a manner contrary to the law.[32] As the Constitutional Tribunal has observed, Article 51(4) reflects the constitutional legislator's conviction that information consistent with reality—and thus the individual's right to prevent or eliminate the circulation of untrue information about them—constitutes a value deserving of the highest constitutional protection.[33] In the digital age, where false content can infringe upon personal rights and damage an individual's reputation, the importance of these constitutional safeguards is clear, as they provide a legal framework enabling individuals to defend themselves against the rapid and widespread dissemination of misleading or harmful information.

Article 61 of the Constitution is equally important, as it sets out a comprehensive right of access to public information and thereby strengthens constitutional guarantees of transparency, accountability and integrity in public life—all of which are essential in preventing and countering disinformation. Article 61(1) grants every citizen the right to obtain information about the activities of public authorities and persons performing public functions. This right also extends to information concerning the activities of bodies of economic and professional self-government, as well as other persons and organisational units, to the extent that they perform public tasks or manage municipal property or state treasury assets. Article 61(2)

[32] Article 54(1) of the Constitution of the Republic of Poland as the source of the 'right to truth' was indicated by the Provincial Administrative Court in Białystok in its judgment of 8 December 2022, ref no II SA/Bk 744/22.

[33] Judgment of the Constitutional Tribunal of 12 May 2008, ref no SK 43/05.

further provides that this right includes access to documents and entry into meetings of collegial public authorities elected in universal elections, with the possibility of recording sound or images. Although Article 61(3) allows for restrictions on this right, such limitations may be introduced solely by statute and only for the protection of the rights and freedoms of others, public order, security or an important economic interest of the state.

In the context of combating disinformation, these constitutional guarantees play a pivotal role. By ensuring openness in the functioning of public institutions and enabling citizens to verify how public tasks are carried out, Article 61 of the Polish Constitution acts as a structural safeguard against the spread of false or misleading narratives concerning public authority. Transparency facilitates informed public debate, strengthens trust in institutions and reduces the space in which disinformation can take root and proliferate. The state, therefore, is obliged not only to respect and protect freedom of expression but also to ensure conditions in which accurate, reliable and accessible public information can serve as an effective antidote to disinformation, thereby upholding truth, the common good and human dignity.

Article 74(3) of the Constitution, which guarantees everyone the right to information on the state of the environment and its protection, also contributes to the constitutional framework relevant to countering disinformation. Environmental matters are particularly susceptible to false or misleading narratives, and effective public participation requires access to accurate science-based data. By obliging the state to provide reliable information in this field, Article 74(3) enhances transparency, supports informed decision-making and strengthens society's resilience to environmental disinformation.

The constitutional importance of truth is further reinforced by the informational duties imposed on key public bodies, including the Supreme Court, the Supreme Administrative Court, the Constitutional Tribunal, the Supreme Audit Office, the Ombudsman and the Council of Ministers, which must provide reliable and accurate reports to the Sejm. This demonstrates that access to truthful information is conceived not merely as an institutional obligation, but as a constitutional right directed towards society. Additional confirmation of this principle appears in Article 41(3) of the Constitution, which requires that a detained person be informed of the genuine reasons for his or her detention, illustrating that truth is an essential safeguard of individual rights. Truth also underpins the broader constitutional architecture of the Republic of Poland: Article 2 of the Constitution embeds it within the notion of a democratic state governed by the rule of law, while Articles 4 and 62 presuppose that citizens must have access to accurate information in order to exercise national sovereignty and electoral rights in an informed manner.[34] Taken together, these provisions demonstrate that the right to truth is firmly rooted in the Polish Constitution and should be recognised as a fundamental constitutional right of the individual.

[34] See also Rakowska-Trela (2015: 12).

4.2 *Statutory Regulations: Fragmented Standards and Practical Limitations*

As mentioned above, disinformation is not explicitly defined as a separate offence in the Polish legal system. However, its consequences may be subject to sanctions under various areas of law. Due to the multifaceted nature of this phenomenon, its regulation is spread across criminal, civil, press, electoral and administrative law. While individual statutes do not expressly refer to disinformation, they contain instruments that enable a legal response to its consequences, particularly in cases involving violations of personal rights, the dissemination of false information, misleading the public or threatening national security. Consequently, countering disinformation in Poland relies on interpreting and applying general provisions that, while not originally designed as a coherent system to protect information, together form a legal framework that limits the manipulation of information in the public sphere.

Although the Criminal Code[35] does not define disinformation as a distinct offence, it nevertheless contains several provisions that may be applied to behaviours commonly accompanying dissemination of disinformation. These include the provisions on defamation (Article 212), persistent harassment (Article 190a), incitement of hatred against social groups (Articles 256 and 257) and insulting a public official (Article 226). Such provisions become relevant when disinformation harms the reputation of an individual or organisation or otherwise infringes on legally protected interests. Article 212 of the Criminal Code is particularly significant in cases where false statements circulated online lower a person in terms of public opinion or undermine the trust essential for their profession or public role, especially when the content is disseminated through mass communication. Article 190a of the Criminal Code addresses forms of digital harassment and identity misuse commonly associated with coordinated disinformation campaigns, including the creation of fake profiles or the fabrication of materials. Articles 256 and 257 of the Criminal Code may apply where disinformation is used to incite hatred, provoke hostility or publicly insult individuals or groups on discriminatory grounds, thereby exacerbating social tensions and threatening public order. They also constitute the primary legal instruments for penalising hate speech in Poland, including forms of online disinformation that disseminate or reinforce such hateful narratives. Article 256 of the Criminal Code criminalises the public promotion of totalitarian regimes and of Nazi, communist or fascist ideologies, as well as public incitement to hatred on national, ethnic, racial or religious grounds or on the grounds of non-religious beliefs. It also encompasses the production, possession and dissemination of materials or symbols intended to promote such content, except when these acts are undertaken for artistic, educational, scholarly or collector purposes. Article 257 of the Criminal Code, in turn, penalises publicly insulting a person or group on account of their national, ethnic, racial or religious affiliation, or their non-religious beliefs, as well as assaults committed on such discriminatory

[35] The Act of 6 June 1997 Criminal Code (Journal of Laws of 2025, item 383, as amended).

grounds. Finally, Article 226 of the Criminal Code becomes relevant when disinformation involves public insults directed at officials or constitutional organs, as such conduct undermines trust in state authority and disrupts the proper functioning of democratic institutions.

Moreover, Article 132 of the Criminal Code introduces an additional, highly specific form of liability by penalising the offence of 'intelligence disinformation'.[36] It provides that a sentence of imprisonment ranging from one to ten years shall be imposed on 'anyone who, while providing intelligence services to the Republic of Poland, misleads a Polish state authority by providing forged or altered documents or other items, or by concealing true information or providing false information of significant importance to the Republic of Poland'. This provision is unique within the European legal landscape and has no direct equivalent in other jurisdictions.[37] Legal doctrine presents differing views regarding the characteristics of the perpetrator of an offence under Article 132 of the Criminal Code.[38] Some authors argue that liability may arise only in the case of a Polish citizen acting intentionally and with full awareness of cooperating with foreign intelligence services. Others, however, allow for criminal responsibility, even in situations involving indirect or less deliberate participation in intelligence-related activities, provided that the perpetrator foresaw the possibility that his or her actions could be used against the Republic of Poland. Given its exceptional nature and the severity of its legal consequences, scholars emphasise the need for a strict interpretation of this provision and for ensuring a balance between safeguarding state security and preserving the procedural guarantees afforded to the individual.

Beyond the sphere of criminal law, additional mechanisms for addressing the spread of false or misleading content are found in sector-specific legislation, particularly in the context of electoral processes. The Electoral Code[39] establishes a special procedure for counteracting the dissemination of false information during election campaigns. According to Article 111 of the Electoral Code, if election materials such as posters, leaflets, slogans, statements or other campaign materials contain false information, the relevant electoral candidate or their representative has the right to apply to the district court for an order to prohibit the dissemination of such information. The court may also order the correction of false statements, the confiscation of election materials, the publication of a response to infringements of personal rights or an apology to the person whose rights have been violated. Additionally, the court may order the party concerned to pay up to PLN 100,000 to a public benefit organisation.

These proceedings are conducted on an expedited basis. The court examines the application within 24 hours, and its ruling, including any obligation to publish a correction or apology in the press or other media, is subject to immediate enforcement. As the Constitutional Tribunal, referring to Article 111 of the Electoral Code,

[36] Chlebowicz (2012: 42); Iwiński, Rosenau (2018: 155).

[37] Hoc (2000: 48).

[38] Chlebowicz (2012: 43), Iwiński and Rosenau (2018: 160).

[39] Act of 5 January 2011 Electoral Code (Journal of Laws of 2025, item 365, as amended).

has indicated, 'One of the most important elements of free elections is free public debate conducted by all interested citizens during the election campaign. Article 2 of the Constitution, which enshrines the principle of a democratic state governed by the rule of law, requires the adoption of legislation ensuring a fair election campaign and enabling citizens to access truthful information about public affairs and candidates. The election campaign should facilitate the free formation of voters' opinions and enable them to make informed decisions on voting day. The very short deadlines for hearing cases in the first and second instances are intended to ensure that a decision is issued in time for voters to familiarise themselves with the court's findings before voting day, and to allow a fair pre-election debate free from false information to take place over a sufficiently long period.'[40]

The Electoral Code also sets out rules governing the conduct of election campaigns on radio and television, ensuring the accuracy of the information provided to voters. This includes the obligation to clearly separate election broadcasts from editorial content (Article 116 §1), the prohibition of campaigning on behalf of other electoral committees (Article 116 §2), equal access to airtime (Articles 117–120) and supervision by the National Broadcasting Council to ensure compliance with technical standards and impartiality in presenting participants' views during debates (Article 122).

In civil law, Articles 23 and 24 of the Civil Code[41] provide for the protection of personal rights, particularly in cases involving violations of an individual's honour, privacy or dignity. Where such rights are infringed upon by disinformation, the injured party may seek injunctive relief and the removal of the effects of the violation, as well as compensation. In one of its rulings, the Supreme Court held that 'The so-called "right to the truth", "right not to be lied to", and "right not to be deceived", as formulated by the complainant, cannot in itself be regarded as a personal right. The right to receive reliable information does not fall within the category of non-pecuniary values closely related to the essence of the individual. The open nature of the catalogue of personal rights does not justify its arbitrary extension without regard for the exceptional nature of the instruments ensuring the protection of such rights. Personal rights are values that are intrinsically linked to the essence of humanity and human nature, independent of human will, and can be clearly specified and objectified.'[42] The Court of Appeal in Warsaw adopted a similar position, stating, 'Contrary to the arguments raised in the appeal, the "right to the truth" is not an individual's personal right, just as the "right to receive true information" is not a personal right protected under Article 24 of the Civil Code. Although the catalogue of personal rights is open-ended and judicial rulings sometimes recognise certain non-pecuniary values as "new personal rights" (for example, the right to revere the memory of a legal person or the right to belong to a particular gender), this does not mean that the catalogue can be expanded at will to include all values and goods that are positively regarded by society, such as "truth" or the "right not to be lied

[40] Judgment of the Constitutional Tribunal of 21 July 2009, ref no K 7/09.

[41] The Act of 23 April 1964 Civil Code (Journal of Laws of 2025, item 1071, as amended).

[42] Decision of the Supreme Court of 19 March 2021, ref no I CSK 343/20.

to", as invoked by the claimant. Personal rights are non-pecuniary values closely linked to the essence of an individual's personality and autonomy. This concept does not extend to logical categories such as "truth" or "falsehood", nor to relationships between individuals, including informational relationships involving the receipt of true or false information from third parties.'[43] These findings support the conclusion that Polish civil courts consistently refuse to recognise the right to truth as legally protected non-material interests of an individual, thereby rejecting the possibility of protecting it under Articles 23 and 24 of the Civil Code.

According to Article 12 of the Press Law Act,[44] journalists have a duty to exercise special diligence and professional integrity when collecting and using press materials. This includes verifying the accuracy of the information obtained and indicating its source. This obligation is intended to prevent the unauthorised dissemination of false information. The requirement of truthfulness is reiterated throughout the Press Law Act. According to its provisions, 'the press is obliged to present phenomena truthfully' (Article 6(1)), 'at the request of the person concerned, the editor-in-chief of the relevant daily newspaper or magazine is obliged to publish a factual correction of inaccurate or untrue information free of charge' (Article 31a(1)) and 'the publication of truthful and reliable reports from public meetings of the Sejm, Senate and local government bodies and their organs, as well as the publication of reliable, socially acceptable negative assessments of scientific, artistic or other creative, professional or public activities, is protected by law' (Article 41).

Under the pretext of press criticism, false or misleading information may not be disseminated, particularly with regard to public figures, including political parties, their representatives and individuals in positions of power. As the Supreme Court stated, criticism of such persons is more widely permitted and they are afforded less protection.[45] For public figures, this narrower scope of protection is the price they pay for their prominent position in society, which naturally entitles the public to take an interest in their actions and behaviour. Indeed, it has been observed that, by virtue of being a public figure, an individual, to some extent, invites others into their private life.

However, at the same time, the case law emphasises that 'the right to criticise cannot be exercised in such a way as to damage the good name or honour of the person criticised' and that 'it is impossible to speak of the protection of the right to criticise when proportionality has not been maintained and the criticism takes the form of unfounded and pointless aggression, thereby undermining the standards of public debate.'[46] When assessing the unlawfulness of press criticism, it is necessary to determine whether the journalistic statement is reliable and whether the presentation of press material—even if it consists of accurate individual information—remains truthful in its overall meaning. It must also be determined whether the material lacks a factual and reliable connection to the facts, creates misconceptions or erroneous

[43] Judgment of the Court of Appeal in Warsaw of 12 December 2019, ref no VI ACa 504/18.

[44] The Act of 26 January 1984: Press Law (Journal of Laws of 2018, item 1914, as amended).

[45] Resolution of the Supreme Court of 18 February 2005, ref no III CZP 53/04.

[46] Judgment of the Court of Appeal in Warsaw of 23 March 2018, ref no I ACa 2078/16.

and harmful judgements, and therefore does not constitute the truthful or reliable use of information. The protection of freedom of expression in the press does not extend to an author or editor portraying a person's behaviour in an excessively abbreviated, simplified or one-sided manner that significantly distorts its actual scope and meaning, thereby misleading the audience.

Finally, administrative law—including the Electronic Services Act[47]—sets out the obligations of internet service providers, who may only be exempt from liability for user-generated content under the conditions specified in Article 14 of that Act. This exemption applies when an entity provides data transmission services ('mere conduit') or temporary data storage ('caching') and acts solely in a technical capacity. This means that it does not initiate the transmission, select the recipient or modify the content. This also means that the entity immediately deletes the data upon receiving notice of its removal or blocking at the source. Similarly, a service provider offering hosting services is not liable for unlawful data if they were unaware of its nature and promptly rendered it inaccessible upon receiving official notification or reliable information.

4.3 *Soft Law and Institutional Practice in Countering Disinformation*

An important source of non-binding norms can be found in soft law instruments. This category includes the Code of Practice on Disinformation,[48] which was published (in the modified version) on 16 March 2022 by the European Commission. It has been endorsed by major platforms, such as Google and Meta. While the Code is not legally binding, it contains voluntary commitments by online platforms to combat fake news, for instance, by collaborating with fact-checking organisations. In Poland, similar functions are performed by media and publishing ethics codes. One example is the Media Ethics Charter, which was signed on 29 March 1995 by representatives of the country's leading media companies and associations. This charter emphasises the obligation of providers to ensure the reliability and truthfulness of information. However, these instruments do not provide for sanctions or appeal mechanisms, which considerably limits their effectiveness.

Polish soft law instruments for countering disinformation play an important role in shaping institutional practice and public awareness in this area. The guide 'How to Counteract Disinformation? (Not Only) for Public Administration', developed by the Research and Academic Computer Network—National Research Institute

[47] The Act of 18 July 2002 on the Provision of Electronic Services (Journal of Laws of 2024, item 1513, as amended).

[48] The original version of the code from 2018, signed at the time by major internet companies – Facebook, Google, Twitter and Mozilla – required necessary changes resulting, among other things, from the COVID-19 crisis and Russian aggression against Ukraine.

(NASK) and published on 17 December 2024, provides practical guidance on identifying, analysing and mitigating the impact of false information, particularly within public institutions.[49] The document promotes communication standards based on transparency, responsiveness and cross-sectoral cooperation. It also (1) explains key concepts, such as disinformation, misinformation and malinformation; (2) identifies the main mechanisms of digital manipulation, including algorithmic amplification, bot activity and coordinated influence operations; (3) outlines practical methods of response, such as monitoring, prebunking, debunking and fact-checking; (4) proposes crisis-communication procedures tailored to public administration; and (5) emphasises the importance of building long-term institutional resilience through education, internal protocols and inter-agency collaboration.

Similarly, the Appeal of the Advisory Council for Resilience to the Minister of Foreign Affairs Against Disinformation, adopted on 28 April 2025, demonstrates a political commitment to coordinated action to strengthen the state's informational resilience.[50] It highlights the importance of public media education, greater transparency in public communication and enhanced collaboration with international partners. In addition, the Appeal stresses the need for public authorities to communicate exclusively on the basis of verified and reliable information, to avoid the use of emotionally charged or manipulative messages and to ensure that institutional communication is timely, responsible and accessible to diverse audiences. It calls for long-term investment in public awareness and media literacy as a means of reducing societal vulnerability to manipulation and emphasises that countering disinformation requires cooperation not only within the state administration but also with academia, civil society, local governments and the private sector. At the international level, the Appeal underscores the importance of closer coordination with partner countries and organisations in order to respond effectively to cross-border influence operations and to strengthen the overall resilience of democratic systems.

The third significant document is the report 'Counteracting Disinformation in Poland: Systemic Recommendations', which was prepared by the Forum for Counteracting Disinformation and published on 8 December 2022.[51] It sets out comprehensive proposals for systemic measures, including developing national analytical structures, strengthening public trust in state institutions and enhancing the accountability of online platforms. While these initiatives are non-binding, they establish standards of good practices and support the implementation of public policies consistent with the principle of information resilience. The report further highlights the need for permanent monitoring of the information environment, coordinated strategic communication across public institutions and the creation of clear procedures for responding to both domestic and foreign influence operations. It also identifies legal,

---

[49] Nakonieczna (2025).

[50] Appeal by the Polish Foreign Minister's Advisory Resilience Council against Disinformation adopted on 28 April 2025 < https://www.gov.pl/web/diplomacy/together-against-manipulation > . Accessed 10 December 2025.

[51] Mierzyńska (2022).

organisational and educational gaps that undermine the effectiveness of counter-disinformation efforts and recommends long-term cooperation between the government, civil society, academia and independent experts. Additionally, the document stresses that resilience requires not only reactive measures, but also preventive actions aimed at building social awareness and reducing susceptibility to manipulation.

Taken together, these soft law instruments illustrate how non-binding norms can nevertheless shape state practice and societal expectations in countering disinformation. Although they lack formal enforcement mechanisms, they provide a coherent set of standards promoting transparency, accuracy and responsibility in public communication, while also encouraging cooperation between public authorities, civil society, academia and online platforms. By offering practical guidance, identifying systemic vulnerabilities and outlining preventive as well as reactive measures, they contribute to building long-term informational resilience and support the lawful, proportionate and coordinated response of state institutions to contemporary information threats.

5 Conclusions and Recommendations

Disinformation, particularly that disseminated through digital platforms, is increasingly recognised in Poland as posing a serious and tangible threat to the rule of law, civil society and public debate. Compared with traditional forms of disinformation, such as leaflets or print media, online disinformation spreads rapidly, is difficult to trace and has a far wider reach. These characteristics significantly amplify its destructive potential, which became particularly evident during the pandemic, the war in Ukraine and in both national and European election campaigns. Public opinion surveys and analyses conducted by state institutions, including reports by NASK, confirm that Polish society is becoming better at recognising disinformation. However, distinguishing it from legitimate, albeit controversial, political criticism remains a challenge.

An evaluation of the effectiveness of existing legal regulations aimed at countering disinformation concludes that their impact is limited. Currently, the Polish legal system lacks a distinct and comprehensive statutory framework that directly addresses disinformation. The application of criminal, civil, electoral or press law provisions is only possible in narrowly defined cases and under restrictive conditions. Further difficulties arise from enforcing national law against foreign entities, particularly digital platform operators, and from the absence of mechanisms enabling a rapid response to emergencies, such as pre-election influence operations or military disinformation campaigns.

One of the main issues is the lack of a clear legal definition of disinformation and a procedural framework to enable a quick and proportionate response. The current body of law, which is largely based on general provisions, is poorly equipped to deal with modern techniques of information manipulation, such as the use of bots, deepfakes, microtargeting and cross-border coordinated campaigns. Another challenge lies in ensuring the adequate protection of freedom of expression without leading to the emergence of preventive censorship. The law must safeguard open public debate and the right to express controversial opinions while protecting individuals and society from manipulation and deception. The most frequently proposed directions for reform include the adoption of a comprehensive anti-disinformation act, the establishment of an independent regulatory authority to monitor the information space, clarification of digital platforms' obligations to remove false or misleading content and strengthening users' rights in appeal procedures.

Finally, effectively addressing disinformation requires the use of non-legal instruments as well, such as media education, public awareness initiatives, the promotion of journalistic ethics and support for professional fact-checking organisations. Legal regulation is just one pillar of a broader strategy that must integrate legal, technological and educational measures. Only a multidimensional approach that balances preserving constitutional freedoms with effectively protecting against falsehoods and manipulation can ensure genuine regulatory effectiveness in the digital transformation of the public sphere.

References

Arce D (2024) Disinformation Strategies. Defence and Peace Economics 35(6): 659–672.

Bader M (2018) Disinformation in elections. Security and Human Rights 29(1–4): 24–35

Bartoszewicz M (2019) Teorie propagandy w obliczu algorytmizacji internetowego komunikowania społecznego. Kultura Współczesna 104(1): 84–98

Basch CH, Meleo-Erwin Z, Fera J, Jaime C, Basch CE (2021) A global pandemic in the time of viral memes: COVID-19 vaccine misinformation and disinformation on TikTok. Human Vaccines & Immunotherapeutics 17(8): 2373–2377.

Bayer J (ed) (2019) Disinformation and propaganda—impact on the functioning of the rule of law in the EU and its Member States, EU. Available at http://www.europarl.europa.eu/supporting-analyses. Access 10 December 2025.

Benkler Y, Faris R, Roberts H (2018) Network Propaganda: Manipulation, Disinformation, and Radicalization in American Politics. Oxford University Press, Oxford

Bień-Kacała A, Kacała T (2023) Dezinformacja – definicja, zagrożenia, reakcja Acta Iuris Stetinensis 44(3): 9–20.

Broda E, Strömbäck J (2024) Misinformation, Disinformation, and Fake News: Lessons from an Interdisciplinary, Systematic Literature Review. Annals of the International Communication Association 48(2): 139–166

Chlebowicz P (2012) Interpretacja pojęcia dezinformacji w świetle art. 132 k.k. Studia Prawnoustrojowe 15: 41–48

Cyuńczyk F (2004) Walka z dezinformacją w warunkach kryzysu praworządności. In Stasiuk-Krajewska K and Wenzel M (ed) Dezinformacja w czasach kryzysu. Adam Marszałek Publishing House, Toruń

Dobrzeniecki K (2020) Prawo do prawdy w perspektywie filozoficznej. Przyczynek do dyskusji. Acta Universitatis Wratislaviensis. Przegląd Prawa i Administracji 122: 73–85

Domalewska D (2024) Dezinformacja jako zagrożenie dla demokracji i regulacje prawne w zakresie jej przeciwdziałania w Polsce i wybranych krajach europejskich. Politeja 92(5): 359–379.

Fetzer JH (2004) Disinformation: the use of false information. Minds and Machines 14(2): 231–240

Florczak-Wątor M (2023) O potrzebie konstytucjonalizacji prawa obywateli do prawdy i konieczności poszerzenia ustawowego zakresu jego ochrony w czasach postprawdy. Przegląd Prawa Publicznego 11: 73–89.

Freelon D, Wells C (2020) Disinformation as Political Communication. Political Communication 37(2): 145–156
Gutiérrez-Coba LM, Coba-Gutiérrez P, Gómez-Díaz J (2020) Fake news about COVID-19: A comparative analysis of six Iberoamerican countries. Revista Latina de Communicación Social 78(78), 237–264
Halagiera D (2024) Dezinformacja w dyskursie nowych mediów (doctoral thesis defended at the Faculty of Political Science and Journalism of the Adam Mickiewicz University in Poznań), available at https://repozytorium.amu.edu.pl/items/f25b17c0-28fe-47aa-8cd1-7e7b6694878c.
Hameleers M, Powell TE, Van Der Meer TG L A, Bos L (2020) A picture paints a thousand lies? The effects and mechanisms of multimodal disinformation and rebuttals disseminated via social media. Political Communication 37(2): 281–301.
Hoc S (2000) Przestępstwo dezinformacji wywiadowczej w kodeksie karnym. Przegląd Sądowy 5: 48
Humprecht E, Esser F, Van Aelst P (2020) Resilience to online disinformation: A framework for cross-national comparative research. International Journal of Press/Politics 25(3): 493–516
Ireton C, Posetti J (2018) Journalism, fake news & disinformation: Handbook for journalism education and training. UNESCO.
Iwiński M, Rosenau D (2018) Odpowiedzialność karna za dezinformację jako forma działań wywiadowczych. Studia z Zakresu Nauk Prawnoustrojowych: miscellanea 8(1): 155–161
Jerit J, Zhao Y (2020) Political Misinformation. Annual Review of Political Science 23(1): 77–94
Jowett GS, O'Donnell V (1999) Propaganda & Persuasion. SAGE, Los Angeles.
Kacała T (2015) Dezinformacja i propaganda w kontekście zagrożeń dla bezpieczeństwa państwa. Przegląd Prawa Konstytucyjnego 24(2): 49–65
Kawka M (2019) Język postprawdy – jak fikcja stała się rzeczywistością. Rocznik Medioznawczy 1: 9–20.
Konieczny MK (2022) Disinformation in legal and criminalistic reality. Studia Prawnoustrojowe 56: 171–196
Lazer DMJ., et al. (2018) The science of fake news. Science 359(6389): 1094–1096
Legucka A (2020) Dezinformacja jako element wojny informacyjnej Federacji Rosyjskiej – założenia i efektywność. Sprawy Międzynarodowe 73(4): 159–186
Lewandowsky S, Ecker UKH, Cook J (2017) Beyond Misinformation: Understanding and Coping with the "Post-truth" Era'. Journal of Applied Research in Memory and Cognition 6(4): 353–369.
Liu PL, Huang LV (2020) Digital disinformation about COVID-19 and the third-person effect: Examining the channel differences and negative emotional outcomes. Cyberpsychology, Behavior, and Social Networking 23(11): 789–793
Łódzki B (2017) Fake news – dezinformacja w mediach internetowych i formy jej zwalczania w przestrzeni międzynarodowej. Polityka i Społeczeństwo 15(4): 19–30.
Martin LJ (1982) Disinformation: An Instrumentality in the Propaganda Arsenal. Political Communication 2(1): 47–64
Mazur J (2021) Informacja i dezinformacja w przestrzeni publicznej. Wprowadzenie do problematyki. Social Space Journal 21(1): 69–95
McIntyre L (2018) Post-truth. MIT Press
Mckay S, Tenove C (2020) Disinformation as a Threat to Deliberative Democracy. Political Research Quarterly 74(3): 703–717
Mierzyńska A (2022) Przeciwdziałanie dezinformacji w Polsce. Rekomendacje systemowe. Available at https://ffb.org.pl/wp-content/uploads/2023/02/Raport_Przeciwdzialanie_dezinformacji.pdf. Accessed on 10 December 2025.
Nakonieczna A. (ed) (2025) Jak przeciwdziałać dezinformacji? Poradnik dla administracji publicznej. Available at https://ochronaludnosci.edu.pl/wp-content/uploads/2025/02/Dezinfo_PoradnikAdministracji-1.pdf. Accessed on 10 December 2025.
Rakowska-Trela A (2015) Prawa wyborców w kampanii wyborczej. Studia Wyborcze 20: 7–34.
Tandoc EC et al. (2018) Defining "Fake News": A Typology of Scholarly Definitions. Digital Journalism 6(2) 137–153

Wachowicz M (2019) Ujęcie teoretyczne pojęcia dezinformacji. Wiedze obronna 266–267(1–2): 226–253.

Wardle C, Derakhshan H (2017) Information disorder: Toward an interdisciplinary framework for research and policy making. Council of Europe.

Zajadło J (2016) Prawda a prawo. In Bator A, Zajadło J, Zirk-Sadowski M (eds) Wielka encyklopedia prawa: Teoria i filozofia prawa. Fundacja 'Ubi societas, ibi ius', Warsaw.

Disinformation in Portugal: Legislating Truth and Unravelling It

Francisco Pereira Coutinho

Abstract Portugal's short-lived statutory "right to protection against disinformation" crystallised post-2016 political anxieties but was swiftly dismantled on freedom of expression and legal certainty constitutional grounds. In its wake, disinformation is addressed through a medium-neutral, ex post legal patchwork spanning electoral, media, consumer protection and civil liability provisions. Case law and media regulator decisions increasingly target deceptive presentation and verification failures by professional media and candidates, while explicitly shielding opinion, satire and value judgements from truth-testing. This chapter reconstructs the rise and repeal of the "right to protection against disinformation" and maps the current toolkit for tackling disinformation through close reading of legislation, judicial decisions and regulatory practice. It argues that the adopted legal framework deliberately eschews direct truth-policing and avoids empowering public authorities to label "disinformation" as such, thereby reducing risks of censorship and politicised enforcement. However, the resulting model remains fragmented, under-enforced and structurally reactive to the speed, scale and strategic amplification of online manipulation.

1 The Portuguese News and Disinformation Landscape

Traditional media still dominate news access in Portugal. Television is used by about two-thirds of the public and remains the main gateway for just over half of audiences. The internet now matches TV in overall weekly reach, but a smaller share of the population names it as their primary source, highlighting TV's continued weight,

I thank Beatriz Neves, Daniela Antão, Joana Moreira and Sara de Almeida for their insightful comments and bibliographical suggestions. All errors are my own.

F. Pereira Coutinho (✉)
Member of CEDIS—I & D Research Center for Law and Society, NOVA School of Law, Lisbon, Portugal
e-mail: fpereiracoutinho@novalaw.unl.pt

P. Passaglia (ed.), *European Legal Perspectives on Online Disinformation*, Ius Gentium: Comparative Perspectives on Law and Justice 140,
https://doi.org/10.1007/978-3-032-25785-7_15

especially among older groups. Among 18–24-year-olds, however, digital channels lead: more cite the open web or social platforms as their main news routes.[1]

News use on social media is concentrated on a few platforms, with Facebook still the leading venue for news.[2] These platforms depend heavily on news brands and professional journalism to supply trusted, high-quality content.[3] This leaves meaningful space for newsroom output on digital platforms, particularly those built around strong visuals or rapid updates, even as creators and influencers gain prominence and sometimes compete with legacy outlets.

Young people's relationship with news is more intermittent and platform-driven, weakening ties to traditional brands.[4] They tend to report lower trust in news and less concern about online disinformation. In response, the government has introduced free digital news subscriptions for 15–18-year-olds as part of wider media literacy efforts, both to build news habits and to encourage a culture of paying for digital journalism.[5]

Portugal faces a growing risk of disinformation.[6] As of 2025, 54% of Portuguese residents trust news overall,[7] placing Portugal among the most news-trusting countries globally.[8] At the same time, distrust has risen sharply, particularly through the COVID-19 period, signalling a broader drift towards scepticism.[9] Around 71% of Portuguese people report being concerned about disinformation.[10] This combination of comparatively high trust, rising distrust, and high concern forms the backdrop to Portugal's legal and policy experiments in tackling disinformation examined in this chapter.

---

[1] Cardoso, G., Paisana, M., Pinto-Martinho, A.: Digital News Report Portugal 2025. OberCom (2025). Available at: https://zenodo.org/records/15599072. Accessed 15 October 2025, p. 24.

[2] Cardoso, G., Paisana, M., Pinto-Martinho, A.: Digital News Report Portugal 2025. OberCom (2025). Available at: https://zenodo.org/records/15599072. Accessed 15 October 2025, p. 133.

[3] Magallón-Rosa, R., Paisana, M., et al.: Disinformation Consumption Patterns in Spain and Portugal. Iberifier (2024). Available at: https://iberifier.eu/2024/05/15/iberifier-reports-disinformation-consumption-patterns-in-spain-and-portugal. Accessed 15 October 2025, p. 37.

[4] Cardoso, G., Paisana, M., Pinto-Martinho, A.: Digital News Report Portugal 2025. OberCom (2025). Available at: https://zenodo.org/records/15599072. Accessed 15 October 2025, p. 154.

[5] Cardoso, G., Paisana, M., Pinto-Martinho, A.: Digital News Report Portugal 2025. OberCom (2025). Available at: https://zenodo.org/records/15599072. Accessed 15 October 2025, p.155.

[6] Pardal, F.: Disinformation Landscape in Portugal V2. EU DisinfoLab (May 2025). Available at: https://www.disinfo.eu/wp-content/uploads/2025/05/20250519_Disinfo-landscape-in-Portugal-V2.pdf. Accessed 15 October 2025, p. 3.

[7] Cardoso, G., Paisana, M., Pinto-Martinho, A.: Digital News Report Portugal 2025. OberCom (2025). Available at: https://zenodo.org/records/15599072. Accessed 15 October 2025, p. 64.

[8] Magallón-Rosa, R., Paisana, M., et al.: Disinformation Consumption Patterns in Spain and Portugal. Iberifier (2024). Available at: https://iberifier.eu/2024/05/15/iberifier-reports-disinformation-consumption-patterns-in-spain-and-portugal. Accessed 15 October 2025, p. 55.

[9] Sousa Guedes, I.: Disinformation Dynamics and Regulation in Portugal: Insights from a Qualitative Study. European Journal on Criminal Policy and Research 31 (2025), pp. 538–539.

[10] Cardoso, G., Paisana, M., Pinto-Martinho, A.: Digital News Report Portugal 2025. OberCom (2025). Available at: https://zenodo.org/records/15599072. Accessed 15 October 2025, p. 18.

2 The Notion of Disinformation

2.1 Definition

Portugal's only codified definition of "disinformation" lived briefly for fifteen months in Article 6 of the Portuguese Charter of Human Rights in the Digital Age (Law 27/2021), which recognises the "Right to Protection Against Disinformation":

> 2. Disinformation means any demonstrably false or misleading narrative that is created, presented, and disseminated to obtain economic advantage or to deliberately deceive the public, and which is liable to cause public harm, notably a threat to democratic political processes, to public policy-making processes, and to public goods.
>
> 3. For the purposes of the preceding paragraph, demonstrably false or misleading information includes the use of manipulated or fabricated texts or videos, as well as practices that flood e-mail inboxes and the use of networks of fake followers.
>
> 4. Mere errors in the communication of information, as well as satire or parody, are not covered by this article.

This concept of disinformation did not emerge in a vacuum. It mirrored the EU's 2018 policy formula, namely the High-Level Expert Group (HLEG) report and the Commission's Communications,[11] which describe disinformation as verifiably false, inaccurate or misleading content that is created, presented and disseminated for profit or to intentionally deceive, and that is liable to cause public harm (e.g., to democratic processes or other public goods), while excluding illegal content, as well as reporting mistakes, satire or parody, and clearly identified partisan news and commentary. Portugal essentially transplanted that approach into statute but did not explicitly carve out illegal content.

The adoption and demise of the statutory fundamental right against disinformation must be read together. Article 6 of the Portuguese Charter of Human Rights in the Digital Age was passed amid post-2016 EU/US debates on election integrity and, domestically, in the wake of the pandemic information crisis. Although approved without opposition,[12] it quickly proved highly contentious. Shortly after promulgation, the President of the Republic referred Article 6 to the Constitutional Court, alleging a breach of the principle of legal certainty (determinability): the provision anchored State action against disinformation in vague, open-ended notions—such as "verifiably false or misleading narrative" and "threat to democratic political

[11] European Commission: Final Report of the Independent High-Level Group on Fake News and Online Disinformation. European Commission (12 March 2018). Available at: https://digital-strategy.ec.europa.eu/en/library/final-report-high-level-expert-group-fake-news-and-online-disinformation. Accessed 15 October 2025, p. 5; European Commission: Tackling Online Disinformation: A European Approach. COM(2018) 236 final, 26 April 2018. Available at: https://eur-lex.europa.eu/legal-content/EN/TXT/?uri=celex:52018DC0236. Accessed 15 October 2025, pp. 3–4; European Commission contribution to the European Council: Action Plan against Disinformation. JOIN(2018) 36 final, 5 December 2018. Available at: https://commission.europa.eu/system/files/2018-12/eu-communication-disinformation-euco-05122018_en.pdf. Accessed 15 October 2025, p. 2.

[12] Diário da Assembleia da República, I Série, 54 (9 April 2021), p. 95.

processes"—without specifying objective criteria or clear evidentiary thresholds; this indeterminacy thus failed to give addressees foreseeable guidance about the scope of the rule and the conduct liable to sanction, opening the door to arbitrary enforcement and a chilling, censorial effect incompatible with the constitutional right to freedom of expression.[13]

Amid sustained public criticism and pressure from several media-sector professional and union bodies,[14] Parliament decided not to wait for the Constitutional Court's ruling and instead repealed the operative parts of Article 6 of the Charter. Law 15/2022 revoked paragraphs 2–6, leaving only an amended paragraph 1 in force. The Constitutional Court later noted that the remaining provision is "emptied of meaning and practical utility",[15] amounting to little more than a general duty to implement the EU Action Plan against Disinformation, with no effective content of its own.

With the statutory text pared back, the Portuguese legal order baseline for disinformation is currently the media regulator's working definition, which ERC (Entidade Reguladora para a Comunicação Social) had already articulated in its 2019 study.[16] ERC adopts the EU/HLEG approach, rejects "fake news" as a catch-all label, and grounds "disinformation" in intentional deception plus risk of public harm, while expressly noting that content can be disinformation even if it is not illegal; conversely, clearly identified partisan news/commentary, mere errors and satire/parody are outside the scope of the concept.[17]

Despite the repeal of the bulk of Article 6 of the Charter, its substantive notion of "disinformation" effectively persists in Portuguese administrative practice through the media regulator's activity. Since 2019, ERC has applied a functional, EU-aligned

---

[13] Presidência da República: Artigo sexto da Carta Portuguesa dos Direitos Humanos na Era Digital (28 July 2021). Available at: https://www.presidencia.pt/atualidade/toda-a-atualidade/2021/07/artigo-sexto-da-carta-portuguesa-dos-direitos-humanos-na-era-digital/. Accessed 15 October 2025. See also: Reis, A. M.: Desinformação e liberdade de expressão. In M. A. de Almeida et al. (Eds.), Estudos em homenagem ao Professor Doutor João Caupers. Vol. I, Gestlegal, 2024, pp. 122–123.

[14] See the statements of the Journalist's Union (Sindicato dos Jornalistas: SJ questiona constitucionalidade do artigo 6.º da Carta dos Direitos Digitais (7 October 2020). Available at: https://jornalistas.eu/sj-questiona-constitucionalidade-do-artigo-6-o-da-carta-dos-direitos-digitais/. Accessed 15 October 2025) and the Press Card Commission (Comissão da Carteira Profissional de Jornalista: Carta Portuguesa de Direitos Humanos na Era Digital (30 June 2021). Available at: https://www.ccpj.pt/pt/deliberacoes/comunicados/carta-portuguesa-de-direitos-humanos-na-era-digital/. Accessed 15 October 2025) calling on the Ombudsperson and the Attorney-General's Office to request the constitutional review of Article 6 of the Charter, Melo Alexandrino, J.: Dez Apontamentos sobre a Carta Digital dos Direitos Humanos. ICJP/ CIDP (2021), p. 1, and Soares Farinho, D.: The Portuguese Charter of Fundamental Rights in the Digital Age: a legal appraisal. Revista Española de la Transparencia 13 (2021), pp. 96–102.

[15] Tribunal Constitucional: Case 66/2023 (7 March 2023), para. 8.

[16] Entidade Reguladora para a Comunicação Social: A Desinformação. Contexto Europeu e Nacional. ERC (2024). Available at: https://www.flipsnack.com/ercpt/estudo-a-desinforma-o-contexto-europeu-e-nacional/full-view.html. Accessed 15 October 2025.

[17] Entidade Reguladora para a Comunicação Social: A Desinformação. Contexto Europeu e Nacional. ERC (2024). Available at: https://www.flipsnack.com/ercpt/estudo-a-desinforma-o-contexto-europeu-e-nacional/full-view.html. Accessed 15 October 2025, pp. 1–2.

conception, operationalising it through enforcing sectoral media-law duties.[18] In short, the statutory fundamental right "to be protected against disinformation" disappeared, but the operative standard endures.

2.2 Distinction Between Close Concepts: Disinformation, Misinformation and Malinformation

In ERC's practice, disinformation is defined by intentional deception and risk of public harm. The regulator applies the concept by focusing on deceptive presentation. In particular, ERC has targeted pseudo-media and news-mimicry,[19] as well as the misuse of reputable outlets' graphics,[20] reinforcing that what matters is the presentation that deceives. This regulatory stance also covers cybersquatting or typosquatting practices—i.e. the registration of identical or deceptively similar (often misspelled) domain names to piggyback on trusted media brands and mislead users as to the origin of the content.

Misinformation (error without intent) falls outside the scope of disinformation and is dealt with as a breach of journalists' professional duties under media law rules. For example, ERC treated as accuracy/verification failures a television broadcast that aired a clip with fabricated subtitles as if true,[21] and another that presented videogame footage as real.[22] Both cases were framed as verification/sourcing breaches that *contribute* to disinformation risks but are not disinformation as such.[23]

Satire and opinion are likewise excluded unless they cross into deceptive impersonation or present fabrications as news. ERC made that explicit in 2025 when assessing Chega's (a populist political party) posts,[24] and earlier when it condemned a fake poll presented in TVI (a free-to-air television broadcaster) branding and the manipulative editing/re-packaging of real news footage.[25]

Malinformation (true information deliberately manipulated or presented out of context to cause harm) is not an autonomous category used by ERC: truthful, lawful content remains protected unless it crosses into illegality or deceptive presentation.

[18] See below Sect. 3.4.2.

[19] ERC/2019/111 (OUT-NET) (10 April 2019); ERC/2023/292 (CONTJOR-NET) (17 August 2023); ERC/2023/341 (OUT-NET) (20 September 2023).

[20] ERC/2023/317 (OUT) (30 August 2023).

[21] ERC/2023/129 (CONTJOR-TV) (13 April 2023).

[22] ERC/2022/282 (CONTJOR-TV) (7 September 2022); ERC/2022/346 (CONTJOR-TV) (19 October 2022).

[23] ERC/2023/129 (CONTJOR-TV) (13 April 2023), para. 67.

[24] ERC/2025/168 (OUT-NET) (14 May 2025) and ERC/2025/167 (OUT-NET) (14 May 2025).

[25] ERC/2024/83 (OUT-NET) (15 February 2024).

2.3 Application of the Notion of Disinformation in the Different Areas of the Portuguese Legal Order

In media law, the Press Law (Law 2/99) and the Journalist Statute (Law 1/99) impose professional duties of accuracy, verification, source identification and independence on journalists. The Television Law (Law 27/2007) adds format-transparency (news vs. opinion vs. advertising) and other editorial obligations. These are the benchmarks ERC uses in disinformation cases where intentionally deceptive, harm-prone material is packaged as journalism.

In electoral law, Law 72-A/2015 on media coverage during elections preserves editorial freedom but sets equity/balance duties for coverage, regulates commercial electoral advertising, and clarifies use of the internet and social media. These are yardsticks against which ERC can qualify deceptive, news-mimicking formats during pre-campaign and campaign periods. In parallel, Law 10/2000 governs opinion polls, requiring prior deposit with ERC, technical transparency and publication timing limits, a framework ERC drew on when classifying a fake "poll" styled in a broadcaster's look as disinformation intended to mislead voters.[26]

In private law, consumer protection/unfair commercial practices (Decree-Law 57/2008, transposing Directive 2005/29/EC) prohibit misleading actions/omissions and blacklist covert advertising and kindred practices. The Advertising Code (Decree-Law 330/90) likewise bans misleading advertising and disguised advertorials. These instruments cover the market-facing layer of disinformation, prohibiting deception irrespective of political content.

For intermediaries and platforms, Decree-Law 7/2004 (e-commerce) requires identification of commercial communications and provides conditional liability shields (mere conduit, caching, hosting), shaping notice-and-action routes when disinformation overlaps illegal content. Since February 2024, the Digital Services Act (DSA) applies EU-wide; Portugal's Decree-Law 20-B/2024 designates ANACOM as Digital Services Coordinator and ERC as a competent authority for media-content matters, adding systemic-risk and transparency duties (including on recommender systems and ad transparency) that widen the public-law toolkit for tackling disinformation. However, Portugal has been referred to the Court of Justice by the European Commission in an infringement procedure for failing to properly implement the DSA, in particular for not granting the Digital Services Coordinator sufficient powers to effectively carry out its tasks.[27]

Finally, Law 82/2021 creates a fast-track administrative notice-and-action mechanism, led by IGAC (the copyright authority), for removal or blocking of online content that infringes copyright. This route can be used where a deceitful item also reproduces or communicates copyright-protected works.

---

[26] ERC/2024/83 (OUT-NET) (15 February 2024).

[27] European Commission: May infringements package: key decisions (Infringement Procedure INFR(2024)2038). Available at: https://ec.europa.eu/commission/presscorner/detail/en/inf_25_982. Accessed 15 October 2025.

In data protection law, the General Data Protection Regulation (GDPR) (Regulation (EU) 2016/679) offers tools that incidentally curb disinformation tactics that rely on unlawful personal data processing (e.g., scraping, covert profiling and political micro-targeting).

Across these regimes, criminal (e.g., defamation) and civil law (general torts, personality rights) remain available where disinformation overlaps illegalities and/or causes individualised harm, while rights of reply/rectification and ERC's sectoral powers provide corrective remedies within the media framework.

2.4 *Specificity (if Any) of Online Disinformation*

"Online" describes the amplification mechanics (scale, speed, algorithmic ranking, inauthentic coordination), not a constitutive element of the concept of disinformation. Neither Portuguese legislation nor case law sets a special, standalone category of online disinformation. In practice, however, the media regulator (ERC) applies a medium-neutral concept of disinformation while providing specific attention to online affordances, especially news-mimicking/brand-impersonation in social media,[28] and pseudo-media sites that imitate news packaging.[29] Portuguese courts have also recognised the online dynamic: the Évora Court of Appeal observed that social-media publications "abound unchecked, are rapidly republished, causing confusion between the true, the opinionated and the false, with often irreparable consequences to those targeted", underscoring why speed, virality and format deception matter when analysing public-harm risk.[30]

2.5 *The Relevance of Illegal Contents on the Definition*

Illegality is not a constitutive element of disinformation in Portuguese administrative practice. In ERC's working concept (aligned with the EU/HLEG approach), content can qualify as disinformation even when it is lawful: what matters is verifiable falsity or misleadingness, intent to deceive (or profit), and being liable to cause public harm, with errors, clearly identified partisan news and commentary and satire/parody excluded. Conversely, when a piece of content is illegal, that illegality is addressed under specific legal regimes without needing the disinformation label. This separation is visible in enforcement: a fabricated "poll" may be disinformation and breach poll-deposit and transparency duties; a deceptive post that reproduces broadcaster

[28] ERC/2023/317 (OUT) (30 August 2023), ERC/2025/167 (OUT-NET) (14 May 2025), ERC/2025/168 (OUT-NET) (14 May 2025).

[29] ERC/2019/111 (OUT-NET) (10 April 2019), ERC/2023/292 (CONTJOR-NET) (17 August 2023), ERC/2023/341 (OUT-NET) (20 September 2023).

[30] Évora Court of Appeal (4 June 2024) (Case 2732/22.3T9STB.E1).

footage/graphics can be removed under copyright rules, but the takedown hinges on infringement, not on the message's misleading nature.

3 The Sources of Law

3.1 Constitutional Law

The Portuguese Constitution protects freedom of expression and information (Article 37), freedom of the press and the media (Article 38), and entrusts an independent administrative entity with safeguarding the right to information and press freedom (Article 39). These guarantees frame any response to disinformation: prior restraints and any other form of censorship are prohibited (Article 37(2)), while ex post responsibilities, including rights of reply/rectification and civil and criminal liability (Article 37(3)-(4)), operate within ordinary law and under independent regulatory oversight (Article 39).

3.2 EU Law and Its Implementation

Portugal's EU-derived framework tackles disinformation through complementary regimes that set duties for platforms and media outlets while preserving freedom of expression.

The e-commerce law (Decree-Law 7/2004, transposing Directive 2000/31/EC) states that intermediaries are not subject to a general monitoring obligation (Article 12) and sets conditional liability exemptions for mere conduit, caching, and hosting (Articles 14–16). Hosts must act expeditiously once they have actual knowledge of manifestly illegal content (Article 16), and service providers must promptly comply with orders from competent authorities (Article 13). This is the legal basis for notice-and-action against clearly unlawful disinformation. The statute also provides a fast, 48-hour provisional dispute-resolution route before the sector supervisor to assess manifest illegality (Article 18), plus reinforced duties introduced later: immediate reporting to the Public Prosecutor when detected content may constitute certain crimes (Article 19-A) and 48-hour blocking duties for child sexual abuse material and grave violations of sexual or bodily privacy (Article 19-B).

Decree-Law 20-B/2024 designates ANACOM as the Digital Services Coordinator and identifies ERC (for media) and IGAC (for copyright) as competent authorities (Article 2), and imposes a general duty to collaborate and comply with their orders (Article 3), creating a national framework to enforce the Digital Services Act (DSA) (Regulation (EU) 2022/2065). This matters for disinformation because very large platforms must assess and mitigate systemic risks (DSA, Articles 34–35), such as coordinated manipulative campaigns, recommender-system amplification of proven falsehoods, or deceptive account networks, which the Portuguese authorities can audit and supervise.

Audiovisual media rules also reach into platform spaces: the AVMS (Directive 2018/1808)-based Television Law (Law 27/2007) extends to video-sharing platform services, requiring providers to embed in their terms and conditions measures against illegal content and content harmful to minors, offer user reporting/flagging and feedback mechanisms, ensure clear identifiability/labelling of commercial communications and provide parental controls (Article 69-C). Compliance is supervised by ERC (Article 69-D).

Decree-Law 57/2008 (Unfair Commercial Practices), which transposes Directive 2005/29/EC, connects directly to "commercial disinformation": it prohibits misleading actions and omissions (Articles 7 and 8), and blacklists practices such as covert advertorials, pretending to be a consumer/astroturfing, and fake or manipulated reviews/endorsements (Annex I of Directive 2005/29/EC).

The GDPR is also relevant where disinformation involves the collection and processing of personal data, targeted amplification, or profiling. The regulation is implemented in Portugal by Law 58/2019, of 8 August, which confers powers on the national data protection authority (Comissão Nacional de Proteção de Dados - CNPD) for supervision, investigation, and corrective measures.

3.3 Legislative Acts

The Digital Rights Charter (Law 27/2021) briefly introduced a "right to protection against disinformation" in Article 6; after Law 15/2022 repealed paragraphs 2–6, only paragraph 1 remains and does not create stand-alone enforcement. Disinformation is thus handled through the general media, advertising, civil/criminal, and regulatory legal frameworks set out below.

The Press Law (Law 2/99) and the Journalist Statute (Law 1/99) supply the day-to-day guardrails that ERC and courts use to separate journalism from deceptive, news-mimicking content. The Press Law guarantees rights of reply and rectification (Articles 24–27 and 32(a)), prohibits disguised advertising by requiring clear identification of ads (Article 28), and anchors civil/criminal liability for unlawful content published via the press (Articles 29–30). The Journalist Statute hard-wires professional duties—rigour and impartiality, separation of facts from opinion, avoidance of unproven accusations and respect for the presumption of innocence (Article 14)—while protecting source confidentiality (Article 11) and safeguarding independence via the clause of conscience (Article 12). Both legal instruments are the levers used to qualify and remedy disinformation when it is packaged as journalism.

The ERC Statutes (Law 53/2005) provide the regulatory backbone. ERC is mandated to promote pluralism and protect the rights to information and press freedom (Article 8), empowered to supervise and sanction (Article 24 and 64), and adjudicate reply/rectification disputes (Articles 59–60), as well as the power to issue non-binding recommendations guiding good practice (Article 63(3)).

In electoral periods, Law 72-A/2015 adds targeted safeguards that curb manipulative messaging. It preserves editorial freedom but requires balanced, representative and equitable coverage (Articles 4 and 6), suspends certain regular opinion slots by candidates to prevent undue influence (Article 5(3)), and bans political propaganda via commercial advertising from the calling of elections, subject to limited exceptions (Article 10). In parallel, Law 10/2000 (opinion polls) requires prior deposit of any poll with ERC and publication accompanied by a technical fiche, with disclosure only lawful after deposit.

Law 82/2021 provides a fast removal/blocking route alongside media-law tools by equipping IGAC with a streamlined, court supported blocking procedure against the unlawful online availability of copyright-protected works, which becomes relevant when fabricated or manipulated media (e.g., deepfakes, stolen footage) also infringe copyright.

The Advertising Code (Decree-Law 330/90) ensures recognisability and truthfulness and bans covert or misleading ads (Articles 7–11), with protections for minors (Article 14) and rules on testimonials/comparatives (Articles 15–16). It directly addresses "commercial disinformation," influencer deception and fake endorsements dressed up as editorial content.

Finally, general liability regimes remain the safety net. The Criminal Code covers crimes against honour (e.g. defamation (Article 180) and insult (Article 181)), discrimination and incitement to hatred or violence (Article 240), public incitement to commit a crime and apology of crime (Articles 297–298), and, where forged materials are used, falsification of documents (Article 256). The Civil Code provides extra-contractual liability (Article 483) and specific protection of reputation/good name (Article 484), while personality-rights provisions allow preventive/cessation measures (Article 70) and non-pecuniary damages (Article 496).

3.4 *The Role of Case Law*

3.4.1 Courts

The Constitutional Court's Case 66/2023 (7 March 2023) unfortunately ended without a merits ruling on the scope of the fundamental right to protection against disinformation. After Law 15/2022 repealed most of Article 6 of the Digital Rights Charter, the Court declined to proceed with an abstract review and expressly noted there was no publicly known record of ERC having sanctioned disinformation under that clause.

Supreme Court case law reinforces that press freedom does not immunise false factual assertions. In the decision of 8 May 2013,[31] the Court held that freedom of the press or of opinion cannot prevail where reported facts are false, equivocal,

[31] Case 1486/03.7TVLSB.L1.S1.

mere suspicions or rumours. This sets a high-level benchmark against which "news-mimicking" disinformation is weighed, especially when content is packaged as fact. On 24 May 2022,[32] the Supreme Court held that a TV broadcaster is liable for airing a false on-screen caption (lower-third) stating that the plaintiff had been detained. Liability arises even if the individual author of the caption is not identified, because the broadcaster controls the message it puts on air. This maps neatly onto common disinformation patterns: brief, highly visible graphics can implant a false factual claim, and outlets remain responsible for the accuracy of those on-air presentations.

Recent appellate case law addresses online virality head-on. The Évora Court of Appeal (4 June 2024[33]) described how social media posting, facilitated by "being behind a screen," proliferates rapidly and is republished in ways that blur the line between truth, opinion and falsehood, often with irreparable consequences for targets. This is directly relevant to online disinformation: the court's reasoning acknowledges scale, speed and re-sharing as aggravating dynamics and supports urgent corrective and compensatory remedies when defamatory or otherwise unlawful falsehoods spread through network effects.

The Lisbon Court of Appeal (19 June 2019[34]) insisted that media, as vehicles of the right to information, are bound by accuracy and truth. The court rejected the argument that citing "reliable sources" suffices, warning that otherwise the right to information would invert into a public duty to accept disinformation. This ruling is directly relevant to online disinformation because it rejects "we just quoted a reliable source" as a defence in fast, hybrid formats (e.g. tweets embedded in articles, quick rewrites, shorts with captions, viral clips). If a media outlet presents a claim as fact, it must still verify core elements (who/what/when/where), check the provenance of images/video, label unverified material, and correct promptly and prominently (not via stealth edits). Otherwise, it risks laundering upstream falsehoods and becoming liable for spreading disinformation.

Systematic judicial coverage is limited because Portugal does not provide open, comprehensive online access to first-instance court decisions, and appellate publications remain selective. The cited rulings nonetheless sketch a consistent approach: strong protection for expression and press, coupled with liability when fabricated or unverified facts are presented as true, an approach that translates naturally to the mechanics and risks of online disinformation.

3.4.2 Supervisory Authorities (ERC)

The most consequential strand of ERC cases regarding online disinformation targets impersonation of trusted news brands. In ERC/2024/83 (15 Feb 2024), ERC held that posting an image in a TV channel's visual identity to promote a fake poll is disinformation because it parasitically exploits the outlet's reputation to make fabricated

[32] Case 14,570/16.8T8LSB.L1.S1.

[33] Case 2732/22.3T9STB.E1.

[34] Case 7623/14.9TDLSB.L1-3.

claims look credible. A similar argument was stated in ERC/2023/317 (30 Aug 2023), which clarified that using a reputable outlet's look-and-feel to lend credibility to false claims may itself constitute disinformation. These rulings speak directly to platform-native tactics, namely cheap fakes and screenshot "graphics" that weaponise familiar branding to deceive at scale.

A second cluster of cases concerns websites that mimic news while disseminating fabrications. ERC identified such behaviour in ERC/2019/111 (10 Apr 2019) and returned to it with more detailed findings in ERC/2023/292 (17 Aug 2023) and ERC/2023/341 (20 Sep 2023), each addressing websites that operate under a news veneer while pushing fabricated narratives. This is central to the online ecosystem, where pseudo-news portals are shared as "sources", and then recycled by influencers or micro-outlets.

ERC has also sanctioned verification failures that put fabricated or manipulated material on air as real. ERC/2022/346 (19 Oct 2022) involved video-game footage broadcast as if depicting real events. ERC/2023/129 (13 Apr 2023) found that airing a social-media clip with satirical, fabricated subtitles as true breached journalists' duties of rigour, source identification, and verification and amounted to disseminating disinformation. These decisions map cleanly onto virality dynamics online: quick takes, stitched clips, and captioned shorts can launder hoaxes unless provenance checks and clear labelling are enforced before amplification.

Because "anti-misinformation" content can itself mislead if sloppy, ERC drew guardrails for fact-checking formats. ERC/2019/288 (16 Oct 2019) set limits for broadcast fact-checks (they must still meet editorial standards and protection-of-minors rules), and ERC/2021/151 (12 May 2021) required accuracy and source diversification, and not reliance on a single expert. The message is that calling a piece a "fact-check" does not relax the legal standards when you present facts to the audience, online or on air.

ERC has also policed everyday editorial practices that can enable disinformation when they erode transparency. ERC/2023/466 (20 Dec 2023) criticised TV reporting that asserted facts without source identification, and ERC/2023/414 (15 Nov 2023) balanced headline freedom against the risk of misleading framings. Applied online, where click-optimised titles, unlabelled embeds, and context-free captions are common, these principles help curb false impressions even when the underlying article is more nuanced.

On elections and polling, ERC flagged a distinct risk vector: fabricated "polls" on social media during electoral periods. In May 2025 it warned of their high disinformative potential and opened inquiries.[35] Applying Law 10/2000, ERC then initiated administrative proceedings after finding a Chega political party post publicising an opinion survey without the mandatory Article 8(2) disclaimer that such a survey does not allow scientific generalisation and reflect only respondents' opinions (ERC/2025/292 and ERC/2025/298, both 10 Sept 2025; ERC/2025/301, 18 Sept 2025).

[35] Entidade Reguladora para a Comunicação Social: ERC alerta para a circulação de falsas sondagens nas redes sociais (9 May 2025). Available at: https://www.erc.pt/pt/a-erc/noticias/erc-alerta-para-a-circulacao-de-falsas-sondagens-nas-redes-sociais-/. Accessed 15 October 2025.

Finally, ERC has clarified the boundary between protected opinion/satire and deceptive formats. ERC/2020/175 (16 Sept 2020) and ERC/2022/92 (23 Mar 2022) emphasised that opinion and satire are not disinformation per se, but when factual premises are presented as facts they must be true. Later decisions—ERC/2025/167 (14 May 2025) and ERC/2025/168 (14 May 2025)—reaffirmed that pure opinion and political mobilisation messages are protected, while impersonation of news brands or the presentation of fabricated facts as true can draw regulatory guidance or censure.

3.5 *The Impact of Soft Law*

3.5.1 Codes of Conduct

The Journalists' Code of Ethics turns broad legal duties into newsroom practice by requiring accuracy and verification and a clear split between news and opinion (Articles 1 and 2), prompt corrections of false or inaccurate material (Article 5), and transparent, responsible use of sources, including not serving as a channel for falsehoods and clearly attributing opinions (Article 7). It also reinforces respect for the presumption of innocence and protection of vulnerable people (Article 8), and sets privacy safeguards and independence/conflict-of-interest rules that reduce hidden commercial or personal biases (Articles 10 and 11). In the online context, where headlines, captions and short clips travel faster than full articles, these operational norms (provenance checks on images/video, clear labelling, visible corrections) are the front-line guardrails that keep hoaxes from being laundered as news.

3.5.2 Other Acts

The Government's National Media Literacy Plan 2025–2029 (PNLM[36]) builds a preventive track against disinformation and "fake news". It designates #PortugalMediaLab—the Government's mission structure for media policy, tasked with coordinating and implementing PNLM activities—as implementing coordinator and sets hard monitoring deadlines: by 31 October each year it must submit the next year's activity proposal, and by 31 March it must file a public annual execution report (with a final evaluation due by 30 April 2029). The plan's anti-disinformation strand prioritises ethical journalism, strengthening fact-checking networks, and nationwide campaigns via public and private media (including local and regional outlets), as well as social influencers, celebrities and content creators so literacy content reaches a wide audience. To bolster accountability, PNLM commits to publishing annual progress reports, supporting research, and maintaining a central website as a transparency hub; it also provides for the participation of GILM (*Grupo Informal sobre*

[36] Approved by Resolution of the Council of Ministers of the Portuguese Government 65/2025 (18 March).

Literacia Mediática)—a long-standing, multi-stakeholder network created in 2009 to promote media education—to accompany execution and contribute to monitoring and evaluation.

4 The Reporting Procedure

4.1 The Abandoned ERC Disinformation Reporting Procedure

Portugal briefly created, then repealed, a bespoke channel for reporting disinformation to the media regulator. In the Portuguese Charter of Human Rights in the Digital Age (Law 27/2021), Article 6(5) granted any person a right to lodge complaints with the media regulator (ERC) against entities that engage in disinformation as defined in Article 6(2)-(4), remitting complaint/decision procedures and the sanctioning regime to ERC's statute. Article 6(6) tasked the State with supporting fact-checking structures created by duly registered media and encouraging the awarding of quality labels by reliable entities with public-utility status. Both paragraphs were revoked by Law 15/2022, leaving only the programmatic Article 6(1) without its own enforcement track.

The legislator's original intent was to give teeth to the "right to protection against disinformation" by coupling a complaint route to ERC with incentives for fact-checking. Citizens could complain to ERC about narratives presented as news but consisting of false or misleading content designed to cause public harm or obtain profit, and the State was to promote media truthfulness by encouraging fact-checking and the awarding of quality labels.

Once the Charter was in force, the governing Socialist Party parliamentary group tabled a bill to operationalise Article 6(6).[37] The proposal restricted public funding support to fact-checking units created by media registered with ERC, barred any State interference in their organisation, methodology or publication, required adherence to international fact-checking principles, and excluded eligibility where public bodies had dominant influence. It also encouraged quality labels to be granted by cultural public-utility entities and identified sector associations that could run such schemes, positioning seals as recognition of service quality rather than State arbitration of truth. The explanatory memorandum of the bill insisted that fact-checking should not belong to any State department and framed the Charter as empowering citizens and independent media, not public authorities.

The model was abandoned amid widespread criticism. In June 2022, the Ombudsman petitioned the Constitutional Court to review Article 6(5)–(6) of the Charter, arguing that the envisioned State intervention in tackling disinformation

[37] Assembleia da República: Projeto de Lei n.º 884/XIV/2.ª (22 June 2021).

posed disproportionate risks to freedom of expression and of the press, and that a generic disinformation complaint procedure lacked solid support in ERC's statute.[38]

ERC itself flagged structural problems in three legal opinions on the Charter submitted to the Portuguese parliament.[39] The regulator warned (i) against vague or expansive definitions of disinformation migrating into enforcement,[40] (ii) cautioned that routing generic disinformation complaints to ERC risked mission-creep from media-law oversight into general truth-policing,[41] (iii) insisted that interventions remain strictly ex post, consistent with the constitutional ban on prior restraints, rather than enabling preventive truth-arbitration,[42] and (iv) urged great care with State-proximate quality labels or publicly supported fact-checking, which could chill lawful speech or look like State-endorsed truth arbitration.[43]

The public debate in the press and Parliament was equally sharp. Critics across the spectrum portrayed the complaint track and the seals scheme as edging toward "state fact-checking" or a "Ministry of Truth",[44] arguing that even indirect State involvement in certifying quality news could amount to censorship by proxy, skew pluralism and chill dissent.[45] Supporters countered that it placed fact-checking in independent newsrooms, ring-fenced it from State control and relied on public-utility bodies for any labels.[46]

The optics nevertheless proved decisive. With Law 15/2022 removing the contested provisions, Portugal reverted to its ordinary toolkit to tackle disinformation rather than a stand-alone, ERC-run specific complaint and certification scheme.

[38] Provedor de Justiça: Provedora de Justiça requer fiscalização da constitucionalidade de normas da Carta Portuguesa de Direitos Humanos na Era Digital (2 June 2022). Available at https://www.provedor-jus.pt/provedora-de-justica-requer-fiscalizacao-da-constitucionalidade-de-normas-da-carta-portuguesa-de-direitos-humanos-na-era-digital/. Accessed 15 October 2025.

[39] ERC/2021/208 (14 July 2021), ERC/2021/221 (4 August 2021), and ERC/2022/195 (21 September 2022).

[40] ERC/2021/208 (14 July 2021), paras. 5–8; ERC/2021/221 (4 August 2021), paras. 13–18; ERC/2022/195 (21 September 2022), paras. 10 and 13–14.

[41] ERC/2021/208 (14 July 2021), paras. 6–9 and 16–18; ERC/2022/195 (21 September 2022), paras. 10 and 15.

[42] ERC/2021/208 (14 July 2021), paras. 5 and 7–9.

[43] ERC/2021/208 (14 July 2021), paras. 12–15, 19 and 22–29; ERC/2021/221 (4 August 2021), paras. 8–9 and 20; ERC/2022/195 (21 September 2022), paras. 8–12.

[44] Barreto, A.: A Inquisição, a Censura e o Estado. Público (29 May 2021). Available at: https://www.publico.pt/2021/05/29/opiniao/opiniao/inquisicao-censura-estado-1964526. Accessed 15 October 2025, Pacheco Pereira, J.: A aliança entre os censores e os que assinam de cruz. Público (29 May 2021). Available at: https://www.publico.pt/2021/05/29/opiniao/opiniao/alianca-censores-assinam-cruz-1964490. Accessed 15 October 2025, and Barata-Feyo, J.M.: A censura má e a censura boa. Público (29 May 2021). Available at: https://www.publico.pt/2021/05/29/opiniao/opiniao/censura-ma-censura-boa-1964302. Accessed 15 October 2025.

[45] João Cotrim de Figueiredo (IL): Diário da Assembleia da República, I Série, 89 (21 July 2021), p. 7.

[46] José Magalhães (PS): Diário da Assembleia da República, I Série, 89 (21 July 2021), p. 14.

4.2 *Reporting Procedure and Other Ways to Tackle Online Disinformation*

Portugal no longer has a single, general "anti-disinformation" act. Instead, several content-neutral frameworks apply across online and offline contexts: media/press duties and remedies, unfair commercial practices and advertising rules, data protection rules, civil and criminal law liability, and platform-governance via the e-commerce law and the DSA's national set-up. Together they curb misleading formats, require transparency for commercial speech, and provide ex-post remedies (reply/rectification, damages, sanctions), without instituting prior restraints or a truth-policing authority.

4.2.1 Subjects Who Can Report

Private individuals may (i) flag allegedly illegal content to online platforms via the DSA mechanisms that require hosting services to provide "notice and action" tools (Article 16 DSA), give recipients access to an internal complaint-handling system for platform decisions (Article 20 DSA), and allow any natural or legal person to lodge a complaint with the national Digital Services Coordinator (Article 53 DSA). They may also benefit from priority handling when reporting through certified trusted flaggers designated under Article 22 DSA. They may (ii) complain to ERC about content from registered media—press, radio, television and their online editions—under the ERC Statute (Article 55). They may (iii) complain to the National Election Commission (CNE) during pre-campaign and campaign under Law 72-A/2015 (Article 9) and raise issues about opinion polls under Law 10/2000 (Article 13). They may (iv) notify IGAC when the same item also infringes copyright, triggering the administrative blocking/removal route in Law 82/2021 (Article 3). They may (v) report misleading commercial practices or advertising to ASAE and, for advertising-specific matters, the Direção-Geral do Consumidor (DGC), which enforce Decree-Law 57/2008 and the Advertising Code. They may (vi) report infringements of data protection law to the Data Protection Authority where the content involves personal data. They may also (vii) lodge criminal complaints with the Public Prosecutor or police for relevant offences in the Criminal Code (Article 242 of the Criminal Procedure Code) and, where appropriate, pursue civil liability actions under the Civil Code.

Public authorities may also initiate proceedings within their remits: ANACOM as the national DSA coordinator for DSA oversight (Article 51 DSA), ERC under Law 53/2005 for media supervision and sanctions, CNE under Law 72-A/2015 during electoral periods, IGAC under Law 82/2021 on copyright blocking/removal (Article 3), and ASAE and, for advertising, the DGC under Decree-Law 57/2008 and Decree-Law 330/90 for unfair practices and advertising. For personal-data issues, CNPD exercises corrective powers over data controllers/processors.

Consumer associations/NGOs may act or report under the class action law (Law 83/95, of 31 August).

4.2.2 Subjects Who Decide on the Report

Private entities decide on user reports via the DSA mechanisms, namely the hosting services' notice-and-action (Article 16 DSA) and, for online platforms, the internal complaint-handling system (Article 20 DSA). They must also comply with authority orders against specific illegal content (Article 9 DSA). Trusted flagger notices must receive priority processing (Article 22 DSA).

In the media sector, ERC decides complaints about registered press, radio and television services (including their online editions), exercising supervision and sanctioning powers under its Statute (Articles 8 and 24) and the Television Law's video-sharing rules (Article 69-D). During pre-campaign and campaign periods, the CNE adjudicates complaints about media coverage and electoral messaging under Law 72-A/2015. Where copyright is also infringed, IGAC may order removal/blocking under Law 82/2021 (Article 3). For misleading commercial practices and advertising, ASAE (and, for advertising matters, the DGC) is the decision-maker in administrative-offence proceedings under Decree-Law 57/2008 and the Advertising Code. In data protection matters, CNPD decides complaints and may order rectification/erasure and other corrective measures against data controllers/processors. Outside these sectoral routes, Decree-Law 7/2004 (e-commerce) frames provider duties, safe harbours and cooperation with authorities, and includes a 48-hour provisional dispute-resolution mechanism before the supervisory authority where illegality is not manifest (Article 18). Self/co-regulatory bodies (e.g., newsroom ombudsmen) provide soft-law correction avenues.

Courts may also be called to adjudicate. Civil courts decide on the protection of personality rights, rights of reply and rectification, and claims for damages under the Press Law and the Civil Code. Criminal courts adjudicate offences such as defamation, insult and incitement or apology of crimes. Administrative courts rule on challenges to administrative decisions, namely those issued by ERC.

4.2.3 Means to Establish the Falsehood of the Contents and the Related Responsibilities

The now revoked Article 6(3) of the Portuguese Charter of Human Rights in the Digital Age listed as "false information elements" the use of manipulated or fabricated texts or videos, inbox-flooding and fake-followers networks; while non-operative today, it usefully frames the artefacts decision-makers still look for when assessing falsehood.

On the platforms' side, falsehood is first screened against the e-commerce standard that ties hosting liability to knowledge and (non-)manifest illegality (Article 16 of Decree-Law 7/2004), and—where illegality is not manifest—allows referral to the supervisory authority for a provisional decision within 48 hours (Article 18).

In the media sector, ERC establishes falsehood by testing content against legally binding journalistic benchmarks (verification, rigour, source identification, separation of fact/opinion) and by checking whether manipulated/fabricated material or brand-impersonation was presented as true. ERC's case practice shows the method: in one case, a satirical clip with fabricated subtitles was aired as fact[47]; in another, an image mimicked a TV channel's visual identity to display invented poll results.[48] For video-sharing platforms, ERC checks compliance with AVMS measures (e.g., flagging/reporting channels, protection-of-minors tools), while the truth/falsity analysis still follows the underlying legal tests where applicable.

During pre-campaign and campaign, the CNE treats as false or misleading electoral "information elements" that fail statutory yardsticks, most concretely, opinion polls that were not deposited or lack mandatory technical data. These obligations apply regardless of medium, including online polls and publication on social media or websites. Silence-period/day-of-reflection rules also apply online to electoral propaganda, with enforcement routed (CNE to ERC) as provided by law.

For commercial claims and advertising, ASAE and, for advertising matters, the DGC determine deception by applying the "average consumer" test, information-duty rules and blacklisted practices. They can demand substantiation of factual claims, order precautionary measures (temporary cessation or prohibition of imminent practices) and prosecute administrative-offence proceedings. Advertising self-regulation may issue non-binding copy-advice and decisions guiding quick corrections.

If the same content also unlawfully communicates protected works, IGAC can establish the infringement irrespective of truth claims by verifying the unauthorised use of copyrighted material and order removal or blocking, acting ex officio or on complaint. Where personal data are processed, CNPD can establish infringements and require rectification/erasure, including search-result delisting where criteria are met.

Courts make the definitive findings of falsehood where rights or crimes are at stake. Civil courts assess evidence to grant reply/rectification and award damages for unlawful attacks on reputation or other personality rights, ordering cessation or correction where appropriate. Criminal courts determine falsity and intent for honour offences, public incitement/apology of crime, and forgery where fabricated materials or documents are used.

Across all fora, responsibilities track mandates: ERC, CNE, ASAE/DGC, CNPD and IGAC verify falsity or other legal unlawfulness within their legal tests and adopt measures or sanctions; the courts adjudicate liability and remedies on the evidentiary record.

4.2.4 Deadlines for the Decision

Under the DSA, certified out-of-court dispute-settlement bodies must make their decisions available to the parties within a reasonable period and no later than 90 calendar days from receipt of the complaint; for highly complex disputes, they may

47 ERC/2023/129 (CONTJOR-TV) (13 April 2023).

48 ERC/2024/83 (OUT-NET) (15 February 2024).

extend once for up to a further 90 days (Article 21). Platforms' internal complaint-handling systems must accept complaints for at least six months from the day the user is informed of the original moderation decision (Article 20(1)–(2)); the DSA otherwise requires timely handling but sets no fixed decision day-count for the internal system.

Under the e-commerce law, when illegality is not manifest in hosting/association cases, the supervisory authority must issue a provisional decision within 48 hours (Article 18(2) of Decree-Law 7/2004). In addition, intermediaries must block within 48 hours the sites on official child-sexual-abuse or intimate-privacy abuse lists (Article 19-B(1) of Decree-Law 7/2004).

Under the IGAC copyright fast-track, the alleged infringer has 48 hours after IGAC's notice to cease availability; failing that, IGAC can go straight to intermediaries in urgent cases (Article 3(1) and 3(5)(a)), and, outside those urgencies, IGAC has a maximum of 10 days to practise the acts foreseen in the law (Article 4(3)). Intermediaries notified by IGAC must comply within 48 hours (Article 5(1)). Urgent blocking measures last no more than 48 hours; other measures may last up to one year (Article 6(1)(a)–(b)).

In the press, the right of reply/rectification must be exercised within 30 days for dailies/weekly papers or 60 days for less frequent publications (Article 25(1) of the Press Law). Once the text is delivered, publication must occur within two days (daily), in the first issue printed after the second day (weekly), or in the first issue distributed after the seventh day (others) (Article 26(2)). If the outlet refuses, it must notify the refusal and reasons within three days (daily) or ten days (weekly or less frequent) after receipt (Article 26(7)). If the right is not satisfied or is unjustifiably refused, the interested party has 10 days to go to court; the media outlet editor then has two days to contest, and the judge decides within the following two days; if the request is granted, publication follows the same Article 26(2) timeframes (Article 27(1)–(4)).

In television and on-demand audiovisual media services, the right of reply/rectification must be exercised within 20 days after the broadcast (Article 67(1) of the Television Law). Transmission of the reply/rectification is, as a rule, made within 24 hours of delivery of the text to the operator (Article 69(1)). If the operator refuses, it must notify the refusal and its reasons within 24 hours of receiving the reply (Article 68(1)).

ERC has a general 30-day duty to decide (Article 58(1) of ERC Statute). For decisions ordering a reply/rectification, right of airtime or political reply, the addressee must comply within the time fixed by ERC or, if none is set, within 48 hours of notification; for non-daily publications, in the first edition finalised after notification (Article 60(1)). Articles 59–60 frame the expedited oversight/appeal mechanics specific to these remedies.

During pre-campaign and campaign, complaints on media coverage are filed with the CNE, which must send them to ERC within 48 hours (Article 9 of Law 72-A/2015). ERC then decides under its own framework.

4.2.5 Forms of Protection for the Authors of Allegedly Illegal Content or Disinformation

Authors benefit from constitutional guarantees of freedom of expression and information (Article 37, including the ban on censorship/prior restraints in Article 37(2)) and freedom of the press and media (Article 38), together with access to law and effective judicial protection (Article 20).

In platform contexts, the DSA requires a statement of reasons whenever content is restricted or removed (Article 17), and gives authors two built-in avenues to contest: the platform's internal complaint-handling system (Article 20) and certified out-of-court dispute settlement (Article 21), without prejudice to lodging a complaint with the Digital Services Coordinator (Article 53) or going to court.

In the hosting/e-commerce track, when illegality is not manifest, the 48-hour provisional mechanism in Decree-Law 7/2004 (Article 18) is an administrative assessment rather than final adjudication, preserving full challenge before the administrative courts.

Before ERC, parties targeted by supervisory or sanctioning proceedings have procedural rights to prior hearing and defence, access to the file, reasoned decisions, and appeal to the administrative courts; in reply/rectification disputes, ERC decisions ordering publication or transmission bind the outlet's timing but remain reviewable. During pre-campaign and campaign, complaints filed with the CNE are forwarded to ERC; authors and outlets keep the same defence and appeal guarantees before ERC and the courts, with the compressed calendar affecting only compliance windows, not the availability of review.

In unfair-commercial-practice and advertising cases, ASAE and, for advertising, the DGC must run administrative-offence proceedings under the general misdemeanours regime, which guarantees the right to be heard, to present evidence and substantiation for claims, to reasoned decisions, and to full judicial appeal on the merits (including proportionality review of sanctions). Precautionary orders (e.g., temporary cessation) are contestable and subject to judicial oversight. Advertising self-regulation allows voluntary correction without prejudice to legal defence.

In the copyright fast-track, IGAC's 48-hour notices and intermediary orders preserve the addressee's ability to contest the underlying order and to seek judicial protection.

Where personal data are involved, data subjects retain GDPR rights. They may lodge a complaint with the CNPD (Article 77 GDPR) and seek effective judicial remedies against controllers/processors (Article 79) and against the supervisory authority (Article 78). CNPD decisions are judicially reviewable.

Across civil and criminal litigation, authors retain substantive and procedural protections. Journalists additionally benefit from professional-duty frameworks, including source protection and professional secrecy.

4.2.6 Sanctions in Case of Detection of Disinformation

Sanctions depend on the legal track that the disinformation triggers. In the media track, ERC may adopt supervisory measures and impose administrative sanctions under its Statute where registered press, radio or television services breach media-law duties. ERC can also order corrective remedies such as reply/rectification or transmissions, and issue recommendations guiding good practice (Article 24). During pre-campaign and campaign, complaints are channelled via the CNE but decisions and sanctions on media coverage ultimately sit with ERC under the sector framework.

Dissemination of false statements that injure reputation or other personality rights may ground compensation for damages (including non-pecuniary) and cessation/correction orders under the Civil Code, together with Press Law remedies of reply/rectification and publication obligations. Criminal sanctions apply where the conduct fits offences.

ASAE and, for advertising matters, the DGC may order precautionary measures and bring administrative-offence proceedings that can result in fines and ancillary measures, applying Decree-Law 57/2008 (Arts. 19–21) together with the Advertising Code (Decree-Law 330/90, notably Arts. 7–11). Advertising self-regulatory bodies may request voluntary withdrawal/correction.

Where the disinformation piggybacks on unlawful use of protected works, IGAC can order removal or blocking and, in urgent cases, impose short-lived blocking measures (Arts. 3, 5 and 6 of Law 82/2021).

For online intermediaries, the e-commerce law couples safe harbours with duties to cooperate with competent-authority orders to remove or disable access (Arts. 12, 13(c), 16). Failure to act with due diligence once aware of manifest illegality may expose providers to liability and regulatory measures under that framework, alongside sector-specific enforcement by the competent authorities designated nationally for the DSA.

In data protection cases, CNPD can investigate, order compliance, and impose fines under the GDPR.

4.2.7 Sanctions in Case of Unfounded Reports or Complaints

On platforms, the DSA allows sanctions for abusive use of reporting and complaint mechanisms: providers of online platforms may suspend the processing of notices and complaints from individuals or entities that frequently submit manifestly unfounded notices/complaints and may suspend users who frequently provide manifestly illegal content (Article 23 DSA).

Knowingly making a false accusation to an authority by imputing an offence to someone is a crime (Article 365 of the Criminal Code). Reporting or creating suspicion of a crime to an authority, knowing it did not occur, is also criminally punishable, including when the false report concerns an administrative offence or disciplinary illicit act (Article 366 of the Criminal Code).

Even when conduct is not criminal, knowingly or negligently lodging groundless complaints that cause harm can generate civil liability under the Civil Code's general tort rule (Article 483), including for reputational damage (Article 484) and non-pecuniary losses (Article 496).[49]

4.2.8 Review of Previous Decisions

Internal appeals to private entities (online platforms). Under the DSA, users must receive a statement of reasons for any restriction or removal (Article 17) and may challenge the decision through the provider's internal complaint-handling system (Article 20). Complaints must be accepted for at least six months from notification of the original decision, handled in a timely manner, and concluded with a reasoned outcome; using the internal system is optional and does not prejudice judicial redress. Users may then escalate to certified out-of-court dispute-settlement bodies (Article 21), which must issue a decision within 90 days of receipt (extendable once, for a further 90 days, in highly complex cases), and/or lodge a complaint with the national Digital Services Coordinator (Article 53). The DSA also preserves access to courts and representative actions (Articles 54–55).

Appeals to administrative bodies. Ordinary administrative remedies under the Portuguese Administrative Procedure Code (CPA) apply ahead of or alongside judicial review.

Appeals to courts. Regulatory acts and omissions by administrative bodies are subject to judicial review, including interim relief where the legal criteria are met. Press-law reply/rectification disputes also have a fast civil-court track to compel publication (Press Law Article 27), while civil liability for personality-rights infringements runs in the civil courts. Criminal prosecutions are heard by the criminal courts under the Code of Criminal Procedure, with the usual defence and appeal guarantees.

4.2.9 Sanctions for Private Entities or Administrative Bodies Who Rendered Erroneous Decisions

Erroneous decisions are reversed on review and may trigger civil liability and other consequences, depending on who decided and under which regime. For private entities (platforms, media outlets), wrongful restrictions/removals are corrected via the DSA redress ladder and may ground civil liability if damage results. For media services, ERC may issue corrective orders and sanctions under its Statute and sector laws; if ERC's own act is unlawful, it is reviewable and quashable.

[49] See Miranda Barbosa, M.: Fake news e fact-checkers: Uma perspetiva jurídico-civilística. Revista de Direito da Responsabilidade (2021), pp. 760–762, and Moura Vicente, D.: Desinformação, Liberdade e Responsabilidade. Revista da Faculdade de Direito da Universidade de Lisboa LXIV (2023), pp. 506–509.

The Constitution (Article 22) lays down the general principle that public entities are civilly liable for losses caused in the exercise of their functions. Under the Regime of the Non-contractual Civil Liability of the State and other public entities (Law 67/2007), the State and other public bodies are liable for damage caused in the exercise of the administrative function by unlawful acts or omissions and by abnormal ("faulty") functioning of the service. The core rules appear in the administrative-function chapter (arts. 7–10): (i) they place exclusive liability on the State/public entity toward the injured party for unlawful administrative acts/omissions (no direct action against the official), (ii) define when illegality exists and what fault/service failure means, and (iii) set out causation and damage requirements. Cases are brought in the administrative courts under the Code of Procedure in the Administrative Courts (Law 15/2002).

Where an administrative body issues an invalid decision that causes loss, the act can be annulled on judicial review. The injured party may also claim State liability under Article 22 of the Constitution and Law 67/2007, and, if intent or gross negligence by an officeholder/agent is established, the public entity may exercise regress against that person (Article 6 of Law 67/2007).

5 Conclusions

Online disinformation is widely perceived in Portugal as a serious risk to democratic deliberation, briefly reflected in the now-repealed statutory "right to protection against disinformation". Its rapid rollback on freedom of expression and legal certainty grounds underscores the limits of attempting to regulate "truth" directly, as vague definitions and open-ended mandates risk chilling effects and prior restraint concerns. What remains is a medium-neutral, ex post model that addresses deception through multiple sectoral legal frameworks. This patchwork is normatively sound, harbouring strong constitutional speech guarantees paired with accountability for deceptive formats, but operationally fragmented, under-enforced and structurally reactive to the speed, scale and strategic amplification of online manipulation.

Portugal's credible way forward is not a sweeping new "anti-disinformation" statute but a coherent, swift and legally disciplined use of existing tools, now reinforced by the DSA, to curb real-world effects at the speed and scale of the online environment. The ongoing infringement procedure over DSA implementation, however, casts a shadow over whether there is real political will to tackle online disinformation effectively.

Online Disinformation and Democracy in Romania

Elena-Simina Tanasescu

Abstract Disinformation is a constantly expanding phenomenon, driven by the rapid development of information and communication technologies. The legal understanding of this concept requires an analysis of the convergence between doctrine, social realities and regulatory mechanisms. From a theoretical point of view, it is therefore necessary to distinguish this concept from other related notions and to discern the different legal consequences that all these notions produce. From an empirical point of view, it is interesting to note the impact that the concept of disinformation has had on the Romanian legal system, both in terms of legislation and case law, particularly with regard to electoral processes.

The rise of the internet combined with the rapid expansion of digital communications and social media have considerably reduced the barriers to accessing and circulating information, while at the same time amplifying the impact and scope of information dynamics. Once described as a "legal paradise",[1] the information space coupled with technological advances specific to the new digital world have gradually transformed into an "information disorder".[2] In this context, disinformation is becoming a constantly evolving and expanding phenomenon, difficult to grasp from a legal perspective, but nevertheless present. This contribution aims to identify the meaning and legal effects of the concept of disinformation in Romanian law, and to explain

[1] Cercelescu, C. M. (2002): Regimul juridic al presei. Drepturile și obligațiile jurnaliștilor. Teora, București, p.60.

[2] Council of Europe (2017): Claire Wardle & Hossein Derakhshan, Information disorder: Toward an interdisciplinary framework for research and policy making. Available at https://edoc.coe.int/en/media/7495-information-disorder-toward-an-interdisciplinary-framework-for-research-and-policy-making.html. Accessed 10 August 2025.

The author thanks PhD student Luca Ciubotaru for the meticulous update of the relevant legal provisions and the scrupulous check of endnotes.

E.-S. Tanasescu (✉)
University of Bucharest, Bucharest, Romania
e-mail: simina-elena.tanasescu@drept.unibuc.ro

P. Passaglia (ed.), *European Legal Perspectives on Online Disinformation*, Ius Gentium: Comparative Perspectives on Law and Justice 140,
https://doi.org/10.1007/978-3-032-25785-7_16

its past impact on elections and its potential influence on the democratic legitimacy of constitutional processes.

1 The Concept of Disinformation

1.1 Definitions

Romanian scholarship has only sparsely considered the notion of disinformation. One possible definition refers to it as a strategic tool aimed at polarising public opinion and deliberately shaping social perceptions.[3] Another one describes disinformation as "part of a specific discursive framework and correlated with the social reality in which it takes place in order to achieve the desired effect [...]", however based on "proven facts and authentic and verifiable sources, but altered by the use of techniques such as lies, seduction, myth or fiction, with the aim of producing the desired effect of informational manipulation".[4] Finally, the concept of misinformation is distinguished from disinformation since it encompasses "false or misleading information circulating without deliberate intent to cause harm, but which may nevertheless produce adverse effects from a legal or social point of view".[5]

It seems that Romanian scholarship follows what has become the classical conceptual framework in this respect, namely the triptych disinformation—misinformation—malinformation. According to Wardle and Derakhshan[6] disinformation refers to verifiably false or misleading information disseminated for economic gain or to intentionally deceive the public, misinformation refers to the dissemination of false or misleading information resulting from misunderstandings or lack of knowledge, and malinformation involves sharing factually correct information but with malicious intent in order to cause confusion or to inflict harm. Another source of inspiration is the Communication of the European Commission of 2018, where disinformation is defined as "verifiably false or misleading information that is created, presented, and disseminated for economic gain or to intentionally deceive the public, and may cause public harm",[7] which includes threats to political and policymaking processes as well as public goods such as the protection of EU citizens' health, environment or security.

---

[3] Mitrea, M. C. (2024): Dezinformarea care traversează frontierele, Revista Română de Drept European 3: 141.

[4] Oprea, B. (2022): Fake News şi Dezinformare Online: Recunoaşte şi Verifică. Manual pentru toţi utilizatorii de internet, 2nd edn., Polirom, Bucharest, 59–98.

[5] Brutaru, V. (2022): Drepturi şi libertăţi. Dreptul la liberă exprimare. Fenomenul fake news. Comunicarea de informaţii false. O schimbare de paradigmă?, Studii şi cercetări juridice 1/2022.

[6] Council of Europe (2017), *op. cit.* pp. 20–21.

[7] European Commission (2018): Communication from the Commission to the European Parliament, the Council, the European Economic and Social Committee and the Committee of the Regions: Tackling Online Disinformation: A European Approach, COM(2018) 236 final, pp. 3–4.

Still, the concept of disinformation lacks a normative definition in the Romanian legal system. As a multifaceted concept, it is analysed in the official legal discourse of public authorities such as the Constitutional Court, the judiciary or specialized regulatory bodies. In decision 70/2023 the Constitutional Court defined disinformation as "*the intentional and voluntary dissemination of false or distorted information with the aim of causing error or deception and producing misleading effects*".[8] The Bucharest Tribunal, defined disinformation as "*verifiably false information that is intentionally disseminated with the aim of misleading the public, generating economic gain, and potentially causing harm*".[9] Article 1 letter f) of the Audiovisual Content Regulation Code, adopted through Decision n°573/2025 of the National Council of Audiovisual, describes disinformation as "*the intentional dissemination of information that can be objectively established to be false or misleading, and which is likely to cause harm to an individual, a social group, an organization, or the public interest*".

1.2 Distinction Between Close Concepts

When addressing issues related to disinformation, Romanian literature operates with other terms as well. Thus, the operational definition of *fake news* includes the intentionality of the false content and the mechanism of dissemination. Tomuş[10] describes *fake news* as the deliberate dissemination of false information in the public sphere, with particular attention for its proliferation in digital environments.

The above mentioned Audiovisual Content Regulation Code distinguishes between disinformation and *inaccurate information*. The latter pertains to the dissemination of false or erroneous content irrespective of intent, particularly when such dissemination poses a risk of harm to the rights and legitimate interests of individuals, groups, or organizations, or when it undermines the public interest (see article 1 letter h).

On the other hand, *propaganda* and disinformation are considered to present "a considerable degree of conceptual overlap, leading to certain redundant connotations",[11] although each term retains its own semantic specificity and analytical relevance. They are both intrinsically linked to the broader notion of 'falsehood' insofar as they refer to the "dissemination of information that is misleading, untruthful or likely to alter perception and understanding".[12]

---

[8] Romanian Constitutional Court, Decision no. 70/2023, Official Gazette, no. 211 (14 March 2023), para. 134.

[9] Bucharest Tribunal, Judgment No. 1323/2021, September 23, 2021, Civil Action for Tort Liability, available at https://sintact.ro/jurisprudenta/1.

[10] Tomuş, A. (2022): Fake news şi război în spaţiul românesc. Cum se raportează românii la tema războiului din Ucraina, Revista Română de Drept al Afacerilor, 5.

[11] Hentea, C (2008), Noile haine ale propagandei, Paralela 45, p. 57.

[12] *Ibidem.*

In this context it is interesting to note that a normative distinction exists between disinformation and *propaganda*, with the latter being expressly acknowledged and subjected to regulation within multiple regulatory frameworks.[13] The legal definition of propaganda refers to the "*systematic dissemination of doctrines, ideologies, theories, or specific opinions, carried out with the deliberate intention of influencing public opinion, capturing, indoctrinating, or recruiting new followers, thereby contributing to shaping beliefs, convictions, and social orientations*".[14]

Finally, *deepfake* refers to any video, audio file or image that has been digitally manipulated using artificial intelligence or specialized software to produce content that appears realistic but is in fact falsified.[15]

1.3 Application of the Notion of Disinformation in the Different Areas of the Legal System

Although it lacks a clear legal definition, the notion of disinformation has been operationalized within a broad range of legislative and regulatory instruments. It sits at the crossroads of criminal law (Article 404 of the Criminal Code—Law n°286/2009), audiovisual regulation (Law n°504/2002 on broadcasting and Article 113 of the Audiovisual Content Regulation Code), competition and consumer protection law (Laws No. 363/2007 and 158/2008) and the regulation of digital services, notably through the implementation of Regulation (EU) 2022/2065 as transposed into national law by Law n°50/2024, thereby exemplifying the intricate and overlapping interplay between public order, media oversight and market regulation.

From a specific standpoint, in instances involving the dissemination of false information regarding the evolution of the COVID-19 pandemic and the related measures of protection and prevention, the notion of disinformation has been regulated under Article 54 of Presidential Decree No. 195/2020, which provides that public authorities are obliged to ensure the dissemination, in the mass media and online, of accurate and objective information, while empowering the National Authority for Administration and Regulation in Communications (ANCOM), prior to notifying affected users, to order hosting and content providers to remove false online content at its source.

Further illustrative examples may be identified within the legislative framework governing substantive public law, particularly in the domains of national defense

[13] Romanian Criminal Code, Law n°286/2009, art. 405; Law n°80/1995 concerning the status of military personnel, art. 28; Law n°47/1992 concerning the organizing and functioning of the Constitutional Court, art. 53, § 3, and art. 64; Law n°360/2002 concerning the Statute of Police, art. 45, lit. a); Law n°17/1990 on the legal regime of the internal maritime waters, the territorial sea, the contiguous zone and the exclusive economic zone of Romania—art. 18, §2; Law n°1/1998 concerning the organization and operation of the Foreign Intelligence Service, art. 15.

[14] Law n°535/2004 concerning the prevention and the fight against terrorism, Article 4, § 9.

[15] National Cybersecurity Directorate (2024), Deepfake Guide. Available at: https://www.dnsc.ro/vezi/document/ghid-deepfake, Accessed 7 September 2025.

and cybersecurity, where disinformation is construed as conduct endangering the *"constitutional order"* (article 3 letter p) of Law n°51/1991 on National Security as amended in 2023).

In Romania, the concept of disinformation has found particular legal relevance with regard to the integrity of electoral processes, as exemplified by Emergency Ordinance n°1/2025, which establishes a framework governing the dissemination of misleading or manipulative content across traditional media, advertising channels and digital platforms. This normative act has been adopted pursuant to the decision 32/2024 of the Constitutional Court, which annulled the entire electoral process for the election of the President of Romania in December 2024,[16] and in accordance with Regulation (EU) 2024/900, which recognizes that political advertising may constitute a *"potential vector of disinformation, particularly where its political nature is not transparently disclosed, is financed by sponsors outside the EU, or is disseminated* via *targeted advertising techniques"*. In decision 42/2025, the Constitutional Court emphasized that *"any violations of law arising from the dissemination of false information must be addressed with both proportionality and specificity, ensuring that such enforcement does not compromise the integrity or legitimacy of the electoral process"*.[17]

Thus, within the Romanian legal landscape, disinformation is a multifaceted notion, regulated across various branches of law, and bearing a particular significance for the protection of the integrity of democratic processes.

1.4 Specificity of Online Disinformation

A document drafted by the Romanian Ministry of Foreign Affairs and submitted for public consultation within the framework of the *Strategic Planning for Enhancing Resilience Against Disinformation and Managing Hybrid Threats*[18] defines the concept of *online* disinformation as the dissemination of false or misleading information through social media, websites, and messaging platforms, thereby posing a substantive challenge to international relations and global stability and underscoring the imperative for coordinated, evidence-based policy and regulatory interventions. Thus, the only distinguishing characteristic of *online* disinformation is the instrument used for the dissemination of the information, namely social media and messaging platforms. At stake it is not so much their attribute of new information and communication technologies (ICTs) as their algorithmic structure, which is designed to

[16] Romanian Constitutional Court, Decision 32/2024, Official Gazette no. 1231 (6 December 2024).

[17] Romanian Constitutional Court, Decision 42/2025 regarding the request for the annulment of the elections for the office of President of Romania held on 18 May 2025, Official Gazette no. 627 (8 July 2025).

[18] Ministry of Foreign Affairs of Romania, Public Policy Proposal for Formulating a Coordinated Response to Online Disinformation within the Competence of the Ministry of Foreign Affairs, April 2024, available at: https://e-consultare.gov.ro/w/2024/03/propunerea-de-politica-publica-pentru-formularea-unui-raspuns-coordonat-la-dezinformarea-online-in-sfera-de-competenta-a-mae/.

maximise users engagement and amplify virality, thus displaying the built-in tension between the commercial motives of their existence and their instrumental utility for the freedom of expression.

A defining characteristic of online disinformation was made clear in Romania in the context of the 2024 electoral process, namely the systematic deployment of coordinated dissemination techniques meant to manipulate recommendation algorithms, thereby creating the appearance of genuine popular support, through *astroturfing*. The Cambridge Dictionary[19] explains this neologism as the practice of publishing opinions or comments on internet or social media that appear to come from ordinary members of the public, but actually come from a particular company or political group as a way to boost the popularity of a specific product or (political) opinion. This type of algorithmic manipulation goes beyond the mere use of bot farms and, in some cases, it may allow for a manufactured popularity to become a genuine one. Coupled with a non-transparent financing of such inauthentic behaviours, the dissemination of propagandistic content has almost succeeded to challenging the democratic process of the election of the Romanian President in November–December 2024. As the Constitutional Court explained in decision 32/2024, the lawful and transparent financing of electoral activities, together with the unequivocal identification of online political advertising, constitutes a fundamental safeguard for the integrity of electoral processes. The Court noted that disinformation and the coordinated manipulation of digital algorithms, particularly of certain social media platforms, had managed to confer an artificial advantage to one of the candidates in that election, who, moreover, had not fulfilled his legal obligations related to the transparency of the financing of his electoral campaign. This behaviour was found illegal with regard to both the European standards pertaining to digital services and the national legislation regulating presidential elections and electoral campaigns. This experience prompted the Romanian Permanent Electoral Authority to adopt in 2025 a *Guide on Combating Disinformation in Electoral Processes*.[20]

1.5 The Relevance of Illegal Contents on the Definition of Disinformation

The Regulation 2022/2065 on a single market for digital services (Digital Services Act) has been implemented through Law n°50/2024. Within the national legal framework the notion of *illegal content,* as defined in Article 3(h) of Regulation (EU) 2022/2065, encompasses any information that is prohibited under Union or national law. It is only the dissemination of illegal content that may attract legal sanctions for internet sites or social media platforms and not the mere signaling of disinformation. Thus,

---

[19] See https://dictionary.cambridge.org/dictionary/english/astroturfing.

[20] Permanent Electoral Authority, Guide on Combating Disinformation in Electoral Processes, 2025, available at: https://www.roaep.ro/prezentare/wp-content/uploads/2025/03/GLFN%20PREZI%2025_3.pdf.

according to article 2 (b) of Law n°50/2024, competent authorities have the obligation to assess the illegal online content and may require intermediary service providers to determine, assess and remove illegal content, provide information concerning individual service recipients, or restore content erroneously removed despite adherence to the provider's terms of service.

Law n°50/2024 designated the National Authority for Administration and Regulation in Communications (ANCOM) as the national Digital Services Coordinator. According to art. 18 of the above mentioned law, ANCOM does not rule on the qualification of online content as illegal, except in cases when ANCOM is the relevant authority. Therefore, the order to take action against illegal content is issued by the relevant authority, according to its competence established by the national legislation.

In the field of audiovisual content provided by audiovisual media service providers, the Audiovisual Content Regulation Code (Decision n°573/2025 of the National Council of Audiovisual) considers *illegal content* any information or conduct that is in violation of national law, regardless of its subject matter or form. Content disseminated online or in the mainstream media may be rendered unlawful by various authorities depending on their competence, such as National Council of Audiovisual for audiovisual content provided by audiovisual media service providers, civil courts in tort claims, police or prosecutor's office if the content or dissemination of the content represents a criminal offence, National Council for Combating Discrimination (NCCD) if the content is discriminatory etc. This is done either on the basis of its intrinsic characteristics, such as the incitement to violence, hatred, or discrimination prohibited under Article 369 of the Criminal Code, or due to the spreading of false information, as regulated under Article 404 of the same law. Furthermore, information may be deemed illegal insofar as it is inherently connected to the promotion or distribution of illicit activities, goods, or services.

2 The Sources of Law

2.1 Constitution

Article 30 of the Romanian Constitution guarantees freedom of expression as a fundamental right. The approach taken has been considered "original"[21] since it encompasses both the formulation and dissemination of ideas and opinions, as well as the creation of intellectual or artistic works, by any medium or in any form, whether oral, written, visual, auditory, or otherwise (Art. 30 §1). It also protects expression from censorship (Art. 30 §2) and it ensures press independence, including the freedom

[21] Verpeaux, M. (2012), La liberté d'expression dans les jurisprudences constitutionnelles, Nouveaux Cahiers du Conseil Constitutionnel, no. 36 (Dossier: La liberté d'expression et de communication), available at: https://www.conseil-constitutionnel.fr/nouveaux-cahiers-du-conseil-constitutionnel/la-liberte-d-expression-dans-les-jurisprudences-constitutionnelles.

to create, organize, and manage publications without arbitrary interference (Art. 30 §3–4), while allowing laws to require transparency of media funding (Art. 30 §5).

Freedom of expression constitutes a fundamental right, whose exercise must be reconciled with the protection of the legitimate rights and interests of individuals, including dignity, honor, privacy, and the right to one's image, as well as other rights recognized by law (Art. 30, §6). Certain forms of expression, such as defamation of the nation, incitement to war, national, racial, class, or religious hatred, discrimination, territorial separatism, public violence, and obscenity contrary to public morals, are expressly prohibited (Art. 30, §7). Civil liability for publicly disseminated information or creative works rests with the publisher, producer, author, organizer of the artistic event, or owner of the means of reproduction, dissemination, or transmission, with specific offenses defined by law (Art. 30, §8).

Article 31 guarantees the right to free access to information of public interest (Art. 31 §1), which is subject to legitimate restrictions protecting minors and national security (Art. 31 §3). It further upholds the regulated autonomy of public broadcasting, ensuring equitable access for major social and political groups, with its structure and parliamentary oversight defined by organic law (Art. 31 §5). Within the framework of national legal doctrine, the right to information is recognized as an autonomous and fundamental right, "inherently complex and continually evolving",[22] indispensable for the development of the individual, the effective exercise of constitutional freedoms, and the guarantee of access to social, political, economic, scientific, and cultural information.[23] Public authorities are obliged to provide accurate and reliable information concerning public affairs (Art. 31, §2). Both public and private media bear a duty to ensure the veracity of information that informs public opinion (Art. 31, §4).

2.2 *EU Law and National Implementation*

In Romania, the EU Regulation 2022/2065, also known as the Digital Services Act has been implemented through Law n°50/2024, which has also amended Law n°365/ 2002 on the electronic commerce. Law n°50/2024 acknowledged the harmonized minimum standards for content removal and information requests while reserving the determination of the underlying legal basis and attendant substantive matters. It designated the National Authority for Administration and Regulation in Communications (ANCOM) as the national Digital Services Coordinator and it incorporated the DSA's sanctioning regime into the national enforcement mechanisms.

[22] Muraru, I. (2008), Comentariu la Articolul 31 in Constituția României: Comentariu pe articole, edited by Ioan Muraru, Elena Simina Tănăsescu, C.H. Beck, Bucharest, p. 299.

[23] Muraru, I. (1999) Protecția constituțională a libertăților de opinie, Lumina Lex, Bucharest, p. 135.

Under the Digital Services Act, the Code of Conduct on Disinformation requires large platforms to ensure transparency and mitigate risks. Romania applies it mainly to political advertising and platform dynamics.[24]

Furthermore, the direct application of Regulation (EU) 2024/900 on the transparency and targeting of political advertising has been reinforced through Emergency Ordinance n°1/2025,[25] which aims at safeguarding free and transparent electoral processes. The Ordinance centralizes responsibility for electoral cybersecurity, the prevention of disinformation, and the promotion of transparency in political campaigns at the level of agencies in charge of electoral processes (Permanent Electoral Authority), audiovisual communications (National Council of Audiovisual and ANCOM) and cybersecurity (National Directorate for Cybersecurity). It requires political actors to ensure the clear identification and disclosure of political advertising, and—where applicable—a declaration regarding the use of targeting or dissemination techniques, thereby mitigating risks arising from cyberattacks, information manipulation, and undisclosed or foreign funding.

Finally, Directive 2000/31/EC on electronic commerce has been transposed through Law n°365/2002 on the electronic commerce,[26] while Directive 2010/13/EU on audiovisual media services has been transposed by means of Law n°190/2022 amending Audiovisual Law n°504/2002.[27]

In addition, the National Artificial Intelligence Strategy[28] provides strategic and regulatory guidance to ensure the consistent application of relevant EU provisions within the Romanian legal order. Thus, Regulation (EU) 2024/1689 on artificial intelligence, establishes enforceable obligations concerning transparency, liability, and the protection of users. These obligations govern commercial communications, audiovisual media services, video-sharing and on-demand platforms, as well as certain AI systems.

---

[24] European Digital Media Observatory (2023), Evaluating the Implementation of the EU Code of Practice on Disinformation in Romania, available at: https://edmo.eu/wp-content/uploads/2023/09/Evaluating-the-Revised-EU-Code-of-Practice-on-Disinformation-in-Romania_v2.pdf. Accessed 3 September 2025.

[25] Emergency Ordinance n°1/2025 on Measures for the Organization and Conduct of the 2025 Presidential and Partial Local Elections, Official Gazette No. 44 (17 January 2025), available at: https://legislatie.just.ro/public/DetaliiDocument/293733.

[26] Law n°365/2002 on Electronic Commerce, Official Gazette no. 365 (29 November 2006) available at https://legislatie.just.ro/Public/DetaliiDocument/37075.

[27] Law n°504/2002—Audiovisual Law, Official Gazette No. 534 of 22 July 2002, available at https://legislatie.just.ro/Public/DetaliiDocumentAfis/214210.

[28] National Strategy on Artificial Intelligence 2024–2027 (2024), developed within the framework of the project "Strategic Framework for the Adoption and Use of Innovative Technologies in Public Administration 2021—2027—Solutions for Increasing Efficiency", available at https://www.adr.gov.ro/wp-content/uploads/2024/03/Strategie-Inteligenta-Artificiala-22012024-1.pdf. Accessed 10 September 2025.

2.3 *Legislative Acts*

Articles 82–84 of the Audiovisual Content Regulation Code (Decision n°573/2025) establish a comprehensive legal framework aimed at safeguarding the fundamental right to accurate, impartial and transparent public information for the audiovisual media service providers. These provisions apply, however, only to audiovisual content offered by audiovisual media service providers. By imposing stringent obligations of integrity, verification and balance upon audiovisual media service providers, they reinforce the essential principles of transparency, pluralism and the free and informed formation of democratic public opinion.

For broadcasting, the Audiovisual Law (n°504/2002) is the main legislative instrument. According to this law, audiovisual media service providers are under the legal obligation to ensure the objective dissemination of information through the accurate presentation of facts and events, thereby safeguarding the free formation of public opinion. The law includes rules on audiovisual commercial communication (chapter III^1), protection of minors (chapter III^2), the right of reply to accusations made in various media (chapter III^3), protection of victims of domestic violence (chapter III^5), regulations for video-sharing platform providers (chapter III^6), audiovisual communication on harmful consequences of drug consumption, and trafficking of human beings (chapter III^7).

Similar measures are implemented with regard to consumer disinformation in order to ensure transparency in commercial communications and to prevent consumer confusion. Consequently, certain advertising practices are expressly prohibited under Law n°363/2007 on Combating Unfair Commercial Practices in Relation to Consumers and Harmonizing Regulations with European Consumer Protection Legislation, which regulates unfair commercial practices in trader-consumer relations and harmonizes national legislation with European consumer protection standards.

As for the area of national security, the identification, prevention, and mitigation of disinformation in cyberspace constitute essential measures, insofar as actions perpetrated by state or non-state actors that impinge upon the constitutional order or compromise the integrity of public institutions are explicitly classified as threats to national security in accordance with Article 3 of Law n°51/1991 as subsequently amended by Law n°58/2023 on the Cybersecurity and Defense of Romania. This provision extends national security concerns beyond the traditional military sphere to the hybrid and informational one. Although Law n°58/2023 on Cyber Defense and Cybersecurity does not directly regulate disinformation, it does focus on institutional and operational cyberdefense, including cyber intelligence, counterintelligence, and preventive informational campaigns promoting *"digital hygiene"* (art. 2 letter m)).

2.4 *Subordinate Acts*

The Supreme Council for National Defense has adopted the National Strategy for Strategic Communication and Countering Disinformation (Decision n°113/2021), which established a binding framework for the identification, prevention and mitigation of false or misleading information capable of undermining national security or public trust[29].

The recently adopted National Defense Strategy for 2025–2030 mentions disinformation among the "*persistent threats, with long-cumulative effects*", together with fake news, manipulation of the information space, malign influences, but also through cyber attacks, part of the hybrid spectrum actions generated by hostile actors[30]. The strategy acknowledges that "*aggressions in the information area aim to shape and/or influence public perception, in order to undermine social cohesion and trust in democratic institutions, in the EU and in NATO. They can also produce polarization and ideological fault lines*".[31]

The Ministry of Research, Innovation, and Digitalization adopted Order n°20.721/May 9, 2024 establishing the Single Contact Point for Receiving Reports Regarding 'Deepfake' Content. This framework operationalizes digital content oversight through a designated point of contact for *'deepfake'* reports under the Digital Services Act.

In accordance with the Romanian Government Decision n°290/2024 for the approval of the Multiannual Strategic Programme for International Development Cooperation and Humanitarian Assistance 2024–2027, Romania's priorities in international development, cooperation, and humanitarian aid include strengthening institutional capacity, mitigating non-conventional security risks, including cybersecurity, protecting critical infrastructure, countering hybrid threats, and combating disinformation, through a unified strategy of proactive, multi-platform communication, public awareness campaigns, and administrative and technological measures to ensure information integrity and promote transparency and open public dialogue.

2.5 *The Role of the Case Law*

2.5.1 Constitutional Court of Romania (CCR)

The CCR has addressed the notion of disinformation in its recent case law, clarifying both its legal scope and relevance for electoral processes. Thus, decision 70/2023

[29] For developments, see Nistor, D. I. A., Institutional Strategic Communication – an essential instrument supporting national security in the current geopolitical context. available at https://gmr.mapn.ro/.

[30] National Defense Strategy of Romania 2025–2030, adopted by Parliament decision no. 48/2025, Official Gazette no. 1092 (26 November 2025), paragraph 47.

[31] *Ibidem.*

clarified the concept of disinformation by reference to the *Explanatory Dictionary of the Romanian Language*, thereby formalizing the concept in legal terms and noting its integration across primary, secondary, and tertiary legislation. The Court declared that "*the concept of disinformation refers to the act of providing false information (in a biased manner), the act of misinforming, and its result, which means intentionally providing false information in a biased manner, misleading others with false information.*" (paragraph 127) It also noted that not any disinformation campaign in cyberspace is targeted by the Romanian legislator, but only those "*that are likely to affect the constitutional order*", i.e. those that "*promote incitement to war, hatred on grounds of race, religion, nationality,* etc., *territorial separatism or public violence, but also to the change of the constitutional democratic regime or the abolition of constitutional institutions*". (paragraph 128).

In Decision 32/2024, which annulled the entire electoral process organized in November–December 2024, the Court further reaffirmed the State's duty not only to ensure the dissemination of accurate information, but also to prevent and counter organized disinformation campaigns capable of undermining electoral integrity. Paragraph 10 explicitly states "*On the other hand, the state also has a duty of neutrality, which includes the obligation to strengthen the resilience of voters, including by raising awareness among the electorate about the use of digital technologies in elections, in particular by providing adequate information and support. Therefore, the state must address the challenges and risks posed by organized disinformation campaigns that could affect the integrity of electoral processes.*" Addressing the phenomenon of voter manipulation through non-transparent uses of digital technologies and undeclared campaign financing, the Court also asserted that the electorate's freedom to form political opinions is intrinsically linked to the right to receive accurate and transparent information, including that disseminated via digital platforms. The Court ruled that any propaganda or disinformation by public or private actors is strictly prohibited, emphasizing social media's duty to ensure transparency and disclose political funding sources.

Finally, in Decision 42/2025,[32] the Court held that disinformation, particularly when disseminated via digital platforms and artificial intelligence technologies, poses a significant threat to the integrity of electoral processes. While participants in electoral processes retain freedom of expression, legal accountability must be applied proportionately to address false information and unlawful conduct, thereby preserving electoral legitimacy.

[32] Romanian Constitutional Court, Decision 42/2025 regarding the request for the annulment of the elections for the office of President of Romania held on 18 May 2025, Official Gazette no. 627 (8 July 2025).

2.5.2 The High Court of Cassation and Justice (HCCJ)

In a landmark decision (n°2230/2021),[33] the HCCJ affirmed the imprescriptibility of crimes against humanity in holding a journalist criminally accountable for the deliberate dissemination of false information that materially contributed to public panic during the 1989 Romanian Revolution.[34] The Court held that while journalists may use limited exaggeration or provocation, this does not justify deliberate disinformation or selective presentation of the truth, noting that the statements made by the journalist were factually inaccurate, materially detached from reality and could not be verified by courts; for a journalist such conduct constitutes intentional manipulation of opinion in that it fails to consider publicly available and reliable sources.

In another decision (n°2193/2025)[35] the HCCJ ruled that electoral disinformation refers not only to the content of the information, but also to the systematic manner of its dissemination, and that individuals may be deemed *"political actors"* even without office or party affiliation if they consistently act to advance a candidate's electoral objectives, with content, frequency, and regularity among the relevant factors. Applying directly Regulation (EU) 2024/900 the Court highlighted that disinformation extends beyond candidates and formal political organizations and stated that: "*individuals who, although they do not hold elected or public office or have political affiliations, may act as* de facto *political actors because they post on their personal accounts, opened on very large online platforms, exclusively for electoral purposes, predominantly and repeatedly, with the potential to influence the electorate, materials whose main purpose is not to exercise their own freedom of expression by promoting their personal opinion, but to promote the political objectives of a single candidate for an elected office*".

2.5.3 Subordinate Courts

Disinformation has been used by subordinate courts either in civil and commercial law or in connection with elections. Thus, according to the Bucharest Tribunal, disinformation is different from fake news and it refers to verifiably false information

[33] HCCJ, Decision no. 2230/2021. The proceedings were definitively closed on November 27, 2019, when the Court rejected the request to reopen the case.—See also: Prosecutor's Office attached to the HCCJ Press Release: Overturning the Dismissal Decisions—Revolution Case, 2019, available at: https://www.mpublic.ro/ro/content/c_21-10-2019-16-10. Public Prosecutor's Office attached to the High Court of Cassation and Justice, "Revolution Case—PICCJ—SPM—Extension and Continuation of Criminal Investigation—Crime Against Humanity," Press Release, April 18, 2018, https://www.mpublic.ro/ro/content/c_18-04-2018-10-04. Accessed 10 September 2025.

[34] Cercelescu, M.: Freedom of speech in times of turbulence, Evrika Publishing, Bucharest, pp. 173–174.

[35] HCCJ, Administrative and Fiscal Litigation Section, Decision no. 2193/2025, April 23, 2025.

that is "*intentionally disseminated with the aim of misleading the public, generating economic gain, and potentially causing harm*".[36]

The Bucharest Court of Appeal held that digital freedom of expression is not absolute and may be limited to protect privacy, reputation, and democratic integrity.[37] The same jurisdiction emphasized that advertising communications must strictly comply with legal provisions, ensure accurate, reliable, and transparent information, and prevent any misleading content that could harm consumers or fair competition, in accordance with Article 93 of the Audiovisual Code.[38]

The same Court of Appeal also stated that, although freedom of expression protects even offensive speech, the electorate can be misled by undeclared electoral materials and manipulated social media algorithms, that allowed disinformation to distort public perception and undermine democratic integrity. It therefore validated content removal from social media platforms under Regulation (EU)2024/900 and Law n°370/2004 on presidential elections.[39]

2.6 *Impact of Soft Law*

It should be noted that the Constitutional Court has expressly recognized the essential role of codes of conduct and interpretative declarations as guiding tools for public authorities facing challenges related to online disinformation. In its decision 32/2024, the Court highlighted the relevance of the Interpretative Declaration on the Code of Good Conduct in Electoral Matters regarding Digital Technologies and Artificial Intelligence, adopted by the European Commission for Democracy through Law.

3 Reporting Procedure and Other Measures to Tackle Online Disinformation

Tackling online disinformation depends on the content of communication and on the possibility to qualify that specific content as illegal, according to the national legal framework.

Article 2 paragraph 2^1 of the Audiovisual Law n°504/2002 granted the National Council of Audiovisual (NCA) supervision of (1) media audiovisual services,

[36] Bucharest Tribunal, Judgment no. 1323/2021, September 23, 2021, Civil Action for Tort Liability, available at: https://sintact.ro/jurisprudenta/1.

[37] Court of Appeal, Decision no. 971/2021, November 23, 2021, Civil Action for Tort Liability.

[38] Court of Appeal, Judgment no. 373/2020, October 16, 2020, Annulment of Act Issued by the National Council of Audiovisual.

[39] Bucharest Court of Appeal (CA), Judgment no. 113/2025, April 22, 2025, Annulment of Electoral Office Decision (Administrative and Fiscal Litigation), available at: https://rejust.ro/juris/4e4ed97ge.

under the editorial responsibility of an audiovisual media service provider; (2) on-demand audiovisual media service (streaming platforms); (3) video-sharing platform providers under the jurisdiction of Romania or under the jurisdiction of a state that is not a member of the European Union, but whose content can be accessed on the territory of Romania. It follows from the above that the NCA is limited to audiovisual content and cannot tackle disinformation that could be qualified as illegal content and spread solely through text or static images.

In the case of video-sharing platform providers, NCA may supervise only the specific obligations these platforms have for: (i) the protection of minors from content that may impair their physical, mental or moral development, (ii) the protection of the general public from content which contains incitement to violence or hatred against a group of persons or a member of a group or (iii) the protection of general public from content which constitutes public incitement to commit offences under Law no. 535/2004 for the prevention and combating of terrorism and or under Law no. 196/2003 on the prevention and combating of pornography or offences of a racist and xenophobic nature.

NCA has no competence regarding the audiovisual content created by individual users, not even when the content of a video-sharing platform infringes the above mentioned provisions. However, when no other effective means are available, in order to prohibit the infringement of these provisions and to avoid the risk of serious harm to the collective interests of the public or the legitimate interests of a person, NCA can request the removal of online illegal content (article 42^9 of Law no. 504/2002).

Law n°504/2002 is the primary normative framework governing the functioning of the NCA, *"an autonomous public authority operating under the supervision of Parliament, vested with the mandate to act as the guarantor of the public interest in the field of audiovisual communication"*.[40] In its role as guardian of the public interest in the audiovisual sector, the Council is tasked with safeguarding the pluralism of ideas and opinions within content disseminated by Romanian audiovisual service providers, as well as ensuring the diversity of information sources accessible to the public. With regard to the regulation of illegal online content, the Council has issued a Practical Guide,[41] which serves as an instrument delineating the procedural framework for the submission of complaints, as well as the criteria and conditions under which the Council is vested with the authority to impose sanctions.

Apart from the NCA, which is competent solely in the area of audiovisual services, online disinformation can be tackled by filing:

- tort claims in civil courts in case disinformation violates the right to private life or the protection of one's image;

---

[40] Law n°504/2002—Audiovisual Law, Official Gazette No. 534 of 22 July 2002, available at https://legislatie.just.ro/Public/DetaliiDocumentAfis/214210. Accessed 20 September 2025.

[41] National Council of Audiovisual, Combating Illegal Online Content—Practical Guide, available at: https://www.cna.ro/IMG/pdf/COMBATERE-CONT-ILEGAL-ONLINE-_GHID-_PRACTIC_CNA.pdf. Accessed 7 October 2025.

- complaints to the National Council for Combating Discrimination (NCCD), the authority responsible for combating discrimination, if the content is discriminatory;
- complaints to the Data Protection Agency, in case of violations of personal data regulations or processing rules;
- complaints to the law enforcement public authorities such as the national police or prosecutor's offices in case the disinformation represents a criminal offence, such as incitement to violence, hatred or discrimination;
- complaints to the Romanian Intelligence Services in case the content represents a threat to national security;
- complaints to the National Directorate for Cybersecurity if the content has direct implications for cybersecurity or information networks and systems (e.g. content promoting cyberattacks, malware or other security threats).

3.1 Subjects Who Can Report

Any person is entitled to submit a report to the NCA in order to denounce any audiovisual content that may be unlawful or harmful.

3.2 Subjects Who Decide on the Report

According to Article 10 of Law n°504/2002, the NCA is established as the *"exclusive authority for the regulation of audiovisual media services"*. It should be clarified in this regard that the NCA does not have jurisdiction over websites that do not contain audiovisual content, including the printed press, as well as online editions of newspapers or periodicals. Its scope of intervention is strictly limited to audiovisual media services and video-sharing platforms.

3.3 Means to Establish the Falsehood of the Contents and the Related Responsibilities

According to the Practical Guide, a complaint or report is defined as *"any communication submitted by a citizen with the purpose of notifying the National Council of Audiovisual of the existence of audiovisual content disseminated online that may contravene applicable audiovisual legislation or compromise public safety"* (Sect. 2). Members of the NCA examine each submission to ascertain whether it falls within their jurisdiction and to determine whether the reported content constitutes a breach of the prevailing legal framework, namely content that is violent or detrimental to minors, unlawful advertising and promotional practices, infringements of privacy, the dissemination of misinformation or manipulative material, and any content prohibited under other statutory provisions.

3.4 Deadlines for the Decision

Requests issued by the CNA on content broadcasted on a video-sharing platform must be executed promptly, within a maximum period of forty-eight hours (Article 429, paragraph 8, of Law No. 504/2002).

3.5 Forms of Protection for the Authors of Allegedly Illegal Content or Disinformation

According to the Practical Guide,[42] very large online platforms have a variable response time, depending on the complexity of the case and the internal moderation procedures implemented, generally set at twenty-four hours.

3.6 Sanctions in Case of Detection of Disinformation

The sanctions depend on the type of illegal content established. They may vary from criminal punishment in case the illegal content represents a criminal offence, to moral damages, in tort claims, to fines applied by specialized agencies (NCCD, Data protection agency) or the removal of online content.

In case of audiovisual content, according to article 42^9 of the Audiovisual Law n°504/2002, NCA can require: (a) video-sharing platform providers to remove the illegal content or to restrict access to it or to display a warning to users when accessing such content or to deactivate the user's account for a period of up to 12 months; (b) service providers providing storage space for video-sharing platforms to remove, deactivate or restrict access to a video-sharing platform; (c) registry operators, which allocate domain names for video-sharing platforms, to remove the domain name of the video-sharing platform. These sanctions are conditioned by the infringement of the obligations of the platforms and by the lack of "*other effective means available to prohibit the infringement of these provisions and to avoid the risk of serious harm to the collective interests of the public or the legitimate interests of a person*".

Accordingly, the NCA is vested with the authority to adopt an official decision, carrying the effect of a removal injunction, which must be sufficiently precise and duly reasoned to allow the provider to identify and implement the necessary measures

---

42 NCA, Combating Illegal Online Content—Practical Guide, https://www.cna.ro/IMG/pdf/COMBATERE-CONT-ILEGAL-ONLINE-_GHID-_PRACTIC_CNA.pdf. Accessed 8 September 2025.

for its enforcement. The competent authority is empowered to require any digital platform, including social networks, that allows the publication or dissemination of content, to remove one or more illegal contents or to restrict access to them, either by deletion or by blocking access, throughout the entire national territory. In accordance with Article 42^8 of the aforementioned law, providers of video-sharing platforms subject to Romanian jurisdiction are obliged to inform users when the content offered contains audiovisual commercial communications.

When a platform fails to comply with a removal order for illegal content issued by the NCA, the Council forwards the decision to the National Authority for Administration and Regulation in Communications (ANCOM). Under Law n°50/2024,[43] ANCOM is vested with the role of *"Digital Services Coordinator"* for Romania and has exclusive competence to ensure the implementation of the Digital Services Act and, in this capacity, exercises strict oversight over large online platforms' compliance with the obligations set out in the Code of Good Practices on Disinformation.

The procedure for handling complaints related to digital services and the violations of Digital Services Act by intermediary service providers was established by ANCOM Decision n°335/2024.[44] Such complaints must concern exclusively violations of the provisions of the Article 53 of the Digital Services Regulation. The review of complaints related to the dissemination of illegal online content without relying on Article 53 of the Regulation falls within the competence of authorities responsible for the supervision of the relevant sector,[45] not ANCOM, except when ANCOM itself is a relevant authority (e.g. technical regulations on electronic communications, audiovisual communications, radio equipment/radio interfaces and postal services).

If the platform persists in failing to fulfill its removal obligations despite notification, the competent Digital Services Coordinator shall promptly inform both the European Commission and the Digital Services Coordinator of the Member State where the platform is established.

3.7 *Sanctions in Case of Unfounded Reports or Complaints*

According to Article 42^9 of Law n°504/2002, any decision issued under this law may be appealed before the competent administrative court, in compliance with the

---

[43] Law n°50/2024 on the establishment of certain measures for the implementation of Regulation (EU) 2022/2065 of the European Parliament and of the Council of 19 October 2022 on a Single Market for Digital Services, amending Directive 2000/31/EC, and also amending and supplementing Law No. 365/2002 on electronic commerce, https://legislatie.just.ro/public/DetaliiDocument/280106. Accessed 7 October 2025.

[44] ANCOM, Decision no. 335/2024 on the procedure for handling complaints concerning digital services, available at: https://www.ancom.ro/uploads/forms_files/Decizie_335_2024_procedura_plangeri1720526272.pdf, accessed 18 September 2025.

[45] ANCOM Annual Report 2024, https://www.ancom.ro/uploads/links_files/Raport_anual_ANCOM_2024.pdf accessed 18 September 2025.

provisions of Law n°554/2004[46] on administrative litigation. This mechanism allows any interested party who considers that their rights or legitimate interests have been infringed by the decision to bring the matter before the administrative court in order to obtain, where appropriate, its annulment or revision.

3.8 Sanctions for Private Entities or Administrative Bodies Who Rendered Erroneous Decisions

Pursuant to Article 14 of Law n°554/2004, the aggrieved party may petition the competent court for the suspension of the execution of a unilateral administrative act, in *"duly justified cases and for the purpose of preventing imminent harm"*, either following referral to the issuing authority or to the hierarchically superior authority or *"within 30 days from the date on which the irrevocable act is brought to their attention"*. Article 18 of the same law provides that, in accordance with the circumstances and subject to the principles of legality and equity, *"the competent court may annul, in whole or in part, the contested administrative act, direct the public authority to issue an administrative act, furnish any requisite document, or undertake any specified administrative measure"*.

4 Conclusions

Although a widely spread and, as of recently, intensively used concept, disinformation does still not have a clear legal definition. Both European and Romanian law prefer to deal rather with its legal effects than to clearly demarcate it from other close or related notions, such as fake news or propaganda. However, the dissemination of false or misleading information in order to deceive the public is not a new phenomenon. What is new is the manner in which this dissemination takes place and the instruments used for this to happen. The rapid expansion of digital communications and of social media have dramatically increased the speed of online dissemination of potentially false or misleading information. At the same time, the algorithmical nature of these new tools has considerably amplified the chances that a coordinated inauthentic behaviour takes place with regard to this dissemination, thus facilitating disinformation on a previously unprecedented scale. Since social media platforms are programmed to elicit instinctive reactions from their users, the free expression that goes along with them, and which is highly valued in any democracy, is often tempered by the inherent possibility of its manipulation and submission to other purposes than the mere manifestation of democratic values.

[46] Law n°554/2004 on Administrative Litigation, Official Gazette No. 1154 of 7 December 2004. https://legislatie.just.ro/Public/DetaliiDocument/57426, accessed 15 September 2025.

This paradox becomes acutely relevant in democratic processes, such as elections, where any disinformation that may be spread during electoral campaigns can easily pass for participation, sometimes even participation of a larger public than the one usually engaged with the process. However, just as the mere organisation of elections cannot be considered evidence of democracy, free expression on social media cannot be considered, in itself, evidence of pluralism or democratic discourse. For values such as freedom of expression or the free election of certain public authorities to come together and lead to an authentic democracy, it is necessary that they be tempered by regulations that serve the public good and not only private interests. That is why the prevention of disinformation, and particularly of online disinformation, is highly relevant for public trust and for the legitimacy of public institutions. But how to achieve this goal when the very concept of disinformation lacks a clear legal meaning although it does bear obvious legal, political and sociological effects.

To date, no comprehensive legal research has systematically evaluated the effectiveness of Romania's existing normative instruments against disinformation in general, whether framed within a general legal regime or a sector-specific one. A first challenge to effectiveness is the fragmented nature of the legal framework and of the responsibilities of public authorities in charge of its implementation. This challenge has been acknowledged by the National Defense Strategy as a risk and a vulnerability,[47] since the rules are dispersed across heterogeneous regimes, including national security, criminal law, audiovisual regulation, and consumer protection, lacking a transversal and integrative legal architecture, for systemic coherence.

At the same time, no single, comprehensive report on the public perception of *online* disinformation has been published, although the issue can be sensed as critical if judged by constitutional and judicial rulings. The Constitutional Court took the extraordinary step of annulling the 2024 presidential elections, on the basis of extensive digital manipulation that undermined electoral integrity. The High Court of Cassation and Justice affirmed the imprescriptibility of crimes against humanity in a landmark case holding a journalist accountable for disinformation that "materially contributed to public panic" during the 1989 Revolution.

Yet, there are still no public policies or mitigation strategies to actively combat (online) disinformation despite the fact that social media platforms have been found technically able to act against cases of coordinated algorithmic manipulation if compelled to do so. The EU Digital Services Act provides for a comprehensive and strong legal framework in this direction. A November 2023 report[48] has analyzed how major platforms in Romania are implementing the EU Code of Practice on Disinformation and found them to be relatively compliant, although slow (and sometimes even reluctant) in making the best efforts to ensure a responsible and trustworthy digital environment.

[47] National Defense Strategy of Romania 2025–2030, adopted by Parliament decision no. 48/2025, Official Gazette no. 1092 (26 November 2025), paragraph 72.

[48] Botan, M. & Stancea, A (November 2023): Evaluating the Implementation of the EU Code of Practice on Disinformation in Romania, available at https://edmo.eu/wp-content/uploads/2023/09/Evaluating-the-Revised-EU-Code-of-Practice-on-Disinformation-in-Romania_v2.pdf, accessed at 9 December 2025.

Recent Romanian legislative measures reflect efforts to address some of the legal issues associated with disinformation and the inappropriate use of artificial intelligence technologies. Draft Law PL-x No. 471/2023[49] establishes a precise legal definition of the term *"deepfake"* and prohibits its dissemination in the absence of an explicit warning. In a similar vein, the draft legislation ratifying Emergency Ordinance no. 5/2025[50] attempts to create a regulatory framework addressing the dissemination of illegal or harmful content on very large online platforms. Also, the recently adopted National Defense Strategy for the period 2025–2030 explicitly mentions disinformation as a threat to the national security, as part of a larger spectrum of hybrid actions.

However, in the long term, both European and national authorities need to devise legal instruments and tools for monitoring and reporting on disinformation of a greater and better calibre than those currently available if a phenomenon such as the one produced in Romania in December 2024 is to be prevented.

References

1. Cercelescu, C. M. (2002): Regimul juridic al presei. Drepturile şi obligaţiile jurnalistilor. Teora, Bucureşti, p.60.
2. Council of Europe (2017): Claire Wardle & Hossein Derakhshan, Information disorder: Toward an interdisciplinary framework for research and policy making. Available at https://edoc.coe.int/en/media/7495-information-disorder-toward-an-interdisciplinary-framework-for-research-and-policy-making.html. Accessed 10 August 2025.
3. Mitrea, M. C. (2024): Dezinformarea care traversează frontierele, Revista Română de Drept European 3: 141.
4. Oprea, B. (2022): Fake News şi Dezinformare Online: Recunoaşte şi Verifică. Manual pentru toţi utilizatorii de internet, 2nd edn., Polirom, Bucharest, 59–98.
5. Brutaru, V. (2022): Drepturi şi libertăţi. Dreptul la liberă exprimare. Fenomenul fake news. Comunicarea de informaţii false. O schimbare de paradigmă?, Studii şi cercetări juridice 1/2022.
6. Council of Europe (2017), *op. cit.* pp. 20–21.
7. European Commission (2018): Communication from the Commission to the European Parliament, the Council, the European Economic and Social Committee and the Committee of the Regions: Tackling Online Disinformation: A European Approach, COM(2018) 236 final, pp. 3–4.
8. Romanian Constitutional Court, Decision no. 70/2023, Official Gazette, no. 211 (14 March 2023), para. 134.
9. Bucharest Tribunal, Judgment No. 1323/2021, September 23, 2021, Civil Action for Tort Liability, available at https://sintact.ro/jurisprudenta/1.

[49] Draft Law on the Responsible Use of Technology in the Context of the Deepfake Phenomenon, PL-x No. 471/2023, available at: https://www.cdep.ro/pls/proiecte/upl_pck2015.proiect?idp=20853. Accessed 7 October 2025.

[50] Draft Law for the Approval of Government Emergency Ordinance No. 5/2025 on Certain Measures in the Social Domain and on the Amendment and Completion of Certain Regulatory Acts, PL-x 96/2025, available at: https://www.cdep.ro/pls/proiecte/upl_pck2015.proiect?idp=22288. Accessed 7 October 2025.

10. Tomuş, A. (2022): Fake news şi război în spaţiul românesc. Cum se raportează românii la tema războiului din Ucraina, Revista Română de Drept al Afacerilor, 5.
11. Hentea, C (2008), Noile haine ale propagandei, Paralela 45, p. 57.
12. Ibidem.
13. Romanian Criminal Code, Law n°286/2009, art. 405; Law n°80/1995 concerning the status of military personnel, art. 28; Law n°47/1992 concerning the organizing and functioning of the Constitutional Court, art. 53, § 3, and art. 64; Law n°360/2002 concerning the Statute of Police, art. 45, lit. a); Law n° 17/1990 on the legal regime of the internal maritime waters, the territorial sea, the contiguous zone and the exclusive economic zone of Romania—art. 18, §2; Law n° 1/1998 concerning the organization and operation of the Foreign Intelligence Service, art. 15.
14. Law n°535/2004 concerning the prevention and the fight against terrorism, Article 4, § 9
15. National Cybersecurity Directorate (2024), Deepfake Guide. Available at: https://www.dnsc.ro/vezi/document/ghid-deepfake, Accessed 7 September 2025.
16. Romanian Constitutional Court, Decision 32/2024, Official Gazette no. 1231 (6 December 2024).
17. Romanian Constitutional Court, Decision 42/2025 regarding the request for the annulment of the elections for the office of President of Romania held on 18 May 2025, Official Gazette no. 627 (8 July 2025).
18. Ministry of Foreign Affairs of Romania, Public Policy Proposal for Formulating a Coordinated Response to Online Disinformation within the Competence of the Ministry of Foreign Affairs, April 2024, available at: https://e-consultare.gov.ro/w/2024/03/propunerea-de-politica-publica-pentru-formularea-unui-raspuns-coordonat-la-dezinformarea-online-in-sfera-de-competenta-a-mae/.
19. See https://dictionary.cambridge.org/dictionary/english/astroturfing.
20. Permanent Electoral Authority, Guide on Combating Disinformation in Electoral Processes, 2025, available at: https://www.roaep.ro/prezentare/wp-content/uploads/2025/03/GLFN%20PREZI%2025_3.pdf.
21. Verpeaux, M. (2012), La liberté d'expression dans les jurisprudences constitutionnelles, Nouveaux Cahiers du Conseil Constitutionnel, no. 36 (Dossier: La liberté d'expression et de communication), available at: https://www.conseil-constitutionnel.fr/nouveaux-cahiers-du-conseil-constitutionnel/la-liberte-d-expression-dans-les-jurisprudences-constitutionnelles.
22. Muraru, I. (2008), Comentariu la Articolul 31 in Constituţia României: Comentariu pe articole, edited by Ioan Muraru, Elena Simina Tănăsescu, C.H. Beck, Bucharest, p. 299.
23. Muraru, I. (1999) Protecţia constituţională a libertăţilor de opinie, Lumina Lex, Bucharest, p. 135.
24. European Digital Media Observatory (2023), Evaluating the Implementation of the EU Code of Practice on Disinformation in Romania, available at: https://edmo.eu/wp-content/uploads/2023/09/Evaluating-the-Revised-EU-Code-of-Practice-on-Disinformation-in-Romania_v2.pdf. Accessed 3 September 2025
25. Emergency Ordinance n°1/2025 on Measures for the Organization and Conduct of the 2025 Presidential and Partial Local Elections, Official Gazette No. 44 (17 January 2025), available at: https://legislatie.just.ro/public/DetaliiDocument/293733.
26. Law n°365/2002 on Electronic Commerce, Official Gazette no. 365 (29 November 2006) available at https://legislatie.just.ro/Public/DetaliiDocument/37075.
27. Law n°504/2002—Audiovisual Law, Official Gazette No. 534 of 22 July 2002, available at https://legislatie.just.ro/Public/DetaliiDocumentAfis/214210.
28. National Strategy on Artificial Intelligence 2024–2027 (2024), developed within the framework of the project "Strategic Framework for the Adoption and Use of Innovative Technologies in Public Administration 2021—2027—Solutions for Increasing Efficiency", available at https://www.adr.gov.ro/wp-content/uploads/2024/03/Strategie-Inteligenta-Artificiala-22012024-1.pdf. Accessed 10 September 2025.
29. For developments, see Nistor, D. I. A., Institutional Strategic Communication – an essential instrument supporting national security in the current geopolitical context. available at https://gmr.mapn.ro/.

30. National Defense Strategy of Romania 2025 – 2030, adopted by Parliament decision no. 48/2025, Official Gazette no. 1092 (26 November 2025), paragraph 47.
31. Ibidem.
32. Romanian Constitutional Court, Decision 42/2025 regarding the request for the annulment of the elections for the office of President of Romania held on 18 May 2025, Official Gazette no. 627 (8 July 2025).
33. HCCJ, Decision no. 2230/2021. The proceedings were definitively closed on November 27, 2019, when the Court rejected the request to reopen the case.—See also: Prosecutor's Office attached to the HCCJ Press Release: Overturning the Dismissal Decisions—Revolution Case, 2019, available at: https://www.mpublic.ro/ro/content/c_21-10-2019-16-10. Public Prosecutor's Office attached to the High Court of Cassation and Justice, "Revolution Case—PICCJ—SPM—Extension and Continuation of Criminal Investigation—Crime Against Humanity," Press Release, April 18, 2018, https://www.mpublic.ro/ro/content/c_18-04-2018-10-04. Accessed 10 September 2025
34. Cercelescu, M.: Freedom of speech in times of turbulence, Evrika Publishing, Bucharest, pp. 173–174.
35. HCCJ, Administrative and Fiscal Litigation Section, Decision no. 2193/2025, April 23, 2025.
36. Bucharest Tribunal, Judgment no. 1323/2021, September 23, 2021, Civil Action for Tort Liability, available at: https://sintact.ro/jurisprudenta/1.
37. Court of Appeal, Decision no. 971/2021, November 23, 2021, Civil Action for Tort Liability.
38. Court of Appeal, Judgment no. 373/2020, October 16, 2020, Annulment of Act Issued by the National Council of Audiovisual.
39. Bucharest Court of Appeal (CA), Judgment no. 113/2025, April 22, 2025, Annulment of Electoral Office Decision (Administrative and Fiscal Litigation), available at: https://rejust.ro/juris/4e4ed97ge.
40. Law n°504/2002—Audiovisual Law, Official Gazette No. 534 of 22 July 2002, available at https://legislatie.just.ro/Public/DetaliiDocumentAfis/214210. Accessed 20 September 2025
41. National Council of Audiovisual, Combating Illegal Online Content—Practical Guide, available at: https://www.cna.ro/IMG/pdf/COMBATERE-CONT-ILEGAL-ONLINE-_GHID-_PRACTIC_CNA.pdf. Accessed 7 October 2025.
42. NCA, Combating Illegal Online Content—Practical Guide, https://www.cna.ro/IMG/pdf/COMBATERE-CONT-ILEGAL-ONLINE-_GHID-_PRACTIC_CNA.pdf. Accessed 8 September 2025
43. Law n°50/2024 on the establishment of certain measures for the implementation of Regulation (EU) 2022/2065 of the European Parliament and of the Council of 19 October 2022 on a Single Market for Digital Services, amending Directive 2000/31/EC, and also amending and supplementing Law No. 365/2002 on electronic commerce, https://legislatie.just.ro/public/DetaliiDocument/280106. Accessed 7 October 2025.
44. ANCOM, Decision no. 335/2024 on the procedure for handling complaints concerning digital services, available at: https://www.ancom.ro/uploads/forms_files/Decizie_335_2024_procedura_plangeri1720526272.pdf. Accessed 18 September 2025.
45. ANCOM Annual Report 2024, https://www.ancom.ro/uploads/links_files/Raport_anual_ANCOM_2024. Accessed 18 September 2025.
46. Law n°554/2004 on Administrative Litigation, Official Gazette No. 1154 of 7 December 2004. https://legislatie.just.ro/Public/DetaliiDocument/57426. Accessed 15 September 2025.
47. National Defense Strategy of Romania 2025 – 2030, adopted by Parliament decision no. 48/2025, Official Gazette no. 1092 (26 November 2025), paragraph 72.
48. Botan, M. & Stancea, A (November 2023): Evaluating the Implementation of the EU Code of Practice on Disinformation in Romania, available at https://edmo.eu/wp-content/uploads/2023/09/Evaluating-the-Revised-EU-Code-of-Practice-on-Disinformation-in-Romania_v2.pdf. Accessed at 9 December 2025.
49. Draft Law on the Responsible Use of Technology in the Context of the Deepfake Phenomenon, PL-x No. 471/2023, available at: https://www.cdep.ro/pls/proiecte/upl_pck2015.proiect?idp=20853. Accessed 7 October 2025.

50. Draft Law for the Approval of Government Emergency Ordinance No. 5/2025 on Certain Measures in the Social Domain and on the Amendment and Completion of Certain Regulatory Acts, PL-x 96/2025, available at: https://www.cdep.ro/pls/proiecte/upl_pck2015.proiect?idp=22288. Accessed 7 October 2025.

The Legal Framework Against Online Disinformation in Slovenia

Matija Damjan and Tjaša Kalin

Abstract This Chapter examines how online disinformation is addressed in the Slovenian legal system, in the absence of a dedicated anti-disinformation act. It first outlines how disinformation is conceptualised in selected government projects and security documents. It then turns to the legal framework, beginning with the constitutional protection of freedom of expression and the rights of correction and reply, and examines how untruthful or misleading content may give rise to consequences under media and audiovisual regulation, electoral law, digital services rules, criminal offences, and civil liability. The analysis shows that Slovenia addresses disinformation indirectly through a dispersed set of rules aimed at protecting other legal interests, which allow many harmful manifestations of disinformation to be tackled but leave gaps for lawful but harmful content and for systemic risks associated with platforms and generative AI.

1 Introduction

The issue of online disinformation has garnered attention in public and political discourse in Slovenia, primarily through awareness-raising projects and references in strategic documents.[1] The Slovenian legal system lacks a dedicated regulatory framework regulating disinformation directly. It does not specifically prohibit or

[1] Project Stop Disinformation – READ, THINK, CHECK of the Slovenian Government Communication Office; project No/Yes of the Slovenian Press Agency; Resolution on the National Security Strategy of the Republic of Slovenia.

The chapter is based on research supported by the Slovenian Research Agency under the research programme P5-0337 "Legal challenges of the information society".

M. Damjan (✉) · T. Kalin
Faculty of Law, Institute for Comparative Law, University of Ljubljana, Ljubljana, Slovenia
e-mail: matija.damjan@pf.uni-lj.si

T. Kalin
e-mail: tjasa.kalin@pf.uni-lj.si

P. Passaglia (ed.), *European Legal Perspectives on Online Disinformation*, Ius Gentium: Comparative Perspectives on Law and Justice 140,
https://doi.org/10.1007/978-3-032-25785-7_17

sanction the creation or dissemination of disinformation. Nevertheless, existing legislation across several areas of law attaches legal consequences to the dissemination of false information or aims to prevent such activity, thereby indirectly addressing disinformation, including online disinformation.

This chapter examines how online disinformation is approached within Slovenia's legal and policy framework. It outlines the constitutional basis for freedom of expression, analyses the main legal areas in which this freedom may be limited, including media law, electoral law, online communications regulation, criminal law, and civil law, and reviews relevant initiatives and soft-law instruments.

2 The Notion of Disinformation

Slovenia has not adopted a legally binding definition of disinformation. It is neither defined in any law or regulation nor listed in the dictionary of Slovenian legal terminology,[2] which indicates that the term does not yet have a fully established meaning in Slovenian legal theory. However, the Slovenian Government has been paying attention to the phenomenon of disinformation. In 2024, the Government Communication Office launched the Stop Disinformation—READ, THINK, CHECK project[3] in cooperation with the Ministry of Digital Transformation. The ongoing project aims to emphasise the importance of verifying information and to share tips on how to recognise disinformation and verify information before sharing it. The Slovenian Government's website devoted to the project defines disinformation as verifiably false or misleading information that is created, presented, and disseminated with the intent to deceive or achieve economic or political gain, and which may cause public harm.[4] Although this is not an official definition, it shows how government bodies generally understand the term disinformation and that they view it as worth paying attention to.

The Government Communication Office's formulation aligns with the European Commission's definition in the Action Plan against Disinformation,[5] which provides the foundation for understanding and addressing disinformation across EU member states. The website offers three key elements of disinformation: deception, purpose and profit or interest. Deception means that disinformation distorts facts, while purpose entails that it is a manipulative deception. Regarding the third element, individuals who create and spread disinformation must be aware of their intentions and the desired outcome.

---

[2] Pravni terminološki slovar, https://isjfr.zrc-sazu.si/sl/terminologisce/slovarji/pravni, last accessed 2025/12/9.

[3] GOV.SI, Ustavimo dezinformacije: PreBERI, preMISLI, PREVERI, https://www.gov.si/novice/2024-05-22-ustavimo-dezinformacije-preberi-premisli-preveri/, last accessed 2025/12/5.

[4] GOV.SI, Dezinformacije, https://www.gov.si/zbirke/projekti-in-programi/dezinformacije/, last accessed 2025/10/14.

[5] JOIN(2018) 36 final, p. 1.

The only legal act in Slovenia that expressly mentions disinformation is the Resolution on the National Security Strategy of the Republic of Slovenia,[6] adopted by the National Assembly on 26 September 2019. Under the Slovenian constitutional order, a National Assembly's resolution is a program document that defines the Assembly's policy in a specific area,[7] but does not have binding effects (Article 153 of the Constitution[8]). The National Security Strategy is the fundamental development and policy document in the field of national security. It aims to define national interests and national security objectives, analyse the security environment, set out the starting points for policy responses to individual security threats and risks, and determine the overall system and organisational solutions regarding the state's overall functioning in ensuring national security. The Resolution mentions disinformation twice: once under the point on hybrid threats and once under the point on information and cyber threats. It emphasises that the state and non-state actors use disinformation and fake news to destabilise democratic institutions, interfere with political processes, weaken constitutionally defined decision-making, and influence public opinion by exploiting vulnerable groups. Disinformation is also depicted as a strategic tool for creating confusion, increasing societal vulnerability, supporting radicalisation, and advancing geopolitical interests. In the cyber domain, the spread of disinformation is identified as a significant threat alongside cyberattacks, espionage, and intellectual property theft, with the potential to undermine critical infrastructure, damage the political system and the state's international reputation, and endanger public safety.

The Communication Office's disinformation project website also differentiates between disinformation, misinformation and malinformation. Misinformation is defined as unintentional false information that someone spreads in good faith without malicious intent, but which can still cause harm. The difference between disinformation and misinformation lies in their primary purpose: misinformation is not intended to mislead deliberately. Malinformation is defined as information that is based on facts but taken out of context and presented in a biased manner. As a result, it is misleading and therefore potentially harmful.[9]

While the project website does not specifically address online disinformation, it emphasises that, with the growing role of social media platforms and the development of artificial intelligence (AI), the potential for spreading disinformation is rapidly increasing. It notes that disinformation has its greatest impact during times of crisis, uncertainty, and widespread dissatisfaction, as it operates on an emotional level and influences people's opinions and decisions. Its purpose is to create confusion, arouse anger and fear, and damage the reputation of individuals, organisations, institutions, and countries. The problem of spreading false information is most pronounced in

---

[6] *Resolucija o strategiji nacionalne varnosti Republike Slovenije*, Official Gazette of the Republic of Slovenia, no. 59/19.

[7] Supreme Court of the Republic of Slovenia, I Up 102/2022, 10. 5. 2023.

[8] *Ustava Republike Slovenije*, Official Gazette of the Republic of Slovenia, no. 33/91, 42/97—UZS68, 66/00—UZ80, 24/03—UZ3a, 47, 68, 69/04—UZ14, 69/04—UZ43, 69/04—UZ50, 68/06—UZ121,140,143, 47/13, 47/13, 75/16—UZ70a, 92/21—UZ62a.

[9] GOV.SI, Ustavimo dezinformacije: PreBERI, preMISLI, PREVERI, https://www.gov.si/novice/2024-05-22-ustavimo-dezinformacije-preberi-premisli-preveri/, last accessed 2025/12/5.

crises, such as the coronavirus pandemic. As for the negative impact of spreading disinformation, the website highlights that since disinformation is used to exaggerate differences in public debates or even to influence political processes, it poses a threat to democracies, as its purpose is to undermine trust in state institutions and the media, thereby undermining confidence in democracy, as it hinders people's ability to make decisions based on reliable data and information.

Since no official definition of disinformation is adopted in Slovenian law, the above definitions suggested by the Communication Office will be used for this chapter.

3 The Constitution of the Republic of Slovenia

Article 39, Paragraph 1 of the Slovenian Constitution guarantees the freedom of expression of thought, freedom of speech and public appearance, freedom of the press, and of other forms of public communication and expression. The freedom of expression is complemented by the right to collect, receive, and disseminate information and opinions freely. Additionally, Paragraph 2 grants everyone the right to obtain information of a public nature in which they have a well-founded legal interest under the law, except in instances provided by law.

The right to freedom of expression, as conceived in the Constitution, derives from the freedom of thought, ideas, opinions, and conscience, and encompasses both the reception and dissemination of information.[10] Dissemination includes statements, messages, ideas, opinions, viewpoints, and other forms of communication.[11] The right should be interpreted broadly to encompass any form of expression of ideas, such as written and spoken words, audiovisual media, images, drawings, pictures, art, satire and all forms of transmitting messages within the framework of private and public communication, expression and information exchange.[12]

No constitutional provision requires expression to be true in order to enjoy the protection under the fundamental right. Therefore, disinformation is not prohibited per se and is not expressly excluded from the scope of free expression.

Nevertheless, the Constitution also provides a specific right to respond to false or misleading information published in the media by means of a correction or reply, which are themselves forms of expression. Article 40 of the Constitution guarantees the right to correct published information which has damaged a right or interest of an individual, organisation, or body, as well as the right to reply to such published information. The terminology used to designate these rights can be misleading, as the right to correction under the Slovenian law corresponds to what is more typically referred to as the right to reply in other legal systems, that is, the right to respond to factually incorrect information published in public media.[13] Most continental European

---

[10] Teršek (2019), p. 374.

[11] Ibid.

[12] Ibid.

[13] Teršek (2019a), p. 390.

legal systems recognise this right in their media legislation, but do not guarantee it at the constitutional level.[14] The Slovenian right to reply, on the other hand, is conceived more broadly as the right to respond to an initial publication regardless of whether it contained untrue statements and to confront it with additional information or opposing views. This concept is largely unknown in other legal systems.[15] The exercise of the right to reply is subject to a public-interest condition detailed in media legislation and extensive case law (see below). Both the right to correction and the right to reply can be used to counter disinformation on online media platforms. However, such defence against disinformation is only reactive rather than pre-emptive, and its activation is in the hands of the affected individuals.

While freedom of expression is broadly conceived in the Constitution, it may be subject to limitations under the general limitation clause in Article 15, Paragraph 3. Under this provision, human rights and fundamental freedoms can be limited by the rights of others as well as in cases specifically prescribed by the Constitution. Online disinformation can severely negatively impact constitutionally recognised values, such as civic discourse and electoral processes in a democratic society, public security, public health, non-discrimination and an individual's privacy and reputation.[16]

Examples of human rights that might justify restricting freedom of speech when disinformation is concerned include the right to equality before the law (Article 14 of the Constitution), the right to personal dignity and safety (Article 34 of the Constitution), and the right to privacy and personality (Article 35 of the Constitution). A direct constitutional limitation of the freedom of expression is contained in Article 63 of the Constitution, which prohibits incitement to discrimination and intolerance, as well as incitement to violence and war. Accordingly, knowingly spreading untrue information in situations where it could infringe other fundamental rights or promote discrimination and intolerance can lead to civil or criminal liability, or to other sanctions under the rules of criminal law, obligations law, and media law that operationalise the abstract constitutional limitations on free speech.

When it comes to grounds for limiting the freedom of expression in the context of elections and referenda, Article 43 of the Constitution guarantees the universal and equal right to vote. Furthermore, Article 44 states that every citizen has the right, in accordance with the law, to participate either directly or through elected representatives in the management of public affairs. Election laws and media laws regulate the expression of political advertising and media reporting on polling data to protect these rights, including rules against misleading or deceptive political campaigns and media reporting on elections.

---

[14] Ibid.

[15] Ibid.

[16] Regulation (EU) 2022/2065 of the European Parliament and of the Council of 19 October 2022 on a Single Market for Digital Services and amending Directive 2000/31/EC (Digital Services Act), OJ L 277, 27.10.2022, pp. 1–102, Recitals 83 and 84.

In the following sections, we will examine how the constitutional principles outlined above are implemented in several fields of law, including the media, audio-visual communications, elections, online environments, and criminal and civil law, and to what extent these rules apply to online disinformation.

4 Media Law

4.1 *The Media as a Means of Spreading Disinformation*

Modern media environments, although central to the circulation of reliable information, can themselves become susceptible to deliberate manipulation, enabling the intentional or inadvertent spread of disinformation through editorial influence, targeted advertising, or other forms of external pressure. According to the OECD, a diverse and independent media sector, and an information ecosystem that supports journalism and facilitates the creation of high-quality news, plays an essential role in enabling open and democratic societies by providing reliable information, bringing issues to the public agenda, facilitating debate, serving as a watchdog for the public interest, and holding public actors accountable.[17] Therefore, pluralistic, independent and trusted media are indispensable for safeguarding information integrity and supporting informed democratic debate.[18]

4.2 *Media Act*

4.2.1 Journalistic and Editorial Autonomy

The Media Act (ZMed-1),[19] adopted in September 2025 and replacing the previous Media Act of 2001, regulates all types of media, except where special legislation applies to audiovisual media. The ZMed-1 lays down the rights, obligations, and responsibilities of media publishers, as well as the measures for protecting the public interest in the media sphere. It aims to ensure freedom of expression, protect the freedom and independence of the media, promote and safeguard media pluralism and protect journalistic and editorial autonomy.[20]

Chapter II of the ZMed-1 is titled "Freedom of Expression and Independence of the Media and Journalistic and Editorial Autonomy." Accordingly, Article 4 provides that media activity is based on the principles of freedom of expression, the inviolability

[17] OECD (2024), Facts not Fakes: Tackling Disinformation, Strengthening Information Integrity, OECD Publishing, Paris, https://doi.org/10.1787/d909ff7a-en, p. 41.

[18] Ibid., pp. 17, 30.

[19] *Zakon o medijih*, Official Gazette of the Republic of Slovenia, no. 69/25.

[20] Article 1, Paragraph 1 of ZMed-1.

and protection of human personality and dignity, the free flow of information, and the openness of the media to diverse options, beliefs, and various types of content. It is also founded on the autonomy of editors, journalists, and other authors in creating programme content in accordance with editorial policies and professional codes, as well as on the personal responsibility of journalists, other authors, and editors for the consequences of their work.

The principle of editorial and journalistic autonomy is established in Article 5 of the ZMed-1, which guarantees that editors, journalists and other contributors may operate independently within the framework of a media outlet's editorial policy and in accordance with the publisher's founding act. Journalists are entitled to refuse assignments that would violate professional or ethical standards, and they are legally protected from retaliation (such as dismissal, demotion or reduction in pay) for exercising this right or for expressing opinions consistent with professional norms. Article 5 also prohibits any unauthorised alteration of journalistic content without the journalist's consent. These provisions reinforce the media's editorial and journalistic autonomy, which is necessary for producing accurate and trustworthy information. Ensuring that journalists can work independently and refuse assignments that contravene professional or ethical standards helps prevent the dissemination of disinformation arising from political, commercial, or editorial pressure.

Correct attribution of all contributors of media content is also required by Article 5. Attributing works to fictitious or non-existent authors is expressly forbidden. Pseudonyms can be used for justified reasons, such as the protection of sources, in which case the contribution must clearly indicate the use of a pseudonym. Signing a journalistic contribution without the journalist's knowledge or against their will is not permitted. This provision ensures transparency in authorship and prevents the deliberate concealment or fabrication of sources.

The confidentiality of journalistic sources is protected in Article 6 of the ZMed-1. Neither journalists nor editors, publishers nor individuals professionally connected to them may be compelled to disclose the identity of their sources or the content of confidential communications, except by a court order and only in cases explicitly provided for by criminal law. The provision also prohibits the detention, investigation or surveillance of such persons, as well as the search or seizure of their premises or equipment, for the purpose of identifying sources without judicial authorisation. In addition, Article 6 explicitly forbids the installation of intrusive surveillance software on devices used by journalists or related persons, again allowing exceptions only by court order. These provisions should strengthen resistance to the spread of disinformation by promoting trustworthy and independent journalism. Protecting journalistic sources promotes independent and credible reporting by enabling sources to disclose information of public interest without fear of retaliation.

4.2.2 Obligations of Media Publishers

Chapter III of the ZMed-1, which regulates the promotion and protection of media pluralism, also addresses the disclosure of conflicts of interest. Under Article 23, a publisher must disclose, at the time of publication of the programme content, any actual or potential conflict of interest that could affect the provision of information to the public. The disclosure must be made in a manner that is clearly understandable and accessible to the public. This provision aims to ensure transparency about media interests, making the audience better aware of the risks of manipulation of media content and the dissemination of false information.

Chapter IV of the ZMed-1 prescribes various obligations and responsibilities of media publishers, as well as certain limitations on media activity, several of which are directed at the spread of untrue or misleading content via media. Article 51 prohibits using media for the incitement to violence or hatred and incitement to commit terrorist offences. It forbids media outlets from promoting hostility against individuals or groups based on personal characteristics such as gender, race, ethnicity, religion, political opinion or other protected grounds. It also bans any form of incitement, glorification or recruitment related to terrorism, including the financing and facilitation of terrorist acts. These restrictions apply equally to traditional and audiovisual media services. This provision helps limit the spread of harmful and extremist narratives that may be fuelled by disinformation.

Further, Article 53 regulates public commenting on media platforms. Media publishers who allow readers to comment on their online publications must establish commenting rules and post them at an appropriate place on the website. These rules must specify the method of signing comments, prohibit incitement to violence and hatred based on personal characteristics such as gender, race, religion, or political opinion, and set out procedures for lodging and handling complaints about comments that fail to comply with the published rules. Upon receiving a notification, the publishers are obliged to remove any violating comments as soon as possible, or at the latest on the subsequent working day. This provision is relevant to the online spread of disinformation and hate speech, as it imposes responsibility on media outlets to moderate user-generated content. The explanatory memorandum to the draft law notes that self-regulation of online hate speech removes the risk of censorship of comments, as media outlets set their own commenting rules.[21] Although the prohibition of disinformation in online comments is not a compulsory part of the commenting rules, requiring transparent rules, traceable authorship and prompt removal of unlawful or harmful comments should help limit the spread of disinformation in digital spaces, promoting commentators' accountability and safer public discourse related to media publications.

Article 56 establishes rules to ensure transparency and ethical standards in advertising. It prohibits covert advertising, i.e. any paid content presented in a way that could mislead readers, listeners or viewers into believing it is editorial or journalistic content. Both the advertiser and the managing editor are liable for such violations,

[21] Republika Slovenija, Ministrstvo za kulturo, Predlog predpisa: Zakon o medijih, 14. 5. 2024, https://e-uprava.gov.si/si/drzava-in-druzba/e-demokracija/predlogi-predpisov/predlog-predpisa.html?id=16268. The memorandum also refers to the decision of the European Court of Human Rights (ECtHR) in the case of Delfi AS v. Estonia, pointing out that the ECtHR thus took the view that the State is permitted to impose stricter liability on the media for allowing the publication of comments of an extreme nature, constituting manifest hate speech and incitement to violence.

and the law presumes intent in cases of covert advertising, placing the burden of proof on the editor to demonstrate otherwise. Article 56 further bans the use of technical methods that prevent conscious recognition of advertisements and prohibits ads that violate human dignity, incite hatred or violence, promote harmful or illegal behaviour, insult religious or political beliefs, harm consumer interests or falsely market products as having medical properties. By prohibiting covert advertising and the deceptive presentation of sponsored material, the law protects audiences from hidden influence and from covert, commercially or politically driven disinformation in advertising campaigns.

As a relatively recent law, ZMed-1 also addresses AI-generated content as an emerging source of disinformation by introducing labelling and transparency requirements. Article 66 of the ZMed-1 requires that any content produced wholly or partially by generative AI systems is clearly marked and easily distinguishable from human-created material. Publishers must also disclose how AI tools are used, especially when they can influence how users interpret or engage with content. The use of AI systems intended for users is considered misleading if, in any way, including through presentation, it deceives or is likely to mislead users and is likely to influence their behaviour or opinions. Article 67 complements the transparency obligations by establishing publisher liability for programme content related to AI systems. The publisher is responsible for the accuracy of statements or data contained in programme content generated or partially generated by AI systems, as well as for ensuring that such content complies with the ZMed-1 and other relevant legislation. In cases where a violation is identified, the publisher must remove the relevant content as soon as possible, no later than within one working day after notification.

The Inspectorate for Culture and Media supervises the implementation of ZMed-1. It is also authorised to impose administrative sanctions on media publishers and their responsible persons for violations of the law's provisions.

4.2.3 The Right to Correction and Reply

Articles 68 and 69 of the ZMed-1 implement at a practical level the right to correction and reply guaranteed in principle by the Constitution (as described above). Very similar rules on correction and reply were already contained in the previous Media Act of 2001.

Article 67 of the ZMed-1 grants every individual the possibility to request the managing editor to publish, free of charge, a correction of any published information that has infringed upon their right or interest. A correction may consist either of denying or rectifying false or inaccurate statements (correction in the narrow sense) or of presenting additional or opposing facts and circumstances that challenge or supplement the published information. This right may be exercised by any natural or legal person affected by the publication, within 30 days of becoming aware of it and no later than three months after the publication date.

The Supreme Court of Slovenia held in 2007 that the right to correction is an integral part of the dialogue that must be made available to the person about whom a particular topic has been raised. The publication of a correction is therefore an integral part of media freedom rather than a legal sanction for a legal violation.[22] Somewhat departing from this view is the position adopted by the Supreme Court in 2022, that the right to correction significantly interferes with media freedom and therefore cannot be unlimited in its content. Instead, the affected person may respond only to the statements in the article that affected them, either by simply denying them or by citing facts and circumstances that refute the decisive statements in the published article.[23] For instance, a person labelled in a television report as an anti-vaccination activist was granted the right to a correction, providing the average viewer with information that was missing from the report and enabling them to form their own opinion as to whether the information that the plaintiff belonged to a group of unconditional opponents of vaccination was justified.[24]

Article 69 of the ZMed-1 regulates the procedure for requesting a correction. The request must be made in writing, either in physical or electronic form, with a qualified electronic signature. It must be evident that it is a correction, indicate the publication to which it refers, the date of that publication and include a title of the correction. If the title is not included or cannot be inferred from the content, the editor determines it. The right to correction also applies when the media ceases to operate. In such cases, the publisher or its legal successor must ensure publication in a compatible outlet.

The right to reply is defined in Article 70 of the ZMed-1 as everyone's right to request that the managing editor publish their response to published information free of charge when the response is in the public interest because it contains verifiable statements that refute, substantially correct, or substantially supplement statements in published information that is of particular importance to the public. The reply must be published without changes or additions; only spelling corrections are permitted. However, the managing editor may ask the person who requested publication of the reply to shorten it before publication. The managing editor may refuse to publish responses with identical content if one has already been published. As already mentioned, the exercise of this right is not contingent on the inaccuracy of the initial publication.[25] Still, it allows any individual to inform the public of any additional information relevant to the topic of the initial publication if the public interest in such information is demonstrated.

If the managing editor refuses to publish a correction or a reply, the affected individuals can enforce these rights by filing a civil lawsuit against the publisher for publishing the correction or reply. To ensure the effectiveness of the correction or reply, the judicial decision must be made quickly. Accordingly, the lawsuit may

[22] Supreme Court of the Republic of Slovenia, II Ips 737/2007, 25. 10. 2007.

[23] Supreme Court of the Republic of Slovenia, II Ips 49/2022, 7. 9. 2022.

[24] Supreme Court of the Republic of Slovenia, II Ips 51/2024, 3. 12. 2024.

[25] The Supreme Court of Slovenia confirmed that the inaccuracy of the facts published in the article for which a correction is requested is not a prerequisite for exercising the right to correction. Determining the (in)accuracy of these facts is also not subject to evidentiary proceedings. Supreme Court of the Republic of Slovenia, II Ips 439/2007, 26. 7. 2007.

be filed no later than 30 days after the expiry of the deadline for publishing the correction or reply and the proceedings before the court of first instance are urgent, and the judgment must be served within three months of the filing of the lawsuit at the latest (Article 72 of the ZMed-1).

A controversial recent judicial case raised the question of whether people can take matters into their own hands when the media refuses to report information they consider essential to the public interest. In 2021, during the pandemic, 20 protesters broke into the premises of TV Slovenija. They managed to enter the news program studio, where they wanted to reveal alleged documents about the dangers of COVID-19 vaccines. The police intervened, escorted the protesters out of the building and charged them with misdemeanour offences for disturbing public order. One of the participants filed a request for judicial protection against the decision imposing a misdemeanour. The Local Court in Ljubljana granted the request and halted the misdemeanour proceedings. The judge considered that the offender had acted in justified extreme necessity to protect the lives and health of people who, as she believed in good faith, had not been informed by the central public media service about the possible serious side effects of COVID vaccines.[26] The decision was harshly criticised.[27] Interestingly, the dispute arose from a situation in which both sides accused each other of misinformation: the media was accused of concealing the truth about vaccination's harmful effects, while protesters were accused of spreading false information about them.

4.3 Audiovisual Media Services Act

The Audiovisual Media Services Act (ZAvMS),[28] which transposes into Slovenian law the Audiovisual Media Services (AVMS) Directive,[29] outlines the rights, obligations, and responsibilities of legal and natural persons providing audiovisual media services and video-sharing platform services, as well as the competences of the national regulatory authority and its cooperation with their counterparts in other EU Member States. Its provisions most relevant to the issue of disinformation are analogous to those found in the general media legislation under the ZMed-1.

Like the ZMed-1, the ZAvMS prohibits incitement to violence or hatred, as well as incitement to commit terrorist offences through audiovisual media services, in line

[26] Local Court of Ljubljana, ZSV 440/2023, 25. 8. 2025.

[27] G. Stražišar, V imenu skrajne sile lahko vdremo v TV-studio, Dnevnik, 13. 11. 2025, https://www.dnevnik.si/novice/slovenija/v-imenu-skrajne-sile-lahko-vdremo-v-tv-studio-2765875/, last accessed 2025/12/9.

[28] *Zakon o avdiovizualnih medijskih storitvah*, Official Gazette of the Republic of Slovenia, no. 87/11, 84/15, 204/21.

[29] Directive (EU) 2018/1808 of the European Parliament and of the Council of 14 November 2018 amending Directive 2010/13/EU on the coordination of certain provisions laid down by law, regulation or administrative action in Member States concerning the provision of audiovisual media services in view of changing market realities, OJ L 303, 28.11.2018, pp. 69–92.

with the requirements of the AVMS Directive (Article 9 of the ZAvMS). Regarding the right to correction and reply, Article 13 of the ZAvMS refers to the application of Articles 68 and 69 of the ZMed-1 (as described above). Under Article 19 of the ZAvMS, audiovisual commercial communications must be clearly identifiable as such. Surreptitious audiovisual commercial communication is prohibited. Audiovisual commercial communications may not use technical means that prevent users from consciously recognising such communications. These provisions are relevant to the broader framework of countering disinformation, as they collectively promote transparency, accountability and respect for factual integrity in audiovisual content.

Article 25 of the ZAvMS prohibits sponsorship of news and informational programme content where the risk of disinformation under the sponsor's potential influence is highest. Sponsorship of other audiovisual media content is allowed in principle. However, there is a strict ban on the promotion of prescription-only medicines or medical services, as well as medicinal products for which the competent medicinal authority has not approved advertising. The latter prohibition, in particular, should prevent the use of sponsorship to promote fake medicines that may be unsafe or lack proven medicinal effects.

4.4 *Code of Conduct of Slovenian Journalists*

The ZMed-1 refers to ethical criteria and standards of journalism in several places. Article 5, for example, stipulates that journalists have the right to refuse to prepare a journalistic contribution or to perform any other journalistic task if doing so would be contrary to the professional and ethical rules, criteria, and standards of journalism. Article 12 stipulates that the public interest in the media includes, among other things, independent, ethical, and credible journalism, as well as the promotion of self-regulation in the media. Article 14 further provides that compliance with professional and ethical standards of journalism is one of the conditions for granting financial support to the media.

Accordingly, the Slovenian Association of Journalists and the Slovenian Union of Journalists adopted the Code of Conduct of Slovenian Journalists,[30] which sets out ethical standards as guidelines and a commitment for the work of journalists and other content creators whose work is published in Slovenian media, regardless of the form of its dissemination. The Code of Conduct was first adopted in 2002 and was last amended in 2025. The Code of Conduct is a form of soft law, meaning compliance with it is voluntary. Violations can be reported to the Journalistic Ethics Tribunal, whose decisions are mainly symbolic.

Several provisions of the Code of Conduct address truthful reporting and the prevention of disinformation in public media. Under Article 1, journalists are required to verify the accuracy of the information they collect and avoid errors. They must

[30] Kodeks novinarjev Slovenije, https://novinar.com/drustvo-novinarjev-slovenije/o-nas/dokumenti/kodeks/, last accessed 2025/12/9.

acknowledge and correct their error, even if it is unintentional. In such cases, the Journalistic Ethics tribunal may determine that the journalist has not violated the Code of Conduct.

When publishing information that concerns serious accusations, Article 3 requires the journalist to obtain a response from the persons concerned, preferably in the same report or as soon as possible thereafter. The same applies when the journalist summarises serious accusations from other media or archives. If the journalist was unable to obtain a response, this must be explained to the public.

A journalist must not withhold information essential to understanding the topic being discussed.[31] When publishing unverified information, rumours or speculations, a journalist must clearly indicate this.[32] A journalist is obligated to distinguish information from commentary clearly.[33] The difference between factual reporting and opinion must be sufficiently evident so that the audience can clearly differentiate between facts and the journalist's view.

These ethical principles are relevant to the issue of disinformation, as they promote accuracy, transparency and accountability in journalistic work. By requiring verification of facts, the disclosure of unconfirmed information and a clear separation between factual reporting and opinion, the Code of Conduct establishes professional standards that help prevent the spread of false or misleading content. Although compliance is voluntary, the Code of Conduct serves as an essential self-regulatory safeguard, strengthening the media's credibility and combating disinformation through responsible, ethical journalism.

When deciding on a damages claim against a newspaper, the Higher Court in Ljubljana stressed that the publication of offensive, false statements is not protected by freedom of expression. According to the code of journalistic ethics and the standards of freedom of expression established by the Constitutional Court and the ECtHR, journalists are obliged to report in good faith and based on established facts.[34]

5 Regulation of Digital Services

5.1 *The Systemic Risk of Spreading Disinformation*

The first report of the European Board for Digital Services of November 2025 notes that several social media platforms, when addressing systemic risks related to civic discourse, the electoral process, and public security, acknowledged the potential role of their algorithmic content recommendation systems in the viral spread of

---

[31] Article 4 of the Code of Journalists of Slovenia.

[32] Article 5 of the Code of Journalists of Slovenia.

[33] Article 15 of the Code of Journalists of Slovenia.

[34] Higher Court in Ljubljana, I Cp 3019/2014, 4. 2. 2015.

misleading narratives. Search engines focused on the risks that disinformation and misinformation may surface in search results due to ranking mechanisms.[35]

The regulation of digital service providers' responsibilities and their liability for illegal or harmful online content is primarily determined by EU law, specifically the Digital Services Act (DSA)[36] and the Terrorist Content Online Regulation (TERREG).[37] The section focuses on how these instruments are applied and enforced in Slovenia, identifying the competent authorities and outlining the responsibilities assigned to them.

5.2 *Rules for Applying the Digital Services Act*

To implement and enforce the DSA in its territory, Slovenia adopted the Act on the Implementation of the Regulation (EU) on the Single Market for Digital Services (ZIUETDS),[38] which entered into force on 13 April 2024. The ZIUETDS designates the competent authorities responsible for implementing and supervising the DSA, and sets out their powers, offences, and sanctions related to its implementation. It also defined the tasks of the digital services coordinator and the ministry responsible for the information society, concerning the creation of a supportive environment for a safe and trustworthy internet, as well as the procedure for cases involving the removal of illegal content.

According to Article 3 of the ZIUETDS, the tasks of the digital services coordinator are performed by the Agency for Communication Networks and Services of the Republic of Slovenia (AKOS), which is an independent body that regulates and supervises the electronic communications market, performs tasks related to radio and television, and regulates and supervises postal services and railway traffic in Slovenia.[39] The second competent authority is the Information Commissioner, an autonomous and independent body that supervises the protection of personal data and access to public information.[40]

Articles 14 to 17 of the ZIUETDS detail how Slovenia enforces the specific mechanisms introduced by the DSA. These provisions establish the procedures for recognising and supervising trusted flaggers, vetted researchers, and out-of-court

---

[35] First report of the European Board for Digital Services in cooperation with the Commission pursuant to Article 35(2) DSA on the most prominent and recurrent systemic risks as well as mitigation measures, 18. 11. 2025.

[36] Regulation (EU) 2022/2065 of the European Parliament and of the Council of 19 October 2022 on a Single Market For Digital Services, OJ L 277, 27.10.2022, pp. 1–102.

[37] Regulation (EU) 2021/784 of the European Parliament and of the Council of 29 April 2021 on addressing the dissemination of terrorist content online, OJ L 172, 17.5.2021, pp. 79–109.

[38] *Zakon o izvajanju Uredbe (EU) o enotnem trgu digitalnih storitev*, Official Gazette of the Republic of Slovenia, no. 30/24 and 95/24 – ZIUETDS.

[39] AKOS website: https://www.akos-rs.si/en/.

[40] Website of Information Commissioner: https://www.ip-rs.si/en/.

dispute settlement bodies, as well as the judicial process for removing illegal online content.

The DSA does not regulate disinformation per se, because most false information is lawful yet harmful.[41] But some disinformation campaigns cross the line into illegality (e.g., election manipulation, public health fraud, coordinated foreign interference, and certain consumer fraud schemes).[42] For these categories, trusted flaggers can identify factual manipulation with high evidential quality, provide high-quality notices to platforms and ensure rapid demotion, removal, or disabling of illegal falsehoods.[43] This reduces the window of virality, which is critical as disinformation often has its strongest impact in the first hours or days. If volumes of trusted-flagger notices spike around a topic (e.g., vaccine hoaxes, hybrid interference operations), very large online platforms must treat this as evidence of heightened systemic risk and adapt their mitigation strategies accordingly.

Under Article 14, AKOS is responsible for granting the status of trusted flagger in accordance with Article 22 of DSA. This status can be obtained by legal or natural persons, including public or private entities and self-employed individuals, provided they meet the criteria set out in the DSA. Applications must include detailed administrative and identification data, as well as evidence demonstrating compliance with the DSA. AKOS also has the power to temporarily suspend or permanently revoke a trusted flagger's status, either on its own initiative or upon the proposal of an online platform, if the entity no longer meets the prescribed conditions or acts in a manner contrary to its obligations. In September 2025, AKOS awarded the first trusted flagger status in Slovenia to the PIP Institute—Legal and Information Centre Maribor[44] for the field of online violence, illegal or harmful speech, and the protection of minors.[45]

AKOS may issue general acts specifying the content and form of applications and reports to ensure uniform procedure. In August 2025, it published recommendations on addressing illegal content on online platforms. The document explains what illegal or harmful content is and recommends appropriate actions for users when they encounter it.[46] Disinformation, along with misinformation and harmful speech, is sorted under the category of harmful content that is not formally illegal but may be considered unethical and socially undesirable. The recommendations point out

---

[41] O Fathaigh et al. (2025), p. 2.

[42] Wilman et al. (2024), p. 271.

[43] Concerning the importance of trusted flaggers in connection to disinformation, see: O Fathaigh et al. (2025), p. 5.

[44] Website of PIP Institute: https://zavodpip.si/.

[45] AKOS, The Agency grants its first trusted flagger status, 3. 9. 2025, https://www.akos-rs.si/en/digital-services/explore/news/news/the-agency-grants-its-first-trusted-flagger-status, last accessed 2025/12/9.

[46] AKOS, The Agency publishes recommendations on how to deal with illegal content on online platforms, 6. 8. 2025, https://www.akos-rs.si/en/digital-services/explore/news/news/the-agency-publishes-recommendations-on-how-to-deal-with-illegal-content-on-online-platforms, last accessed 2025/12/9.

that such content may violate the terms of service and can be reported directly to the platform.[47]

Article 15 of the ZIUETDS introduces the status of vetted researcher, which may be granted by AKOS either *ex officio* or upon request, in accordance with Article 40 of the DSA. This status enables researchers to obtain access to platform data for the purpose of studying systematic risks, such as disinformation. This article defines the formal requirements for applications.

The certification of out-of-court dispute settlement bodies is regulated in Article 16 of the ZIUETDS. In line with Article 21 of the DSA, AKOS issues certificates to applicants who meet the prescribed conditions and may later revoke the certificates if the body ceases to fulfil the conditions set out in the DSA. Furthermore, AKOS is authorised to define the content and format of both reports and certificates under the general acts.

Finally, Article 17 of the ZIUETDS outlines the judicial procedure for removing illegal content when all other remedies under the DSA have been exhausted. Jurisdiction lies with the District Court in Nova Gorica. The court may order the removal or restriction of access to illegal online content, including the disabling of hosting services or deletion of domain names. It must respect the constitutional guarantees of freedom of expression and information, as well as the principle of proportionality. In every case, the court must select the least intrusive measure necessary to achieve the intended goal and must make this decision within 30 days of receiving the petition.

5.3 Rules for Applying the Terrorist Content Online Regulation

The purpose of TERREG is to ensure the rapid removal of terrorist content, not harmful or misleading information more broadly. However, certain forms of disinformation are part of terrorist propaganda, such as fabricated narratives, manipulated media for radicalisation or false news to intimidate or destabilise societies.[48] Such disinformation can be classified as terrorist content, not because it is false, but because it forms part of a terrorist group's recruitment, intimidation, or provocation strategy. Because TERREG relies on one-hour removal orders, it provides a much faster mechanism than ordinary notice-and-action regimes under the DSA. In hybrid influence operations linked to terrorist actors, this short response time can prevent the rapid spread of false claims used to mobilise or spread fear.

---

[47] AKOS, Kako ravnati v primeru nezakonitih vsebin na spletnih platformah?, https://www.akos-rs.si/fileadmin/user_upload/Digitalne_storitve/Priporocila_o_ravnanju_v_primeru_nezakonitih_vsebin.pdf, p. 3.

[48] Albus (2025), p. 210.

The Act on the Application of the Regulation (EU) on Addressing the Dissemination of Terrorist Content Online (ZIUORTSV)[49] was adopted on 23 September 2024 and entered into force on 23 November 2024. The Act designates the competent authorities responsible for implementing and supervising TERREG, sets out their respective powers, and outlines the offences and sanctions related to its implementation. Under Article 3 of the ZIUORTSV, jurisdiction for enforcing and reviewing removal orders for terrorist content lies with the District Court in Nova Gorica, which acts as Slovenia's central judicial authority under TERREG. The court is also required to establish a contact point responsible for communication, coordination and exchange of information with other member states and the European Commission. AKOS is the competent authority for assessing the exposure of hosting service providers to terrorist content, in accordance with Article 5 of TERREG, as determined by Article 4 of the ZIUORTSV. It is also responsible for supervising the implementation of TERREG, including the monitoring of specific measures adopted under Article 5 of the Regulation.

6 Electoral and Referendum Law

Very large online platforms and search engines have reported systemic risks to voting and electoral processes stemming from the large-scale dissemination of false or misleading content. These systemic risks may include disinformation and misinformation about election dates, candidate eligibility, voter registration processes, or the delegitimisation of democratic processes, e.g. via unfounded claims of electoral fraud, procedural flaws, interference, or institutional biases in favour of or against certain persons, political parties or opinions. Providers and civil society organisations also highlighted systemic risks stemming from generative AI, particularly that generative AI chatbots may answer election-related questions incorrectly, for instance, by presenting incorrect election dates or incorrect information about candidates.[50]

Freedom of expression in connection with elections and referenda in Slovenia is regulated by the Election and Referendum Campaign Act (ZVRK).[51] It regulates the issues related to election campaigns for the election of members of the National Assembly, members of the European Parliament from the Republic of Slovenia, the President of the Republic, members of representative and individually elected bodies of local communities, and issues relating to referendum campaigns. Chapter II contains provisions on election and referendum campaigns in the media.

---

[49] *Zakon o izvajanju Uredbe (EU) o obravnavanju razširjanja terorističnih spletnih vsebin*, Official Gazette of the Republic of Slovenia, no. 95/24.

[50] First report of the European Board for Digital Services in cooperation with the Commission pursuant to Article 35(2) DSA on the most prominent and recurrent systemic risks as well as mitigation measures, 18. 11. 2025, p. 20.

[51] *Zakon o volilni in referendumski kampanji*, Official Gazette of the Republic of Slovenia, No. 1/07, 103/07, 11/11, 28/11 and 98/13.

Article 5 of the ZVRK regulates the publishing of opinion polls and surveys concerning candidates, political parties and referendum questions. To ensure transparency and unbiased public information, media publishers must disclose essential methodological details, including the client, payer, and provider; the period and method of data collection; the sample and response rates; the questions asked; and any measurement errors. The publication of such polls and surveys is prohibited during the twenty-four hours preceding the voting day and until the closing of polling stations, thereby ensuring the integrity of the election silence period.

The obligations of media publishers regarding the presentation of candidates and political parties during the campaign are set out in Article 6 of the ZVRK. Media outlets are required to establish and publish clear rules regarding the scope, conditions, and method for using airtime or print space for campaign presentations within fixed deadlines prior to the election or referendum day. The public broadcaster, Radiotelevizija Slovenije (Radio and Television Corporation of Slovenia),[52] must allocate airtime in accordance with its statutory provision on political propaganda. Additionally, other media in majority public ownership are obligated to provide equal conditions and treatment for all campaign organisers. However, they may differentiate between parties already represented in the National Assembly or local representative bodies and those that are not.

Finally, Article 7 of the ZVRK introduces a general transparency requirement for campaign advertising. All media advertising content related to elections or referendums must indicate the name of the customer commissioning the publication. The same applies to printed and electronic materials, including posters, pamphlets, banners, and telecommunications messages, which must visibly display the commissioner's name. Additionally, posters must bear a serial number.

These provisions, although not directly addressing disinformation, contribute to reducing its impact in the electoral context. By imposing strict transparency and disclosure requirements on opinion polls, campaign advertising and media coverage, the ZVRK limits the spread of misleading or manipulative information and enhances the accountability of campaign actors.

[52] Radiotelevizija Slovenije is a public institution of special cultural and national importance. It performs a public service in the area of radio and television activities, for the purpose of providing for the democratic, social and cultural needs of citizens. Its activities are regulated by Radiotelevizija Slovenija Act (Official Gazette of the Republic of Slovenia, no. 96/05, 109/05 – ZDavP-1B, 105/06 – odl. US, 26/09 – ZIPRS0809-B, 9/14 in 163/22).

7 Criminal Law

7.1 General

The dissemination of disinformation is not, as such, a criminal offence under Slovenian law. The Criminal Code (KZ-1)[53] does not explicitly prohibit the creation or dissemination of disinformation. Nevertheless, certain criminal offences may capture elements of disinformation, particularly when false statements or deceptive content cause concrete harm to individuals, public safety or democratic processes. These provisions, although not directly aimed at combating disinformation, can operate indirectly as legal mechanisms that address its harmful forms. In this regard, the boundaries of freedom of expression are most visibly delineated through criminal law. Offences such as slander, defamation, and others mark the points at which the protection of freedom of expression gives way to the protection of other fundamental rights and public interests. Criminal law thus functions as a legal instrument through which freedom of expression is limited in cases where it would cause serious harm, and it may serve as a tool to address certain forms of disinformation only insofar as it has all the elements of one of the incriminated offences.

7.2 Offences Against Honour and Reputation

The first type of criminal offences that involve elements of disinformation consists of offences against honour and reputation. The protection of honour and reputation is founded upon human dignity, which belongs to everyone without distinction.[54] The protection in criminal law is closely connected with freedom of expression.[55] The Slovenian legislator considers that the protection should be ensured through a combination of criminal law and civil law remedies[56] (as detailed in the following section). The dual system is believed to provide adequate protection.[57]

Article 159 of the KZ-1 incriminates slander. Whoever issues or circulates any false information about another person that could tarnish that person's honour or reputation, and which they know to be false, shall be punished by a fine or imprisonment for up to six months or up to one year, if it is committed through mass media,

---

[53] *Kazenski zakonik*, Official Gazette of the Republic of Slovenia, no. 50/12—official consolidated text, 6/16, 54/15, 38/16, 27/17, 23/20, 91/20, 175/20—ZIUOPDVE, 195/20, 95/21, 186/21, 206/21—ZDUPŠOP, 105/22—ZZNŠPP, 16/23, 107/24—odl. US.

[54] Šorli and Čeferin (2023), p. 979. Article 34 of the Constitution grants everyone the right to personal dignity, Article 35 protects personal rights of people which include the right to honour and reputation.

[55] Ibid., p. 981.

[56] Ibid., p. 984.

[57] Ibid.

and up to two years where the conduct may cause grave consequences for the injured party. With slander, the element of false information is present, as in disinformation.

The offence of slander requires the dissemination of false information that damages another person's honour or good name, and that the perpetrator knows to be false. The element of false information, combined with the intent to harm, resembles the core of disinformation, which also involves deliberate creation or circulation of false content. However, the purpose and protected legal interests differ. While Article 159 of the KZ-1 protects the individual's honour and reputation, the concept of disinformation primarily concerns the protection of the public sphere, democratic processes, societal trust and information. While slander can occur online through online platforms or social media, its criminalisation is tied to personal harm.

The next possible criminal offence related to disinformation is defamation, as enshrined in Article 160 of the KZ-1. Whoever claims or circulates anything false about another person that could tarnish their honour, or reputation shall be punished by a fine or imprisonment for up to three months, or up to six months if committed via mass media, websites or at a public gathering, and up to one year in aggravated cases involving grave consequences for the injured party. However, if the perpetrator proves the veracity of their claims or that they had a valid reason to believe in the truthfulness of what they claimed or circulated, they shall not be punished for defamation; however, they may still be punished for insult or for the false and contemptuous accusation of a criminal offence. When it comes to claims that a person has committed a criminal offence that is prosecuted *ex officio*, the truthfulness of such a claim may only be proved by means of a final judgment. Other evidence may be used only when prosecution or a court trial is not possible or permitted. If the defamation entails that the injured party has committed a criminal offence, in the circumstances set in Paragraph 3 of Article 158 of the KZ-1,[58] the perpetrator shall not be punished for defamation even without a final judgment if they can prove the existence of a valid reason to believe that the disseminated claim was true.

The offence of defamation, as outlined in Article 160 of the KZ-1, and the concept of disinformation share a common element: the dissemination of false information. However, defamation allows for the defence of truth: a person is not criminally liable if they can prove that their statements were true or that they had reasonable grounds to believe them to be true.

Another criminal offence in the chapter of offences against honour and reputation is a contemptuous criminal accusation from Article 162 of the KZ-1. It criminalises conduct whereby a person, with the intention of exposing someone to contempt, accuses them of having committed or having been convicted of a criminal offence, or communicates such information to a third person. The sanction is a fine or imprisonment of up to three months, or up to six months if the act is committed through mass media, websites or at a public gathering. At first glance, the elements of this

[58] The circumstances of Article 158, Paragraph 3 in the sphere of defamation entail that it happened in a scientific, literary or artistic work, in a serious review or in the performance of official duties, in a journalistic work, in the course of a political or other social activity, or in defence of a right or the protection of justified benefits.

criminal offence may be met in cases where the spread of disinformation involves a false accusation that a person concerned has committed a criminal offence. However, if the person did not commit the accused offence or if it was not committed at all, then the elements of contemptuous criminal accusation are not met. Then such an accusation can still be considered defamation, depending on the circumstances.

In connection with all the mentioned criminal offences against honour and reputation, Article 166 determines the consequences for editors, publishers, printers or manufacturers for the public notice of criminal offences against honour and reputation. The managing editor (or a person acting in their place) may be punished within the limit of the sentence prescribed for the underlying offence where the public notice was committed by publication in periodical or online media and the author is unknown, the information was published without the author's consent or the author cannot be prosecuted for legal and factual reasons. The editor is not liable for live broadcasts they could not prevent or for websites that enable real-time user content without prior control. Similar rules apply to publishers, printer and manufacturers of non-periodical printed and audio-visual publications.

7.3 *Public Incitement to Hatred, Violence or Intolerance*

Public incitement to hatred, violence or intolerance is incriminated in Article 297 of the KZ-1. The provision criminalises public incitement based on a broad range of personal characteristics, including nationality, race, religion, ethnicity, gender, sexual orientation or any other personal circumstance, where such conduct may jeopardise or disturb public law and order or involves threats, verbal abuse or insults. The basic sanction is imprisonment of up to two years. The same punishment applies to anyone who in the same manner publicly disseminates ideas of racial supremacy, provides support for racial activities, or denies, diminishes the significance of, approves, justifies, derides, or advocates genocide, holocaust, crimes against humanity, war crimes, aggression, or other criminal offences against humanity. Where the offence is committed by publication in the mass media or on websites, the editor or person acting as editor is liable, except in case of live broadcasts they cannot prevent or publication on a website that enables users to publish content in real time or without prior review. If the offence is committed by coercion, ill-treatment, endangering security, desecration of ethnic, national, or religious community symbols, damaging the movable property of another person, or desecration of monuments, memorial stones, or graves, the sanction increases to up to three years of imprisonment. If the offence is committed by an official through abuse of power the sanction is up to five years. In all cases, the materials and objects bearing such messages and the devices intended for their manufacture, multiplication and distribution must be confiscated or their use disabled. Online disinformation may fall within the scope of this provision when false content is intentionally disseminated to incite hatred, hostility or intolerance against individuals or groups based on their personal characteristics.

A defendant was found guilty of committing this criminal offence because, as the managing editor of a magazine, he allowed an author to publish an article claiming, among other things, that *"immigrants of other races have more radium in them and that it is sufficient to create a microorganism that will attack only immigrants due to its radium content; God will create such a microorganism that will not tolerate the DNA of immigrants, and migrants will fall ill and die; it is possible to create a virus that only makes certain people, races, and groups of people with certain characteristics sick; this is targeted elimination, in the same way that people target certain types of natural pests, moulds, and weeds; this is not racism, but purification, the removal of weeds, which is necessary for a good harvest."* The court held that such statements constitute a clear and public dissemination of the idea of the superiority of one race over another and approval of genocide, thus fulfilling the legal criteria for a criminal offence under the second paragraph of Article 297 of the KZ-1. The Supreme Court also confirmed that the statement in question must be excluded from the protection of the right to freedom of expression, based on its content, as reflected in the ECtHR's case law on hate speech.[59]

7.4 Other Offences Involving Disinformation

Turning to other criminal offences that might cover some forms of disinformation, Article 239 of the KZ-1 regulates the abuse of the financial instruments market. Under the third point of Paragraph 1, whoever, with the intention of procuring illegal proceeds for themself or for a third person, abuses the market in financial instruments by means of a prohibited action, namely by spreading incorrect or misleading information on financial instruments or related spot commodity contracts, and with the same intent, spreading rumours, incorrect and misleading information via media, online, or in any other similar manner shall be sentenced to imprisonment for up to three years. Under Paragraph 2, the sanction increases to up to five years if the abuse results in substantial pecuniary gain or material harm and the perpetrator intended such gain or harm. The abuser must be aware that the information is false or misleading and they spread it with the intention of creating a false or misleading impression about the demand and prices of a financial instrument.[60] The dissemination of false information is carried out by the abuser through traditional or electronic media in order to influence the price of financial instruments.[61] Before that, however, they had already acquired a certain quantity of such financial instruments to sell them at a higher price after the market price rose, a practice known as scalping.[62] The abuse of financial market instruments represents a specific, economically oriented form

[59] Supreme Court of the Republic of Slovenia, I Ips 32326/2021, 8. 10. 2024.

[60] Ferlinc (2023), p. 1168.

[61] Ibid.

[62] Ibid.

of disinformation, characterised by the use of false information to distort financial markets.

Article 283 of the KZ-1 regulates false criminal complaint. Whoever reports that a person has committed a criminal offence, prosecuted *ex officio*, knowing the accusation is false, or plants traces of such an offence or otherwise causes criminal proceedings to be initiated shall be sentenced to imprisonment for up to two years. If an official makes such a report through abuse of office, he or she shall be sentenced to imprisonment for up to three years. Additionally, whoever falsely reports that they have committed a criminal offence that is prosecuted *ex officio*, or reports such an offence knowing that it has not been committed is punished by a fine. In the context of disinformation, this offence could apply when false or misleading information is deliberately disseminated with the intent to trigger criminal proceedings or fabricate allegations of criminal behaviour.

The last criminal offence that could encompass some forms of disinformation is abuse of distress and warning signals under Article 309 of the KZ-1. Whoever abuses a distress or warning signal or makes an unwarranted call for help, or provides false information on a threat, thus causing a state body or other authorised organisation to act without due necessity or unjustifiably use protection, rescue or assistance resources, shall be sentenced to imprisonment for up to three years or up to five years, if the abuse obstructs or hinders the work of judicial or other state bodies and results in significant material harm. This offence resembles certain forms of disinformation, as it criminalises the deliberate dissemination of false information about threats or emergencies. Both involve the intentional spread of falsehoods capable of causing concrete harm. This provision could, for example, apply when disinformation abuses distress and warning signals by spreading false warnings online about natural disasters, public health emergencies, or terrorist attacks.

8 Civil Law

As already mentioned, civil law provides private enforcement remedies against infringements of individuals' honour and reputation, which may also be committed through the spread of disinformation. The Code of Obligations (OZ)[63] governs the reimbursement of material damage arising from defamation or calumny under Article 177. Any person who defames another or asserts or disseminates untrue statements on the past, knowledge or capability of another, even though the former knows or should have known that they were untrue, and thereby inflicts material damage on the latter, must recompense such damage. However, any person who reports anything untrue about another without knowing that such was untrue shall not be liable for the damage inflicted if there was a genuine interest in so doing for the former or the person to whom the report was made.

[63] *Obligacijski zakonik*, Official Gazette of the Republic of Slovenia, No. 83/01, 28/06, 40/07, 97/07 and 64/16.

The OZ does not define the term defamation. Consequently, both the civil courts and the legal theory rely on the definitions provided in the KZ-1, in the chapter on criminal offences against honour and reputation.[64] Statements that harm a person's honour and reputation may be either true or false.[65] If the statements are false, the injured party may choose either to prove their falsity or to claim that they are offensive.[66] In the latter case, the burden shifts to the defendant, who must demonstrate that the statements were true or that there was a justified reason to believe in their truthfulness.[67]

The courts have held that, when assessing the unlawfulness of disputed statements, a distinction must be made between statements of fact and comments or value judgments. In the case of facts, it is important whether they are true or not. There is no unlawfulness if the defendant proves the truth of the published facts, or, in the case of published untrue facts, that they had reasonable grounds to believe in their truth. In the case of value judgments or opinions, a sufficient factual basis is sufficient to ensure the proportionality of the intervention. A negative value judgment is inadmissible only if it has no basis in facts to support it or if it goes beyond the subject of the discussion and turns into personal defamation and humiliation.[68] The Constitutional Court held that not only journalists but also other individuals who participate in public debate must act in good faith, i.e., they must have a sufficient basis to believe that the facts they publish are true.[69]

The Constitutional Court also held that a lawsuit against a newspaper publisher may be justified if the title of a published article contains false or misleading statements concerning potential corruption (the taking of a bribe by a political party), even if the article as a whole does not report that an illegal act was committed. The title's meaning and communicative weight must also be assessed separately from the article.[70]

9 Conclusion

Slovenia does not regulate online disinformation through a single, dedicated instrument, but through a dispersed framework built around freedom of expression, media and audiovisual rules, EU digital regulation and general criminal and civil law. This allows many harmful manifestations of disinformation to be addressed indirectly, especially where they overlap with hate speech, reputational attacks, electoral manipulation, terrorist content or financial market abuse. At the same time, key safeguards,

[64] Jadek Pensa (2003), p. 1014.

[65] Ibid.

[66] Ibid.

[67] Ibid.

[68] Higher Court in Ljubljana, I Cp 2792/2015, 23. 3.2016, and I Cpg 18/2022, 24. 1. 2023.

[69] Constitutional Court of the Republic of Slovenia, Up-515/14, 12. 10. 2017.

[70] Constitutional Court of the Republic of Slovenia, Up-530/14, 2. 3. 2017.

such as constitutional rights of correction and reply, professional self-regulation and the implementation of DSA and TERREG, place growing emphasis on transparency, accountability of intermediaries and protection of public-interest journalism.

However, the current approach remains fragmented and largely reactive. It is strongest where clearly illegal content or individualised harm can be shown, but less suited to tackling lawful but harmful content, coordinated influence operations and systemic risks linked to platforms and generative AI. Rather than introducing broad new speech offences, the main challenge for Slovenia is to improve coordination between existing instruments, strengthen institutional capacities and support independent fact-checking and media literacy, so that disinformation governance becomes part of a broader strategy for democratic resilience and digital environment.

References

Albus V (2025) Eyes Shut, Fingers Crossed: The EU's Governance of Terrorist Content Online under Regulation 2021/784. In: Gsenger R, Sekwenz M-T (eds) Digital Decade: How the EU Shapes Digitalisation Research. Nomos Verlagsgesellschaft mbH & Co. KG.

Ferlinc A (2023) Zloraba trga finančnih instrumentov, 239. člen. In: Korošec D, Filipčič K, Devetak H (eds) Veliki znanstveni komentar posebnega dela Kazenskega zakonika (KZ-1), 2. knjiga, Posodobljena izdaja. Uradni list Republike Slovenije : Pravna fakulteta Univerze v Ljubljani, Ljubljana.

Jadek Pensa D (2003) Posebej o povrnitvi premoženjske škode pri žalitvi časti ali širjenju neresničnih trditev. In: Plavšak N, Juhart M (eds) Obligacijski zakonik (OZ) s komentarjem, 1. knjiga: Splošni del. GV Založba, Ljubljana.

Ó Fathaigh R, Buijs D, Hoboken J van (2025) The Regulation of Disinformation Under the Digital Services Act. Media and Communication 13:. https://doi.org/10.17645/mac.9615.

Šorli M, Čeferin R (2023) Osemnajsto poglavje: Kazniva dejanja zoper čast in dobro ime. In: Korošec D, Filipčič K, Devetak H (eds) Veliki znanstveni komentar posebnega dela Kazenskega zakonika (KZ-1), 1. knjiga, Posodobljena izdaja. Uradni list Republike Slovenije : Pravna fakulteta Univerze v Ljubljani, Ljubljana.

Teršek A (2019) 39. člen (svoboda izražanja). In: Avbelj M (ed) Komentar ustave Republike Slovenije. Del 1: Človekove pravice in temeljne svoboščine. Nova univerza, Evropska pravna fakulteta, Ljubljana.

Teršek A (2019a) 40. člen (pravica do popravka in pravica do odgovora). In: Avbelj M (ed) Komentar ustave Republike Slovenije. Del 1: Človekove pravice in temeljne svoboščine. Nova univerza, Evropska pravna fakulteta, Ljubljana.

Wilman F, Kalėda SL, Loewenthal P-J (2024) The EU Digital Services Act, 1st edn. Oxford University Press.

Online Disinformation: Impact Factors, Resilience Patterns, and Legal Solutions in the Spanish System

Teresa Rodríguez de las Heras Ballell and Pedro Aránguez Díaz

Abstract This chapter provides a systematic legal analysis of online disinformation in Spain, situating national developments within the broader European framework while identifying the specific legal choices made at domestic level. It clarifies the notion of disinformation as employed in Spanish law and policy, distinguishing it from the colloquial and imprecise concept of "fake news", and traces the evolution of Spain's institutional understanding of the phenomenon. The chapter then examines the constitutional foundations governing communicative freedoms, focusing on the role of the Constitution and the jurisprudence of the Constitutional Court and the Supreme Court. It analyses the interaction between EU law and the Spanish legal order, including the influence of EU soft law and binding digital regulations, as well as the fragmented legislative and regulatory instruments indirectly addressing disinformation. Particular attention is paid to procedural mechanisms, reporting structures, remedies, and safeguards for fundamental rights. The chapter concludes by assessing current reform proposals and likely trajectories of the Spanish legal framework.

1 Setting the Scene: Notion of Disinformation, Milestones and Consumption Patterns

Modern societies are becoming increasingly vulnerable. Social, political and economic complexity, intense dependence on technology, and exposure to disinformation, as a pernicious effect of a paradoxically over-informed society, are factors that explain this growing vulnerability. Interestingly, these vulnerability factors are

T. Rodríguez de las Heras Ballell (✉) · P. Aránguez Díaz
Universidad Carlos III de Madrid, Madrid, Spain
e-mail: teresa.rodriguezdelasheras@uc3m.es

P. Aránguez Díaz
e-mail: pedrojuan.aranguez@uc3m.es

T. Rodríguez de las Heras Ballell
European Law Institute, Vienna, Austria

P. Passaglia (ed.), *European Legal Perspectives on Online Disinformation*, Ius Gentium: Comparative Perspectives on Law and Justice 140,
https://doi.org/10.1007/978-3-032-25785-7_18

interconnected and feed into each other aggravating and amplifying the exposure to risk and the intensity of such vulnerability. One of the most distinctive factors in the modern profile of a vulnerable society is its difficulty in building a common vision of reality. Such a failure is the result of geopolitical, technological, and societal factors. Therefore, disinformation needs to be framed within these coordinates.

Disinformation is definitively not a new phenomenon. The concerns brought about by the fluid and imprecise term of 'fake news' are not unique to present times but a constant throughout history. However, as a historical phenomenon, it has constantly evolved according to the characteristics of each society, the means of access to information, the forms of producing and spreading information, and the consumption patterns. Therefore, disinformation cannot be separated from cultural, political, societal, and ideological reasons. Hence, it is intriguing to discover whether as a global phenomenon, there are still distinctive domestic features in its intensity and criticality, its conceptualization, the social perception of its effects, or the legal and regulatory responses to counter its consequences.

Nevertheless, domestic or national characteristics do not hide the fact that disinformation is today a global phenomenon with a rather singular profile compared to previous manifestations throughout the history. Its current profile is strongly and decisively defined by the technological transformation of contemporary societies. That means that disinformation today cannot be either explained or properly combatted without appreciating this intimate link with digital technologies—from social networks to artificial intelligence (AI). Not surprisingly, the national diagnosis of disinformation in a particular country is, to a certain extent, significantly determined by technology adoption levels, digital consumption patterns, and cultural features, as well as by domestic legal responses to technology (electronic means, digital medium, platforms, AI, data).

Against such a backdrop, this national report of online disinformation in Spain is subject to those three determinants. First, the globality of the phenomenon leads to identifying common features in the problem. The notion of disinformation or its adverse effects on democratic societies are common and should rarely differ among countries, at least, those sharing similar cultural, socioeconomic, and political backgrounds in the present time. Second, the dependency on technology entails that online disinformation is a historical phenomenon that presents unique and distinctive features in contemporary societies. Therefore, disinformation is going to be contextualised in a specific technological state of our societies and linked to key components and actors of the present digital economy (digital intermediaries, social networks, platforms, AI systems, influencers, deep fakes, etc.). Hence, the interaction of citizens with technology in a particular country largely defines disinformation consumption patterns, risk perception, exposure to fake news, and resilience. Nevertheless, cultural reasons and political or socioeconomic circumstances can occasionally or more permanently shape disinformation features in a country or a region. Thus, third, the cultural, political, and socioeconomic situation in a country can add specificities or particularities to the analysis. In fact, political turmoil, a deep polarisation of society, economic crises, societal tensions, low social cohesion or cultural, ethnical, or racial division stoke disinformation and may give the phenomenon special characteristics, intensity, or extent.[1] Therefore, peaks of concerns about disinformation, higher gravity of its influence on citizen's opinion and behaviours, or reactions from authorities or lawmakers can be easily associated to health crisis, natural catastrophes, disruption of public services, election campaigns, or other milestones perceived as highly controversial (enactment of a piece of legislation, celebrations, court decisions, appointment of political positions).[2] Then, despite the numerous commonalities of disinformation in Spain with other countries, in particular, in the EU, as a contemporary phenomenon, some domestic factors may be unique to a country and explain the timing, the approach or the scope of specific regulatory or legislative responses or justify other relevant specificities.

Within the above framework, this introduction sets the scene of online disinformation in Spain by addressing three aspects.

Firstly, the notion of disinformation in Spain. As explained under 1(a), domestic notion of disinformation and national conceptualisation of online disinformation do not differ from common definitions and general understanding of the phenomenon in the EU. The global character of disinformation reduces appreciably the variability in definitions. However, it will be interesting to trace how the popularity of the term "fake news" to capture the problem in the political debate and in the public opinion has not crystallised in the legislative and regulatory actions that systematically resort to a terminology underpinned by the notion of "disinformation" (disinformation campaigns, online disinformation, disinformation risks). Chosen terminology is also transpiring which triggers have denotated the concerns and the urgency to react in a country. Thus, as it will be expounded below, main concerns have been evolving from disinformation in the context of "hybrid warfare" to disinformation as a destabiliser of democratic societies, especially in electoral periods, to disinformation as a symptom of lack of pluralism, of independence, and of transparency of informative, communication, and media ecosystem. Secondly, despite the commonalities, disinformation can present cultural or social characteristics. Thus, under 1(b) a brief overview of disinformation consumption patterns in Spain is provided. Thirdly, it explores the legal, regulatory, and procedural landscape to detect and combat disinformation in Spain (*infra* 2).

These three angles pivot on a theory developed in previous works to fully capture the modern profile of online disinformation, conceptualise it, and effectively disassemble into its distinctive components. This theory connects the distinct characteristics of today's disinformation and the seriousness of its demolishing impact on democracies with the thesis that our society is an "omnimetric society".[3] Responses to online disinformation in contemporary legal systems should acknowledge and properly embrace this *omnimetric* character of our society. Otherwise, it is our understanding that disinformation-countering measures and legal and regulatory actions risk being ineffective, useless or simply misfocused.

---

[1] Alendete D (2019); Badillo A (2019); Badillo A et al. (2023).

[2] Detailed analysis of cases in Moreno-Castro C et al. (2023).

[3] As formulated in Rodríguez de las Heras Ballell T (2023). The development and the detailed explanation of the theory is referred to this cited contribution.

1.1 Notion, Definitions, and Approach to Disinformation

The term "fake news" has become extraordinarily popular to describe many different contexts of misinformation and disinformation, but also to denote pure illegal content, defamation, parody, or simply offensive content. As a consequence, 'fake news' is useful to direct attention towards a well-identified social problem, although the concept is, in essence, vague, imprecise, and to certain extent confusing to be employed in legal analysis. On the one hand, "fake-news" phenomenon certainly comprises more than news. It encompasses any visual, graphical, or textual content produced and disseminated on a digital format likely to misinform or disinform. Furthermore, 'fake news' label is used to tag a wide array of mis- and disinformation types, including manipulated content, false content, misleading content or fabricated content. With such an impreciseness, the term is unsuitable for delimiting the scope of application of any legislative response or regulatory action.

The term "fake news" both in original English and less frequently in Spanish (*noticias falsas*) is used in Spain to denote disinformation-related concerns in social, political, and media discourses. It is a term well-recognised and understood by public opinion to capture a vaguely define informative phenomenon. Nevertheless, save for rare, scarce references in certain texts, the term used in legal, regulatory, and consultative instruments is "disinformation" (*desinformación*). In fact, as further detailed below, once the phenomenon is perceived and formally addressed in successive reports, guides, action plans, and regulations, disinformation is properly defined and adequately delimitated from specific tools, such as fake news, and other challenges, such as cybersecurity attacks, propaganda, misinformation, illegal content amounting to criminal offences, and so on.

Hence, the terminological choices are also revealing an evolution in the comprehension of the problem, in the perspectives, and in the type of responses. A quick overview of the main milestones is traced below to spot the notions used, the definitions, where available, and the approaches.

In Spain, the perception of disinformation as a security problem did not arise from national experience but rather from that of third parties, especially through the initiatives of the Council, the European Union External Action Service or the European Parliament.[4] The general perception that the circulation of false information had become a large-scale problem arose in the second half of the 2010s, centred on two events: the Russian invasion of Crimea in 2014 and the 2016 US presidential election.[5] The first event reveals the role of disinformation as one of the core components of the modern "hybrid warfare" or "complex irregular warfare".[6] The second event acted as a catalyst of the perception that disinformation campaigns combined with cybersecurity attacks are serious threats to democratic societies. It was the catalyst of a chain of events that evidenced the potential of disinformation campaigns to

[4] European External Action Service (2019); European Commission (2018); European Parliament (2022)

[5] Badillo A, Arteaga F (2024).

[6] Hoffman FG (2017); Mattis JN, Hoffman FG (2005).

destabilise democracies, alter electoral processes, and influence on public opinion. Spanish public and private reaction towards disinformation did not mobilise until the end of 2017, detonated by disinformation campaigns in relation to domestic political events (referenda, elections).

From that point on, Spain's initiatives to combat disinformation start taking shape following the EU's responses. The first steps taken showed that disinformation was initially linked to technological risks, cybersecurity and hybrid threats. Hence, responsibilities were initially attributed to *Consejo Nacional de Ciberseguridad*[7] and to the Ministries of Defence (*Mando Conjunto de Ciberdefensa*) and Foreign Affairs (ambassador for cybersecurity and hybrid threats). This conception of disinformation as part of hybrid warfare is maintained in the Action Plan against Disinformation[8] of the European Commission. Spain participated in the initiatives at the EU level (*Hybrid CoE*), but it had not formally assumed the threat of disinformation.

A genuine national response to disinformation begins in February 2019 with the elaboration of the first report about disinformation in Spain by the National Cryptological Center (CNI, *Centro Criptológico Nacional*).[9] From the title of the document (*Desinformación en el ciberespacio*), it was revealed that the analysis was focused on online disinformation. Thus, and consistently, the notion of disinformation, the identification of main sources and enablers, and the vulnerability of the Spanish society (90% of the population aged between 16 and 65 used internet at that time) to disinformation impact were essentially defined and linked to technology factors.

Unlike the European Commission's definition that essentially associated disinformation with "fake news", the Spanish Guide adopted a broader approach and rightly identified a constellation of tools, actors, and components of the online disinformation landscape: fake news, deep fake news, malicious headline approaches, digital platforms dedicated to disinformation, controlled discussion forums, malicious digital profiles and automated accounts, false identities, guest stars, paid advertisements, algorithmic confirmation biases.

This notion of disinformation as a phenomenon that goes beyond "fake news" permeates the subsequent actions taken in Spain. The term used is consistently "disinformation" and often references are to "disinformation and 'fake news'". Thus, in the *Comisión Mixta de Seguridad Nacional* (Mixed Commission of National Security), several public hearings were organised to address "disinformation and 'fake news'" (2019, 2020, 2023),[10] qualified by the potential to cause "disruptive effects on society". Concerns about disinformation are mainly linked to electoral periods and intimately associated to cybersecurity.

---

[7] Centro Criptológico Nacional (n.d.).

[8] European Commission (2018).

[9] CCN-CERT (2019), Gobierno de España (2019).

[10] Sádaba Chalezquer MR, Santos Sánchez DJ (2023); Rodríguez de las Heras Ballell T (2023).

The term "disinformation" is the one included in the regulations governing the procedure to fight against disinformation[11] and in the National Security Strategy 2021.[12] Interestingly, the National Security Strategy pivots around the notion of "disinformation campaigns", identified as the main threat to National Security, that is expressly differentiated from "fake news" (false information) and erroneous information (misinformation). In fact, it is acknowledged that disinformation campaigns do not necessarily consist of fake news, but are characterised by the intention to distort reality by manipulated content. Thus, "disinformation campaigns" are basically defined by several intentional and operational elements:

- the intention to create confusion and undermine social cohesion;
- the coordinated use of different media to create and disseminate content aimed at a wide audience; and
- the malicious intent to discredit or influence the target of the attack.

Yet, in the Foreign Policy Strategy 2021–2024 (*Estrategia de Acción Exterior*),[13] disinformation is identified as one of vectors contributing to the political and governance fracture. The Strategy recognises four deep fractures in our world: a socioeconomic fracture, an ecological fracture, a technological fracture, and a political and governance one. Disinformation is stressed as a key accelerator of the loss of the citizenship's confidence in the institutions and the debilitation of the solidity of democratic systems. In this context, other concepts are framed within the disinformation challenge: 'fake news', the increasing and worrying questioning of expert knowledge, and *post-truth (postverdad).*

The last stage in this process does not question the term or the notion that remain labelled as "disinformation" but the approach in two senses. Firstly, a shift from detecting to fighting against disinformation in Spain. Secondly, the actors involved in the procedure to counter and fights against disinformation (citizens, media and platforms, verifiers, trusted flaggers and fact-checkers, pubic administration).[14] This inclusive and proactive approach against disinformation crystallised in the creation of the *Foro contra las campañas de desinformación* that is composed of four members representing the Ministries of Foreign Affairs, European Union and Cooperation, Defence, Interior, and Economic Affairs and Digital Transformation, appointed by each of the corresponding Ministries and ten members representing civil society, academia and the private sector.

---

[11] Orden PCM/1030/2020 (2020) por la que se publica el procedimiento de actuación contra la desinformación aprobado por el Consejo de Seguridad Nacional. Boletín Oficial del Estado no. 292, 5 Nov 2020.

[12] Real Decreto 1150/2021 (2021) por el que se aprueba la Estrategia de Seguridad Nacional 2021. BOE num 314, 31/12/2021.

[13] Gobierno de España (2021).

[14] Orden PCM/541/2022 (2022) por la que se publica el Acuerdo del Consejo de Ministros de 31 de mayo de 2022, por el que se crea el Foro contra las campañas de desinformación en el ámbito de la Seguridad Nacional y se regula su composición y funcionamiento. BOE no. 142, 15 Jun 2022.

1.2 Differential Factors and Consumption Patterns

As explained above, Spain joined the political debate on disinformation and its consequences for democracies slightly later than other European countries, despite the fact that various factors might render Spanish society particularly vulnerable to this risk. Among these vulnerabilities, scholars[15] underline the following characteristics of Spanish society as aggravating factors in the exposure to disinformation.

Political systems with greater freedom of expression are also more vulnerable than autocracies or dictatorships to disinformation campaigns generated by external actors, as free movement of information exposes democratic systems to interference, external influence, and overinformation/disinformation/misinformation.[16] As per the annual study by Reporters Without Borders (RSF) on the state of press freedom around the world, Spain has remained in the top quarter of countries with the best conditions for journalism and freedom of expression over the last twenty years, with slight setbacks between 2003–2006 and 2008–2010. The trend has shown stabilisation and a constant improvement from 29th out of 139 in 2002 (21st out of 100), Spain has moved up to 32nd out of 180 (18th out of 100) in the latest RSF ranking 2025.[17] Other indicators show that Spain has experienced a stabilisation in democratic conditions for years.

A second factor that amplifies the potential vulnerability of Spanish society to disinformation campaigns is the high penetration of technology (fixed and wireless infrastructures) and an intense and widespread use of digital technologies by the population. In particular, Spanish young generations highly rely on social media (49% over the average of 42% in the EU) to access political content. Nevertheless, young people declare to be more aware of their exposure to disinformation (more often than the EU average).[18]

Furthermore, the surge of social media networks as the primary news and information source takes places in a fertile traditional media sector in crisis. To the crisis of media business models (due to several factors such as the global economic crisis, and the decline in advertisement investment), media has faced a major crisis of trust. As in many countries in southern Europe, the evolution of media systems in a process of "polarised pluralism" has undoubtedly contributed to the perception of the media not as reliable autonomous agents of the political system responsible for a task of public service, but as highly biased, ideology-driven instruments of political game.[19] Data on confidence in traditional media in Spain are low and, as a consequence, population becomes intensely exposed to disinformation catalysed and amplified by social media and alternative sources.

These vulnerability factors are dramatically aggravated by the current political polarisation stoked by a growing political tension that reduces the ability and, more

---

[15] Badillo A, Arteaga F (2024).

[16] Fried D, Polyakova A (2018).

[17] Spain is in the position 23. Reporters Without Borders (2025).

[18] Eurobarometer (2024).

[19] Badillo A, Arteaga F (2024).

importantly, the desire to verify the accuracy, veracity, and reliability of content and information confirming own biases. Thus, information is weaponised, and citizenship loses critical capacity and critical will.

Yet, another decisive factor of vulnerability is the language. Pursuant to the most recent report of the *Instituto Cervantes* (Spanish in the World, 2025),[20] the number of Spanish speakers has grown by 30 million in 2025, 5% more than the previous year, reaching 636 million potential speakers. It is the second most widely spoken mother tongue in the world (after Mandarin Chinese) and the third or fourth most widely spoken language overall (after including Hindi). The reach of Spanish makes it an ideal common linguistic space for cultural and informational circulation in the 21 countries around the world that share it. Thus, Spanish population is more directly and effectively targeted by disinformation campaigns created to affect any Spanish-speaking country, in addition to disinformation produced in English that has a global and natural impact in most countries around the globe.

2 The Sources of Law

2.1 The Constitutional References

The Spanish legal regime applicable to disinformation is fundamentally anchored in the Spanish Constitution of 1978, which provides a comprehensive framework for the protection of freedom of expression and freedom of information, while simultaneously allowing for their limitation when they collide with other constitutionally protected rights and interests. The Constitution does not contain any express reference to disinformation, misinformation, or fake news. Instead, disinformation is legally addressed through the constitutional architecture governing communicative freedoms and their limits, as interpreted by constitutional and ordinary courts.[21]

The pivotal provision is Article 20 of the Constitution, which enshrines the freedom to express and disseminate thoughts, ideas and opinions, as well as the freedom to communicate or receive truthful information by any means of dissemination. Article 20 also expressly prohibits prior censorship, thereby excluding, as a general rule, preventive administrative or judicial control over the circulation of information. This prohibition has profound implications for any regulatory strategy aimed at combating disinformation, as it severely restricts the possibility of ex ante content control by public authorities. The constitutional relevance of this prohibition has been repeatedly emphasised by the Spanish Constitutional Court, which has consistently held that systems allowing public authorities to prevent the dissemination of content before publication are incompatible with the constitutional order,

---

[20] Instituto Cervantes (2025).

[21] García Rubio F (2022).

except in extremely exceptional circumstances expressly provided for by law and justified by overriding constitutional interests.[22]

The requirement of veracity contained in Article 20(1)(d) of the Constitution does not operate as a general obligation to communicate objectively true information. Constitutional case law has clarified that veracity must be understood as a duty of diligence in the verification of facts, particularly applicable to professional journalism. The Constitutional Court has consistently rejected the idea that the Constitution protects only objectively true information, recognising instead that the protection of freedom of information would be seriously undermined if journalists were exposed to liability for mere inaccuracies, provided that they acted with due professional diligence.[23] This doctrinal construction is particularly relevant in the context of disinformation, as it prevents the automatic exclusion of false or misleading content from constitutional protection and requires a contextual assessment of intent, diligence, and social relevance.[24]

Other constitutional provisions frequently invoked in legal disputes related to disinformation include Article 18 of the Constitution, which protects the right to honour, personal and family privacy, and one's own image. Disinformation that harms individual reputation or disseminates false factual allegations about identifiable persons may therefore be subject to civil or criminal liability without infringing Article 20, provided that the restriction is proportionate and necessary.[25] Article 10 of the Constitution, which proclaims human dignity as the foundation of the political order and social peace, also plays an interpretative role, particularly in cases involving hate speech or degrading narratives targeting vulnerable groups.

Furthermore, Article 23 of the Constitution, guaranteeing the right to participate in public affairs, acquires particular importance in electoral contexts, where disinformation may distort democratic processes and undermine the free formation of the popular will.[26]

The constitutional framework thus establishes a model in which disinformation is not treated as an autonomous legal category, but rather as a phenomenon assessed through the balancing of fundamental rights. The decisive question is not whether information is false as such, but whether its dissemination unjustifiably infringes other constitutional rights or protected interests.[27]

---

[22] STC 6/1988, FJ 5; Espaliú-Berdud C (2022).

[23] STC 159/1986, FJ 6; STC 21/2000, FJ 8.

[24] Rodríguez de las Heras Ballell T (2020).

[25] Ley Orgánica 1/1982, 5 May 1982, de protección civil del derecho al honor, a la intimidad personal y familiar y a la propia imagen, BOE num 115, 14/05/1982 (LO 1/1982), arts. 7–9; STC 14/2003, FJ 6.

[26] Sabater-Quinto F, Belmonte-Martín I, Lloret-Irles D (2025).

[27] García Rubio F (2022).

2.2 EU Law and Its Implementation

European Union law constitutes a decisive normative layer in the Spanish approach to disinformation. Although the regulation of freedom of expression remains primarily within the competence of Member States, EU law has progressively shaped national responses through a combination of soft law instruments, sectoral regulation, and, more recently, binding digital governance rules.[28]

Article 11 of the Charter of Fundamental Rights of the European Union guarantees freedom of expression and information in terms closely aligned with Article 10 of the European Convention on Human Rights. Any national measure addressing disinformation within the scope of EU law must therefore comply with the Charter, which requires that limitations on fundamental rights be provided for by law, respect their essential content, and be proportionate to legitimate objectives.

The EU's strategic response to disinformation has been characterised by a preference for cooperative and non-punitive instruments. This approach is reflected in the 2018 Action Plan against Disinformation, which conceptualises disinformation as a systemic risk to democratic societies rather than as a category of illegal content per se. The Action Plan promotes institutional coordination, strategic communication, media literacy, and cooperation with online platforms, while explicitly cautioning against measures that could undermine freedom of expression.[29]

Spain has aligned itself closely with this EU strategy. The most significant manifestation of this alignment is Order PCM/1030/2020, which establishes the national procedure against disinformation. This instrument was expressly adopted to implement the EU Action Plan within the Spanish legal order and to integrate Spain into EU coordination mechanisms such as the Rapid Alert System.[30] This choice reflects a conscious decision by Spanish authorities to avoid criminalisation or administrative censorship and to rely instead on soft governance mechanisms compatible with constitutional guarantees.

More recently, Regulation (EU) 2022/2065 on a Single Market for Digital Services, commonly referred to as the Digital Services Act (DSA),[31] has introduced binding obligations for online intermediaries, including large online platforms,[32] with regard to systemic risks such as disinformation. Although the Digital Services Act does not require Member States to prohibit disinformation as such, it obliges platforms to assess and mitigate systemic risks affecting civic discourse and electoral processes.[33] Spain, like other Member States, must ensure the effective application of these obligations through national authorities, thereby reinforcing the regulatory

---

[28] Espaliú-Berdud C (2022).

[29] European Commission (2018), pp 2–4.

[30] Orden PCM/1030/2020.

[31] Regulation (EU) 2022/2065 of the European Parliament and of the Council of 19 October 2022 on a Single Market for Digital Services (Digital Services Act, DSA) [2022] OJ L 277/1.

[32] In a fundamental shift of the EU legal response from online intermediaries to platforms, Rodríguez de las Heras Ballell T (2021).

[33] Arts 34–35 DSA.

environment in which disinformation is addressed without directly restricting lawful speech.[34]

2.3 Legislative Acts

Spanish legislation does not contain a single, comprehensive statute devoted to disinformation. Instead, disinformation is addressed indirectly through a fragmented set of legislative acts belonging to different branches of law. This legislative choice reflects both constitutional constraints and a deliberate policy preference for sectoral regulation.[35]

In criminal law, the Spanish Penal Code does not criminalise the dissemination of false information as such. However, disinformation may fall within the scope of several criminal offences depending on its content, context, and intent. The Spanish Attorney General Office ("Fiscalía General del Estado") has explicitly acknowledged that so-called fake news (interestingly, unlike other regulatory instruments in Spain using systematically 'disinformation', the popular term of 'fake news' is employed in this context) may constitute hate crimes, offences against public order, fraud, crimes against honour, or offences against public health, provided that the constituent elements of those crimes are met.[36] This approach reinforces the principle of ultima ratio in criminal law and avoids the risks associated with broadly framed offences targeting false information.

In civil law, Spanish law on the protection of honour, personal and family privacy, and one's own image provides remedies against disinformation that harms individual reputation. This legal framework allows courts to order rectification, cessation, and compensation without engaging in general content regulation.[37] In the electoral sphere, the Spanish law on the general electoral regime contains specific rules aimed at safeguarding the integrity of electoral processes, including provisions on campaign communication and media neutrality, which may indirectly address disinformation during electoral periods.[38]

Media and audiovisual legislation also plays a role, particularly through obligations imposed on broadcasters and audiovisual service providers regarding accuracy, pluralism, and the protection of minors. However, these obligations are framed in

[34] Comisión Nacional de los Mercados y la Competencia (2024).

[35] Moreno-Castro C et al. (2023).

[36] Fiscalía General del Estado (2020).

[37] LO 1/1982, arts 7–9.

[38] Ley Orgánica 5/1985, 19 June 1985, del Régimen Electoral General (LOREG), BOE num 147, 20/06/1985, arts 50 and 53.

professional and sectoral terms rather than as a general prohibition of disinformation.[39] Among recent legislative acts of indirect relevance to the regulation of disinformation, Real Decreto 444/2024 merits particular attention. Adopted in implementation of Article 94 of the General Audiovisual Communication Act, the Decree establishes the criteria under which users of video-sharing platform services may be classified as "users of special relevance". Although the instrument does not regulate disinformation or false content as such, it reflects a legislative strategy that addresses risks linked to large-scale dissemination of information by focusing on audience reach, influence, and systemic impact rather than on the truthfulness of individual messages. By identifying highly influential users and subjecting them to enhanced transparency and responsibility obligations within the audiovisual regulatory framework, the Decree contributes to the broader legislative environment in which disinformation is indirectly addressed through structural and sectoral regulation, consistent with constitutional constraints on content-based intervention.[40]

2.4 *Subordinate Acts*

At the level of subordinate legislation, the previously mentioned Order PCM/1030/2020 occupies a central position. Adopted by the Ministry of the Presidency and approved by the National Security Council, the Order establishes an institutional framework for the prevention, detection, and analysis of disinformation affecting Spain, creating coordination mechanisms among public authorities and channels of cooperation with EU institutions and private actors.

Importantly, the Order does not establish sanctions, nor does it confer powers to remove or block content. Its focus lies on strategic communication, situational awareness, and inter-institutional coordination. This design has been interpreted as an attempt to reconcile national security concerns with constitutional and European standards on freedom of expression. At the same time, the Order might be criticised for its reliance on national security structures and for the lack of explicit safeguards regarding transparency and oversight, particularly in light of the absence of parliamentary involvement.[41]

---

[39] Ley 13/2022, 7 July 2022, General de Comunicación Audiovisual, BOE num 163, 8/7/2022, arts 4 and 89; Rodríguez de las Heras Ballell T (2020).

[40] Real Decreto 444/2024, 30 April 2024, por el que se regulan los requisitos a efectos de ser considerado usuario de especial relevancia de los servicios de intercambio de vídeos a través de plataforma, en desarrollo del artículo 94 de la Ley 13/2022, de 7 de julio, General de Comunicación Audiovisual, BOE num 106, 1/5/2024.

[41] ARTICLE 19 (2021).

2.5 *Acts Passed by Territorial Autonomies*

Spain's regional governments (*comunidades autónomas*) have not adopted specific legislative frameworks targeting disinformation. Regional competences in areas such as media, education, and public health have occasionally led to initiatives aimed at promoting media literacy or countering misinformation in specific contexts, but these measures remain programmatic and non-coercive.[42]

Any autonomous regulation directly affecting freedom of expression would, in any event, be subject to strict constitutional scrutiny due to the State's exclusive competence over the basic conditions guaranteeing equality in the exercise of fundamental rights, based on the Spanish Constitution territorial competence division.

2.6 *The Role of Case Law*

In the absence of a comprehensive statutory framework, and the need to analyse each situation in an individual basis, case law plays a decisive role in shaping the Spanish legal regime applicable to disinformation.

2.6.1 The Constitutional Court

The Constitutional Court has developed a sophisticated doctrine on the relationship between freedom of expression, freedom of information, and their limits. Its jurisprudence consistently emphasises that freedom of expression protects not only inoffensive or accurate speech, but also ideas and opinions that may shock, disturb, or offend.[43] False factual statements are not automatically excluded from protection, although their dissemination may lose constitutional protection when it unjustifiably infringes other fundamental rights.[44]

In dealing with the dissemination of falsehoods in social networks, the Constitutional Court has recently noted the importance of online disinformation (without using such express terms) in considering the negative impact and reach such falsehoods can have. The Court reasoned that social networks fundamentally transform the circulation of information because of their immediacy, speed, and lack of effective prior filters, which allows content to spread on a massive and largely uncontrollable scale. This amplifies their capacity to shape public opinion well beyond that of traditional media, while at the same time increasing the risk of unjustified harm to personality rights. For this reason, the assessment of potential infringements of honour, privacy, image, or data protection must take into account contextual factors

[42] Sabater-Quinto et al (2025).

[43] STC 235/2007, FJ 4.

[44] STC 14/2003, FJ 6.

such as the reach of the account, the public or private status of the person involved, the existence of multiplier effects, and the speed of dissemination.[45]

The Court's case law on veracity, public interest, and the distinction between facts and value judgments has become a cornerstone for lower courts dealing with disinformation-related disputes. This jurisprudence effectively constrains legislative and administrative action, ensuring that the fight against disinformation does not erode the constitutional core of communicative freedoms.

2.6.2 The Supreme Court

While the Supreme Court does not conceptualise "disinformation" as an autonomous legal category, its case law is useful to the Spanish legal treatment of false statements because it repeatedly operationalises the criteria that determine when false or misleading assertions remain protected speech and when they become actionable interferences with legally protected interests.

In civil matters, the Supreme Court has consistently built its reasoning around the distinction between verifiable statements of fact and non-verifiable value judgments, treating this as decisive for evidentiary analysis and for the balancing exercise in conflicts between personality rights and communicative freedoms. The Court stresses that value judgments, as such, lie "outside" proof of truth, while factual assertions can be tested for accuracy and are therefore capable of being false in a legally relevant sense.[46] Where the contested content is factual, the Supreme Court's balancing approach typically asks whether the communication concerns a matter of public interest and whether the author acted with sufficient diligence in verifying the factual basis before publication, while accepting that minor inaccuracies do not necessarily defeat the requirement of "veracity" in this jurisprudential sense.[47] When these conditions are not met, dissemination of false factual allegations about identifiable persons may constitute an unlawful interference with the right to honour and trigger civil liability and remedies under Spanish law.[48] In this sense, the Supreme Court's civil jurisprudence does not treat "falsehood" as a standalone wrong; rather, falsehood matters insofar as it feeds into a structured proportionality-type assessment that asks whether the interference with honour (or privacy or image) is justified in light of public relevance and the author's diligence.[49]

In criminal law, the Supreme Court's relevance to disinformation emerges through its interpretation of offences where falsity and the element of mens rea are central. For defamation offences (so-called *calumnia* and *injuria*), the Court's case law reiterates that criminal liability is not triggered by falsity alone, but by the offence's specific subjective requirement, namely that the imputation is made with knowledge

[45] STC 8/2022, FJ 3.

[46] STS 250/2023, 14/02/2024.

[47] Ibid.

[48] LO 1/1982, arts 7–9.

[49] STS 250/2023.

of falsity or reckless disregard for the truth.[50] The same structural approach informs the Supreme Court's treatment of other disinformation-relevant offences such as fraud, where deception must be "sufficient" and causally connected to patrimonial disposition, and public-order offences where false alarms only become criminally relevant when the statutory thresholds of endangerment or disturbance are satisfied rather than because the information is false in the abstract.[51]

In administrative and regulatory disputes concerning digital services, the Court's jurisprudence can indirectly affect new duties on online intermediaries, as the Court has reaffirmed that intermediary responsibility under Spanish and EU rules (liability exemption) turns on contextual assessments of neutrality, knowledge, and control, and that imposing broad ex ante control duties risks becoming an impermissible general monitoring obligation. In its judgment concerning a hosting platform required by a regional administration to block or suppress listings, the Supreme Court framed the key questions as including whether such requirements amount to a general supervision duty contrary to the e-commerce framework.[52] In a closely related register, the Supreme Court's case law on intermediary legal status and liability exemption has also engaged with the "neutral host" versus "active role" distinction and with the compatibility of national measures with EU constraints against general monitoring.[53] This jurisprudential background might be relevant, by analogy, to disputes about false online content in the platforms[54] when channelled through notice-based and knowledge-based liability logics under the EU framework, mainly the DSA.[55]

2.7 *The Impact of Soft Law*

Soft law instruments exert significant influence on the Spanish legal regime for disinformation. This influence is particularly pronounced because Spain has historically lacked a comprehensive statutory "anti-disinformation" framework and because the constitutional sensitivity of regulating communicative freedoms pushes institutional practice toward coordination and strategic communication tools.[56] As described in the introduction (*supra* 1), tracing back the national response to disinformation in Spain show this primary trend to rely on these kinds of actions and tools and the preference for coordination and preventive mechanisms aligned with and triggered by EU moves.

[50] STS 2074/1998, 27/01/2001.

[51] Fiscalía General del Estado (2020).

[52] STS 238/2019, 30/12/2020.

[53] STS 923/2019, 27/6/2019.

[54] Whether the transition from a digital economy to a platform economy required a new legal framework and, in particular, whether the liability exemption rules should apply straightforward to platform operators, are discussed in Rodríguez de las Heras Ballell T (2017)

[55] Rodríguez de las Heras Ballell T (2023).

[56] Moreno-Castro C et al. (2023).

As previously expounded, policy instruments such as the EU Action Plan against Disinformation and platform-focused cooperation frameworks have shaped Spanish policy choices. Spain's national procedure approved in 2020 expressly presents itself as implementing the 2018 EU Action Plan against Disinformation, and it is assessed as prioritising communicational strategies and coordination structures rather than setting a direct restriction procedure for disinformation content.[57]

The reliance on soft law is often defended as flexible and more compatible with freedom of expression, but it has also drawn criticism for opacity and accountability risks, particularly where coordination is anchored in national-security structures and where the language of "verified" or "truthful" information might invite overreach.[58]

2.8 *Influence of Foreign Legal Solutions*

Foreign legal solutions have exerted a limited influence on the Spanish approach to disinformation. This influence is primarily indirect and mediated through European Union initiatives and comparative academic debate rather than by legislative transplantation. Spanish debate has tended to observe more interventionist foreign models with caution, and there has been sustained resistance to approaches that would empower administrative bodies to decide truthfulness as such, given the constitutional emphasis on legality, judicial guarantees, and the protection of communicative freedoms. In this sense, foreign solutions function mainly as reference points in policy discussion rather than as sources of binding legal norms.[59]

2.9 *Possible Legal Reform*

The question of legal reform in the field of disinformation remains open in Spain. There is a legislative proposal to tackle disinformation in Spain.[60] The legislative bill proposes a far-reaching reform of the Spanish media and information landscape by framing the fight against disinformation primarily as a structural and institutional problem rather than as an issue of isolated false content. Its core objective is to guarantee the constitutional right to receive truthful information by strengthening pluralism, transparency, and professional independence in the media sector. To this end, the proposal introduces strict limits on concentration of media ownership based on audience thresholds across television, radio, print, and digital press, and creates extensive transparency obligations concerning ownership structures, financial

57 See also Rodríguez de las Heras Ballell T (2018).

58 ARTICLE 19 (2021).

59 Moreno-Castro C et al. (2023); European Commission and High Representative (2018).

60 Proposición de Ley Orgánica de garantía del derecho a la información veraz y lucha contra la desinformación, 122/000107 ('Legislative Bill 122/000107').

interests, and sources of income, including public advertising. These measures are complemented by internal transparency duties for larger media outlets, such as the adoption of editorial independence mechanisms and the public disclosure of governance and financial information, reflecting the view that structural conditions of the media system are a key factor in preventing disinformation.

A central feature of the bill, put forward by the mixed parliamentary group in the Spanish Parliament (*Grupo Mixto*),[61] is the creation of a new independent body, the *Consejo del Derecho a la Información*, conceived as the primary authority responsible for safeguarding the right to truthful information. This body would have broad competences, including the detection of false news disseminated by media outlets, the maintenance of public registers relating to media ownership and sanctions, and the exercise of sanctioning powers. The bill establishes a detailed administrative sanctioning regime, including fines, publication obligations, loss of access to institutional advertising, and, in severe or repeated cases, revocation of licences. At the same time, it seeks to protect journalistic integrity by addressing labour precarity in the media sector, restricting outsourcing of news production and reinforcing employment stability for journalists. Overall, the proposal articulates a comprehensive and interventionist model that combines media pluralism rules, institutional oversight, and administrative enforcement as tools to combat disinformation.

Terminologically, the bill's title refers to 'disinformation', a term that is employed in the text as the ultimate aim of the legislative action, but adds references to '*noticias falsas*' and 'false statements' as it is focused on ensuring pluralism in the media space. Therefore, references to falsity in news, and statements is intimately linked to the personal scope of application of the bill. Pursuant to Article 2, the bill is aimed to apply to natural and legal persons providing communication services who carry out their activity directly, or participate in the share capital of such service providers in any of the following areas: television, radio, print media and digital media.

So far, the proposal has not been adopted and there is no political leeway at the moment to reach an agreement on its approval or an amended successful version. But the political and intellectual dialogue that accompanied its debate can serve as the foundation for future reforms under a different configuration of Congress (*Congreso de los Diputados*).

Likely reform trajectories concern governance and accountability rather than criminalisation, including clearer competence allocation and oversight in the domestic operationalisation of EU digital regulation, stronger transparency and human-rights safeguards around institutional coordination mechanisms, and resilience measures (media literacy, research access, and structured cooperation). In this respect, the Spanish regime appears more likely to evolve incrementally, driven by EU legal developments and constitutional doctrine, than through the creation of a singular "disinformation offence" or an administrative truth-determination model.[62]

---

[61] *Grupo Mixto* refers to a parliamentary group formed by all members of the Spanish Parliament who do not meet the essential requirements to form their own parliamentary group, according to the Spanish Constitution, Spanish law, or the internal regulations of parliament.

[62] Badillo A (2024); Sabater-Quinto F et al. (2025).

3 The Regulation

3.1 Reporting Procedures and Other Ways to Tackle Online Disinformation

Spanish law does not create a single, unified disinformation reporting procedure applicable across online environments. Instead, it offers a plural architecture that depends on whether the contested content is merely false or misleading (and therefore often lawful), or whether it also amounts to illegal content under existing categories of Spanish law such as offences against honour, hate crimes, fraud, unlawful processing of personal data, or breaches of regulated-sector duties.[63] Outside of coercive enforcement, reports might activate institutional and coordination mechanisms linked to national security.[64]

At EU level, the most relevant reporting framework for online environments is now found in the Digital Services Act (DSA). The DSA strengthens notice-and-action mechanisms for illegal content and introduces procedural rights surrounding platform content moderation decisions. For very large online platforms and very large online search engines, it also treats disinformation as a systemic risk that must be assessed and mitigated through risk-management duties, rather than through state decisions on truthfulness.[65]

Accordingly, Spain tackles online disinformation through a combination of platform governance, increasingly structured by EU rules; civil and criminal remedies for specific wrongs linked to falsehood; and administrative intervention only in those domains where the legislature has conferred competence, such as audiovisual regulation, data protection, consumer protection, public health communications, and electoral guarantees. The overall orientation is preventive and remedial rather than punitive, and it is shaped by a consistent preference for ex post accountability and procedural safeguards, rather than ex ante filtering.

3.1.1 Subjects Who Can Report

In practice, the first reporting actor is often the user. Private individuals can report content directly to platforms using internal reporting tools, particularly where the content allegedly violates platform rules on disinformation, harassment, hate speech, manipulated media, or coordinated inauthentic behaviour, based on the DSA.[66]

Private individuals may also report or challenge disinformation through remedies aimed at correcting or neutralising false factual statements, especially when their personal rights are implicated. The most time-sensitive and specific remedy is

[63] Badillo A (2024).

[64] Orden PCM/1030/2020.

[65] Arts 16 and 20–21 DSA.

[66] Arts 16, 49 DSA.

the right of rectification for media under a specific Spanish law, which allows any natural or legal person to demand rectification of factual information that refers to them, is considered inaccurate, and may cause harm.[67] The reporter must first send a rectification request to the media outlet and, if refused or not published properly, they can bring a streamlined action before a court of first instance. The availability of this instrument matters for online disinformation insofar as digital-native outlets, and sometimes broadcasters' online services, disseminate factual narratives that can be rectified without the claimant having to prove a criminal offence.

Where disinformation takes the form of reputational harm, individuals may proceed through civil protection of honour, privacy, and image, or through criminal complaint for defamation (*calumnia* or *injuria*) where the statutory thresholds are met. In criminal procedure, private individuals can file a criminal complaint. This reporting route is not designed for disinformation in general; it is tied to the specific offence alleged, and the criminal-law principle of legality pushes adjudication towards narrow typologies and intent requirements rather than broad truth-control.[68]

Public servants and public bodies also act as reporters, but again only within limited legal mandates. Police and prosecutors can act upon information that disinformation is being used to commit offences such as hate crimes, fraud, or public disorder.[69] Sectoral administrations may forward matters to prosecutors where criminal elements appear, or they may open administrative proceedings where they have competence: for instance, data protection when personal data are unlawfully used, or consumer authorities where misleading practices affect consumers.[70]

3.1.2 Subjects Who Decide on the Report

Decision-making authority depends on the chosen forum. Where the report is submitted to a platform, the platform is the first-instance decision-maker. In these cases, the decisive criteria are usually the platform's internal rules and its assessment of legality risks. Under the DSA, when platforms take certain moderation actions, they must provide a statement of reasons to the affected recipient of the service, thereby introducing a minimum procedural framework for decisions that can otherwise feel opaque.[71]

[67] Ley Orgánica 2/1984, 26 March 1984, reguladora del derecho de rectificación, BOE num 74, 27/3/ 1984 (LO 2/1984), arts 1–6.

[68] Fiscalía General del Estado, Circular 2/2022, 20 December 2022, sobre criterios para la actuación del Ministerio Fiscal en los delitos contra el honor, BOE num 2, 3/1/ 2023; Serrano Hoyo G (2003); Hernández Ramos M (2022).

[69] Real Decreto of 14 September 1882, por el que se aprueba la Ley de Enjuiciamiento Criminal, Gaceta de Madrid, 17/9/1882.

[70] Real Decreto Legislativo 1/2007, of 16 November 2007, por el que se aprueba el texto refundido de la Ley General para la Defensa de los Consumidores y Usuarios y otras leyes complementarias, BOE num. 287, 30/11/ 2007.

[71] Arts 17, 20 DSA.

When the report is framed as a rectification request to the media under Spanish law, the "decision-maker" at first instance is not a public authority but the director or responsible person of the media outlet, who must publish the rectification within three days if the legal conditions are met. If the outlet refuses, fails to publish, or publishes incorrectly, the decision then moves to a judge of first instance through a rapid procedure that may culminate in a decision delivered immediately or the next day after the hearing.[72]

Where the report takes the form of a civil claim for protection of honour, privacy, or image, the decision-maker is the civil judiciary. Where it takes the form of a criminal complaint, the decision-maker is first the investigating judge (akin to the investigating role of prosecutors in many countries) and later the criminal court. In these contexts, "truth" is not declared in the abstract; it is assessed as evidence relevant to statutory elements, defences, and proportionality.

Administrative bodies decide only on narrow grounds within their legally defined competence. A data protection authority may decide whether personal data have been unlawfully processed or disseminated. An audiovisual regulator may decide whether regulated entities have breached duties imposed by audiovisual legislation. Consumer authorities may address misleading commercial practices. Spain does not have a specialised administrative authority empowered to determine truthfulness of online content in general.

3.1.3 Means to Establish the Falsehood of the Contents and the Related Responsibilities

Spanish law does not adopt a single evidentiary method for establishing falsehood in disinformation cases. Instead, proof rules follow the forum and the underlying cause of action. In civil contexts, courts assess evidence under ordinary civil procedural standards. In honour-related disputes, the key move is usually to distinguish facts from value judgments, and then to determine whether a factual assertion is verifiable and, if so, whether it was communicated with adequate diligence and within a matter of public interest. Falsehood is therefore relevant, but it is embedded in a broader balancing test linked to constitutional rights and civil liability doctrines, rather than being treated as a standalone element.[73]

In criminal contexts, falsity operates as an element of certain offences or as part of the required *mens rea*. For *calumnia*, Spanish Criminal Code defines it as the imputation of an offence "with knowledge of falsity or reckless disregard for the truth", and the Penal Code specifies penalties, particularly when publicity is involved.[74] For *injuria*, the Criminal Code similarly makes falsity relevant where insults consist

[72] LO 2/1984, arts 3–6.

[73] Del Hierro JL (2014); de Verda R, Beamonte R, Parada Vaca O (2012).

[74] Código Penal (Ley Orgánica 10/1995, de 23 de noviembre), BOE num 281, de 24 de noviembre de 1995, arts 205–206.

of the imputation of facts and are carried out with knowledge of falsity or reckless disregard.[75] Fraud, which can be committed through disinformative narratives designed to induce error, depends on the existence of "sufficient deception" leading to patrimonial disposition.[76]

3.1.4 Deadlines for the Decision

Because there is no unified disinformation procedure, deadlines are heterogeneous. The clearest and most specific statutory deadlines appear in the rectification regime for media. A rectification request must be sent to the director within seven days of publication or diffusion of the information, and, if properly exercised, the director must publish the rectification within three days of receipt. If rectification is refused or mishandled, the affected person may bring an action within seven working days, and the judge must convene a verbal hearing within seven days of the request, with the judgment delivered immediately or the next day.[77]

In administrative proceedings, including those that may incidentally involve disinformation, decision-making deadlines are governed by the general framework of Spanish administrative procedural law rather than by any disinformation-specific rules. Law 39/2015 establishes a general obligation for public administrations to issue and notify an express decision in all administrative procedures, regardless of how they are initiated.[78] The same statute sets default maximum time limits for resolving procedures and regulates the legal effects of administrative silence in proceedings initiated at the request of an interested party, distinguishing between positive and negative silence depending on the nature of the powers exercised and the interests at stake.[79] These provisions are particularly relevant where allegedly disinformative content triggers administrative action within a specific regulatory domain, such as data protection, consumer protection, or audiovisual regulation.

For platform reporting, the DSA does not impose a single deadline for all platforms in all cases, but it does require that notices be processed and decisions taken diligently, and it strengthens procedural expectations by requiring explanations and internal complaint-handling.[80] In practice, platforms often rely on tiered urgency systems, especially for election-related integrity issues, but those operational details typically sit in platform policies and codes of practice rather than in Spanish statutory deadlines.[81]

---

[75] Ibid, art 208.

[76] Ibid, art 248.

[77] LO 2/1984 arts 3–6.

[78] Ley 39/2015, de 1 de octubre, del Procedimiento Administrativo Común de las Administraciones Públicas, BOE núm 236, de 2 de octubre de 2015, art 21.

[79] Ibid, art 24.

[80] Arts 16, 20 DSA.

[81] E.g., Commission Guidelines for providers of Very Large Online Platforms and Very Large Online Search Engines on the mitigation of systemic risks for electoral processes pursuant to Article 35(3)

3.1.5 Forms of Protection for the Authors of Allegedly Illegal Content or Disinformation

In Spain, the core protection for authors of allegedly illegal content is constitutional and procedural: public authorities cannot impose prior censorship, and any restriction on speech must be grounded in law and applied ex post with judicial guarantees, including adversarial process and (in criminal matters) the presumption of innocence.[82] For reputational disputes, an additional safeguard is that rapid correction mechanisms such as rectification are narrowly framed and do not function as a punitive finding of falsity, but as a time-sensitive right to publish a reply under judicial control if contested.[83]

The main practical vulnerability for authors today lies in private content moderation, so legal protection increasingly takes the form of DSA due-process rights against platform decisions.[84] Platforms must give users a statement of reasons for key moderation measures and provide an internal complaint-handling system enabling review of removals, suspensions, and other restrictions.[85] Users also gain access to certified out-of-court dispute settlement bodies, which adds an external review layer beyond the platform's own appeal system.[86]

Order PCM/1030/2020 has been debated in Spain precisely in regard to safeguards for authors. The Order's non-sanctioning, non-removal design can be read as a built-in protection for authors: it deliberately avoids giving the administration power to block or punish speech.[87]

3.1.6 Sanctions in Case of Detection of Disinformation

Sanctions arise only when disinformation overlaps with a legally defined wrong. For instance, the official memorandum from the Spanish Attorney General makes clear that fake news may be relevant insofar as it is used to commit hate crimes, fraud, offences against honour, or public order offences, among others.[88] Criminal sanctions therefore depend on the offence. In the sphere of honour, *calumnia* and *injuria* crimes can be sanctioned with fines and potentially imprisonment as provided

of Regulation (EU) 2022/2065 (2024) Official Journal of the European Union C/2024/3014, 26 Apr 2024; Shahi GK, Tessa B, Trujillo A, Cresci S (2025).

[82] Presno Linera MA (2020).

[83] LO 2/1984, arts 1–6.

[84] Rodríguez de las Heras Ballell T (2018).

[85] Arts 17, 20 DSA.

[86] Ibid, art 21.

[87] Orden PCM/1030/2020.

[88] Fiscalía General del Estado (2020).

by statute.[89] Fraud can entail imprisonment, beyond restitution, where the deception is sufficiently serious and leads to patrimonial harm.[90]

Civil remedies consist of rectification, cessation, and compensation. In practice, where the main harm is reputational, the civil path is often preferred because it allows targeted correction and compensation without extending criminal law into the regulation of discourse. The rectification regime for media is a paradigmatic example of this remedial logic and demonstrates that Spanish law aims at restoring informational integrity in a proportionate way.[91]

Administrative sanctions are possible only within regulated domains. If disinformation is packaged as a misleading commercial practice or unlawful advertising, consumer authorities may apply administrative sanctioning powers. If it involves unlawful processing of personal data, administrative penalties may follow under data protection law. If regulated audiovisual service providers breach duties of integrity or protection of minors, sanctions can follow under audiovisual regulation.[92]

Finally, a separate sanctioning track concerns platforms themselves. Spanish law follows the EU rules for intermediary liability. The Spanish law established liability limitations for hosting providers where they lack effective knowledge of illegality or act diligently to remove or disable access once they have such knowledge.[93] The DSA now overlays this with harmonised obligations and a stronger enforcement architecture at EU and national level, including potential penalties for systemic non-compliance.[94] The practical shape of sanctions for platforms depends on enforcement designations and procedures in each Member State, and penalties target non-compliance with regulatory duties rather than the communication of falsehood as such.

3.1.7 Sanctions in Case of Unfounded Reports or Complaints

Spain does not have a bespoke offence for false reporting of disinformation specifically. However, general legal mechanisms can apply when reporting is weaponised. The clearest is the offence of false accusation or complaint: a person who imputes

---

[89] Código Penal (Ley Orgánica 10/1995, de 23 de noviembre), BOE núm 281, de 24 de noviembre de 1995, arts 206 and 209.

[90] Ibid, art 248.

[91] PwC Spain (n.d.).

[92] García Rubio F (2022); Real Decreto 1/2007, of 16 November, por el que se aprueba el texto refundido de la Ley General para la Defensa de los Consumidores y Usuarios y otras leyes complementarias, BOE num 287, 30/11/ 2007; Ley Orgánica 3/2018, 5 December 2018, de Protección de Datos Personales y garantía de los derechos digitales, BOE num 294, 6/12/2018.

[93] Ley 34/2002, of 11 July, de servicios de la sociedad de la información y de comercio electrónico (LSSI), BOE num 166, 12/7/2002, art 16, 14.

[94] Arts 16, 20–21 DSA.

criminal facts to another before officials with a duty to investigate, acting with knowledge of falsity or reckless disregard for the truth, can be punished under Spanish criminal law.[95] Similarly, the simulation of offences or the making of false complaints that provoke proceedings can be punished.[96]

In Spanish civil litigation, courts routinely impose costs on the losing party as a general rule, and this can include costs consequences for unfounded actions; costs are normally awarded against a party whose claims are wholly dismissed unless the court finds serious doubts of fact or law, and although the statute does not expressly provide for a separate abuse of process sanction, courts may interpret and apply the costs regime to curb objectively vexatious or bad-faith litigation and may consider abusive conduct when allocating costs, reflecting a procedural check on unfounded claims.[97] However, in administrative contexts, Spanish law does not provide for a general sanction for knowingly false complaints as such.

Within platforms' own systems, abusive reporting is usually addressed by internal governance tools, such as deprioritising habitual abusers, limiting reporting functionality, or treating repetitive unfounded notices as non-credible. The DSA's proceduralisation of notices may indirectly deter abuse by requiring that notices contain specific elements and by linking certain legal effects to the quality of notices.[98]

3.1.8 Review of Previous Decisions

Because decision-makers vary, review paths also vary. For the specific procedure of rectification disputes in media, it provides a streamlined judicial track. Decisions in the rectification process are generally designed to be swift and final, though limited appeals exist in specified cases and within very short time limits.[99]

For criminal decisions, review follows ordinary criminal procedure, including appeals against certain decisions and judgments depending on competence and procedural stage. For administrative decisions, Spanish law provides administrative appeals and, ultimately, judicial review before the contentious-administrative courts.

For platform decisions, the DSA requires internal complaint-handling systems for certain moderation outcomes and introduces the possibility of out-of-court dispute settlement via certified bodies.[100] Users may also pursue judicial remedies where private moderation intersects with contractual rights, consumer law, or data protection, though those routes are complex and fact-dependent.

---

[95] Código Penal (Ley Orgánica 10/1995, of 23 November), BOE num 281, 24/11/1995, art 456.

[96] Ibid., art 457.

[97] Ley 1/2000, of 7 January 2000, de Enjuiciamiento Civil, BOE num 7, 8/1/ 2000, art 394.

[98] Art 16 DSA.

[99] LO 2/1984, art 8.

[100] Ibid, arts 20–21.

3.1.9 Sanctions for Private Entities or Administrative Bodies Who Rendered Erroneous Decisions

Spain does not provide a special sanctioning regime for wrong disinformation decisions. The relevant legal controls are again general. For administrative bodies, the main accountability mechanism is the regime of state liability. Spanish law establishes that individuals have the right to be compensated for injuries to their goods and rights resulting from the normal or abnormal functioning of public services, subject to the statutory conditions.[101]

For private entities, including platforms, erroneous moderation may trigger civil liability only in limited scenarios, since platforms generally act within contractual and regulatory frameworks that allow content moderation, and claims must navigate contractual terms, consumer law, and freedom of enterprise.[102] The DSA nonetheless increases the visibility and contestability of platform errors by requiring reason-giving and complaint-handling.[103] Additionally, Spain's previous intermediary liability framework has tended to avoid imposing general monitoring duties, focusing instead on knowledge-based responsibility and diligent action once illegality is known,[104] in full alignment with the EU Directive on Electronic Commerce.[105]

3.2 Regulations Concerning Disinformation in General, Therefore also Applicable to Online Disinformation

No regulation in Spain concerns disinformation in general. The proposed legislative bill for a disinformation law has not received parliamentary approval yet and there are no certain prospects that it will be approved or, if approved, that it would be with its current content and form.[106] The bill proposes a comprehensive reform that addresses disinformation by restructuring the media system rather than targeting false content in isolation. It seeks to strengthen the right to receive truthful information through limits on media concentration, enhanced transparency of ownership and financing, and safeguards for editorial independence. A new independent authority would oversee compliance, maintain public registers, and exercise sanctioning powers. The proposal

101 Ley 40/2015, de 1 de octubre, de Régimen Jurídico del Sector Público, BOE num 236, 2/10/2015, art 32.

102 Van der Sloot B (2015).

103 Arts 17, 20 DSA.

104 LSSI, art 16.

105 Directive 2000/31/EC of the European Parliament and of the Council of 8 June 2000 on certain legal aspects of information society services, in particular electronic commerce, in the Internal Market ('Directive on electronic commerce') OJ L 178, 17.7.2000, pp. 1–16.

106 Proposición de Ley Orgánica de garantía del derecho a la información veraz y lucha contra la desinformación, 122/000107.

thus advances an interventionist model combining media pluralism, institutional oversight, and administrative enforcement to prevent disinformation.[107]

4 Conclusions

4.1 *Perception of Disinformation Risk and Effectiveness of Countering Measures and Policies*

As evidenced by Iberifier Fact-checking partners over the course of the past 3 years, information flows in Spain have been exposed to mis-/ disinformation regarding foreign events and followed the general trends in relation to typologies, formats and intentionality frameworks.[108] In particular, the combination of traditional disinformation campaigns with AI applications (*deep fakes,* artificially manipulated content, false account, chatbots, AI-generated video, voice, and images) has alarmingly aggravated the impact of disinformation and reduced the effectiveness of detecting mechanisms. Population is seriously exposed to sophisticated disinformation content with significantly lower capacity to respond.

Data of Eurobarometer has been showing high level of risk perception of Spanish population regarding the criticality of threat of disinformation to democracy. In the report of 2018,[109] the percentage was 84%, the second highest in Europe. These concerns, however, have not implied more robustness and effectiveness in identifying "fake news". On the contrary, percentages were below the European average according to the Eurobarometer data. Besides, Spaniards showed a majority trend (51%, the second highest in the EU) to attribute responsibility to national authorities in fighting disinformation.[110]

In this societal context, it should be taken into account the transition in the Spanish society towards information consumption patterns that typically characterise an omnimetric society. The radicality of such a shift from traditional media consumption to social media consumption is a key calibrator of the exposure to online disinformation. In that regard, data reveal an exponential growth in the number of internet users and the number of social network users. Access to information and news through news aggregators has acted as an amplifier of the risk for accidental consumption of dis/misinformation. Aggregators, recommenders and other intermediary services enlarge the distance between the content consumer and the source and hide most of the credibility indicators that primary sources provide. Therefore, consumption patterns revealing intensive use of news aggregators and similar services

---

[107] Ibid.

[108] Magallón-Rosa R, Paisana M et al (2024).

[109] Flash Eurobarometer (2018).

[110] Complete data and detailed analysis in Magallón-Rosa R, Paisana M et al (2024).

in addition to social media do normally evidence a social landscape more fertilised for disinformation.

As previously discussed, country-specific features, such high political tension and polarisation, or concrete events with strong impact on citizens –the impact of catastrophes (the DANA), electoral periods, corruption cases, pending judicial decisions– stoke disinformation campaigns, and more decisively, increase permeation of disinformation into the public opinion. Polarised countries are more vulnerable to disinformation as confirmation bias neutralises any attempt to verify content. Credibility indicators are replaced by affective, and highly ideological factors. Thus, content consumers are less willing to verify information, and more exposed to manipulated content arousing their fears, anxiety, and prejudices.[111]

4.2 *Future Actions and Proposals*

Fighting against disinformation shall not be fully successful and effective unless it takes into account the societal, political, and technological factors that underpin online disinformation in contemporary societies. As explained in this paper, that means to consider global aspects as well as country-specific characteristics.

As a global phenomenon, disinformation shows common features that outline the unique profile of today's disinformation. Beyond acknowledging the profound and intimate connection with technology, it should be framed within the singular conditions of an omnimetric society. In this regard, an effective implementation of the EU instruments on platforms (primarily DSA, and, to a certain extent DMA) in Spain is crucial.

As a country-specific phenomenon, socioeconomic, political, and cultural conditions are also decisive in devising and deploying the right measures and actions. At the moment, there is a legislative bill[112] that approaches the fight against disinformation as a structural and institutional problem in the Spanish media and information landscape. Disinformation is not targeted as a standalone challenge but as a by-product of a malfunctioning media sector. Therefore, it is focused on preserving and fortifying the constitutional right to receive truthful information by strengthening pluralism, transparency, and professional independence in the media sector. The current political terrain does not allow one to predict its approval.

In 2024, the Action Plan for Democracy[113] was presented by the Spanish Government as a roadmap with 31 measures to be implemented over the next three years to improve the quality of government information, ensure media plurality and increase the transparency of the legislative branch and the electoral system. The Action Plan

[111] The Edelman Trust Barometer pictures Spain as a polarised country and alerts about decreasing optimism in the population. Edelman (2023).

[112] Legislative Bill 122/000107.

[113] Gobierno de España (2024).

pivots on three axes. Each one will entail implementation actions, various measures, and certain legislative actions.

References

Alendete D (2019) *Fake news. La nueva arma de destrucción masiva*. Deusto, Madrid.

ARTICLE 19 (2021) Spain: ministerial order establishing the national procedure against disinformation. https://www.article19.org/wp-content/uploads/2021/09/SpainDisinfoMinisterialOrder-ENG.pdf.

Badillo A (2019) La sociedad de la desinformación: propaganda, fake news y la nueva geopolítica de la información. Real Instituto Elcano, Madrid.

Badillo A et al (2023) *Analysis of the impact of disinformation on politic, economic, social and security issues, governance model and good practices: the cases of Spain and Portugal*. IBERIFIER, Pamplona. https://doi.org/10.15581/026.002.

Badillo A, Arteaga F (2024) El impacto estratégico de la desinformación en España. IBERIFIER, Pamplona.

CCN-CERT (2019) Desinformación en el ciberespacio. Ministerio de Defensa, Madrid

Centro Criptológico Nacional (n.d.) Consejo Nacional de Ciberseguridad. https://www.ccn.cni.es.

Comisión Nacional de los Mercados y la Competencia (2024) El Ministerio para la Transformación Digital y de la Función Pública designa a la CNMC como coordinador de servicios digitales de España. CNMC, 24 Jan 2024. https://www.cnmc.es/prensa/coordinador-servicios-digitales-20240124.

del Hierro JL (2014) Verdad y veracidad informativas: el ejemplo español. Eunomía. Revista en cultura de la legalidad 7:41–56

de Verda R, Beamonte R, Parada Vaca O (2012) La colisión entre el derecho al honor y la libertad de información (deber de veracidad y reportaje neutral). Revista Boliviana de Derecho 14:122–139.

Edelman (2023) Edelman Trust Barometer 2023. https://www.edelman.com/es/2023-edelman-trust-barometer.

Espaliú-Berdud C (2022) Legal and criminal prosecution of disinformation in Spain in the context of the European Union. Profesional de la información 31(3).

Eurobarometer (2024) Youth Survey 2024. https://europa.eu/eurobarometer/surveys/detail/3392

European Commission (2018) Tackling online disinformation: a European approach. COM(2018) 236 final, Brussels, 26 Apr 2018.

European Commission (2018) Joint communication to the European Parliament, the Council, the European Economic and Social Committee and the Committee of the Regions: action plan against disinformation. JOIN(2018) 36 final

European External Action Service (2019) Countering disinformation. https://eeas.europa.eu/topics/countering-disinformation_en

European Parliament (2022) Report on foreign interference in all democratic processes in the European Union, including disinformation. A9–0022/2022

Fiscalía General del Estado (2020) Tratamiento penal de las fake news. Fiscalía General del Estado, Madrid, pp 1–3. https://www.fiscal.es/documents/20142/954527/Tratamiento+penal+de+las+fake+news.pdf.

Flash Eurobarometer (2018) Fake News and Disinformation Online. https://data.europa.eu/data/datasets/s2183_464_eng?locale=en.

Fried D, Polyakova A (2018) Democratic defense against disinformation. Atlantic Council, Washington, DC

García Rubio F (2022) El régimen jurídico de la lucha contra las fake news en España. Actualidad Administrativa no. 9:1–22.

Gobierno de España (2024) Plan de acción por la democracia. https://www.mpr.gob.es/prencom/notas/Documents/2024/2024-3002_Plan_de_accion.pdf.
Gobierno de España (2021). Estrategia de acción exterior 2021-2024. Madrid.
Gobierno de España (2019) Informe del plan de lucha contra la desinformación. Madrid
Hernández Ramos M (2022) El conflicto entre la libertad de expresión y el derecho al honor en las redes sociales. Derecho Privado y Constitución 36:213–244.
Hoffman FG (2017) Conflict in the 21st century: the rise of hybrid wars. Policy Studies
Instituto Cervantes (2025) El español en el mundo. In: Anuario del Instituto Cervantes 2025. https://cvc.cervantes.es/lengua/anuario/anuario_25/el_espanol_en_el_mundo_anuario_instituto_cervantes_2025.pdf
Magallón-Rosa R, Paisana M et al (2024) Disinformation consumption patterns in Spain and Portugal. IBERIFIER, Pamplona. https://doi.org/10.15581/026.007.
Mattis JN, Hoffman FG (2005) Future warfare: the rise of hybrid wars. U.S. Naval Institute Proceedings 131.
Moreno-Castro C, et al (2023) *IBERIFIER report on political and legal aspects of disinformation in Portugal and Spain.* IBERIFIER, Pamplona. https://doi.org/10.15581/026.004.
Presno Linera MA (2020) La libertad de expresión en internet y las redes sociales: análisis jurisprudencial. Revista Catalana de Dret Públic no. 61:65–82
PwC Spain (n.d.). Derecho de rectificación 2.0: las nuevas reglas del juego en medios digitales. https://www.pwc.es/es/newlaw-pulse/entretenimiento-medios/derecho-rectificacion-2-0.html.; LO 2/1984.
Reporters Without Borders (2025) RSF index 2025. https://rsf.org/en/index?year=2025.
Rodríguez de las Heras Ballell T (2023) Trust in an omnimetric society? Reputational systems in platforms as tools for assessing contractual performance and applying remedies. In: Bussani M, Cassese S, Infantino M (eds) *Comparative legal metrics.* Brill, Leiden, pp 266–28.
Rodríguez de las Heras Ballell T (2023) Solving the platform liability quandary: continuity and innovation in the DSA. https://doi.org/10.17875/gup2023-2502.
Rodríguez de las Heras Ballell T (2023) Hearing before the Congress of Deputies of Spain. Congreso de los Diputados. https://app.congreso.es/AudiovisualCongreso/audiovisualdetalledisponible?codSesion=18&codOrgano=319&fechaSesion=28/03/2023&idLegislaturaElegida=14. Accessed 11 Jan 2026
Rodríguez de las Heras Ballell T (2021) The background of the Digital Services Act: looking towards a platform economy. ERA Forum. https://rdcu.be/ce8dM.
Rodríguez de las Heras Ballell T (2020) La responsabilidad de las plataformas en el control de las noticias falsas: modelos para mitigar la desinformación. In: Rodríguez Ayuso JF, Atienza Macías E (eds) Retos jurídicos ante la crisis del COVID-19. Wolters Kluwer, Madrid, pp 299–321.
Rodríguez de las Heras Ballell T (2018) Credibility-enhancing regulatory models to counter fake news: risks of a non-harmonized intermediary liability paradigm shift. Journal of International Media and Entertainment Law 8(2):129–178.
Rodríguez de las Heras Ballell T (2017) The legal anatomy of electronic platforms: a prior study to assess the need of a law of platforms in the EU. The Italian Law Journal 3(1):149–176.
Sabater-Quinto F, Belmonte-Martín I, Lloret-Irles D (2025) Respuestas públicas a la desinformación en la UE y España (2015–2023): una cuestión abierta. Revista Mediterránea de Comunicación 16:8–9.
Sádaba Chalezquer MR, Santos Sánchez DJ (2023) Hearing before the Senate of Spain. Senado de España. https://www.senado.es/web/actividadparlamentaria/sesionescomision/detallecomisiones/sesionescomision/sesioncelebrada/index.html?lang=gl_ES&legis=14&id=G020004&idSes=6&idConv=1. Accessed 11 Jan 2026
Serrano Hoyo G (2003) Procedimiento para el enjuiciamiento de los delitos de calumnias e injurias. Revista de Derecho Penal y Criminología 11:305–334
Shahi GK, Tessa B, Trujillo A, Cresci S (2025) A year of the DSA Transparency Database: what it (does not) reveal about platform moderation during the 2024 European Parliament election. arXiv. https://arxiv.org/abs/2504.06976.

van der Sloot B (2015) Liability of internet intermediaries for privacy violations in Europe. Journal of Intellectual Property, Information Technology and Electronic Commerce Law (JIPITEC) 6:63–83.

Sweden: Between Prevention of Online Disinformation and Freedom of Expression

Carl Lebeck and Victoria Al Haj

Abstract This chapter covers the main aspects of the Swedish regulation concerning online disinformation. Sweden has chosen a very limited approach to prevention of disinformation focusing on particular instances of disinformation regardless of technical form rather than any general regulation of disinformation online. That largely reflects a long tradition of strong protection of freedom of expression where the courts have (with certain exceptions) avoided to arbitrate on issues of truth and falsehood. That means that most measures aimed at countering disinformation in Swedish law are either directed to specific forms of disinformation (such as swindles, defamation, denial of genocides etc.) or dependent on measures of EU law. The reticient approach to the regulation of disinformation in Swedish reflects a view where the use of freedom of expression in and of itself is seen as a way to protect against disinformation of various kinds.

1 Introduction

This chapter aims to give an account of Swedish law on online disinformation, focusing on legislation that prohibits or restricts dissemination of incorrect information in various specific contexts. It should be noted that legislation aimed at online disinformation in general is very limited in Swedish law, meaning that legislation regulating disinformation in most cases also regulates other things. Most legislation and case law discussed here hence concern disinformation offline as well as online in particular contexts. It also means that Swedish regulation on disinformation is fragmented, and the account here seeks to provide an overview of central legislation, which however is not exhaustive. Online disinformation as a concept has loomed large in public debates as well as in debates on law and policy during the last decade.

C. Lebeck (✉)
Department of Law, Stockholm University, Stockholm, Sweden
e-mail: Carl.Lebeck@juridicum.su.se

V. Al Haj
Ramberg Advokater, Stockholm, Sweden

P. Passaglia (ed.), *European Legal Perspectives on Online Disinformation*, Ius Gentium: Comparative Perspectives on Law and Justice 140,
https://doi.org/10.1007/978-3-032-25785-7_19

Swedish law with regard to disinformation has remained very limited which reflects the traditionally strong protection of freedom of expression and freedom of the press in Swedish law. In Swedish law there is hence no general concept nor any general prohibition of disinformation, neither offline nor online. It is clear that, prohibition of dissemination of disinformation (in and of itself uncommon) in Swedish law, does not extend to prohibition of possession of disinformation. The restrictions on disinformation in Swedish law therefore only indirectly concerns freedom of information. The Swedish regulation of freedom of expression gives a privileged place to printed media (through Freedom of Press Act (Tryckfrihetsförordningen)) and traditional radio- and television (through the Freedom of Expression Fundamental Law (Yttrandefrihetsgrundlagen)), whereas most online communications fall outside the special regulation to protect freedom of expression and hence being subject to general criminal law and the general protection of freedom of expression. Online webpages may acquire a so called "editorial certificate" (*utgivningsbevis*) which means that they are covered by the Freedom of Expression Fundamental Law.[1] Most online communications fall however within the scope of general protection of freedom of expression under the Instrument of Government (Regeringsformen).[2] Sweden has gradually adapted certain legislation to EU law which in some instances has limited the scope allowed for disinformation, in particular contexts. Considerable parts of Swedish legislation on particular instances of disinformation aim to enable application of EU law in Swedish law.

In Swedish law there is a general distinction between private individuals (i.e. natural and private legal persons) and public authorities. Private individuals are protected by freedom of expression[3] whereas public authorities are bound by a general duty to provide correct (objective) information.[4] That means that there is a general obligation on every public authority to only provide correct or at least well-founded information and a general prohibition on public authorities to disseminate disinformation. That obligation applies in relation to information concerning particular individuals[5] and in relation to information to the public at large.[6]

[1] 1:4–1:5 Freedom of Expression Fundamental Law.

[2] 2:1 Instrument of Government.

[3] 2:1 Instrument of Government.

[4] 1:9 Instrument of Government (concerning the obligations of public authorities to be truthful, objective and impartial).

[5] Justitieombudsmannen (Parliamentary Ombudsman), Annual Report, JO 2007/08 s. 439.

[6] Justitieombudsmannen, decision 19th January 2026, nr. 1017–2025. JO 2020/21 s. 573, JO 2019/20 s. 445, JO 2019/20 s. 54, JO 2014/15 s. 146, JO 2010/11 s. 616.

1.1 Definitions of Disinformation

There is neither any formalised nor general definition of disinformation in Swedish law. There are however, as discussed below, rules prohibiting certain kinds of disinformation under criminal, administrative and private law.

In some contexts, a distinction is made between false information and true information presented in a misleading way (i.e. *disinformation*), and harmful if true information (i.e. *malinformation*). Information may be false in the sense of being factually incorrect and disseminated to mislead. In other cases, information may be correct but presented in a way which is misleading. However, as information which is misleading in a particular case but not false, contains correct information, there may be a general interest in protecting also such expressions. True information which may be harmful to someone, may also be important and beneficial to others. That is the reason for why harmful information is often if not always protected under freedom of expression. (E.g. information on the corruption of elected politicians or civil servants is obviously harmful to the persons concerned but may be a benefit to the public and to the public debate.) It is therefore clear that information which is harmful to individuals but which is of strong public interest is normally protected under freedom of expression. It is clear that neither disinformation nor malinformation are generally regarded as illegal in most contexts in Swedish law, although it may still be regulated and limited.[7]

1.2 Distinctions Between Notions of Misleading Information

There are few formal definitions of disinformation, regarding the content of the misleading information, but there are different rules prohibiting false or misleading information in particular contexts, in Swedish law.

1.3 Application of the Notion of Disinformation

There are rules on particular kinds of disinformation concerning e.g. swindles or fraud and spreading of false rumours in wartime as opposed to general rules on disinformation in Swedish law.

---

[7] Ronan Ó Fathaigh, Natali Helberger & Naomi Appelman, The perils of legally defining disinformation. Internet Policy Review, 10(4). (2021). https://doi.org/10.14763/2021.4.1584.

1.4 *Specificity of Online Disinformation*

There is little specific legislation in relation to online disinformation although there are rules concerning liability for misleading information in different contexts, including online. There is certain legislation concerning responsibility for so called "bulletin board systems" i.e. webpages that provide a forum for discussion among users, where the person responsible for the bulletin board may be held responsible for certain unlawful content.[8]

1.4.1 The Relevance of Illegal Contents to the Definition

There are examples albeit few that expressly makes certain content unlawful, online or otherwise in Swedish law. With regard to criminalisation of content of information in Swedish law, such criminalisation exists, but it does seldom directly focus on disinformation.[9] It is however clear that certain online information may be prohibited from being disseminated in Sweden on the basis of EU-law.[10]

2 The Sources of Law

2.1 *Constitutional Framework of Freedom of Expression and Freedom of the Press*

The Swedish constitutional framework concerning freedom of expression rests on three pillars, the protection of freedom of expression in the Instrument of Government, the Freedom of the Press Act and the Fundamental Law of Freedom of Expression. The reason for this tripartite structure of Swedish protection of freedom of expression, is that certain parts of the regulation of freedom of expression under Swedish law depends on the technical medium of expression, giving printed media, radio and television as well as certain online media a privileged status.

[8] 1§ lag (1998:112) om ansvar för elektroniska ansvarstavlor (Bulletin Board Act).

[9] Examples of criminalisation of possession of content of information may be found in relation to criminalisation of dissemination and possession of pictures and films of child pornography (16:10a Brottsbalken (Criminal Code)), and with regard to dissemination and possession for the purpose of dissemination of pictures and films of extreme violence (16:10c Criminal Code). Under Swedish law there are also prohibitions against dissemination of certain content, e.g. defamatory statements that may but do not necessarily need to be disinformation. Prohibition against dissemination of fraudulent information exists. These issues will be discussed more closely in Section 2.

[10] Lag (2023:319) med kompletterande bestämmelser till EU:s förordning om åtgärder mot spridning av terrorisminnehåll online (Law with complementing regulations to EU's regulation against dissemination of terrorist content online). Regulation (EU) 2021/784 of the European Parliament and the Council of 29 April 2021 on addressing the dissemination of terrorist content online.

2.1.1 General Constitutional Protection of Freedom of Expression

2:1 Instrument of Government provides for that everyone in Sweden may provide information to other and to express thoughts, opinions and feelings. The protected expressions include all kinds of expressions, such as written or printed materials, oral statements, whether in private conversations or in public speech, demonstrations, theatrical productions, paintings, sculptures, musical performances, and electronic media that are not connected to printed media.[11] Databases related to printed media or having applied for so called voluntary protection under the Fundamental Law of Freedom of Expression fall under the Freedom of Expression Fundamental Law.

The understanding of what counts as expressions protected by freedom of expression in Swedish law is essentially content-neutral. It also means that lies and disinformation are in most cases understood as protected expressions. Whereas general constitutional protection of freedom of expression (although not the specific protections of freedom of the press) includes commercial speech, the threshold for limiting commercial speech, as illustrated inter alia by the Marketing Act (Marknadsföringslagen) is low. The fact that expressions are protected does not exclude that they may be limited.

Freedom of expression may be limited through statutory legislation adopted by the parliament (except concerning official secrecy which may be amended by delegated legislation).[12]

Limitations on freedom of expression may be adopted to serve a number of stated purposes as well as other important reasons.[13] Among the general purposes considered as legitimate grounds to delimit freedom of expression in Swedish law are protection of national security, protection of public order, protection of provisions of goods, privacy, reputation of individuals as well as prevention, prosecution and punishment of crimes.[14] It should be noted that among the grounds for restricting freedom of expression mentioned in 2:23 Instrument of Government, protection against disinformation is not expressly mentioned. It does not necessarily rule out that protection against disinformation may be a ground for such restrictions as 2:23 Instrument of Government also allows for other grounds for restrictions on freedom of expression in cases where there may be other particularly important grounds for restricting it. However, it is an indication that protection against disinformation per se as opposed to disinformation that endangers national security, violates privacy or is used to further fraud, has not been regarded as main reason for restricting freedom of expression in Swedish law.

---

[11] See further, Petrén G. & Ragnemalm H., Sveriges grundlagar, Liber Förlag, Stockholm (1980), 43–44. Bull, T. & Sterzel, F. Regeringsformen – en kommentar, 3rd ed., Studentlitteratur, Lund (2023) 63–64.

[12] 2:20 Instrument of Government. Bull, T. & Sterzel, F. Regeringsformen – en kommentar, 3rd ed., Studentlitteratur, Lund (2023) 96–97.

[13] 2:23 Instrument of Government. Bull, T. & Sterzel, F. Regeringsformen – en kommentar, 3rd ed., Studentlitteratur, Lund (2023) 100–103.

[14] 2:23 Instrument of Government.

Restrictions on the freedom of expression may not go further than what is necessary to attain the purpose that has motivated the adoption of the restrictions.[15] Restrictions on freedom of expression have to be necessary, not just in general, but also in the particular case.[16] The criterion of necessity in Swedish law is not distinguished from, but includes a requirement of rationality of restrictions on freedom of expression. Restrictions on fundamental rights, including freedom of expression, may never be so extensive as threaten to undermine the free formation of political opinion being a fundamental part of democratic self-government.[17]

Whereas there is no formal requirement of proportionality in the strict sense in the sense of balancing between public interest and individual rights provided for in the text of the Swedish Instrument of Government, there has been a development in case law towards recognition of proportionality-requirements also for restrictions on freedom of expression.[18] It is clear that proportionality-requirements include a certain, if limited, balancing of interests in this regard. Restrictions on disinformation are hence also subject to requirements of necessity and proportionality in Swedish law, generally as well as in the particular case.

2.1.2 Constitutional Protections Concerning Freedom of the Press

The Freedom of the Press Act concerns printed media, which are subdivided in periodical and non-periodical publications.[19] The Freedom of the Press Act provides for so called crimes of the freedom of the press, and crimes concerning use of freedom of expression in printed publications are only punishable insofar as the Freedom of the Press Act provides for it.[20] Such crimes have to be provided for in both the Freedom of the Press Act and the Criminal Code.[21]

The Freedom of the Press Act also posits a central principle of exclusive responsibility meaning that there is only one person who may be held responsible for crimes under the Freedom of the Press Act.[22] That person in relation to periodicals may

---

[15] 2:21 Instrument of Government.

[16] NJA 2012 s. 400.

[17] 2:23 Instrument of Government.

[18] The Swedish supreme courts have held that the principle of proportionality is generally applicable concerning a variety of rights, such as property (judgements of the Swedish Supreme Administrative Court, RÅ 1996 ref. 40 and RÅ 1999 ref. 76 and Swedish Supreme Court in NJA 2018 s. 753), freedom of movement (HFD 2024 ref. 5) and detention (HFD 2016 ref. 44, NJA 2018 s. 1051 and NJA 2024 s. 81). There are also number of cases where the Swedish Supreme Court has held that restrictions on freedom of expression, regardless of the technical form of expression, are subject to requirements of proportionality, in the last decades. See inter alia, NJA 2012 s. 400, NJA 2020 s. 1083, NJA 2021 s. 215, NJA 2021 s. 498 and NJA 2023 s. 246.

[19] Chapters 4 and 5 Freedom of the Press Act.

[20] 1:9 Freedom of the Press Act.

[21] 7:1 Freedom of the Press Act.

[22] 1:9, 8:1 and 8:6 (respectively) Freedom of the Press Act.

be the,[23] and then in lieu of the publisher or the publisher's deputy, the owner,[24] the printer[25] or the distributor of the periodical, in that order.[26] For non-periodic publications, the author is responsible, in lieu of the author (if the author is unknown or wants to remain anonymous), the publisher, the printer or the distributor in that order.[27] The main reason for this order is to provide for possibilities for persons who want to remain anonymous to publish and disseminate information, while still ensuring that someone may be held legally responsible for the publication. The requirement of editorial independence precludes that any other actor has any superior editorial role in decision-making on publishing, whether off-line or on-line.[28] The approach to the freedom of the press as it has been understood traditionally in Swedish law, emphasised the technical form of publications thereby avoiding the distinction between mass media as a protected institution and other actors publishing and disseminating materials.

In relation to the substantive limits to what is allowed to publish, the Freedom of the Press Act, and Freedom of Expression Fundamental Law, reflect the Criminal Code, which means that defamation and agitation against minorities are both prohibited. The scope of application of the Freedom of the Press Act is however not unlimited. Certain crimes that are committed through printed media fall outside the scope of the Freedom of the Press Act. That includes crimes such as fraud, swindles or blackmail.[29]

In relation to the Freedom of the Press Act there is also an absolute prohibition on censorship, i.e., the review of lawfulness of materials prior to publication.[30] The Freedom of the Press Act and the Fundamental Law on Freedom of Expression are also characterised by their character as constitutional criminal legislation, i.e. criminal law at the hierarchical level of constitutional law. It also means that rules concerning punishment of freedom of expression crimes, are normally interpreted in a restrictive manner (as is generally the case with provisions of criminal law).

The main difference between the Freedom of the Press Act and the Fundamental Law of Freedom of Expression on one hand and general law regulating expressions in other media than printed media on the other, is that the Freedom of the Press Act and the Fundamental Law of Freedom of Expression, both provide for a special criminal procedure in trials of printed media and a special catalogue of crimes. The special criminal procedure includes the use of a jury (otherwise not existing in Swedish law), which consists of laymen (normally politically appointed)[31] determining whether the court should try or reject the case.[32] In the case that the jury rejects the case, it

[23] 8:1 Freedom of the Press Act.

[24] 8:3 Freedom of the Press Act.

[25] 8:4 Freedom of the Press Act.

[26] 8:5 Freedom of the Press Act.

[27] 8:7–8:10 Freedom of the Press Act.

[28] 8:2 Freedom of the Press Act.

[29] Axberger, H-G, Tryckfrihetens gränser, Liber Förlag, Stockholm (1984) 39–61.

[30] 1:8 Freedom of the Press Act.

[31] 12:7 Freedom of the Press Act.

[32] 12:4 Freedom of the Press Act.

does so without any reasons and without any possibility for appeal. In such cases a prosecution against an author/editor (of a non-periodical publication) or a publisher (of a periodical publication) have failed and the defendant has been acquitted.[33] With regard to especially serious crimes (mainly connected to national security) responsibility may also concern others than the author or publisher of a publication, although that is uncommon.[34]

In addition to the constitutional rules concerning freedom of expression under the Instrument of Governance and freedom of the press, there are also specific provisions to protect freedom of expression in television, radio and electronic media that are connected to printed media, and secondly electronic media that have acquired certain protection (and responsibilities) under the Freedom of Expression Fundamental Law.[35]

2.2 *Legislative Acts*

In general, Swedish law has traditionally assumed an approach to freedom of expression which means that disinformation has generally been protected as expression, whereas specific kinds of disinformation have been criminalised or otherwise regulated by law. A part of the reason for this very liberal approach has been the strong tendency of the Swedish legislator to avoid to *generally* differentiate between false and true statements with regard to freedom of expression. The absence of a general prohibition on disinformation means that Swedish law does not generally distinguish between degrees of protection of freedom of expression related to quality of the content of expression. The legislation that concerns disinformation (including misleading information) hence concerns specific instances of misleading information in relation to, in particular defamation, fraud, swindles or misleading marketing practices.

Traditional broadcasting of radio- and television are subject to licensing-requirements.[36] They may be revoked by courts on the basis of serious crimes against the Freedom of Expression Fundamental Law with regard to local[37] and commercial radio.[38] The government may set general licensing requirements for tv- and radio requiring them to adopt an approach of objectivity.[39] However that requirement does not extend to online materials.

With regard to various forms of technologically sophisticated forms of disinformation it seems clear that insofar they are made for purposes of fraud or swindles, or

[33] 12:4 Freedom of the Press Act.

[34] 7:22–23 Freedom of the Press Act.

[35] 1:1 Fundamental Law of Freedom of Expression.

[36] 4:2 Radio- och tv-lag (2010:696) (Radio and Television Act).

[37] 18:3 Radio and Television Act.

[38] 18:5 Radio and Television Act.

[39] 4:8 Radio and Television Act.

for the purposes of defamation and slander, they are covered by criminal and to some extent administrative law. The kind of disinformation that is generally protected under freedom of expression concerns false information in relation to political, religious, artistic and other forms of expressions.

2.2.1 Criminal Law Concerning Disinformation

In Swedish general criminal law there are a number of crimes instituted, that at least in some cases concern disinformation. These crimes are however typically generally applicable and include but are not specifically related to online disinformation.

5:1 Criminal Code criminalises defamation in Swedish law. Defamation concerns cases where individuals have accused other individuals of crimes or acts that make individuals appear as reprehensible, or other information that may expose the individual to the contempt of others. Such acts are not defamatory insofar as the person making the statements are legally obliged to disseminate the information or insofar as it was justifiable to do it under the circumstances in the case. Defamatory false information disseminated in bad faith always gives rise to criminal responsibility. The criminalisation of defamation is a protection of the personal sphere and as such a restriction on 2:1 Instrument of Government. It is justified by the need to protect the personal sphere and the good name of individuals.

9:1 Criminal Code criminalises fraud which consists of the use of misleading information (regardless of technical means) to make someone else to commit or omit acts which harm the persons committing them and benefit the individual that misled. In a similar way, the person which provides false information in relation to automatic processing of information (e.g., in relation to computers) in a manner which is beneficial for the person providing the information and harmful to someone else is responsible for fraud. Similar criminalisation of misinformation includes falsified bills[40] as well as for fraudulent use of identification information of legal persons (e.g., companies, associations or public bodies) etc.[41] These varieties of fraudulent acts include dissemination of misleading information which may include but are not limited to online information. Fraud also falls outside the scope of protection of freedom of the press. 1:4 Act on Punishment of Market Abuse in the Securities Market (Lag (2016:1307) om straff för marknadsmissbruk på värdepappersmarknaden), prohibits the spreading of disinformation in order to affect the price of a security, which is punishable by imprisonement. This legislation to some extent overlaps with criminal law on swindles.

Under 9:9 Criminal Code, a person that disseminates false or misleading information to the public, in order to affect the valuation/prices of assets or goods, is liable for swindle. The difference between frauds and swindles is that swindles are directed towards the public at large, i.e., a swindle by definition includes an element of disinformation directed towards the general public and not only in relation to a

---

[40] 9:3a Criminal Code.

[41] 9:3d Criminal Code.

particular individual or group of individuals. Like fraud, swindles fall outside the protection of freedom of the press.

Under 16:8 Criminal Code, there is a general prohibition of agitation against minorities. That prohibition does not in and of itself focus on dissemination of disinformation, but it is clear that the 16:8 Criminal Code also criminalises hateful and untrue statements about ethnic and religious groups as well in relation to groups defined by sexual orientation. Recently 16:8 Criminal Code was also amended to include denials of holocaust and certain other genocides among the criminalised acts.[42] Within the framework of agitation against minorities, it is hence clear that certain forms of disinformation are included among the criminal acts. In the preparatory works to 16:8 Criminal Code, it was clarified that the criminalisation does not cover scholarly and scientific studies of ethnic and religious groups nor aims to prevent objective discussions of social and other issues.[43]

In wartime dissemination of false or misleading information to soldiers or military personnel or mislead them to induce defeatism, is prohibited as treason under 22:1 Criminal Code and 7:17 Freedom of the Press Act (if committed through printed media). In wartime, dissemination of *false* rumours or *false* statements of (purported) facts, in private, among the general public or to a foreign state that create dangers for the security of the realm is criminalised under 22:5 Criminal Code[44] and 7:19 Freedom of the Press Act (if committed through printed media).

A medium that emerged early in the history of internet was so called "bulletin boards" where individuals could engage in dialogue on various issues as well as to disseminate information and views.[45] Bulletin boards accept contributions by participants, but do not provide channels of communication exclusive to a particular user. In 1998 the first Swedish statute on electronic bulletin boards was adopted, which meant that responsibility for moderating bulletin boards and remove unlawful contented rested with the owner of the bulletin board, i.e. the person controlling which contributions/messages that were published.[46] The responsibility of the owner/operator of a bulletin board meant that such a person had to be named, unlike anonymous contributors.[47] Responsibility extended only to certain particular crimes, whereas the individual contributor would be responsible for other crimes and not directed against disinformation in general.[48] Responsibility under the act does not concern bulletin boards that are subject to regulation under DSA,[49] nor for such boards as

[42] Prop. 2023/24:93, En tydligare bestämmelse om hets mot folkgrupp, 37–42.

[43] Bäcklund, Agneta et al., 16 kap. 8 § Brottsbalken, Brottsbalken: en kommentar, JUNO Norstedts Juridik Stockholm, (2025) (online version, visited 29 November 2025).

[44] Bäcklund, Agneta et al., 22 kap. 5 § Brottsbalken, Brottsbalken: en kommentar, JUNO Norstedts Juridik Stockholm, (2025) (online version, visited 29 November 2025).

[45] 1§ Bulletin Board Act.

[46] 4 and 5 §§ Bulletin Board Act.

[47] 3§ Bulletin Board Act.

[48] 5§ Bulletin Board Act.

[49] 4a§ Bulletin Board Act.

those that are subject to the Freedom of the Press Act or the Freedom of Expression Fundamental Law.[50]

2.2.2 Administrative Law Concerning Disinformation

Administrative law concerning disinformation remains limited in Swedish law. 2 § Marketing Act (Marknadsföringslagen (2008:486)) provides for that Marketing Act is applicable when businesses market goods and services to consumers or when businesses seek to purchase goods and services in their business. It includes digital goods and services as well as communication between businesses and consumers by electronic means. The Marketing Act prohibits various forms of marketing on- as well as offline. It covers marketing that uses disinformation and is misleading as well as marketing that includes threats, violence, harassment, coercion or the use of other aggressive means of pressure against potential customers.[51]

Misleading practices of marketing are also prohibited. Misleading marketing includes, misleading and incorrect comparisons between goods and services[52] and misleading information on the character of the sale[53] (e.g., misleading information on final sale[54] or sale due to bankruptcy[55]). It also includes misleading information on the conditions of a transaction[56] as well as misleading information on the character of the goods in question.[57]

4:16a, Securities Funds Act (Lag om värdepappersfonder 2004:46) prohibits misleading factsheets about securities funds from the companies setting up and providing for such funds. 9:14 Securities Market Act (Lag om värdepappersmarknaden (2007:528) prohibits misleading marketing materials from securities institutes. However, in Swedish administrative law the main legal restrictions that concern (information judged to be) disinformation stem from EU law. That includes in particular regulation under the Digital Services Act[58] (DSA), the Digital Markets Act[59] (DMA) and the European Media Freedom Act[60] (EMFA). Swedish law generally

[50] 2 § 3 Bulletin Board Act.

[51] 6–8 §§ Marketing Act.

[52] 18 § Marketing Act.

[53] 17 § Marketing Act.

[54] 16 § Marketing Act.

[55] 15 § Marketing Act.

[56] 12 § Marketing Act.

[57] 13-14a §§ Marketing Act.

[58] Regulation (EU) 2022/2065 of the European Parliament and of the Council of 19 October 2022 on a Single Market For Digital Services and amending Directive 2000/31/EC (Digital Services Act).

[59] Regulation (EU) 2022/1925 of the European Parliament and of the Council of 14 September 2022 on contestable and fair markets in the digital sector and amending Directives (EU) 2019/1937 and (EU) 2020/1828 (Digital Markets Act).

[60] Regulation (EU) 2024/1083 of the European Parliament and of the Council of 11 April 2024 establishing a common framework for media services in the internal market and amending Directive 2010/13/EU (European Media Freedom Act).

accepts the primacy of EU law, which means that measures under the DSA and the EMFA will be applied within Swedish law. In cases where there is discretion left to the member states with regard to implementation of EU law, Swedish authorities and courts will take into account Swedish constitutional norms concerning freedom of expression.

The DSA, DMA and EMFA are EU-regulations and hence have direct effect. The Swedish legislator has however adopted specific statutes concerning the implementation of some of these EU-regulations in Swedish law, with regard to Swedish authorities.

The DMA is primarily aimed to safeguard competition in digital markets and on digital platforms of various kinds.[61] However it sets limits to acts of platforms and put them under oversight of EU institutions and national authorities, which may indirectly affect the regulation of disinformation.

Concerning the DSA the Swedish legislator has adopted a specific act with additional rules governing the implementation of the DSA by Swedish public authorities.[62] Swedish authorities under the Swedish implementing legislation are authorised to decide on prohibition of unlawful content and mandate publication of correct information.[63] With regard to the DSA, the Swedish implementing act has not included any obligation for platform providers to actively search for disinformation.[64]

With regard to the EMFA the Swedish legislator has adopted a statute providing for implementation of the EMFA which mainly concerns competition law in the media sector and administrative regulations.[65] The EMFA was adopted in 2024 and aims to protect the role of (traditional) mass media in European societies. The Act does not aim to infringe upon the rights and freedoms under the EU Charter of Fundamental Rights.[66] It aims *inter alia* to prevent disinformation and polarising messages in media outlets.[67] It includes mass media which are commercial actors, as well as public service media of various kinds. It should be noted that mass media is understood as a special category of commercial actors given particular protection, as well as certain specific responsibilities.[68] Art. 18 EMFA provides for requirements of transparency for very large online platforms, which seems to aim to restrict influences on online-platforms, not just by third countries but also by actors that may be economically dependent on such countries as well as political parties. It also seeks to enforce a principle of editorial independence, outside traditionally edited media.

---

[61] Preamble, recital 7, Digital Market Act.

[62] Lag (2024:954) med kompletterande bestämmelser till EU:s förordning om digitala tjänster (Act with complementing rules to the EU Digital Services Act).

[63] Chapter 2, 1–3 §§ (Act with complementing rules to the EU Digital Services Act).

[64] Prop. 2023/24:160 Kompletterande bestämmelser till EU:s förordning om digitala tjänster, p. 20.

[65] Lag (2025:1242) med kompletterande bestämmelser till EU:s mediefrihetsförordning (entry into force on 1 January 2026) (Act with complementing rules to the European Media Freedom Act). See government bill, Prop. 2024/25:197 Kompletterande bestämmelser till EU:s mediefrihetsförordning.

[66] Preamble, recital 8, European Media Freedom Act.

[67] Preamble, recitals 4 and 6, European Media Freedom Act.

[68] Art 2(1) and Art. 4 European Media Freedom Act.

With regard to Swedish law and the implementation of in particular the EMFA, there are ambiguities with regard to rules of responsibility and editorial independence, as editorial responsibility and editorial independence by Swedish law is vested with one single person, the responsible publisher (*ansvarig utgivare*), or the author of a publication.[69]

Regulation (EU) 2024/900 of the European Parliament and the Council of 13 March 2024 on the transparency and targeting of political advertising, inter alia seeks to restrict dissemination of disinformation in EU law. The requirements of transparency concerning political advertisment have traditionally not existed in Swedish law, as the responsibility for printed media has rested with author, and the author is unknown with the publisher, printer or the person disseminating it, in that order. With regard to online media, anonymous communications has remained largely accepted. EU law is now accepted as a possible limitation on Swedish law, including on fundamental rights, but it is clear that EU law adopts a different approach to requirements of transparency for political advertisement than what was traditionally the case in Swedish law. EU has also adopted specific regulations on market abuse and prospectuses for securities. The Market Abuse Regulation provides for prohibition of false or misleading information that may affect the price of securities. The EU has also adopted similar legislation concerning markets for cryptoassets.[70] The Prospectus Regulation concerns requirements for publication of information concerning securities in relation to initial public offering of securities[71] as well as powers of national regulatory authorities of powers of national regulatory authorities of publication of information in some contexts.[72] The Swedish legislator has adopted implementing legislation concerning them which however has not changed their character.[73]

---

[69] 8:1 and 8:6 (respectively) Freedom of the Press Act.

[70] See inter alia Art. 12 and 22 REGULATION (EU) No 596/2014 OF THE EUROPEAN PARLIAMENT AND OF THE COUNCIL of 16 April 2014 on market abuse (market abuse regulation) and repealing Directive 2003/6/EC of the European Parliament and of the Council and Commission Directives 2003/124/EC, 2003/125/EC and 2004/72/EC. Art. 6, 7 and 14 Regulation (EU) 2023/1114 of the European Parliament and the Council of 31 May 2023 on markets in crypto-assets, and amending Regulations (EU) No 1093/2010 and (EU) No 1095/2010 and Directives 2013/36/EU and (EU) 2019/1937.

[71] Art. 22, REGULATION (EU) 2017/1129 OF THE EUROPEAN PARLIAMENT AND OF THE COUNCIL of 14 June 2017 on the prospectus to be published when securities are offered to the public or admitted to trading on a regulated market, and repealing Directive 2003/71/EC.

[72] Art. 20, REGULATION (EU) 2017/1129 OF THE EUROPEAN PARLIAMENT AND OF THE COUNCIL of 14 June 2017 on the prospectus to be published when securities are offered to the public or admitted to trading on a regulated market, and repealing Directive 2003/71/EC.

[73] 3:4 Act with Complementing Rules to the EU Market Abuse Regulation (Lag (2016:1306) med kompletterande bestämmelser till EU:s marknadsmissbruksförordning) provides for that the Swedish Financial Supervisory Authority may publish information to correct information given by actors that is deemed incorrect, if it has been published in conjunction violations of Art. 15 Market Abuse Regulation. 3:7 Act with Complementing Rules to the EU Prospectus Regulation (Lag (2019:414)med kompletterande bestämmelser till EU:s prospektförordning) also provides also for that the Swedish Financial Supervisory Authority may publish information to correct information given by actors that is deemed incorrect. 2:6 Act (2024:1159) with complementing rules to the EU regulation on markets for cryptoassets (Lag (2024:1159) med kompletterande bestämmelser

2.2.3 Private Law Concerning Disinformation

To some extent disinformation may be regulated through private law. If individuals enter into contracts on the basis of misleading information, that may give rise to contractual tort claims, and contractual sanctions of various kinds, including reduction of prices for goods and services or that contracts are declared void.[74]

Disinformation may also give rise to liability on the part of private actors. In Swedish law, tort liability for economic damages on the part of private (as opposed to public) actors may only arise in conjunction with damages to bodies and things,[75] or in conjunction with crimes.[76] The practical role of tort law in relation to protection against disinformation in Swedish law has thus typically remained limited.

The Consumer Sales Act which concerns the sale of goods to consumers (i.e., non-commercial users), including sale of digital services, prohibits consumer contracts that are misleading.[77]

Following 37 § Marketing Act, businesses may be liable for economic damages that follows from misleasing marketing practices. 2:1 Act on Company Names (lag 2018:1653 om företagsnamn) provides for that company names may not be registered if they may mislead the public. A similar rule exists in 2:7 (2) Trademark Act (2010:1877) concerning registration of trademarks that may mislead the public with regard to the character of a good or service concerning its character, quality, geographical origins or other circumstances. That may also be a basis for rescinding a registration of a trademark under 3:1 Trademark Act (Varumärkeslagen (2010:1877)). A certain liability for mistranslations and incorrect summaries of prospectuses exist in chapter 2, 15 § Act on trade with financial instruments (lag 1991:980 om handel med finansiella instrument). Under 3:3 Tort Act, Swedish public authorities (i.e., national authorities and local governments) may be liable for damages that have been brought about by misleading information by public authorities. In such cases, the public authorities to be liable must have negligently or purposively misled the public or individuals.

---

till EU:s förordning om marknader för kryptotillgångar) provides for supervision of markets of cryptoassets, where the Swedish Financial Supervisory Authority it may publish information on actors in the case that it deems information published by actors that are under their supervision, incorrect. Similar provisions exist in 2:5 Act (2024:1085) with complementing rules to the EU regulation on green bonds (Lag (2024:1085) med kompletterande bestämmelser till EU:s förordning om europeiska gröna obligationer).

[74] 30 § Avtalslagen (1915:218) (Contract Act).

[75] 2:1 Skadeståndslagen (1972:207) (Tort Act).

[76] 2:2 Tort Act.

[77] 4:1–4:4, 4:7–4:8 and 4:11 as well as Chapter 9, Konsumentköplagen (2022:260) Consumer Sales Act, see in addition concerning consumer services, 33 § Konsumenttjänstlagen (1985:716), Consumer Services Act.

2.3 *Subordinate Acts Concerning Disinformation*

There are no subordinate acts directly related to prevention of dissemination of disinformation, although certain government agencies such as the Psychological Defense Agency[78] and the Swedish Civil Defence Agency (previously the Swedish Civil Contingencies Agency)[79] have respectively been charged with tasks to counter disinformation and provide authoritative information in crises. The Swedish Institute (being a government agency working on public diplomacy) is charged with enhancing resilience against disinformation concerning Sweden abroad under 1§ (2) Executive ordinance with instruction for the Swedish Institute (Förordning med instruktion för Svenska institutet 2015:152). Their powers are however limited to provide information to the public.

2.4 *Case Law*

The role of case law with regard to disinformation has generally been limited. Issues related to disinformation may arise in different contexts, including in criminal law.

2.4.1 Supreme Courts

There are few instances of case law that directly concern issues of disinformation in Swedish law. Regarding regulation of hate speech, agitation against homosexuals (in an offline environment) has been held to be criminal.[80] There is little case law concerning swindles and defamation that have concerned acts committed on line, decided by the supreme courts.

2.4.2 Subordinate Courts

With regard to disinformation, subordinate courts have applied rules against agitation against minorities in some cases. Historically there has been prosecutions of hate speech that occurred offline that included disinformation of various kinds.[81]

Statements made online that the cultures of certain religious and ethnic groups are characterised by parasitism and inability to maintain democratic governance have

---

[78] 2§ Förordning (2021:936) med instruktion för Myndigheten för psykologiskt försvar. (Executive ordinance with instruction for the Agency for Psychological Defence).

[79] 15 § Förordning (2008:1002) med instruktion för Myndigheten för civilt försvar (Executive ordinance with instruction for the Civil Defence Agency).

[80] NJA 2006 s. 467.

[81] See inter alia, RH 1991:20.

been regarded as agitation against minorities.[82] Cases concerning agitation against minorities have also concerned statements about Muslims and their relation to non-Muslim groups, where courts of appeals have found that certain statements as such constitute agitation against a (religious) minority.[83] In Swedish law, denial of the holocaust has been prosecuted in courts, although not in relation to disinformation online.[84] Svea Court of Appeal has stated that with regard to disinformation there are historically well established facts whose rejection amount to agitation against minorities.[85] A number of cases concerning defamation on the internet have occurred but they have normally not directly concerned disinformation.[86] There are hence cases where disinformation, on- as well as offline have been prosecuted, however such prosecutions have not concerned the issue of disinformation per se but cases where disinformation has been prohibited for some other reason. The Patent- and Market Superior Court has adjudicated repeatedly on misinformation connected to misleading marketing practices, as well as lower general courts on swindles, both which at least partly take place online.

2.5 *Soft Law*

There is little or no soft law aimed at regulating the issues of disinformation in Swedish law. There is a system of self-regulation related to traditional Swedish media, in particular newspapers, which includes an Ombudsman and a Board of Complaints for Media where individuals subject to negative publicity may file complaints.[87] However, that is not directly aimed at preventing disinformation, and only to a limited extent connected to online-media, and not at all to social media (except for channels connected to traditional print and broadcasted media).

2.6 *Influence of Foreign Regulation*

Swedish law has been marked by an unusually strong protection of freedom of expression, but there has been limited influence with regard to protection of freedom of

[82] Court of Appeal for Scania and Blekinge, case B 2033–12, judgement 13 June 2013.

[83] RH 2017:14.

[84] Court of Appeal for Scania and Blekinge, case B 592–19, judgement 9 October 2019. Svea Court of Appeal, judgement 7 June 2023, case B 609–23.

[85] Court of Appeal for Scania and Blekinge, case B 592–19, judgement 9 October 2019.

[86] RH 1997:61 and RH 2008:60.

[87] Rules on publicity for press, radio and television, have been adopted on a voluntary basis by the private institution the Media Ombudsman, a body of media self-regulation. Medieombudsmannens och Mediernas Etiknämnds årsredovisning 2024. https://medieombudsmannen.se/det-har-ar-medieombudsmannen/arsberattelser/ (visited 14 November 2025).

expression, concerning disinformation by foreign law. The criminalisation of denial of certain genocides (in particular the holocaust) has however clearly been influenced by the development of hate speech regulation in the EU.[88]

3 The Regulation

3.1 Regulations Applicable to Online Disinformation

As discussed above, there is apart from EU law, very limited regulation specifically of online disinformation in Swedish law. The analysis here will focus on the extent to which general rules on disinformation are applicable to online-contents.

3.2 Regulations Concerning Disinformation in General, Therefore also Applicable to Online Disinformation

There are no general provisions with regard to protection against disinformation as such in domestic Swedish law and hence no particular authorities overseeing such disinformation. With regard to media channels which require licenses of various kinds, i.e., national and local radio- and tv-broadcasting (as well as materials provided for by broadcasters on the internet), there is a supervisory authority in the Media Authority (Mediemyndigheten).[89]

3.2.1 Subjects Who Can Report

The Consumer Protection Ombudsman can bring cases to the Patent- and Market Courts concerning misleading marketing practices. Anyone may report content of national and local radio- and tv-broadcasting to the Media Authority, or other public authorities charged with overseeing disinformation in their respective fields. There are no special rules concerning reports by civil servants. Other printed media is subject only to jurisdiction of general courts under the Freedom of the Press Act, where cases may be reported to the Office of the Chancellor of Justice by aggrieved parties or anyone else, and to courts by aggrieved parties and the Office of the Chancellor of Justice. That is also applicable to online media attached to print and

[88] See Swedish government bill, Prop. 2023/24:93 En tydligare bestämmelse om hets mot folkgrupp.

[89] 1–3 §§ Förordning (2023:844) med instruktion för Mediemyndigheten (Executive ordinance with instruction for the Media Authority).

broadcasting media. Social media in general are subject to general rules on prosecution in the general courts, meaning that anyone may report them to prosecutorial authorities and cases may also be brought by public prosecutors or victims of crime.

3.2.2 Subjects Who Decide on the Report

The Patent- and Market Court decide on cases on prohibition of misleading marketing practices. The Board of review for radio and television, which is a part of the Media Authority may review whether media under its authority have acted contrary to requirements of objectivity.[90]

There is an Ordinance complementing the implementation of the DSA (Förordning med kompletterande bestämmelser till EU:s förordning om digitala tjänster (2024:958)) providing for the Consumer Protection Authority to be the public authority charged with reviewing misleading online information to consumers, and the Media Authority is responsible for reviewing cases of online disinformation which is not directed towards consumers. There is an Ordinance complementing the implementation of the EU regulation on political advertisement (Förordning (2025:1410) med kompletterande bestämmelser till EU:s förordning om politisk reklam) that provides for that the Media Authority is responsible authority for applying the EU regulation on political advertisement. In other cases, it is clear that it is the authorities charged with enforcing the legislation in question that are responsible for initiating decisions. With regard to online materials that are covered by the Freedom of Expression Fundamental Law, the Chancellor of Justice is the exclusive prosecutor of such materials (except for individuals concerned).[91] With regard to online materials which are not subject to the Freedom of Expression Fundamental Law, provisions of general criminal law apply. In both cases prosecutorial authorities decide on whether the case should be brought to the courts, and cases are ultimately decided by general courts for civil and criminal law (although individuals concerned may also bring cases).[92]

3.2.3 Means to Establish the Falsehood of the Contents and the Related Responsibilities

There are no special administrative procedures to determine the falsehood or truth of statements in Swedish law. In the case that issues of disinformation become a matter of judicial proceedings, it may be so in the general courts (either in criminal or civil cases) or administrative courts (e.g. in cases of appeals against administrative

[90] 16:2 Radio and Television Act (this control is limited to licenced broadcasting, which is not subject to the supervision of the Office of the Chancellor of Justice).

[91] 9:2 and 12:1 Freedom of the Press Act read in conjunction with 10:1 Freedom of Expression Fundamental Law.

[92] 19:1 Rättegångsbalken (Code of Judicial Procedure).

sanctions of and/or prohibitions unlawful marketing practices). As there are no legal rules of evidence in Swedish law, the courts are bound to determine the correctness of the statements independently of previous judicial or administrative assessments of facts.[93]

3.2.4 Deadlines for the Decision

Both the Office of the Chancellor of Justice as well as courts, prosecutorial authorities and administrative authorities are bound to respect the requirements of trials within a reasonable time (2:11 Instrument of Government), but otherwise there are no general rules connected to deadlines on whether to make decisions about disinformation. Concerning criminal prosecution of disinformation, the general rules of statutory limitations apply, after which an alleged crime may not be prosecuted.

3.2.5 Forms of Protection for the Authors of Allegedly Illegal Content or Disinformation

Unless there are specific instances of legislation against false information, which are uncommon, authors of disinformation are protected by constitutional protection of freedom of expression.[94] As discussed above, criminalisation of disinformation is limited to disinformation committed for economic gain,[95] defamation, specific instances of offences against public order, such as agitation against minorities, including denial of (certain) genocides[96] or spreading of false rumours in wartime.[97] As noted above in particular cases, disinformation may have certain legal effects in, criminal, private or administrative law, but the common denominator in such cases is that the disinformation also would need to be covered by criminalisation, administrative prohibitions or private law prohibitions which concern other matters than mere disinformation. Authors and publishers of allegedly illegal content or disinformation can normally rely on general protection of freedom of expression.

3.2.6 Sanctions in Case of Detection of Disinformation

Sanctions concerning disinformation will ensue in the case that disinformation is criminalised or administratively prohibited. Criminal punishments are provided for in the Criminal Code concerning defamation, fraud, swindles as well as with regard

[93] 35:1 Code of Judicial Procedure.

[94] 2:1 and 2:23 Instrument of Government.

[95] 9:9 Criminal Code and 2 § Marketing Act.

[96] 16:8 Criminal Code.

[97] 22:5 Criminal Code.

to agitation against minorities and in special criminal legislation for market manipulation. The criminal punishments consists of fines or imprisonement. Treason is punished by imprisonement from ten years to life and spreading of false rumours with fines or imprisonement. As discussed above criminal responsibility may also ensue under the Freedom of the Press Act and Fundamental Law of Freedom of Expression.

There is also a plethora of administrative sanctions concerning specific kinds of disinformation.

29§ Marketing Acts provides for monetary sanctions for violations of the Marketing Act, which includes various forms of disinformation.

12:1 Securities Funds Act (2004:46) provides for sanctions for depositary institute and securities funds that do not comply with their obligations, including if leaving misleading information to the public. The Swedish Financial Supervisory Authority may order the fund to take certain action or prohibit certain action, or in grave cases revoke the licence to operate, including under 12:1a Securities Funds Act (2004:46) if the fund repeatedly fails to comply with requirements concerning factsheets on funds or other required information.

25:1 Securities Market Act (2007:528) provides for sanctions against securities institutes or marketplaces for securities, where the Swedish Financial Supervisory Authority shall order the subject concerned to take certain action to reduce risks in the operations of the subject or prohibit certain action (e.g. the payment of dividends), prohibit the execution of a decision, make a remark or give warning. They are however restricted to aggravated cases of intentional or grossly negligent action on the part of the institute or its leadership. In such cases, measures mentioned may be combined with monetary sanctions.

3:23 Act with complementing rules to the EU Digital Services Act provides for sanctions for violations of the DSA but not connected to sanctions in this regard. There are no specific rules on sanctions in the Act with complementing rules to the European Media Freedom Act.

5:3 Act with Complementing Rules to the EU Market Abuse Regulation provides for that the Swedish Financial Supervisory Authority may order an actor to cease with certain actions, it may decide on return of profits for marketmanipulation to the state, or impose monetary sanctions 5:4 of the Act with Complementing Rules to the EU Market Abuse Regulation provides for that the Swedish Financial Supervisory Authority can prohibit an actor to engage in proprietary trade of securities for those engaging in market manipulation, including through disinformation or prohibit individuals to have be member of the board or chief executive officer in a Swedish securities institute. 5:1 and 5:4 Act with Complementing Rules to the EU Prospectus Regulation provides for that the Swedish Financial Supervisory Authority may reject a prospectus for sale of securities, make a remark on the conduct of the business, order an actor to adopt measures to provide correct information or impose monetary sanctions for incorrect information.

3:2. Act (2024:1159) with complementing rules to the EU regulation on markets for cryptoassets provides for that the Swedish Financial Supervisory Authority may make remarks on the operation of a company concerned, warn the company or ultimately withdraw licence to operate, under 3:3 the same act may remarks and warnings be combined with monetary sanctions. Under 3:1 and 3:4 Act (2024:1085) with complementing rules to the EU regulation on green bonds, there are similar provisions, with misconduct on institutes that originate green bonds, including misinformation concerning green bonds.

11–15 §§ Act with complementing rules to the EU-regulation on political advertisement (Lag (2025:1408) med kompletterande bestämmelser till EU:s förordning om politisk reklam) contains rules on monetary sanctions for those publishing or disseminating political advertisement that do not meet the mandated standards on transparency with regard to the origins of political advertisement. These sanctions are imposed in an administrative manner which may be subject to judicial review. However, this kind of rules are in principle difficult to combine with the view that printed media and online-media clearly attached to printed media in Swedish law are exclusively under the supervision of the Office of the Chancellor of Justice and may only be prosecuted under the Freedom of the Press Act.

There are criminal sanctions for infringing upon corporate names (5:1. Act (2018:1653) on Company Names) and on trademarks (8:1 Trademark Act (2010:1877)).

There is hence no traditional of general criminalisation of false information in Swedish law.

3.2.7 Sanctions in Case of Unfounded Reports or Complaints

There are no sanctions aimed specifically at unfounded reports or complaints concerning disinformation. However, there are criminal sanctions concerning defamatory statements that are false or unjustified,[98] there are also sanctions in relation to unfounded prosecutions[99] as well as about unfounded reports or complaints about crimes to prosecutorial authorities or police.[100]

3.2.8 Review of Previous Decisions

Since there are no special decisions on dissemination of disinformation and the only decisions rendered are through the ordinary system of courts or public authorities, review will take place through review of courts or Judgements from the Patent- and Market Court (decided after complaints from the Consumer Protection Ombudsman) may be appealed to the Patent- and Market Superior Court, which is the final instance.

With regard to review of decisions relating to administrative measures, such can mostly be appealed from to administrative courts. However as there is no general right

[98] 5:1 Criminal Code.

[99] 15:5 Criminal Code.

[100] 15:6 Criminal Code.

to judicial review in Swedish law, right to appeal concerning decisions relating to particular forms of disinformation may be limited by the relevant statutes. The general rule (to which each act contain exceptions) provided for under 14:1 Securities Funds Act (2004:46), 26:1 Securities Market Act (2007:528), 6:1 Act with Complementing Rules to the EU Market Abuse Regulation, 6:1 Act with Complementing Rules to the EU Prospectus Regulation, 4:1 Act (2024:1159) with complementing rules to the EU regulation on markets for cryptoassets as well as 4:1. Act (2024:1085) with complementing rules to the EU regulation on green bonds is that decisions under the respective acts may be appealed to general administrative courts.

The same rule applies under 20:1 Radio- and Television Act and 18-19 §§ Act (2025:1408) with complementing rules to the EU-regulation on political advertisement.

With regard to criminal prosecutions for particular kinds of disinformation the normal rules on appeal in criminal cases apply.

3.2.9 Sanctions for Private Entities or Administrative Bodies Who Rendered Erroneous Decisions

There are no specific sanctions for private entities or administrative bodies who rendered erroneous decisions concerning disinformation. However, such decisions may give rise to criminal liability for involved civil servants under 20:1 Criminal Code, or tort liability with regard to exercise of public authority under 3:2 Tort Act, or liability for incorrect information disseminated by public authorities under 3:3 Tort Act. In relation to sanctions on private bodies such are limited insofar as allegations concerning disinformation are also typically protected by freedom of expression, although certain statements about (natural) persons may be regarded as defamatory.

3.2.10 Their Use in Practice

The main difference in application of legislation regulating freedom of expression concerns printed media protected under the Freedom of the Press Act and online media protected under Freedom of Expression Fundamental Law and online information covered by general criminal law concerns the procedure.

With regard to online materials protected under the Freedom of the Press Act and the Freedom of Expression Fundamental Law, prosecutions are brought exclusively by the Chancellor of Justice (or individuals concerned) and reviewed by a jury, that may reject a case and acquit the defendant without providing any reasons. In order to decide that a case should proceed, six out of nine members of a jury must agree for the case to be materially decided by the court. If the jury finds that a case should be allowed to proceed to the court, the court may still acquit the defendant. This means that materials protected under Freedom of the Press Act and online media protected under Freedom of Expression Fundamental Law are rarely held to be unlawful. Prosecutions of materials not protected by special constitutional rules on freedom of expression is more common but still relatively limited, but follows the general (adversarial) criminal procedure. In cases concerning administrative law regulating disinformation, such cases are subject to review by administrative courts under the general Administrative Judicial Procedures Act (Förvaltningsprocesslagen).

4 Conclusions

4.1 *The Degree of Perception of* Online Disinformation *as a Problem*

The Swedish approach to online disinformation has been characterised by caution on the part of the legislator to adopt legislation against disinformation. That reflects partly a longstanding tradition in Swedish law and of the Swedish legislator to be neutral in relation to different expressions in the public sphere. (The Swedish government has historically sought to influence public discourse but mainly done so through public information and public service media rather than through any extensive restrictions on the dissemination of information and opinions.) The considerations on disinformation in Swedish law have traditionally been cursory, the underlying assumption has been that freedom of expression furthers both dissemination of information as well as the free formation of political opinion in society that are both necessary for democratic self-government. The underlying assumption seems to have been that in general restrictions on disinformation were neither necessary nor desirable.

The traditional approach in Swedish law to disinformation hence normally allows for dissemination of falsehoods with certain exceptions such as defamation, agitation against minorities, swindles, fraud and misrepresentation in economic matters, which are prohibited. Dissemination of false statements concerning military defence are criminalised in times of war, but not otherwise.

Since the issue of disinformation has not received much attention in relation to regulation of freedom of expression in Swedish law, it seems clear that disinformation except for certain clearly defined areas was not regarded as an important issue. The underlying view was that insofar as dissemination of disinformation occurred, the effects of such falsehoods would be limited in a society marked by wide freedom of expression and attendant rational enquiry. In these regards, Sweden for a long time may be regarded as an example of an uncommonly consistent liberal approach to protection of freedom of expression, which has also been reflected in that liability for defamation does not protect corporations, that protection of privacy in relation to mass media has been relatively weak, and that constitutional law for long time favoured protection of freedom of expression over data protection.[101]

One may summarise the traditional Swedish approach to disinformation as one that with exceptions that concern tangible harm to individuals or the public order, does

[101] E.g. NJA 2001 s. 409.

not criminalise, prohibit or sanction disinformation in general. Swedish legislation traditionally relied on the notion that uninhibited public debate was the best way for society as well as for individuals to find truth and exercise political autonomy. The traditional approach in Swedish law has been that censorship and suppression of speech carry far greater risks to society than disinformation normally does, an approach which is clearly different from the approach to freedom of expression, in particular in online contexts, of current EU law.

4.2 The Perceived Effectiveness of the Overall Regulation (Specific and General) of Disinformation

It is difficult to assess whether the traditionally liberal approach to disinformation in Swedish law has subjected Sweden to greater degrees of disinformation than legal orders adopting a more restrictive approach. There seems not to be any evidence for the view that Sweden is uncommonly subjected to or harmed by disinformation. The regulation of disinformation under national law in Swedish law is fragmented and in general not connected to disinformation online specifically, but rather to forms of disinformation that may be disseminated online as well as offline.

4.3 Main Critical Issues

The legal, in particular constitutional issues concerning regulation of disinformation in Swedish law are connected to the tendency of law preventing disinformation to restrict freedom of expression as it has traditionally been understood. Swedish domestic legislation has remained limited with regard to online disinformation, and measures against such disinformation has largely been limited to measures by public authorities to provide their point of view on issues where disinformation exists. The tendency in EU law towards greater restrictions on online disinformation, therefore raises questions concerning the constitutional limits to restrictions on freedom of expression in Swedish law.

4.4 **De Jure Condendo**

There is little domestic legislation planned to delimit disinformation, albeit the development of legislation to combat perceived disinformation at EU level obviously affects (and potentially conflicts with) Swedish law. The traditional Swedish approach and the approach of EU to disinformation are different and may create tensions between Swedish constitutional law where freedom of expression is regarded as self-sustaining and protecting society against dangers of governmental abuse of powers and the current view in EU law which presupposes that free expression, in particular on the internet may be a danger to society due to risks associated with disinformation from foreign as well as domestic actors.

References

Avtalslagen (1915:218) (Contract Act).
Axberger, H-G, Tryckfrihetens gränser, Liber Förlag, Stockholm (1984).
Brottsbalken (Criminal Code).
Bull, T. & Sterzel, F. Regeringsformen – en kommentar, 3rd ed., Studentlitteratur, Lund (2023).
Bäcklund, A. et al., Brottsbalken: en kommentar, JUNO Norstedts Juridik Stockholm, (2025) (online version, visited 29 November 2025).
Court of Appeal for Scania and Blekinge, case B 2033-12, judgement 13 June 2013.
Court of Appeal for Scania and Blekinge, case B 592-19, judgement 9 October 2019.
Court of Appeal for Southern Norrland, RH 1997:61.
Court of Appeal for Southern Norrland RH 2008:60.
Förordning (2008:1002) med instruktion för Myndigheten för civilt försvar (Executive ordinance with instruction for the Civil Defence Agency).
Förordning (2021:936) med instruktion för Myndigheten för psykologiskt försvar. (Executive ordinance with instruction for the Agency for Psychological Defence).
Förordning (2023:844) med instruktion för Mediemyndigheten (Executive ordinance with instruction for the Media Authority).
Justitieombudsmannen (Parliamentary Ombudsman),Annual Report, JO 2007/08 s. 439.
Justitieombudsmannen (Parliamentary Ombudsman),Annual Report, JO 2010/11 s. 616.
Justitieombudsmannen (Parliamentary Ombudsman),Annual Report, JO 2014/15 s. 146.
Justitieombudsmannen (Parliamentary Ombudsman),Annual Report, JO 2019/20 s. 54.
Justitieombudsmannen (Parliamentary Ombudsman),Annual Report, JO 2019/20 s. 445.
Justitieombudsmannen (Parliamentary Ombudsman),Annual Report, JO 2020/21 s. 573.
Justitieombudsmannen decision 19th January 2026, nr. 1017–2025
Konsumentköplag (2022:260) Consumer Sales Act.
Lag (1991:980) om handel med finansiella instrument, (Act on trade with financial instruments).
Lag (2004:46) om värdepappersfonder (Securities Funds Act).
Lag (2007:528) om värdepappersmarknaden (Securities Market Act).
Lag (2018:1653) (Act on Company Names).
Lag (2023:319) med kompletterande bestämmelser till EU:s förordning om åtgärder mot spridning av terrorisminnehåll online (Law with complementing regulations to EU's regulation against dissemination of terrorist content online).
Lag (2024:954) med kompletterande bestämmelser till EU:s förordning om digitala tjänster (Act with complementing rules to the EU Digital Services Act).
Lag (2024:1085) med kompletterande bestämmelser till EU:s förordning om europeiska gröna obligationer (Act with complementing rules to the EU regulation on green bonds).
Lag (2024:1159) med kompletterande bestämmelser till EU:s förordning om marknader för kryptotillgångar (Act (2024:1159) with complementing rules to the EU regulation on markets for cryptoassets).
Lag (2025:1408) med kompletterande bestämmelser till EU:s förordning om politisk reklam (Act with Complementing Rules to the EU Regulation on Political Advertisement).
Medieombudsmannens och Mediernas Etiknämnds årsredovisning 2024. https://medieombudsmannen.se/det-har-ar-medieombudsmannen/arsberattelser/ (visited 14 November 2025).

Ó Fathaigh R., Helberger, N. & Appelman N. (2021). The perils of legally defining disinformation. *Internet Policy Review, 10*(4). https://doi.org/10.14763/2021.4.1584.
Petrén G. & Ragnemalm H., Sveriges grundlagar, Liber Förlag, Stockholm (1980).
Proposition 2023/24:93, En tydligare bestämmelse om hets mot folkgrupp.
Proposition 2023/24:160 Kompletterande bestämmelser till EU:s förordning om digitala tjänster.
Radio- och tv-lag (2010:696) (Radio and Television Act).
Regeringsformen (1974:152) (Instrument of Government).
REGULATION (EU) No 596/2014 OF THE EUROPEAN PARLIAMENT AND OF THE COUNCIL of 16 April 2014 on market abuse (market abuse regulation) and repealing Directive 2003/6/EC of the European Parliament and of the Council and Commission Directives 2003/124/EC, 2003/125/EC and 2004/72/EC.
REGULATION (EU) 2017/1129 OF THE EUROPEAN PARLIAMENT AND OF THE COUNCIL of 14 June 2017 on the prospectus to be published when securities are offered to the public or admitted to trading on a regulated market, and repealing Directive 2003/71/EC.
REGULATION (EU) 2021/784 OF THE EUROPEAN PARLIAMENT AND OF THE COUNCIL of 29 April 2021 on addressing the dissemination of terrorist content online.
REGULATION (EU) 2022/1925 OF THE EUROPEAN PARLIAMENT AND OF THE COUNCIL of 14 September 2022 on contestable and fair markets in the digital sector and amending Directives (EU) 2019/1937 and (EU) 2020/1828 (Digital Markets Act).
REGULATION (EU) 2022/2065 OF THE EUROPEAN PARLIAMENT AND OF THE COUNCIL of 19 October 2022 on a Single Market For Digital Services and amending Directive 2000/31/EC (Digital Services Act).
REGULATION (EU) 2023/1114 of the European Parliament and the Council of 31 May 2023 on markets in crypto-assets, and amending Regulations (EU) No 1093/2010 and (EU) No 1095/2010 and Directives 2013/36/EU and (EU) 2019/1937.
REGULATION (EU) 2023/2631 of the European Parliament and of the Council of 22 November 2023 on European Green Bonds and optional disclosures for bonds marketed as environmentally sustainable and for sustainability-linked bonds.
REGULATION (EU) 2024/900 of the European Parliament and the Council of 13 March 2024 on the transparency and targeting of political advertising.
Rättegångsbalken (1942:740) (Code of Judicial Procedure).
Skadeståndslagen (1972:207) (Tort Act).
Svea Court of Appeal, RH 1991:20.
Svea Court of Appeal , RH 2017:14.
Svea Court of Appeal, case B 609–23, judgement 7 June 2023.
Swedish Supreme Administrative Court, RÅ 1996 ref. 40.
Swedish Supreme Administrative Court, RÅ 1999 ref. 76.
Swedish Supreme Administrative Court, HFD 2016 ref. 44.
Swedish Supreme Administrative Court, HFD 2024 ref. 5.
Swedish Supreme Court, NJA 2001 s. 409.
Swedish Supreme Court, NJA 2006 s. 467.
Swedish Supreme Court, NJA 2012 s. 400.
Swedish Supreme Court, NJA 2018 s. 753.
Swedish Supreme Court, NJA 2018 s. 1051.
Swedish Supreme Court, NJA 2020 s. 1083.
Swedish Supreme Court, NJA 2021 s. 215.
Swedish Supreme Court, NJA 2021 s. 498.
Swedish Supreme Court, NJA 2023 s. 246.
Swedish Supreme Court, NJA 2024 s. 81.
Tryckfrihetsförordningen (Freedom of the Press Act).
Yttrandefrihetsgrundlagen (Fundamental Law of Freedom of Expression).